*One Step Ahead in China*

# One Step Ahead in China

## GUANGDONG UNDER REFORM

# EZRA F. VOGEL

*With a contribution by John Kamm*

HARVARD UNIVERSITY PRESS
*Cambridge, Massachusetts*
*London, England*
*1989*

*Library of Congress Cataloging-in-Publication Data*

Vogel, Ezra F.
   One step ahead in China : Guangdong under reform / Ezra F. Vogel.
      p.   cm.
   Bibliography: p.
   Includes index.
   ISBN 0-674-63910-3
   1. Kwangtung Province (China)—Politics and government.
   2. Kwangtung Province (China)—Economic conditions. I. Title.
   II. Title: 1 step ahead in China.
DS793.K7V64 1989                                                    89-31695
951'.27058—dc20                                                     CIP

# Contents

*Preface*   *vii*

*Introduction: Fieldwork in a Changing Province*   *1*

## PART I   The Winds of Change

1   *The Cultural Revolution: Disaster Strengthens the Reform Impulse*   *15*

2   *Hong Kong: Outside Progress Shapes the Reform Impulse*   *43*

3   *A Decade of Reforms*   *76*

## PART II   Patterns of Change

4   *Special Economic Zones: Experiment in New Systems*   *125*

5   *The Inner Delta Counties: Flexible Local Initiative*   *161*

6   *Guangzhou: Rebuilding an Old Capital*   *196*

7   *Prefectural Capitals: Outposts of Change*   *220*

8   *The Mountain Counties: Moving Development Uphill*   *251*

9   *Hainan Island: Accelerated Frontier Development*   *275*

## PART III   Agents of Change

10   *Entrepreneurs: Statesmen, Scramblers, and Niche Seekers*   *313*

11   *Reforming Foreign Trade*   by John Kamm   *338*

PART IV   Perspectives on Change

     12   *Society in Transition: Between Planning and Markets*      395

     13   *The Takeoff of the Guangdong–Hong Kong Region*      426

         *Appendix    Provincial Structure and Statistics*      453

         *Notes*      467

         *Selected Bibliography*      481

         *Acknowledgments*      493

         *Index*      497

# *Preface*

In June 1989 the massacre of students in Beijing's Tiananmen Square stunned China and the rest of the world. It was not the first time that China's rulers had ordered soldiers to slaughter unarmed civilians. Throughout the country's long history countless emperors have tried to keep the Mandate of Heaven by annihilating those who threatened their rule. Chiang Kai-shek's troops in 1927 ruthlessly killed thousands of Communists and in 1947 did away with thousands of Taiwanese. In 1967, in the midst of the Cultural Revolution, rampaging Communists murdered thousands of urban Chinese. But the 1989 massacre was the first such atrocity played out under the vigilant eye of modern telecommunications, and it was thereby instantly and dramatically accessible to people everywhere. It marked the definitive end to an era in which the Chinese state could monopolize the flow of information in and out of China.

Chinese military leaders, frightened by the deterioration of political control, underestimated the popular passion for change and sought to enforce a pattern of authoritarian rule that was no longer tenable. This tragic miscalculation escalated the conflict between military and political leaders over the desirability of economic and political reform and made it difficult for any group to attain the power necessary to steer a course of peaceful reform. The noble attempt of millions of Chinese to modernize was placed in jeopardy.

This book is the story of one province's efforts at reform in the decade from 1978 to 1988, when the government in Beijing pursued more enlightened policies. The sixty million people of Guangdong

Province made remarkable use of their chance to lead the nation in opening to the outside world and in promoting internal reform. At the time of writing, it is not clear to what extent the progress of that province, and of Hong Kong across the border, will be allowed to continue. Although the citizens of Guangdong have been more interested in economic advances than in political reform, and although most have been remote from the political conflicts in Beijing, they cannot entirely escape the impact of distant events. Guangdong is dependent on interactions with outside businesses, and foreign investors look for a predictable environment. The developments in Guangdong in the first decade of reform demonstrate how much its citizens can achieve and suggest how much they may continue to achieve in the years ahead—if political circumstances give them the opportunity.

June 1989

*One Step Ahead in China*

# Introduction

# *Fieldwork in a Changing Province*

When I first visited Guangdong Province in 1973, even the model factories shown to visitors had old machinery that was not always working. Factory grounds were poorly maintained, with little regard for safety, and work was often stopped because of shortages of equipment, supplies, and energy. Few managers in either factories or offices had specialized knowledge, and workers displayed little interest in their work. Universities had not been operating regularly since 1967. In Guangzhou, the province's capital and largest city, formerly known to foreigners as Canton, goods were transported mostly by smoky diesel tractors or in carts pulled by bicycles. Large, locally made trucks also hauled goods or people, who stood in the open bed; there were few buses and almost no cars. Many stores were no longer operating, and the few items available for sale were simple and of poor quality. Vegetable markets were small and quiet. There were virtually no signs of construction. A model commune, Pingzhou, had a few small factories, including an agricultural machinery repair shop, but most of the work was done by hand. In the countryside most goods were transported by diesel tractor, water buffalo, or carrying pole; few roads were smooth enough for bicycles. People were frightened to be seen with foreigners, let alone talk frankly with them.

When I visited the same area in 1979 and 1980, not much had changed. In 1978 the average annual per capita rural income was only 193 yuan, scarcely more than $100, and for urban residents it was only 402 yuan. In 1980, almost 80 percent of the province's population was still rural.

In annual visits to Guangdong since 1980, however, I have seen striking changes each time. By 1987 in Guangzhou, bicycles pulling carts had virtually disappeared and diesel tractors had been banned. Buses were more widespread, and almost no one traveled standing in a truck bed. The streets were jammed with taxis, vans, cars, and motorbikes, in addition to bicycles. Stores, filled with goods and customers, lined the streets. Open food markets were large and noisy, with a far greater variety of goods for sale than before. New buildings and construction sites could be found in all parts of the city, and dozens of factories had modern production equipment. Pingzhou Commune's headquarters had been transformed into a built-up town, with large new factories, a modern hotel, and new apartment buildings. It, too, was bustling with activity. More roads in the countryside were paved, and the number of bicycles per rural household in the province as a whole had increased from 0.55 in 1978 to 1.39 in 1986. Trucks and vans had largely replaced the diesel tractors on rural highways. By 1987 the average per capita rural income had more than tripled to 645 yuan, an average annual increase of 11 percent after adjusting for inflation. Per capita income among salaried urban residents had increased to 1,233 yuan.[1] And many were prepared to talk openly about their lives and their government.

These changes had been sparked by a new coastal strategy and by reforms introduced by Deng Xiaoping in December 1978, two years after the death of Mao Zedong, to get the economy moving. Previously, to equalize wealth and reduce the risk of exposure to foreign attack, Mao had taken resources from coastal areas to build up the poorer provinces of inner China, often at great cost and with little effect. But Deng decided to allow the coastal areas to move ahead more rapidly, to experiment with new systems and become engines of growth for the rest of China. Among the coastal provinces Guangdong had unique advantages. Located far from Beijing in China's southeast corner, with a coastline of 2,400 kilometers, it could experiment with little worry that the impact of political or economic disruptions would threaten the nation's capital. Because it then made only minor contributions to China's heavy industry and national income, the risk to the national economy would be small. And in its location next to Hong Kong, Guangdong had the best access in China to world developments and was most able to test the usefulness of foreign technology and management. China therefore allowed Guangdong to take the lead in experimenting—"to walk," as the slogan put it, "one step ahead" *(xian zou yibu)*.

Guangdong began to move ahead at a time when the Soviet Union and East European countries were thinking of reform. Aware that they had fallen behind many capitalist countries in their goal of enriching their people, these nations were ready to consider changing socialism as they knew it, including the long-term planning system and even the patterns of Communist Party rule. China's General Secretary, Zhao Ziyang, diplomatically stated at the Thirteenth Party Congress in 1987 that socialist countries were not in a race to reform but were all pursuing reform in their own way. But China had in fact begun economic reforms several years before Gorbachev began *perestroika* and had pushed them further than any other socialist country. Within China, Guangdong pursued reforms more vigorously than any other province. If it was one step ahead of most of China, it was perhaps two steps ahead of the rest of the socialist world.

A semitropical province the size of a major European nation, Guangdong on the eve of reform had an area of 212,005 square kilometers (see map) and a growing population already numbering nearly sixty million. (See the Appendix for basic data.) Guangdong's foreign trade dates from the eighth century; the province has long been on the forefront of China's relations with the outside world. After 1699, when the British established a regular trading base in Canton, it was a center for the China trade, and from 1760 until the end of the Opium War in 1842, Canton was the only Chinese port open to the outside. The city remained at the center of the interaction between China and the West until 1949.

More often than other Chinese, Guangdong residents have gone abroad and brought in Western ways. Sensing the outside world's economic and military power, Guangdong patriots led the effort to strengthen China's response to the Western challenge. The Opium War, initiated by local Chinese resisting the British, was fought in Guangdong. The 1898 effort to reform the Qing Dynasty (1644–1912) was led by Liang Qichao and Kang Yuwei, both Guangdong natives. The 1911 Revolution was led by Sun Yat-sen, also a Guangdong native, and he established his Republican government in Canton. Chiang Kai-shek served as commander at the Huangpu (Whampoa) Military Academy on the outskirts of Canton and built his early base of power around the academy's graduates. Mao Zedong got his start at the Peasant Training Institute in Canton and there developed his plans for rural revolution.

But the spiritual center of the Communist Revolution of 1949 was not in Guangdong, or in other coastal areas, but in inner China. As

# GUANGDONG PROVINCE, 1984

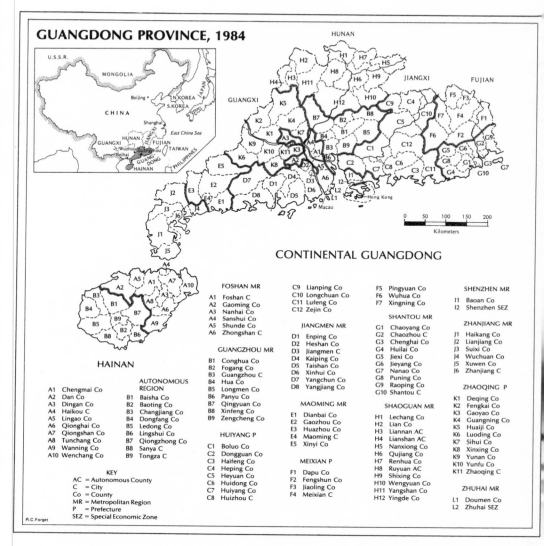

## CONTINENTAL GUANGDONG

### HAINAN

| A1 | Chengmai Co |
| A2 | Dan Co |
| A3 | Dingan Co |
| A4 | Haikou C |
| A5 | Lingao Co |
| A6 | Qionghai Co |
| A7 | Qiongshan Co |
| A8 | Tunchang Co |
| A9 | Wanning Co |
| A10 | Wenchang Co |

### AUTONOMOUS REGION

| B1 | Baisha Co |
| B2 | Baoting Co |
| B3 | Changjiang Co |
| B4 | Dongfang Co |
| B5 | Ledong Co |
| B6 | Lingshui Co |
| B7 | Qiongzhong Co |
| B8 | Sanya C |
| B9 | Tongza C |

### KEY

AC = Autonomous County
C  = City
Co = County
MR = Metropolitan Region
P  = Prefecture
SEZ = Special Economic Zone

R.C. Forget

### FOSHAN MR

| A1 | Foshan C |
| A2 | Gaoming Co |
| A3 | Nanhai Co |
| A4 | Sanshui Co |
| A5 | Shunde Co |
| A6 | Zhongshan C |

### GUANGZHOU MR

| B1 | Conghua Co |
| B2 | Fogang Co |
| B3 | Guangzhou C |
| B4 | Hua Co |
| B5 | Longmen Co |
| B6 | Panyu Co |
| B7 | Qingyuan Co |
| B8 | Xinfeng Co |
| B9 | Zengcheng Co |

### HUIYANG P

| C1 | Boluo Co |
| C2 | Dongguan Co |
| C3 | Haifeng Co |
| C4 | Heping Co |
| C5 | Heyuan Co |
| C6 | Huidong Co |
| C7 | Huiyang Co |
| C8 | Huizhou C |

| C9 | Lianping Co |
| C10 | Longchuan Co |
| C11 | Lufeng Co |
| C12 | Zejin Co |

### JIANGMEN MR

| D1 | Enping Co |
| D2 | Heshan Co |
| D3 | Jiangmen C |
| D4 | Kaiping Co |
| D5 | Taishan Co |
| D6 | Xinhui Co |
| D7 | Yangchun Co |
| D8 | Yangjiang Co |

### MAOMING MR

| E1 | Dianbai Co |
| E2 | Gaozhou Co |
| E3 | Huazhou Co |
| E4 | Maoming C |
| E5 | Xinyi Co |

### MEIXIAN P

| F1 | Dapu Co |
| F2 | Fengshun Co |
| F3 | Jiaoling Co |
| F4 | Meixian C |

| F5 | Pingyuan Co |
| F6 | Wuhua Co |
| F7 | Xingning Co |

### SHANTOU MR

| G1 | Chaoyang Co |
| G2 | Chaozhou C |
| G3 | Chenghai Co |
| G4 | Huilai Co |
| G5 | Jiexi Co |
| G6 | Jieyang Co |
| G7 | Nanao Co |
| G8 | Puning Co |
| G9 | Raoping Co |
| G10 | Shantou C |

### SHAOGUAN MR

| H1 | Lechang Co |
| H2 | Lian Co |
| H3 | Liannan AC |
| H4 | Lianshan AC |
| H5 | Nanxiong Co |
| H6 | Qujiang Co |
| H7 | Renhua Co |
| H8 | Ruyuan AC |
| H9 | Shixing Co |
| H10 | Wengyuan Co |
| H11 | Yangshan Co |
| H12 | Yingde Co |

### SHENZHEN MR

| I1 | Baoan Co |
| I2 | Shenzhen SEZ |

### ZHANJIANG MR

| J1 | Haikang Co |
| J2 | Lianjiang Co |
| J3 | Suixi Co |
| J4 | Wuchuan Co |
| J5 | Xuwen Co |
| J6 | Zhanjiang C |

### ZHAOQING P

| K1 | Deqing Co |
| K2 | Fengkai Co |
| K3 | Gaoyao Co |
| K4 | Guangning Co |
| K5 | Huaiji Co |
| K6 | Luoding Co |
| K7 | Sihui Co |
| K8 | Xinxing Co |
| K9 | Yunan Co |
| K10 | Yunfu Co |
| K11 | Zhaoqing C |

### ZHUHAI MR

| L1 | Doumen Co |
| L2 | Zhuhai SEZ |

China closed its doors to the capitalist world and turned inward after 1949, there was no role for a go-between with the outside. The Communist leaders brought to Guangdong the same political structure, the same policies, the same campaigns they brought to the rest of the country. Not only was new economic investment in the 1960s and early 1970s directed toward inner China, but politically as well

China became more introspective and nativistic. People who were too Westernized or too capitalistic, or who had overseas relatives and other contacts, were suspect and on the defensive. No province was better suited as a target for criticism than Guangdong, and no province was more completely wrenched by China's closing to the outside world.

The reforms after 1978 allowed Guangdong to resume its historical role of helping to meet the foreign challenge and enrich the nation, but the context was greatly changed. China was by then a strong, independent nation, and leadership was firmly in the hands of the Communist Party. Guangdong's role was not to push China to stand strong against foreigners but to lead the modification of the socialist system. The new context involved expanded competition in world trade and much higher levels of technology and education. Although Guangdong's new role had a historical base, reopening in the 1970s was perhaps as much a jolt to the system as closing had been in 1949. Leaders accustomed to propounding Maoism had to study Western management and technology, those engaged in political struggle joined the struggle for industrial efficiency, and those who had been denouncing capitalism began to learn from those they had been de-nouncing. The transition was by no means easy or universally wel-comed, and not all foreign ways were looked on with favor. One of Guangdong's roles was to sift out what was useful from a plethora of foreign practices.

Guangdong leaders sensed great opportunities, but many also feared making errors in complex new situations for which they had almost no experience. They aimed to bring a closed province of poor and poorly educated people into the modern world. The first decade of reform was dynamic but chaotic, with continuous economic, social, and political change.

In 1987 I spent seven months in Guangdong at the invitation of the provincial government in order to study and report on developments since reforms had begun. My host unit was the Provincial Economic Commission, responsible for Guangdong's overall economic devel-opment. I was told that my wife and I were the first such foreign guests in Guangdong and the only foreigners invited for a long-term stay at the provincial guest house. I am not aware of other foreigners who have been given a comparable opportunity to study a Chinese province.

Guangdong officials had several reasons for asking that such a study be undertaken. They were aware that the climate for foreign investment in Guangdong was not satisfactory. Yet they believed that the progress and openness of their province had been greater than most foreigners realized, and that an account of their recent experience, if told objectively, would improve the climate for foreign investment and better inform investors of the nature of their opportunities. They realized that their own propaganda was easily discounted, and they felt a foreign academic would have more credibility. Even more important to some of my hosts was their search for a vision of society that fit both China's tradition and world realities, and they welcomed the perspective of an outsider with more experience studying relevant countries than they had themselves.

From my conversations with provincial officials, I believe there are three major reasons I was invited to Guangdong. First, since I was the one foreign academic who had specialized in Guangdong's overall development, working with me required less effort. Only a handful of their officials spoke English, but I could read materials in the original Chinese and conduct my interviews in Mandarin. A few members of the provincial government had read my earlier book, *Canton under Communism: Programs and Politics in a Provincial Capital, 1949–1968,* either in the original or in a version translated for internal circulation. They did not agree with everything in the book, but they acknowledged it as a serious scholarly effort and knew that I was familiar with their basic organization, their policies, and their cities and counties. They knew also that the three months I had spent at Zhongshan University (Guangzhou) in the summer of 1980, as reforms were beginning, had provided me with an initial baseline perspective against which to chart changes.

Second, I had developed personal relationships of trust with several key Guangdong leaders. The Commonwealth of Massachusetts and the Province of Guangdong, drawing on their links in the old China trade, had established a sister-state relationship in 1983. As a member of the Massachusetts committee, I had helped host a number of leaders, including Governor Liang Lingguang, Vice-Governor Yang Li, and Economic Commission Director Zhang Gaoli (later vice-governor), and Deputy Director Yang Mai. When Governor Michael S. Dukakis in turn visited Governor Liang for a week in 1987, I served as his guide and interpreter in Guangdong.

Third, some officials had read the Chinese edition of my book *Japan as Number One.* They believed it played a role in making Japan's success known to the rest of the world, and they hoped that a book on Guangdong might help the world learn about their success.

When I received the invitation in 1985 I wanted very much to accept it, for I had continued to follow major provincial developments so that I might someday write a sequel to *Canton under Communism*. I realized that in no society are people entirely open with outsiders, and that despite Guangdong's increased freedom, there was much that was not easily accessible to foreigners, but I knew that this invitation would make it much easier to see many places and interview key people. It turned out that the willingness of officials to show me places and to discuss Guangdong's problems, though not unlimited, far exceeded my expectations.

My biggest concern in accepting the invitation was whether I would have the independence to conduct my research and write up my results in a way that met academic standards of objectivity. I spent a week in the summer of 1986 in Guangzhou to explore this with provincial officials. I explained that I could not be like Edgar Snow, Rewi Alley, and other foreign observers who reported only the favorable side of China's developments; I had to have the freedom to report negative aspects as I saw them. The officials responded that times had changed and that China's policies had changed as well. As a result of the Great Leap Forward (1958–1960) and the Cultural Revolution (1966–1976), leaders had increasingly come to understand the dangers of blind followers, and they encouraged me to describe Guangdong completely in my own terms. I was to pay all my direct expenses in China to help preserve this independence, and the officials agreed not to review what I wrote to see whether my conclusions were acceptable to them. The manuscript would reflect my personal findings, and they acknowledged that these might differ from their own views. I spent June through December of 1987 in Guangdong carrying out the fieldwork. I returned for three weeks in the summer of 1988 to round out and update my research. I made the end of 1988, ten years after reforms began, the cut-off year for this book and have incorporated the latest statistics then available.

In ten weeks of traveling throughout the province in 1987, I visited and interviewed officials in all fourteen of Guangdong's prefectures and prefectural-level units and in all three special economic zones. I traveled through over seventy of Guangdong's one hundred counties and interviewed officials in thirty of them, including some that were very poor. I did not have time to go to all the province's counties, but I visited every one that I asked to see. I saw not only state factories, farms, mines, and commercial and service enterprises but collective enterprises and individual enterprises. Before each trip, I tried to learn about the locality by reading relevant materials and getting the perspective of provincial officials, and then selected certain key issues to explore in detail. Local officials were told before my arrival that I was a friend of China and that they were to be frank and provide the information I desired. I traveled with my research assistant from the Provincial Economic Commission, who had helped me arrange my schedule.

In a typical local area, I received several three-hour briefings from the leaders of the local economic commission, which was under the provincial commission, and from the deputy head of the county or prefecture in charge of economic work. These briefings provided an overview of developments in the locality, and I had ample opportunity to raise questions. Although the briefings were informal, following local protocol I was received as an official from the Provincial Economic Commission. I then visited several key factories, construction projects, markets, and other noteworthy local spots. During the course of a day I had opportunity to socialize with a number of people of varying ranks and specialties. All interviews and conversations were in Mandarin, and in the few cases in rustic areas where I had trouble understanding local accents or where officials did not speak Mandarin, my assistant translated between their Cantonese and my Mandarin. In the evening I dictated a summary of all my notes and observations for the day, and these tapes were sent back to Boston to be transcribed. I was usually given some statistics and written reports about the locality, and in this book all data without specific citation come from these reports, mostly unpublished.

In the five months I spent in Guangzhou, I typically had one or two three-hour interviews each day with working-level provincial officials in charge of various aspects of the economy. Many of the interviews were suggested by my host unit, but visits were arranged to see specialists in every area I requested except in military affairs. Since 1980 I have had the opportunity to interview a governor, two provincial first Party secretaries, five vice-governors, and a mayor of Guangzhou as well as hundreds of other provincial, prefectural, county, town, and village officials and ordinary citizens. Some were franker than others. They did not volunteer information about intra-Party disagreements that had not already been made public, and many understandably tried to portray the province's development in a favorable light. On the whole I found those I spoke to remarkably candid in admitting problems, far more so than when I had visited Guangdong earlier. I have chosen to keep all these sources anonymous to avoid any risk to them in case of changing political currents. In my fieldwork I thought of myself as an anthropologist, trying constantly to get a broad sociological overview of major developments in the province.

I spent the rest of my time in Guangzhou reading materials, making site visits in and around Guangzhou, preparing for interviews and visits, and typing up my notes. I had ample opportunity to socialize with Chinese I knew outside of official circles, including those I had come to know at Harvard, to talk with other foreigners in Guangzhou, and to walk along the streets. I learned a great deal through my wife, Charlotte Ikels, who speaks Cantonese and was gathering information for her own research in visits to two hundred ordinary families in Guangzhou. Before and since the fieldwork, I have also learned from Chinese students from Guangdong studying in the United States. I spent several weeks in Hong Kong interviewing Chinese and foreign businesspeople, officials, academics, and others who had had experience, not necessarily pleasant, in Guangdong. Hong Kong periodicals in Chinese and English that comment, often critically, on Guangdong affairs provided another useful source.

Foreign trade has been central to Guangdong's development, and I was fortunate that John Kamm, the foreigner who knows it best, was willing to write about it for this book. Aided by his fluency in Cantonese and Mandarin and his training in anthropology and East Asian studies, he was the first foreign businessman to establish an office in Guangzhou. He has been traveling to all parts of the province for over a decade from his home in Hong Kong. He not only has written Chapter 11 and worked closely with me to integrate it into the book but has been an invaluable guide and critic.

A few comments about procedures should also be mentioned. I have adopted the pinyin system of romanization (e.g., Guangdong, rather than the former transliteration, Kwangtung) used in mainland China, except for names of well-known Chinese living in Hong Kong, Taiwan, or overseas, for which I used the most common transliterations. All dollar amounts refer to U.S. dollars. From 1978 until 1981 the official yuan-dollar exchange rate fluctuated from 1.49 to 1.71 yuan to one U.S. dollar. In January 1981 the rate was set at 1.53 yuan to the dollar and this was raised on January 1, 1985, to 2.80; on October 30, 1985, to 3.20; and on July 5, 1986, to 3.70. Since then it has been unchanged. (See Chapter 11 for black market and internal market exchange rates.) All weights given in tons refer to metric tons. I have at times used the masculine personal pronouns to include both men and women to simplify the style and because a majority of cadres, including almost all in top positions, are men, but there are substantial numbers of women cadres at working levels, particularly in areas such as public health, education, and neighborhood organization.

Ever since collectivization and nationalization were completed in 1956, there have been Chinese leaders who urged a change in their nation's basic system. Some raised questions in 1956–57 but were squelched by the anti-rightist campaign. Some spoke out in 1959–1962, after the Great Leap Forward collapsed, but they were silenced by Mao Zedong. His death in 1976 removed a powerful obstacle, but by that time the proponents of reform had in any case become much stronger. In Chapter 1, I consider what happened in the Cultural Revolution to create a ground swell for reform that was strong enough to overcome the kinds of resistance that have thwarted change in other socialist countries. I trace its course both to understand the motive force for reform and to describe the baseline from which Guangdong's reforms began.

When its relationship with the Soviet Union deteriorated after 1969, China began to turn to the capitalist world and was increasingly exposed to developments abroad. Chinese Communist Party leaders, schooled in fraternal socialism, took notice of discussions of reform in other Communist countries, but they were moved even more deeply, especially in Guangdong, by the industrial success of their East Asian neighbors. Despite their professions of patriotism, many in China had nagging doubts that Chinese culture might again undermine their efforts to industrialize. Was industrialization the preserve of white Westerners? As word spread of the success of Japan and other East Asian powers, many mainland Chinese gained confidence that if people of Chinese ancestry in Taiwan, Singapore, and Hong Kong could succeed, they could too. China had to learn how they had achieved so much, even if this meant new policies, new management, and new organization. They could gain this information from many sources, but most came from the *nan damen,* the large southern gateway, Hong Kong. This was especially true for Guangdong. How that gateway, a bastion of free market capitalism, shaped the province's reforms is the topic of Chapter 2.

After these two chapters on the sources and nature of the reform impulse, the reforms themselves are described in Chapter 3. Chinese leaders realized that they suffered from the same systemic problems found in other socialist countries and that to liven up the economy, they needed fundamental reforms in virtually every area: in the city and the countryside, in industry and agriculture, in society, even in the political system. But what were the critical areas and how could they pace and guide reforms to keep them moving without being derailed, as had happened in other socialist countries? They acknowledged that they were groping and experimenting, but they nevertheless pushed ahead with a series of bold reforms.

Chapters 4 through 9 trace what happened in the first decade of reforms as their impact spread to various parts of the province. Changes were felt early in the newly created special economic zones, especially Shenzhen and Zhuhai (Chapter 4), but in fact some of the greatest transformations came not in these zones but in certain counties in the Inner Pearl Delta (Chapter 5). The Inner Delta, for reasons of history and proximity to Hong Kong, grew more rapidly than other parts of the province, but paradoxically the great capital of the Inner Delta, Guangzhou, lagged slightly behind them because remaking the old city proved very difficult (Chapter 6). As change spread throughout the province from the Inner Delta, the prefectural capitals (Chapter 7) helped guide developments in the more backward parts of each prefecture, the mountainous areas of continental Guangdong (Chapter 8). Development began last in remote Hainan Island (Chapter 9). It remained part of Guangdong until 1988, when it was made a separate province to help speed its modernization.

Chapters 10 and 11 analyze the immediate forces, internal and external, that drove Guangdong forward. Chapter 10 describes how entrepreneurs, both political and economic, helped Guangdong take advantage of new opportunities, and Chapter 11 relates how Guangdong was propelled by its efforts to produce for international markets.

Chapters 12 and 13 seek to provide perspective and analysis. Chapter 12 looks at the nature of Guangdong society amid reform; Chapter 13 compares the broad pattern of development in Guangdong and in the emerging Guangdong–Hong Kong region to that of other East Asian industrializing economies.

PART I

*The Winds of Change*

# 1.

# The Cultural Revolution: Disaster Strengthens the Reform Impulse

"How can I explain to my children," asked the first Party secretary of a county in Guangdong, "what happened in the Cultural Revolution?" While still in his early twenties, he had just returned from a stint in the army to become an official in his home county when the Cultural Revolution broke out. When Red Guards began attacking "those in authority," he was at first criticized for shielding some of his superiors. After passing scrutiny, however, he was selected as one of a handful of civilians to join a small core of army officials in running the county. "I myself," he added, "have trouble believing what happened and understanding how we could have been so mistaken."

Guangdong residents are still trying to understand what went wrong in the turbulent decade that began in May 1966. By the time the Cultural Revolution was over, it had derailed the modest reforms of the early 1960s, mobilized thousands of youth, created mass warfare, terrorized the vulnerable, disrupted the economy, and fundamentally altered the course of Chinese development. The initial attack on "old culture" and the launching of the Red Guards paved the way for Chairman Mao's real purpose, the purge of leading Party bureaucrats, but the resulting chaos led to military control of civilian institutions, the dispersal of the mass organizations, and finally the gradual rehabilitation of those purged. At its worst it was a reign of terror, and many later wondered how they could have been so cruel. Knowledgeable officials and intellectuals, looking back, have diverse explanations, personal, political, and historical, for what occurred, but they keep returning to a number of themes.

One common explanation stresses the importance of Chairman Mao's hold on the masses. When he fully employed the propaganda apparatus at his disposal, no one could stop him. A vice-governor and former top aide to Tao Zhu, Guangdong's preeminent leader from 1952 until the Cultural Revolution, put it this way: "Mao Zedong did not create the Great Leap Forward. We all did. We lacked experience, we lacked knowledge. Mao may have lit the spark, but he could not have done it alone. We all joined in. China was so poor. We had so little and hoped for so much. We did not have the experience to judge what was objectively feasible. But the Cultural Revolution? Mao created it. We cadres were not with him, but he had a hold over the masses and he used it fully."

Soviet specialist Robert Tucker has examined the unusually strong "hold over the masses" that various leaders have had in different countries, and he has determined that in all cases the populace had experienced disasters and believed the great leader responsible for its rescue. In pre-1949 China, the years of turmoil, internal war, foreign exploitation, and continuing poverty created a desperate longing for a leader strong enough to end what the people regarded as oppression by both foreign powers and their own capitalist and landlord classes. The identification of Mao with the victory in 1949, the expulsion of foreign "imperialists," the dethroning of exploitive capitalists and land-lords, the effort to defend and ennoble the common person, and the improvements in agriculture and industry made him a popular hero. Even those who later renounced Mao acknowledged his contributions to China before 1957 and believed in his patriotism and his desire to improve the livelihood of the masses. Knowing little of the outside world, however, Mao pushed for a pattern of development not in keeping with world realities, and from the 1960s on he faced an additional struggle against growing numbers of cadres (*ganbu,* that is, state officials, working in administrative positions; they are frequently but not necessarily Party members) who wanted to alter his approach.

Mao enhanced his image through a powerful propaganda apparatus, and the study of his Little Red Book early in the Cultural Revolution made emulating him a veritable cult. Even cadres who nourished serious doubts about his leadership after 1957 remained silent—sometimes out of fear, sometimes because they saw no alternative, and sometimes because they thought that public belief in Mao facilitated their task of uniting and governing the world's largest nation, so recently a "loose sheet of sand." Many youth and even some cadres, lacking broader experience or education, had no basis for evaluating the impact of Mao's willingness to sacrifice economic growth for ideological goals, his stress on "reds" over "experts," his attacks on intellectuals, and his commitment to continuing the class struggle. They simply accepted what they were told.

In 1966, when he wanted to fight the growing number of high-level cadres upset by his rule, Mao could not count on the support of ordinary cadres; they feared that they, too, might eventually be implicated. He therefore, with military support from Lin Biao, called upon the youth to attack those who did not share his purer vision. The estimated eleven million Red Guards he greeted during the eight rallies held in Tiananmen Square between August 18 and November 26, 1966, were powerfully moved; millions of others who saw movies of the dramatic events were equally affected. At that time they had no knowledge that would have given them a more critical perspective, and they stood ready to confront selfish officials and carry out Mao's wishes to create a better China. In 1967–68 some Red Guards, told to submit to those whom they had formerly been told to attack, became disillusioned. And in 1972, after it was publicly announced that Lin Biao, earlier chosen by Mao himself to be his successor, had been killed while trying to escape after a failed coup attempt, many people began to wonder privately about the Chairman's leadership. Doubts had increased by 1976, as disasters continued. Nevertheless, many of these doubters had been touched by Mao's magic a decade earlier.

Mao's explanation for launching the Great Proletarian Cultural Revolution struck a responsive chord. Many workers and peasants in 1966 were unhappy that the higher levels of cultural and educational institutions were still dominated by members of the pre-1949 bourgeois classes and their children. Ordinary people often believed in Mao's efforts to ensure that he would be succeeded by those committed to his vision of an egalitarian sovereign China, and they thought that officials who issued arbitrary commands, enjoyed special perquisites, and lacked concern for the welfare of the masses deserved to be criticized. When lurid stories of bureaucratic excesses appeared, people clamored for the punishment of those involved.

Furthermore, the long years of earlier political campaigns had left strong resentments. People who had undergone months or years of mental torture in endless rounds of accusation known as "criticism" or "struggle sessions," in labor reform, or in reeducation did not easily forget those whom they considered responsible. Although these campaigns had had specific mottoes and targets, within neighborhood and work units individuals tended to defend their friends and attack their enemies. It was not always possible to know what had been placed in one's dossier or by whom, but many who had been affected had their suspicions and were ready to act on them.

Cadres and intellectuals who opposed the Cultural Revolution were afraid to say so. Ever since the anti-rightist campaign of 1957, everyone had understood that it was more dangerous to be considered a "rightist," that is, one who raised questions about high-level policies and about mass mobilization, than a "leftist," one who eagerly followed orders. Those labeled rightists had been subject to "struggle sessions" and sent to labor camps where the examination of their thoughts continued. Many never came back. Cadres had been under pressure since 1957 to refrain from criticism and to declare publicly their support for Chairman Mao. As young people were declaring themselves Red Guards and revolutionary rebels, cadres wanted to prove that they too supported the masses. Anyone who resisted was in danger of being "struggled against" in mass demonstrations and hauled off by the crowds with no certainty of safe return. Almost no one was ready to take such risks.

Moreover, few believed that the struggles would go on so long. Having seen previous campaigns, cadres thought that if they promptly sided with the masses, the struggles would soon be over. Provincial, municipal, and county leaders handed over the symbols of office, the chops for certifying documents, because they believed that once they proved their commitment they would be allowed to return to their posts. They underestimated Mao's willingness to purge so many high-level cadres and to push China to the brink of chaos in order to assert his own control and select his successors. Even Mao did not realize how much resistance he would encounter, how long the disorder would continue, and how difficult it would be to both maintain order and keep his vision alive. Once the masses were involved and battle lines were drawn, the struggles took on a life of their own that no one could fully control.

A final contributing factor often mentioned was the personal loyalty of some to Mao, whether out of conviction or opportunism. These included military officers like Lin Biao (until 1970); propagandists like Mao's wife, Jiang Qing, and Yao Wenyuan; and sizable numbers of cadres at the local as well as national level who hoped to position themselves for a role in the post-Mao leadership.

Whatever their explanation of its origins, all agree that during the Cultural Revolution, the country veered out of control.[1]

## The Cultural Revolution in Guangdong, 1966–1976

*The Launching of the Red Guards, Summer and Fall 1966.* On June 2, the *People's Daily* reported that Chairman Mao had approved a wall poster at Beijing University by Nie Yuanzi, a Party secretary in the philosophy department. The poster criticized the university's Party committee and called for an attack on revisionists. University and middle-school students (ordinarily ages twelve to eighteen) were told to attack "bourgeois culture" and to help create an appropriate new culture through the Great Proletarian Cultural Revolution. Youth in Guangdong, as elsewhere, responded immediately. They demonstrated, held mass rallies, wrote posters and news sheets, and struggled against targets selected for attack. When Mao signified his support for the movement by donning a Red Guard arm band on August 18, after the Eleventh Plenum of the Eighth Party Congress, Red Guards blossomed everywhere.

Young people in China had been much less exposed to the wider world than had those in many other countries. Television was not yet common, and radio had been tightly controlled. Few youth thus had any basis for challenging what they were told. Nor did many have a well-developed notion of Red Guard goals, and they eagerly sought out those who came from the North with more reliable information about what was expected. Mao relied not only on his own personality cult but on the young people's grievances. Once mobilized, they acted on some of their own complaints against red tape, bureaucratism, excessively tight control over their lives, political study, the lack of opportunities to pursue higher education, and, above all, being sent to the countryside with return at best uncertain.

Schools and universities organized their own Red Guard groups, which then affiliated with similar groups locally and nationally. Schools closed a month early in June 1966 and remained closed during the 1966–67 academic year to allow students to support the revolution.

Activity was greatest in the larger cities and in the elite schools. In the early months, membership was mostly restricted to the children of "good social classes" (workers, peasants, and revolutionary cadres). Theoretically they were attacking the "four olds" (ideology, culture, habits, and customs), but in fact they usually began by attacking the hapless targets of earlier campaigns—former landlords, capitalists, Kuomintang members, and rightists and their friends, relatives, and sympathizers. Some activity, such as taking down street signs and mementoes that implied a connection with capitalism or lecturing neighborhood capitalists, was harmless. But students also struggled against teachers and school administrators, sometimes physically as well as verbally, for not adequately supporting the revolution. And when masses of students gathered in the streets, the more radical often gained control, defacing or tearing down stores, temples, churches, and statues that could be seen as remnants of bourgeois culture. While collecting evidence, they grilled, abused, and sometimes struck those whose homes they inspected.

Local youth, told to *chuanlian* (link up with other Red Guards around the country), took to the trains and roads, and similarly Red Guards from elsewhere came to Guangdong. Students were given free train rides, access to public buildings to lay out their bedding at night, and free meals prepared by various institutions in towns and cities throughout the country. Some enjoyed the unprecedented opportunity for free travel and sightseeing, but others were deadly earnest about struggling against authorities who were said to be resisting the wishes of Chairman Mao.

Local people were especially frightened by those who were from outside the province and therefore less constrained by personal connections. Ordinary citizens behaved cautiously, as they had during the warlord struggles of the 1920s and 1930s, during the War of Resistance against the Japanese, and during the Civil War between the Communists and the Kuomintang. They stayed close to their homes, boarded up their doors, and avoided being out on the streets in the evening. Even during the day they moved around no more than necessary to get to work and to do minimal shopping. They took few risks, and by wearing badges and placing signs in their windows they tried to show that they too supported the revolution. Rural people, as they had in the turmoil before 1949, organized self-defense groups to protect themselves both against groups of traveling youth who might attack them and against looters who might take advantage of the turmoil.

*Storming the Headquarters, October 1966 to January 1967.* Beginning in October 1966 the target gradually shifted from the "four olds" to the "power holders [*dangquan pai*] taking the capitalist road," that is, the top Party leaders in every unit. Not only youthful Red Guards but "revolutionary rebel" cadres in offices and factories everywhere were encouraged to join in the attack. Leading Party officials in Guangzhou were publicly paraded about and struggled against in large accusation meetings. Although communication was highly imperfect, local Red Guard leaders observed who was singled out in Beijing and suggested similar targets nearby; the news spread by word of mouth and by informal Red Guard news sheets. Local guards then attacked, sometimes with outside help.

On the eve of the Cultural Revolution, as noted above, even the highest level of cadres in Guangdong and Beijing did not believe that Mao would eventually push out virtually every top Party official in the country. Only later could they see Mao's determination to whip up the youth to topple the major leaders of the Party everywhere. Since the Communist Party was the bedrock of authority, it was hard for people in Guangdong to believe that their chief local Party leaders, Tao Zhu and Zhao Ziyang, would be forced out. Tao Zhu left Guangzhou in May 1966 to become vice-premier and head of the Party's Propaganda Department in Beijing, and close friends of his report that he had no idea what he was getting into and no trepidation about going. With other high Party figures he was attacked in Beijing in the fall of 1966 and, on January 3, 1967, was taken into custody by the Red Guards. Although his fate was not widely known until December 1978, when a moving letter from his daughter, Tao Siling, was published, he was struggled against, isolated, denied medical attention when ill, and died in prison in 1969.[2]

Zhao Ziyang, long second in charge in Guangdong under Tao Zhu, became the top leader there after Tao's departure for Beijing. Beginning in October 1966, Zhao Ziyang was paraded about and publicly struggled against in more than twenty mass demonstrations. He was injured in the process. The best-known pictures at the time show him, like high officials in Beijing, wearing a dunce cap and bowing to the masses as if in apology for his errors. Witnesses of the struggle sessions report that he remained erect and dignified despite the shouts of the crowd. After disappearing from public view in 1967, he did not reappear until 1973; he became premier in 1980 and after 1987 Party general secretary of all China.

Many high-level cadres were injured during the unpredictable mass criticism sessions. Zeng Sheng, former mayor of Guangzhou and a hero of the War of Resistance against Japan while commander of the East River Guerrillas, was struck on the head by his accusers; he was reportedly the first Guangdong official to be badly wounded. He was so affected by the bruises and by his subsequent four years of isolation that he had difficulty communicating for over six months after his release from prison several years later, and he never fully recovered.

Even as late as January 1967 local leaders could not imagine that all major offices would be taken over and Party activities suspended. Yet on January 22, following the national pattern, all major Party and government offices in Guangdong were occupied by revolutionary rebels, with the tacit support of the army, and officials handed over the symbols of office. Officials later reported that they had wanted to show their cooperation with the revolutionary rebels and had no idea that it would take several years or, in some cases, a decade or longer before their names were cleared and they were allowed to return to work. They could not know that some would return but not be allowed to work, and that many would never return at all.

Guidance for the takeovers came through the Cultural Revolution Group *(wenge xiaozu)* headquartered in Beijing, but mass organizations had considerable independence. In June 1966, local Party officials had guided the attacks, and the children of elite cadres, especially of military officers, had dominated the Red Guard movement. But as the Party lost control of the movement to the Cultural Revolution Group in late summer, Red Guard members were no longer exclusively from the "good social classes." Expression of correct attitudes *(biaoxian)* became more important than class background *(chengfen)*. The children of bourgeois intellectuals—in addition to the children of peasants and workers—came to be the leaders of the most prominent Red Guard groups. These "rebel" Red Guards, long distraught that their parents' background had cast a shadow over their education and career opportunities, had been further upset in the summer of 1966 when their heritage kept them out of the movement. They remained furious at local officials who had treated their families like enemies of the people, and in late 1966 when they were allowed to join the Red Guards, they were thus more motivated to attack local power holders than were the children of local cadres and army officers. In the months leading up to the January takeover in Guangdong, several thousand Red Guards from the North also played a crucial role in attacking local officials and in bringing information from Beijing.

Yet confusion was rampant. It was not always clear to local Red Guards or cadres which Red Guard group was dominant in Beijing or what leaders there wanted them to do. Local leaders under siege also helped launch Red Guards who were in fact defending them, but all claimed to be supporting Mao and the Cultural Revolution. The Cultural Revolution Group complained that some were deliberately creating confusion by "waving the red flag to fight the red flag."

Within the radical groups supporting the January takeover, there were some who tried to protect key leaders from excessively severe attacks. Soon after the takeover, word came from Beijing through the local military that several hundred of the very highest leaders in Guangdong, including Zhao Ziyang, jailed under military custody, were to be "protected from the masses." Though Zhao was paraded before the masses many times thereafter, the military generally protected him from physical attack. Many who underwent "thought examination" and criticism sessions in locations unknown to friends and relatives regarded the term "protected by the military" as a euphemism. Still, many of the top cadres who were taken to Meihua Yuan, the military headquarters on the northeastern outskirts of Guangzhou, where they were placed in barracks prepared for their arrival, felt that the military was more disciplined and fundamentally more conservative, and therefore less wild, than the worst mass organizations. Even if they were struggled against and isolated, those held by the military were allowed to sleep and received three meals a day.

Many cadres were not so fortunate. They remained in their homes or in special housing in their units, in hospitals, or in other public buildings, where they were subjected to verbal and physical abuse far less controlled and far less predictable. Those not taken away also lived under the threat of unannounced visits by groups that ransacked their homes for incriminating materials.

*Military Takeover, Mass Struggle, and Revolutionary Alliance, February 1967 to April 1969.* After the Party headquarters were taken over, some officials in Guangdong and elsewhere tried to maintain their influence through cadres still on the job, in what rebels later called the "February adverse current." Disorder was too great, however, as supporters of power holders clashed with their accusers, and Mao called in the troops to maintain order. By March 15, the Provisional Military Control Commission was established. Local military officials, led by Huang Yongsheng, head of the Guangzhou Military Region, were responsible for maintaining order and tended to crack down on warring Red

Guard groups. Middle-school and university students were assigned to military training under the direction of the military. Even this, however, did not stop the continuing chaos.

In Guangzhou, as elsewhere, struggles between Red Guards took on a life of their own as many groups became more intent on attacking each other than on attacking those in authority. Most groups tended to be affiliated in some loose way with one of the two great factions, the Red Flag and the East Wind. Former participants interviewed in Guangdong and other areas in the 1980s believed there was no pattern of who belonged to which group other than personal predilection, but Stanley Rosen's careful analysis shows that Red Flag (rebel) members more often came from "have not" intellectual and "bad class" backgrounds, while the East Wind (conservative) members were more often children of officials, workers, and soldiers.[3]

In April 1967, as the radicals gained ascendency in Beijing, the military was encouraged to support the rebel Left in order to preserve the gains made in getting rid of Party power holders through mass struggle. One way of supporting leftist groups was to supply weapons to them, but as they began to use them, other Red Guard groups used their contacts with different military or public security groups to acquire guns or at least spears of their own. Some in Guangzhou stormed a public security warehouse to seize weapons for themselves. Armed clashes occurred between the factions, both inside offices and on the street. At one point, one group was meeting in Sun Yat-sen Memorial Hall while opponents met nearby in the Yuexiu Stadium. Both groups were armed with long spears, and when some from the stadium attacked those in the hall, many were injured. In another incident, a group occupying the headquarters of the General Union building on the north bank of the Pearl River, not far from Shamian, was set upon by others who had been occupying the nearby Aiqun (then called Chongzhong) Daxia, the famous prewar hotel. In Sanyuanli, just north of where the railway station was later built and near where local Chinese resisting the British touched off the Opium War, parading Red Guards were fired upon by some rural militia and upwards of thirty people died. At the entrance to Zhongshan University one morning, the bodies of senior history professors were found hanging from the trees where they had been lynched.[4]

Between April and August, not only Red Guards but various groups throughout the province took advantage of the anarchy to settle accounts with old enemies, whoever they might be. In Haifeng, along the east coast of Guangdong, some descendants of the early revolutionary leader Peng Pai were killed, which set off several rounds of attack and counterattack. In places like Guangning, Yangjiang, and Dianbai counties, poor areas in western Guangdong, thousands were killed in clashes.

No one attempted to keep an accurate count of how many were killed, and some authorities clearly tried to downplay the numbers. Nor did anyone carefully investigate to see which suicides could be attributed to the Cultural Revolution. But from various accounts of witnesses, it is clear that tens of thousands died in various parts of Guangdong in the confrontations and from suicides related to the intense pressure that individuals were under. Groups affiliated with Li Yizhe collected a list of forty-two thousand people said to have been killed in armed clashes, but another, more conservative, estimate placed the number at nearer to thirty thousand.[5] Still, in Guangdong there was less violence than in places like Guangxi, where officials estimated that over a hundred thousand died and unofficial estimates ran as high as three hundred thousand.

The turning point in the Cultural Revolution was the Wuhan Incident of July 20, 1967, when high-ranking leftist officials sent out from Beijing to support the rebels in Wuhan were detained by the local military commander there. In the fall of 1966 Mao had urged people not to fear disorder, but in the spring of 1967 many military officials, called in to keep a modicum of order, were not happy about allowing certain favored youth groups to run rampant. The Wuhan commander, Chen Caidao, refused to reopen the struggle. Clashes in Guangzhou reached their peak in the weeks after Chen detained the Beijing officials. In late August and early September, Mao, Lin Biao, and the Gang of Four (Jiang Qing and three of her associates) had no choice but to make peace with local military commanders and allow them to control some of the greatest excesses. Mao and the others tried to consolidate their gains the best they could. In line with the new efforts, Zhou Enlai received representatives of different Guangzhou Red Guard factions in Beijing in a series of peace talks from late August until mid-November. This made it possible to hold Guangzhou's semiannual trade fair in the fall of 1967, albeit a month later than usual. In the meantime the Provisional Military Control Commission in Guangdong began collecting weapons and cracking down on those who were creating too much disorder.

In September 1967 the Military Control Commission moved in

force in Guangzhou to establish firmer control, but even then theirs was not an easy task. When they went to Zhongshan University to take several faction leaders into custody, for example, other students protected them and the military had no way to find or identify them. By late September most of the armed outbreaks were under control, however.

Groups of soldiers were put in charge of every important unit throughout the province. In a county of roughly a million people (in a province that then had almost fifty million in almost one hundred counties), for example, several hundred soldiers took charge and divided themselves into groups to lead each major government office, commune, factory, and school. These soldiers tended to be lower in rank and younger than those in large municipal and provincial offices. At the county level, the military generally criticized a smaller portion of Party officials than it did at higher levels. One county official reported that no one was executed in his county, only one person died in a mass struggle, and fewer than twenty committed suicide, some of which may not have been related directly to the Cultural Revolution.

Offices, factories, and schools were reorganized along military lines. Workers and students were given military training and expected to follow military discipline. Not only did soldiers lack specialized training to run offices and factories, but some were scarcely literate and virtually none had university training. They were told to investigate thoroughly every member of their work unit, examining his or her history, connections, and attitudes to ensure that each was committed to the revolution. They had a mandate to criticize anyone with capitalist tendencies. Commonly the soldiers concentrated on this political work and allowed other cadres, within limits, to continue the operation of the offices. If nothing else, fear led people to comply.

Once order was restored, the local military began trying to form alliances with select cadres and representatives of mass organizations in order to rebuild the political and economic order. The key ruling group within each work unit was a "revolutionary committee," which combined Party and administrative functions. Preparatory revolutionary committees were set up for each province, municipality, and county in the fall of 1967, and the Guangdong Provincial Revolutionary Committee and the Guangzhou Revolutionary Committee were formally established on February 21, 1968. Although rebels had a sympathetic ear in Beijing from late March to early June 1968, the most radical tended to lose out when the military reestablished local order. Those told to stop the struggle believed they were being punished for what they had been encouraged to do a year or two earlier. As the military authorities began cracking down, the most determined rebels staged armed resistance during the summer of 1968, but by August the mass organizations had largely been dismantled.

At the Ninth Party Congress in April 1969, Mao and Lin Biao endeavored to stabilize the new leadership and declare an end to the Cultural Revolution. Tensions between Lin and Mao later erupted in 1971, however, and conflicts between Zhou Enlai and Deng Xiaoping on one side and the Gang of Four on the other made it impossible to provide the Party and government with any clear direction until after the fall of 1976, when Mao died, the Gang of Four was captured, and the Cultural Revolution finally ended.

*The Rustication of Youth and the Establishment of May Seventh Cadre Schools, Spring 1968.* To reestablish order in 1968, cadres and representatives from mass organizations had to be screened by the local military to ensure that they would go along with the new leadership. Some college students were assigned to work in factories, in an effort to quiet down the cities. Because there were few urban employment opportunities, however, most former Red Guards, the "intellectual youth" (*zhishi qingnian,* students in grades 8 through 12) were sent to the countryside. A small minority from military and select cadre families were able to find opportunities in the cities. In all, some 994,000 Guangdong urban youth were sent to work in rural areas. The largest group, about 100,000, went to state farms on Hainan Island. Since the gaps between rural and urban life were great, few urban youth wanted to stay away from the cities, but military and state control was sufficiently tight that they felt they had no choice but to comply. Having originally responded to Mao's call, many were by then thoroughly disillusioned with the leadership and discouraged about their own future.

On May 7, 1968, the second anniversary of Mao's jotting a note in the margin of a book he was reading that it would be good for cadres to combine study and physical labor, Guangdong, like other provinces, began establishing May Seventh Cadre Schools. In early 1969 over four hundred of the approximately eight hundred cadres in the Central South Bureau of the Party, which supervised a six-province region and had its headquarters in Guangdong, were sent to a barren wilderness in Shangcao, Lian County, in northwestern Guangdong, once used by Taiping rebels as a granary. Guangdong provincial officials were sent to large state farms in Yingde and Lechang counties, a few hours north of Guangzhou on the North River. Guangzhou municipal officials were sent to Conghua, just above the city. Counties set up their own May Seventh Cadre Schools for their cadres, usually located near the county seat. There all cadres in government and Party offices spent their term of months or years, engaging in physical labor and studying Mao's *Thoughts* under the guidance of soldiers. Cadres judged to have no political problems in accepting the new leadership of their work units were sometimes allowed to return after several months. Others who were judged politically questionable remained until the late 1970s. Cadres became cynical about the blatantly political goals of their study, and those allowed to return quickly were deeply relieved.

Teachers, university professors, and other intellectuals generally stayed longer. Even in the late 1980s, less than 1 percent of Guangdong's adults were college graduates and less than 8 percent were high school graduates. In the 1950s almost anyone with a high school education was regarded as an intellectual, and even in the late 1980s, although education had expanded considerably, all college graduates were considered intellectuals and intellectuals from diverse fields felt a common bond. Since nearly anyone who was able to afford a high school or university education before 1949 came from a "bad class" background, nearly all who had completed their training before 1949 had long been suspect. Only slowly were they allowed to return to work, and many did not come back until 1975. Most universities were not fully functioning until the fall of 1977, after the resumption of entrance examinations.

*The Economy under Military Occupation, 1967–1976.* In work units, because some people were constantly being struggled against and many with specialized knowledge were removed after January 1967, work was at best chaotic, sometimes almost nonexistent. Although cadres were sent to May Seventh Schools in rotation, those who remained behind did not always have the expertise or information required to do their assigned work.

Long-term planning was virtually impossible between 1966 and 1976, and in 1966–67 even annual plans were suspended. No effort was made to have a real multiyear plan between 1966 and 1971, and the fourth five-year plan, which began in 1971, was not based on the usual detailed planning procedure.

The Provincial Revolutionary Committee combined the work of

Party and government organizations. Under it a political group *(zhengzhi gongzuozu)* managed political affairs. The Provincial Planning Commission, Economic Commission, Science and Technology Commission, and Agricultural Commission were collapsed into a Production Group *(shengchanzu)*, which after 1967 tried to make annual plans and ensure that they were met. But because of the chaos in supply lines, the Production Group concentrated on only the most essential goods and tried to maintain at least minimal levels of production and distribution.

The policy for the countryside by the early 1970s was cautious: to grow enough rice to avoid starvation. Even local areas that had formerly specialized in other crops and had imported rice were expected to become self-sufficient in grain. Some areas that had previously produced little grain had to dig up land planted in specialized crops in order to grow rice, even if the soil was not suitable. Most rural cadres and farmers complied for fear of being attacked as bourgeois, though some areas not supposed to grow specialized crops got away with it by in addition increasing rice yields enough to meet quotas. Production teams were expected first to meet grain quotas, then other procurement quotas, and only then could they produce for their own needs. Private plots were extremely limited and private markets were at best highly restricted, in some areas nonexistent. Prices were tightly controlled, and goods were of poor quality and limited variety. Pork, chicken, fish, and sugar rations allowed each person only a few ounces a month. Since farmers no longer made private sales and received only salaries from collective work, their income plummeted. The attention to rice ensured that there was basically no starvation, unlike conditions during the Great Leap Forward, but the experience taught people how important the markets had been.

In government offices, a small number of people were usually selected by the military to handle administration. The military did not really look after productive tasks, and work was thus at best chaotic and in some cases came to a halt. The military's task, as already noted, was to check the "thought" *(sixiang)* of each individual and struggle against key targets. Many were terrified of arbitrary and vindictive soldiers, but others found some to be quite decent individuals, conservative in their basic attitudes and desirous of preserving order. One highly placed bank official who worked closely with the military in running the Bank of China offices in Guangdong said, "We received such impossible orders from higher-level units that while I made some kinds of accommodation to the military in our bank, they made even more accommodations to us. By the end we had quite a good mutual understanding and a workable relationship."

Most middle- and low-level cadres who returned to their offices after their stint at the May Seventh Cadre Schools continued their style of life much as before. Absenteeism, even among those allowed to return to offices, was high, because those who stayed away from work were often not disciplined. There were almost no promotions or salary raises during the Cultural Revolution.

The Beijing government decentralized and gave considerable authority to lower levels during this period, but local units operated under tight constraints. Each locality was responsible not only for meeting its own grain needs but for meeting its industrial needs as well. Communes, counties, and cities, unable to buy from elsewhere within China, let alone from outside, were expected to produce the industrial goods they required. Counties without their own raw materials sometimes had to do without, even if that forced production to cease. Within large factory, university, or government office complexes, the compound was a self-sufficient, independent economic entity. Units often grew vegetables for their mess halls, had their own handicraft team to make repairs, and ran their own kindergartens and schools. Telephone and transport service had stagnated, and communication and transportation between localities was difficult at best. The devolution of authority to lower-level units was, from one perspective, an adjustment to the reality that the higher levels were unable to communicate and transport goods in a timely fashion to meet local needs.

Some figures were adjusted to show progress, but cadres later acknowledged that in fact production declined during these years. Anything a factory produced, including the many rejects of poor quality that never left the warehouse, was included in production data, and sometimes figures were further inflated. It was not until several years after the Cultural Revolution had ended that planning officials had confidence that statistics were sufficiently reliable to be useful.

Factory production of consumer goods was neglected, because priority was placed on meeting basic industrial needs. Many shelves, even at the Nanfang Department Store, the biggest and best in Guangdong, remained empty. When the amount of consumer goods began to increase after the Cultural Revolution, the quality of even the simplest products was still marginal. Light bulbs flickered, clothes had tears, plates had chips, and hot water bottles leaked.

Not only had production stagnated and sometimes stopped; the economy had retrogressed from its position as a system with a moderate amount of regional trade and specialization to one that was more primitive and self-sufficient. This was to make the contrast with the other economies of East Asia, which were in the same period achieving their great takeoffs, all the more dramatic when China was reopened to the outside.

*Top Leadership, 1967–1978.* Huang Yongsheng, the professional military officer and commander of the Guangzhou Military Region who became the dominant official in Guangdong after the January 1967 military takeover, also became the first director of the Guangdong Provincial Revolutionary Committee. Known to be a close follower of Lin Biao, he remained in his position until reassigned to join Lin in Beijing in July 1969. It was later widely rumored that Lin's contingency plan, if his 1971 coup had failed but he had survived, was to establish a base at the Nanhu Lake resort next to a military base just north of Guangzhou, where Huang would protect him. Officials in high positions at the time find this implausible, for Lin and his supporters lacked a broad base of power and even the resort in question was not fully controlled by Huang. Huang in fact was sometimes criticized by local rebel Red Guards for not supporting them. He clearly preferred the more conservative East Wind faction, and officials under him considered him more concerned with preserving order than with making revolution. He was succeeded by other military officials, Liu Xingyuan and Ding Sheng, selected by Mao. Ding was especially disliked in Guangdong for his role in attacking civilian leaders. It was not until Zhao Ziyang took over the Revolutionary Committee in April 1974 that Guangdong returned to civilian leadership.

Zhao served as provincial chairman of the Revolutionary Committee and as first Party secretary until October 1975, when he was transferred to Sichuan Province. Although Zhao was highly respected for his work in Guangdong before the Cultural Revolution and was to play a great role in bringing reforms to Sichuan, while in Guangdong in 1974–75 he did not yet have sufficient leverage with the military or a broad enough mandate to bring about significant reforms. Therefore, despite his many abilities, he accomplished little during his term. He was succeeded by a military official, Wei Guoqing, who, though not considered objectionable, also did not advance the reform process. Only in December 1978, when Wei was replaced by Xi Zhongxun and Yang Shangkun, did reform begin in Guangdong.

*Rehabilitation and Reassessment, 1973–1980.* As the Cultural Revolution drew to a close, questions about those who had been struggled against were very difficult to resolve. Individuals who were still in labor camps or detention, and especially those who had endured mental and physical abuse, had scores they wanted to settle. Many of those responsible for their suffering were still in power and were understandably reluctant to give potential challengers any opportunity. Yet other cadres in power, convinced that many who were not yet rehabilitated had been unjustly accused, wanted to clear their records and criticize the officials who had risen under Lin Biao and the Gang of Four.

The clearing of names was a slow and painful process. Each person's record had to be examined, and when someone was cleared this reflected poorly on the original accuser and meant the return of someone who bore him a grudge. Yet for those who wished to return to work or school, rehabilitation was a prerequisite. And rehabilitation was not just for the living, but for the honor of those who had died under detention or in labor camps. The effort to clear names continued from 1973 through 1980, trailing off thereafter. Even then relatives and friends of the deceased, cheered in 1980 by the posthumous clearing of the names of Liu Shaoqi, formerly second only to Mao, and Tao Zhu, still pushed to have names of their loved ones cleared.

The living who were cleared referred to their release as "liberation." Many detainees, without access to the outside world, had lost their sense of time and place and had no idea when they might be freed, let alone what was happening outside. For them release often came suddenly, and they hardly knew where to begin. Sometimes they found their homes locked up, sometimes other family members were still under detention in unknown places, and sometimes it took time to find a new work assignment.

Some liberated cadres were too old to return to work, and many of those still of working age were so debilitated emotionally that they found it hard to follow routines. It took years for many people to take a real interest in their work, and fears had not fully dissipated a decade later. Even the fall of the Gang of Four in 1976 and Deng's policy speech at the Third Plenum of the Eleventh Party Congress in 1978, major landmarks in reducing apprehensions, were not enough. Most people were returned to their old units, and former accusers and accused had to learn to live with each other. Occasionally someone with especially bitter experiences was allowed to choose a different unit. Some were released so late that their jobs had been filled, and they too were assigned elsewhere.

Although youth were illegally trickling back home or escaping to Hong Kong in the early 1970s, the majority of them began to return to the cities in 1975, as soon as they were allowed to do so. Those sent to the countryside in 1968 had been supposed to stay for life, and they often had more trouble getting back their urban registration than did those sent later, who had been assigned only for a term of several years. Only a handful, usually those who had married someone in the countryside, chose not to return. An estimated four hundred thousand youth returned to the cities of Guangdong in 1975–1977, and only a small number found opportunities for regular long-term employment or returned to school.[6]

Public criticism of the excesses began slowly and cautiously. While Zhao Ziyang was Guangdong's first Party secretary from April 1974 to October 1975 he, like Deng, granted a certain permissiveness to those who had suffered in the Cultural Revolution, even to Red Guard rebels who had criticized him and others in power in the fall of 1966. The best known among those who spoke out in Guangdong were three people who wrote under the code name of Li Yizhe. They had already begun to work together in late 1973, and in 1974 they wrote an extensive critique of military rule under Lin Biao, with criticism of Jiang Qing and her followers, then still in power, clearly implied. Li Yizhe raised broader questions about the basic system, including the need for the development of law and the protection of individual rights. As the first great public critique of the Cultural Revolution, their writings had an explosive impact, even though their own activities were circumscribed and one of the three remained in jail long afterward. They were a little ahead of their time; their views were later reflected in the brief period of Beijing's Democracy Wall and in the official media as discussion became more open.[7]

By 1977 most people had returned to their offices, and the reassessment gradually expanded from Lin Biao, the Gang of Four, and their associates to include Mao and the Cultural Revolution itself. Some of the most biting criticism came initially in fiction. Most famous in the late 1970s in Guangdong, as elsewhere, was the short story "The Scar" ("Shanghen," sometimes translated as "The Wounded"), by Lu Xinhua, published in August 1978. The story began in the early part of the Cultural Revolution. Its central character was a young woman who tried to prove her loyalty to Mao by denouncing her mother and her deceased father and by volunteering to go to the countryside. While living there she even refused to read the letters her mother sent her. In 1973 when she began to have some doubts about what she had done, she finally opened one of these, and found that it asked her to return because her mother was ill. She rushed home, finally tracking down her mother's whereabouts only to discover that she had just died. The "scar" was not only the alienation of mother and daughter and the years of suffering, but the daughter's guilt for having added pain to someone unjustly accused.[8]

For several years "scar" literature captured the mood of the country. People became engrossed in telling and listening to each other's accounts of horrors, although some found certain experiences too painful to relate. They felt anguish not only because of their own suffering but because they regretted making concessions to authorities to defend themselves or felt they should have tried harder to defend their loved ones. In Beijing, as cadres returned, official accounts followed the literary revelations and spelled out more tragedies. Public criticism of Mao was at first muted, but gradually even the official media acknowledged that the Cultural Revolution had been a disaster, and Mao was criticized for having made serious errors after 1957.

People's efforts to free themselves from these pains did not end in the 1980s, but by the early part of the decade many wanted to forget the scars. It was necessary, they said, to go on with their lives. Their views were like those of a young official, who said, "We all suffered. If we continue to settle accounts, it will perpetuate the evils of the Cultural Revolution. People should not be held fully responsible for their excesses under the pressures of the time. We should clear the names of and help those who suffered. We should acknowledge the errors of Mao in causing the Cultural Revolution tragedies, but we should stop excessively recalling the past and concentrate on building the future." Bad memories and enmities, however, were not so easily erased. Over a decade later, work of all kinds and at many levels could still occasionally break down because those who had suffered could not forgive their former attackers who remained in positions of power. Some of the grudges were passed down to the next generation.

## The 1978 Starting Line

After the Cultural Revolution ended in 1976, two years were required before the new leadership had consolidated its power sufficiently to launch a reform program. Although some changes began to take place in 1977 and 1978, the most significant reforms began after the Third

Plenum of the Eleventh Party Congress in December 1978. The situation then was in many ways ahead of that of 1952, when the new Communist government had first begun socialist construction. According to provincial statistics, the average per capita income in Guangdong in 1978 was four times that of 1952, and since 1952 the retail price index had risen only 15 percent.[9] In the intervening years Guangdong had fashioned a political structure capable of supervising rural production, offering basic education to over 90 percent of the youth, providing public health services, supervising a birth control campaign, and providing a modest welfare network. Enough highways and rail lines had been built to ensure that distribution of food was adequate, except from 1959 to 1961, to meet minimal requirements. A base of heavy industry had been built, including the opening of several major mines and steel, chemical, machinery, and rubber factories.

If one asks what might have been possible by 1978 had policies of the early 1960s continued, the answer must be that the losses from the Cultural Revolution were vast but immeasurable. The biggest costs were not from physical damage to buildings, factories, or transport facilities. A few buildings and rail lines had been damaged and many historic relics and buildings had been defaced, but the impact of this on the economy and on people's livelihood was minor. Nor did officials concerned with future development regard missed opportunities for increases in production or the stagnation of the standard of living as the biggest loss of the Cultural Revolution.

Neglected infrastructure was a more serious problem. People in factories, stores, and economic units had had so many problems with supply, energy shortages, missing personnel, and political pressures that they had concentrated on meeting their immediate targets. Long-range planning for new roads, railways, bridges, levees, sewage, power plants, communication networks, and forest preservation had all been postponed, further taxing the existing facilities, which themselves were not well maintained. The problems had existed before 1966, but they were much worse in 1976.

Aged machinery further deteriorated. The housing stock, already under great pressure in the early 1960s due to the lack of new construction, also degenerated. By the end of the Cultural Revolution, because of population growth and lack of repairs, people lived in housing more dilapidated and crowded than at any time since 1949. In the counties, new roads had been built to aid agriculture and industry, but in the cities, road repair, bridge building, and the supply of electricity to the populace, classified as helping consumption rather than industry, were given low priority and thus were neglected. Guangzhou, for example, had twenty-nine thousand telephones in 1952. By 1978 its population had almost doubled to over three million, but the city still had the same number of telephones, now in a worse state of repair.

Guangdong did not fare well in national priorities set during the turbulent decade. Top Communist leaders, being from inner China, had long favored their home areas over the richer cosmopolitan coastal areas, but the latter suffered further after the Sino-Soviet split in 1960 and during the Vietnam War because of worries about the coast's vulnerability to attack. In the 1960s and early 1970s, investment was concentrated in remote parts of China, in the "big third front."[10] Guangdong, as one of the most exposed areas, not only received little new investment during the Cultural Revolution but had some of its existing facilities moved inland—some to other provinces and some from Guangzhou to remote areas in Shaoguan Prefecture, where facilities and personnel were less adequate. Within greater Guangzhou, some facilities were moved from the city proper to rural counties like Hua and Conghua. These locations, though still in Guangdong, required longer supply lines and were an extra burden for the province.

Problems in the infrastructure were organizational as well as material. Because of supply shortages, factories had resorted to stockpiling goods that they might later need and did not always report this to higher levels—they considered not being able to meet output quotas a greater risk than being discovered for false reporting. Because of inadequate record keeping and constant changes in personnel, financial branches of the government and financial institutions, notably banks, could not supervise the enterprises under them. Because basic reporting systems had suffered from neglect, economic units could not provide meaningful coordination. Because higher levels could not supervise the felling of trees, soil was badly eroded. Population planning and its implementation were slow in getting started, even though specialists were concerned that the increase in food resources was falling slightly behind population growth.

But the really monumental loss in the Cultural Revolution was in human resources. Upon assuming power in 1949, Chinese Communist leaders had wanted to promote people from peasant and worker families, but they found that so few among them were well trained that they had to use individuals from "bad class" backgrounds, particularly for specialized intellectual activities. Mao and his fellow leaders, fearful that these individuals might have great influence and undermine faith in the regime, tried, through political campaigns and regular study and supervision, to contain their potentially subversive effect.

"Bourgeois intellectuals" had thus been under siege before 1966, but the Cultural Revolution raised the siege to a new level. Subject to constant mental pressure for so many years, they were emotionally drained by the time they were released. Most remained apathetic and fearful, just wanting to survive on a personal level and visit family and friends. They took some solace in the material compensation they received, though at times it was scarcely more than a token. They wanted to avoid risks, and all public life seemed risky. Yet who could replace them? China had far too few citizens, young or old, with such training or education.

In Guangdong, people with overseas connections had problems similar to those of intellectuals. Some leaders estimated that as many as 60 percent of Guangdong cadres had a relative or a close friend overseas. Those with such connections not only were more subject to criticism but had more trouble becoming Party members, getting into good schools, and joining the army. All these problems had been raised to new levels after 1966.

During the Cultural Revolution young cadres who might otherwise have been gaining supervised experience to prepare them for later responsibilities had been given no such guidance. They had concentrated on what was then most immediate, political struggle and political survival. There had been no training programs and little written material to aid even the ambitious who were willing to work on their own. Many of the best and brightest in this group were given high positions after reforms began, but they lacked the relevant administrative experience and maturation process enjoyed by their peers in other countries.

Those in their teens in 1966 had little opportunity to advance their education in the following years. Although middle schools mostly remained open except for the 1966–67 school year, many of the best teachers in the best schools had been sent away or were under siege. Some institutions of higher learning were open part of the time between 1969 and 1977, but the training was at best substandard and irregular. Since there were virtually no books in the countryside, most of the 994,000 Guangdong youth sent there had no way to study on their own. In 1977 and 1978 some of the lucky ones passed entrance examinations or attended special courses to make up for what they had missed, but reopened institutions had to lower their standards because examinees were so poorly prepared. Most young people removed from school and sent to the countryside, however, were never able to return to school. In 1976 the generation that had reached adulthood in the previous decade felt used by political leaders. Their personal lives had been disrupted, and many were confused, troubled, undisciplined, untrained, and bitter. Those who were the oldest children in their families often had to accept poor jobs while their younger brothers and sisters acquired better training and employment. They came to be known as the "lost generation."

Even the fortunate students who were given the best chance at the universities in the late 1970s were often disappointed. Most faculty had been away from academic work for much of the decade, and they were not only drained and cautious but out of touch with recent developments in their fields. There were almost no up-to-date Chinese textbooks and almost no funds to buy foreign books or to pay for foreign travel. Students, eager to make up for lost time and aware that new opportunities would await them after graduation, were frustrated. "Using books from the 1950s, faculty of the 1960s were teaching students in the 1970s to prepare them for the 1980s," some complained.

The children of parents under detention or away at cadre school had commonly been left with relatives or friends, but sometimes these care givers were themselves under siege or sent away. Some children had no choice but to fend for themselves. Even if their parents or guardians were around, they were often so distracted with the emotional strain of having spouses or relatives under detention that they could provide little guidance or discipline. As they grew older, those who had been untended or little attended as children were especially confused and troubled.

It was not easy to get China back on track. In work units, for example, there was considerable sympathy for those who had suffered during the Cultural Revolution and for older people who, now close to retirement, had received no pay raise for over a decade. But all those who suffered were not necessarily good workers, and sympathy for the sufferers made it difficult to maintain high standards of performance.

Power during the Cultural Revolution had been distributed not on the basis of standard criteria but on the basis of personal relations. The exercise of power, cloaked in terms of ideology, was in fact based on kinship and friendship. Power, not subject to universal standards, corrupted, and leaders were able to use political measures against those who challenged them. They also sometimes acquired perquisites like housing, use of cars, scarce goods, and access to entertainment.

The spirit dominating the workplace during the turbulent decade had been one of getting by, avoiding responsibility, doing little or no work, taking no initiative, acquiring as many privileges as possible, and using whatever influence one had to obtain jobs for friends or relatives. When supplies or energy resources were unavailable, workers sometimes waited weeks or months with no work to do. There was not enough stability for managers even to attempt to maintain discipline, quality, or efficiency. With permanent salaries guaranteed by the state, workers saw no advantage in exerting themselves. Hong Kong managers at the time, aware of those ingrained work attitudes, did not want to hire new émigrés from the mainland.

Cadres and factory managers trying to reorganize their work after the Cultural Revolution found files in disarray, personnel whose political cases needed attention, rivalries and mutual antagonisms from the previous years not entirely dissipated, and many decisions about organization and leadership still pending. In many factories, if employees worked efficiently they ran out of their allotted raw materials by the end of the morning and spent the afternoon in study and discussion. Workers demanded that bonuses still be given out since the problems were not their fault. With bloated staff they could not fire, lacking people with technical and managerial expertise, and short of supplies, managers found new incentive systems insufficient to solve their problems.

The human resources problem involved far more than a lack of training and experience. For years people had been called upon to work selflessly, to sacrifice themselves for the common good. By the end of the Cultural Revolution, the public had heard these appeals from too many officials concerned with their own power and perquisites. Exhortations to further sacrifice invited skepticism and ridicule.

Many people in Guangdong, as elsewhere, spoke of the spiritual vacuum and the crisis of confidence. Belief in Mao had provided a

secular form of faith that had given hope to many, and their disillusionment extended beyond individual leaders to the system they represented, including the Communist Party and the socialist system.
Some Party leaders escaped the full brunt of public anger, for they
too had been victims. But because Communist cadres had been in
charge and had led China through the disastrous Great Leap Forward
to the Cultural Revolution, at the very least the Party had lost the
aura it had once enjoyed. Even the excitement of economic progress
could not fully restore the faith or fill the spiritual void.

People had little in which they could take pride. In the early days
of Mao, even the poor had a sense of moral superiority and dedication.
But now their decades of sacrifice seemed foolish. They could not take
pride in the appearance of their clothes, their homes, or their jobs.
Government officials and service personnel were paid the same
whether or not they gave proper attention to the public. Having been
taught that workers were the new masters, many bureaucrats conveyed
an attitude to the public that said, "Why should I serve you? You are
a bother. Go away."

Called on too long to make sacrifices, people wanted, after 1978,
to know how much they would be paid and what goods they would
be given. The Cantonese had been traditionally regarded by others in
China as thinking only of material possessions. But many of them had
responded in the 1950s to the appeals to work selflessly, and many
had accepted the discipline of the earlier years. Like others, they now
insisted on seeing the material benefits before they would exert themselves. At best it would take a long time to reestablish pride in work
and a level of discipline that would make discussions of responsibility,
efficiency, and productivity in the workplace meaningful.

## The Passion for Change

In 1957, after collectivization, some Chinese leaders argued that the
socialist transformation had been pushed too far, and they became
influential enough in 1961 after the failure of the Great Leap Forward
to make modest reforms in the system. During the Cultural Revolution
the worst features of the Chinese system reached such an extreme that
the voices in favor of basic change became stronger everywhere, including in the leading organs of the Communist Party. Too many
people believed the words that appeared on Beijing's Democracy Wall

in 1978: "East Germany isn't doing as well as West Germany, North Korea as well as South Korea, or China's mainland as well as Taiwan." In the 1960s Chinese leaders were confident that despite their problems they had a better system, but in 1976 they were not.

In an address on August 8, 1977, Deng Xiaoping spoke of the need for systemic reform, and at the Third Plenum of the Eleventh Party Congress in December 1978, he was in a position to push it forward. Although many issues remained to be settled, Deng was able to marshal widespread support for certain fundamental views that had been present but not dominant before 1966:

More attention had to be given immediately to improving the general population's livelihood. People had suffered too much. There had been enough talk of "isms"; China had to find what worked.

The socialist system was too tight and needed to be loosened. Excess planning had made the economy lifeless and destroyed motivation. Markets had to be revived and allowed to flourish in order to enliven production and satisfy people's needs. China had gone too far in copying socialism from the Soviet Union and needed to move away from that path.

Class warfare and political campaigns that attacked so many people had to cease, and individuals needed to be protected from unpredictable assaults. Moreover, intellectuals and specialists deserved to be treated as patriotic Chinese; China had too few of them and badly needed their help.

Tight controls over people's lives had to be relaxed. Urban youth should not be forced to stay in the countryside against their will, nor should anyone be forced to engage in public works projects over a long period of time without compensation. People ought to be allowed more freedom to speak their minds, to read and watch what they wanted, and to travel freely.

The Communist Party had to relax its grip over the everyday economic system. Disasters had resulted when it had tried to run daily affairs. The Party, too, had to give more attention to what worked and to promote individuals more on the basis of their ability and performance and less on the basis of their political loyalty.

China needed to expand its contacts with foreign countries and, in particular, take advantage of increased commerce with other countries to learn from their technology and their experience. In Guangdong, this meant opening its doors to Hong Kong.

\* \* \*

This is not to say that there was no resistance to economic change. Resistance was overcome, however, because after the Cultural Revolution the idea of reform had become unstoppable. The previous decade had been so devastating that many wept not just for fallen comrades and relatives but for the fate of China. Yet they also echoed a view expressed by a former vice-governor of Guangdong: "We must be thankful for the Cultural Revolution. Without it, we could never have undertaken such fundamental reform. It took the Cultural Revolution for us to realize the weaknesses of our old system. And in the long run, China will be better because of it."

# 2.

# *Hong Kong: Outside Progress Shapes the Reform Impulse*

The Chinese were so preoccupied with their internal struggles during the Cultural Revolution that they had little energy to consider the outside world, even if they had the opportunity. As the turbulence decreased, they acquired the energy and, thanks to changes in the international situation, the opportunity. Relations between China and the West improved both because China began looking outside the Soviet bloc and because the United States wanted to overcome the legacy of the Korean War and normalize relations with China in order to gain its cooperation in ending the Vietnam War. These changes made possible a new opening to the outside world for the first time since America had begun the embargo of Chinese ports in 1950.

This opening occurred just as China's neighbors in East Asia were reaping the benefits of some of the most rapid economic growth and social transformation the world had ever seen. A controlled Chinese press had not prepared its people for the scale of these changes. They were shocked to see how far they had fallen behind, and this deepened their doubts about their own past leaders and their own system. How, they wanted to know, had other East Asian countries succeeded, and how could China learn their secrets?

Unlike people in many parts of China who had nowhere to turn, Guangdong had its own special gate to the outside: Hong Kong. As in other countries divided by artificial political barriers, the people of Hong Kong wanted to reestablish their connections with relatives and friends on the other side. Hong Kong was under British rule, but the population was overwhelmingly made up of Cantonese migrants and

descendants of migrants who had come from southern and northeastern Guangdong over the course of 150 years. Nostalgic and curious,
they hoped to renew their ties with their native villages. Hong Kong
businesspeople had visions of goods they could sell to Guangdong
and of goods that could be made in Guangdong and sold elsewhere.
Labor-intensive manufacturing firms in Hong Kong, concerned about
the growing shortages and higher costs of labor that were hurting
their competitiveness in world markets, saw an unlimited supply of
cheap labor. And as it became clear after 1982 that Hong Kong would
revert to Chinese sovereignty in 1997, many there wanted to prepare
for the years ahead by learning about and strengthening their personal
and business connections across the border.

As the border became more porous, people in Guangdong began
to think more about how Hong Kong's technology, economic expertise, business connections, and financial resources could help them in
their own development. They did not think everything in Hong Kong
was worth imitating, but Hong Kong became for them the symbol
of modernity. No other place did more to shape their views about
what they wanted and the changes they had to make. What precisely
did Guangdong people see when they began to renew their contacts
with Hong Kong? What had happened to Hong Kong since 1949,
when it and Guangdong had gone their separate ways? What had it
acquired that was now accessible to Guangdong?

## Hong Kong's Loss of Its Hinterland, 1950

The Chinese had the military power to take Hong Kong in 1949, but
many Chinese Communist leaders had been stationed there in the late
1940s and realized Hong Kong's value as a source of foreign supplies
and as a place to earn foreign currency. To help preserve Hong Kong,
moreover, Great Britain was willing to grant diplomatic recognition
to Beijing, and Beijing considered that an important aid to China's
quest for standing in the international community.[1]

The border between Hong Kong and Guangdong did not close
immediately after the Communists took over the province in October
1949. Communist underground workers and patriotic youth from
Hong Kong found their way into Guangdong. From Guangdong,
businesspeople who feared the loss of their enterprises, landlords who
feared the loss of their land, Kuomintang supporters who feared the

loss of their lives, and young people expecting to find greater job opportunities flooded into Hong Kong. Traders and relatives continued to go back and forth across the border.

With the outbreak of the Korean War in 1950, the United Nations, on the initiative of the United States and its allies, imposed a blockade against China. The Chinese in turn built a giant fence along the border to Hong Kong. While China took a socialist path and expanded Communist Party control, Hong Kong remained one of the world's most open economies. Smuggling across the border continued on a substantial scale in the early 1950s because China needed outside supplies during the Korean War, but the legal trade between Hong Kong and China collapsed and the role of Hong Kong as a lively commercial entrepôt center, where goods were transshipped between China and the outside world, abruptly ceased.

For the Communists, who wanted a planned economy, tight political control, and individual service to the nation, Hong Kong became a symbol of the evils of capitalism they were fighting against: selfish businessmen, anarchy, corruption, and pursuit of individual pleasure. For those in Hong Kong who sought freedom to make money in their own way, communism was a system that appropriated private wealth, persecuted successful businesspeople, and eliminated freedoms. Their worst fears were confirmed in the Korean War. China then launched the campaign against counterrevolutionaries, and in 1951 Guangdong began its land reform and the three and five "anti" campaigns against capitalists. Hong Kong residents learned that friends and relatives in Guangdong were being terrorized, publicly humiliated, beaten, and in some cases killed.

Hong Kong had long been a haven for those out of power in China, and the British tried to maintain an even hand between the Kuomintang and the Communists. Many local Chinese, never quite sure who was an agent for the Kuomintang, Communists, British, or Americans, shunned political activity, but the Kuomintang and the Communists and their sympathizers continued their struggle just short of open warfare. The world was divided between labor unions, schools, magazines, newspapers, movie theaters, and even restaurants and stores that were Communist (locally known as "patriotic"), and those that were anti-Communist or non-Communist. The Communists urged their adherents to hoist their flags on their national day, October 1, while the Kuomintang supporters hoisted their flags on their national day, October 10.

A certain modus vivendi developed between China and Hong Kong. British troops and officials steadfastly maintained that they were prepared to defend Hong Kong, but most observers believed it impossible. "How," went the local joke, "would China take Hong Kong?" Answer: "By phone." One announcement of China's intention, and Hong Kong would fold. The British were careful not to provoke the Communists. Other countries were allowed to use Hong Kong as a base for China watching, but they had to be discreet so as not to provoke a reaction from across the border.

As part of the implicit agreement that allowed Hong Kong to remain under British rule, the British demanded civil obedience of the local Communists but otherwise made no effort to restrain local Chinese Communist publications, the Bank of China, China Resources (composed of China's state foreign trade corporations), Chinese-run department stores, China Merchants Steamship Navigation Company, the patriotic schools, and labor unions.

The colony received most of its produce and, by the 1970s, much of its water supply from Guangdong. China in turn used Hong Kong as a base for gathering information, technology, supplies, and foreign currency. With few exports to offer the outside world, China earned a quarter or more of its foreign currency through food and other daily necessities sent to Hong Kong.

A trickle of legal immigrants crossed into Hong Kong each day, and tens of thousands of Hong Kong residents were allowed to cross the border to visit their native villages on annual holidays. One could change trains at the border, and trucks with special border permits brought goods into Hong Kong. Many Hong Kong residents corresponded with relatives, but contact by phone was virtually impossible. Those in Hong Kong often sent remittances to relatives and served as a conduit for people in Taiwan and elsewhere who were afraid to contact mainland relatives and friends directly.

British prudence and Chinese interests enabled Hong Kong to remain politically viable. In the early 1950s the question was whether Hong Kong could remain economically viable enough to support not only its old residents but the huge influx of immigrants. Its population had reached 1.3 million in 1940 but had dipped to 600,000 by 1945, after many had fled to the Chinese countryside during Japanese rule. By the mid-1950s many of these people had come back and over a million new immigrants had arrived as well, making the population twice as large as in 1940.

Because of Hong Kong's mild climate, migrants could sleep on the hillsides. They erected squatters' huts, technically illegal, but in fact tolerated. Except during the typhoon season in the summer, the most urgent problem was not shelter; instead it was food, health care, and jobs. Temporarily, Protestant and Catholic service agencies helped provide food. Like the Chinese population they served, these agencies found refuge in Hong Kong from all over China. The sponsoring churches in Europe, North America, and Australia that had once funded missionary activity throughout China easily generated funds sufficient to make a big difference in Hong Kong. Yet even they could not provide enough money if the economy remained weak. Hong Kong needed more new jobs to make up for the loss in the entrepôt trade and the rise in the population.

## The Growth of Manufacturing, 1950s and 1960s

Before World War II, the great center of Chinese manufacturing and international finance was not Hong Kong but Shanghai. Shanghai's Yangtze River area had a far larger population, with much more industry and better developed services, than the Guangzhou–Hong Kong area. Shanghai had an international settlement with some three hundred thousand foreign residents—French, British, Americans, and Japanese. Although the Japanese had built a formidable manufacturing base in China's Northeast, only Shanghai had the breadth and depth of resources to supply a large manufacturing plant with the needed machines, supplies, parts, personnel, and industrial services. In 1949, Shanghai businessmen fled to many different countries. Some industrialists, largely in textiles, regarded Singapore and Taiwan as too politically controlled and believed they could do better in Hong Kong.

Shanghai textile leaders had begun to prepare for the modernization of their industry after World War II by ordering new equipment from England. Some of it was en route when the Communist troops moved toward Shanghai, and the industrialists notified the ships at sea to deliver the machinery instead to Hong Kong. They and their managers moved to Hong Kong and, before long, built factories in Tsuenwan, in Hong Kong's sparsely settled New Territories. Most Shanghai textile people escaped from China with little but their expertise, but British and other international bankers in Hong Kong, desperate to keep their economy viable and looking for promising ventures, recognized their potential and supported them. Tsuenwan, with its core centering around textiles, grew from a village of 5,000 in 1945 to a city of 750,000 in 1985.

People from Shanghai did not assimilate easily, however, and Hong Kong, with all its international flavor and diverse Chinese groups, remained essentially Cantonese. Shanghai textile managers ate in Shanghai restaurants, established associations of Shanghai business-people, and socialized with those from Shanghai. Their work force was sharply split between highly paid workers from Shanghai and poorly paid local workers. Sizable numbers of Chaozhou people from Shantou (formerly transliterated "Swatow") Prefecture, Amoy and Fuzhou people from Fujian, and Hakka from mountainous places like Meixian in northeastern Guangdong had long been in Hong Kong. But their influence was weak, and they increasingly assimilated into Cantonese culture. Shanghai émigrés, whether financiers, shopkeepers, workers, White Russians, or Jews, regarded Shanghai as superior, and few deigned to learn Cantonese. Hong Kong's Cantonese lumped most northerners together as Shanghainese whether they came from Ningbo and elsewhere in Zhejiang, from Jiangsu, and sometimes even from places far from Shanghai.

Immigrants eager for employment provided a seemingly inexhaust-ible supply of cheap labor, and Shanghai industrialists offered wages the market would bear. In dealing with their workers, textile plant owners were more like the harsh Japanese textile factory owners at the turn of the century than the Japanese managers of the 1950s who, to ensure the loyalty and dedication of their workers, made long-term commitments to them and granted them a range of secondary benefits. Traditional Chinese family and locality associations and Western mis-sionary relief organizations provided the welfare net in Hong Kong, in effect indirectly subsidizing the textile enterprises there.

Although the Shanghai industrialists did not fit into the local busi-ness community and paid non-Shanghai workers marginal wages, their factories played a critical role in providing an economic base for Hong Kong just as the bottom fell out of the traditional entrepôt trade. Some enterprising workers in these and other factories observed how the industries were organized, and they left to set up tiny cottage industries and apparel shops or to establish other niches in tailoring or the garment industry. The availability of these tiny shops and many additional hungry refugees provided "surge potential." When huge orders from American buyers came in, businesses confidently accepted them, knowing they could quickly expand capacity by additional hiring and subcontracting.

A second wave of industrial growth came in the late 1950s and early 1960s as entrepreneurs seized new opportunities to produce artificial flowers, other plastic goods, watches, toys, and additional labor-intensive consumer goods. And by the late 1960s entrepreneurs had created a third wave of industrial growth in low-grade electronic goods, replacing Japanese products as Japan moved up the manufacturing scale. As in the second wave, the third wave of industrial leadership was local, but this time the leaders were often graduates of U.S. or Taiwanese colleges in engineering or business who, upon their return, with family help and connections to the outside world, started enterprises that required more technology and international expertise. With intense local competition and a changing international market, some fell by the wayside, but many shrewd businesspeople, with financial backing and a measure of luck, led companies that grew at explosive rates.

Outside observers sometimes describe Hong Kong as a showcase of a pure laissez-faire market economy practicing free trade, in contrast to Japan, Korea, and Taiwan, which protected infant and growing industries. Indeed, though certain institutions like the stock market were tightly controlled by a small circle, government procurement was not entirely by competitive bidding, and accreditation in medicine and accounting followed British rather than international standards, Hong Kong markets for agricultural and industrial products remained remarkably open. Unlike those other economies, Hong Kong had no significant market of its own in which even to consider protecting infant industries until they could develop economies of scale.

But in fact the government of Hong Kong played an important role in economic development. Talented colonial administrators and enlightened policies helped Hong Kong to become the world's only industrialized colony. As Britain surrendered the reins of government in its other colonies, it brought some of its most talented colonial servants from those places, trained them in Cantonese, and assigned them for a term as basic-level district officers with high standards of service. Beginning in 1953 when a major fire broke out in the Shep Kip Mei squatters' area, the government increasingly accepted responsibility for building minimal public housing.

The Hong Kong government had long been one of the few in Asia that provided a system of law under which international businesspeople felt they could get fair treatment on the basis of clearly specified laws. The government not only provided public transportation, the water supply, the sewage system, health care, and schooling but controlled the land supply and selected certain small industrial sectors that it deemed desirable to support. The scarcest resource of all was land. It was government policy to put up land for lease when it was reclaimed and became available, but it was made available at such a slow pace that demand exceeded supply, thus generating enough income from leasing land to provide a high proportion of the government's budget. Although the land was generally made available in public auction to the highest bidder, certain land was set aside for which only firms in certain sectors—tanning and electronics, for example, which could not have afforded to compete against large land developers—could bid, in order to preserve their viability. The government also developed land for other sectors. Its action allowed industrialists to concentrate their funds not on expensive land and land development but on manufacturing equipment, and thus helped industrial expansion.

Although the aura of Western superiority had been punctured when the Japanese overwhelmed British defenses in 1941, social life in Hong Kong remained highly stratified in the years immediately after World War II. The Western community remained very much at the top, figuratively and literally, with their residences high on the Peak. British government and business officials could take the Peak tram or drive down from their homes to the Government Secretariat or to their businesses nearby. Not far below the Secretariat was a green, where well into the 1970s men could play cricket and assemble at the nearby Hong Kong Club. Westerners, including managerial staff, university faculty, merchants, and even sailors and garrison troops and their families, together constituted only 1 or 2 percent of the population.

Some local Chinese, as their businesses expanded, began to acquire luxurious styles of life, which created enormous gaps between them and ordinary workers. Yet in the 1950s only a few, mostly those who had been in Hong Kong for two or three generations, were accepted into the social circles of the Western business and government leaders and until then few Chinese lived on the Peak, except as servants of British families. The Chinese were mostly congregated in downtown Hong Kong, in Kowloon, and in the largely rural New Territories, where they worked mostly as merchants, artisans, and transport or construction coolies. By the late 1970s, however, as the Chinese gained in wealth and worldly sophistication, social barriers between Chinese and Westerners began to disappear.

Hong Kong University brought faculty mostly from England and other Commonwealth countries. Bright Chinese youths were selected and trained there, primarily to serve in administrative and clerical positions in government or business firms—for example, as managers for the British trading companies, popularized in James Clavell's *Tai-pan* and *Noble House*. They also provided specially trained manpower in other fields, such as medicine, in which they could provide services for the local population.

Like first-generation entrepreneurs in many countries, Hong Kong's Chinese businesspeople trusted only a small group of relatives and close friends. Some of these, or their offspring, might be educated abroad and welcomed back into the business, but other employees, it was assumed, would leave to start their own competing companies as soon as they learned the business. It seemed best to discourage them from acquiring such skills, and therefore company owners were slow to develop a managerial and professional staff. Throughout the 1960s ordinary college graduates of Hong Kong universities found few attractive managerial opportunities in Chinese companies; only positions as low-level clerical staff or as industrial workers were available. But by the 1970s the great growth of multinational companies serving Southeast Asia from Hong Kong had created a large new white-collar class.

On average, Chinese workers in Hong Kong in the 1960s were not as dedicated to their jobs or as well educated as Japanese or Korean workers. Many Chinese relied on physical labor to survive. They accepted low wages because continuous numbers of newer refugees were willing to work in their stead. Lacking job security, they were responsive to material incentives, and they did what needed to be done.

The gaps in income, material possessions, and style of life were huge. Public housing policy after 1953 provided only minimal housing facilities for squatters and others who could not afford private housing. Few private land developers in the 1960s found it profitable to build housing for low-income workers, and the government, though it built on a vast scale, had trouble keeping up with the continued influx and the baby boom that began in the 1950s. A whole family of workers was not infrequently crowded into a single room, at rents that in the early 1960s were scarcely 1 percent of what well-to-do families in private housing paid in the better residential districts.

## The Emergence of a Common Civic Culture, 1967–1975

Chinese immigrants to Europe and North America had often gone originally as "sojourners," intending to return eventually to their home villages. After they had been abroad for a decade or two, many realized that their home was now in their new country, and they began to adapt accordingly. Many Chinese émigrés who fled to Hong Kong similarly first regarded it as a temporary way station. Some were still considering returning to China, if the right opportunity opened up, and many hoped to go abroad. Few were ready to make long-term commitments. Builders of apartment houses sold the units even before the buildings were complete in order to get a quick return on their investment, and shopkeepers and manufacturers had a similar perspective. Hong Kong was, as journalist Richard Hughes described it in the title of his book, a "borrowed place" living on "borrowed time."

Yet by 1967, like the sojourners who remained abroad, many people expected to stay in Hong Kong and they began to think of putting down roots. When the chaos of the Cultural Revolution spilled over into Hong Kong in the middle of that year and mobs of Communist demonstrators and supporters caused damage to life and property, there were those who tried even harder to find greener pastures overseas, but many were galvanized to defend a community that they had begun to consider their own. Some refugees who had fled China illegally feared for their lives if the Communists took over, and others feared for their livelihood. They knew they needed the British to maintain Hong Kong's separation from China, and after 1967 they were increasingly prepared to work with each other and with British government officials for the good of Hong Kong. By international standards Hong Kong was not yet a stable settled community, but many governmental and private leaders wanted to help it move in that direction.

The experience of living in Hong Kong had gradually helped create a common mass culture. Many immigrants had arrived as single people, but most married and began to rear children. Residents began reading the same newspapers, listening to the same radio programs, and they were just beginning to watch the same television programs. This was particularly true for the second generation, born in Hong Kong in the early 1950s. The Hong Kong government expanded its educational system, and children were receiving a longer standard education, commonly through lower middle school (grade 9). People in Hong Kong began to feel proud of their progress, a pride that was reinforced with the contrasts between their lives and those of the new flow of migrants from China in 1972–1975.

And yet, unlike Taiwan, where public commitment to Confucian ideology and Sun Yat-sen's Three Principles remained strong, Hong Kong did not have an explicit public value system to counter the drive for material acquisition. Wealth had been the basic measure of rank, and shopkeepers did not always feel shame at outsmarting customers, even if it required deception. The spirit of Hong Kong clearly remained pragmatic and short term, with everyone expected to look out for himself, ever ready if necessary to get into a public argument. It was difficult to define what it meant to be a Hong Kong native in a way that transcended this spirit, a common mass media, and the mere fact of living there. National symbols, common religious beliefs, and a consciously taught tradition were absent. Government schools taught decency and manners, but, afraid of divisiveness, they did not teach twentieth-century Chinese history. Few studied or even identified with the Chinese classics. Hong Kong had a modernized folk tradition, but it lacked a high culture.

The enormous gaps in income began to decline in the 1960s as the demand for ordinary workers increased, forcing wages up. Average personal income in Hong Kong did not reach U.S. $5,000 per year until the mid-1980s, but from the 1950s, when the average income was several hundred dollars per year, wages rose rapidly and steadily. The very rich, engaging in a conspicuous display of wealth that had gone out of style in many countries, continued to employ maids and chauffeurs, ride in luxury cars, and wear great quantities of jewelry. By the mid-1970s, however, ordinary workers were beginning to be able to afford the new "standard" possessions: a television set, refrigerator, stove, washing machine, tape recorder, and camera; some could replace electric fans with air conditioning. Those who had not yet acquired these goods expected to within a few years. A consumer culture was created on a mass scale that had never before existed in China or Hong Kong. And the size and quality of Hong Kong housing continued to improve rapidly. As a sizable portion of the local population entered into a middle-class style of life, the chasm between the lives of rich and poor narrowed.

The Hong Kong government, which had been slow in the 1950s in responding to the need for public services, began rapidly expanding its public works program. Many political émigrés from China, who feared for their lives under Communist rule, believed their future depended on continued British commitment to Hong Kong and did not demand full-scale suffrage. Still, many local Chinese wanted more recognition and consultation, and British officials in Hong Kong, sensitive to the worldwide rejection of colonialism, tried to modify their style of rule to gain greater popular acceptance. They consulted with and honored leading local Chinese and increased their commitment to public facilities and human services. With substantial income from the auctions of seventy-five-year land leases, the government moved quickly to catch up with the need for roads, tunnels, port facilities, airports, and public parks and laid plans for subways and better train service. They showed more sensitivity to the views and aspirations of local Chinese, more of whom were becoming their friends as social barriers and economic differences declined.

The great governor of Hong Kong from 1947 to 1957, Sir Alexander Grantham, wrote in *Via Ports* that when he retired from Hong Kong government service and sailed with his family for England in the late 1950s he did not know whether he was going home or leaving home. By the late 1960s many British civil servants, after serving as district officers in the New Territories and as higher officials working for Hong Kong development for many years, did know the answer. Talented civil servants like David Akers-Jones and Jack Cater, who had dedicated most of their working life to Hong Kong, decided that their homes were there and that they would remain after retirement, even after 1997.

Cleavages between regional subgroups within Hong Kong also began to decline. People who had originally been prepared to look after their own families and others from their home town or village were increasingly prepared to think about Hong Kong as a whole. The term "Hong Kong old-timer" *(lao Xianggang)* came to be used for someone who had lived in Hong Kong for twenty years or so, regardless of which social group he came from. Hong Kong residents who had moved on to North America or other Western cities by the late 1960s thought of themselves as primarily from Hong Kong; their identification with the original town or village in China from which their family descended had become less important.

One reflection of the new civic identification was the campaign in the early 1970s to keep Hong Kong clean. Although spitting and littering did not disappear as quickly as in Singapore, where fines were more strictly enforced, and many Hong Kong streets remained smelly, disorderly, and unadorned, public cooperation and government determination led to a considerable improvement in cleanliness. In many places garbage was picked up twice daily.

At the same time the Independent Commission against Corruption (ICAC) began to take action against corruption, especially in the police force. Problems did not disappear, however, and there was considerable resistance by policemen who forced the government to back down on some of its reform ambitions. Secret societies were not totally ended, massage parlors and "love hotels" remained havens for prostitution, gambling remained widespread, and extortion did not end. But progress was made in reducing the worst of these practices. Taxi drivers and employees of service institutions became more courteous. People were more willing to stand in queues while waiting for public transportation, with less argument. As their lives began to improve, they were prepared to support efforts to create a more livable environment.

Hong Kong business leaders, even into the 1980s, maintained personal control over their companies. They resisted the regularization of rules about employment and insisted on their right to hire and fire at any time. Many employees were still ready to leave the moment they had another good opportunity, and the owners treated them accordingly. The owners might seek advice and weigh alternatives, but they were not afraid to take risks. In contrast, they saw Japanese and even Taiwanese business leaders as indecisive and unable to act quickly.

The splits between those from Shanghai, Chaozhou, and Guangzhou and its environs began to decline in the 1960s. The naked pursuit of wealth, while hardly abandoned, was tempered by the desire to be respected in the community. Many selected to the Government's Legislative Council and Executive Council and those knighted were wealthy, but not all were, and no one was chosen for wealth alone. Those chosen for these highest honors had also performed social service for and been respected by the Hong Kong community. By the early 1970s many leading businesspeople were making sizable donations to art museums, civic centers, universities, hospitals, welfare institutions, and scholarship funds for Hong Kong as a whole. Although they might have joined the boards of these institutions originally because of the honor involved, Chinese leaders who met together on charitable, university, and other community boards shared a sense of responsibility to the entire community. Many were not above trying to outsmart each other, and plenty of Hong Kong businesspeople were prepared to take advantage of those from Guangdong, who were less knowledgeable. But among themselves the business leaders preferred no written contract, and when they gave their word everyone understood that their honor and standing in the community were at stake should they fail to deliver.

The growing ease of air travel helped bring together an international overseas Chinese business community. Chinese business leaders from Taiwan, Singapore, the United States, and elsewhere saw each other frequently over the years. Hong Kong business leaders sought to make Hong Kong not only a successful business site but also an attractive place that they could be proud of when they encountered Chinese leaders from elsewhere. This concern for their standing in the global Chinese business community also strengthened their willingness to help Hong Kong.

## A Global City

When they lost their hinterland in 1950, Hong Kong business leaders, with a limited local market, had no choice but to find a new role in world markets. Their British colonial heritage, school training, and frequency of contact with English speakers gave them, like those in Singapore, an advantage over their Japanese, Korean, and Taiwanese counterparts. Even ordinary citizens who had not received a good English education but who worked in hotels, restaurants, or their own shops often learned enough "street English" to communicate with foreign businesspeople and the large number of foreign tourists. The rich who sent their brightest children and young relatives to the best business schools in North America and Europe apprenticed them in the financial markets of London and New York. This access to English language and to Western business practices made it easy for those in Hong Kong to take part in global business activities. It also made Hong Kong an attractive city for international businesses that wanted to locate regional offices where they could rely on a predictable legal system and where there were cosmopolitan business circles in which their Western executives could feel more comfortable than in Tokyo, Taipei, or Seoul.

Although British firms had dominated Hong Kong's prewar business community, after World War II European and U.S. multinationals gradually encroached on the former proprietary spheres of British companies. The U.S. Chamber of Commerce in Hong Kong grew rapidly after it was established in 1969; by the 1980s 150 foreign banks had branches or offices there. In the early 1950s Japanese manufacturers began using Hong Kong as an important base for gaining world market share in consumer electronic goods, which they sold not only to local Hong Kong residents but to tourists. Signs for Japanese electronic goods came to dominate small shops and the billboards on the skyline. American servicemen and other Americans connected with the Vietnam War were prominent among tourists in the 1960s; by the 1980s they were superseded by rich Japanese tourists who came by the planeload. The British often maintained excellent and profitable trading companies, but their share of the Hong Kong economy declined compared to that of other foreigners and of local Chinese. As the local Chinese gained a larger share of the Hong Kong market, they also became more cosmopolitan and more knowledgeable about world markets.

As the Association of Southeast Asian Nations (ASEAN) grew stronger, modern air transport and telecommunications helped Hong Kong strengthen the network of relationships with overseas Chinese business leaders in Thailand, Indonesia, Malaysia, Singapore, and the Philippines. In the prewar period Cantonese had been the lingua franca of the Chinese business network in East and Southeast Asia, and even after the war as Mandarin gained strength in Southeast Asia, Cantonese remained an important language in business circles. Hong Kong companies thus retained a significant regional role, even though the content of the trade and service network changed rapidly.

Although Hong Kong expanded its manufacturing activities, when it is compared to Japan, Korea, or Taiwan, its advantage has not been in manufacturing efficiency or productivity. Hong Kong, like England, did not place as much emphasis on technical and engineering training as did Japan or Korea. Whereas the Japanese became especially skilled in managing large professional staffs and the Koreans in obtaining a disciplined response within large organizations, Hong Kong's special talent lay in trading, marketing, and identifying access to world resources. Hong Kong had a high proportion of small companies that were quick to respond to world markets. The Japanese continued to move boldly, but they preferred solid, long-term development; in contrast, Hong Kong businesspeople were prepared to take more risks. Although Hong Kong proved innovative in developing computer software in the late 1980s, its manufacturers in textiles, plastics, and electronics kept up not by generating their own technology but by rapidly identifying and absorbing world technology and using it to supply world demand. They learned to gather critical bits of information, use shrewd methods of bargaining, and move quickly to form international alliances when those suited their purposes.

Part of this resourcefulness stemmed from the fact that Hong Kong could not, with its small population base, compete with Japan or even with Korea in its universities and research institutes. Instead, it relied more on the great universities and research centers of the world, particularly in the United States, except in fields which require British certification.

The Hong Kong markets, sensitive both to changes in world markets and to political winds from China, remained volatile, far more so than those in many other nations. Even shrewd business leaders with extraordinary records of success floundered in Hong Kong when the markets suddenly changed in ways beyond their ability to anticipate. Fortunes were made and lost quickly, which contributed to an unusual intensity in those who were addicted to success.

In finance, shipping, and construction, Hong Kong's achievements were as remarkable as the best achievements of Japan, Korea, Taiwan, and Singapore in their own areas of strength. In the early 1980s this colony of little more than five million people had become the third-largest financial market in the world, after London and New York. It was not passed by Tokyo until the mid-1980s. Though shaken in 1983 by concern about 1997 and in 1987 by the exposure of the stock market's domination by a self-interested clique, Hong Kong leaders moved quickly to restore confidence. In the manufacturing of watches, toys, wigs, and high-fashion apparel, Hong Kong was a major factor in the world markets in the late 1980s. In shipping, Y. K. Pao and C. Y. Tung, originally from Ningbo, had already surpassed the Greeks in the 1960s to become the leading shipping magnates of the world. In the early 1980s Hong Kong overtook New York to become the second-busiest container port in the world, and in 1987 it moved up again, past Rotterdam, to become the busiest. The construction of high-rise office and apartment buildings proceeded at an unparalleled pace. Using construction equipment from Japan, builders worked at a speed unsurpassed anywhere.

Hong Kong's postwar success stood out in bold relief to the fate of the other foreign-led territory south of China, Macau, which fell far behind Hong Kong beginning in the 1950s. To be sure, Hong Kong had natural advantages in its deeper harbors, which had already begun to be important in the early part of the century as larger ships came to call, and in its more stunning vistas, which attracted tourists. The English language also made Hong Kong more accessible to the international community than did Portuguese. Most important, the British government was led by a professional meritocratic civil service, while Macau was led by short-term political appointees from Lisbon. Officials in Macau did not develop the continuity, long-term perspective, commitment, and infrastructure that would have made Macau more attractive to foreign business. By contrast, in Hong Kong the arrival of the Ningbo industrialists, foreign tourists, and financial services provided a critical mass that made it attractive to everyone—to China traders, to multinational businesses, and to Chinese émigrés seeking jobs. With this critical mass, Hong Kong kept up its momentum and even had to close its doors to immigrants. While Hong Kong became a world center, Macau, though it had room to welcome outsiders without fear of being inundated, remained a small regional center for the West River area until the 1970s.

Even the modernization of Macau after the 1970s derived less from internal development than from spillover from Hong Kong. When hydrofoils reduced travel time between Hong Kong and Macau to one hour, Hong Kong developers helped build modern gambling casinos in Macau, not permitted in Hong Kong, so that they could travel there on weekends. Only when international multifiber quotas on textiles were established did Hong Kong textile companies, shrewdly stretching their quotas by getting special quotas for Macau, establish modern textile factories in Macau. In 1989, Hong Kong ceased to receive preferential treatment in the U.S. market because it was no longer considered a lesser developed country, and Hong Kong businesses were prepared to take advantage of Macau's status as a lesser developed area. Compared to the vitality in Hong Kong, Macau was still far behind. Although official documents and policy pronouncements from Beijing referred to "Gangao" (Hong Kong/Macau) as if they were of equal status, people in Guangdong, looking for models, used only the term "Xianggang" (Hong Kong).

In the 1980s one could argue that Hong Kong had become the most truly international city in the world. People of many races and nationalities felt at home there. It had no trade barriers, and it traded more each year than it produced. Its business leaders were all oriented to world markets, and they were able to respond to developments elsewhere with lightning speed. In this combination of qualities only Singapore was in its league.

## The Reopening of Guangdong

In the aftermath of its 1969 border clashes with the Soviets, China began in 1970 to turn to the outside world. Relations with Canada and with some West European countries were soon normalized. Visits to China by the U.S. ping-pong team and Henry Kissinger in 1971 and by President Richard Nixon and Prime Minister Kakuei Tanaka in 1972 followed. The opening of China proceeded, at first slowly and cautiously, and then, with U.S. recognition in 1979, more rapidly.

The opening gained momentum as new transport and communication facilities improved to meet demand. Border crossings between Hong Kong and Guangdong, mostly involving Hong Kong residents visiting China, increased from a few hundred thousand a year in the early 1970s to over ten million in the late 1980s. Until the late 1970s the 158-kilometer train ride from Hong Kong to Guangzhou was an all-day affair. People left Hong Kong early in the morning, got off at the border at Luohu, ate a leisurely lunch, and then caught the afternoon train from Luohu to Guangzhou, arriving in late afternoon. On April 4, 1979, daily nonstop service between Hong Kong and Guangzhou was inaugurated, reducing travel time to 2 hours and 59 minutes. By 1987, daily service included four nonstop trains departing Hong Kong and four departing Guangzhou, each with fourteen cars. Airplane service between Hong Kong and Guangzhou, which had begun in 1978 with a daily flight, similarly expanded in the 1980s to several flights per day, and a daily hydrofoil service, almost as fast as the train, was also added. By the 1980s hydrofoil, ferry, and freight service to and from Hong Kong, virtually nonexistent in the early 1970s, linked Hong Kong directly to all nearby cities and towns in Guangdong.

In the early 1980s the overland trip from Macau to Guangzhou took at least a full day; it included five ferryboat rides, often with several hours' wait at each river. By 1988, when the last and largest of the necessary bridges was finished, the trip took three to four hours, traffic around Guangzhou permitting. By then road time from Hong Kong to Guangzhou had also been reduced from a lengthy day's drive to four hours, and a superhighway was under construction to cut the time to two hours.

As late as the early 1980s an advance reservation and often a several-hour wait were required to make a phone call from Hong Kong to Guangzhou. By the mid-1980s telephone calls between Hong Kong and Guangzhou hotels, businesses, and government offices could be dialed directly. These new links brought Hong Kong and Guangdong far closer than they had been before 1949, and Hong Kong now had far more to offer in terms of entrepôt trade.

Within Hong Kong, the enmities between the "patriotic Chinese" and the Kuomintang supporters gradually began to erode. As the sense of danger dissipated, mutual denunciations became less militant and some people in the two camps, at first discreetly and carefully, began to have more direct contact. Some former refugees, aware that China considered them deserters and kept a dossier on their activities, waited many years before making their first return visit. Until 1987, when Taiwan publicly dropped its objections to visiting relatives in China, many Hong Kong residents who had friends and relatives in Taiwan were reluctant to travel to China. The thaw could not suddenly change the feelings of everyone who had lost friends or relatives at the hands of the other side. But increasingly people became more philosophical about the broad historical forces that had pulled China apart and more prepared to be benevolent toward former enemies.

As much as those on both sides of the border wanted to renew contact, relations did not always proceed smoothly. Visitors from Hong Kong felt obliged to bring large gifts every time they came, and some relatives in China made not only large but specific demands for material goods. Hong Kong residents complained that those in China seemed not to realize how hard they had worked for what they had. They felt sorry for their friends and relatives in the mainland, many of whom had suffered political pressure as well as physical deprivation. But in addition, proud of their own new material possessions and urban sophistication, people from Hong Kong tended to look down on their "country cousins" on the other side of the border. From the perspective of those who had become more materially advanced and secure, their mainland relatives seemed grasping, selfish, and materialistic—just as they themselves had once been when they felt so deprived of the wealth they saw about them.

Before the collapse of the Maoist world view in the late 1970s, those in China felt more virtuous than their Hong Kong brethren, whom they derided as selfish and superficial. Proud of building a moral society of greater equality and security, they were prepared to make sacrifices. Even those who received financial aid from relatives in Hong Kong regarded it as a city where there were few values beyond wealth and where sexual immorality, crime, corruption, and lavish waste were rampant. Some accepted the picture the Chinese mass media drew of Hong Kong as a place where colonialists and capitalists oppressed the common workers, where many had no place to sleep but on the streets, and where workers were perpetually insecure about their future.

Even before the mid-1970s some in Guangdong—those who received secret reports from relatives, and cadres in the Xinhua News Agency, Communist Party Liaison Department, Foreign Affairs Ministry, or intelligence organizations—had some sense of the economic progress of the outside world. They were reluctant to talk to others, however, for fear they might say something that would get everyone in trouble. And despite the fact that Guangdong residents had a far better sense than residents in other provinces had of outside developments, almost none of them realized the true scope and depth of what had occurred. It was a great shock, for example, to learn that Hong Kong had far surpassed the economic level of Shanghai.

In the 1970s, with the criticisms of Mao and excessive leftism and the acceptance of material wealth as a legitimate goal in order to achieve modernization, the people of Guangdong lost their moral grounds for defending their sacrifices and taking pride in their own way of life. Their value system, already strained by the failures of the Great Leap Forward and the Cultural Revolution, collapsed, and with it went their ability to resist the lure of Hong Kong's material goods. Wealth emerged as the preeminent measure of success, and those who pursued it were no longer targets of public criticism.

Yet looking up to Hong Kong proved very painful. Those in Hong Kong, being richer, were in the more powerful position. People in Guangdong found it hard to believe that Hong Kong had achieved its success by superior virtue or effort, but they at least had to swallow their pride and accept the reality that they had become, in effect, supplicants to their friends and relatives across the border.

## The South Wind into Guangdong

"Where did you get that television set?" asked one 1980s Guangdong resident of another. "The South Wind," his friend replied—that is, through a connection in Hong Kong. The South Wind brought material goods but, even more important, an alluring world of style, freedom, comfort, capital, technology, and expertise that roused Guangdong to change. In its transformation since 1949, Hong Kong became a veritable treasure trove of inspiration and services for the development of Guangdong. Guangdong's desire and ability to learn from Hong Kong, however, did not arise immediately upon China's opening to the outside. Gradually, as connections across the border grew, people came to see the value of Hong Kong's achievements for their own lives. By the end of the 1980s the atmosphere in Guangzhou was free enough that *Nanfeng chuang* (The window to the South Wind), a fashionable magazine, was explicitly introducing ideas and styles from Hong Kong.

Virtually all towns and villages in southern Guangdong had abundant private connections with Hong Kong. As the province became receptive to it, the South Wind brought information and perspective not only on Hong Kong but on the entire outside world, at a trustworthy personal level. Overseas Chinese in North America, Southeast Asia, and elsewhere who had roots in Guangdong usually had a network that led to their native province through Hong Kong. The thousands of visitors who entered Guangdong each day via Hong Kong were bearers of goods, currency, and, more important, foreign ways of thinking. In Guangzhou's better hotels where foreigners stayed, local residents, unlike in most cities in China, were permitted to enter and observe the modern architecture, efficiency, cleanliness, and levels of customer service that were beyond what they had ever known. Pilot factories and farms introduced through Hong Kong similarly brought completely new concepts of efficiency and organization as well as modern technology. Even middle- and small-sized Hong Kong entrepreneurs who invested in China had a new approach to management, and in their Guangdong factories some of the more talented local workers acquired skills that would eventually be useful beyond these enterprises.

The impact of Hong Kong in Guangdong extended far beyond the world of business. Some of the richest businesspeople believed they could make more money in Hong Kong than in the mainland in a given amount of time, with fewer bureaucratic hassles, and in a milieu they preferred. Still, desiring the good will of the mainland, they chose to make substantial donations to China, often for educational or special training programs. Two of Hong Kong's billionaires, Li Ka-shing and Henry Fok, for example, donated large sums for new universities in Guangdong, modeled in good part after universities in Hong Kong. Some business leaders, anticipating retirement before 1997 and thus believing it not worth the effort to establish their own personal connections with China, nevertheless encouraged their children, who would be doing business after 1997, to nourish such contacts, even beyond immediate business interests. One group of second-generation business leaders, for example, established the Peihua ("Cultivation of China") Foundation to support training programs in which they introduced modern Western practices in areas like business management, accounting, telecommunications, computers, and mining management.

Until the 1970s leaders in China were quite innocent about matters of international trade, finance, market development, and packaging, despite the fact that Communist Chinese organizations such as the Xinhua News Agency, China Resources, China Merchants, China Travel Service, Yuhua Department Stores, the Bank of China, trade unions, and the Communist Party already had large staffs stationed in Hong Kong. The leaders were from many parts of China, but the rank-and-file cadres hailed mostly from Guangdong. During the Cultural Revolution, mainlanders working in Hong Kong were seen as almost inevitably tainted by capitalism. For those in China, fear of this contamination and the criticism it would bring was an effective barrier to learning about Hong Kong. As the thaw progressed, the work of those stationed in Hong Kong was seen more positively and their responsibilities and their numbers exploded. New organizations such as Yuehai (Guangdong Enterprises) were added. Their main offices in Guangdong sent senior cadres to Hong Kong, not simply to check up on branches there and to acquire personal belongings, but to understand foreign developments.

Some of these organizations—the Bank of China, for example—established special training programs for mainland colleagues, which made it easy for staff from Guangdong to acquire in their native language an understanding of the outside world that would take more time, trouble, and far more funding elsewhere. Some newer organizations, established in Hong Kong since the opening of China, were more flexible than older ones. China International Trade and Investment Corporation (CITIC), a large mainland-based corporation originally given an estimated one billion dollars in seed money by China and directed by China's favorite in-house capitalist, Rong Yiren, not only bought property in Hong Kong but took part in joint business dealings with capitalist organizations. CITIC was able to issue bonds, purchase shares in such Hong Kong-based enterprises as Cathay Pacific Airways, administer a fund that acquired shares in the Japanese stock market, and take the lead position in a consortium to develop Hong Kong's second harbor tunnel. Everbright, a smaller-scale entrepreneurial firm led by Wang Guangying, a Tianjin capitalist and brother-in-law of Liu Shaoqi, also used "capitalist methods" in Hong Kong to help achieve China's goals.

By the mid-1980s thousands of Chinese cadres were visiting Hong Kong each week. In the late 1970s such a trip was like visiting an exotic, tempting, and slightly sinful house of treasures. By 1987 it had become routine and even ordinary people from Guangdong could get permission to join tour groups to Hong Kong organized by Chinese travel agencies. They naturally passed on the wonders of what they saw.

Many children of high-level cadres from Beijing as well as from Guangdong were able to find work in Hong Kong or in nearby Shenzhen, a domesticated version of Hong Kong. Their parents might be critical of the excessively bourgeois life their children led in Hong Kong, but that did not mean the elders were immune to its influence.

The influence of books, magazines, and newspapers from Hong Kong had always extended beyond the personal network,[2] but television's impact was even greater. In all East Asian countries television, introduced just as industrialization was beginning, played a major role in transmitting foreign ideas. More than any earlier medium it provided a powerful link to the outside world and made possible a more vivid and intimate understanding of foreign life and foreign ways of thinking. As television became more common in China in the early 1980s, the government permitted it to show a broader range of programs. Coverage was selective but included worldwide news, travelogues, foreign dramas, and advertising. To a public that had regarded the outside world almost as another planet, television brought an unprecedented first-hand awareness.

The impact of television was even greater in Guangdong than elsewhere in China. The number of television sets was higher, because of the higher standard of living: surveys in the Pearl River Delta revealed that by the mid-1980s over 90 percent of the households there had access to television. As the first families in towns and villages in more remote areas of Guangdong acquired sets, neighbors and relatives came to gaze at the marvels they revealed.

After sets became available, Guangdong was also the one place in China where sizable numbers of people had direct access to outside television. Authorities, aware of the appeal of Hong Kong stations, made periodic efforts to curb the large "fish-bone" *(yugu)* antennae in Guangzhou that picked up Hong Kong programs, but many households within a fifty- to hundred-mile radius remained able to receive the programs without extra equipment. Their friends and relatives from the north also eagerly viewed Hong Kong television when visiting. To limit this, authorities used domestic broadcast frequencies that interfered with outside reception, allowed substantial amounts of attractive Cantonese programming, and even purchased selected Hong Kong programs to be rerun on Guangdong stations. Whether viewing the more attractive local programs designed to compete with Hong Kong television or watching it directly, viewers could never again be ignorant of outside progress.

The South Wind brought not only technology and expertise useful for the modernization of China as a whole but opportunities for the acquisition of wealth and privilege for individuals and their friends. In the 1980s, some people in Guangdong found the goods so attractive and so beyond the realm of anything they could acquire through their own incomes that they were willing to bribe, smuggle, extort, deceive, and use nepotism to achieve their aims. And some became victims of Hong Kong businesspeople ready to mislead and deceive their less-informed Guangdong friends and business partners for personal gain. In short, the South Wind had many fragrances and odors. Perhaps above all it gradually brought an awareness that with effort Guangdong could hope to achieve what Hong Kong had.

## A New Entrepôt Role and New Workers

The opening of China permitted a new era of economic relations between Hong Kong and Guangdong. Veterans in Hong Kong businesses who had survived the earlier collapse of the entrepôt trade believed that this loss, by stimulating Hong Kong to develop its own manufacturing and an acute sensitivity to world markets, had in the long run benefited Hong Kong. It was thus not only a more modern but a stronger and more diversified Hong Kong that began a new era of entrepôt trade after a hiatus of almost thirty years.

Customs figures did not distinguish where in China trade originated, but most Chinese trade with Hong Kong was to and from Guangdong. The rapid growth of Hong Kong's entrepôt trade in the late 1970s is reflected in data on trade between China and Hong Kong (in billions of U.S. dollars):[3]

|  | 1980 | 1987 |
|---|---|---|
| Trade to Hong Kong from China | | |
| Direct | 3.5 | 4.3 |
| Indirect | 0.9 | 10.7 |
| Total | 4.4 | 15.0 |
| Trade from Hong Kong to China | | |
| Direct | 0.3 | 3.6 |
| Indirect | 0.9 | 7.7 |
| Total | 1.2 | 11.3 |
| Total HK–PRC trade | | |
| Direct | 3.8 | 7.9 |
| Indirect | 1.8 | 18.4 |
| Total | 5.6 | 26.3 |

While two-way direct trade between Hong Kong and China (goods produced in Hong Kong and destined for China and goods produced in China destined for Hong Kong) roughly doubled between 1980 and 1987, entrepôt trade (indirect trade, passing through Hong Kong to and from China) exploded, increasing to about ten times its 1980 level.

Many mainland officials, including those in Guangdong, wanted to deal directly with foreigners and avoid middlemen, especially condescending Hong Kong capitalists who would sooner or later be sure to get a good share of the profits. Yet China needed those capitalists for their knowledge of business and technology, their access to finance, their skill in managing large projects, and their control of the transportation and telecommunications infrastructure. Chinese managers might complain about profiteering by those in Hong Kong. But when held accountable for bewildering tasks like shipping goods to world markets, marketing, insuring, guaranteeing delivery, servicing, and handling errors, they usually chose to pass the responsibility to a Hong Kong agent. Some in Guangdong learned the hard way that they could not quickly acquire the necessary skills. Guangdong Province established some thirty commercial companies to operate in Hong Kong in the 1980s, but by the end of the decade virtually all were in debt, unable to compete successfully.

When it experienced a foreign currency shortage, China often cut purchases from Hong Kong firms before it reduced purchases from the large multinational Western and Japanese firms whose technology and goodwill it badly needed. Yet because Hong Kong businesspeople had unique advantages, they outperformed foreigners in Guangdong in the first decade of its reopening. Many Westerners were reluctant to invest in Guangdong and other parts of China, because they doubted it would be easy to hire and fire workers, repatriate funds, avoid unanticipated costs, and solve problems if the Chinese should fail to deliver on their assurances. After listening to their lawyers point out all the risks that result from lack of legal guarantees, many foreign investors preferred to err on the side of caution. Their Hong Kong counterparts also sought legal assurances when possible, but they had superior access to an informal network of friends and relatives inside China. They might lack leverage when pressures in China were severe and they might be cautious about substantial investments, but under ordinary circumstances their network provided a measure of security that Westerners could only seek through legal guarantees. This gave Hong Kong something close to a small captive market in Guangdong, a hinterland that, though under a different political system, proved to be not unlike what Japanese, Korean, and Taiwanese industries enjoyed in their own countries.

In the 1980s no city in China could quickly acquire Hong Kong's skills, infrastructure, and cosmopolitan nature. Hong Kong towered above Shanghai, Guangzhou, and Beijing, even after a decade of reforms in those cities. Its position linking economic relations between China and the outside world remained unique. At the end of the 1980s, Hong Kong, with one-half of 1 percent of China's population, had roughly the same amount of foreign trade as all of China combined.

For Hong Kong industrialists, the new labor supply in Guangdong was even more important than new markets. There are no accurate data on the flow of immigrants from Guangdong to Hong Kong, because refugees have had to elude officials on both sides of the border, but according to estimates, tens of thousands flowed to Hong Kong each year during the 1960s and 1970s, with surges in 1962, 1976, 1977, and 1978. After 1978, cooperation between Hong Kong and Guangdong authorities and tighter controls almost stopped the flow, and Hong Kong manufacturing, still growing and with no new immigrants, soon absorbed all its excess labor supply. By 1988 unemployment was below 2 percent, which enabled Hong Kong workers to bargain for higher wages and better working conditions. Although their wages lagged far behind those of Japan and slightly behind those of Singapore, their rise was so rapid that labor-intensive industries making toys, plastic flowers, low-grade textiles, and electronics, unable to meet international competition, were in danger of being wiped out. For the owners, building factories and hiring workers on the other side of the border provided the answer. Although Guangdong laborers were less skilled, less disciplined, and less efficient, they were willing to learn and keep at their jobs without complaining. In the early 1980s they were producing goods at about one-fifth of Hong Kong's labor cost. As many as ten laborers applied for each opening in Guangdong. Hong Kong businesses thus acquired the world's most inexhaustible supply of workers.

During the first decade of reforms, Hong Kong businesses, having little confidence in managers or engineers in China, commonly planned and designed the products to be produced in Guangdong. They shipped materials into China and there, under the guidance of managers from Hong Kong, goods were processed and returned to Hong Kong. Managers were sent in not only because of their management skills but because they had more independence and were less susceptible than local managers to pressures from local Chinese officials. The large gaps between the incomes of the Hong Kong managers and the Guangdong workers created jealousies, and the relationship was not always an easy one. But Guangdong's workers were happy to have the jobs, their managers had no language barrier, and together they were able to get the job done. In the summer of 1987, when the governor of Hong Kong, David Wilson, announced his estimate that over one million workers in Guangdong, more than Hong Kong's entire manufacturing labor force, were processing goods for Hong Kong businesses, China's Xinhua News Agency promptly phoned him with its estimate of *two* million.

The inexhaustible supply of mainland labor gave Hong Kong businesses trying to meet rapid increases in world demand a "surge capacity" even greater than what they had once enjoyed when Hong Kong had its own excess labor supply and cottage industries. By the mid-1980s this new source had spurred more growth in Hong Kong. Hong Kong, despite its nervousness and stock market woes, thus seemed to have more vitality than ever in spite of, or perhaps because of, the approaching union of 1997.

## The Shadow of 1997

Unlike many countries that have been suddenly united or divided without notice, Hong Kong and China began to grow together some fifteen years before they were to be united officially as the Chinese "resume sovereignty." Hong Kong was tense during the first years of this process, especially during 1982–1984 when the British and Chinese negotiated their future.

Until 1982, when British officials decided to broach the subject of 1997 with China, Hong Kong was thriving, despite some anxiety about the future. Most people were optimistic that in 1997, when the ninety-nine-year lease on the New Territories expired, Hong Kong would remain prosperous. But as more questions arose about long-term investments and as bankers extending their usual fifteen-year loans sought reassurance about repayments after 1997, British officials felt it prudent to raise the issues to ensure a stable transition. Prime Minister Margaret Thatcher journeyed to Beijing to meet with Chinese leaders, who used the occasion to assert full sovereignty over Hong Kong and to announce that all of Hong Kong, including the portion ceded after the Opium War, would revert to China in 1997. Deng Xiaoping set a two-year deadline for reaching a basic agreement on the transition to Chinese rule, through diplomatic negotiations aimed at securing the continued stability and prosperity of Hong Kong. Chinese and British discussions began that led eventually to the Sino-British Joint Declaration on the Question of Hong Kong in September 1984.

The Hong Kong mood, the stock market, the housing market, and the value of the Hong Kong dollar plummeted three times during the talks—shortly after the Thatcher visit in September 1982, in September 1983 when talks almost broke down over the issue of whether the British would have a role after the Chinese resumed sovereignty, and after May 1984 when Deng announced that Chinese troops would be stationed in Hong Kong after 1997. The Chinese were firm in their insistence on sovereignty and on the absence of a British role after 1997. But in the Joint Declaration, registered with the United Nations, they showed that in the two years of negotiation they had acquired a far better understanding of what was needed to maintain prosperity in Hong Kong and far more flexibility than many observers believed possible two years before. In the declaration the Chinese agreed that Hong Kong could maintain a separate capitalist system for fifty years. Under the policy of "one country two systems," they basically agreed to continue Hong Kong's own common law system; they allowed Hong Kong-born Chinese to continue to use British passports for travel abroad; they agreed that Hong Kong should have its own air services agreements and its own shipping register. They also approved the continuation of existing leases until 2047, and they set up a Sino-British Joint Liaison Group to continue until 2000 to help ensure the smooth transfer of government.[4]

A committee of thirty-six Chinese and twenty-three Hong Kong leaders was formed to draft the basic laws for governing the Hong Kong Special Administrative Region from its inception in July 1997. The Basic Law, the first version of which was issued in 1988 for consultation with the people of Hong Kong, was to be promulgated in 1990.

It proved impossible to ease Hong Kong's anxieties completely. The Communists' record of making promises as they took over mainland cities and altering them as political circumstances changed could not be erased. Would mainland China really permit an open Hong Kong that included horse-race betting, Taiwanese political activity, anti-Communist publications, mini-skirts, massage parlors, and flagrant financial speculation? Would Communist leaders resist the temptation to tap Hong Kong's resources to help other areas at Hong Kong's expense? Would international financiers still find Hong Kong attractive under Communist rule? Many Hong Kong people were pleasantly surprised at the flexibility China showed in 1984 but were nonetheless disappointed that the 1988 draft of the Basic Law did not specify more procedures to guarantee local political autonomy.

The great British trading house of Hong Kong, Jardine Matheson, announced in March 1984 that it was moving its headquarters to Bermuda. Many middle-class intellectuals and well-to-do businessmen and their families sought citizenship or permanent residence cards in England, Canada, the United States, Taiwan, Singapore, Australia, or New Zealand. Only after they had established an alternative did some return to give Hong Kong a try. Wealthy parents sent children abroad for university training for a new reason, expecting them to establish themselves and to be prepared to look after aged parents who might later join them. Expectant mothers flew to the United States to give birth to babies who would have U.S. citizenship and thus could go to America at any time and bring their parents. Businesspeople in Hong Kong quietly began diversifying their assets to Swiss banks, to the New York and Tokyo stock exchanges, and to real estate in Los Angeles, Toronto, and London, even while continuing to invest in a buoyant Hong Kong.

Many people in Hong Kong expected to leave before 1997, and more were keeping their options open. Some were planning to depart for reasons similar to those of many others who had left that part of China for the last 150 years: to find better economic opportunities and to join friends and relatives who had previously emigrated. Some planned to leave because they did not want to adjust to the constraints and risks in their personal or professional lives that they expected to face after 1997. The number of actual emigrants varied, depending on the residents' opinions on both their local long-range prospects and the likelihood of their gaining foreign citizenship or permanent residence. In 1987, when some were disappointed that Hong Kong could not gain more guarantees for the shape of post-1997 autonomy, the number of emigrants doubled to fifty thousand a year. Many were middle-class managers and professionals, some of whom were experienced China traders who considered their Chinese counterparts, arriving in Hong Kong in increasing numbers, to be bureaucratic, unpredictable, and arbitrary. So many academics and managers in multinational corporations were leaving or talking about leaving that universities and banks were seriously concerned about staff shortages.

The panics between 1982 and 1984 and China's decision to resume full sovereignty over Hong Kong in 1997 strengthened the leverage of China over those in Hong Kong. Residents believed that despite the various guarantees given by China on Hong Kong's status after 1997, the political power of China would nonetheless be very strong. By the mid-1980s the cadres from the mainland assigned to work in Hong Kong had come to be known as *biaoshu,* an uncle not in the direct patrilineal line. In Hong Kong the term implied a "country bumpkin," but it took on another meaning based on *The Red Lantern,* a popular Cultural Revolution opera about the anti-Japanese guerrilla forces. It described the underground Communist political commissars who showed up in a unit in preparation for the Communists' later takeover. In the 1980s people in Hong Kong had leverage over those from China because of the superior wealth and knowledge of the modern world, but the eventual transfer of political power gave the *biaoshu* a counter-leverage that kept the relationship from being lop-sided.

## Two-way Anticipatory Socialization

Social scientists have coined the term "anticipatory socialization" to describe how people, knowing they will become members of new organizations, begin to acquire the appropriate attitudes and skills even before they join. After 1982, those in Hong Kong who chose to remain began to socialize themselves for their post-1997 roles as citizens of Communist China. In a similar way, the Chinese were already increasing their investment in Hong Kong and learning how to take part in the capitalist world. Perhaps never have two territories facing reunion had such a long period of preparation.

In Hong Kong many began to study Mandarin, which they realized they would need for business in China. They started to read more mainland publications and pick up the current vocabulary of mainland organizations. In areas related to their work, they purposefully explored how to get things done in China. Businesses that were able established ventures across the border and built up personal networks and expertise. Privately, too, businesspeople gradually considered what their own lives would be like after 1997.

The Beijing government had no regular government representative in Hong Kong. By the late 1970s, however, a small group within its Hong Kong Xinhua News Agency branch had been assigned to function in effect as a protogovernment. A decade later this group included some seventy officials. In recognition of the growing importance of Hong Kong, China upgraded this Xinhua office in 1983 and appointed as head Xu Jiatun, a former provincial first Party secretary who had helped bring modern reforms to Jiangsu Province. When he arrived in Hong Kong, local people colloquially referred to him as the "governor" or the "ambassador" and regarded his pronouncements as semiofficial statements of the government that would someday rule them. He became the head of a growing network of Communist organizations that were playing an increasing role in the financial, commercial, tourist, and even manufacturing life of Hong Kong. By nourishing a broad range of contacts in Hong Kong, showing understanding of local sensitivities, and publicly praising Hong Kong's capitalism, he helped calm local anxieties about mainland intentions.

In July 1988, the Joint Liaison Group making plans for post-1997 government chose Hong Kong as its principal base, even while continuing to meet once each year in London and Beijing. Four out of the five regular members of the Chinese team moved to Hong Kong, with a sizable support staff. Mindful of their "liaison" role and cautious lest they awaken local fears of mainland interference, they tried to keep a low profile. Nevertheless, they acquired an aura of power in the eyes of local people.

Not only the business community but people in every walk of life in Hong Kong, including workers, shopkeepers, newspaper reporters, and academics, sought to deepen their ties with their counterparts across the border. Some complained that others in Hong Kong were too eager to please their future leaders and were making too many concessions to every hint from China about what it wanted in the future.

Some of the elite assigned to Hong Kong by China in the 1980s went there with an air of self-confidence and even superiority. Some were more preoccupied with opportunities for personal gain than with their national responsibilities. But once there they soon became aware that they had much to learn from Hong Kong, and in their work as well as their personal lives they began to acquire ways of thinking and behavior better adapted to non-Communist society.

The same kind of adjustment was taking place on Guangdong's side of the border. In the late 1970s few there had much sense of what had been required to gain the technology and material goods that Hong Kong had. Like generations of prerevolutionary Chinese, those in Guangdong initially wanted to enjoy the material benefits without greatly altering their way of doing things, but gradually they learned how much change was needed to acquire and spread the benefits of modern industry. Sometimes this required a complete reorientation of one's behavior or way of thought. Guangdong cadres who casually dropped in to Hong Kong for long leisurely visits on workdays were jarred, for example, by the attitude of their Hong Kong business hosts, who thought of time as money, to be organized and carefully apportioned. Many assumptions in Hong Kong about good service, efficiency, profitability, and modern technology startled people from Guangdong and set off endless waves of rethinking. As the 1980s progressed, such new ideas and patterns of behavior, along with new styles, flowed into Guangdong almost as if the border did not exist.

It was one thing for the people of Guangdong to hear that people somewhere in the world had access to such possessions, and quite another to learn that their own friends and relatives, less than a hundred miles away, had them. The objects no longer seemed beyond reach. If anything, the problem was that the exposure was too intense and the gap too great to bridge easily. Even those who preferred the economic security of the socialist system found the immediacy of foreign goods irresistible. Although Guangdong was so large and so poor and Hong Kong so rich that many efforts to bridge the gap in the first decade of reopening were doomed to frustration, what the city cousins achieved led the country cousins to keep trying. At the government and Party level, planners were concerned with such questions as how to restructure basic systems to allow goods to flow more freely, to permit factories and stores to function more efficiently, and to provide people more incentives for better performance. What they saw in Hong Kong, for all its dangers of graft and corruption, gave them a sense of immediacy, urgency, and direction as they wrestled with the issue of what reforms to introduce and how.

# 3.

# *A Decade of Reforms*

As the turmoil of the Cultural Revolution receded, China's leaders focused on a goal that had eluded their predecessors for over a century: enriching the nation. To achieve it they relentlessly introduced fundamental reforms that shook up the stagnant old system.

The negative lessons of the Great Leap Forward and the Cultural Revolution, and the newly discovered successes in the outside world had given most Party leaders a new sense of direction. Workers and work units needed more incentives to make them more dynamic. Specialists deserved respect and more freedom to pursue their work. Goods had to circulate more freely to meet consumer and industrial needs. The tilt toward heavy industry had to be altered toward light industry, particularly consumer goods. New management skills and technology from Japan and the West were required. After Mao died in 1976, however, leaders disagreed on how to realize these ambitions. Three major approaches dominated discussions over the next few years.

The first, an effort to achieve rapid growth with few systemic reforms, was played out from 1976 to 1978, during and immediately after the rule of Mao's immediate successor, Hua Guofeng. Convinced that investment was the key to growth, Hua and his planners moved quickly to make up for lost time. They increased the leeway of local governments to collect revenue, to borrow, and to make their own investment decisions. These policies sparked rapid growth, but uncontrolled investment and inadequate planning caused budget deficits and enormous waste. A great deal of new equipment and even many whole plants were not usable because of quality problems, shortages of energy and supplies, untrained manpower, and poor management. Critics denigrated the 1977–1979 spurt as the *yang yuejin* (the Western-style Leap Forward). It used new terminology, technology, and loans from the West, but, they complained, like the earlier *tu yuejin* (the rustic Leap Forward), it also suffered from optimism detached from reality and veered out of control. The 1979 annual plans had called for capital investment of thirty-six billion yuan, but actual investment reached fifty-four billion. In 1979 there was a national budget shortfall of seventeen billion yuan and in 1980 of twelve billion, very serious for a small economy.[1] It was clear that more had to change before investment and Western advice could be effective.

A second view was championed by Chen Yun, who in the 1950s had been a father of the relatively successful first five-year plan. He believed that China still needed socialist planning—that the failures of the previous two decades came not from the system per se but from mistakes, inadequate controls, and poor implementation. China was too poor and its population too large to be able to produce enough goods to meet demand. Opening the market too widely would lead to uncontrollable inflation and to the misallocation of resources to projects of low priority instead of to projects crucial for national development. China therefore should continue to rely on price controls. The lesson Chen drew from the disastrous Leap Forward and the Cultural Revolution was the need for caution, to ensure that the economy was on solid ground even if it grew at only a modest rate.[2] In his view the budget deficit had to be controlled and debts from abroad limited; investment reduced to avoid supply shortages; and spending at smaller plants curtailed to ensure supplies for larger, more essential ones.

The third view, which won the day in 1978, was that of Deng Xiaoping. Formerly secretary general of the Party, twice out of favor, he had wide experience in top circles in Beijing and a broad-based following when he succeeded Hua Guofeng in early 1978. By December he had sufficiently consolidated his power and organized his thinking to set out guidelines for a concerted multiyear reform effort at the Third Plenum of the Eleventh Party Congress. He forthrightly acknowledged that there were fundamental systemic problems, irrational rigidities that blocked progress. He believed reforms were needed to lay the foundation for several decades of solid progress toward the goals he popularized as the "four modernizations" (in agriculture, industry, science and technology, and national defense).

Deng acknowledged that China's leaders would be experimenting in uncharted territory. They would, as he said, "Take a step, then take a look" *(zou yibu, kan yibu)*. As it turned out, China took several bold steps in almost every year of the next decade. The leadership looked around after each change and tried to correct its worst side effects. Sometimes they decided a small step backward was necessary, but overall they continued to move ahead. Deng and Zhao Ziyang, who became premier in September 1980, were ready to accept some disorder, which they saw as the price of reform.

Although the reforms were to touch virtually all areas and all Party and government organs, the most critical area was "system reform" *(tizhi gaige)*. This was distinguished from "structural reform" *(zhidu gaige)*, in order to make it clear that the basic leadership structure was not being attacked, thereby minimizing high-level opposition. The group in Beijing charting this course was the Economic System Reform Commission (Jingji Tizhi Gaige Weiyuanhui, sometimes translated as the Commission for Restructuring the Economy), headed first by Zhao Ziyang, and then by Li Tieying and Li Peng, all very powerful leaders. Parallel commissions, composed of dedicated reformers with a broad mandate, were established in Guangdong and elsewhere for provincial-level reforms. The commissions were interagency groups without independent power; they worked with various branches of the government in recommending reforms in their respective spheres.

Deng and his commission quickly began to spell out the content of reform. They wanted to give a larger role to markets, give more initiative to smaller work groups in the countryside, get rid of the "iron rice bowl" *(tie fan wan)* that gave security to workers regardless of their performance, permit more private and collective-run enterprises, liven up state enterprises by creating more incentives, and loosen the tight state control over microeconomic management. But they were determined to be pragmatic. They did not start by announcing a well-developed program; instead they discussed general topics and then allowed local areas to take the initiative, within an acceptable range, to find out what worked. Formal reform policies were issued only after they had been tried in many locations, usually with many variations. Even then, Deng was willing to consider later revisions.

To move ahead Deng needed the backing of conservative cadres as well as committed reformers, and in March 1979 he set forth a political platform designed to gain broad support for the reform program. China was to retain socialist ownership; leadership was to remain in the hands of the Communist Party; the authority structure was to remain stable; and Marxism-Leninism and Mao Zedong Thought were to guide policy.[3] These four principles were not defined so precisely that they could test who was complying; rather, they were general assurances to conservatives that Deng was not tampering with what many considered sacred.

At least initially, China was to retain socialist planning. Markets would be expanded, but they would be subordinated to and not allowed to interfere with state plans, which still controlled all basic commodities and most manufactured goods.

From what they had heard about crime and social disorder in places like the United States and Hong Kong, cadres believed that China was better served by the Party's selection of a core of elite leaders dedicated to the public good than by "bourgeois democracy." In this they were scarcely different from leaders in Taiwan and Singapore who also doubted the wisdom of choosing top rulers strictly by public elections. Some Chinese Communist leaders could imagine that elections might play a greater role in advanced countries with a more knowledgeable citizenry, but they thought that at best it would take several decades before China had a public sufficiently informed even to consider such a step. To prevent the kind of unpredictable assaults that had occurred during the Cultural Revolution, cadres wanted a legal framework, but they also wanted power to remain firmly in the hands of the Communist Party.

Criticisms of Chairman Mao within Party circles had been far more severe than the Chinese public had been told. Many who had been hurt by his policies felt that in his later years Mao had been a disaster for China, and on October 1, 1979, the thirtieth anniversary of the Communist victory, Marshal Ye Jianying, speaking for the Party and the government, presented a major overall critique of Mao's role in the Cultural Revolution. Yet even he and other leaders who had suffered felt that Mao had been dedicated to China, to ordinary workers and peasants; that Mao had made valuable contributions in uniting the nation; and that his Thoughts, with their respect for China, for ordinary peasants, and for the idea of sacrifice, were still useful guidelines. Even those who were more skeptical of Mao's value acknowledged that given his mass following and the number of cadres who had been involved in carrying out his orders, it would be too disruptive now to engage in broad-scale public criticism. He was seen by the public as a Communist Party leader, and an attack on him would further damage the image of the Party. Similarly, rather than attacking Marxism-Leninism directly, leaders felt it wiser to avoid divisiveness by saying that historical circumstances had changed and then proceeding with the reforms.

Anyone studying Chinese reforms since the Cultural Revolution is frustrated in trying to pin down the process. It is easy enough to find documents announcing reforms and even to find summaries of decisions not fully released to the public. It is difficult, however, to distinguish reforms from other decisions and administrative actions, and there was no single list of reform measures. Since announcements of reforms were made only after considerable experimentation, it is often hard to determine when provincial policy on a given issue changed from disapproval to passive acceptance, from passive acceptance to approval, and from approval to broad implementation. When practices were declared successful and codified, many localities claimed to have originated them, and there is no way to determine who was first. It is difficult to ascertain to what extent reform directives were implemented, for foot-dragging is not easily uncovered. To compare reforms in Guangdong systematically with those of other provinces would require original research elsewhere that is beyond the scope of this work. And yet by following documents, making visits, and talking with cadres and ordinary people about their experiences, it is possible to speak with some confidence about the main outlines of the reform program in Guangdong and to provide impressions of how they compared with those elsewhere.

## Granting Guangdong and Fujian a "Special Policy"

Deng's decision to allow experiments in order to get the economy moving gave all the provinces more freedom. When authority had been decentralized previously, guidelines and Party control had been so tight that local areas had little room to maneuver. Deng now realized that if control was too tight, it would nip the new spirit in the bud. He wanted to get rid of the vicious circle described in a saying popular among cadres: "Things were lifeless, so open up; once opened up, there's chaos; once chaos, pull back; once pulled back, things are lifeless" *(si, jiu fang; yi fang, jiu luan; yi luan, jiu shou; yi shou, jiu si)*. "You can't grow fish," went the old proverb, "in clear water." Beijing was prepared to crack down if a serious problem developed, but the reform period was purposely more permissive.

The greater latitude created a gray area used masterfully by local officials like Ren Zhongyi, the first Party secretary in Guangdong after November 1980. "If something is not explicitly prohibited," Ren told his associates, then "move ahead," and "if something is allowed, then use it to the hilt." Local leaders everywhere sensed that Beijing would be especially tolerant of those who helped their localities become more successful economically. Once goals were announced but before specific directives came out, officials at lower levels introduced programs that were arguably within the spirit of the goals. The art of divining what higher levels would not oppose and finding explanations to justify one's actions, long a skill of Chinese bureaucrats, flourished. Guangdong enjoyed especially good communication with Beijing during the reform era. With sources of information through Hong Kong, where many children of Beijing's highest cadres were located and where magazines often broke stories of developments in China not yet circulated within the country, Guangdong officials ascertained the limits and acted accordingly. They generally believed in reform; as one vice-governor put it, "We made full use of our opportunities."

Yet Beijing had enough leverage in the provinces that their reforms, including Guangdong's, could not have succeeded without Beijing's wholehearted support. The Communist Party had been reconstituted after the Cultural Revolution, and members everywhere followed the wishes of the Party Central Committee in Beijing. The highest Party officials at each level were appointed by the next higher level; top Party officials in Guangdong were assigned and removed directly by Beijing. After a policy was enunciated by the national government, Guangdong did not oppose it publicly. Furthermore, the building of railroads, bridges, ports, telecommunication systems, and other infrastructure required personnel as well as technical help from the capital. Many basic goods were allocated by Beijing, and the work of economic officials at the provincial level was thoroughly interwoven with the work of those at the center.

Guangdong not only had an advantage in its skill at determining and fully using Beijing's limits of tolerance; it was also administered under a special policy that allowed it more leeway than other localities were given. Historically, Cantonese, the dominant group in Guangdong, were not particularly loved in Beijing or elsewhere in China. Many Chinese regarded them as cunning, opportunistic, and materialistic. But there were compelling political and economic reasons for the special freedom and support given to Guangdong. For the same reasons a similar policy was applied to Fujian, although in the 1980s Guangdong was more economically advanced and moved more rapidly.

One reason for this support was to encourage national unification. Beijing then claimed sovereignty over three territories over which it did not yet exercise de facto rule: Hong Kong, Macau, and Taiwan. In 1979, three years before Margaret Thatcher visited China, Beijing was already considering these issues. To maintain the prosperity of Hong Kong and Macau after reunion, China needed the positive cooperation of the people there. And because Beijing now wanted foreign help to modernize, it could not afford to alienate countries that would not tolerate the use of force to regain Taiwan, a project that therefore also required the positive cooperation of the Taiwanese. Since Hong Kong and Macau were inhabited by people originally from Guangdong and Taiwan by people from Fujian, what more could China do to win over the people of these three territories than to allow their native provinces special flexibility to gain their goodwill? Reform in Guangdong and Fujian thus served an important political goal.

Beijing's approach to Guangdong and Fujian also relieved the state's financial burden. When leaders at the center contemplated the requirements for modernization in 1979, they were acutely aware of their financial constraints, exacerbated by the huge budget deficits that had resulted from the extravagant, poorly planned investments under Hua Guofeng. Horrendous bottlenecks in transport, electric power, energy, communications, manufacturing, and technology required attention. Bureaucrats everywhere wanted greater financial resources for their sector or their locale. China had to find ways to modernize without straining its pitifully small and overcommitted national budget.

Guangdong and Fujian presented a special opportunity. Almost 80 percent of the Chinese who had migrated overseas had come from Guangdong, and the next largest number had come from Fujian. Many began earning their living abroad through one of the "three knives" (cooking, hair cutting, or construction) but rose to become one of the "three highs" (intellectuals, owners, or white-collar employees). Some starry-eyed Guangdong officials estimated that the financial assets of overseas Chinese totalled $200 billion. The feelings of overseas Chinese and "compatriots" (those in the territories claimed by China, and hence not considered "overseas") toward China had been strained by the suffering inflicted on their relatives during political campaigns since 1949. But they retained a reservoir of goodwill toward their homeland. Even during the Cultural Revolution, they had continued to send financial support to relatives in China. In 1979 they sent some 745 million yuan to Guangdong through deposits in branches of the Bank of China in Hong Kong, Macau, and overseas. Taiwanese sent funds indirectly, but Fujianese in Southeast Asia sent them directly. With flexible policies, compatriots and overseas Chinese would invest in China and help relieve the national budget. Where better to attempt changes that would encourage investment than in Guangdong and Fujian?[4] The essence of the bargain between Beijing and Guangdong was captured by the pun of the time. "If you won't give us *qian* [money]," said Guangdong, "how about *quan* [power]?"

The special policy could also reduce strains on national resources and the transportation system, problems some planners considered as serious as the shortage of funds. With an increased ability to cooperate with the outside, Guangdong might generate enough foreign currency to purchase more resources from abroad. Cooperation with Hong Kong could also attract technology to support Guangdong's efforts to expand light industry. Any import of resources would also help relieve the transport burden. Guangdong could play another key role in increasing China's foreign exchange earnings, badly needed for the purchase of technology and machinery. If the province had the flexibility not only to produce light industrial goods for the international market but also to reorient its agricultural policy to capture an even larger share of the Hong Kong food market, it could gradually switch to higher-quality food products and to more food processing.

Guangdong was far away from Beijing, which reduced the risk that its changes would cause political unrest in the central government. Areas like Shanghai, Tianjin, and the Northeast, moreover, played such a large role in China's basic industry that national officials were not inclined to tamper with them. Guangdong's contribution to China's treasury was modest, and thus any failure on Guangdong's part would not greatly upset the national budget.

Perhaps most important, Beijing's reform-minded leaders, above all Zhao Ziyang, who had served in Guangdong for over two decades beginning in 1952, knew that Guangdong cadres were more receptive than others to trying new programs, and had access to world technology and management systems through Hong Kong. Beijing believed that if Guangdong could demonstrate some successes, it would be easier to persuade more conservative cadres elsewhere to implement the same policies.

In short Guangdong and Fujian, because of their special relationship to the outside world, were targets of opportunity for China. Given the rigidities of state planning and the state bureaucracy, leaders realized that more changes would be required to interface with compatriots, overseas Chinese, and foreigners than could readily be made nationwide. The new special policy was an effort to give Guangdong the flexibility to make those changes and take advantage of its special proximity to the outside world. In the new atmosphere after the Cultural Revolution, this was a logic that even conservatives found hard to oppose.

Even before the Third Plenum of the Eleventh Party Congress in December 1978, key Guangdong officials and those in Beijing concerned with Guangdong had been given hints about the new policy, and they thus had time to consider how to apply the policies of the Third Plenum to the province. A small task force under the State Council began to work on the details of what were to become the guidelines for Guangdong's special policy.

There were many issues to be considered—the nature and extent of the new policy, and its application to a multitude of areas, including agriculture, industry, commerce, banking, foreign trade, and budgeting. Discussions proceeded apace, and in May 1979 a small task force led by Gu Mu of the State Council came to Guangdong for a round of meetings and site visits in an effort to finalize the new guidelines. Gu Mu, an experienced Party technocrat who had joined other intellectuals in the Communist movement in Beijing in the 1930s, had been concerned with economic matters for most of the years since 1954.[5] A minister of the State Capital Construction Commission, vice-premier of the State Council, and secretary in the Party Central Committee Secretariat, he was the major liaison with Guangdong in the development and implementation of its special policy, including the special economic zones. With solid support in Beijing, a thorough knowledge of national policy and the national bureaucracy, an open and direct manner, and a commitment to finding new approaches that would make Guangdong and the special economic zones a success, he was highly successful at his task.

It was a measure of how far national unification had proceeded since 1949 that the two high-level officials Gu Mu brought with him to represent the central government and help draft the report, Gan Ziyu and Li Hao, had originally come from Guangdong, and that the leading official representing Guangdong in the drafting, Yang Li, was originally from Shanghai. After a few days of discussion, Yang Li drafted a statement, secured the approval of the Guangdong leaders, and on June 6 issued it on behalf of the Guangdong Provincial Party Committee.[6] The Fujian Provincial Party Committee issued a similar statement on June 9. Gu Mu made the necessary rounds to obtain the approval of Beijing officials, and on July 15 the Party Central Committee and the State Council issued a joint announcement officially endorsing the guidelines that had been drawn up by the two provinces.

Leaders wanted to move ahead boldly. Yet, shaken by their failures in the Great Leap Forward and the Cultural Revolution and acutely aware of their own lack of experience in creating a new system for a modern complex economy, both national and provincial leaders were cautious about becoming locked into policies that might not work. Perhaps the most common words used to describe the new policy toward Guangdong and Fujian were *mosuo* (groping), *tansuo* (testing), and *shiyan* (experimenting). Officials did not create a reform program all at once, but set guidelines that they expected to evolve into concrete policies. The guidelines for Guangdong, quite similar to those for Fujian, were as follows.

In administering agricultural, industrial, transport, commercial, educational, cultural, technical, and public health activities, the province was given more independence to respond to its own needs. China did not, however, follow the suggestion of Xi Zhongxun, then provincial first Party secretary, of using the model of American states for Guangdong's new role. Central government ministries still supervised Guangdong branches in their respective spheres, but provincial authority in all these areas was significantly increased.

The province was given more freedom in managing foreign trade. Many Guangdong branches of national trading companies were allowed to split off and become independent. For export goods manufactured in Guangdong, Guangdong could basically make its own decisions, including determining prices. Guangdong could set up its own organizations in Hong Kong and Macau for trade promotion and information gathering. The increased foreign currency income (including funds from processing assembly, compensation trade, and joint manufacturing enterprises) that sales abroad generated would largely remain in Guangdong.

Guangdong was given new fiscal independence. Beginning in 1980, instead of sending to the central government a certain percentage of taxes collected, Guangdong would pass on, in addition to customs fees and fees collected directly by Beijing, a fixed sum *(baogan),* which would stay the same for five years.

The province was given increased financial independence. Banks in Guangdong were given more leeway to make their own investment decisions. When the province planned to use foreign currency, it would notify the central government, rather than ask for permission, and the banks would make payments accordingly. The province was permitted to set up an independent provincial investment company that could deal directly with overseas businesses and financial institutions.

Guangdong was given more authority to determine the distribution and supply of materials and resources within the province. It could not acquire materials and resources on the state plan beyond a certain agreed amount, but it could decide how to use those it did acquire without obtaining central government approval.

The province was given increased authority in managing commercial activities, including taking over as independent companies the Guangdong branches of five state companies formerly supervised by the central government.

Guangdong was given greater flexibility in determining wages. It could raise salaries above the national guidelines and decide how to adjust wages, including the proportion of salary to be paid out in bonuses.

The province was given increased leeway to set prices in certain categories and to allow the market to determine certain other prices.

An "experimental export district" was to be established. This was the initial formulation of what became the special economic zones (see Chapter 4).[7]

These guidelines enabled Guangdong, and especially its special economic zones, to be at the cutting edge of introducing reforms. Guangdong did not lead China in all reforms; many were introduced in more than one province almost simultaneously, and some came to Guangdong after they were in place elsewhere. Guangdong officials believed that most of their rural reforms began at about the same time as in the national models of Sichuan Province under Zhao Ziyang, then its first Party secretary, and Anhui Province, under its first Party secretary, Wan Li. Despite conflicting claims about the initiation of specific reforms, even officials outside Guangdong later acknowledged that Guangdong moved, on the average, more boldly than other provinces. Their "thinking was more liberated," it was said, and with their special policy they were in any case more able to put their reform instincts into practice.

## The Launching of Reforms in Guangdong

Beijing chose some of China's most senior leaders to head its work in Guangdong. On December 11, 1978, just when Deng was launching reforms at the Third Plenum, Xi Zhongxun was sent to Guangdong to be first Party secretary and governor, and Yang Shangkun was sent as second Party secretary. Xi had already been chairman of the Shensi-Gansu Border Region in Yanan in 1934 and had been selected as vice-premier of the State Council in 1959. He had been arrested and jailed later that year, initially because of questions connected with his earlier role in Yanan, which had received great publicity in new, recent publications. Yang Shangkun had served as Zhou Enlai's deputy as early as 1933, as the secretary general in the Eighth Route Army Headquarters in Yanan from 1940 to 1946, and as a leader in the Party Secretariat for many years, where he served directly under Deng Xiaoping. He had been a major early target of the Cultural Revolution, along with Peng Zhen, Lo Ruiqing, and Lu Dingyi, and had spent many years in detention.[8]

In 1952, when Beijing had sent Tao Zhu and the Southbound Work Team to take over the leadership of Guangdong, they had been accompanied by thousands of outside officials, who before long dominated all major sections of the government. The leaders they replaced, drawn from the local guerrilla forces during World War II and the war against the Kuomintang, felt besieged. The split between locals and outsiders had remained strong until all were threatened by new outsiders during the Cultural Revolution.[9]

In 1978 when Xi came to Guangdong, in contrast, he brought one personal secretary. He and Yang, and Ren Zhongyi and Liang Lingguang after them, were not part of a large outside takeover. They fit into an established provincial structure by then firmly under the control of Beijing. There was no struggle between locals and outsiders.

Xi and Yang were gone before two years had passed. Having suffered for many years in detention themselves, they played a major role in rehabilitating Guangdong cadres still under a cloud from the Cultural Revolution. They managed the conflict over local demands for more democracy by walking a fine line between preventing "bourgeois democracy" and granting leniency to Li Yizhe and others. Xi played a role in expanding rural markets and launching the special economic zones, and Yang was instrumental in getting the cooperation of the local military forces, some of whom had originally been followers of Lin Biao's local military leaders, Huang Yongsheng and Ding Sheng. But despite their support for reforms, Xi and Yang, perhaps because of their lack of experience in guiding regional economies, did not live up to the hopes of many in getting the economy moving.[10]

Their successors, Ren Zhongyi and later Liang Lingguang, proved popular among local cadres and enormously successful in effecting economic change. Provincial first Party secretary Ren Zhongyi had been highly regarded as a leader in the Northeast for over three decades, particularly for his skill as first Party secretary of Liaoning Province. Liang Lingguang had become mayor of Xiamen (Fujian) as early as 1952. He had experience in economic issues not only in Fujian but as minister of light industry from March 1978 until he was sent to Guangdong. His experiences were particularly appropriate for Guangdong, which in its new strategy was stressing light industry. An enthusiastic supporter of reforms, he began in Guangdong as first Party secretary of Guangzhou, and then served, from May 1983 until August 1985, as governor.

The reputations of Ren and Liang preceded them, and on November 16, 1980, a week after they arrived in Guangdong, they were welcomed by an enthusiastic crowd of over five thousand cadres at the Sun Yat-sen Memorial Hall.[11] Soon after he arrived, Ren spent a great deal of time dealing with issues of morale. He listened well and gave talented and trusted subordinates freedom to act on their own initiative.

A broad propaganda effort helped gain public support for reforms. Ren gave many addresses to key groups in Guangzhou and throughout the province. Because of Beijing's policy of retrenchment after the loose spending under Hua Guofeng, he had to begin by stressing readjustment in the economy.[12] Articles were prepared for the press and for television, then just becoming a major media vehicle. There were, of course, new slogans: "To the outside, more open; to the inside, looser; to those below, more leeway" *(duiwai, gengjia kaifang; duinei, gengjia fangkuan; duixia, gengjia fangquan)*. People were to use more "flexible tactics" *(linghuo cuoshi)*.

There were of course propagandists who, having passed on doctrine for decades, mouthed slogans as before; they talked about "flexible tactics" without becoming more flexible, and hailed the new "four managements" (of planning, commodity prices, bonuses, and economic discipline) without changing their management style. But propaganda was becoming less doctrinaire. There were still illusions about how close China's technological level was to that of Europe; about the degree to which the people of Hong Kong, oppressed by British colonialism, would welcome liberation by China; and about the speed with which Chinese economic levels could surpass Hong Kong's ("by the year 2000," it was thought). But through their contacts in Hong Kong and with overseas visitors, Guangdong leaders were gradually making a more accurate assessment, and their propaganda began to have a greater ring of truth.

When a major change in policy is undertaken in China, there is, in addition to political education, criticism of those resisting policy change. Beginning with a special meeting in April 1981, provincial Party leaders redirected the momentum from criticizing leftist excesses of the Cultural Revolution to a new target: leftists who were resisting reform. People were criticized for being unwilling to accept modern technology; for mistakenly thinking that competition, individual enterprise, and "commodity economics" were the same as capitalism; for failure to recognize that whether a particular state enterprise survived was not equivalent to whether the nation survived; for reluctance to open their markets to people from other provinces and other countries; for lack of enthusiasm in studying foreign developments; for excessive fear of capitalist restoration; and for unwillingness to get rid of old methods.[13] Like Deng, Ren wanted to avoid the familiar cycle of creating new victims who would later "settle accounts," and he therefore made the campaign milder than earlier ones.

As part of the new "special policy," Beijing approved setting a fixed sum—one billion yuan per year for five years—to be turned over to the central government from Guangdong's revenues, beginning in 1980. Other provinces were envious of this system, which capped a province's payments to the center and gave it more flexibility, and several years later some were allowed to adopt the same system.[14] Other localities, especially Shanghai, considered Guangdong's payments low, but the figure did represent an increase in revenues paid to Beijing. In 1979 Guangdong officially had paid Beijing 0.89 billion yuan, but with various deductions it actually sent only 0.68 billion. Payments from Guangdong were lower than from northern industrialized cities because of the evaluation of industrial assets, an important revenue component. In 1980, because some older sources of provincial revenue (iron, coal, petroleum) in Guangdong were reassigned so that these monies were collected directly by the central government, the actual payment was 0.78 billion yuan. Beijing had serious revenue shortfalls, however, and tried to get Guangdong to increase its payments. Guangdong, like other provinces, was reluctant to agree to the principle of making up shortfalls, but a compromise was reached on November 15, 1982, whereby Guangdong "lent money" to Beijing on a one-time basis, knowing that the amount would not be repaid. In 1986 Beijing negotiated another such loan from Guangdong. Guangdong remained happy with the system, nevertheless. In 1981 it had decided to collect from its prefectures and counties in the same fashion.

To help leaders draw up plans for changes, groups in every branch of the government began preparing reports. New research centers and ad hoc groups were set up to work on special problems. Although not all top Party and administrative leaders were enthusiastic about reform, they at least gave it lip service. Local areas were encouraged to try out experiments, then go on to little reforms and then to bigger reforms *(shi gai, xiao gai, da gai)*.

The most fundamental reforms were recommended by the Guangdong Province System Reform Office (Tizhi Gaige Bangongshi), established in December 1980. After Ren had been told he would be going to Guangdong, he asked his predecessors there to set up the office, some two years before the national System Reform Office was organized in Beijing, to help guide reforms upon his arrival. Though the provincial office was small and much of their discussion phrased in Marxist theory, the officials were committed to reform and their perspectives were broad-gauged. The office was attached directly to the provincial government, and its head, Wang Zhuo, advised top officials on economic reform. Wang, a pragmatic political economist, had previously drafted economic documents for Tao Zhu at the Central South Party headquarters in the early 1960s. In Guangdong, with a small staff that consulted with relevant branches of government, he provided a cogent and acceptable rationale for far-reaching reforms. The overall goal was to enliven the economy by increasing the role of market mechanisms. The key issues were how to manage the transition, pace various reforms to prevent excessive imbalances, retain the political support of key groups, and keep the economy moving forward.

# The Reforms

There is no simple list of Guangdong's reforms. What follows is an effort to summarize the most important system reforms in the decade after 1978. Changes in foreign trade, a somewhat separate issue, are dealt with in Chapter 11. (See also the statistical overview and output data in the Appendix, Tables A.2 and A.3.)

## *Agriculture*

Guangdong followed Beijing's strategy of pushing agricultural reforms first, to generate support for reforms in other areas.

In 1978, on the eve of the new reforms, the organization of agriculture in Guangdong, as in most parts of China, was essentially as it had been in the early 1960s. The province's 9,200,000 farm families were divided into 309,000 production teams,[15] which were the basic accounting units. Teams were grouped together in some 25,365 brigades, and they in turn were in 1,882 communes.[16] The team leaders, under direction from above, decided how much land was to be planted in which crop in order to meet state quotas in primary crops like rice, sugar, and peanuts. Each day they assigned groups of team members to perform various tasks as needed. Although practices varied by team, commonly each day a team worker was given work points for his or her work. After the harvest, which in most areas occurred twice a year, when the produce was sold to the state, various team expenses and reserve funds were deducted from the proceeds and then the profits of the team were distributed to team workers on the basis of their points. Farmers had small private plots where they could raise secondary products like vegetables, pork, and fowl, some of which they could sell on the open market.

Perhaps the two biggest changes in rural Guangdong between 1962 and 1978 were the great increase in the number of people in each team and the increase in the area planted in rice in order to feed the larger population and gain local self-sufficiency in accord with changes in national policy. In 1962 Guangdong had 32 million rural residents, but by 1978 it had 47 million. In the meantime, in line with the philosophy of the earlier Dazhai model of larger, more socialist units, the number of production teams decreased from 411,000 to 309,000.[17] This meant that the average population of a production team almost doubled, from 78 to 152. The total land farmed was virtually unchanged, but the number of mou (one-sixth of an acre) planted in spring rice had increased from 28.1 million mou to 30.8 million and in the fall crop from 33.2 million mou to 34.1 million.[18]

Although Lin Biao and the Gang of Four were later accused of emphasizing only rice, in fact the land area devoted to other crops was not greatly reduced during the Cultural Revolution. Secondary crops were destroyed during the period, but this was later exaggerated to discredit Lin Biao's followers; in fact, with the tacit cooperation of many rural cadres, there had been a significant "second economy" involving many agricultural goods sold outside approved channels.[19] The amount of pork procured from teams by the state had also remained fairly steady.[20] Still, farmers feared criticism for spending too much time on private plots and marketing, and this affected the supply of many goods. Some fruit trees had been cut down, and many more suffered from neglect. The quantities harvested of fruits such as bananas, lychee, and tangerines fell off sharply in the early 1970s.[21] Vegetables and other produce grown on private plots were even more affected, as were the numbers of chickens and ducks raised.

Collective agriculture had originally been introduced to ensure enough grain collection to feed the cities as well as to permit larger irrigation projects, more rational land use, economies of scale, and mechanization. But large-scale mechanization brought less advantage to rice-paddy agriculture than it had to larger collectives in the Soviet Union, and collective management had destroyed incentives and proved unpopular with peasants. Production teams had been reluctant to allow peasants to spend too much time on private activity for fear they would neglect collective tasks.

The new system that was eventually approved in 1982 assigned responsibility for meeting production quotas of basic goods, such as rice, cotton, edible oil, and sugar, down to the household. Reformers knew, however, that peasants could meet their quotas and still have more time for other crops and marketing. Realizing that this would make more rural labor available, they could then allow towns and rural enterprises to grow in order to absorb these workers. At the same time, to help ensure that peasants who could earn more by producing fresh vegetables, fish, and fowl for markets would still produce their quotas of key goods, reformers would raise the prices at which the state procured the produce from the collectives. The new system was still too controversial in 1979, in Guangzhou as well as in Beijing, and therefore a series of smaller reforms and growing permissiveness preceded the really big decision that ended collectivization and introduced the household responsibility system.

A key goal of provincial agricultural planners after 1978 through all stages of rural reform was to keep the supply of rice and other crops stable while increasing the supply of secondary agricultural produce and gradually releasing rural labor for other activities. Although rice acreage decreased more than planners would have liked, rice production actually increased. Between 1980 and 1984 the total mou in Guangdong in the two crops of rice declined from 62.5 million to 59.0 million, but in 1984 there was an all-time high rice production of 17.9 million tons, compared with 16.2 million tons in 1980. Although it declined slightly after 1984, rice production remained basically steady and rose again in 1987. Once farm families were made responsible for quotas, they met their requirements, and members of their households were free to seek income elsewhere. The sources of rural income changed accordingly, as may be seen in the following percentages:

|  | 1980 | 1985 |
| --- | --- | --- |
| From agriculture | | |
| Crops | 60 | 51 |
| Forestry, livestock, fish, rural industry | 40 | 49 |
| From all sources | | |
| Primary (agriculture) | 69 | 58 |
| Secondary and tertiary | 31 | 42 |

One of the earliest steps in agricultural reform was deceptively simple: farmers were allowed to sell more goods in the market. As earlier, there was still fear that farmers would spend too much time on marketing, and the impact of this change was modest at first because the teams were still cautious about allowing them too much free time, and the farmers wanted to avoid possible criticism. The effect eventually began to accelerate, however, as fears receded and reorganization proceeded.

The first steps in agricultural reorganization in Guangdong, taken in 1978, were modest ones designed to reduce objections to the procurement system. That year the provincial government, like many others, replaced mandatory quotas with contracts, designed to allow rural units some bargaining room before they accepted quotas. Under the new system the state contracted with communes, which in turn contracted with brigades, and the brigades with teams. To be sure, the price the state contracted to pay for the rice was still below a true market price, and higher-level units had considerable leverage over lower-level units. But as part of the new agreements, the higher-level units agreed to supply goods such as fertilizer, diesel fuel, plastic for covering crops, and insecticides that were needed for production. And the "contract" allowed local units to bargain for the amount supplied and to reduce the amount of grain turned over if higher levels failed to deliver the amount contracted.

A major early reform, approved for Guangdong at a meeting in Shunde in January 1979, before spring crops were planted, was that the team, still the basic accounting and production unit, was allowed to divide tasks among smaller, more stable work groups. At that time the larger number of workers per team, 62 in 1978 compared with 36 in 1962,[22] had made crop management more difficult. Under the new system, "the responsibility system linked to output" (*lianchan chengbao zerenzhi*), the work group guaranteed to turn over to the production team a certain fixed output for the fields it managed. In return it was given greater freedom to divide up its work as it chose. The system was sometimes called the "five fixes and one reward" (*wu ding yi jiang,* a term also used in the early 1960s). The work group had a fixed membership on a fixed area of land. To meet its fixed production quotas it was given a fixed amount of supplies. For meeting quotas it was given a fixed number of work points, which became the basis for calculating its share of team profits. If the work group exceeded its quotas, it was rewarded in proportion to its surplus.[23]

In 1980 it was still not clear to local reformers whether reforms would stop with the system of smaller work groups or whether they would fully decollectivize and assign production targets to the household. Actual practice varied widely. Once stable work groups became acceptable, many teams tended to create smaller and smaller work groups until they began to approach the size of the household. There were occasional reports that some local teams, with at least the tacit approval of local cadres, had assigned responsibility for targets to the household.

One of the first moves toward family agriculture came over the winter of 1978–79, when individual families in certain poor areas were allowed to "borrow land" (*jiedi*) from the production team to use over the winter season between the fall rice harvest and spring transplanting. This had also been done in 1959, when food was short as a result of the Great Leap Forward. In 1979, once families in effect had their own land during the short winter season, they wanted the practice to continue the next winter.

In early 1979 Guangdong provincial officials received reports that in very poor areas like Haikang County (Zhanjiang Prefecture) and in remote mountainous areas *(sanshanqu)* like Zijin County (Huiyang Prefecture), local teams had taken the initiative on a wide scale in assigning land to households even during rice-growing season. Official policy did not yet permit this, and local officials tried to clamp down. In Zijin, higher-level cadres went down to villages to stop it in March, June, and September 1979, and yet over the year, as they later discovered, the number of teams practicing it increased from 1,300 to 3,700. An investigation of the situation there and in nearby Heyuan and Heping counties began on June 10, 1980, led by the head of the Provincial Agricultural Commission, Du Ruizhi. At meetings from June 19 to 25 the team members discussed their findings with officials. Du reported back to the province that assignment of land to individual families was even more widespread than previously reported, that the peasants were pleased, and that despite bad weather, production had improved substantially. Nevertheless, Du could not persuade the province to approve the practice openly. Some feared that Beijing might disapprove, some feared loss of cadre authority in the countryside, some feared difficulty in collecting grain, and some feared that after success the first year, production of basic crops would later fall off and that once land was distributed it could not easily be taken back.

Du, a rural Party leader for over thirty years who had worked very closely with Zhao Ziyang on provincial agriculture, had in 1955 been an enthusiastic supporter of collectivization. He had kept close to the rural scene and described events there as he saw them, however, and had served six years in jail from 1966 to 1973 for having spoken bluntly about commune problems in May 1959. Even though he could not get full support from the province, he said in front of the 899 officials at the Huiyang prefectural meeting that, though it was desirable to strengthen the collective, peasants engaged in private agriculture were increasing production and that it would destroy their enthusiasm to clamp down hard. The implication was clear; they could continue.[24] Without provincial approval, he could not advocate the policy, but he did not stop teams that practiced it. He had stretched his authority to its limits, but no one publicly disagreed.

It was difficult for die-hard supporters of collectivized agriculture to oppose decollectivization in mountainous areas like Zijin, where farmers did not have enough food to meet China's minimum nutritional standards. At the national level, moreover, the Fourth Plenum of the Eleventh Party Congress, on September 28, 1979, had already permitted the practice in areas that were especially poor.[25] Once it was allowed in mountainous areas, contracting to the household spread to other areas. At a forum of provincial and municipal Party secretaries called by Beijing in September 1980, it was announced that not only mountainous areas but other areas in difficult straits, where the peasants wanted it, could contract down to the household.[26] Knowing the practice was permitted in poor areas and that the head of the Provincial Agriculture Commission did not oppose it, other teams in Guangdong felt less risk in doing the same.

Compared to the great fanfare that had accompanied collectivization, when cadre work teams had gone down to the villages from higher levels, decollectivization took place quietly. The household responsibility system was so popular in the countryside that farmers eagerly divided up almost overnight, without help from higher levels. One survey of rural practices in the Pearl River Delta, which was not a poor area, conducted in 1981 and published in 1982 by Graham Johnson, a Canadian sociologist, reported that by 1981 often 20 percent or more of the teams had already divided their work using the household responsibility system. This was particularly true for crops like sugar and fruit, which did not require a great deal of labor or input of fertilizer and other materials.[27] With this initiative from the peasants, leaders who opposed decollectivization had no hope of successfully resisting the policy change.

In 1982, when Beijing clearly supported the household responsibility system, provincial and lower-level officials could openly support what many had tacitly begun to allow. Teams that had decollectivized could be more open about what they had done, and others followed quickly. By 1983 the household responsibility system was virtually universal throughout Guangdong. Land was still owned by the state, but it was assigned by the team to a family, which was responsible for turning over a set quota of output to the team after harvest. The team had the right to reassign the land if the household did not meet quotas or after the guaranteed term ended. Agricultural planners did not believe that the state could afford to buy rice if the price were determined by the market, and therefore believed that quotas were needed. The contract that a farm household made each year to produce a set amount of rice at a set price ensured that those quotas would be met.

Even before a January 1984 national directive made it official, cadres began giving peasants guarantees that they could work the same land for many years, not uncommonly fifteen to twenty, so that they would give the land the inputs it needed. The new issue faced by rural planners was how to maintain some form of collective organization in order to keep the benefits of collective irrigation, health service and welfare, and economic cooperation for joint purchasing, mechanization, and marketing.

The freeing of excess household labor was a great boon for subsidiary crops and rural industry. Rural markets were allowed to grow larger and to add handicrafts and manufactured goods. As with decollectivization, this began even before formal permission for the expansion of markets was granted by the province in September 1980. In 1978, of the 193 yuan average annual per capita rural income in Guangdong 48.4 percent was from work in the collective, 39.8 percent from family sideline work, and 11.8 percent from other miscellaneous work. In 1982, per capita rural income had risen to 382 yuan, with 40 percent from collective income, 47.5 percent from family sideline work, and 12.5 percent from other work.[28] Officials privately acknowledged that these figures understated income from family sideline work, which was actually substantially higher than officially reported, but it was clear that farmers were responding to the new permissiveness to produce more for direct sales.

Among Guangdong farmers, decollectivization and the reopening of the markets was commonly known as "the second liberation." It was an opportunity to earn more, but many peasants considered this less important than their new freedom to work where and when they wanted to in their own way.

The formal abolition of higher-level rural units, communes and brigades, begun in the fall of 1983, was a change of lesser importance than was the allocation of team responsibility to households. By August 1984 the 1,982 communes in the province had been replaced by 1,836 *qu* (districts) and 163 *zhen* (townships), the 26,583 brigades had been replaced by 19,955 *xiang* (administrative villages, often composed of several small natural villages) and 346 *zhen,* and the 386,924 teams had been combined into 96,982 *cun* (village) councils.[29] (See also Table A.1 in the Appendix.) The term *qu,* used before 1958, was unique to Guangdong and was temporarily used because Guangdong communes had been larger than elsewhere. The process of regularizing local administrative structure by national standards, however—making all larger rural communities into *zhen* or *xiang*—

began almost immediately. The *qu* that had 2,000 or more nonagricultural residents (who were entitled to rice coupons) were allowed to become *zhen*. Because this classification brought some benefits to the community, in *qu* that otherwise would have had less than the numbers required, residents who had no regular household registration were also counted, if they agreed to provide their own rice. *Qu* that had fewer nonagricultural residents became *xiang*. When asked what changes they made when communes were abolished, cadres not uncommonly said simply, "We hung up a new sign," meaning that they changed in name only. Although a small number of former brigade and team cadres lost their jobs, most of them were absorbed in new economic units. Though the political and economic units had been divided officially by the abolition of the communes, Party units at all levels in the countryside were basically unchanged.

After 1982 the availability of agricultural products in urban markets increased annually by leaps and bounds. Provincial agricultural officials allowed rural markets to expand, and the number of agricultural goods with set procurement quotas and prices was rapidly reduced. By the mid-1980s, reflecting their new knowledge of world developments, cadres were using a fashionable expression to describe their new role: *hongguan guanli* (macroeconomic management). They were to reduce their microeconomic management, increase the role of the market in agricultural goods, and ensure that the transition went smoothly. In fact, however, they did not give up microeconomic management so easily.

The benefits of rural reform, as Beijing leaders had hoped, were broadly shared, both by peasants who grew freer and richer and by urban consumers who had available more food of greater variety and higher quality. In 1927 Mao had advocated that the revolution begin in the countryside and then encircle the cities. In 1984 in the "second rural encirclement," the tide of rural reform brought large-scale reform to the cities.[30] The success of rural reform raised the confidence of leaders in Beijing and increased political support for the idea that opening markets and contracting for production had lessons that could be fruitfully applied to urban areas.

## Enterprise Reform

Most reforms were hard to carry out singly; they interlocked like pieces of a puzzle. Enterprise reform in particular seemed to touch virtually all other aspects of the economic structure, for it was insep-arable from reforms in price, financial systems, wages, hiring, supply systems, and governmental organization. But two major efforts aimed directly at enterprise reform can be distinguished: one was simple, quick, and successful; the other complex, continuous, and less suc-cessful. The simple one involved granting permission to expand indi-vidual and collective enterprises. The more complex task was to enliven state enterprises.

*Growth of Independent Enterprises and Collectives.* In 1955–56, large corporations had been made into state enterprises, and small indepen-dent urban stores, artisans, and service shops were reorganized into collectives. Over the years these collective facilities had atrophied, especially during the Cultural Revolution when many were criticized for bourgeois tendencies. Certain essential operations, such as bicycle repair shops and a few small stores that sold daily necessities, were available in urban areas even during the height of the Cultural Rev-olution. But so many shops providing daily necessities, repair, and other services had closed down that even families of the most ardent opponents of capitalism found it hard to bear. After collectivization in 1957, 620,000 people in the province were still working in urban individual enterprises. By 1978, although the urban population had almost doubled, the number of workers in individual enterprises had declined to 170,000.[31]

Individual enterprises, like the rural household responsibility sys-tem, first expanded in an area hardline Communists found it difficult to oppose—among "youth awaiting employment" (*daiye qingnian;* the term "unemployed" was still politically sensitive). By 1974 many of the 994,000 young people sent to the countryside had begun to return, but state enterprises and government offices, already over-staffed, had too few openings. At the time of the annual Spring Festival holiday in 1974, there was a huge demonstration on Baiyun Mountain (Guangzhou), estimated by some to involve 100,000 peo-ple.[32] Leaders, fearing social unrest, knew change was urgently re-quired in order to place thousands of youth, some of whom had been awaiting employment for several years. Allowing them to set up in-dividual and collective enterprises to sell daily necessities, repair goods, and serve drinks and fast foods seemed, even to many who opposed liberalization, a solution to the problem, and political opposition was not significant.

More independent stalls and shops, almost always staffed by young people, had begun to reappear almost immediately after the fall of the Gang of Four in 1976, and by October 1980 it was official policy that the monopoly of state enterprises had ended. Even individual enterprises employing more than the previous limit of seven nonfamily members were to be permitted. Distasteful terms like "capitalist" were replaced by more attractive labels like "individual enterprise house- hold" (*geti hu;* see Chapter 10). Many doubted that entrepreneurs would be tolerated for very long, but by 1980 newspaper articles began to appear praising people who were getting rich through in- dividual enterprises. To be a *wanyuan hu* (a household earning ten thousand yuan a year) was upheld as glorious. Socialism, it was ex- plained, did not mean poverty. Later articles criticized cadres who had discouraged individual enterprises, which demonstrated both that not all cadres had gotten the message and that high-level cadres were determined to make the new system work. Shops, stalls, and artisans began to increase, at first slowly, and by 1982–83 very rapidly. Many old services were reestablished—barber and tailor shops, delivery and transportation services, carpentry and repair workshops—and many new services, for information, research, and computer assistance, were opened for the first time. By mid-1984 it was estimated that 700,000 in the province were working in some 530,000 individual commercial enterprises, and that over 100,000 additional people were engaged in providing individual transport services.[33] To encourage larger enter- prises, a new attractive category, "private enterprise" *(siying qiye)*, was created in April 1988 for businesses with more than seven people.

New "collective" enterprises were established by the local govern- ment rather than by groups of private individuals. In some cases state enterprises that had been run by higher levels of government were passed down to local governments to become collectives. Local gov- ernments were encouraged to establish new collectives either by them- selves or in cooperation with other local governments. There was a continuum from large collectives, run by cities and counties, to tiny ones, run by urban districts and villages. In urban areas administrative responsibility was divided between the No. 1 Light Industry Bureau (which generally included larger collectives in sectors such as metal- working, hardware, and electronics, where planning controls were considered necessary), and the No. 2 Light Industry Bureau (which generally included smaller enterprises that used few materials and products needing planning controls).

Unlike state enterprises, these collective enterprises were more independent of the bureaucracy and less subject to rigid rules about position, status, salary, and welfare payments. State factory managers and higher-level cadres considered collective enterprises prone to loose business ethics, profiteering, and bribery. Local officials sponsoring them regarded them as an important source of income[34] and more efficient than state enterprises. Local power brokers considered them opportunities for gaining loyal supporters in exchange for finding people new work assignments.

In the countryside, the former commune and brigade industries were turned over to the townships and administrative villages. Some of the tiniest were leased or sold to individual households. In the five years after 1980 the rural collective enterprise work force expanded almost as much as it had in the previous twenty-three years. In 1957 there were 1,240,000 workers in these rural collective enterprises; in 1980, 1,710,000; and in 1985, 2,126,000.[35]

By the early 1980s most people recognized that small firms provided a vast new range of goods and services, and that in management, efficiency, hard work, and service, small independent enterprises were outperforming the collectives and that collectives in turn were outperforming state enterprises (the Chinese slogan was *guoying buru jiti, jiti buru geti*). Their success distressed not only conservative ideologues but also cadres supervising or working in state enterprises. Reformers at the highest levels saw this competition as a useful way to goad state enterprises to better performance. But even these high-level cadres assumed that individual enterprises would not ordinarily exceed a certain size, though this was not clearly defined. Almost no private enterprise became as large as even middle-sized private enterprises in the West. Some cadres and some ordinary consumers believed that the larger collective and state enterprises had a greater sense of responsibility to the public at large. News articles appeared, for example, describing how some entrepreneurs sold meat from animals that were clearly diseased. Many consumers felt that state enterprises, despite their poor service, were in some ways still more reliable than independent enterprises, where narrow self-interest was too blatant. Yet because they wanted the goods and services they had for so long done without, consumers continued to patronize the entrepreneurs.

*Reforms in State Enterprises.* The rationalization of state enterprises, a key goal from the beginning of reforms, proved to be one of the most stubborn problems to resolve. Some of the earliest targets were wasteful and unprofitable factories. Small county plants, expanded during the Cultural Revolution to promote economic independence in the event of being cut off by war, often wasted resources, especially electricity, and contributed to shortages that were becoming more acute with growing demand. The most prominent examples were small-scale nitrogenous fertilizer plants. In 1979 Guangdong had eighty-eight, almost one per county. As part of the economic readjustment in 1980, an effort was made to consolidate them, improve efficiency, increase usable output, and conserve electricity. By 1987 only thirty-five remained. Military-related plants that had been relocated in remote mountainous areas safe from attack, mostly in Shaoguan Prefecture and in central Hainan, were at best a drain on the transport system and resources and at worst virtually inoperative because of lack of supplies and personnel. Some plants were moved, and in the early 1980s, some 269 such enterprises in Guangdong were closed or merged.[36] Most inefficient plants remained in operation, however, and efforts at rationalization continued.

In the late 1970s, as leaders began to realize how far behind their factories were in comparison to those of other East Asian countries, nearly everyone, including factory managers themselves, wanted changes, but it was difficult to know where to begin. They had too many poorly qualified and poorly motivated staff members and too much backward technology, poor organization, and low-quality output. Many managers believed the solution lay in persuading higher-ups to give them modern plants and equipment, but perhaps the key issue, debated in Beijing as well as in Guangdong, was motivation. Workers who had an "iron rice bowl" and "ate from the big common pot" (*chi daguo fan,* that is, received the same salary regardless of what they did), were hard to motivate. From the worker's perspective, the question was, why bother? Years of political strife and frustrations, lack of supplies, lack of proper machinery, lack of trained technicians, inability either to reward workers who contributed more or to punish the lazy, and lack of responsiveness to requests for help from higher levels had led most managers, like most employees, to give up the struggle. It was easy for each cadre to feel that the problem was beyond his or her control and that responsibility for the problem lay elsewhere.

There was wide agreement that the solution lay in giving enterprises more independence, making them more responsible for their own profits and losses, and then in turn linking employee benefits to enterprise performance. But state enterprises had been, in effect, the lowest level in a state economic bureaucracy, and therefore many decisions had been made, not in the unit, but at various levels above. Thus even the simplest move to make the enterprise responsible for its own profits and losses proved difficult to implement. An effort to achieve this desirable but seemingly elusive goal was at the heart of most of the enterprise reforms.

One approach was to simplify requirements within the firm. Formerly, an enterprise was tied down not only with production targets but with wage targets and materials targets, to say nothing of ideological targets. Designed to provide a system of proper controls for a large national planning system, targets had become so numerous that they hampered the flexibility of the manager trying to improve overall effectiveness. After 1980, just as rural reforms gave farm households independence as long as they met grain targets, so most enterprises were granted considerable independence as long as they met output and, increasingly, profit targets.

Financial targets became increasingly important as a way to reduce the state budget and push plants to become more efficient. Formerly plants with high national priority had received funding from higher levels regardless of their performance, and plants of lower priority, such as those making consumer goods, not only had received no help but had turned over all their earnings, no matter how profitable they were. With the reforms, profitable firms were allowed to retain more of their profits and officials tried to reduce allocations to inefficient operations. In 1979 one hundred of the largest state enterprises in Guangdong, which provided over 60 percent of the province's profits, were given greater autonomy, and became theoretically responsible for their own profits and losses. If they surpassed their targets, they could use their additional income to increase wages, build housing, or expand production as they chose. This scheme was extended to county-run state enterprises and, in July 1980, to most state-run enterprises in the province.[37] In fact, however, higher levels of government usually still came to their aid when they suffered losses.

One of the earliest efforts to stress profit targets came from a successful experiment in Qingyuan County, where factories were given bonuses for exceeding profit targets *(chao jihua lirun ticheng jiang),* and factories passed on a fixed amount of revenues to higher levels. Qingyuan, a poor county north of Guangzhou to which both Tao Zhu and Zhao Ziyang had personally come to supervise experiments in rural organization, in 1978 had seventeen state industrial plants, many of which were operating in the red. The biggest problem was the ammonia factory. In October county officials allowed it, a fertilizer factory, and a cement factory to receive a bonus if they met their profit targets. The scheme was very successful and was picked up by the Economic Commission of Shaoguan Prefecture (of which Qingyuan was then a part) and by the Provincial Economic Commission; during 1980 and 1981 it received national attention as a model. Although many provincial officials supported it, in the end the experiment was shot down by the officials of the Provincial Finance Bureau, who felt that it limited their revenues.[38] They preferred taxation, and in 1983 when the Finance Bureau carried the day within the provincial government, the experiment came to an abrupt end, a blow to those trying to provide greater financial incentives to enterprises.

In 1983 profit retention was replaced by taxation *(li gai shui)*; the new system was codified into national law in October 1984. The goal was to reduce further the arbitrary sharing of profits by higher units and give the enterprises some leeway to decide how to use their profits. Taxation at first was too tightly administered and gave less incentives to enterprises than had the system of bonuses. When Beijing permitted it in 1985, some enterprises in Guangdong were allowed to revert to the bonus system, but taxation remained the basic long-run approach to revenue collecting.

The results of these efforts proved disappointing. In reality, when managers who were grappling with poor equipment, shortages of electricity, shortages of supplies, inadequate funds to buy new equipment, workers accustomed to getting paid for a light work load, and no leeway to hire and fire employees were told that they could retain profits, they still did not know where to begin. A great many factors, such as whether the factory would receive new machinery, supplies, or technical staff, and how the supplies and enterprise products would be priced, were beyond their control, and changes in these areas usually overwhelmed whatever improvements they might attempt. Even if profitable enterprises were able to raise wages and improve worker housing more than other enterprises could, workers found it hard to believe that their own efforts were crucial in increasing enterprise profits.

Furthermore, higher-level officials found it difficult to crack down on factories that were not profitable. This problem, a familiar one to analysts of socialist plans everywhere, has been referred to as a "soft budget constraint."[39] No matter how poor an enterprise's performance, government officials, to maintain employment, avoid dislocations, and keep production flowing, came to the aid of operations within their sphere of responsibility. Guangdong, like other provinces, tried to warn enterprises by letting one or two go bankrupt. But enterprises correctly discerned that higher officials were not yet prepared to permit any major enterprise to fail. In 1984 roughly one-fourth of Guangdong's state enterprises were operating in the red, reflecting the province's limited success in placing pressure on them to reduce their losses.

In 1987 and 1988, hope for enlivening state enterprises was placed in giving their general managers the power, salary, prestige, and independence to carry out a more entrepreneurial role. The Party secretary had previously been the most powerful person in an enterprise, but even in the early 1980s the plant head or general manager in most enterprises had already gained in independence, relative power, and salary. Engineers had formerly received higher salaries than the general manager, but in the early 1980s this was reversed, reflecting recognition of the importance of overall management. By 1987 some thought that, as in Hong Kong or the West, a top manager who made the whole plant more effective deserved far more reward than an ordinary salaried employee. New courses and lectures on enterprise management stressed the importance of the entrepreneur who could keep all parts of an operation running smoothly and take advantage of new market opportunities. An effort was made to locate such managers, regardless of their background. According to the new scheme, managers signed several-year contracts. If they succeeded in meeting their targets, they were to be handsomely rewarded. If not, they were to be replaced.

These new approaches still did not have the impact reformers hoped for. Few workers felt working hard was worth it or even that they could benefit from a more efficient plant. Party leaders still had the key power of personnel appointments, and their views were still dominant. Experienced managers with a sense of efficiency were hard to find, and few were willing to risk pushing potentially indignant workers, especially those who were Party members. The manager given leeway and out to prove himself did not necessarily inspire other employees, who did not earn nearly as much as he did. Some experienced managers feared that, not unlike earlier generations of political activists, they might alienate fellow workers who did not want to be used for someone else's successes. For these reasons, some enterprises experimented with electing managers from a small selected slate in the hope that the manager chosen by his workers could work well with them.

It was, as Deng had suggested, a time for experimentation, and some successes had been achieved by the late 1980s in increasing concern for efficiency, profitability, and quality. But perhaps in no other area was there such great effort in continued and varied reform experiments, with such modest results.

## Wages and Employment

Wage reforms were designed as a critical part of improving motivation in state enterprises. Nothing seemed more central to solving this problem than giving greater rewards to those who made greater contributions. The first major effort was the establishment of a large-scale bonus system, beginning in 1979 and 1980.

Bonuses were enthusiastically welcomed by workers, most of whom had received no wage increases for twenty years, but they soon strained companies' resources and failed to achieve the goal of providing incentives for hard work. Popular demand for bonuses was so strong that most managers gave in to workers' requests, regardless of the enterprise's ability to pay. Workers, allowed to decide how to distribute bonuses among themselves, awarded them mostly on an egalitarian basis. Sometimes they humanely offered more to senior workers, who had waited the longest for raises, or to those who had suffered most in the Cultural Revolution. When the State Council imposed a ceiling on bonuses in January 1981, Guangdong was criticized for offering too many and told that annual bonuses could not exceed two months' pay. In the early years of reform, "bonuses" became in effect an across-the-board wage increase, making it impossible to reward efficiency.

A later experiment linked the total bonus package to the overall profits of the firm. This had some success where it was tried. However, there were so many extrinsic factors that might have accounted for the success of the firm that profitability could still only be said to be marginally related to incentives.

Another experiment paid some workers by piece rate. Not all jobs, especially those done collectively by large groups, as on assembly lines, and those done by cadres and office workers, were easily amenable to piece-rate wages. But for packing boxes, sewing garments, or similar jobs, piece rates were highly effective in improving performance.

By the mid-1980s the program considered most promising for

improving labor mobility and worker incentives, in Guangdong and elsewhere, was the labor contract system. Guangdong began to try this on a large scale in 1984 after experiments in Qingyuan and Shenzhen. It was not feasible to get workers already granted permanent employment to accept term contracts, but after a July 1986 State Council decision, new workers in state enterprises were hired on this system, which theoretically eliminated the iron rice bowl. By the end of 1986, 520,000 Guangdong workers, about 7 percent of the province's state and collective work force, were part of the system. Workers commonly received contracts for terms ranging from one to five years, and they could leave or be terminated at the end of the contract. Nevertheless, it was still not easy to dismiss a worker at the end of this contract period, for the ethos did not yet support it.

Two of the most successful changes in getting abler people into better jobs were the circulation of information about job openings and the requirement that applicants take examinations. People in critical positions could sometimes still control the news of the pending exam or grade exams to favor personal connections, but as news of job openings and examinations spread by the late 1980s, that became more difficult.

These new systems were slowly beginning to have some effect in some plants, but the fact that so many other factors essential to efficiency were still missing meant that even in the late 1980s the two major efforts, the bonus and the contract system, were not as effective as planners had hoped.[40] Reformers remained dissatisfied, and new efforts continued.

## *Reducing Planning and Increasing Markets*

Reformers recognized that the complex planning system imposed many rigidities that strangled the vitality of the firms and the economy. Guangdong's effort to reduce the role of planning and increase the extent to which goods could be sold on the market began as early as 1979. Wang Zhuo, as head of the Provincial System Reform Office, provided the theoretical framework, not only in his articles in national journals but in his advice to local leaders: China had put too much emphasis on "product economics" *(chanpin jingji)* and needed to put more on "commodity economics" *(shangpin jingji)*, the circulation of goods and services. If production were driven by demand and market, then higher quality and more appropriate products would result. The government would achieve its overall social goals best by using its leverage over macroeconomic measures to strengthen market forces that would move in the desired direction.

The biggest worry was inflation, the beast that in the view of China's leaders had eaten away at public support for the government after World War II and caused the collapse of the Kuomintang. Those concerned with macroeconomic policies were therefore cautious about eliminating planning and pricing controls and using market mechanisms too quickly. The key issue in their view was pacing, taking goods off plan when officials could count on enough supply to keep market prices from skyrocketing. This was especially important for consumer staples like rice and vegetables. The reformers believed they had to take some risks to achieve the breakthrough to a market economy that East European countries found so difficult, but they wanted to retain controls that would enable them to keep down prices, especially for daily necessities.

The opening of markets moved furthest and fastest in secondary agricultural goods. The first major change began in October 1980 with the ending of the state monopoly in rural marketing and the reduction of compulsory sales to the state. Gradually the number of goods to be purchased through quotas from the rural areas was reduced, and for the goods still on quota, the amount of the quota was gradually reduced. Producers could sell their surpluses on the market. The number of agricultural items with procurement quotas was reduced from 110 to 26 in 1980, to 13 by 1984, and to 5 by 1987.[41]

The biggest risk was taken during the winter of 1980–81. Quotas and price controls were removed on many agricultural items, including daily vegetables, pond fish, and fruit. Prices did rise, and local consumers and Beijing officials criticized local leaders for letting prices get out of hand. Local leaders, afraid of consumer unrest, gave a special supplement to salaried workers in 1981 to help them cope, even though they knew this would add to inflation.

But provincial officials basically held their ground, and their efforts proved a great success. They chose to end controls over vegetables at the beginning of the winter because in Guangdong, with a very mild climate and the added availability of paddy land on which produce can be grown over the winter, vegetables are much more plentiful at that time. The growing cycle is as short as six to eight weeks for some. Officials were confident that if prices went up, local peasants would quickly produce more vegetables. The response was just as predicted.

The cycle for pond fish is longer; many farmers had not been accustomed to turning fields into ponds, and were therefore hesitant to take that step. The price of a typical variety of fish had risen from less than 2 yuan per catty (0.5 kilogram) before the opening of the market in 1980 to 5 yuan per catty within weeks afterward. By 1982 pond fish had fallen to 3 yuan a catty and were much more plentiful than before, and by 1986 a typical fish cost the consumer 1.6 yuan a catty, about the same as before decontrol. But consumers were eating roughly four times as much fish as they had in 1980. Pond fish became the classic Guangdong story illustrating the virtues of successful market deregulation.

By 1982–83 under the household responsibility system, farmers were bringing plenty of goods to the market, inflation rates were below those of the nation, and even officials who had criticized Guangdong acknowledged its success. Even in the case of fruit, where the growing cycle was several years, Guangdong managed well. The price of bananas was high in the early 1980s but began to fall by 1987 as more became available. For reasons of convenience some farmers still chose to sell to rural procurement stations, but farm families mostly marketed their own produce or sold to a new layer of middlemen. Guangdong farmers had always been aided by their warm climate, but officials outside the province acknowledged that Guangdong was also bold and successful in pacing the decontrol of secondary agricultural products.

To encourage the growth of the physical marketplaces for agricultural and other consumer products in towns and cities, provincial officials urged banks to lend money to local communities to build them. In these new markets people could rent stalls or shops, which provided more income that allowed communities to repay their loans within several years. In addition to these fixed stalls, more places were set aside on the street where individual farmers and others could bring their mats or stalls and sell their produce.

After the 1984 all-time high in the rice harvest yields of both Guangdong and the nation, procurement quotas on rice were gradually reduced and production beyond the quotas could be sold on the market. Farmers naturally met quotas with ordinary rice and sold their best rice on the private markets. In 1985, as part of the new strategy, the province was permitted to produce slightly less rice and more of the crops that could be sold on the market to bring higher returns and more foreign currency. Some provincial officials hoped that

Guangdong might buy rice from other provinces like Hunan at lower state prices, but because Guangdong was richer, other provinces objected and Beijing encouraged Guangdong to pay higher negotiated prices.

An effort was also made to decontrol industrial goods. Like agricultural goods, industrial goods had long been divided into three categories: category one for goods strictly on state plans, category two for goods local governments could allow to be marketed after local plans were fulfilled, and category three for goods off plans. Manufactured goods in categories one and two were in turn classified into three types: (1) production supplies, (2) consumer goods for daily use, and (3) consumer handicrafts. In 1980 there were still 95 production supplies in category two, but by 1985 there were only 22; the rest had been opened to the market. The number of consumer goods still in category one (including cotton yarn, cotton cloth, kerosene, and edible oil) was reduced in November 1980 to 9 and those in category two (including nylon, silk, artificial fiber, soap, sewing machines, bicycles, and televisions) to 42.[42] Consumer handicrafts had been open to market prices from the beginning. The number of goods in category two overall was reduced from 160 in 1983 to 128 in 1984.[43]

As goods began to appear in greater quantity, rationing was gradually dropped. Except for rice and cooking oil, rationing of most agricultural products was eliminated in the early 1980s, and in 1981 cloth rationing was reduced and in 1983 eliminated. Guangdong was able to reduce restrictions on cloth before the rest of the country because of its rapid expansion in local production of synthetic fibers.

The decontrols on production supplies proceeded much more slowly. Especially in heavy industry, there was a shortage of raw materials, parts, and equipment. Officials feared offering these goods on the open market because they thought this would not only increase their price but also divert them from areas considered high priority. Yet controls meant that many state enterprises, not allowed to raise the prices of their products, found it difficult to make a profit. Beijing's solution was to allow state enterprises, whether supervised by the central, provincial, municipal, or county government, to sell a portion of their production on plan at low fixed prices and to sell the rest at higher market rates. It was a highly complex solution to a difficult transitional problem. Enterprises naturally tried to acquire as many goods as they could on state plan, at lower prices, and sell as much as possible off plan, at higher prices. Higher-level officials could also greatly affect a firm's profitability in their decisions about how much was to be produced on or off plan, and to some extent they had to police firms to make certain that supplies acquired on plan were in fact used to produce goods on plan.

Because Guangdong's profits were increasing, it could afford to buy more goods off plan and also to purchase more supplies abroad than other provinces could. In the case of steel, for example, by 1983 of the 1.5 million tons used for basic construction in Guangdong, 5.8 percent was purchased on the national plan, 8.3 percent on the provincial plan, and 85.9 percent on the market.[44] With its concentration on producing consumer goods, virtually all off plan, Guangdong had a lower percentage of products on state plan and was buying and selling a much higher proportion of its goods off plan than were other provinces. Many enterprises preferred the security of being on a state plan, but province officials continually tried to increase the proportion of goods off plan.

Some of the biggest efforts to reduce the role of state planning came in the military and the defense industry. The military was encouraged to open its service establishments, hotels, restaurants, and stores to the general public to earn income to supplement the national budget. Factories producing military equipment were encouraged to produce civilian goods in their areas of competence—electronic equipment, machinery, and clothing—in order to earn extra income. Military bands sponsored popular entertainment, military hospitals and recuperation centers were opened to paying customers from Hong Kong, and even firing ranges charged customers who wanted to practice shooting. The military began sending officers to business schools and to work in foreign trade. In adapting to markets, the military and defense industries thus reduced their financial burden to the state and gave greater attention to efficiency.

The reduction of the scope of planning did not always work well because firms that were sole producers or that produced goods still in short supply could charge high prices, "monopoly rents," without feeling market pressure for better performance. The expansion of markets may have seemed slow by the standards of Westerners who would have counseled greater openness. But for socialist bureaucrats embedded in a different system and worried about all that might go wrong, the pace seemed incredible; many were proud that they had moved so quickly without greater dislocation.

*Pricing*

As an indicator of value and as the critical factor in determining the profit and loss of enterprises, pricing was one of the most central and complex issues facing reformers. Reformers aimed to allow the market a greater role in determining prices and to allow domestic prices to move toward international market prices. They tried to pace price adjustments and decontrols with other reforms and economic developments so that the supply of goods would be adequate to avoid high inflation rates (see Appendix, Table A.4). Price deregulation was not the same as eliminating planning, for some goods off plan still had price controls and some planned goods were allowed more leeway in adjusting prices.

Managing the transition smoothly was an enormous, painstaking task for the Pricing Bureau, which took on many new officials and began detailed studies of actual market conditions. To hedge their risks, reformers moved in stages. For some goods taken off plans, they still sometimes set a range of prices within which they could fluctuate according to market forces. For goods still on plan, they tried to adjust set prices gradually in order to reflect actual costs and market forces more accurately. They allowed lower levels of government more authority to adjust prices to market circumstances. Even after decontrolling, they gave special incentives to ensure the production of goods that might have been in short supply and timed the release of state stockpiles of key goods to reduce sudden swings in prices.

Guangdong decontrolled prices, especially for agricultural products, more rapidly than other provinces did. But for goods on state plans affecting markets in other provinces, they could not decontrol prices and increase procurement prices too much faster than was occurring elsewhere. For goods still partly on state plan, Guangdong negotiated price changes with Beijing and, for certain products, with other provinces as well.

To reduce the risk of urban unrest, Guangdong officials tried to contain price increases of staples like rice and to peg price increases with wage increases. While raising the price of rice procured from farmers to encourage them to meet their quotas, government officials provided subsidies to keep down the price charged to consumers. Government leaders considered rice supply and retail price stability so important that rice subsidies grew to consume a major portion of the government budget. In 1986, for example, the province paid out 1.3 billion yuan in rice subsidies.

Prices of agricultural goods were decontrolled more rapidly than prices of industrial goods. Of 118 types of agricultural products with prices administered by Beijing or Guangdong at the beginning of reform, only two, rice and tobacco, had administered prices in 1988. Prices of consumer products were decontrolled more quickly than prices of producers' goods. Of 392 types of consumer goods originally controlled, only a handful of items like salt and sugar were still controlled in 1988. Of 1,446 types of production goods with price controls, over 1,100 were still controlled in 1988, but government units were allowed to sell many of these items off plan after plan targets were met. The price was negotiated *(yijia)* between units and reflected market forces but also special circumstances and higher-level government advice. Since Guangdong state enterprises moved off state plans quickly, its enterprises used "negotiated prices" on a broad scale. By 1988 most prices in Guangdong were no longer administered.[44]

At the Thirteenth Party Congress in October 1987, leaders in Beijing, buoyed by the success of reforms, announced their intention to pursue further price decontrols. Top leaders in Beijing believed that if they could persevere through three to five years of inflation and some unrest, they could achieve the basic transition to market prices, and many were prepared to take the risk. Guangdong leaders, believing they could complete the process in two to three years, started, between the Party Congress and the middle of 1988, to dismantle remaining controls, beginning with sugar, alcoholic beverages, and tobacco. However, inflation in many Chinese cities, including Guangzhou, aroused severe consumer anxiety, especially among low-paid salary workers. In June 1988, Guangzhou residents, having been told about impending price rises on large consumer items, rushed to the banks to withdraw funds to make purchases. On one day the banks did not have enough liquidity to allow people to withdraw all they wished, but by the next day monies were made available and calm returned.

Official estimates showed inflation rates in Guangdong in 1988 to be over 20 percent, and some estimated that the actual rate was twice as much. The sources of pressure on prices in Guangdong were for the most part similar to those elsewhere. The People's Bank had expanded the currency in circulation since 1980, and loans increased rapidly. Firms with monopolies or oligopolies on products had raised their prices when decontrol was effected, and many individual entrepreneurs were quick to raise prices when shortages arose. In addition, since Guangdong was richer and had to buy a higher portion of goods off state plan and to import a larger number of higher-priced goods from abroad, it had not only greater purchasing power but higher costs than other provinces. Guangdong also moved ahead of the nation in raising the retail prices of rice and edible oil as a step toward eliminating the state subsidy that filled the gap between the high procurement and low retail price.

Guangdong officials in 1988 believed that they could continue to decontrol prices without causing severe problems. They reasoned that Guangdong's living standard was further above subsistence than other localities' were, that consumers were less anxious since they had surmounted the earlier round of price increases in secondary agricultural products, that bank savings remained high, and that subsidies to low-paid salary workers could reduce anxieties. In mid-1988 Beijing officials, concerned about panic over inflation, ordered national efforts to tighten price controls, to limit credit, and to reduce large construction projects. Guangdong officials, realizing that their economy was still closely linked with the national economy, cooperated with Beijing in holding back on further price decontrols. As inflation slowed down slightly in late 1988, ordinary citizens in Guangdong, as elsewhere, were relieved. Many of the province's officials, however, still believed price decontrol desirable and awaited an opportune time to continue the process.

*Finance*

Financial controls had been very lax during the Cultural Revolution, and in the late 1970s control over spending was placed in the hands of the local bank branches that were responsible for the accounts of the local state enterprises. Part of the early post-1978 efforts, therefore, involved not weakening but strengthening supervision of money spent by enterprises.

In 1979 the People's Bank of China began to transform itself into a central bank, supervising other banks rather than lending directly to other institutions. Its funds were dispersed to form anew or strengthen seven specialized banks: the Bank of China (for foreign exchange); the Agricultural Bank of China; the Industrial-Commercial Bank of China; the People's Construction Bank of China; the People's Insurance Company; the Transportation Bank of China (whose Guangdong branch opened in 1987); and the China International Trust and Investment Company.

In 1980 Chinese banks became more active in attracting deposits and in providing basic investment and working capital for enterprises. Until 1979 China had been very conservative in its monetary policies and had financed basic construction with allocations from the state budget. After that year, in contrast, the government increasingly financed such construction with loans, in which the Agricultural Bank, the Industrial-Commercial Bank, and the Construction Bank played the central role. This gave them a great deal of authority, of course, and meant a corresponding loss of authority from units that had formerly made fiscal outlays. As banks acquired experience they began, like banks elsewhere, to give key consideration to the borrower's ability to repay.

In order to begin Guangdong's banking independence with loans linked to deposits, the People's Bank agreed in 1980 to assign 400 million yuan per year to Guangdong for three years. Guangdong officials tried to be prudent, however, and in the end they used only what they considered necessary, 700 million yuan rather than 1,200 million. From then on banks in Guangdong were allowed to link lending to deposits and expand loans as they acquired deposits. Between 1981 and 1983 they authorized new loans for industry and infrastructure of some 5.2 billion yuan, of which 4.5 billion came from deposits, and 700 million from bank funds collected from other sources. In the same period the banks released 7.17 billion yuan to assist village and town *(xiangzhen)* industry.[45] The Agricultural Bank, the richest of the seven institutions because most of the population was rural and the growth of rural enterprises and private marketing of rural goods created more savings, not only financed rural industry but, in collaboration with other banks, lent some to other sectors. (In July 1984 the Rural Credit Cooperative, which had borrowing and lending offices in the countryside under the supervision of the Agricultural Bank, began to play a much larger role not only in collecting deposits from increasingly rich farmers but in financing local rural development projects.) Decisions on actual lending were decentralized in large part from the provincial-level bank offices to those at the municipality, prefecture, and county levels. This greatly sped development, but in the early 1980s it led to some careless lending and waste until those authorizing the loans acquired more experience. It also allowed some officers to lend to those with whom they had special relationships or who gave them payoffs. Banks tried to counter this by setting up better control systems.

To speed the development of infrastructure desperately needed by industry, Guangdong pioneered within China the granting of loans to supplement local budget allocations to build bridges and roads. The loans were to be repaid through tolls. When the first toll bridge was erected between Guangzhou and Foshan, even many Guangdong officials still thought that bridges and roads were public facilities that should be open to everyone without payment. The toll experiment was later judged so successful, however, that by 1984 Guangdong had built twelve such bridges, and counties began following suit. By the late 1980s it was the new conventional wisdom throughout China that to hasten development it was quite appropriate for the user to pay the cost of certain expensive roads and bridges.

Leaders continued to search for new ways to raise funds for investment without diverting funds from other projects they considered important for development. In late 1985 Guangdong and five of its larger municipalities were allowed to become experimental areas with new flexibility in financial markets. They were theoretically allowed to issue stocks and shares in companies. As of 1988, however, stocks and shares had not begun to play an important role; banks were still the dominant institutions.

## Role of the Communist Party

In 1978 most Chinese Communist Party members lived in rural areas and had not completed high school; nearly half had been admitted during the Cultural Revolution, when priorities were different. Deng Xiaoping recognized that a new focus was required. To help raise the educational and skill level of cadres, he decreed in 1980 that all cadres employed in the Party and administrative hierarchies would retire at age sixty, except for ministerial-level officials or, in the provinces, the governor and vice-governors, who could serve until age sixty-five. By the mid-1980s this meant that virtually everyone who had served in the guerrilla forces and the army prior to 1949 had to retire, and that a high proportion of the employees in Party and government offices who were the least educated and the least prepared for the complex tasks of modernization were gone. The Party rectification campaign, beginning in 1983, though milder and more orderly than many earlier rectification campaigns, also weeded out some younger cadres who had supported the Gang of Four and perpetrated some of the excesses of the Cultural Revolution.

In their place, during 1982–1984, the Party admitted many new members who were younger, better educated, and more specialized.

The Party could not quickly overcome the legacy of the poor education many had received during the Cultural Revolution or the decades of selecting bureaucrats on the basis of political criteria rather than meritocratic tests. In Guangdong roughly half the Party members had no more than a junior high school education in 1980, but those promoted to the highest positions after that tended to be members with high school or university training. The Party still valued those of proven loyalty, but those made heads of factories were commonly former engineers. Among new deputy heads in each county, at least one usually had training in engineering.

In counties and townships, where work had long centered on agriculture, first Party secretaries traditionally spent most of their time on rural work. After reforms, the new first secretaries usually had received more schooling but still came from a rural background and felt comfortable guiding rural work. The new government heads of counties and townships, in contrast, usually younger and better educated, often had a more industrial and urban background and therefore tended to concentrate on those areas. The first Party secretary remained the *diyi bashou* (the "number one power"), but usually the independence of the county head was increased so that informally his relative status rose and his authority was expanded over matters in which he had more experience, commonly industry and the economy. At lower levels, however, even where administrative units like brigades and teams had been abolished, Party committees and branches remained.

The division of responsibilities between government and Party officials was sharpened. Party branches at every level and in every unit and enterprise had been the ultimate authority, supervising others. In times of stress like the Great Leap Forward and the Cultural Revolution, when Party leaders were prone to bypass administrators and govern directly, their lack of specialized expertise had had disastrous consequences. After the mid-1980s local Party leaders were therefore enjoined to stay out of administration and concentrate on policy, propaganda, personnel, and mass organizations. Party "work departments" that duplicated government organs were dismantled and cadres assigned elsewhere, which gave the government clear authority in agriculture and industry. The scope of the Party Organization Department was reduced, but Party approval was still required for key personnel appointments; this ensured that the Party, though specialized, retained crucial leverage. Although they granted greater autonomy to government officials and managers than before, Party officials could still use their leverage to maintain diffuse control that went beyond formal definitions of power. Even the technocrats who rose in stature had to work through these informal power networks.

Guangdong Party leaders decreed that all cadres under forty who expected to have a position in the Party or administration at the provincial bureau level or above should have university training. Aspirants who did not could attend night school or special courses. The schools they attended, however, including Party schools, did not generally have the academic levels of the better universities. There was thus an element of credentialism, but the new attention to education did help expand the horizons of cadres and create an atmosphere in which those who were well educated received more respect than they had before. Although educational standards were still low by international standards, the situation was improving rapidly.

## Government Reorganization

All leaders recognized that the government was too large, with too many layers and too many units. Over the years units had continued to expand, and provincial units that had ceilings on their numbers still often found ways to enlarge by having people attached to them who were really on the payroll of another unit. In the reform process an effort was made to reduce the size of units, primarily by retiring more people and by not replacing all who retired.

Leaders also recognized that enterprise vitality required greater autonomy and a change in the direction of the government's role from providing microeconomic supervision to giving macroeconomic guidelines. Before the reforms, each government enterprise had been assigned to one supervisory government bureau *(zhuguan)*, colloquially known as the enterprise's *popo* (the "mother-in-law," that is, the most powerful person in the family). The problem, as all cadres knew, was that there were too many *popo*.

One way of dealing with a *popo*, begun in late 1982, was to remove it from the government budget and make it into a "controlling company" *(zong gongsi)*. The new controlling company became in effect the company headquarters, and the companies the bureau formerly supervised became its subsidiaries. In experimental areas like Qingyuan County and Jiangmen City all economic bureaus supervising economic units were eliminated, a streamlining move that left government supervision in the hands of commissions, the layer formerly above the bureaus. Leaders hoped the new controlling company would earn its own keep. But too frequently the bottle changed without changing the wine. Former cadres were now called managers, but often little was new except the title and the increase in their salary. Controlling companies were to be eased off the government budget after a brief transitional period, and then they were to charge other units for services. Although the transitional period was sometimes extended, this change did eventually relieve the government's budget burden. The problem, however, was that controlling companies lacked skills desired by the subsidiaries and thus had few services they could justifiably charge for. Instead they used their position of power to extract surcharges on subsidiaries, without always performing a useful economic function.

The bureaucracy also grew, despite efforts to contain it, through "temporary" offices, which were set up to deal with new problems but which tended to become semipermanent. By the late 1980s there were over seventy "temporary" units at the provincial level that somehow proved more persistent than the reformers trying to simplify them.

Another important governmental reorganization was at the prefectural level. With roughly one hundred counties, the provincial government, like the Kuomintang and the Qing Dynasty before it, commonly supervised the counties through prefectural-level units that were officially branches of the provincial government. The number and boundaries of the prefectures changed from time to time, but generally there had been about twelve, and by 1979 a prefecture averaged about five million people. With the exception of Guangzhou, most of the population in each prefecture was rural, as was the focus of the prefectural administration. Within the prefecture there was a capital city or large town, but the administration of that city was an independent unit that generally had little direct contact with the counties in the prefecture (see Chapter 7).

To prepare for modernization and industrialization, the province decided that when urbanization reached a certain stage, former prefectures *(diqu* or *zhuanqu)* would be split into smaller units and treated as metropolitan regions. (The Chinese term, *shi,* literally means "city," but because these *shi* have replaced the prefecture and include surrounding counties, while other *shi* do not, I have chosen to use the term "metropolitan region" for the large multicounty units.) Thus in 1984 Zhanjiang Prefecture was split into Maoming and Zhanjiang Metropolitan Regions, and Foshan Prefecture into Jiangmen and Foshan Metropolitan Regions. The city administration of the prefectural capital, formerly separate from the prefectural government, was merged with the former prefectural staff into a single staff for the whole metropolitan region. This reorganization had two distinct advantages. By giving cadres experienced in urban and industrial issues a broader geographical area of responsibility, their talents could help guide the work of counties as they began to move from farming to more commercial and industrial activities. It also helped increase the horizontal linkages between enterprises located in the city proper with those located in nearby counties, connections that had been almost impossible under the old cellular bureaucratic structure. Some former rural enterprises thus became subsidiaries or subcontractors to larger enterprises located in the city proper.

"Horizontal linkage" *(hengxiang lianxi)*, indicating links between units across administrative boundaries, became a new buzzword, part of an effort to expand the freer flow of goods and services. If a single governmental unit supervised two enterprises and the two had a disagreement, the unit could easily resolve it. But because in China there were few legal bases for agreements and contracts were simple at best, such problems were not easy to solve if two enterprises were under different units. As trade and markets expanded, the problem of vertical and horizontal linkages *(tiaotiao kuaikuai)*—that is, too many separate lines of authority—seemed more constraining. Some officials at all levels were specifically assigned to promote horizontal linkages across geographical and jurisdictional boundaries. In the early 1980s the focus was on grouping together failing industries, but by 1985, when the horizontal linkage boom began, the focus was on new, more creative linkages, such as trade associations of companies in the same field, specialized service companies, enterprise groupings, and technology and information exchange associations. Reformers hoped these would be voluntary associations organized by enterprises, but in the late 1980s the initiative still often came from cadres. Since progress in horizontal linkages could weaken the *popo,* resistance to giving up too much authority to new linkages was not unknown. But though bureaucratic power remained strong and markets were not yet well developed, horizontal linkages nevertheless played an important role in extending economic links beyond local communities.

## Windows of Opportunity

In early 1982, when huge cases of smuggling and profiteering, detailed in Chapters 9 and 11, came to the surface, many cadres in Guangdong feared that the new special policy for Guangdong and the reforms might come to an end. Irregularities had become serious, and this had made Guangdong vulnerable to attack. On January 11, 1982, Beijing launched a full-fledged campaign against smuggling and illegal trafficking *(zousi, fansi)*, with Guangdong as the major national target.[46] The capital sent down cadres to investigate and summoned Guangdong's leaders to give explanations. Local cadres were examined and reexamined, and some were punished. A similar campaign was launched in 1984 to eliminate corruption, particularly in Hainan. In mid-1988, as part of a national effort to contain public distress about inflation and cadre corruption, Beijing cracked down on Guangdong's wasteful investments, loose financial controls, and excessive price increases.

Opponents of Guangdong's special policy, who had been forced to remain silent while high-level officials spoke of Guangdong's special needs, were then given an opportunity to have their say. Leaders of other provinces, who resented Guangdong's ability to buy up goods at top prices in their markets, complained about interference in their markets. Beijing cadres in various ministries, who disliked the concessions they had to make to Guangdong because of its special policy, tried to reduce the disruptions the province caused in their efforts to provide the supplies and outputs for national plans. Senior Beijing leaders, guardians of the faith, who believed that the Kuomintang had failed because of corrupt officials, passionately railed against the dangers of Guangdong's decadence.

But in each case, officials in Guangdong moved forcefully to respond to complaints and to retain the support of major leaders in Beijing. Senior Beijing leaders like Zhao Ziyang, Wei Guoqing, Xi Zhongxun, and Yang Shangkun, who had served in Guangdong, and Gu Mu, the great reform era go-between, were of great help in maintaining Beijing's support. And top leaders who had more doubts about Guangdong's policies were neutralized after they inspected Guangdong's accomplishments.

Throughout the first reform decade, except for these three pauses in 1982, 1984, and 1988, leaders at all levels relentlessly introduced fundamental changes at a dizzying pace. Reforms touched every major sphere and every locality in Guangdong. They scored so many successes and gained such popular support that fundamental policy reversals in most areas became unthinkable.

A systematic comparison of Guangdong reforms with those elsewhere must await further research on other provinces. But Guangdong unquestionably took the lead in decontrolling prices for secondary agricultural products, financing roads and bridges to be repaid by tolls, making revenue payments to Beijing by fixed annual sums, and allowing selected county governments and individual factories to engage directly in foreign trade. During this first decade after the Third Plenum of the Eleventh Party Congress, reform was in the air everywhere. Beijing and many provinces were simultaneously discussing and trying similar reforms, in agriculture, enterprise management, wages, prices, and planning. Other provinces undoubtedly moved sooner and further on many individual reforms in these areas, but Chinese officials acknowledged that no other province pushed the overall reform effort as far as Guangdong did—to the very limits of Beijing's tolerance.

In October 1987 the Thirteenth Party Congress gave the reform program a rousing endorsement and encouraged Guangdong to take another step ahead. In January of the next year, Guangdong announced that it was planning further major reforms for the second decade and, to help guide the effort, began developing a vision *(guihua)* for the province for the year 2000. New financial institutions, such as a provincial development bank and a stock market, were planned. Leaders agreed to allow enterprises to contract for overall profit levels and manage their own operations more flexibly. They began to expand markets in land and housing. They aimed to simplify government administration further and facilitate the mobility of cadres. They intended to allow factory managers to assume more power than the Party secretaries.

The reforms at the end of the first ten years were thus incomplete. Markets were not fully open, bureaucracy remained bloated and cumbersome, local prices did not reflect world prices, conservative officials interfered with development, bottlenecks proliferated, and corruption was widespread. Confusion, contradictory practices, and inconsistent regulations abounded. But for all these imperfections, reformers had broken down barriers to progress. Perhaps more important than all the individual reforms was the spirit of overcoming obstacles and finding new solutions. At the very least, these incomplete reforms provided new windows of opportunity, which enterprising residents in all parts of the province eagerly seized.

# PART II

## *Patterns of Change*

# 4.

# *Special Economic Zones: Experiment in New Systems*

As China considered how to modernize, areas known as export-processing zones, where foreign companies could bring in supplies to produce goods for export without tariff barriers, seemed to have much to offer. Wanting to expand exports after World War II, all countries in East and Southeast Asia except Japan, Hong Kong, and Singapore had established such zones. Japan, confident of its prewar technological head start and hypersensitive to foreign domination, felt it could catch up through education, licensing technology, and reverse engineering, without inviting foreign factories to a special zone. Hong Kong and Singapore had such small domestic markets that there was no point in protecting their home markets with trade barriers, and therefore they required no separate zones. Unlike Japan, China had been isolated from advanced world technology for so long that its industry had little chance of reaching world levels quickly without inviting in foreign manufacturers. And unlike Hong Kong and Singapore, China's internal market was certainly large enough to gain from protecting its infant industries. In short, China's situation was like that of countries with zones.

When it emerged from the Cultural Revolution, China lacked personnel sufficiently knowledgeable about foreign economic developments to inform leaders about the experience of other countries with export zones. Moreover, the two with the most relevant experience, Taiwan and South Korea, were closed to China for diplomatic reasons. In order to learn about the Taiwanese and Korean zones as well as others, the Chinese turned to businesspeople and academics in Hong

Kong. Documents from Taiwan, written in Chinese, were readily accessible there, and now that China's leaders wanted to compete with Taiwan economically as well as politically, they focused on its three zones: Kaohsiung (established in 1966), Nantse (1970), and Taichung (1971).

The ability of zones to provide jobs, experience with new technology and management practices, and foreign currency earnings seemed attractive. Some knowledgeable officials realized that to reassure and attract foreign companies China would have to provide tax incentives and other guarantees. But on the whole in 1978 Chinese leaders, long cut off from international markets, underestimated how much they would have to improve their infrastructure, upgrade cadre training, and fundamentally alter their way of thinking to be competitive with other countries.

From the Third Plenum in December 1978 to China's official establishment of four "special economic zones" (three in Guangdong) on August 26, 1980, and even through the two years thereafter, there were many debates about how to structure the new areas. On July 15, 1979, the Party Central Committee and the State Council announced that they would try three "special export zones." By the time the dust settled and Shenzhen and Zhuhai were operating, it was clear that Chinese leaders had renamed them "special economic zones" (SEZs) because they wanted to achieve far more than other countries had through their export-processing zones.

One goal was to contribute to the return of Hong Kong, Macau, and, it was hoped, Taiwan to China. If the Chinese could manage a place near Hong Kong and Macau that incorporated capitalist practices like those used in Hong Kong and Macau, they would not only gain experience useful for managing the different systems of Hong Kong and Macau but also help reassure people in Hong Kong and Macau about their future. Furthermore, it was expected that the standard of living in this zone would be higher than in Guangdong overall and could thus provide a kind of buffer, reducing the gap between Hong Kong and the rest of Guangdong.

Beyond Hong Kong and Macau, Chinese were also thinking of Taiwan. By learning how to run a different system and making a success of it, they might have a better chance of winning over the minds of the Taiwanese and promoting closer relations and eventual reunion with the mainland.

Because the Chinese were experimenting with reform just as the special economic zones were established, many leaders also looked to them to try bolder experiments with system reforms. The zones had distinct borders, and thus if problems developed in the experiments, they could be sealed off from the rest of the country. They could, as Premier Zhao Ziyang put it, be a place for sifting out practices useful for all of China.

Unlike export-processing zones elsewhere, China's zones, after observing customs regulations and other formalities, were allowed to sell some products within the country. An effort was made, however, to limit the amount.

It followed that the zones that were to play this larger role would be not simply factory sites, as in other countries, but much larger geographical areas with broader functions—political, cultural, educational, and technological, as well as economic. Another key addition was tourism, which seemed a promising way to earn foreign currency, especially from nearby Hong Kong. The area of Shenzhen's zone alone was 327.5 square kilometers. By 1984 Zhuhai's area was 15.2 square kilometers, Xiamen's (in Fujian, the only one not in Guangdong) was 129.9 square kilometers, and the central government had approved expansion of Shantou's to 52.6. Taiwan's three export-processing zones, in contrast, together constituted less than 3.0 square kilometers.

The newly established zones were the first places in China where foreign capitalists established their own factories and enterprises. The discussion of the zones thus became a focal point for the controversies over the proper direction for China's future.

The issue was especially sensitive because the zones reminded many of the "treaty ports" that had been opened along the coast after the Opium War by foreign countries, who used military force to demand sites for foreign trade. There, backed by their soldiers, foreigners made their own rules to support their privileges, to the outrage of patriotic Chinese. By the 1970s the basic history lesson, studied by a generation of Chinese, described how foreigners had exploited the Chinese in treaty ports and how the Communist leaders had thrown out the exploiters. Were they now being invited back? Although the Cultural Revolution had wounded China's sense of righteousness, many cadres were still morally repulsed by the return of foreign capitalists to coastal cities. Ordinary citizens, grown increasingly cynical, suspected some cadres were inviting in foreigners for their own personal gain, and many of the top leaders were worried about the corruptibility of lower-level cadres. Hong Kong and Macau had long been symbols of crime and decadence. And financial speculation and profiteering, even if not considered crimes in the West, were repugnant to many socialist planners. How could China voluntarily invite the return of such a world?

The zones remained vulnerable to political attack. Hunan's provincial secretary, Mao Zhiyong, for example, refused to allow zone newspapers into Hunan until, at Deng's request, he took a trip to the zones to observe their progress.[1] The planner Chen Yun was "too ill" to visit from Beijing, and when he called for a "summing up" of the zones' experience in 1982, not just foreigners but many cadres in Guangdong and Beijing worried that the zone might not be allowed to continue.

Chinese leaders who supported the zones tried hard to minimize their vulnerability to criticism. The experiment that was being tried, they made clear, was not capitalism but "state capitalism," in which the state was firmly in control. When the name "special economic zone" was chosen, it was to make clear that only the economy would be treated as special. To appeal to Marxist-Leninists, reformers used an elaborate theoretical rationale, describing how Lenin's New Economic Policy of the 1920s was important for the Soviet Union at a certain stage of development. China, they explained, had not yet passed that stage. When the USSR established its New Economic Policy, power remained firmly in the hands of the government, the workers, and the peasants. Now, they made clear, power remained firmly in their hands, not in the hands of the capitalists. Officials dealing with foreigners were under great pressure to demonstrate that they were not allowing themselves to be taken advantage of. Many had seen while growing up that being a leftist was less risky than being a rightist, and when they were uncertain they instinctively wanted to err on the side of being tough with the capitalists.

Gu Mu, who had been in charge of granting Guangdong its special policy, was placed at the top of both the State Council's Special Economic Zone Office in Beijing and the Foreign Investment Control Commission. He made frequent inspection tours of the zones. One of his many virtues was that he not only had the confidence of Zhao Ziyang but had especially strong connections with Chen Yun and Bo Yibo, two of those most concerned with the dangers of weakening socialism and socialist planning. Many of China's highest leaders visited the zones in the initial years to ensure that they were developing in a satisfactory manner, and generally they were impressed with what they saw. Once they had visited, consulted with local officials, and appeared in public in the zones, they had become identified with them, thus providing high-level support for their continuation. Shenzhen also came to be seen as a desirable place for young cadres to go. Many children of high-level cadres arranged to be sent to Shenzhen, which made it more difficult for top cadres to oppose the zones.

At the time of the Opium War, the Qing Dynasty considered the interaction with foreigners that occurred in Guangdong too important to leave to local leaders. They dispatched strong officials from Beijing and took a very active role in supervising those areas. Similarly, when the special economic zones were developed after 1979, Beijing considered them too important to leave to local bureaucrats. They sent cadres from Beijing and assumed a prominent role in directly supervising the zones.

It still required considerable courage for so many leaders and lower cadres to push through this development. Deng Xiaoping acknowledged that "when you open the door some flies will get in." Beijing was prepared to tolerate some flies in the special economic zones, but local cadres were expected to exercise vigilance to ensure that not too many got through to China.

## Shenzhen Special Economic Zone

The Shenzhen SEZ towered so far above China's other three special economic zones that for some Chinese as well as for foreigners it alone became virtually synonymous with SEZs. When the zones were first established, the two other SEZs in Guangdong, Zhuhai and Shantou, covered only 6.8 and 1.6 square kilometers compared to Shenzhen's 327.5. In 1986 Shenzhen's total industrial output was 3.5 billion yuan, slightly more than that of the three others combined (Xiamen's was 2.6 billion, Zhuhai's 0.7 billion, and Shantou's 0.2 billion). Because it bordered on Hong Kong to its south, Shenzhen had an immediate political significance and a nearby economic stimulus far beyond that of Zhuhai, which bordered on Macau, or of Shantou and Xiamen, which bordered only on the Pacific Ocean further up the coast. Shenzhen was the main site visited by Beijing leaders evaluating zone policy, by foreign capitalists considering investing, and by comrades from socialist countries contemplating reforms in their own systems. The zone began with developments in Shekou, and we too will begin there before examining the subsequent urban planning for

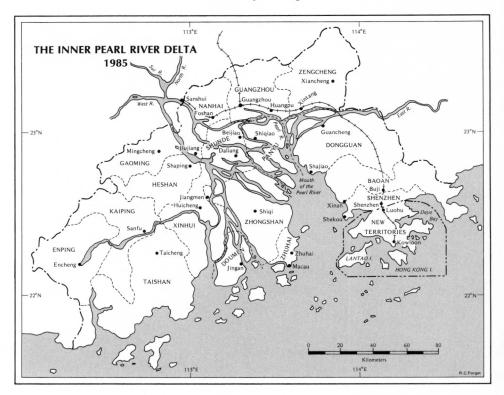

the Shenzhen SEZ (see the accompanying map of the Inner Pearl River Delta).

## Shekou Industrial Zone

In late 1978 the China Merchants Steam Navigation Company, Ltd. (CMSN), under Beijing's Ministry of Communications but based in Hong Kong, proposed to establish a base in the southwestern corner of Baoan County, an area later to be incorporated into the Shenzhen special economic zone that was then already under discussion. Having just been granted independence in enterprise management to help speed the four modernizations, CMSN hastened to make use of the opportunity. The Central Committee of the Chinese Communist Party and the State Council granted CMSN its request on January 31, 1979, shortly after Baoan County was reorganized as Shenzhen Municipality but almost eighteen months before the zone was established by dividing the region into the SEZ, the more urban area, and Baoan County, the more rural area. The site was on a small peninsula shaped like the head of a snake with an open mouth and therefore called Shekou ("snake mouth"). The spot was only seven kilometers across a bay from Hong Kong's New Territories. Only a few years before it had been heavily patrolled; it had been a favorite spot for escapees attempting to swim to refuge in Hong Kong.

Originally known as the Public Bureau of China Merchants Steam Navigation, CMSN was founded in 1872 by the Qing Dynasty. Under the leadership of a highly entrepreneurial viceroy, Li Hung-chang, it made great progress in helping China catch up with the rest of the world in the purchase and production of steamships. It led the modernization of the Chinese navy and shipping fleet, but thereafter went through various ups and downs and reorganizations. In January 1950 its major branch in Hong Kong decided to cast its fate with Beijing rather than with Taiwan. CMSN became a state-owned company, but a large branch remained in Hong Kong, staffed by high-level officials assigned by Beijing.

After 1950 the branch focused its activities on shipping, and it grew and modernized with Hong Kong's explosive growth. The company still controlled slightly more than a 10 percent share of the shipping in and out of Hong Kong when it made its proposal to Beijing in 1979, and had in the meantime expanded into related areas such as dock management, marine machinery and engineering, warehousing, surveying, tourism, hotels, banking, and investment. Keeping pace with the competition, it had installed modern communications equipment and computer systems. Until 1979 it had not been appropriate to expand these business operations into China itself, but that year, as part of the new climate, CMSN began to put its expertise to work inside China with a substantial investment.

The CMSN leader from Hong Kong who made the proposal to Beijing, Yuan Geng, could hardly have had a more appropriate background. He had originally come from Baoan County and therefore knew the Shenzhen area well. In his youth he had served as a fighter in the anti-Japanese East River Guerrillas under Zeng Sheng, who was also from Baoan County. He had distinguished himself as a soldier in the War of Liberation in the Huai-Hai battle. In 1945 he had been dispatched to Hong Kong as the Communist representative to discuss postwar naval arrangements with the British and the Kuomintang.

After 1949 he had worked in the International Liaison Department of the Communist Party, and later headed international liaison work under the Ministry of Communications. Serving in such places as Vietnam and Cambodia, he developed a broad range of contacts with overseas Chinese—some of whom, in 1979, could be viewed as prospects for investment in China. He frequently visited Hong Kong on ministry business, and in 1978 he was spending a good part of his time there, making good use of his close relations with local Chinese businesspeople. He himself had little business experience, but he knew how to select and use talent. When he presented his proposal, he was supported by CMSN's parent ministry and his former employer, the Ministry of Communications, which was then headed by his friend and former commander Zeng Sheng, who had been in favor of the Shenzhen project from the start.

Yuan proposed that a large facility be established in Shekou to scrap old ships that were in a poor state of repair. CMSN had originally thought of carrying on this activity in the New Territories, but the dismantling of ships required a large area and land in Hong Kong had become so expensive that there was no affordable site of the size needed. In 1979 Hong Kong was in the midst of a building boom that required a great deal of steel, and the steel from the scrapped ships could be sold to Hong Kong construction companies at high prices. The CMSN plan was an opportunity to offer substantial numbers of jobs to the plentiful workers in China and, by selling the products in Hong Kong, to make considerable sums of money, in foreign currency.

Once Beijing had approved the project, CMSN moved quickly to clear the land in Shekou for construction. In the 1960s and 1970s, when no city in the world had more new construction than Hong Kong, companies there had honed their skills and capacity to use the most modern equipment, and all this was available to CMSN. In July, with preparatory work out of the way and construction plans moving ahead, it began building harbor facilities and putting in the necessary infrastructure of electricity, roads, and sewage systems. It purchased a large electric furnace from Denmark to smelt the iron. An aluminum factory was to be built to make use of aluminum scrap.

By 1982, when a considerable amount of infrastructure had been put in and the furnace had arrived, the project no longer made economic sense. Hong Kong's hopes for 1997 had plummeted after Margaret Thatcher's 1982 visit to Beijing. The bottom fell out of the

Hong Kong real estate market, construction dropped off, and the demand for scrap steel plunged. In the meantime, the demand for old ships had greatly increased, and it was no longer possible to buy them at such a low price. The demand for electricity in Guangdong was growing much faster than the supply, moreover, and because the project would place heavy demands on electric power, it seemed impossible and perhaps even unwise to guarantee a reliable power source. Shenzhen was also developing a new ecological consciousness, out of tune with the considerable industrial pollution that the project would inevitably produce, just when China was beginning to envision Shenzhen as an urban showcase for the outside world. There seemed to be no way to make the project a success.

If the project had been led by a typical Chinese industrial unit, it is hard to imagine that it would have had the leeway, expertise, or resourcefulness to resolve the problems expeditiously. Yuan Geng and CMSN, however, responded quickly. They canceled the ship dismantling project and searched for a buyer for the furnace. Hunan Province needed one and bought it. Hardly missing a beat, the developers made new plans for their site in Shekou as an industrial zone within the SEZ. In place of the original sizable steel facility, they built a much smaller steel mill. They purchased ingots and melted them into rolled steel to meet the demands of plants moving to Shekou. Aluminum ingots were purchased from elsewhere and rolled into aluminum sheeting to be used as siding on the refrigerators and other new consumer products the newly established SEZ would produce. Although the new SEZ policy required plants to export most of their products and the steel and aluminum plants did not export directly, officials were flexible enough to approve the projects quickly because their output would be used by nearby factories that did produce for export.

In the meantime, Beijing allowed Shenzhen enterprises the authority to pioneer in attracting foreign companies, fully owned subsidiaries as well as joint ventures, to bring in capital and technology in order to produce for export. As the first industrial zone in Shenzhen, Shekou could point to industrial sites already in place and to a physical infrastructure, including shipping facilities, nearing completion. By 1987 the port facilities at the Chiwan docks had twelve berths and could dock ships up to thirty-five thousand tons, including container ships. An outer harbor along the outside of the breakwater was being built that would soon be capable of docking ships up to seventy thousand tons. Apartments far above ordinary Chinese standards were built for cadres and workers; attractive apartments and villas were erected for sale to foreign executives. To attract foreign businesspeople on a long-term basis, Yuan Geng even invested a considerable sum of the zone's own capital to build an international school for foreign children.

At first Shekou's promoters naturally turned to companies in areas where they already had close business relations, and one of the first sizable factories to settle in Shekou was a joint venture with a Danish company to produce cargo containers, both for Hong Kong and for the domestic Chinese market. Another built yachts and another produced paint.

Shenzhen had hoped to attract foreign direct investment in areas of high technology, but it soon became apparent that to get investors who would move in quickly to produce for export, it would have to accept companies that did not use particularly high technology. One of the first successes was Kader Industries, which made a hit with its Cabbage Patch dolls, produced there in great quantity. Hong Kong businesses also began to establish textile plants.

CMSN used its experience in the travel business to attract tourists, especially from Hong Kong. In addition to the commercial pier, a passenger ship terminal was developed, and by 1987 hovercraft were making seven round trips daily, taking only forty-five minutes to reach Hong Kong's Kowloon pier. Next to the Shekou passenger terminal was a new "Five Star Hotel," a joint venture with Miramar Hotels of Hong Kong, to service the weekend vacationer as well as the business traveler.

A problem in all rapidly expanding areas, the timing and matching of various facilities, was compounded in Shenzhen, where so many cadres lacked relevant experience. Projects were delayed and poorly synchronized. Even in 1988 some basic facilities were still under construction, and financial and commercial facilities in Shekou were much larger than its population of twenty-five thousand required.

Still, in the eyes of Beijing, of Western businesspeople, and of young people seeking employment, Shekou was a success. Beijing was pleased that Shekou cost the government nothing, operated at a profit, and earned substantial amounts of foreign exchange. Visitors from Beijing to Shenzhen, especially from 1983 to 1985, were disturbed at the rampant commercial speculation and opportunism in many parts of Shenzhen, but they always reported that Shekou was a success. In 1984 Shekou was given an opportunity to make a profit on the purchase of vans from Hainan, before the issue became an incident (see Chapter 9), but its management committee turned it down. Shekou, already making adequate profits, saw its role as one of building industries that would be useful for the country, not just making money. Such decisions were dear to the hearts of Beijing's leaders, concerned about capitalist decadence. Foreign businesspeople had a reservoir of stories about Chinese bureaucrats who excelled in inefficiency, bureaucratism, personal profiteering (as discussed in Chapter 12), and a poor understanding of the needs of international business, but they saw the leaders of the Shekou industrial zone as exceptions who understood international business and were reliable, responsive, and honest.

For youth looking for a future, Shekou was seen as a very desirable place to work; the average age of a Shekou employee in 1987 was twenty-six. Shekou companies were getting their pick of young people and employing what was for China an unusually high proportion of high school and university graduates. As an early front runner, Shekou thus became a model for and the envy of the other industrial zones established in the Shenzhen special economic zone.

## Comprehensive Urban Planning

In the decades after World War II rapid economic growth in East Asia was accompanied everywhere by explosive urban growth. Westerners familiar with urban development in places like Tokyo, Seoul, Taipei, Hong Kong, and Singapore were astounded by the speed of their new construction, but none of these cities approached the growth rate of Shenzhen's special economic zone. The Shenzhen SEZ's population in 1980 was seventy thousand; in 1986 it was five hundred thousand; and by 1990 it was expected to be eight hundred thousand. In a single decade, farmland was replaced by infrastructure, industrial sites, public facilities, and private housing adequate for a new population the size of a city like Boston.[2]

The Shenzhen SEZ was a pioneer in experimenting not only with enterprise management but with urban planning. As a major site for a modern city, Shenzhen attracted some of the most talented planners and architects in China. The work was under the direction of the Municipal Planning Bureau (Shenzhenshi Guihuaju), and they had a senior planning committee (*guihua weiyuanhui*) to advise them in their work. Visitors and advisors came not only from all major centers in China but from all over the world.

It would later become clear that as of the late 1980s the Shenzhen SEZ had built too many attractive hotels, restaurants, commercial centers, and office buildings and had occupancy rates below break-even points. Given the tight constraints on capital, Shenzhen was criticized by many Chinese for putting up too many new buildings and too few factories.

The overly rapid construction resulted from the innate difficulty in predicting future needs that will really be determined by market demands in a new era, but this was compounded by lack of experience, powerful local ambitions, decentralization of operational authority, and the easy availability of loans from government banks. Even Singapore, one of the best-planned cities in Asia though it was for many years short of hotel space, in the mid-1980s suddenly suffered from a vast excess capacity. Viewed negatively, Shenzhen planners wasted money and left many units in the city saddled with excessive capacity and debt. Viewed positively, considering Chinese experience and the realities planners confronted, they moved with considerable skill and almost miraculous speed to create what became arguably China's most attractive and livable city.

The plan went through three major stages between 1980 and 1986. It began with an effort to estimate the macroeconomic growth of the city. Planners then drew up physical plans for urban development that accorded with these estimates of growth. In reality, the estimates for economic production in 1990 had already been reached by 1987.

The Shenzhen SEZ, located in a southern strip of what was formerly Baoan County, covers forty-nine kilometers from east to west and an average of seven kilometers north to south. When administrative reorganization was completed in 1982, what had been Baoan County had been renamed Shenzhen Metropolitan Region and was divided into two parts: the Shenzhen SEZ and the rural remains of the old county, which, though smaller, was still referred to as Baoan County. When boundaries were drawn, communes were not split down the middle but placed on one side of the border or the other in order to minimize disruption. Most were in Baoan County, so that as few people as possible would have to be displaced by industrial and commercial expansion. The zone included fifteen former communes, most very small in size, and two towns. The old Shenzhen town, with slightly more than twenty thousand people and by far the larger of the two, was located along the railroad between Hong Kong and

Guangzhou and became both the nucleus for the new SEZ and also the administrative center of the Shenzhen Metropolitan Region.

Shenzhen was one of the few large cities in China to be built using a comprehensive plan for the infrastructure. Various slogans were used to describe the process and encourage those involved in the change: "three pathways and one leveling" *(san tong yi ping)* or "five pathways and one leveling" *(wu tong yi ping)*. The pathways were roads, electricity, telecommunications, gas, and sewage, and the leveling was of large tracts of land. By 1987 some 48 square kilometers, mostly along the southern and western parts of the zone, had either been developed or were under development. By the year 2000 it was planned that about one-third of the entire zone, about 121 square kilometers, would be developed. Most of the rest was mountainous, to be preserved as tourist sites.

Final plans called for three major roads along the length of the zone from east to west. The road furthest to the north was for transport of goods; it was to relieve pressure on the middle road, reserved exclusively for passenger traffic. The road furthest south, along the coastal areas, was to be used for both goods and passengers. Not only the major roads but the other "pathways" were basically in place before the developers began site development.

Some housing construction began almost immediately after the decision to create a special zone. The first large housing developments, located just north of the Luohu border crossing, were modeled after Hong Kong's Shatin, but many later thought that the buildings were too close together. By the time these buildings were well under way, the city planners decided to give more consideration to the experiences of Singapore, which seemed to them the best urban model because it had such effective public order and was so attractive physically. Many from Shenzhen, including Mayor Liang Xiang, visited Singapore, and the father of Singapore's economic miracle, Goh Keng Swee, became an advisor to China's special economic zones. Like Singapore, Shenzhen decided to leave large green areas between buildings, much more than had been left in Luohu, and trees, shrubs, and flowers were planted throughout the city.

Within China, the Army Engineer Corps (Gongcheng Bing) had an excellent reputation for civil engineering. After the major earthquake in Tangshan in northern China in 1976, Tangshan's reconstruction was China's largest urban project. In 1980, as large-scale construction began in Shenzhen, the Army Engineer Corps of some twenty thousand officers and soldiers was moved from Tangshan to Shenzhen. They were known for their willingness to work hard, and they formed the core of the Shenzhen civil engineering staff. As part of army retrenchment, the entire Corps was demobilized in 1983. Nearly all remained in Shenzhen as civilians, however, and they became key employees in many of the sizable construction companies, more than a hundred in number, then operating in Shenzhen. Shenzhen in a sense had the best of both worlds—dedicated low-cost workers from China and modern construction equipment from the West by way of Hong Kong.

Architects had an opportunity to design dozens of major new buildings as well as hundreds of apartment houses over twenty stories high. Not only could they use more imaginative designs than China had ever before permitted, but they could incorporate new materials not yet widely used in China and could assume that modern machinery from Hong Kong would be used in the construction process. The finest architects of China, such as Wu Liangyang, chairman of Qinghua University's architecture department and favorite student of the famous architect Liang Sicheng, came as advisors.

One experiment tried in China for the first time was a system of taking bids on buildings. After the municipality had agreed to allocate land to a certain unit or company for a building, planning officials developed the desired specifications, and then architects, working with construction companies, submitted their designs for the building. A committee of architects under the city then examined the bids, usually three to five per major building, and made the selection. The contract included clauses that provided penalties for delays. Beijing leaders, just beginning to experiment with how to make the most efficient use of capital, liked the idea of companies competing to cut costs. They were also impressed that as buildings went up faster, even with the same rate of interest, capital could circulate more quickly and thus accomplish more.

To develop the city so rapidly, no single committee could make a decision on every site and every building. Consortia of outside developers were each assigned to develop huge industrial zones. Next to Shekou's port facilities at Chiwan, a large site to be used for oil exploration was developed by Nanshan Development, a consortium of mostly mainland Chinese companies led by Nanhai East. Several other industrial zones were developed by consortia of foreign businesses, mostly from Hong Kong.

This division of responsibility not only brought in some of Hong Kong's most experienced developers but gave them a stake in spreading the network to attract companies to build plants in Shenzhen. The negative side of decentralizing planning in this way was that it was difficult to control the duplication of services, especially of first-class hotels, revolving restaurants, and stores designed to attract foreign visitors and earn foreign currency. In the mid-1980s there was still a shortage of services for ordinary residents and visitors from inner China who had difficulty affording Shenzhen's high prices geared to Hong Kong and the West.

Objective outside observers rated the performance of construction companies in Shenzhen as below the average of those in Hong Kong, although much higher than in other parts of China. Many construction workers, freshly recruited from the countryside, were inexperienced in new construction techniques. Roofs sometimes leaked, plumbing facilities were not always properly installed, and walls were not always neatly finished. And because many units were later saddled with debts from low occupancy, funds were not always available later to make needed repairs. During construction, companies with foreign capital often found it just as cheap and far more reliable to bring in materials from Hong Kong. But furnishings, as much as possible, were supplied by mainland manufacturers, and they did not always meet first-class international standards. Even in the late 1980s Shenzhen, its old unattractive buildings not yet cleared and its beautiful but flawed buildings not yet repaired, was not entirely a finished city.

Yet by 1987, as more facilities were completed, residents began to enjoy living in their Shenzhen apartments. These were not only far better than those in inner China but provided more space per capita and almost as many facilities as ordinary Hong Kong apartments. As the plants and trees grew, residents increasingly found their city attractive. Many young people who had some choice about where to live considered Shenzhen the most desirable city in the country.

If China's prior experience in modern city planning, architecture, and construction is taken into account, Shenzhen's development was an impressive accomplishment. China's best architects had reached advanced world standards, and planners and architects from many parts of the world came to Shenzhen to observe. When the Chinese planners and architects returned home, they were not often given the resources and opportunities to apply the most advanced lessons they had learned, but they used their Shenzhen experiences in teaching their students, which helped to raise the levels of performance and expectation throughout China.

## Links with Inner China

One of Shenzhen's key purposes was to provide the links within China that, as in the case of city planning and architecture, would enable successful new technology and management practices to be rapidly diffused throughout the rest of the country.

From 1979 until about 1982, however, it was mostly Shenzhen that sought the linkages. Its leaders wanted units in other parts of China to invest in Shenzhen's development and to cooperate to help raise Shenzhen's level of technology. They sent cadres to visit advanced research and technology centers in various parts of China, especially in Beijing, Shanghai, Tianjin, and the Northeast.

Central government leaders were favorably disposed to help Shenzhen, and Gu Mu, with a small group he headed directly under the State Council, provided a critical liaison to make this possible. His strong identification with the zones' success made it easy for local officials to confide in and work with him. He proved well suited to the new era of bold experiments; he wanted results and was a natural troubleshooter who sought solutions to difficult issues.

In Guangdong Vice-Governor Wu Nansheng initially acted as a similar liaison between Shenzhen and Guangdong Province, but soon passed this role to Liang Xiang, who in October 1981 officially became first Party secretary and mayor of Shenzhen. When he took these new posts, Liang Xiang, already active in provincial politics as a vice-mayor of Guangzhou in charge of industrial development, became concurrently a vice-governor of Guangdong, and this enabled him to play a key part in coordinating affairs with the province. Guangdong helped to get Shenzhen started, but as Shenzhen gained its footing and was made an independent planning unit under Beijing it acted more independently, and this made its relation with Guangdong awkward. Liang Xiang proved to be an ambitious official who moved quickly and decisively to take advantage of the new wide-open era in Shenzhen. Although not all of his ideas, such as the establishment of Shenzhen's own currency, were approved by Beijing, he was later chosen as the first governor of Hainan when a similar role was required.

By 1981, as Shenzhen began to take shape, many units in other parts of China were eagerly responding to the call of Beijing to establish branches there. In part this was because Beijing had created special rules for Shenzhen. Branches in Shenzhen paid far lower taxes, ordinarily around 15 percent, and they were allowed to keep up to 90 percent of the foreign exchange they earned and far more of their profits than was allowed in inner China. State enterprises in inner China, trying to adapt to reforms under which they were held responsible for their own profits and losses, could see the advantages of a branch in Shenzhen. Companies also found that it was an attractive base for the final preparation of goods for export and for gaining information about new technology and new export opportunities. Most cadres were happy to be assigned there for a period of time; they could learn new technology and management practices, earn more, and often, one way or another, acquire appliances they might not otherwise be able to own. By 1987 over two thousand "domestic link" ventures, under some twenty-five different central government ministries, had established Shenzhen offices.

Before long, regional governments were also setting up offices in Shenzhen. By 1987, twenty-seven of China's twenty-nine provinces and many municipalities had established offices and their own provincial guest houses. These in effect were a modern version of the traditional *huiguan,* the locality association meeting halls that provided a gathering place and assistance to people who had originally come from the same locality. Now they were organized by provincial and municipal governments and guided by governmental purposes, stimulated by the new linkages between economic areas made possible by the reforms. Officials from the regions who came for government or commercial business could stay overnight at rates far below Shenzhen's high commercial prices. Local staff of the provincial office could arrange appointments for these visitors in Shenzhen. Compared to those who gathered at traditional *huiguan,* they were now more concerned with learning about technology and international markets. Provinces also had Hong Kong offices, but Hong Kong was even more expensive and required special permission to visit. Shenzhen rapidly became a great gathering place for people seeking information about the outside world. Some provincial offices, under pressure not to be a financial burden to the province, experimented with charging fees for their rooms and other services. By the end of 1985, 29,609 (11,850 from governmental units) of Shenzhen's 63,684 cadres were working for "domestic link" enterprises and units.[3]

The enterprises that responded most eagerly to the call to set up branches in Shenzhen were generally "third front" enterprises, those that in the 1960s and early 1970s had been moved inland when Chinese leaders, preoccupied with foreign tensions, feared establishing industry in coastal areas. After reforms began, the government was not only reluctant to make new investments in poorly located inland plants but encouraged them to move or establish branches elsewhere to help achieve profitability in the new era of more open markets. Shenzhen afforded an opportunity to set up a branch that could absorb new technology and pass it on to its old inland plant. The branch could also obtain better information about market opportunities abroad and sometimes could package and market the company's products or get the home plant to adapt products accordingly.

Many of the talented engineers and managers working in third front industries had originally come from coastal cities like Shanghai and Tianjin before they had been required to move inland, and they were looking for opportunities to return. Because their original cities usually had strict residence controls, few received permission to move back. Shenzhen was an attractive alternative; as a growing city it could offer residence permits or at least temporary permits for specialists from other parts of China, and it provided more urban facilities than did cities inland. Even cadres who had grown up in inner China and wanted to return generally looked upon a term of two to five years in Shenzhen as an opportunity to further their careers.

Some factories in Shenzhen, responding to enterprise independence and rewards for profitability, were not enthusiastic about transferring technology to companies in inner China that might become their competition. But there was a growing awareness that technology was a commodity and that firms in Shenzhen with new technology could make it available for sale. Whether through sales, friendships, or brotherly company assistance, considerable technology and expertise was acquired by the third front branches and transferred to inner China. It would be an exaggeration to say that information from Shenzhen branches radically changed many home companies, but it did play a continuing role in stimulating new practices and the adaptation of inland factories to the international markets. By 1987, 2,658 enterprises in Shenzhen had some kind of inner link.

The national government investment in the special economic zones and the effort to construct enough infrastructure to attract foreign investors made planners vulnerable to criticism from inner China, which felt disadvantaged. The success of Shenzhen in providing useful services to enterprises and governments in other provinces thus played a very critical role in maintaining enough political support in Beijing to keep the zones going.

## Links with Outside Capital

From its inception as a special economic zone, Shenzhen was expected to rely primarily on foreign capital and to import modern technology. It was allowed to set up joint ventures, wholly foreign-owned ventures, and processing contracts. These goals proved to be far more difficult than planners initially expected, and the difficulties led many in Beijing to evaluate the Shenzhen experiment negatively. Many joint enterprises and wholly foreign-owned ventures did not go smoothly, and both Beijing and foreign companies regarded them as at best frustrating, and at worst failures. Considering the unrealistic hopes that Beijing had for attracting the latest technology at virtually no cost, the political pressures on Shenzhen not to make concessions to foreigners, and Chinese officials' low level of technical and international experience, it is perhaps surprising that any of these ventures worked at all. Shenzhen was a critical early learning experience regarding what might be expected from foreign direct investment for leaders and observers in many parts of China.

Many looked to China as a market for their products. The potential of a market with the world's largest population continued to dazzle foreign businesspeople as it had for generations, and taking advantage of that potential remained almost equally as elusive as it had been for earlier entrepreneurs. By 1979 most foreign multinationals seeking production sites in East Asia had found them outside of China and were quite satisfied. Goods could be produced at low cost within a fast, predictable delivery time, with a minimum of red tape. For the most part they did not believe that China could significantly improve on the record of operations elsewhere. If foreign companies were to establish plants in Shenzhen, they wanted them to be bases to sell to inner China. Yet the guidelines China developed for Shenzhen called for foreign plants to produce goods primarily for export.

Chinese companies sought modern technology, but foreign companies had little incentive to provide it. China lacked technical staff who could use, maintain, service, and repair modern machinery, let alone install, adapt, improve, and redesign it as personnel in plants in other East Asian countries could. Given mainland China's lack of ability to absorb the technology, lack of patent protection, desire to use technology to export its own products, and reluctance to repatriate profits in foreign currency, it was initially very difficult for them to find many takers among foreign businesses.

Many basic issues that foreign investors considered essential had not been fully resolved when Shenzhen opened. China badly needed foreign currency, and it was not always clear how much of its earnings a foreign company could repatriate in foreign currency. It was not clear whether foreigners could hire and fire workers whenever they chose. Although direct labor costs were much cheaper than in other East Asian countries, foreign companies were commonly asked to pay the Chinese unit (the enterprise or the local government, not individual workers) for labor costs; the unit charged far more than local labor costs and used the rest to cover construction or overhead costs. It was not clear whether foreigners could set salaries as they chose. It was not clear how easy it would be for foreign executives or their employees to come and stay at their sites and how much they would be charged if they did. It was not clear how many unanticipated fees foreign businesses would be asked to pay. It was not clear whether the Chinese side could deliver all the items contracted for in a timely fashion and what recourse a foreigner might have if the Chinese failed to deliver.

Provincial and national officials tried to provide regulations giving the assurances that foreigners wanted without sacrificing Chinese interests, but they had few staff members experienced in international law and they were cautious about giving away too much. As in other areas, the first announcements reflected general policy but offered little precise guidance about what would be permitted. The first regulations, passed by the National People's Congress in August 1980, established guidelines for the special economic zones; in November 1981 a series of regulations for them was passed concerning entry and exit, labor and wages, business registration, and land regulation. In late 1983 Guangdong passed special legislation on the management of property in Shenzhen. Since these regulations were not always considered adequate protection by foreign businesses, new rules were passed on economic contracts and technology imports in January 1984, and in December 1984 more specific regulations were issued by Shenzhen itself on land-use fees. In late 1986 Shenzhen officials followed up the new leeway granted in state guidelines to simplify various kinds of paperwork.

These successive changes established some framework, but because interpretations by local officials were not always consistent they were still not enough to reassure foreign companies. Some Chinese officials, eager to attract business to their locality, gave assurances when negotiating, but because of jurisdictional problems within China it was not always clear that other officials in different units could or would honor them. Some Chinese negotiators were overly cautious in order to avoid possible charges that they were sacrificing the nation's interests to those of capitalists. Others required the foreigner to give them special gifts or finance the study of relatives abroad.

Chinese officials, trying their best to represent their nation's interests, sometimes devised techniques to offset their lack of knowledge of international markets or bargaining practices. They took bids from several companies and shared the lowest bid with the other companies to push them to offer still more favorable terms. They learned to express interest at an early stage and get a letter of intent, and then, after a foreign company had made an investment of time and energy, test how far the limits could be pushed. Sometimes they waited until a company became impatient and then made demands they thought the foreigners, in their hurry to finish the transaction, would not resist. Sometimes they concluded an agreement and then, as the foreign company began to go into production, notified it of extra charges. Sometimes they tried to cut costs by buying only hardware, hoping they could handle all the software themselves; when they could not, they asked the foreign partner to explain how to resolve these problems but expected to pay nothing further. Some, not sure of international practices, refused to accept those commonly agreed to by those accustomed to doing business worldwide.

Many Western or Japanese businesses decided the risks were too great. But as discussed in Chapter 2, the Hong Kong Chinese, whose greater confidence was based on their finely tuned understanding of the culture, their personal connections in China, their ability to send in on-site managers and supervisors, and their readiness to give presents, moved more quickly to invest. As of 1987 over 90 percent of the foreign investment in Shenzhen was from Hong Kong. But even Hong Kong companies were cautious. Their investments were quite small and they too sought assurances, formal as well as informal.

Despite problems, creative Chinese officials and foreign businesspeople with a long-range perspective peeled away at the layers of problems to find ways to meet the needs of both parties. They sometimes agreed that if a foreign company would export a certain amount, it could also sell a certain amount within China. When opportunities for additional domestic sales presented themselves, the Chinese joint venture partner would find ways to allow the company to exceed the contracted percentage for domestic sales. For foreign companies ready to bring in some modern technology and prepared to make substantial investments over a long period of time, the Chinese were flexible in offering incentives beyond the minimal ones stated in the regulations. And Shenzhen officials were empowered to make investment decisions up to $50 million per project, far more than those in other localities were allowed, even after the 1984 expansion of open cities. And as much as they wanted higher technology, they often accepted small contracts from Hong Kong companies that used low-priced local labor to process materials brought from Hong Kong.

By the end of 1986 some 760 foreign enterprises had industrial contracts in Shenzhen, and there were 3,000 additional agreements for export processing. Although foreign investment in industrial plants had still not caught up with investment in hotels and other service-sector facilities, already over $600 million had been invested in industry. And as Shenzhen negotiators were becoming more attuned to international practice and more knowledgeable about international markets, their offices were continuously bustling with foreign businesspeople who had come to discuss possible investments.

### Recession, Readjustment, and Beyond

The years 1984 and 1985 were tough economically for China as a whole, but they were even tougher for Shenzhen. In 1985, because China suffered from a trade imbalance and a serious shortage of foreign currency, there was a national tightening of imports and new investment. In Shenzhen much of the infrastructure was by then complete, but some units that had been planning to build interrupted, slowed, or even abandoned plans because of lack of funds. Much of the dynamism and demand for services in Shenzhen in the early 1980s had been fueled by the fantastic construction activity, and as this began to slow down, it took a toll on Shenzhen's economy.

In 1984, Beijing opened fourteen coastal cities to foreign investment. The decision was an affirmation, even a tribute, to Shenzhen's success, for it was an extension of many aspects of Shenzhen's experiment. But the tribute created new problems for Shenzhen. Just when it was changing its focus from infrastructure to foreign industry, fourteen cities stood ready to offer attractive terms to foreign investors. Many of the newly opened cities, such as Guangzhou and Shanghai, had a broader base of resources, technology, and personnel than did Shenzhen.

Shenzhen also had new competition from nearby rural areas. Shenzhen's wages had risen rapidly to attract workers during its construction boom and for its many new industrial plants. The higher pay benefited its workers but created a large wage gap with nearby rural areas. In 1981 many Hong Kong investors who wanted a site across the border for a small processing plant happily set up shop in Shenzhen, but by 1984 they had often decided that it made more sense to invest in a nearby county that offered to make the goods at far lower labor costs than Shenzhen could.

The coup de grace in 1984–85 came from Beijing. Much of Shenzhen's income in 1983 and 1984 came from sources that Beijing found distasteful. Foreign currency was in very short supply, and there was a thriving black market in Shenzhen for those willing to pay more than the official exchange rate. Speculators came from all over China. The official value of the U.S. dollar in 1985 was 2.8 yuan, but the semiofficial dual rate was almost twice as much and the black market rate even higher. Speculators in badly needed goods were beginning to hold them for later resale and to transport them some distance, where they could command prices and earn profits that many regarded as excessive. Furthermore, many consumer items that were still prohibited from ordinary sale in mainland China were coming into Shenzhen. Hotels and restaurants serving foreigners, for example, were given special permission to buy some consumer items from abroad, and foreigners working in Shenzhen and overseas Chinese visiting relatives were allowed to bring in a certain amount of goods. Some of these goods and some smuggled goods found their way to private stalls that did a substantial trade. Many of the so-called companies set up in Shenzhen existed in name only *(pibao gongsi)* in order to carry on these shady practices. Those in inner China eagerly sought opportunities to go to Shenzhen on business trips, and then not uncommonly returned with a consumer item or two, perhaps smuggled, for their unit or their family.

In 1982 the authorities, already concerned about the impact of the

Shenzhen SEZ on such black markets, had decided to erect a "second border," separating Shenzhen from the rest of China, in addition to the one separating Shenzhen from Hong Kong. Construction had gone slowly, but as the eighty-six-kilometer fence neared completion in 1984, border control became easier. The completion of the fence, with its six gates for customs inspection, enabled officials to clamp down on these unsavory developments.

The 1984 crackdown helped clean up "decadent capitalist" influences, but it caused problems for many in Shenzhen, including restaurant and hotel keepers and their bankers. The planners may have overestimated the original demand for facilities, but when fewer Chinese visitors came to Shenzhen because it was no longer possible to buy or obtain goods as before, the bottom fell out of the demand for products and services. Hotels and even office buildings suffered from serious excess capacity. Units defaulted on loans, and since many were waiting to be paid back before they could repay their loans, circles of debts became a serious problem.

Beijing also became stricter with Shenzhen. Disappointed that Shenzhen had spent far more foreign currency than it had earned and had spent more on lavish buildings than on manufacturing technology, Beijing demanded that Shenzhen abandon low-tech processing industries in favor of higher technology and concentrate on the export market rather than on less demanding and more eager domestic consumers. Beijing did not object if nearby counties attracted simple processing industries. But since it had invested 3.4 billion yuan in Shenzhen from 1979 to 1984[4] with the goal of attracting advanced and export-oriented industries, it insisted that Shenzhen concentrate on this more difficult task. Beijing leaders realized that their crackdown would cause several years of difficult adjustment for Shenzhen, but they were convinced that the moral health of the nation and continued political support for Shenzhen required it.

Foreign observers who looked at hotel occupancy rates, profit levels, and debt repayment schedules were quick to pronounce Shenzhen a failure, and even some young cadres, including children of high-level officials, abandoned Shenzhen in the 1984–85 downturn. Yet there were several reasons why the vast majority of Shenzhen officials chose to stay and why they remained positive about Shenzhen's future. Shenzhen's nearness to Hong Kong provided convenient access to international markets, an information base, and a sensitivity to international trends far beyond anything that other cities in China were likely to achieve in the foreseeable future. The new links between Hong Kong and Guangdong were vitalizing the entire region, which in the late 1980s was growing at breakneck speed. Hong Kong offered world-class facilities in transportation and communication that were unlike anything other Chinese cities were likely to achieve in this century, and Shenzhen, with access to these links, would continue to play an important role for mainland businesses and people who found it too expensive to set up in Hong Kong.

One way to conceptualize developments in Shenzhen is as a natural expansion of a metropolitan region centered in Hong Kong, an idea that will be pursued in Chapters 11 and 13. As Hong Kong industry and services expanded, new transport and other facilities were required beyond Hong Kong's borders. As land prices in Hong Kong rose astronomically, Hong Kong investors sought land at lower rates. As labor costs increased rapidly in Hong Kong, where unemployment was below 2 percent, businesses looked for new sources of labor. Shenzhen was able to supply that land and that labor at lower costs. As border controls loosened, the natural process of metropolitan expansion would continue to overcome boundaries and different political systems.

By the mid-1980s Hong Kong residents were already going to Shenzhen in large numbers on the weekends. Shenzhen's earliest efforts to persuade those in Hong Kong to live in more attractive buildings at lower costs than in Hong Kong got off to a slow start because Shenzhen lacked many of the amenities, but as these improved, more people from Hong Kong found them attractive.

Shenzhen could not compete with nearby counties for processing industries seeking the lowest-cost labor. But it had higher levels of technical and administrative ability with better connections throughout China, and many businesses that wanted these resources came to Shenzhen rather than to the nearby counties. Nor could Shenzhen compete with Shanghai or Tianjin as a center of science and technology. But its managers learned quickly about the international markets and made timely use of their knowledge.

Results after late 1985 lent some support to this optimism. New foreign investment fell off from 1984 to 1985, but it picked up substantially in 1986. Even in 1985, with new plants completed from earlier investment, industrial production rose over 50 percent above 1984 levels and increased at comparable rates again in 1986. According to official figures from 1980 to 1987, industrial production grew

an average of about 80 percent a year and was continuing to grow
rapidly.

Shenzhen continued to attract thousands of talented young people
in China seeking higher salaries and a freer atmosphere. In 1984 thirty
students from high schools in Shenzhen passed the very difficult exam
to the top national universities; in 1985 over three hundred passed,
and the number continued to rise rapidly each year. This reflected the
talented families moving to Shenzhen and the rising educational levels
in local schools. Shenzhen remained behind Hong Kong in efficiency,
and in the late 1980s wage increases sometimes shot ahead of productivity increases to the detriment of Shenzhen's ability to attract
new investment. But Shenzhen industry was still much more efficient
than most of China. Many young cadres who had trouble accepting
the bureaucratic constraints in other Chinese cities found a place in
Shenzhen. Shenzhen remained more vulnerable than other places in
China to the vagaries of the international market. But this is the kind
of vulnerability that stimulated others in East Asia in the postwar era
and that also sparked the young people of Shenzhen.

Shenzhen was not necessarily beloved by outsiders. Westerners
much preferred Hong Kong, with its greater sophistication and variety. In the late 1980s Hong Kong and foreign businesspeople still
found Shenzhen decision making slow and the workers less motivated
than their own. Within China many considered the people of Shenzhen materialistic, arrogant, decadent, and sometimes corrupt. There
were well-known stories of senior cadres who cried upon visiting
Shenzhen, feeling that all they fought for during the socialist revolution was being lost. Even some younger cadres who visited found
Shenzhen too materialistic, prices beyond their means, and foreign
businesspeople treated too well. Many denigrated Shenzhen's accomplishments, convinced that its industry had not been very successful
and that the attractive construction was not a product of local skill
and hard work but of enormous national investments and favorable
policies. Shenzhen was vulnerable to criticism, but after its first few
years many Chinese provinces and enterprises had a stake in its success,
and many bright young people in Shenzhen believed that Shenzhen
had made it. It was evolving its own style, far more northern and
national, far more Mandarin, than either Hong Kong or Guangzhou,
and yet far more open and international than other cities in China.
And even Beijing officials disgusted with Shenzhen's decadence and
misuse of funds acknowledged that it still had a role sifting new

technology and management practices and helping to reintegrate Hong Kong into China.

## Shenzhen Experiments

The Chinese may disagree among themselves about where which reform first began on what scale, but from 1980 to 1985 Shenzhen's ability to open new offices and new factories and its access to world developments through Hong Kong gave it unusual opportunities to try new system reforms. It became a great laboratory for determining which Western practices were most suitable for China. No place was inspected more often by top leaders to see how reforms were going. Marshal Ye Jianying visited in 1980 and 1981; Premier Zhao Ziyang visited in 1980 and several times thereafter; Party General Secretary Hu Yaobang visited in 1983; Deng Xiaoping visited in 1984. Because of its role in training cadres in new ways of thinking, Shenzhen was called "Deng Xiaoping's High Cadre University."[5] In 1984, for example, the Shenzhen government had over a hundred thousand visitors from the North. Among them were a high number of top officials from the central government, provincial, and municipal units. They were encouraged by Beijing leaders to go not only to gain political support for the SEZs and reforms but to gain ideas that could be applied in their own locale. In addition to innovations in city planning and architecture and the opening of China to foreign enterprises, Shenzhen applied several system reforms.[6]

*Employment and Labor Payments.* Shenzhen experimented with a wide variety of flexible payment systems to increase work motivation. Shenzhen was among the first to offer bonuses to workers on the basis of their performance and later to link bonuses to the overall profitability of a company. It was among the first to pay workers by their job, not simply by their rank. It was among the first to try out the labor contract system, in which people in large enterprises were not hired for life; instead employment could be terminated, either by the employer who found the employee's work unsatisfactory or by the employee who gave one month's notice. Yuan Geng, disappointed that cadres sent to work in Shekou by the Ministry of Communications lacked knowledge about foreign developments and international business, began in 1980 to require examinations and to recruit able engineers, international business specialists, and even ordinary workers.

*Simplification of the Economic Bureaucracy.* Most provinces and municipalities had two layers of bureaucracy between enterprises and the top local government: administrative offices over major areas and large bureaus or departments under them. Beginning in 1981, Shenzhen reduced this to one layer, the administrative offices. In the economic sphere, it had only four administrative offices: industry, planning, finance-trade, and communication. By 1984 it had only sixteen municipal bureaus, far fewer than other cities of its size had. Because these offices did not try to make detailed plans for the companies under them but concentrated primarily on macroeconomic management, they could operate with a far smaller bureaucracy. They privatized government bureaus and made them controlling companies that integrated the work of factories in their respective spheres.

*Democratic Restraints on Management.* Concerned that cadres too frequently developed cliques and exercised arbitrary authority that dampened the enthusiasm of workers, Yuan Geng tried various procedures for election of cadres in Shekou's governing bodies and factories, and Shekou leaders believed this helped make cadres more sensitive to their workers.

*Enterprise Autonomy.* Enterprise autonomy was being tried in many parts of China. Because Shenzhen's enterprises were less subject to detailed state plans, had less bureaucracy supervising them, had more opportunities for direct access to funding, and could make more decisions about labor, enterprise autonomy was in fact much greater there than elsewhere. The firm was responsible for profits and losses. In state and collective firms, the manager was held responsible for the success of the firm, and in joint ventures with foreign firms, the manager was responsible to the board of directors.

*Banking Services.* By 1986 twelve foreign banks had branches in Shenzhen and nine more had representative offices. In addition to offering capital for foreign investors, they were beginning to have a freer hand in accepting deposits, offering interest rates higher than Chinese banks, and offering a variety of customer services. This created pressures on Chinese banks to offer more attractive customer services, to allow more freedom to Chinese customers in withdrawing deposits without questions asked, and to move toward offering more interest-rate flexibility.

*Horizontal Linkages between Local Firms.* In inner China, enterprises were basically linked vertically to the supervisory unit responsible for managing them. In Shenzhen, where the role of the supervisory unit had been greatly weakened, many enterprises found themselves too small to compete in international markets. Shenzhen thus pioneered in developing "enterprise groups" *(jituan)* which provided horizontal linkages between companies and were more under the control of the companies than of government bureaucrats. One type of enterprise group linked different firms in a particular sector. In the electronics sector, for example, the Electronics Enterprise Group (Dianzi Jituan), composed of about thirty electronics companies, developed a common brand name (Saige) for the export of goods that met certain agreed-upon standards and sponsored certain common information and export promotion services. Another type of enterprise group was composed of all the companies in Shenzhen that had once been related to the Ministry of Aeronautics. Although companies from this ministry existed in all major Chinese cities, the branches in Shenzhen were the first to form an enterprise group.

*Freedom in Land Use.* More urban property was put up for long-term lease in Shenzhen than in most other cities, and Shenzhen experimented with using urban property as a mortgage for bank borrowing. In 1987 Shenzhen, seeking ways of generating badly needed capital and inspired by the Hong Kong example, auctioned off land on a fifty-year lease for the first time, a practice it expected to continue.

*The Changing Role of Shenzhen.* After its problems in 1984, Shenzhen lost some of its magic as a national example. Some officials felt Shenzhen was so different that it was not worth studying except as a convenient place for learning from Hong Kong. They thought it better to study the Delta counties and simply visit Shenzhen. In any case, by the time major reforms spread to inner China in the mid-1980s, Shenzhen had largely completed its mission as a testing ground for the admission of foreign capital, modern urban planning and architecture, and other key system reforms. Its national significance in the years ahead, leading up to 1997, was likely to be as a buffer for the reabsorption of Hong Kong into China. In this role, it was expected to act as a crucial go-between in educating people in China about world capitalist practices and in training people in Hong Kong how to operate within the Chinese Communist system.

## Zhuhai Special Economic Zone

The Zhuhai special economic zone, created at the same time as Shenzhen's, was in most ways precisely parallel.[7] Just as Shenzhen was located immediately north of Hong Kong at the eastern end of the mouth of the Pearl River, Zhuhai was located immediately north of Macau at the western end of the mouth, thirty-six nautical miles away from Hong Kong. Zhuhai could conduct trade overland through Macau, then a city of almost four hundred thousand, just as Shenzhen could through Hong Kong, and Zhuhai administrators could prepare for taking over Macau, just as Shenzhen anticipated the repatriation of Hong Kong. And similar to the organization of the Shenzhen SEZ and Baoan County under Shenzhen Metropolitan Region, the Zhuhai SEZ and Doumen County to its west were part of Zhuhai Metropolitan Region.

But just as Macau fell behind Hong Kong, Zhuhai could not keep up with Shenzhen. In 1844, as Macau began to lag commercially, its Portuguese leaders began to rely heavily on gambling as the major source of government funds. In 1963 Macau put up its first modern gambling hotel, and more first-class hotels and restaurants followed. In the 1970s as new hydrofoils and hovercraft cut Hong Kong–Macau travel time from four hours to one, tourism and gambling exploded. In 1985, with some 58 percent of its public revenues coming directly from gambling, Macau was the gambling capital of the Asian Pacific region.[8]

Zhuhai has some beautiful hills and vistas, and it was quite natural that Zhuhai planners began to develop tourist facilities to gain foreign currency. By 1982 there were several attractive hotels around a tourist center at a small, centrally located mountain, Shijingshan, and at several other scenic spots. It became clear, however, that Zhuhai could not duplicate Macau's success at tourism unless it had gambling facilities. Although some Zhuhai planners entertained the idea of allowing gambling for outsiders but not for locals, officials, worried about moral degradation, chose to do without gambling even if it meant a slower development of tourism.

From the beginning Zhuhai had planned to set up industrial zones, and by 1982 when much of the infrastructure was in place and it was clear that tourism would not produce as much revenue as had been hoped for, leaders concentrated their attention on industrial development. Everbright, a Hong Kong–based company under the direction of Wang Guangying, the former Tianjin mayor and brother-in-law of Liu Shaoqi, played an entrepreneurial role. But no company in Zhuhai played the pioneering role that CMSN had played in Shekou. Zhuhai's overall guidance was directed by two development companies under the SEZ Economic Commission and by several development companies under the Foreign Economic Relations and Trade Commission.

Because Zhuhai's development lagged two to three years behind Shenzhen's, it drew heavily on Shenzhen's experience. It too had a centrally integrated plan that began with electricity, roads, sewage, and telecommunications, on which it moved very quickly. It also designed attractive new buildings, though because Zhuhai planners believed Shenzhen had expanded too rapidly, with too many tall buildings, they built fewer skyscrapers. Apartments were large in size but more spread out, with more attention to style. Zhuhai moved more slowly in construction to avoid the problems of underutilization and tying up of badly needed capital. It also tried to keep tighter controls on speculation and the smuggling of foreign consumer goods.

Compared to Shenzhen, however, Zhuhai had several clear disadvantages. Its harbor, like Macau's, had shallow water, and even by the late 1980s it had only one berth that could dock a ten thousand ton ship. The highway linking Zhuhai and Guangzhou was operative by 1987, about the same time that the highway from Shenzhen to Guangzhou was completed, and planning for the limited access high-speed road linking Zhuhai to Guangzhou kept pace with the planning for the link from Guangzhou to Hong Kong. But Zhuhai was not connected to a railroad, and at China's stage of development railroads were still important. Zhuhai was much smaller (15.2 square kilometers compared to Shenzhen's 327.5) and hence did not have the critical mass to support a university, a research center, or financial and informational services comparable to Shenzhen's. Above all, it was adjacent to Macau instead of Hong Kong. The easy flow of people and information between Shenzhen and Hong Kong gave Shenzhen an incomparable advantage.

In fact Zhuhai became more closely linked to Shenzhen and Hong Kong, both little more than an hour away by hydrofoil, than to Macau. Zhuhai cadres concerned with industrial development met constantly with cadres from Shenzhen, and for investment and technology they turned overwhelmingly to Hong Kong. The industrial zones in Zhuhai (Xiawan, Jida, Beiling, and Nanshan) closely followed the development of such zones in Shenzhen.

Zhuhai did not pioneer experiments in system reforms the way Shenzhen did. Its reforms basically followed those of Shenzhen, modified in implementation to avoid mistakes. On January 29, 1984, when Deng Xiaoping was in Zhuhai just after visiting Shenzhen, he inscribed a scroll that read: "The Zhuhai SEZ is good [*Zhuhai jingji tequ hao*]." When asked, he did not describe Shenzhen in the same way. It was clear he believed Zhuhai to be morally superior to Shenzhen, to have less smuggling and speculation, even though Zhuhai had looked to Shenzhen as the innovative model.

By the late 1980s Zhuhai had also begun to take off. In 1980, in the area that became the Zhuhai zone, there were only ten individuals who had university-level training in technical fields. In 1986 alone, 1,700 such people came to Zhuhai. In 1981 its industrial output was 0.038 billion yuan; in 1987 it reached 1.2 billion and was on target to reach its goal of 3.6 billion by 1990. Like Shenzhen, Zhuhai had offices from virtually every province in the nation, and it ranked with Shenzhen in attracting talented young cadres. Efforts begun in 1982 to bring foreign companies to Zhuhai began to pay off in 1985, and over the next several years, the number of new factories—making products such as compressors for refrigerators and air conditioners, electronic equipment, glass, beer, videocassettes, computer diskettes, synthetic fibers, printed circuit boards, and televisions—increased rapidly.

Although its industrial production lagged far behind Shenzhen's, Zhuhai had many similarities to Shenzhen. Zhuhai brought in a great deal of investment from inner China as well as from Hong Kong. Its technical personnel and top several hundred administrative cadres were overwhelmingly from the North, and many of the enterprises were led and established by units from inner China. Zhuhai had become, like Shenzhen, more a northern city. In 1980 the combined population of Zhuhai City (127,000) and Doumen County (about 240,000) had been almost exactly the same as Shenzhen City and Baoan County, and because its labor demands grew more slowly than Shenzhen's, it could obtain the workers it needed by hiring locals. Since there was a substantial local labor surplus at the time the Zhuhai SEZ was started, there was a conscious policy to hire ordinary workers from the local population; Shenzhen had required far more workers from other counties and even from other provinces. Yet by the late 1980s, as labor demands for Zhuhai had increased, it began to absorb some labor from the neighboring West River area, mostly from the rural areas of Jiangmen and Zhaoqing Prefectures, to whose economies the zone proved to be a great stimulus. While Shenzhen, like Hong Kong, was on its way to becoming a global city, Zhuhai thus used its international connections to become the center of a regional economy.

## Shantou Special Economic Zone

Shenzhen, Zhuhai, and Xiamen (across the straits from Taiwan and outside Guangdong) geographically faced the outside territories to which they hoped to provide a bridge. The only special economic zone that faced no such territory was Shantou. Why should it be given special status? Although Shantou had been only a fishing town until the middle of the nineteenth century, it was made a treaty port (known then as Swatow) and before 1949 within the province was second only to Guangzhou as a trading center. Though closed down after 1949, it retained its potential as a major port city.

A large group from the Shantou area had emigrated before the Communists took power, and they came to dominate much of the business of Southeast Asia. With their own language (Chaozhou, known in various parts of Southeast Asia by other transliterations, such as Tiuchew) and culture, they retained a fierce regional loyalty. As China's reforms were instituted in the late 1970s, they clamored for increased development of Shantou, and as successful entrepreneurs, they were prepared to invest in a zone in their home area.

Just what form the opening of Shantou would take was more difficult to resolve than in the case of Shenzhen and Zhuhai. Even its initial designation as a special economic zone lagged some months behind the other two. Both Shenzhen and Zhuhai had been, at best, small towns with heavily rural populations. They therefore required completely new cities, with new housing for those moving in. Shantou, in contrast, was already a densely populated urban area. A major issue was whether to create only a small SEZ, which would be somewhat like an export-processing zone in other countries, or whether to open up all of Shantou or at least a major portion of it as the SEZ. Although many local people wanted to open up the entire city, higher authorities initially designated only a very small zone of 1.6 square kilometers. In 1984, when fourteen coastal cities were declared open, many in Shantou felt it too should be declared an open city. But since it already had a special economic zone, it was felt that opening the entire city would interfere with the SEZ development that was just getting started. At that time the Shantou zone was expanded, however, to include the entire Longhu area, 22.6 square kilometers (including the original SEZ), and the Guangao area, 30 square kilometers across the bay to the south.

The zone organizers felt from the beginning like a deprived younger brother. Investment of all kinds—from Beijing, from Guangdong Province, from other units in China, and from overseas Chinese— lagged behind Shenzhen and Zhuhai. By 1987 the total investment in the Shantou SEZ was only 385 million yuan, far less than in the other areas. In part this was because Shantou had a narrower mission. It did not have the undeveloped mountainous areas found in Zhuhai and Shenzhen appropriate for tourism. It was not close enough to Hong Kong to attract weekend travelers. Nor was it close enough to Hong Kong that inland Chinese companies would find Shantou a useful listening post for information about foreign trade, technology, and management techniques.

Shantou also had more difficulty attracting foreign capital. Transport lines from Hong Kong and Macau were much more distant. Although only about five hundred kilometers away, in the 1980s Shantou was still usually a ten-hour road trip or a twenty-four-hour boat trip from Hong Kong, the closest spot in the outside world. Language was another consideration. The dominant group in Hong Kong spoke Cantonese. They considered Chaozhou people clannish and felt more comfortable dealing with the Cantonese-speaking areas of Guangdong. The one-fourth of Hong Kong's citizens who traced their ancestry to the Chaozhou-Shantou region had a more limited range of businesses that they could expand to Shantou. Southeast Asian businesspeople originally from Chaozhou-Shantou also had far less economic incentive to invest there, despite their localist loyalties, because cheap labor was already available where they were. Because the Shantou zone was of such a small scale and the area had so many of its own talented bureaucrats, it needed few outside cadres. Shantou retained a local flavor compared to the more cosmopolitan, all-China flavors of Shenzhen and Zhuhai. Thus the Shantou SEZ had to be content in the 1980s with the development not of a comprehensive second system but of a more limited export-processing zone, not unlike that of other countries.

In the early 1980s the Shantou area began developing infrastructure for development that provided better port and road support (see Chapter 7). The zone also developed its own small port facility as well as its own administrative service sector, including its own hotel. Its administrative infrastructure was essentially the same as that of the Shenzhen and Zhuhai SEZs. Shantou, acknowledging its weak position in competing for foreign investment, decided it would be necessary to accept export-processing contracts. Given its constraints, it did an excellent job of recruiting new industries, and by 1987 had several hundred factory buildings with 18,800 employees. Its industrial production was 300 million yuan a year, almost 10 percent of the production of the entire Shantou City area. The zone factories included processing projects from Hong Kong in carpets, textiles, ceramics, embroidery, and canning.

After the rest of the Longhu area was added in 1984, a decision was made to expand its industrial area to a total of 3.6 square kilometers and to open an agricultural area of 2.0 square kilometers. The industrial addition permitted the expansion of existing projects and the addition of a few new ones.

Shantou was known for its high-quality agriculture. It had long produced the highest rice yields in the province, and its tangerines were especially sweet. It had many highly trained agricultural technologists. Building on this base, in its new agricultural area it began creating fish ponds for shrimp and eel already contracted to the Japanese, developing new vegetable crops with export potential like broccoli and asparagus, and experimenting with new fruit strains. The SEZ in essence became an agriculture experimental station for the surrounding region, trying out new crops and advising nearby farmers on the preparation of crops for export. In the late 1980s it was just beginning to turn to food processing, developing facilities for canning and the preparation of frozen foods that would then be expanded beyond the SEZ.

Shantou zone officials hoped that at a later stage they would be able to attract more capital-intensive industries. The Guangao area was added with the idea of developing a large petrochemical complex. Because it was located across the bay and away from large population centers, it was felt that this development would not affect the quality of the environment in the major urban area. With this expanded area the zone in the 1990s would encompass a major part of the modernization efforts of the entire city.

The Shantou special economic zone helped bring new industry to the city and to stimulate the agricultural modernization of the surrounding region. However, unlike Shenzhen and Zhuhai, new cities with comprehensive new systems that brought new economic vitality to an entire region, the zone in the 1980s was only a small appendage to Shantou City, dedicated to producing for export.

By the time the Shenzhen, Zhuhai, and Shantou special economic zones began taking off, they were in fact no longer so special, despite their name; other coastal cities were also opening up. Zhuhai and

Shenzhen still had a foreign policy role in the reabsorption of Hong Kong and Macau into China, but they had played out their historical role in trying out new experiments and had become more like other local development zones, including Shantou, that were bringing industry to their localities.

# 5.

# *The Inner Delta Counties: Flexible Local Initiative*

In February 1985, the cities and counties of the Inner Delta were officially grouped together as the Pearl River Delta economic development zone. The zone included four small cities (Foshan, Jiangmen, and two former counties administratively reorganized as cities, Zhongshan and Dongguan) and twelve counties (Doumen, Baoan, Zengcheng, Panyu, Nanhai, Shunde, Gaoming, Heshan, Xinhui, Taishan, Kaiping, and Enping); see the map in Chapter 4. The zone included the central core of the Delta, except for Guangzhou, and was called the Inner Delta *(xiao sanjiazhou)* to distinguish it from the Greater Delta *(da sanjiazhou)*, which in December 1987 was defined to include twenty-eight counties and cities. Long the richest part of the province and closest to Hong Kong, the Inner Delta area had already greatly benefited from the openings to the outside in the mid-1970s. After 1985 it was allowed to offer more special tax and other incentives to attract foreign investment and encourage foreign trade.[1]

Compared to the special economic zones, the Inner Delta had many disadvantages. Shenzhen and Zhuhai received significant help from talented technical and administrative cadres from the north. They had generous support from national ministries and the companies under them to build local facilities. National and international architects participated to make Shenzhen in particular a world-class modern city. In contrast, the Inner Delta counties were the country cousins, encouraged to rely on their own strength.

But these disadvantages had a positive side, which the country cousins used to their advantage. The sixteen counties and cities in the

Inner Delta had an average of almost six hundred thousand people each, but the number of top cadres administering a county at most numbered several hundred. In line with policy, most had local roots and, having grown up near Hong Kong, had a good sense of how to use Guangdong's opening to the outside. Many county-level cadres had been promoted from below and had known each other from earlier days, when they had all attended meetings for commune leaders. They had been through many campaigns together and, except for a small number of the highest level of cadres, they had not particularly suffered during the Cultural Revolution. They shared a long-standing identification with their community, a knowledge of its history, and a commitment to its future. The new openings gave them a chance to work toward long-cherished dreams of local development.

The county officials did not have the SEZs' problem of strangers from diverse backgrounds working together or Guangdong Province's and Guangzhou City's problem of many bureaucratic layers and compartments, each with its own ethos. Nor did they need to clear as many decisions with higher authorities. The counties were primarily working outside state plans, and even if higher-level permission was required, officials generally responded more quickly because county requests were for smaller sums. In contrast to higher levels of government, the counties and small cities of the Inner Delta were like small companies run by a single owner, embarking on a new venture without established rules. They were not always thorough in their staff work, but they were ready to respond quickly and flexibly.

Many favorable geographical and historical factors helped the Inner Delta move ahead of the rest of the province to take advantage of opportunities that had been dormant since 1950.

The Pearl River Delta is formed by the conjunction of several major rivers. From its small beginnings in Fujian, the East River flows through Mei County in northeast Guangdong down through eastern Guangdong for several hundred kilometers. At Shaoguan in northern Guangdong, the Wu and Zhen rivers come together to form the North River, which runs down through the northern part of the province. From Guangxi through the western part of the province rushes the West River, biggest of them all. On their way, these rivers pick up tributaries, and at Guangzhou they unite to form the Pearl River, which flows out through a wide mouth into the ocean. But near Guangzhou, these rivers also split off into eight major outlets, all of which flow to the sea and into many little branches that interlace the entire Delta area.

The Pearl River Delta, along with the smaller Han River Delta in Guangdong's northeast, has been the most fertile part of the province. With a warm climate and ample water for irrigation, it has been an excellent area for paddy rice, its major crop for centuries. Over the years as silt accumulated in the Delta and the population grew, ambitious projects were undertaken to reclaim more land from the sea and to prevent it from flooding. Yet despite this reclamation and the general fertility of the land, public health advances from the middle of the nineteenth century caused population to grow even faster than food production.

When foreign trade began to grow in the middle of the eighteenth century, people along the riverways and coasts of the Delta built small ports, linking their towns with larger posts and ultimately with international markets. Communities even farther away began making products that could be transported overland or by river to the larger ports and from there to the outside world. At the beginning of the twentieth century a railroad linked Hong Kong through Guangzhou along the North River to Shaoguan and north China, and a small local track ran from Guangzhou through Foshan to Sanshui, a river port a few miles northwest of Guangzhou where the North, West, and Sui rivers came together. Another one ran southwest from Guangzhou to Taishan, but it was never rebuilt after its destruction in World War II. Although transport before 1949 was still largely by boat, the Delta bustled with commerce and light industry alongside agriculture.[2]

From 1950 until 1970, just as the closing of the border deprived Hong Kong of its entrepôt role, the Inner Delta lost the outlet for most of its exports. Some agricultural goods were still supplied to Hong Kong, and a substantial illegal trade evaded border controls during the Korean War, but ordinary commercial exports were drastically reduced. To stop the smuggling and reduce the risks of enemy infiltration, Chinese authorities closed down most of the coastal and river ports and vastly reduced the scale of those that remained. Only fishing boats were left, and even they were carefully monitored.

Markets within the Inner Delta contracted further in the late 1950s after collectivization and communization, and they shrank still more after the Cultural Revolution. Except for some meat and fresh vegetables, little was available through private marketing. During the 1960s and 1970s agricultural products such as grain, sugar cane, peanuts, pork, soy beans, potatoes, and hemp continued to flow through official channels between production teams, brigades, communes, and county capitals via boat, cart, and tractor. Some farm implements and a few consumer goods were sold by the state stores and cooperatives, but supplies were limited. The factories and work-shops that remained were run by counties, communes, and brigades in order to repair and produce items needed in agricultural produc-tion—fertilizer, cement, agricultural tools and machinery, and irriga-tion pumps.

Legal emigration from the Inner Delta, including from the "four counties" (Si Yi) of Taishan, Xinhui, Kaiping, and Enping and the city of Guangzhou, which since the nineteenth century had been the great source of immigrants to North America, came to a halt in 1950. Some, mostly daring young men, fled to Macau and Hong Kong, but population control within China was tight; those found in counties other than their own could be arrested. Most of the escapees, therefore, were from counties adjacent to the border (Baoan and Zhongshan) or along the rivers and coast closest to Hong Kong or Macau (Panyu, Dongguan, and Xinhui). At least several hundred thousand escaped to Hong Kong between 1950 and the late 1970s. Once there, they had little or no contact with the villages they had left. That the Inner Delta, long known for its commercial dynamism, could be transformed so completely into the same system of collective communes, state commerce, and tight border controls as that put into effect elsewhere testifies to the strength of the Communist control system at its height.

## The Reopening of the Inner Delta

As reforms began in 1979, the Inner Delta had almost 9.5 million people in 21,500 square kilometers, an area over half the size of Taiwan and almost as densely populated.[3] At the time it was still overwhelmingly rural, with 7.3 million still living in the countryside.[4] It was still backward by the standards of newly developing economies. Almost three-fourths of the population earned their living by agricul-ture without benefit of mechanization, and the richest counties had an annual per capita income of only four hundred to five hundred yuan (see the data on all Guangdong's counties in the Appendix, Table A.5).

Even during the Cultural Revolution, however, Inner Delta income had remained substantially above the provincial average. On the eve of the reforms it had 16 percent of Guangdong's population but generated 25 percent of its income. Its superior soil, the opportunity it had to market some agricultural products in Hong Kong and Guangzhou, the ease of water transport, and its technical expertise all helped it maintain its lead over other areas. Officials understood that these same factors and links with overseas relatives and compatriots in Hong Kong and Macau would in a freer reform period give the region an even greater edge. Indeed, in the latter part of the Cultural Revolution, when production in many state factories stopped, some of the rural workshops, geared toward agriculture, were allowed to produce consumer goods, which gave them a head start when reforms began.

Growth took off without long-range planning, and therefore the physical infrastructure proved woefully inadequate. In the 1950s and 1960s the government had invested in reclaiming coastal land and building embankments to prevent water damage, but it had done little other basic construction. Even when planners began to address the issues in the 1980s, their estimates of growth were still far too low, and Beijing and local units took a long time to agree on how to share the costs of construction. Roads, bridges, electric power, sewage systems, and telephone service lagged badly behind demand. As the number of bicycles, tractors, trucks, vans, and motorbikes grew, bottlenecks at river crossings and at key routes into cities took hours to negotiate. Factories, short of electric power, often had to close two or more days a week; they suffered from blackouts. Consumers endured chronic power shortages. The problems only worsened until the late 1980s, when new methods of finance, loans to be repaid by tolls for roads and bridges, and rapid construction gradually began to ease the situation.

Counties, at the apex of rural organization, theoretically had the power of coordination even before the late 1970s, but in reality they were under such constraints that there was little room for initiative. The new loosening of guidelines, the availability of loans, and the fixing of multiyear lump-sum total revenues to be passed to higher levels gave the counties room to maneuver, and the counties in turn set lump-sum revenue quotas for townships under them. In addition, as its nonagricultural work force grew, a county could petition to become a city and thereby receive an urban organization, with more economic and industrial cadres and fewer agricultural cadres. Zhongshan County became a city in 1984 and Dongguan in 1987, and in 1988 they were detached from their metropolitan regions to become independent cities.

To help increase revenues in poor prefectures, any Inner Delta county that was physically adjacent to a poorer prefecture was assigned to it in the early 1980s. Rich Dongguan remained part of the poorer Huiyang Prefecture, and Panyu and Zengcheng remained part of Guangzhou Metropolitan Region to balance the poorer counties in the north. Although Foshan Metropolitan Region included the rich adjacent counties of Zhongshan, Shunde, and Nanhai, it also included Sanshui, then a poorer county outside the Inner Delta, and Gaoming which, though in the Inner Delta, was much poorer. Jiangmen Metropolitan Region not only included the old Si Yi—Taishan, Kaiping, Xinhui, Enping, and Heshan (formerly part of Enping)—but also two poorer counties, Yangjiang and Yangchun.

Economic growth in the Inner Delta was disorderly and went in many directions. It is possible nevertheless to identify several patterns that help clarify the dynamics and structure of the process. One area of growth, in markets for agricultural products, did not require a great deal of planning. Other areas of growth, centering on industrial development—township and village enterprises, export processing, comprehensive metropolitan modernization, and large modern factories—required more capital and planning.

## Markets in Agricultural Products

Once the household responsibility system was introduced and the farmers of the Inner Delta were confident they could produce and market without criticism, they quickly took the initiative in responding to the demand for agricultural products in Hong Kong, Macau, Shenzhen, Zhuhai, and Guangzhou. These markets experienced explosive growth after 1982. Given the limits of transport and refrigeration at the time, Inner Delta farmers had practically a captive market in all these cities except Hong Kong, which also imported a substantial amount of food from overseas.

The demand for food supplies increased rapidly in the 1980s as the population grew, the Chinese standard of living rose, and Inner Delta farmers increased their share in the Hong Kong market. By the end of the decade Guangzhou had about 3 million urban inhabitants, Hong Kong and Macau 6 million, and Shenzhen and Zhuhai together had another million. The Inner Delta's 7.3 million farmers were thus supplying not only the food required for themselves and the 2.2

million town and city dwellers of the Inner Delta but most of the food for the 10 million urban residents nearby. Roughly, in this area of 20 million people, the rural population, less than 40 percent of the total, was supplying almost all the food needed for themselves and for the 60 percent of the population that was urban. Throughout China as a whole, in the late 1980s, about 75 percent of the population was rural and supplied food for themselves and the 25 percent that was urban. Productivity per farm worker in the Inner Delta, still low by Western standards, thus represented a considerable advance over the rest of China.

The demand for higher-quality food was perhaps even more signif-icant than the overall increase in demand. The Cantonese are known for their love of food, and by the end of the Cultural Revolution there was a tremendous pent-up desire for meat, fish, and better and more varied vegetables. As produce became available in Guangzhou and Delta towns in the early 1980s people rushed to buy it, even if they had to wait in line and pay higher prices. Banquet entertaining and marriage feasts, long subdued, blossomed as a wider selection of food became available and urban incomes rose. The rapid rise in Hong Kong's standard of living led to a demand for even fancier produce than in Guangdong. After the reforms, with better channels for getting to the Hong Kong market, farmers could respond more quickly to its demands. The same was true on a lesser scale in Macau and in the special economic zones.

While responding to new market opportunities, farm families could not entirely neglect the rice crop, even if they could earn more else-where, because they still had quotas to meet. The amount of acreage in rice dropped about 10 percent within a decade, but total output remained fairly stable, peaking in 1984 and 1987. During his 1984 visit to the Delta, Zhao Ziyang encouraged farmers to concentrate on cash crops in order to expand their income. Some local areas experi-mented with allowing farmers to make cash payments in lieu of rice quotas, and Guangdong did import some rice from Hunan and Guangxi as it had before it became self-sufficient in the 1970s. There was never enough surplus available from elsewhere to lower the area's quotas significantly, however, and local officials still generally required each farm household to meet a minimum rice quota in order to keep the land assigned to it under the household responsibility system.

Most families found ways to meet their grain quotas and still pro-duce other goods for the free market. When the price of fish in the

Guangdong market went up in 1981, for example, the area devoted to fish ponds expanded rapidly. As the government raised the procurement price for sugar cane over several years, farmers increased their acreage, although the impact was delayed because of its eighteen-month growing season. Fruit trees took several years to mature and therefore involved more risk, but by the late 1970s the planting of fruit trees had also greatly expanded. Overall farmers became more deft at discovering which markets paid which prices at which time, and they began to calculate annual profits a field could generate if planted in a particular crop. They responded quickly to changing demand, which maximized individual income and reduced price differentials in different localities.

In the early 1980s, because of the absence of refrigeration, consumers in Guangdong wanted live fish and fowl in order to be assured of their freshness, and vegetables were delivered daily from the fields to retail markets. The three major Delta urban centers (Guangzhou, Zhuhai–Macau, and Hong Kong–Shenzhen) were located almost at the points of the Delta triangle, and therefore farmers in most parts of the Inner Delta could get fresh vegetables, fowl, and fish to at least one of the centers daily and sometimes even more than once a day.

Other products began to be transported over longer distances. By 1984 Inner Delta farmers had realized, for example, that they could not make as much profit on pigs as on other crops, and they reduced their involvement in that market. Using the better transport system that had begun to develop, farmers in Hunan and Guangxi sent in pigs to the Delta to satisfy demand. Varieties of fruit that could not be grown in the South came in from the North, and southern fruit was shipped in the other direction. By the late 1980s the Shantou area sent vegetables overnight for the Delta markets. The geographical area covered by food markets was thus expanding, but Inner Delta farmers still dominated Delta markets in fish, fowl, and vegetables.

The move to cash crops enabled the value of agricultural production in the Inner Delta to rise much more rapidly than elsewhere; it doubled from 2.85 billion yuan in 1978 to 5.63 billion in 1984.[5] By 1984, though it had only 10 percent of Guangdong's arable land, the Inner Delta grew 27 percent of the value of the province's agricultural produce.[6]

By the mid-1980s the bustling economy of the region gave some farm dwellers opportunities to earn even more income outside agriculture. Some families were willing to give up rights to their farmland, but the vast majority wanted to keep the fields because of the security they offered. In some localities, farmers took higher-paying jobs off the farm and hired people from poorer localities to do their agricultural work. A more common solution was for some family members, often the elderly and the housewives, to do the farming, which released other members to get more lucrative jobs elsewhere. In the prereform production teams, in a family with three adult workers, for example, all three had worked for the team; they had had no other option. Under the household responsibility system, two people could easily handle all the farm work on the fields the family was allotted. The third person was freed to work elsewhere.

New specialists emerged to take advantage of the new opportunities. Farmers could market their own product in nearby towns and cities, but many of them found it was more efficient either to take the goods to market and sell them all at once to a middleman who would then resell them at retail prices or, better still, to let someone with a vehicle transport their goods to market on their behalf. Some individuals bought a tractor and wagon from a production team that was selling off its goods and specialized in transporting goods to and from markets or construction sites.

With more money in the countryside, demand for rural housing, considered by many the most secure long-term investment a family could make, exploded. Much of the Inner Delta had large amounts of red-clay soil, suitable for brick making. Farmers could dig up the soil, bake the bricks in a simple, locally built kiln, and build their own homes, usually in collaboration with neighbors. This created a new demand for workers to transport the bricks and other supplies. Specialists were needed to give technical advice on home building, to perform the most complex construction tasks, and to supply fixtures and furniture. Newly built small brick homes, though rustic and modest by Western standards, began to dot the countryside of the Inner Delta. Rural housing, as a result, became far more satisfactory than urban.

With rural income increasing, savings shot up. At the end of 1978 the bank assets of those who lived in large villages, towns, and cities in the Inner Delta were 0.48 billion yuan. At the end of 1984 the figure was 4.17 billion yuan, almost nine times as much, far surpassing the provincial average.[7] Most of the savings were deposited in the Agricultural Bank of China or the Rural Credit Cooperative, and the money there could be recycled for investment, particularly for township and administrative village industries. But the individual accounts also reflected the increase in family income and the ability to purchase more bicycles, televisions, electric fans, refrigerators, and washing machines, thus fueling the growth of new stores and a burgeoning consumer industry.

The new household responsibility system was not without its problems. The role of the rural collective in providing care for the sick and the aged was not fully replaced after households became the key economic unit for agriculture. The increase in rural wealth and market opportunities led many rural communities to use farmland for the construction of new buildings, both for residences and for commercial or industrial purposes, without adequate controls to preserve the maximum amount of arable land for farming. Market controls were not always adequate to prevent sellers from deceiving their customers.

Yet the benefits of the new reforms were enormous and widely dispersed. By the early 1980s both farmers and city dwellers had no difficulty deciding whether the reforms were a good thing or not, and their convictions grew stronger as progress continued. One can understand how in 1958 cadres and peasants, never having experienced communes, did not resist when they were told that communes were good. After rural cadres and peasants had experienced twenty years of collectivization and then ten years of reforms, it was impossible to believe, even with worries about inflation, criticisms of individual policies, and cynicism about corruption, that they would ever passively accept any basic reversal in reform policy. Even cadres nostalgic for the purer days of the past could not imagine turning back from this "second liberation."

Perhaps most important, the increased market for consumer goods supported the introduction of modern production machinery. It was the breakthrough from handicrafts to industry that was to create the real leap in Delta living standards and to bring a fertile agricultural area into the modern world. Aside from the basic reform policies, little government coordination had been required to expand cash crops and agricultural markets. Although the government did help to ensure that the markets had adequate physical space, vendors were properly registered, the market was clean and orderly, and prices and sales were fair, the changes were largely from the response of individual farm families and marketers to new opportunities. Industrial growth, however, required far more coordination and planning.

## Township and Village Industry

Once most communes had been transformed into townships *(zhen)* and brigades into admininstrative villages *(xiang)* and even before a March 1, 1984, national directive on the subject, cadres focused on how to expand rural community industries.[8] On the average, a township in the Inner Delta had about sixty thousand to seventy thousand people, and the administrative village from four thousand to five thousand. Typically, the township had a town headquarters, with a nonagricultural work force of several thousand, and the administrative village a much smaller nonagricultural settlement.

Township and village enterprises changed their orientation from aiding agriculture to responding to market demand. It was true that as farm households received land-use rights, some wanted more agricultural equipment, machinery, and other producers' supplies to raise their output or efficiency, and this maintained and even increased demand for these goods. But the explosive growth in industrial demand came from the growing desire for consumer products. State factories were encouraged to help meet this new demand, but the township and village enterprises, despite having less technical talent and capital, responded with greater speed and agility. Some township and village enterprises made parts to be assembled in state factories; in the Inner Delta, however, many of the townships were large and prosperous enough to make their own products, though with modest levels of investment and low levels of technology initially. By the early 1980s these rural enterprises had the full support of higher levels of government, including favorable tax treatment, even more than that received by urban, collectively owned enterprises, which in turn received more favorable treatment than did state enterprises.

Township and village enterprises were officially classified as operating under "collective ownership," as opposed to state ownership, but in fact they were run and financed by the township and village governments. They grew out of the old commune and brigade enterprises, and there was considerable continuity in personnel. The Party organization was basically unchanged. As a World Bank study of these enterprises shows, township and village budgets depended heavily on these enterprises, and this fact gave local officials strong incentives to ensure their success.[9]

Like counties, township and villages had great flexibility in managing their enterprises and were initially very free of bureaucratic constraints. As the Inner Delta township industries grew, however, the skills required to run them exceeded those available locally. Unable to get talented urban cadres to move to small towns, townships in part bridged the gap by turning to county, prefectural, and provincial government specialists in various departments for advice on accounting and taxes, measuring demand, training management, and acquiring appropriate technology. Unlike earlier periods, when higher-level officials passed out orders, the initiative came largely from local communities, anxious to increase their revenues. Those at the province level unofficially served not only as consultants but as a clearinghouse for knowledge of developments in other townships.

Before 1979, the government had made it very difficult for rural dwellers to migrate to towns and cities. With the reforms, however, towns in the Inner Delta needed more workers. Although officially household registration remained tight, in practice restraints were relaxed on new migrants. Rural reforms allowed households to release excess laborers, who flowed to jobs in the Inner Delta towns and cities. In this the Inner Delta area was quite different from other areas, such as Jiangsu, which had successful township enterprises but whose county cadres, wanting to keep wages higher than in surrounding areas, chose not to welcome outside laborers.[10]

The Agricultural Bank of China held the bulk of Guangdong's household savings deposits, and with reform it began to invest more in rural community industry than in agriculture. Because the Agricultural Bank had branches in every county, its officials quickly became familiar with local community enterprises. Concerned with repayment, they were able to be firmer in rejecting poor credit risks than local governments, with their "soft budget constraints," could be. The bank's total lending was linked to deposits, but it could move funds around from one county to another to make promising loans. In making its decisions, the bank commonly consulted with appropriate higher-level officials both about the quality of the local enterprise's leadership and the market potential for its products.

Although the Agricultural Bank was the key source of initial investments in rural enterprises, once an enterprise was successful, it could generate its own funds for expansion. The local community could also draw on the profits from one enterprise to invest in other local enterprises. Market forces thus quickly replaced government priorities in rural community investment decisions.

Shunde County, known within Guangdong for having successful township enterprises, can illustrate their development. All fourteen of Shunde's townships in the mid-1980s were relatively prosperous, but Beijiao's enterprises were particularly successful. Beijiao Township in 1987 had a population of 75,000, 58,000 of whom lived in the countryside. It had 15,000 industrial workers, of whom roughly 11,000 worked in the town and 4,000 in some of the nineteen villages *(xiang)* within the township. Roughly 2,400 workers were employed in construction, 500 in transport, 400 in commerce, 250 in education, and 360 as town cadres. In addition there were a small number of teachers and school administrators and about sixty cadres in the town who were on the state budget rather than on the local community budget. Basic statistics for Beijiao Township were as follows:

|  | 1979 | 1986 |
| --- | --- | --- |
| Production (million yuan) | | |
| Industrial | 14 | 305 |
| Agricultural | 30 | 55 |
| Acreage (mou) | | |
| Rice | 37,000 | 36,000 |
| Fish pond | 16,000 | 21,000 |
| Sugar | 21,000 | 18,000 |

The former Beijiao Commune had an Industry and Transport Office that changed its name to the Agriculture, Industry, and Commerce Federation when the commune became a township, and in 1986 it became a controlling company *(nonggongshang lianhe gongsi)*. It then had twenty-eight cadres, including a general manager and four deputy general managers, and it charged management fees to the companies under it. There was a separate labor service company, a monopoly that grew out of the former labor office of the commune and became similarly self-supporting by charging fees for assistance in labor placement. Although theoretically independent companies, these new firms still had a quasi-governmental function in supervising the township enterprises.

The best-known factory in Shunde was the Yuhua Electric Fan Factory (Yuhua Dianfengshanchang), which in 1987 employed 1,200 people, producing 1.2 million fans a year (about 4 percent of all the electric fans produced in China), valued at approximately 100 million yuan. The factory manager, Ou Jianchang, was honored in 1987 in

Beijing as one of the ten great national entrepreneurs from a peasant background. The factory had originally been a commune factory that made soy sauce and plastic tops for thermos bottles. Ou attended technical high school *(zhongzhuan)* in 1957–1959 and went to work in this factory upon graduation. He held a position as an accountant there until he became head in 1967.

Yuhua had begun to make a variety of plastic goods while still a commune factory, but in the 1970s it lacked sales outlets for these products. Toward the end of that decade, Ou decided to move into plastic electric fans, and by 1982 Yuhua was producing seventy thousand a year. They originally learned the basic technology from a state factory in Guangzhou but later gained new technology from Hong Kong. Ou himself went to Hong Kong frequently to get advice about technology and markets from people he had met through personal channels. In the early 1980s three thousand firms in China produced electric fans, but by 1987, as some expanded and competition grew keener, the number had fallen to five hundred. Some of Yuhua's fans were sold to a foreign trade corporation for export to Southeast Asia. Although the factory itself did not receive foreign currency directly, it was allowed in 1984 to use some of the foreign exchange it had earned to purchase foreign-made machinery. With this new equipment it was able to produce 1.2 million fans in 1985, an annual level it then maintained.

Having achieved success in electric fans, Ou moved ahead to produce air conditioners and microwave ovens. He was convinced that microwaves, because they use less electricity than conventional ovens, had a great future in China, and he therefore planned to use some of his company's earnings along with some borrowed funds to expand into microwave production. Banks, knowing his reputation as a successful entrepreneur, were prepared to offer loans, though not as large as he would have liked.

In addition to the Yuhua factory, Beijiao was the site of the Meide Electric Fan Factory, with seven hundred workers, and the Nanfang Electronics Factory, with eight hundred workers. There was also the Pige Furniture Company, linking five factories, which together employed some two thousand people. The furniture factory grew out of an old commune cement boat factory, which turned to furniture when the market for cement boats dried up. The company worked through the state Arts and Crafts Corporation to produce tubular furniture, partly for export. It was allowed to use some of the foreign currency it earned to import materials that its workers then finished and prepared for sale as exports.

Beijiao Township was one of the few townships with a considerable amount of imported manufacturing equipment. By the late 1980s, however, all townships in the Inner Delta had industrial enterprises that played a similar role in providing employment to local workers freed from agriculture, in earning local township income, and in helping meet the demand for consumer products. The better factories, like those in Beijiao, rapidly upgraded their technology and expanded their scale of production. By Western and even by Hong Kong's standards, most of these township and village enterprises were in 1988 not yet well run or very efficient, but the rate of growth and change in one short decade was high, even by the standards of the fastest-growing newly industrializing economies. Such progress could be attributed to local entrepreneurs, to the accessibility of Hong Kong technology and information, and to the judgment of higher officials about which town enterprises could make good use of foreign currency to purchase appropriate technology.

## Export Processing

Many of the Inner Delta's township and village enterprises, like those in Beijiao, developed from local initiatives. But many other township and village workshops there represented a confluence of local and Hong Kong initiatives. The classic case is Dongguan County, which in 1985, because of the success of its workshops, became Dongguan City.

By the late 1980s all the counties in the Inner Delta had export-processing factories that made goods using materials received from Hong Kong and shipped the finished products back to Hong Kong to be sold on the world market. Dongguan City had so many such factories that it became a national symbol for export processing. In 1987 the city, whose population of 1.2 million was distributed in thirty-two townships, received approximately 2.4 billion yuan in processing fees. Industrial production in Dongguan, during the reform decade that began in 1978, grew at over 40 percent per year.[11]

With planning, designing, marketing, and sales handled in Hong Kong and labor-intensive work done cheaply in China, small and middle-sized Hong Kong companies were able to continue faring well in international competition. In the late 1970s, once Chinese townships saw that such arrangements provided good jobs for their cadres and the general population, good income for their township governments, and rapid progress in enriching their communities, they sought out Hong Kong partners.

Dongguan had several advantages. Only Baoan County was closer to Hong Kong, and by the early 1980s transportation from Dongguan to Hong Kong was readily available, by ship and especially by truck. The roughly six hundred thousand people in Hong Kong who had come from or who had descended from those from Dongguan County provided easy and reliable links between Hong Kong and their native county. Dongguan officials estimated that 20 percent of their young people had escaped to Hong Kong in the decades before reforms began, primarily because there were so few local opportunities. "We have changed our view of these youth," said a former commune Party secretary, who scarcely more than a decade earlier had been responsible for preventing escapes and apprehending those who tried. "We saw them as bad but now see them as adventuresome and capable, unlike the more restrained obedient ones who stayed behind." Ten years later he was a county official, with the job of contacting former escapees in Hong Kong to encourage them to invest in Dongguan.

Dongguan officials estimated that about half their contracts on the Hong Kong side were with former Dongguan residents. Even Hong Kong businesspeople who were not from Dongguan sometimes looked for a worker from Dongguan in their company and asked him to help smooth relations with local Chinese officials. Although ordinary Dongguan residents until 1987 had difficulty obtaining visas to go to Hong Kong, officials from towns negotiating contracts had no such difficulty and often worked through Dongguan friends in Hong Kong to find export-processing contacts.

The contracts themselves were relatively simple in the late 1980s. The Hong Kong side supplied the *lai liao* or *san lai*—the materials, the model of what was to be done, and the equipment that must be imported into China. Hong Kong managers remained on site or commuted daily or weekly to train the workers and ensure close attention to management. When necessary, personnel were sent from Hong Kong to repair the machinery or redesign the product to fit changing market conditions. The Chinese side supplied the building, electricity, and other local utilities, and the labor, which it hired. Hong Kong did not pay the workers directly; lump sums were paid for a certain quantity of goods contracted, with final payment when the products were completed. Contracts covered the production of a spec-ified item for a set term, commonly one year. They were commonly renewed and separate contracts added for additional items, often be-tween the same Hong Kong company and Dongguan factory. In some contracts the machinery brought in from Hong Kong reverted to Chinese ownership after a specified period, typically about ten years.

In 1987–88, the factories were generally simple brick structures, several stories high, which appeared from the outside much like apart-ment buildings. Most factories did not require heavy machinery, but if it was needed it was located on the ground floor. Inside, the building was usually divided into large rooms, typically holding fifty to a hundred desks. Some work, such as the making of plastic bags or the assembling of simple radios, required assembly-line work, but more commonly each person working at a desk turned out single pieces and was paid on a piece-work basis. In each room all were usually engaged in the same work. For example, young women might take a specially shaped sponge and sew onto it a small piece of material already cut, making a furry toy animal. In another workshop workers might sew shirts or blouses, and in others comb hair for wigs or artificial hair for dolls. Other factories made incense, firecrackers, candles, and candy and other food products.

The workers in a given workshop were usually all the same sex, although a single factory often had several workshops in which young men and women were separately engaged in similar work. Women were considered nimbler in producing toys, apparel, and electronic products, and slightly more than half the workers in Dongguan work-shops were women. Workers had to be at least sixteen years of age. A high proportion were junior high school graduates who had had to wait a year or longer after leaving school before becoming old enough to work. The workers were almost all young, the average age in most workshops being under twenty-five. Many of the rooms had the flavor of a senior high school class, with a workshop manager instead of a teacher. The rooms were generally bright and airy, and although air conditioning, as in homes, was still rare, they had large electric fans.

Because workers were paid by the piece, income varied considerably. In some factories, when rushing to meet big orders, workers could be asked to work twelve-hour instead of eight-hour shifts. Average in-come in 1987 was around 200 yuan per month. For farm families, whose annual income per worker a decade earlier had been scarcely that much, this was initially seen as a very attractive salary.

Dongguan managers earned much more than workers, commonly

350 to 400 yuan a month. Factories were generally located in the vicinity of former commune and brigade headquarters. In poor mountain counties with very little economic activity, some former brigade, commune, and team cadres, declared redundant as reforms thinned bureaucratic ranks, had little choice but to go back to full-time farming, a move most found unattractive. In Dongguan, however, cadres had the option of becoming managers in export-processing factories. There, some controlled factory personnel decisions, just as they had in communes or brigades. As brigade or commune cadres they had typically made about 100 yuan a month, about one-quarter of what they came to make as factory or workshop managers. Dongguan factory managers were, not surprisingly, enthusiastic supporters of reform.

Most local cadre managers had supervised people, but few had experience in business. In the initial formation of a factory, they played a very important role. With their local contacts, they knew how to locate appropriate factory sites and how to arrange for electricity, water, and other equipment. A loan from a local bank was generally required to finance the building and the equipment furnished by the Chinese, and cadres knew how to arrange for these. They knew whom to contact to obtain the most reliable labor force possible and how to select workers and lower-level managers. But once these essential formative steps were taken, the local Dongguan managers had little day-to-day responsibility compared to the job of the experienced business managers sent in from Hong Kong. In a sense, they continued to receive attractive salaries as troubleshooters, well connected with local community leadership.

As pleased as the workers were to find jobs with good wages, many found it difficult to adjust to the pressure. Many young workers, especially those who came from small communities, were not used to working with strangers and felt lonely. Many found it constraining to be at a desk for so many hours with such rigid time requirements, and most found it hard to handle the pressure of keeping up when paid by the piece. In the mid-1980s as people learned more about Hong Kong, many came to believe that its citizens had to work too hard. Some young people in Dongguan were not even sure the money was worth it.

The work in these factories demanded little skill, and training was at best brief. The workers did not acquire specialized skills, but they learned how to work in a large organization and developed a sense of efficiency, something they and their elders had not previously had.

They gained a sense of how a company operates, how to organize work, how markets change, and what efficient management is like. Some workers were innovative in thinking of better ways to organize their work, but many tasks were repetitive and some began to find them boring.

One advantage of the processing industry was that it spread wealth. By 1987 every township in Dongguan was thriving. Virtually every young person in Dongguan looking for work had an opportunity to find employment. In fact, Dongguan's labor supply was exhausted in the early 1980s, and labor began flowing in from elsewhere. Dongguan towns decided that they would derive economic benefit from factory expansion even if it required outside workers. Migrants working in factories on the outskirts of the county capital of 120,000 people generally found housing in the city, but many small towns built dormitory facilities for their workers.

In mid-1987 county officials acknowledged that they were not able to keep an accurate count of the new migrants. They estimated that about 250,000 young workers from other counties were then working in Dongguan, the vast majority of whom had migrated since the early 1980s. Some young male migrants to Dongguan were employed in construction work, and a few worked in agriculture, but the vast majority were in processing plants. In 1987, in a county of 1.2 million including the outsiders, an estimated half million people were employed in these processing factories, which had been of minor importance a decade before. The best jobs went first to locals, and the least desirable jobs, particularly in construction, went overwhelmingly to outsiders. "A few years ago," observed one county official, "our youth went to Hong Kong and sent back money to their poor relatives in Dongguan." "Now," he added, "poor mountainous areas send their youth to Dongguan and these youth send back money to their poor relatives."

Since most of the profits from the export-processing fees went to the townships, villages, and Dongguan City, these entities became far richer than those in neighboring counties that had less export processing. Dongguan paved its roads, mostly with cement, so quickly that in the late 1980s it had more miles of paved roads than any other county in Guangdong. From a county considered poor a decade before, it had become one of the richest in the province.

The amount of new housing construction going on in Dongguan's 530 villages in this period was staggering. In many villages, by the end of the decade, all of the hundreds of houses were at most several years old. Thousands of the new homes were three-story family dwellings; and many who had originally built two stories had later added a third. It was not uncommon for towns to set up their own lot plan, to work out with each family how much space it would be assigned, and to determine where each home would be located. Construction was simple enough that families and their friends put up their own homes, as described above. Construction workers who came from the outside worked not on private homes but on roads or on public buildings, which were also going up at a prodigious rate.

Although factory wages initially seemed high, new opportunities developed so quickly that some of the most ambitious factory workers left for new work in private enterprises. It was difficult for youth from other counties to develop the contacts and obtain the permits required to open private businesses, so those taking advantage of these more attractive opportunities were almost always locals. Some originally left the farms to work in factories, but as the price of fruit rose and their family converted its land allotment to banana and orange trees, they sometimes left the factories for the fruit groves, where they could earn as much in less demanding work.

Social changes followed. Young people, proud of earning their own incomes, acquired more independence and became more conscious of changes in fashion. New styles in clothing and new electronic products from Hong Kong reached Dongguan far more quickly than in nearby Huiyang counties. Because female workers were in as much demand as males were and could often earn as much, the status of women improved. Formerly it had been expected that when a couple married the groom's family would contribute more to set up the household. By the late 1980s the young woman was expected to bring one or two pieces of furniture or a major appliance, such as a refrigerator or a washing machine. In return, if her family's contribution had been closer to that of the man's, she expected to be treated more equitably by her husband's family.

The wealth also enabled Dongguan's towns to build new hotels and restaurants in addition to roads. The county had no trouble financing a 36,000-kilowatt power station and contracting with the provincial electricity grid for 50,000 kilowatts of power in the early stages of financing the large Shajiao Electric Power Station. As a result, they experienced fewer power shortages than poorer counties did.

The town of Humen, where opium was first burned on the eve of the Opium War, has a wonderful natural harbor; in 1987 it began to be developed into a large commercial port. It had such excellent natural conditions that it hoped to become a major port in the area. If it could dock large ships that would then go directly abroad, the cost of reprocessing through Hong Kong could be avoided. New factories were also built in order to take advantage of the new harbor. Such developments began to transform this formerly rustic area.

Not all Chinese economic planners were enthusiastic about export processing. Some criticized it as a system in which foreign capitalists reaped the benefits of low-priced Chinese labor. They sometimes used the term "exploit," a word that to Chinese cadres had very strong connotations. Cadres in Dongguan learned to live with such criticism. "We welcome such exploitation," said one high official without any hesitation, "for we benefit from it."

Nevertheless, many questioned the future of export processing. What would happen to a community that had tailored a large factory site to a Hong Kong manufacturer if the manufacturer did not renew his contract after a year? In the late 1990s, when the workers would be in their thirties and even older, would they still be welcome in these factories or would they be replaced by younger workers? As Dongguan wages rose and as transportation continued to improve within Guangdong, would they be replaced by cheaper inland workers and, if that occurred, could cast-out workers find a new niche? Would world markets continue to welcome their products?

Planners in Guangdong or Beijing therefore did not find Dongguan processing nearly as attractive as the more modern factories being put up elsewhere. But as much as Guangdong wanted to acquire modern technology, the brutal fact was that its most promising niche in the world economy in the late 1980s was in labor-intensive industry. By 1988 top leaders in Beijing like Zhao Ziyang acknowledged the value of export processing as a way of enriching people and teaching them good work habits. Most poorer counties in Guangdong did not expect to acquire large modern factories quickly. For them the Dongguan model seemed the best to which they could reasonably aspire, and they worked hard to prepare their transport and electric power infrastructure in order to attract Hong Kong companies to process exports in their county.

## Comprehensive Metropolitan Modernization

Unlike Dongguan, Foshan had long been a leading center of both light industry and government administration. Located twenty-five kilometers southwest of Guangzhou on the Fen River, Foshan (Buddha Mountain) was a temple town from at least the time of the Tang Dynasty (628–960), and the Foshan Ancestral Temple *(zumiao)* remained a major tourist site. By early in the Ming Dynasty (1368–1644) Foshan was known as one of the four great Chinese market towns, famous for ceramics and secondarily for metalwork. In modern times the harbor on the Fen River could dock ships of a thousand tons and was linked with other ports in the Delta area. At the beginning of the twentieth century, Foshan became the midpoint in the short railway linking Guangzhou and Sanshui. It remained a major market town with a sizable ceramics industry into the 1950s, and then continued to grow as a major political center.[12]

In 1954 Foshan City became the capital of Foshan Prefecture, which then oversaw most of the Inner Delta counties. By the late 1970s the city population approached three hundred thousand, second only to Guangzhou in the Inner Delta. Though its markets lost vitality during the Cultural Revolution, the Foshan area remained more prosperous than most areas of Guangdong. During the turbulent decade, though traditional ceramic handicraft designs were forbidden, production centered instead on inexpensive souvenirs celebrating Mao and other revolutionary heroes. Its factories and workshops aiding agriculture were among the best in the province, and its consumer industries made a good start in the latter part of the Cultural Revolution. It had begun to benefit from China's opening as early as 1973 when it became an export production base, described in Chapter 11. Soon afterward a new highway was begun linking it to Guangzhou. Although its housing was as run down as that of other communities, Foshan already had a base for industry and foreign trade when reforms began.

With support from the province and from Beijing, Foshan was the first large community in Guangdong to take off after 1978. It was run by a collective leadership, as was typical, headed by First Party Secretary Tong Mengqing, who strongly supported reforms, and it had an entrepreneurial mayor who became a catalyst and symbol for development.

Bold and controversial, Mayor Yu Fei was a creative problem solver who was not afraid to push projects even when not everyone favored them. Originally from Jiangsu, he had been assigned to Guangdong in 1946 by the Fourth Division to work with the East River Guerrillas. After demobilization he served in Nanhai County, which surrounds Foshan and had its offices inside Foshan. He married a local Cantonese woman, raised his family in Foshan, and remained there. After holding a variety of economic posts in Nanhai County, he became its deputy head and then was transferred up to Foshan City. Beginning in 1973 he served as head of the Commerce Bureau, from 1977 as head of the Finance Office, and after 1979 as mayor of Foshan City. In 1983, when Foshan City was amalgamated with half of the original prefecture (the other half going to Jiangmen) to become Foshan Metropolitan Region, containing 3.5 million people, Yu Fei remained as mayor of the region. He served there until November 1985, when he was promoted to become Guangdong's executive vice-governor. Before becoming mayor, he had long been thinking about how to develop Foshan. Assuming power just as reforms began, he and his associates had an opportunity to carry out their visions, first in Foshan City and then in the metropolitan region.

His predecessor as mayor, Yang Deyuan, had been an able leader who had helped lay the groundwork for modernization before moving on to become a vice-governor. Yang Deyuan had the reputation of keeping tight control over finances to ensure they were used wisely. If any unit in the city was prosperous, it was said, somehow 80 percent of its funds would flow into the city treasury and it would still have to apply to Yang Deyuan for approval of major expenditures. In this new era, when provincial superiors showed greater tolerance for variations and decentralized power, Yu Fei delegated authority and encouraged his trusted subordinates to take the initiative. He was known as one who did not blame others, even during the Cultural Revolution; when difficulties arose he took responsibility and protected those below him. With his support, therefore, they were prepared to act boldly.

During the campaign against bribery and smuggling in 1982, many Beijing officials came to investigate Yu Fei, known as a deal maker who did what was necessary to get something done. He was open in explaining what he had done, however, and he was never publicly criticized or accused of wrongdoing. He had gone out of his way to encourage Gu Mu and other high-level leaders to visit Foshan and to keep them informed of Foshan's development; it was understood that he enjoyed their support. His rank had been too low for Premier Zhao Ziyang to know him well when Zhao was provincial Party secretary, but Zhao was well informed about Foshan, visited there on trips to Guangdong, and approved of Foshan's main lines of progress.

Yu Fei had no formal training in finance, but he learned on the job and saw finance as the critical lever for realizing his plans for Foshan development. "When he sat in meetings discussing urban construction," recalled a former subordinate, "he had a pad, calculating what each item would cost." Many leaders were cautious about using personal connections, for fear of criticism, but Yu Fei believed in using them openly for public goals. His wife was head of the Foshan branch of the Bank of China, and several members of her immediate family were leaders of the Hong Kong financial community who helped educate Yu at a time when almost no officials were adequately trained.

Foshan was not the only Delta community to go to Hong Kong for financing. But Yu Fei went with a keener understanding of the Hong Kong business mentality, better-prepared public relations, a carefully tailored tax and incentive program, and more ambitious requests. In one large meeting in Foshan alone, some one hundred Hong Kong businessmen were shown investment opportunities. It was estimated that while he was mayor, Foshan received commitments in foreign currency of $710 million, of which $512 million was actually used during his tenure. These were not enormous amounts by American or Japanese standards, but they were huge by Chinese standards, especially for a small city. With Yu's prompting, Foshan attracted and was willing to use more capital investment than Guangzhou, which had ten times Foshan's population. By the late 1980s, however, while Guangzhou was beginning to prosper, Foshan was straining to service its debts.

When Chinese banks began lending money early in the reform period, many officials, schooled to think of debts as dangerous risks, were reluctant to take them on. Yu Fei, more confident because of his financial background, borrowed before others thought it safe. Called by newspapers "the mayor with the burdens of debt," Yu Fei not only borrowed but worked out new arrangements pairing the Agricultural Bank, which had large deposits, with the Industrial-Commercial Bank in the joint management of funds in order to make available new monies from the countryside to help industry.

Yu typically moved ahead in new situations before it was made clear what was and was not acceptable. He allowed individuals to buy shares (*gufen*) in companies. Foshan was the first to borrow funds to build a major bridge and then to charge tolls in order to use that income to repay loans and finance further construction projects.

Sensing the need for marketing as they moved from plan to market, Yu Fei, in a political climate accustomed to naming model farmers and model workers, was the first leader bold enough to add model salesmen *(tuixiaoyuan)*. It was known that some products Foshan imported from abroad were resold at higher prices, with profits going for investment. In Yu Fei's view, the profits had gone for a good cause, the financing of industry. As higher officials began to take a dim view of this and the gray area became black, Foshan quickly ended the practice and escaped criticism.

Yu Fei first used funds to finance the modernization of industrial plants. Foshan worked closely with foreign advisors in Hong Kong, and foreign entrepreneurs considered him to be someone with whom they could do business. Foshan also worked closely with the Provincial Economic Commission, which kept well informed about developments in production technology and presided over a modest budget to help finance plant modernization.

The essence of Yu's industrial investment strategy was to import the critical minimum of production equipment needed to make modern products. Foshan built factory facilities using whatever local machinery it could and then imported the remaining equipment required to create a full production line. Rather than use a single foreign company to supply all needed foreign equipment, Foshan hoped to save money by negotiating the best buy for each machine. Since Foshan lacked technical personnel, it contracted with foreigners to train local people to operate all new equipment purchased abroad, and it insisted on clauses requiring that machinery be installed and operate successfully for some months. This strategy was not unknown in other counties, but Yu Fei pursued it systematically and on a bigger scale. He also insisted that some products be used as compensation trade, sold abroad, not only to help repay foreign investment but to be sure that products met international standards. Despite these efforts, however, some problems remained. In particular, local technicians, even several years later, still did not have the breadth of training and experience needed to continue to improve and adapt the machinery purchased from abroad.

Under the new national guidelines of the early 1980s, local communities were allowed to make decisions locally on plots up to 10.0 mou in size. Foshan placed a workshop on 9.9 mou of land, and before long other workshops related to the first workshop were also built on plots of 9.9 mou. In this way a large factory was put together with local initiative and no red tape. Foshan was allowed to make investments up to $5 million, and at one point Yu Fei underwent some mild public criticism for building a number of plants near each other, each worth under $5 million, but totalling far more. "You said we could not make an investment of more than $5 million," he reportedly told Gu Mu, "but you did not say how many times we could make such investments."

Yu Fei was aware that any enterprise classified as a "state enterprise" had access to state support, supplies on state plans, talented workers, and a worker welfare net. But he felt that state enterprises were embedded in red tape that made a timely response to the market impossible. Until 1979, modern plants of any size had been state enterprises assigned to some government unit, while "collectives" operated in the less modern sector with lower wages and security. Foshan, under Yu Fei's guidance, pioneered a new approach in which the category of "collective" was stretched to include enterprises that had thousands of employees and that were often more modern and larger than many state enterprises. In his view it was then the only way to gain the flexibility needed for enterprises to adapt to market forces. To be sure, his plants received loans from government banks, were led by Party officials, were tied to the municipal government, and had frequent contact with higher officials. But the "collective" category still insulated local plants from regulations and higher-level administrative procedures. In 1986, within Guangdong, 60 percent of the value of industrial production was from state enterprises. In Foshan Metropolitan Region it was 29 percent, with 66 percent produced by collective enterprises and the rest by small private enterprises.

By relying on collective plants, Foshan developed a highly diversified group of medium-sized factories that did not require higher-level approval for investment. The diversity reduced the risks for a small city producing for unknown markets when the city had little money and banks were cautious. But it also made economies of scale difficult to obtain. Foshan's strategy was to move ahead of other localities wherever there was a promising new market to enter. It was not clear how this strategy would look in the 1990s, when Foshan would face competition from larger factories with larger economies of scale, but for the first decade it worked very well. In 1988, despite some strain to meet their debts, Foshan factories were planning to expand their scale.

By far the largest group of factories built by Foshan were in textiles and apparel, a sector where Hong Kong had very good advice to offer. The factories used a broad range of materials, including polyester fibers, cotton, and silk, and covered all phases of the production process. The next largest group focused on electronics. This included factories for assembling television sets and videocassettes as well as liquid crystal displays, audiocassettes, personal computers, circuit boards, and lower-technology products like electric fans and radios. Many of the more complex components were bought from abroad or produced in cooperation with foreign companies, but where possible local enterprises bought foreign production machinery and produced the goods themselves. Foshan's third largest area of concentration was in plastic goods, including handbags, gloves, and shoes. They also produced many household consumer goods, especially watches, light bulbs, cans, wine, and toys.

Ceramics, the area of Foshan's traditional strength, also grew, although in value of production it did not keep pace with textiles, apparel, and electronics. Realizing that it was not immediately possible to reach international standards in ceramic tableware, Foshan concentrated in two areas: handicraft ceramics and ceramic tiles for construction. After the Cultural Revolution, factories began to resurrect their traditional handicraft objects but also began to create many new designs for international markets. With technical assistance from Italy, they advanced rapidly in ceramic tiles as the booming construction industry in Guangdong and other parts of China opened a large new market. By the late 1980s there were several tile factories, with a total of several thousand employees and a nationwide sales force.

These industries, which mostly produced consumer items, found a growing market as Delta incomes rose. In the mid-1970s even people in the Inner Delta were so poor that they could afford little more than basic necessities. Their relatives from Hong Kong and overseas bought them presents when they visited, however, and initially played a major role in creating demand. By the early 1980s as Foshan factories moved into production, the new agricultural sales by farmers, export-processing sales, and new investment from Hong Kong increased consumer purchasing power in the Delta. Foshan took the lead, not only ahead of other Delta areas but ahead of most parts of China, in identifying and responding to this demand.

When Foshan's factories were first established, average wages, approaching two hundred yuan per month, were considered high and many rushed to apply. By the mid-1980s new opportunities, as in Dongguan, led energetic young people to form individual enterprises in which they could make far more money. There was still an ample supply of new workers from poorer areas, but there was more labor turnover than Yu Fei and his managers desired and no easy solution except to expand training. Yu Fei believed that an enterprise could not run if incentives were geared strictly to individual performance, because there would be inadequate incentive for workers to cooperate and work for the enterprise as a whole. From the beginning Foshan enterprises linked wages to the profitability of the enterprise as a whole. At first the idea was somewhat ahead of its time; higher-ups who knew about the practice tacitly approved but opposed publicity for fear of arousing opposition.

In addition to reinvesting in industry, Foshan used its profits to transform the city. Though it was not wealthy enough to afford the huge modern buildings designed by famous architects in Shenzhen, its urban renewal far outpaced that of Guangzhou and other comparable cities. It expanded the city into former farm areas, building broad boulevards with bike lanes like those in other large modern cities and vast numbers of what for China were relatively modern apartment buildings. By the late 1980s, unlike Guangzhou, virtually all apartments in the city enjoyed running water. The city arranged temporary housing as whole areas were being torn down and rebuilt.

Foshan's development was not limited to its urban center. Some Chinese communities concentrated on only some of the "five wheels of development"—the county, township, village *(xiang)*, small village *(cun)*, and individual enterprise—but Yu Fei promoted all five. As the capital of the most prosperous prefecture in the province, Foshan pioneered an approach that became the model of what a metropolitan region should be, even before it was so designated. In the early 1980s it was far ahead of Guangzhou in looking out for its counties, and placed many of the new factories there rather than in the city proper. Foshan supported the expansion of cash crops by farmers and helped sponsor the construction of physical infrastructure needed for new markets and stores. People were encouraged to move from the countryside to Foshan's new apartments. Of those employed in the primary sector in Foshan Prefecture as a whole in 1980, 35 percent had moved into the secondary and tertiary sectors by 1985, and in the same year only 47 percent of the labor force of the metropolitan region remained in agriculture. In a 1986 sample survey of five thousand households in Foshan Metropolitan Region, the average per capita annual income was 1,050 yuan. In 1980 it had been 265 yuan. By 1985 official data showed that in Foshan City districts per capita annual income was 3,286 yuan, well above Guangzhou's, which was 2,602.[13]

Foshan also modernized and greatly expanded its department store, which began to rival even the Nanfang Department Store in Guangzhou in scope of products offered. Setting the pace for other communities, Foshan placed on the top floor a large amusement center and a large restaurant, which in the evening doubled as a night club, featuring disco. Foshan also pioneered the practice of leasing state stores to individuals, who were then responsible for turning over certain preset profits to the state. It also built large new shopping areas where individual proprietors could rent space.

After reforms had begun in 1979, most Guangdong prefectures moved to establish their own "universities," whose role was not unlike that of American community colleges. Foshan, among the first, arranged to set aside fifty million yuan and a site for its university. By 1986 it had a thousand regular full-time students and about six hundred part-time evening students.

Within the Inner Delta, Foshan was thus unique in two respects. First, it was the largest urban area that moved with the same speed and unity as the more rustic counties. Second, its leaders had a broad vision of modernization and successfully converted its industrial base into a program of comprehensive development for a metropolitan region as the core city became an engine of growth that helped pull along the surrounding rural areas.

## Large Modern Factories

In 1979 Guangzhou City was negotiating with a foreign company for the establishment of a polyester fiber plant. An Indonesian Chinese businessman was prepared to provide financing and, with the advice of Hong Kong textile specialists, modern European manufacturing machinery had been selected. But the Guangzhou City discussions were stalled in bureaucratic red tape, and Provincial Economic Commission officials who wanted to see plans move forward were frustrated by the delays. Suddenly, officials from Xinhui County offered to take over negotiations and locate the plant in their area. They perfectly demonstrated the quicker response so often shown by Inner Delta counties.

Xinhui, a county of eight hundred thousand, was one of the Si Yi counties that had sent so many of its people to America.[14] Dotted across it were large impressive residences, commonly of gray brick and several stories high, built by rich overseas Chinese who had returned in the decades before World War II. The buildings often had a watch-tower on top, used in the prewar period to defend against gangs of bandits who roamed the countryside. In the late 1970s many of these houses were emptied and returned to the families of their original overseas Chinese owners as part of China's effort to make amends for the horrendous treatment of local overseas Chinese families before reforms began.

In 1979 Xinhui was especially ready to make a move. It could see that nearby Foshan, Nanhai, Shunde, and Zhongshan had organized much more quickly and were already one or two steps ahead; it wanted to catch up. Although residents of Xinhui had many overseas relatives, they were mostly far away, not in Hong Kong. Xinhui was just distant enough from Hong Kong that in the 1960s and 1970s escape from there had been more difficult than from Dongguan, Baoan, and Zhongshan. For the same reason, it was also not as convenient for the Hong Kong businesspeople who were just beginning to set up export-processing factories across the border.

When Xinhui leaders first thought about expanding exports, they focused on their traditional industries. They put a great deal of effort into upgrading the factories in their specialty, the making of hand fans from *kui,* a kind of palm tree. Xinhui had long cultivated these trees, which still lined many of the streets of its towns. But by 1979, observing the limited markets and the already low price of *kui* fans, cadres doubted whether they could rely on the fans to bring their county economic prosperity. Electric fans were becoming available and destroying the demand for the hand fan of an earlier era. The same was true for silk, another Xinhui product; it was becoming expensive to produce, and with so many new fibers that could be washed in washing machines, world demand for silk had fallen off. Guangdong demand for tractors from the Xinhui tractor factory had also stagnated. It was clear to Chen Shuihong, director of Xinhui's Economic Commission and an especially farsighted planner, that they had to look elsewhere.

Two other visions of change had not come to fruition. Xinhui cadres had begun working with an electronics firm in Hong Kong to establish a factory in the county, but by 1979 it was becoming clear that they would not be able to reach an agreement satisfactory to both sides. And the hope that Xinhui's tractor factory might begin producing cars or even motorbikes was little more than a pipe dream for the foresee-able future, given the factory's level of technology, the capital require-ments, and the low level of Guangdong's purchasing power.

The new reform policy had resolved earlier ambivalence about automated manufacturing. In the mid-1970s, many Chinese planners had doubted whether, given China's vast labor supply, it was wise for China to move to automate production. By the end of the decade, however, planners had decided that improving the standard of living required modern manufacturing, and that if necessary they would solve the employment problem by increasing the numbers hired in the tertiary sector. When the opportunity for the polyester plant came up, Xinhui officials were therefore ready to take action.

The agreement came quickly. The Indonesian businessman, Chen Yunkang, agreed to invest $10 million for modern machinery, imported primarily from Switzerland with some from West Germany and Japan. Chen Shuihong, who negotiated on the Chinese side, persuaded Chen Yunkang to agree to purchase 30 percent of their product each year to ensure that they would be able to pay off the debt even if the domestic market developed slowly. Construction began in 1981 on the site of a *kui* fan factory that had been closed down, and the opening ceremony was held September 27, 1983. The plant soon produced 5,000 tons of *dilun* (dacron) a year. By the end of 1986 the original investment in this plant had been repaid, Chen Yunkang was earning substantial amounts of income, and an additional plant producing 7,500 tons a year was in operation. When the two were completed they represented a total investment of 127 million yuan, including a total foreign investment of $19 million. In 1986 their output was worth 256 million yuan, and managers expected to repay the entire original investment by 1989.

The success of the plants surpassed even the planners' expectations. As the standard of living began to improve in the Delta people wanted more clothing of more varieties. Garments made from polyester fiber in Hong Kong, beginning to come into Guangdong, seemed very stylish. Many Inner Delta residents were beginning to afford simple washing machines, and polyester fiber washed well in them. Cotton was in short supply within China at the time, and spinning and weaving plants in Guangzhou were having trouble obtaining enough cotton fiber to keep their machinery busy. Beijing officials had originally withheld approval for Guangzhou to purchase polyester fiber production machinery from abroad because they were trying to develop indigenous equipment and wanted to wait until it was ready. But in 1979 with its new special policy, Guangdong had the freedom to make its own decisions. Provincial officials' support of Chen Shuihong allowed Xinhui to move ahead despite Beijing's reluctance. As it turned out, problems developed with the domestic technology and Beijing also eventually turned to the technology used in the Xinhui factories. In the meantime, Xinhui's new plant produced fiber not only quickly but cheaply.

The polyester fiber plants proved so successful that by 1985 a small factory in Xinhui making other fibers brought in new modern equipment, and by 1986 it was producing five thousand tons a year of *binglun* (polyethelene) fiber a year. In November 1985, a Xinhui nylon factory with the capacity to make four thousand tons of synthetic fiber a year went into operation. These new plants brought wealth to Xinhui. With its profits, the county could afford to build modern hotels, expand its roads, and improve the upkeep on its parks; with a vastly improved infrastructure, it could then go to Hong Kong and elsewhere for further joint ventures.

Xinhui's success helped drive Guangdong's textile and apparel industry. Elsewhere in the province, in places like Haikou and Lechang County in Shaoguan, similar plants were soon installed, bringing employment and wealth to their communities. By 1987 seventeen similar synthetic fiber plants had been established elsewhere in China.

Perhaps no other kind of factory had such a large impact in the Inner Delta in the first decade of reform. But particularly successful plants of various sorts had a large impact on the success of an entire county. For counties that were slightly slower in getting started, the idea of betting heavily on certain larger factories, pioneered in Xinhui, became in effect a late developer's approach to acquire economies of scale and catch up with some of the more advanced counties.

## Layers of Change

Among the twelve counties and four cities in the Inner Delta, one could distinguish three tiers at the end of ten years of reform. The first tier comprised those closest to Hong Kong; their economies were most integrated with Hong Kong's. This tier included Dongguan, Baoan, Doumen, and in the late 1980s was beginning to include Panyu. Their ready accessibility by truck and boat to Hong Kong (and in the case of Doumen, to Macau) and the presence in Hong Kong of recent migrants from these counties made it easy for them to develop export-processing arrangements with Hong Kong. They were overwhelmingly export-oriented. All made rapid advances, but the speed and thoroughness with which they took advantage of their situation appeared to depend most on the *sixiang* (thought, i.e., attitude) of the county leaders. Counties with a unified leadership, committed to make the best of the opportunities, as in Dongguan, moved more quickly than those that were equally close but in the early 1980s did not make that commitment, as in Panyu. Doumen, west of Macau and farthest from Hong Kong, grew much more slowly than the other counties. The varying growth rates are reflected in the following data on county industrial-agricultural output (in millions of yuan). The growth revealed in tier one, especially for Dongguan, is understated, because in export processing only process fees were counted, not the total value of the final product.

| | 1980 | 1985 | Percent change 1980–1985 |
|---|---|---|---|
| Tier One | | | |
| Baoan | 158 | 494 | 312 |
| Dongguan | 902 | 1,941 | 215 |
| Doumen | 204 | 372 | 183 |
| Panyu | 599 | 1,268 | 212 |
| Tier Two | | | |
| Foshan | 861 | 2,623 | 305 |
| Nanhai | 992 | 2,546 | 256 |
| Shunde | 997 | 2,772 | 278 |
| Xinhui | 584 | 1,344 | 230 |
| Zhongshan | 927 | 2,329 | 251 |
| Tier Three | | | |
| Enping | 188 | 336 | 179 |
| Gaoming | 98 | 144 | 146 |
| Heshan | 154 | 324 | 210 |
| Jiangmen | 653 | 1,261 | 193 |
| Kaiping | 358 | 635 | 178 |
| Taishan | 431 | 1,019 | 236 |
| Zengcheng | 233 | 378 | 162 |
| Total | | | |
| Inner Delta | 8,341 | 15,293 | 237 |
| Guangdong | 36,732 | 69,449 | 189 |

In the second tier were places like Foshan, Nanhai, Shunde, Xinhui, and Zhongshan, which were relatively close to Hong Kong but not as close as the first tier. These areas, being slightly more distant from

Hong Kong, initially found it less easy to attract simple processing plants. But they had larger towns, a history of more light industry, and more experienced artisans than the first tier had. They were also closer to Guangzhou and could make use of its expertise and its network of access to internal Chinese markets. Tier two counties therefore took more initiative and aimed higher than processing goods for Hong Kong. They produced for the world market, but far more than the first tier they also produced for the rest of Guangdong and gradually other provinces as well.

The second tier developed more entrepreneurship, because it faced more complex issues of capital, technology, and marketing than did the first tier, which relied on ongoing management by Hong Kong. They pursued many different routes to attract and build industry. Nanhai moved early and established many fairly small village industries. Shunde relied heavily on large townships, and with the help of Hong Kong capital established several industries on a larger scale than those in Nanhai. Zhongshan, with more of its population already centered in the county capital, relied more on bigger, county-run state factories. In the late 1980s Zhongshan and Shunde began to converge in their approaches. Zhongshan, impressed with the vitality and local initiative of neighboring Shunde's town industries, decided to set up more town-led industries. Shunde County, impressed that Zhongshan government received more income from its state industries and could undertake more countywide projects like road building, decided to develop more state enterprises.

In the third tier were counties farthest away from Hong Kong: Taishan, Jiangmen, Heshan, Kaiping, Enping, Gaoming, and Zengcheng. They had less convenient transportation to Hong Kong, and fewer Hong Kong entrepreneurs originated from them. Except for Zengcheng, a poor agricultural county with little industrial expertise, they were also farther from Guangzhou. Although all but Gaoming had sent many migrants to North America, in the 1980s the stimulus for development from overseas relatives was far less than that for development from Hong Kong to nearby counties. The cadres were initially slower than those in the second tier in working to bring industry to their areas. Poorer to begin with, they were often less willing to take risks for fear that they would be in deep trouble if the projects failed. By the mid-1980s, however, as transportation improved, making them more accessible to Hong Kong just as the cost of labor was rising in the first and second tiers, they sensed more opportunities and began to build up their infrastructure. By the late 1980s they too had experienced an infusion of Delta dynamism and their industry was growing at double-digit rates. They had carefully studied the example of the first two tiers and, though a half step behind, were following in their footsteps. This was especially true of Jiangmen, the seat of a metropolitan region and, next to Foshan, the second-largest urban center in the Inner Delta.

By the mid-1980s, most Hong Kong businesspeople found the Inner Delta, with its cheaper labor and more responsive local cadres, more to their liking than the Shenzhen SEZ. Local communities elsewhere in Guangdong and throughout China found the Inner Delta a more realistic target to emulate. The Inner Delta was also far more integrated into the provincial economy than were the SEZs. The Inner Delta, and especially Foshan, became, in effect, the provincial model and one of the key national development models. Major national leaders, including Deng Xiaoping, Zhao Ziyang, Hu Yaobang, and Li Xiannian, visited and followed developments closely as they thought about urban reform. Thousands of cadres from all over China took a standard tour, from Guangzhou through Nanhai, Foshan, Shunde, Zhongshan, and Zhuhai, across by boat to Shenzhen, and back through Dongguan. Cadres throughout Guangdong followed Foshan and other Inner Delta experiences in study sessions. Outside cadres came to Foshan and other parts of the Inner Delta to serve internships in government offices and factories. Within the Provincial Economic Commission, for example, forty-three counties sent over two hundred high-level officials to spend a year or more working in Foshan in order to gain knowledge and experience that they could then use in their counties. Many other cadres originally assigned to the Inner Delta were sent out to bring the same dynamism to other parts of the province.

# 6.

# *Guangzhou: Rebuilding an Old Capital*

"Compared to the counties of the Pearl River Delta," observed one of Guangzhou's leading economic officials, "Guangzhou is like a tired old man." After reforms, the counties could establish new factories on former marshes or farm land without dislocating very many people or facilities. Guangzhou, in contrast, was overcrowded—its large population was difficult to move and its heavy industrial plants, with their 1950s equipment, expensive to replace. The plants had aged workers less amenable to innovation and retired workers who required housing and welfare. Farm families could build two- or three-story brick housing quickly, basically by themselves; replacing Guangzhou's run-down housing would require a large capital investment, new infrastructure, and difficult decisions about financing and priorities. Compared to the small, usually cohesive, group of county leaders who could act quickly, Guangzhou was slowed down by complex issues and four layers of bureaucracy above its enterprises: top officials, commissions and administrative offices, bureaus, and large public corporations. Counties had little responsibility beyond their boundaries, but Guangzhou, as the capital of its own metropolitan region, with eight counties before 1988, and as the provincial capital, had to serve a broader area. Revenue payments from a city or county to higher levels were generally set for five years, using one year's production as a base line. This meant that counties or small cities that began with hardly any industry and grew rapidly had virtually a tax holiday for five years. As a large city beginning with a large base that was being slowly replaced, Guangzhou had no such advantage.

Many problems Guangzhou confronted after 1979 were also found in other large Chinese cities, because national policy had for too long neglected urban infrastructure and housing. Beginning in 1954 and continuing through the Cultural Revolution, the motto and practice had been to change Guangzhou from a "consumption city" to an industrial city and, from 1958 on, to the industrial base for South China. Within manufacturing, the production of basic industrial goods was favored over the production of consumer goods. When a factory was built, the policy had been "production first, livelihood later" *(xian shengchan, hou shenghuo)* that is, build the factory first and worry about facilities for the workers later. Leaders hoped that once heavy industry succeeded there would be benefits for people's livelihood, but in 1979, three decades after the Communist takeover, these benefits had still not arrived. "We failed to realize," leaders acknowledged in a 1987 reevaluation, "the role of consumption and commerce in stimulating production."[1]

Priorities in construction before 1979 had followed the emphasis on heavy industry. A road built in the countryside could more easily be defined as necessary for production. If it were built in the city, it was defined as benefiting people's livelihoods. The same was true for bridges, electricity, sewage systems, and telephone service. Needs were great when reforms began. Traffic, for example, had grown considerably since 1949. In 1950, when a bridge was built across the Pearl River in downtown Guangzhou to replace one destroyed during the Communist victory, Guangzhou had two bridges. Because no new bridges were built from then until 1984, however, dozens of tiny ferries shuttled people back and forth across the river. In the early 1950s there were twenty-nine thousand telephones. In 1984 there was still the same number, virtually all over thirty-five years old.

Most of the housing stock had badly deteriorated by the 1980s. Except for some new cadre housing in eastern Guangzhou and apartments to house workers at newly built factories, almost no new housing was constructed between 1949 and 1979. Since residents had little capital, few materials, and no incentive to repair housing they did not own, they had made almost no repairs for over forty years. Most houses had running water, but many lacked plumbing. Since the population had doubled in the meantime, there was an acute shortage of space.

Simple brick factories had been built in the 1950s along the southern bank of the Pearl River so that their products could be transported directly along the waterways (see map of Guangzhou). After those areas filled up, similar factories were built southeast of Guangzhou proper toward Huangpu, along the Pearl River or its tributaries. Equipment, introduced mostly in the 1950s and 1960s by domestic factories, the Soviet Union, and Eastern Europe, was by world standards already outdated when installed. After the poor maintenance during the Cultural Revolution, much of the machinery was in shambles. Apartments had been built to house the workers on factory compounds, and the state had promised workers retirement benefits, including lifelong use of the housing. Thus by the 1980s, the factories were antiquated and the original residents aged. The housing needed repair, and many factories lacked space and funds to build housing for their new workers.

The Communists took over the old government buildings that had been used by the Kuomintang in the north central part of the city, an area where the Ming and Qing dynasties had also once located their government offices. As the municipal and provincial administrations and Party offices enlarged to staff the entire bureaucracy, covering all aspects of political, economic, and military activity, the government built many new office buildings to the east and northeast. New apartments were built nearby in neighborhoods where officials and more affluent businesspeople, often with overseas financial help, had lived before 1949. Even these newer apartments were cheaply constructed and often needed repair. As workers retired but remained in the buildings, new buildings were again needed for new workers.

Guangzhou was also a "tired old man" in its role as the spiritual leader of the Cantonese region. For centuries Guangzhou had had no rival as the center for Cantonese culture, cuisine, and politics. If anything this was even truer after 1949, because power and capital were even more centralized in Guangzhou. Even after the reforms Guangzhou remained the unrivaled political center, with responsibility for leading the province and providing infrastructure and public services. But the rise and increased accessibility of Hong Kong and the development of Shenzhen meant that Guangzhou was no longer the only major center of Cantonese life. Local areas had formerly looked to Guangzhou as the sole source of investment, but after China's opening the possibility of attracting foreign investment, earning foreign currency, and purchasing foreign goods held greater appeal. For new ideas about economic matters, technology, and management, better information came from Hong Kong or its satellite Shenzhen.

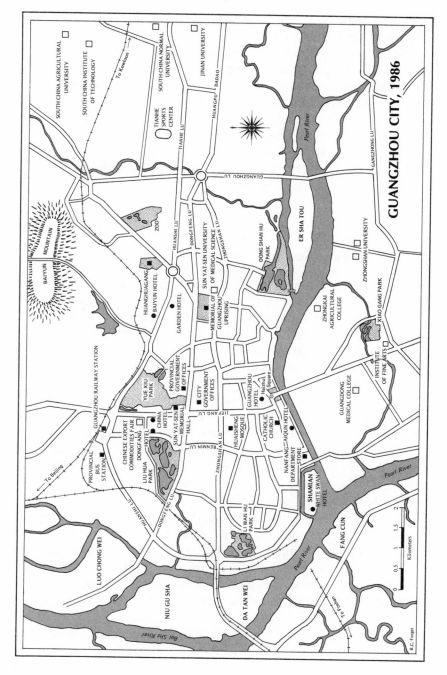

GUANGZHOU CITY, 1986

SOUTH CHINA AGRICULTURAL UNIVERSITY

SOUTH CHINA INSTITUTE OF TECHNOLOGY

SOUTH CHINA NORMAL UNIVERSITY

JINAN UNIVERSITY

To Kowloon

TIANHE SPORTS CENTER

TIANHE LU

HUANGPU DADAO

Pearl River

GANGZHONG LU

GUANGZHOU LU

BAIYUN MOUNTAIN

ZOO

HUANSHI LU

DONGFENG LU

ZHONGSHAN LU

SUN YAT-SEN UNIVERSITY

MEMORIAL OF MEDICAL SCIENCE

ER SHA TOU

DONG SHAN HU PARK

ZHONGSHAN UNIVERSITY

HUANGHUAGANG

BAIYUN HOTEL

GARDEN HOTEL

MEMORIAL OF GUANGZHOU UPRISING

GUANGZHOU RAILWAY STATION

YUE XIU PARK

PROVINCIAL GOVERNMENT OFFICES

CITY GOVERNMENT OFFICES

GUANGZHOU HOTEL

Haizhu Square

ZHONGKAI AGRICULTURAL COLLEGE

XIAO GANG PARK

INSTITUTE OF FINE ARTS

CHINESE EXPORT COMMODITIES FAIR

DONGFANG HOTEL

CHINA HOTEL

SUN YAT-SEN MEMORIAL HALL

JIEFANG LU

RENMIN LU

ZHONGSHAN LU

HUAISHENG MOSQUE

CATHOLIC CHURCH

GUANGDONG MEDICAL COLLEGE

To Beijing

PROVINCIAL BUS STATION

LIU HUA PARK

NANFANG-AIQUN HOTEL

DEPARTMENT STORE

HUANSHI LU

DONGFENG LU

LI WAN HU PARK

SHAMIAN WHITE SWAN HOTEL

Pearl River

LUO CHONG WEI

NIU GU SHA

DA TAN WEI

FANG CUN

Pearl River

To Foshan

Bai Sha River

0    0.5    1    1.5    2

Kilometers

R.C. Forget

Young people who sought new fashions in clothing, hair styles, cuisine, house furnishings, or store displays looked to Hong Kong. In television, popular songs, and popular culture too, Hong Kong had great allure. An embarrassing symbol of the changed position came each summer when Guangzhou, following Beijing, went on daylight savings time, and Hong Kong did not. In the 1980s all the counties nearest Hong Kong and even some farther away began to follow Hong Kong rather than Guangzhou.

And yet, though Guangzhou lagged behind, the general dynamism of the region and the determination of its leaders enabled Guangzhou to undergo rapid change, first in tourist facilities and then in commerce and industry.

## Expanding Facilities for Overseas Visitors

As the southern gateway to China, Guangzhou wanted to make a good impression on visitors, especially those who might help with modernization. "It was necessary," some of the more sophisticated local cadres were soon saying, to "improve the investment climate." This required making amends to overseas Chinese relatives and improving tourist facilities, an effort that brought the earliest round of changes as reforms began.

Officials estimated that as many as one-third of the families in Guangzhou proper had overseas connections. And overseas Chinese whose ancestral homes were in other parts of Guangdong and even elsewhere in China commonly entered China through Guangzhou, where they often paused for a brief visit. Sometimes local relatives came from the countryside to greet their visiting relatives in Guangzhou, where facilities were better.

With the opening, relatives could personally bring in presents or foreign currency. China had long maintained "friendship stores," where people with foreign currency could buy goods not generally available. Beginning in the late 1970s, these and other state stores catering to overseas visitors and local residents who received funds from abroad rapidly expanded, serving the visitors while accumulating foreign currency and increasing savings deposits.[2]

High-level officials had long tried to walk a tightrope between showing special consideration to local relatives of overseas Chinese and criticizing those who displayed improper bourgeois behavior, which inevitably included these same people. Officials responsible for overseas Chinese affairs generally favored more consideration, while the guardians of public morality, working in Party propaganda and public security, were less tolerant of their "decadence." During the Cultural Revolution the purists and the less controlled Red Guards under them had the upper hand, but with the reforms and the opening to the outside, those favoring special consideration dominated. In the late 1970s the Guangzhou Overseas Chinese Affairs Office began improving and expanding the city's hotels, restaurants, shops, reception centers, and even hospitals and museums for overseas visitors.

It was impossible for China to undo the harsh treatment suffered by local people with overseas connections, but the best way to ease the estrangement was by returning the property that had been taken away. This was much easier in the countryside, where farm families retained de facto control of their homes, than in the cities, where housing after 1949 was appropriated by the state, and living space was assigned by the Housing Management Bureau. Often high officials had been placed in the homes. In addition, some property had been damaged or destroyed, ownership rights were not always clear, and heirs were numerous and dispersed throughout the world. After 1979 new policy guidelines were developed, and complicated negotiations, sometimes lasting years, were required to determine who was to receive what property or compensation. Only after this was complete were many overseas Chinese, embittered by the earlier treatment of their relatives or friends, willing to consider contributing to China and repairing the property where their relatives lived.

Some overseas Chinese businesspeople had continued trade with China even in the worst years, but their activities in China were, as in the classic China trade, highly circumscribed in time and place. Contact was normally restricted to the nationwide Export Commodities Fair held in Guangzhou since 1957. At it, twice a year for one month (later twenty days), beginning in mid-April and mid-October, foreign buyers chose goods from Chinese export displays. Originally a modest exhibition site existed in Haizhu Circle, centrally located on the north bank of the Pearl River, with several hotels within easy walking distance. In 1973, as China was beginning to open more widely to Western countries, it built a huge exhibition hall a few kilometers north of the old site and began fashioning an area appropriate for foreign trade. It greatly expanded the nearby train station and added a large tower to the outdated Dongfang Hotel, then the best hotel in the city and across the street from the new trade center. Gradually new office buildings, exhibition halls, and more modern foreign tourist services were added.

In the late 1970s, as detailed in Chapter 11, contacts were allowed to expand far beyond the trade fair. Foreign businesspeople could go directly to other cities as well as to Guangzhou, but overall trade grew rapidly enough that the fair continued to attract many visitors, albeit for a shorter period of time. Guangzhou, wanting to make full use of its facilities to gain foreign currency, set up smaller specialized exhibits throughout the year.

In 1979, with the new special policy, Guangzhou could also begin to make use of foreign investment. Officials in contact with foreigners knew that Guangzhou needed better hotels and higher-quality tourist services to respond to complaints about the poorly equipped buildings, the awful service and the inadequate communication facilities. Plans were laid for newer and better facilities.

Although progress was rapid, it still took several years to finance, plan, and build modern hotels, but transportation within Guangzhou was changed almost overnight. Until that point, each hotel had a few cars but did not always manage them well. A guest could go from the hotel to another destination, but without special prior arrangement, he had no way to find a car to return to the hotel. In September 1979, Guangzhou officials signed a contract with a Hong Kong company, which then purchased and brought 270 Japanese-made taxis to Guangzhou. Guangzhou City set up an independent company to operate the vehicles. Since drivers, who paid a fixed fee to lease taxis, earned whatever revenue they took in, they picked up as many passengers as possible, a striking contrast to drivers in other Chinese cities, who were paid set salaries. As the cabs brought in income, Guangzhou bought them on installment. Within three years, the Hong Kong investors had been repaid with handsome interest, and then the cabs, entirely owned by Guangzhou, were used for several more years. The instant success of this venture brought more contracts, and by 1987 there were some eight thousand taxis in Guangzhou. Guangzhou was then the one major city in China where taxis were conveniently waiting at all major points and could be readily hailed on the streets, by local people using local currency as well as by foreign visitors.

The demand generated by businesspeople at the trade fair, tourists, and the personnel connected with the oil explorations of the early 1980s created a substantial revenue base for more modern hotels.

Three major modern hotel complexes, each with over a thousand beds, were undertaken with the cooperation of Hong Kong businessmen. Henry Fok helped finance the White Swan, located on Shamian Island, the old center for foreigners prior to 1949; a consortium that included Hong Kong's Regent Hotel and Hopewell put up the China Hotel; and the owners of Hong Kong's Lee Garden Hotel helped finance and build the Garden Hotel. The revolving restaurant at the Garden Hotel became the new symbol of modernity and was quickly imitated by Inner Delta counties who wanted to show that they too had arrived. The White Swan sent large numbers of personnel to Hong Kong for training, and in the other two hotels, fleets of managers came in from Hong Kong. By the mid-1980s, with new apartment wings as well as hotel rooms, with a modern communication system, with distinguished architectural design, and with service that visitors to Guangzhou only two to three years earlier would not have believed possible, Guangzhou was transformed into a city with world-class tourist facilities.

Guangzhou became the first major city in China to allow ordinary people without special permission in the front doors of the first-class hotels for foreign guests, as noted in Chapter 2, because it was awkward to exclude or check all local relatives of overseas guests. Henry Fok insisted that local residents be allowed in his White Swan Hotel, and after that the other hotels quickly followed suit. The large numbers of visitors coming to Guangzhou thus brought new services and set new standards that began to reverberate throughout the city and the Delta.

## Reviving Guangzhou's Commerce

The reformers enabled Guangzhou to move rapidly in developing a commodity economy, reviving its historical role as a commercial city. In the 1950s many cadres, observing that China's commercial history had not brought modernization, believed what they were taught, that changing Guangzhou from a commercial city into an industrial one was the path of progress. Although many small shops were closed or combined during the socialist transformation in 1955–56, Guangzhou still had 3.8 stores per 100 people in 1957. In 1978, this had dropped to 0.3 per 100 people.[3] By that time it was all too obvious that two decades of relying only on large state organizations had destroyed incentive and failed to benefit consumers. The simplest things—eating, washing, going to the bathroom, finding clothes, and getting a hair-cut—had become "big difficulties" *(danan)*. After 1978 leading economic officials began to argue that the commodity economy was not only compatible with industrial development, but that it could help drive industrialization. Guangzhou residents, pushed close to their limits by appeals for self-sacrifice, were hopeful they would again be able to buy what they needed.

As noted in Chapter 3, as part of the effort to solve the problem of the tens of thousands of young people, mostly returned from the countryside, who were "awaiting employment," in 1978 and 1979 many were given permits individually and collectively to establish small snack bars, restaurants, and sundry goods stores. These youth could thus earn their own living and meet some of the public demand for more services. By 1984 the number of commercial establishments in Guangzhou had increased to 1.5 per 100 people.[4] By the next year there were officially 37,521 independent enterprises with a total of 52,059 workers,[5] and in fact there were many more who were without set stores or stalls and therefore not officially counted.

Many of the stores that had formerly lined the streets of downtown Guangzhou had been turned into little workshops in the 1950s or had been used simply as dwelling units. After 1979 more and more were again rented out as commercial establishments. The former shop-keepers were rarely still around to resume their work, but a new generation of young people learned for the first time how to operate small enterprises.

New markets expanded throughout the city. A specialized market for agricultural products, four blocks long, for example, was established on Qingping Road, just north of Shamian Island. By 1988 it sold products from forty-three Guangdong counties and twenty-three other provinces. Huge areas like Huanghua were set aside for night markets, each several blocks long, with room for thousands of entrepreneurs to sell their wares. Open markets were allowed on many streets, and some streets permitted the erection of permanent wooden stalls. On the outskirts of the city, farmers put up stalls on their own land near the road. Just as local factories established outlets in other cities, so factories in other provinces and cities began to set up sales outlets in Guangzhou. State factories and even government units, to supplement their own budgets, opened to the general public facilities formerly open only to their own employees: restaurants, stores, and

other service establishments. Even twenty-four-hour stores began operating. These changes were paralleled all over China, but it is doubtful
that any other city's new markets were operated on a larger scale or
with more verve than in Guangzhou, with its commercial history,
new-found wealth, and close relations with Hong Kong.

Most of these stores and stalls employed only a handful of people.
Most had so little capital that they could not stock a large amount of
goods. The owner was usually also the manager, but sometimes the
capital was borrowed from friends and relatives. Sometimes a person
with a little savings bought rights to a stall and in fact rented out the
space to someone else or hired a salesperson. As they prospered, they
improved their facilities; by the late 1980s most shops in Guangzhou
had new signs.

State stores felt the pressure of the competition but it was still not
easy for them to become more efficient. One solution was for the state
to lease the smaller stores to an individual family, which would then
become an agent selling the goods on behalf of the state. This arrangement took a variety of forms. The family could guarantee to sell a
certain quantity of goods for the state, turn over a certain amount of
money, and then make a high proportion of profit on anything sold
beyond that amount. Or a family might promise to pay the state a
certain amount for all the current inventory and then, when new goods
were needed, buy the goods from the factory directly; the family would
then continue to turn over a certain amount of rent or profit to the
state for goods sold, and became in effect an independent entrepreneur
in a state-owned building. The Municipal Commercial Bureau, impressed with the vitality of the small-scale independent commercial
sector, eventually gave up trying to establish new small state stores.
In addition to renting out its smaller stores to private agents, it
concentrated on establishing larger and more specialized stores.

The Nanfang Department Store, long preeminent in Guangzhou,
became a national leader among state stores in offering new incentive
systems and improving quality and service. The store was a direct
descendent of a large department store founded by a Malaysian
Chinese businessman along the north bank of the Pearl River near
Shamian Island in 1918. The store was destroyed by fire in the 1930s
and was not completely rebuilt until 1954. During the Cultural Revolution, as mentioned earlier, many of its shelves were bare. Certain
key items like thermos bottles, dishes, and towels were available, but
the amount and variety of goods was limited and quality was poor.

The attitude of store personnel, as in other state stores, was at best indifferent.

After 1979 the store was given new autonomy, and Deng Hanguang, who had become general manager in 1977, began to work with his staff to make good use of this freedom. Hong Kong department stores, including those owned by Communists, had been catching up with world standards in range of goods and services, and it became a matter of pride to demonstrate that Guangzhou could run an equally good store. The store began to make its own contracts with factories. Previously, all the store's goods had come from the twentyeight specialized state wholesale companies, which had simply accepted products from factories and passed them on to Nanfang. By 1980, Nanfang buyers were going to factories and selecting items. When Nanfang gave notice that orders would be cut if goods did not meet its specifications for type and quality, some factories responded. Before long, manufacturers, concerned about profits, began to send their representatives to Nanfang to talk with salespeople in the relevant departments about customer preferences.

In 1985 Nanfang organized its top one hundred factory suppliers into the Industrial-Commercial Friendship Association (Gongshang Lianyihui). Once or twice a year these factories exhibited their goods within Nanfang and supplied factory representatives to explain the goods to the customers. In addition buyers from Nanfang expanded their travel in China to select goods, and by 1987 they were purchasing forty thousand products from over two thousand different factories.

In 1983 the Nanfang, like government units, agreed to turn over to the state a set amount of revenues for the next four years. Its general manager had a contract for this four-year period and was responsible for meeting targets. Using 1986 as a base year, new targets were set for another term that began in 1987. Within that target, the store passed on 55 percent of its profits to the municipality, but beyond the target only 30 percent was to be passed on and the rest was retained by the store, to be used for expansion, bonuses, or welfare as the store management decided.

The responsiveness of Nanfang personnel to customer preferences was aided by setting profit targets for each division. By 1984 the thirteen divisions within the main store and three divisions elsewhere each had profit targets. The salary of cadres working in a division depended on meeting targets and was raised in accordance with the degree to which these were surpassed. Bonuses for ordinary sales personnel were based on sales within each work station, with some leeway for ratings by the superior based on the individual's work attitude and maintenance of the stock.

Nanfang was the first Chinese department store to pioneer such techniques, and in 1983 and 1984, though Guangzhou was China's eighth-largest city, Nanfang was first in the nation in sales. Department stores elsewhere came to study its experience, and by 1987 it had been surpassed by a department store in Shanghai and one in Beijing. Because those cities had much larger populations and because other new department stores in Guangzhou, especially the Huaxia established just next door, had begun to imitate Nanfang, it had little hope of regaining the lead; its sales, however, continued to grow rapidly. Some felt the responsibility for falling behind was Deng Hanguang's. He had moved quickly in the early 1980s but had not done enough to continue adaptations as management issues became more complex, and he was later found guilty of sloppy management and indiscretions.

Nanfang advertised and had some special sale items to attract public interest, but it did not compete with other department stores by lowering its prices to lure customers away from competitors. Nor, if goods were in short supply, would it raise prices to take advantage of the situation. The Municipal Consumers' Council might raise objections if it did, but more important was the sense of the proper role of a state enterprise. As Guangzhou's largest and most successful department store, Nanfang was closely tied to the Municipal Commerce Bureau and had a sense of responsibility for the city's commerce. In 1982, for example, Nanfang sent a group of executives to establish a new department store in Shipai, a rapidly growing suburb that needed such facilities, and turned the store over to a separate company once it was running smoothly.

In 1978, Nanfang's best year until that point, it had sales of fifty-two million yuan. In 1983 sales surpassed three hundred million, and they have continued to grow since. Using its own profits, the store rebuilt and added new floor space, expanding from 6,400 square meters in 1978 to 18,600 by the mid-1980s. The quantity, variety, sophistication, and display of consumer goods in Guangzhou still lagged considerably behind that of Hong Kong, where incomes were much higher and tourists from other countries far more numerous. But Nanfang sent personnel to learn from Hong Kong stores and, through Guangzhou's sister relationship with Fukuoka, Japan, from the Iwateya Department Store there, and its commercial spirit was not far behind. The gap between Guangzhou and other cities or between Guangzhou in the late 1980s and Guangzhou a decade earlier was enormous. The Chinese had long agreed that, "For eating, it's Guangzhou" *(shi zai Guangzhou)*, but by the late 1980s many consumers elsewhere acknowledged that "For shopping, it's Guangzhou" *(shangpin zai Guangzhou)*.

## Rebuilding the City and Its Industry

Ameliorating the neglect of urban construction for three decades required so much work that catching up with basic needs would at best take several decades. In the fourth five-year plan, from 1971 to 1975, Guangzhou spent 1.6 billion yuan on urban reconstruction; in 1976–1980, 3.7 billion. This doubled again in 1981–1985, and was expected to double again in 1986–1990. But most of the rebuilding remained to be done.

A portion of the added funds came from the increase in the revenue base, with about 7 percent of the municipal budget going for basic construction in each of the five-year plans. A small part of the increase derived from the fact that certain fees—for telephone and water, for example—that had formerly been collected by the central government started to go directly to Guangzhou. Although Guangzhou grew slowly compared to the counties surrounding it, after late 1978, the combined value of industrial and agricultural output grew an average of 11 percent per year. From 1978 to 1985 the value of the Guangzhou Metropolitan Region output grew as follows (in millions of yuan):[6]

|                | 1978  | 1985   |
|----------------|-------|--------|
| Agriculture    | 1,000 | 1,510  |
| Light industry | 4,832 | 11,140 |
| Heavy industry | 2,874 | 5,898  |
| Total          | 8,706 | 18,548 |

Most of the construction after 1978 was financed by loans. In line with the new policy, formally enunciated in 1983 but actually in practice earlier, banks could lend money to enterprises that had prospects of repaying loans from their own income. Construction for nonproductive investments like schools and hospitals still came entirely from the government budget.

Because the infrastructure was so deficient, serious bottlenecks continued throughout the 1980s. Electric power shortages caused days off at factories, and demand increased so rapidly that even when new power facilities were completed, shortages stopped only temporarily. In accord with long-range plans, in the early 1980s, the province began introducing modern telephone switching equipment and then, in the middle of the decade, began a rapid expansion of telephone service. From the twenty-nine thousand telephones of 1984, it expected to reach two hundred thousand by 1990. By the mid-1980s modern telephone service was available in key government offices, hotels, and modern enterprises, but people still had great difficulty reaching those connected by older equipment. "What impressed me about Hong Kong," said a young cadre allowed to visit there for the first time in the mid-1980s, "was how easy it was to make a phone call."

Road paving, repair, and extension in Guangzhou continued on a large scale throughout the 1980s. Several major roads were widened to make room for two cars each way with a separate strip for bicycles. It was expected that bicycles would be a major means of transportation for some decades at least. Despite road construction, the ban on tractors, and the virtual disappearance of bicycles pulling carts, the increase in cars, vans, trucks, buses, bicycles, and motorbikes was more than the city could handle. As roads from Guangzhou to Shenzhen and to Zhuhai were completed, the vastly increased traffic flowing into Guangzhou was subject to hours of delay during peak periods. Planners hoped that new bypass highways scheduled for completion in the 1990s, by keeping through traffic out of the city, would relieve some of the congestion found in key arteries.

Before 1980, only a handful of buildings had elevators and were more than eight stories high. There were some apartment buildings of eight or nine stories, but they had no elevators. By the late 1980s, as some of the older buildings in downtown Guangzhou, commonly two and three stories high, were torn down, they were replaced with buildings ten stories high or higher. Gradually residents became willing to climb the stairs to tenth-floor apartments, and taller buildings began using elevators. By the late 1980s dozens of buildings over ten stories high, mostly apartment buildings, were under construction at any one time. As at Shenzhen, modern construction equipment was brought in, but both newer and older techniques and workmanship of both acceptable and unacceptable quality continued to coexist. Tens of thousands of youths, mostly from poorer counties, slept in shacks and under canvas-top shelters at the construction sites during the months they were working on a given project.

The proportion of people living in modern housing in Guangzhou in the late 1980s lagged far behind the proportion in Foshan. Guangzhou City proper, which had 3.8 square meters per person in 1980 and had built vast amounts of new housing to achieve its rate of 5.6 square meters per person by 1985, had little hope of achieving Foshan's 1985 level of 12 square meters per person before the year 2000. It was expected, however, that during the seventh five-year plan, ending in 1990, Guangzhou's ten thousand residents who in 1985 still did not live in at least 2 square meters of housing per person would be relocated to meet this minimum standard. The thirty million yuan allocated for this project alone was more than all the money spent for housing in Guangzhou during a typical year of the Cultural Revolution.

Housing might have gone up even faster except for the difficulty of resolving the issue of who was paying for it. State work units were still responsible for providing housing for their personnel, but the rents paid only a tiny fraction of actual building costs. For structures built before 1949 the low rents were not as critical a problem, although they did not cover costs of repair. More serious was that because there was no means to finance and recover costs, few enterprises could afford to put up new buildings. State industrial and commercial units that, with reforms, had to compete with private and collective enterprises on product price had little incentive to build new housing. Virtually no one but the richest of entrepreneurs and the recipients of the largest gifts from overseas relatives could afford to pay the actual cost of new housing like the Donghu Xincun (East Lake New Village) project developed in 1982. To pay the full cost of their housing would have required an entire reform of the wage system, including raising wages far higher than offices and enterprises were able to pay. Experiments were under way in the late 1980s to increase rents gradually and to move in the direction of making housing a commodity rather than a perquisite. One of the most promising intermediate efforts was for work units to give housing vouchers to workers to cover a high portion of the rents workers had to pay on the open market. Nevertheless, the gap between salaries and rents remained so great that there was little hope of fundamentally solving Guangzhou's housing problem in the twentieth century. The city was therefore trying to help subsidize reconstruction in limited areas and ensure that all buildings going up were tall ones, to help reduce overcrowding.

Guangzhou's investment in industry, especially heavy industry, was also severely constrained by shortages of capital and readily accessible raw materials. Large industrial plants making steel, ships, tires, machinery, and chemical fertilizer were decades out of date, and modernization required heavy investment. Considerable foreign machinery was required, and foreign currency was in short supply. Guangzhou planners gave light consumer industry higher priority than heavy industry, because it could bring greater returns and more foreign sales. Hong Kong investors also wanted quicker returns and showed little interest in capital-intensive industries. Furthermore, Guangzhou's lack of resources required that they be brought in from long distances, creating a heavy strain on the national transport system. Planners therefore tried only to modernize heavy industry producing industrial goods needed by local industry. Given the limited availability of funds, fully modernizing heavy industry was another goal unlikely to be achieved before the twenty-first century.

To obtain foreign exchange and a high return on investment, the strategy for the sixth and seventh five-year plans (1981–1990) concentrated on investment in consumer industries such as textiles, bicycles, watches, tires, refrigerators, televisions, air conditioners, beer, and Chinese medicine. Metropolitan region guidelines called for these factories to be located on the outskirts of Guangzhou City and for apparel factories using a low level of technology and some food processing to be moved farther out into the rural areas. The investment required in light industry was far less than needed in heavy industry, but even this sector could not modernize on a broad scale because new technology required foreign currency. A small county or city might be able to gather enough funds so that a small number of urban people could find employment; it was quite another matter for a large city of over three million to transform itself quickly. Although its visible progress was less impressive than in some nearby Delta counties, Guangzhou was nonetheless able, as we have seen, to double the value of its light industrial production between 1978 and 1985.

## The Guangzhou Economic and Technological Development Zone

Guangzhou's long-term development plans, developed in the mid-1980s, called for the city's industry to expand to the southeast toward Huangpu, 35 kilometers from the city center. The development of this area between Guangzhou and Hong Kong seemed natural because of the growing economic nexus between Guangzhou and Hong Kong. New highways through Huangpu to Shenzhen, 114 kilometers southeast of Guangzhou, linked the area to Hong Kong; the railway between Hong Kong and Guangzhou passed through it; and the broadening and deepening of the Pearl River channel at Huangpu made it convenient for ocean-going vessels. The old portion of Huangpu Port, the major port in South China, was remodeled and a new portion added to make it the fourth-largest port facility in China, after Dalian, Tianjin, and Shanghai. It had the ability to dock ten ships of 10,000 tons or more simultaneously and to turn over 1,600,000 tons of freight annually, a capacity still far from fully utilized in 1988. Although its facilities were not yet fully modernized, the port could handle containers and had a very efficient coal-unloading operation capable of absorbing the additional coal that began to come from Shanxi in 1989. When Guangzhou was given permission to open its own industrial zone, it naturally chose a location adjacent to this new port within its jurisdiction.

Guangzhou leaders had long wanted their own zone to attract foreign business, and some had been disgruntled when Shenzhen had been earmarked for projects that might just as easily have been located in Guangzhou. From 1979 to 1984 Shenzhen was able to bring in $650 million in overseas investment compared to Guangzhou's $340 million. In the same period, exports from Shenzhen rose from $1.4 million to $260 million while Guangzhou's rose from $160 million to $250 million. Annual output per worker in Shenzhen rose from 7,215 yuan to 28,000 yuan, surpassing Guangzhou's which rose from 14,000 to 19,000 yuan.[7] Guangzhou officials could accept some division of labor in which Shenzhen was oriented to the outside world and Guangzhou was oriented to its regional responsibilities, but they wanted direct access to foreign technology, expertise, and capital. And they found it far more satisfying to start afresh in a new location than to deal with the troublesome problems of old organizations, old equipment, displacing population, and coping with retraining and reassignment.

Guangzhou was thus very enthusiastic when it was given permission to build its own industrial zone in 1984. The Shenzhen special economic zone was several years old by then, and its experience had much to teach Guangzhou. The positive lessons included how to manage large construction projects, contact potential foreign investors, and coordinate activities with other institutions. In addition to avoiding corruption, planners hoped to do better than Shenzhen in two key respects. First, they wanted to concentrate in areas of higher technology. Higher officials had from the beginning encouraged Shenzhen to attract new technology, but as noted, the pressure to make rapid progress caused it to build many tourist and commercial operations as well as labor-intensive processing operations. To signify its different intent, Guangzhou called its site the "economic and technological development zone." In a sense, the model was not Shenzhen as a whole but the Shekou industrial zone within Shenzhen.

Second, planners hoped to manage better the pace of their development. They wanted to move quickly but to avoid overbuilding and excess capacity. As in Shenzhen, they began by blocking off large areas, leveling the ground, and putting in electricity lines, sewage systems, telecommunications, and roads. In Huangpu, where the project centered around reclaiming marsh land, they brought in landfill and pumped out massive amounts of water into the Delta through long drainage pipes. This was accomplished in good time, but it cost roughly three hundred million yuan, and required considerable help from the central government. Zone planners built their own 19,000-kilowatt power station as a backup to the provincial electricity grid, and they brought in microwave telecommunication equipment. Rather than investing extensively in developing sites that might lie idle, they developed small tracts. Only when factory contracts were in hand and only when the tract sites were filled did they develop a second area.

Unlike Shenzhen, which was guided directly by Beijing and recruited cadres nationally, the Huangpu zone was strictly under Guangzhou City and recruited talented cadres, mostly young college graduates, from within the Guangzhou government. The first head of the zone was Zhu Shenlin, a 1949 graduate of Huanan Engineering University. Zhu was then a rising star in Guangzhou and was experienced in managing technological projects. While head of the zone he also served as deputy secretary of Guangzhou's Municipal Party Committee, and in early 1986 he was called from the zone to become mayor of Guangzhou. In 1988 Lei Yu, then deputy mayor, was put in charge. Their appointment to the zone reflected the importance Guangzhou attached to the project and the close involvement of its top leaders in the zone's development. To spur development and provide it with a financial base, the city allowed the zone to pay no taxes to the municipality for five years and to use proceeds from rents and other fees for further development of the zone.

Because the area was strictly for industrial development, the zone, at 9.6 square kilometers, was only a fraction of the size of Shenzhen. The first portion to be opened for development was a tract of 2.6 square kilometers, 1.06 square kilometers of which was for commercial areas, dormitories, guest houses, schools, and other support space. Most of the buildings in the support center were in use by 1987.

To help attract foreign companies, planners wanted to reduce the red tape caused by jurisdictional boundaries, and therefore they centralized authority in an Administrative Committee (Guanli Weiyuanhui), which had broad decision-making powers. The Administrative Committee was empowered to make decisions on all operations involving $10 million or less, including decisions about hiring, wages, rent, and other fees. This eliminated most jurisdictional problems, although some higher-level governmental agencies were still beyond the ability of the zone to control. For example, it was not easy for companies settling in the zone to resolve questions of charges for electricity supply; these were determined by the provincial electric power company. As in Shenzhen and other special zones, the Guangzhou zone offered special tax advantages and allowed goods from abroad that were to be used for production to enter without customs charges. Instead of establishing government bureaus to administer the zone, service companies were set up to provide such services as job placement, technology transfer agreements, construction, and commerce. Because these organizations were starting fresh, it was easier for them to limit lethargic bureaucratism, which remained strong elsewhere.

The zone, hoping to draw investment quickly, interpreted its mandate to attract "high technology" to include foreign companies that had fairly modern manufacturing equipment regardless of the product as long as it caused no pollution. Although many foreign companies still preferred to deal with counties, whose administration was even simpler, by 1987, scarcely more than two years after construction had begun, foreign companies had selected sites for eighty-two industrial plants, forty-two of which were under construction or completed by mid-1987. By then five hundred million yuan in investment had been committed by foreign firms, including an Australian processing plant for goose liver, an Italian ceramics factory, an integrated circuits factory and a plastics factory from the United States, and a malt-producing plant from Denmark, as well as plants producing apparel, toys, and yogurt. If one interpreted "technology" narrowly, it remained to be seen in the late 1980s whether technology from the zone could easily be transferred to other parts of Guangdong and China. But managers, staff, and workers were acquiring new experience in using modern production equipment to produce goods of quality, priced to meet international competition. There could be no doubt that people working in the zone were acquiring general skills required in modern business organizations.

Perhaps even more difficult than attracting foreign capital was the task of persuading skilled technicians and managers from Guangzhou to work in the zone and in other areas east of the city. Because of overcrowded roads, at least two hours were required in 1987 to travel from the center of Guangzhou to the zone, a distance of thirty-five kilometers. Guangzhou relied on paying "outskirt supplement" bonuses to encourage workers to travel the long distances, and expected to have to do so for some time.

## Promoting the Development of Guangzhou's Counties

Of the various layers of Guangzhou Metropolitan Region's administrative responsibility prior to administrative reorganization in 1988 (four urban districts, four suburban districts, and eight counties), perhaps the one that required the most attention in the mid-1980s was the county level. Guangzhou officials who were concerned about industry had thought until then almost exclusively of the urban districts and the southeastern suburbs. Foshan, for example, gave much more initial attention to county industrial development than did Guangzhou.

In keeping with the new conceptions underlying reform, those places allowed to develop first were expected to become engines of growth for other areas. In the early 1980s province and metropolitan

*Patterns of Change*

region leaders began to give more attention to the role of Guangzhou in developing its surrounding counties. As part of the plan for richer areas to help poorer ones, in 1983 the province added two poor counties, Qingyuan and Fogang, located just north of the former Guangzhou Region, to Guangzhou's six other counties. Of the five counties in the Foshan Metropolitan Region, only one, Sanshui, was not in the rich Inner Delta area. In 1985 the other four had an annual per capita income above one thousand yuan. In contrast, of the eight counties under Guangzhou, seven were poor, north of the city; only one, Panyu, was in the richer Inner Delta area and had a per capita income above one thousand yuan a year. Only one other county in Guangzhou Metropolitan Region, Hua, was as well off as Sanshui. The other six had annual per capita incomes under six hundred yuan,[8] and five of these not only contributed no income to Guangzhou Metropolitan Region but received financial assistance from it to help with their administrative, educational, and welfare services.

The tax burden for supporting its counties was thus much heavier for Guangzhou than for Foshan, which exacerbated Guangzhou's problems with the tax system. By 1985 Foshan's industrial production was already worth 10.8 billion yuan, over half of Guangzhou's, but because Foshan had started in 1980 from a low tax base, it was paying less than one-third of what Guangzhou paid in taxes. The problem is reflected in the following data comparing the two metropolitan regions in the amount of revenues passed on to higher levels, total fixed investment during the sixth five-year plan (1981–1985), and total agricultural-industrial output in 1985 (figures in millions of yuan). Foshan's tax burden was low in comparison to its fixed investment.

| | Revenues paid to higher levels | | Total investment | Production |
|---|---|---|---|---|
| | 1980 | 1987 | 1981–1985 | 1985 |
| Foshan | 50 | 500 | 2,500 | 10,800 |
| Guangzhou | 400 | 1,800 | 1,500 | 19,400 |

The decision in 1984 to make Guangzhou and six other cities separate line items *(danlie)* on the state plan gave Guangzhou increased financial independence from Guangdong. According to the accompanying agreement, until it achieved its profit targets, Guangzhou was permitted to keep 34 percent of its profits and had to hand over 66 percent to higher levels. When it surpassed its quota, it kept 60 percent and handed over only 40 percent. The new arrangements did not fundamentally alter Guangzhou's financial plight, but it did help marginally and allowed Guangzhou to permit enterprises to keep as much as 45 percent of their profits, far more than in other cities, thus greatly increasing the ability of successful firms to reinvest in plant and equipment.

Although Guangzhou began to increase its financial assistance to its counties in the mid-1980s, perhaps the most important change was assigning industrial cadres from the metropolitan region to assist their counterparts in the counties. Guangzhou had moved quickly to form groups of companies *(jituan)*, and new *jituan* linked enterprises in Guangzhou with those in the counties. This not only provided the counties with more access to technology and expertise but broadened their vision and made their approach to industrial development more realistic. In the mid-1980s Guangzhou concentrated on building up the roads and infrastructure in Panyu, because it was well situated for economic development and with rapid growth it could help finance more backward counties. In 1988, with the completion of a critical new bridge, Panyu was moving rapidly to narrow the gap with its neighbor Nanhai, which had spurted ahead earlier.

By the late 1980s another county, Zengcheng, was poised for takeoff. Although it included poor mountainous areas to the north, it also stretched southeast to the East River, where its southwestern part bordered on Huangpu and its southeastern part on Dongguan. When Lei Yu, of Hainan Island fame, went to Zengcheng as county magistrate in early 1987, he helped to focus its planning to speed up development. After the usual first month of visits to the various towns and consultations with local officials, he was convinced that subordinates who identified the transportation system as the key bottleneck were correct. He and his fellow officials focused on building two key bridges and paving and widening eight roads, because they believed that then the southern part of Zengcheng would be ripe for the same kind of export-processing explosion that had hit Dongguan. Lei Yu quickly gathered the project support necessary from Guangzhou Metropolitan Region and Guangdong Province. His actions also helped lay the groundwork for another new industrial zone, Xintang, on the north bank of the East River, opposite Dongguan.

Zengcheng's success came more from its initiatives than from Guangzhou's, but Guangzhou's cooperation and support were critical.

Zengcheng's success stimulated the other counties in the metropolitan region to move more rapidly to take advantage of similar opportunities. A number of poorer counties north of Guangzhou had mountainous areas, and officials from Guangzhou helped them develop a lumber industry and downstream industries that made use of the lumber. They also helped these counties, all heavily agricultural, expand their food-processing industries. Qingyuan County, which had clay soil especially suitable for making pottery, was given assistance to develop ceramics and porcelain factories. Guangzhou also helped make the connections that led in 1987 to a large joint venture with American Standard for producing porcelain bathroom fixtures.

These efforts had already begun to have considerable impact by the late 1980s. To be sure, the natural vitality of the Inner Delta and of Guangzhou proper had a considerable spillover effect on these counties. But the role of government remained central for improving the infrastructure, for making key introductions, and for enabling these developments to take place.

Despite all of Guangzhou's problems, the collective and private sector had developed enough dynamism by the mid-1980s not only to absorb the 400,000 youth returning from the countryside but to provide employment for over 100,000 new migrants a year. By 1987 Guangzhou had 1,100,000 temporary residents, constituting 33.2 percent of the population, by far the highest percentage in any large Chinese city. A few were dependents living with relatives, but almost two-thirds were employed. According to a 1987 sample survey, roughly one-half of the workers were in construction; of the other half, a third were in industry, and two-thirds were in commerce and other services. Housing, of course, was strained—construction workers lived on-site, factory workers were squeezed into already overcrowded dormitories, and many others were accommodated by suburban farmers who put up simple dwellings on their land to earn additional income.[9] Poorer areas saw Guangzhou as a haven, and by Spring Festival 1988 Guangzhou had to turn away many who came looking for work.

Not only had the collective and private sector taken on a new dynamism, but in 1988 an unusually able team of top leaders, including Zhu Shenlin and Lei Yu, began pushing the government to play a more active role in rejuvenating the city. Their vision called for attention to foreign markets to increase foreign currency and to help with technological progress. They wanted to continue focusing on light industry and modernizing the infrastructure. But as they studied cities abroad, they noted the growth of the service sector and wanted to help make Guangzhou a provincial center and a national leader in information, finance, education, and tourism. They planned to push forward vigorously, and they expected that even housing and heavy industry, the most intractable problems, would undergo fundamental transformation within two to three decades.

# 7.

# *Prefectural Capitals: Outposts of Change*

By the mid-1980s the new vitality had significantly transformed every township in the Inner Delta. This area and its adjoining cities, Shenzhen, Zhuhai, and Guangzhou, then contained one-fifth of Guangdong's population but was producing almost two-thirds of its industrial output. The rest of the province did not yet have the margin of extra resources, convenient markets, contacts in Hong Kong, optimism, and vision needed to make such a breakthrough. Yet in contrast to their impoverished condition in 1979, all parts of the province had begun to make progress by the middle of the next decade. To be sure, work on issues like health care, education, pollution, and corruption had scarcely begun and still loomed large as the 1990s drew closer. But food had become more plentiful, markets livelier, people better dressed, and bicycles more common. More locally made goods were available, and more consumer products made elsewhere could also be purchased. In all counties construction was booming; there were new roads, new houses and apartments, and new public buildings.

In part the growth outside the Delta area was internally generated by decollectivization and the opening of markets. But it was the effect of the Delta dynamism—its expanding markets, its overall demonstration of what was possible, and the new efforts of provincial leadership to extend that vitality—that brought the biggest changes to the rest of the province. These local and outside forces together set off a reaction in regional centers, which in turn helped spread development to the remote areas of the province.

## Transport and Market Expansion

As the Delta economy grew, its increased purchasing power sucked in goods from elsewhere in the province, just as its new job opportunities sucked in young laborers. Those who sent goods and family members to the Delta earned new income with which they improved their standard of living. Increased trade between the Delta and the rest of Guangdong would not have been possible, however, without the improvement of roads and the greater freedom granted to individuals and cooperatives to market and transport a wide range of goods over long distances.

Boats continued to operate along the coast and on some of the rivers; in many boats, diesel engines had replaced oars. But outside the Delta area, water transport declined not only relatively but absolutely. Parts of many key routes—the North and East rivers and their major tributaries, for example—had become largely impassable in dry seasons because of diversion of water for irrigation and because of silting caused by the lack of soil conservation.

Rail lines were not greatly expanded during the early reform period. Double tracking on the major north-south route from Guangzhou through Shaoguan was finally completed in 1988. The route from Maoming through Zhanjiang to southwestern China had been in place before the reforms, but the route from Sanshui to Maoming, which linked Guangzhou with southwestern China, was delayed by jurisdictional and funding problems and not scheduled for completion until 1990. Aside from these lines, there were only short rail routes in spots in Hainan and from Mei County through Xingning to Longchuan: hardly sufficient for such a large population, especially since transport by rail was at that time calculated to be cheaper than by truck.

The biggest growth came in roads and bridges. Although it is difficult to obtain accurate information on the quantity of goods transported, the increasing importance of the roads is reflected in data on passengers traveling on public buses. In 1978, 15 percent of passengers using public transportation traveled by rail, 15 percent by water, and 70 percent by road. By 1986 this had altered to 10 percent by rail, 6 percent by water, and 84 percent by road. During those eight years the number of passenger trips on public vehicles using roads grew from 121.9 million to 330.4 million per year.[1] Much of this increase was on privately or collectively owned bus lines, usually operating with second-hand buses, which provided public transportation between many towns and villages for the first time in history.

Throughout the decade there was a tremendous increase in paved roads, which ran the gamut from simple asphalt pavement without proper undergirding to well-paved cement highways that could meet standards anywhere. Except for major provincewide roads, there were great differences between counties because each county planned and financed its own routes. Eventually nearly all large administrative villages in Guangdong were linked by all-weather roads. At the end of the reform decade, however, there were still no roads in Guangdong that compared with international highways, and even on the best roads, usually two lanes wide, vehicles traveling at the top speed of 70 kilometers per hour shared the road with slow-going tractors, bicycles, and pedestrians. The first limited-access throughway, the Zhuhai-Guangzhou-Shenzhen superhighway, was under construction in 1988. Road planning was not always well coordinated, and cars speeding into cities not infrequently waited some hours for ferry boats, as in Shantou or Zhanjiang, or at traffic bottlenecks. Bridges were also built at a prodigious pace: between 1978 and 1986, 1,436 permanent bridges went up in the province, with a total length of 62,500 meters. Most large towns had been located on rivers, and in many towns these new bridges made possible, for the first time, vehicle traffic between the two banks as well as uninterrupted long-distance travel.

As reforms began, there were only a few thousand cars and trucks in Guangdong. By 1986 there were 100,000 registered passenger vehicles and 162,000 trucks,[2] still a small number by international standards. Most of the new vehicles were purchased by government units, which used their foreign currency to acquire Japanese vehicles rather than domestically produced vehicles that required frequent and troublesome repairs. Only a few of these vehicles were owned by private individuals, who began purchasing small used trucks and traded them in for bigger and newer ones as their enterprises grew. Within counties, tractors transported heavy goods, and by 1985 73,000 of the 188,000 tractors used for transport[3] were privately owned, mostly purchased from brigades and teams that sold them off with decollectivization. Motorbikes began to be popular in the mid-1980s, carrying passengers or, more often, goods on the back seat or in a side car; they were nearly all privately owned. To be a driver was still a valued occupation, now open to anyone who paid for the training, not just former soldiers considered to be good security risks.

Within townships and cities, bicycles could be used to carry goods as well as people. The number of bicycles per rural household increased from 0.55 in 1978 to 1.39 in 1986.[4] By 1986 the average number of bikes per household was 2.2 in the towns and cities of Guangdong, 1.5 in the rural flatlands, 1.4 in the rural hilly areas, and 1.1 in rural mountainous areas.[5] Within a decade, both the use of carrying poles, balanced on the shoulder, and the use of cows to pull carts were virtually eliminated.

In the early 1980s, many enterprising individuals with access to vehicles brought in goods from elsewhere that were unknown in their area and made a great personal profit. By the late 1980s it was hard to find such opportunities, for with the expansion of the transportation system, highly desired goods had become more widely distributed, and with competition, large price differentials had been reduced. With better roads, more vehicles, and the chance to respond to demand, many goods circulated over a much broader geographical area.

## Government-Led Growth

In Guangdong the government played a much larger role in shaping development beyond the Delta area than would have been the case in a nonsocialist country. Government offices still approved all major construction projects and the purchase of new equipment, especially those requiring foreign currency. The banks providing loans were government banks, and even if higher levels allowed local branch offices to make decisions, government policy and the views of local government offices had a great impact on bank decisions. The larger enterprises were still all state enterprises and even in collectives, local officials had great leverage and sometimes ran the enterprises directly.

Regional government centers therefore became much more influential than they would have with only market forces operating.[6] Three newly created cities—Shenzhen, Zhuhai, and Tongza (Hainan)—suddenly became important centers, primarily as the result of administrative decisions rather than economic forces. Economic considerations affected the selection of a site to be a prefectural capital, but once it was selected, investment expanded far more rapidly there than elsewhere in the prefecture. Government units located in the prefectural capitals channeled investment into construction to widen the streets and to put up large new public buildings, cadre housing, and other support facilities. Larger factories were placed in these capitals, and then market forces began to operate, making them commercial as well as public and industrial centers.

## The Seven Centers of Regional Growth

In the 1980s several prefectures were reorganized as metropolitan regions, but they retained considerable continuity as regional administrative centers between the province above and counties below them. Some of the fourteen prefecture-level capitals in Guangdong were subdivided in 1988. Until then, however, five (Guangzhou, Foshan, Jiangmen, Shenzhen, Zhuhai) were located in the Inner Delta area, already discussed. Hainan Island had two (Haikou and Tongza), discussed in Chapter 9. If the Inner Delta is the hub of a wheel, the remaining seven (Zhaoqing, Huizhou, Shaoguan, Zhanjiang, Maoming, Shantou, and Meixian) can be thought of as nodes part way out along the spokes of half a wheel (the other half of which is in the water). (See the province maps in the Introduction and at the end of this chapter.)

All seven prefectural capitals were originally important water transport centers: Huizhou, Zhaoqing, Shaoguan, Maoming, and Meixian are on rivers; and Shantou and Zhanjiang are the great ports of northeast and southwest Guangdong, respectively. All were administrative centers before 1949 except Maoming, which was later made an administrative center because of oil development.

The capitals' growth depended on the economic status of the areas they served as well as on administrative decisions. Each served at least some poor rural counties, which naturally contributed less income to the prefecture and were less able to help the prefecture finance investment. In both vitality and proximity to the Inner Delta, these capitals can be divided into three groups: cities most closely linked with the Inner Delta (Huizhou, Zhaoqing, and Shaoguan); cities more distant from the Delta but with a good regional base for development (Maoming, Zhanjiang, and Shantou); and an isolated mountain area with limited opportunities for short-term development (Meixian).

### Huizhou: From Cultural Capital to Modern Technology

By the late 1980s Huizhou, the administrative center of the East River area, was the capital most affected by the growth of the Inner Delta. It was linked to Delta information, styles, and business, and its standard of living was rising rapidly. It was a city of 188,000, of whom 122,000 were urban residents, and presided over Huiyang Prefecture, whose population numbered 7,730,000, second largest after Shantou. The prefecture encompassed Dongguan and ten other counties; its thirty-two thousand square kilometers made it then the largest of any of Guangdong's prefectures and almost as large as Hainan Island.

Huizhou was already the prefectural capital in the Song Dynasty (960–1276), when Su Dongbo, the designer of the more famous West Lake in Hangzhou, was sent to Huizhou and designed its West Lake. Huizhou's West Lake was 50 percent larger than Hangzhou's and gave it a beautiful setting. More than any other of Guangdong's prefectural capitals, the city retained a sense of history and culture. Aside from Zhaoqing's Seven Star Park, Huizhou became the most attractive prefectural capital for tourists visiting Guangdong.

Located closer to Hong Kong than any other non-Delta prefectural capital, Huizhou was the only one of these seven prefectural cities to be overshadowed by one of its counties in industrial production and standard of living. Indeed, Huizhou's industrial production in 1986, 0.26 billion yuan, was scarcely one-eighth of Dongguan County's 1.96 billion yuan. Huizhou's population was only about one-fifth the size of Dongguan's, and in 1986 the average per capita income in Dongguan was almost twice that in Huizhou. The rise of Dongguan, which is only one county closer than Huizhou to Hong Kong, reflected the explosive impact that Hong Kong and Shenzhen had on the hierarchy of wealth and power. In the early 1960s, the combined value of Dongguan's agricultural and industrial production was about the same as that of another Huiyang county, Lianping. Lianping also grew economically, but in 1986 it was the poorest of Huiyang's ten counties, and its combined agricultural and industrial output was 0.097 billion yuan, about 4 percent of Dongguan's 2.61 billion yuan.

As a center of influence in the area, Huizhou was displaced not only by Dongguan but even more by Shenzhen, which in 1979 was a small town in Baoan County, Huiyang Prefecture, administered from Huizhou. By the late 1980s many Huizhou people looked to the Shenzhen SEZ for employment opportunities, up-to-date technology, information about world markets, and fashion.

By 1984 the travel time by motor vehicle between Huizhou and Hong Kong had been halved to only three hours, and Huizhou officials, though one step behind Dongguan, began working with Hong Kong businesses to establish factories. With reduced transport time, Hong Kong manufacturers looking for new sites saw opportunities in Huizhou. In 1988 construction began on the first portion of the new Guangzhou-Shantou railway passing through Huizhou, and the new superhighway had the potential to reduce the Huizhou–Hong Kong trip to two hours by 1990. Rural counties in Huiyang Prefecture seemed less attractive because they had a less educated labor pool, mostly Hakka and, in two counties, Haifeng and Lufeng, Chaozhou people. The Huizhou populace, on the plains near Guangzhou, were not only closer and better educated but mostly Cantonese-speaking, which made contact with Hong Kong much easier.

Huizhou, while ready to accept some labor-intensive processing plants, began working in the late 1980s to surpass Dongguan in higher-technology manufacturing. Like other regional cities in the province, it had lost educated youth to Guangzhou and Shenzhen. But as the old cultural center of the region, it still had more young people with good educational backgrounds than Dongguan did, and prefectural planners were determined to use these more skilled workers to attract companies in high-technology fields. By 1987 Huizhou had erected one nine-story building, under the sponsorship of the Huiyang Development Company, which housed several high-tech partnerships with companies like Phillips, Shinwa (of Japan), and General Scanning (of the United States), producing goods like car radios, semiconductors, and electrocardiogram machines. In 1988 they expanded to a nearby building, employing five thousand people on the two sites, and the city was developing two additional industrial parks.

In nearby Dongguan, the export-processing plants usually hired junior high school graduates and gave them simple tasks that required virtually no training; in Huizhou, however, high school graduates working for these firms received additional training and supervision, and a few were sent abroad for further instruction. Although in value of production Huizhou could not compare with Dongguan, it could at least make use of its higher educational levels to acquire a leadership position within the prefecture in higher-technology manufacturing. And because it was defined as a promising location, other Hong Kong enterprises were ready to set up plants there by the late 1980s, thus providing further technology and management skills to help it develop.

## Zhaoqing: From River Port to Light Industry

Located 106 kilometers west of Guangzhou on the north bank of the West River, Zhaoqing was second only to Huizhou in profiting from the new activity in the Pearl River Delta. In 1986 Zhaoqing Prefecture, including the city proper and its ten counties, had a population of 2,934,000. The city's residents numbered 194,000, of which 42,000 were farm and 152,000 were nonfarm population.[7] Close to the industrializing counties of the Inner Delta and with new transport links to Guangzhou and Hong Kong, Zhaoqing City began to alter its identity from a river port known chiefly for transporting agricultural supplies and commodities to a city with diversified industry and modern transport links to the outside world.

The West River, by far the broadest and deepest river in Guangdong, carries far more freight than the North and East rivers. It runs from beyond Wuzhou on the Guangxi side of the border through the length of Zhaoqing Prefecture, down to Sanshui, where it joins the North and Sui rivers, and on down to the South China Sea. Throughout history the West River has been the great and busy pathway through the western part of the province, and this remained true in modern times although road paving in the area began in the 1950s.[8] In the late 1980s the Zhaoqing harbor still took ships of up to a thousand tons; they could go east to Guangzhou and the sea. Of the sixteen ports on the river, the only other port that could handle vessels of this size was Liudu, which serviced the mines at Yunfu, twenty kilometers to the south. Ships of five hundred tons could go all the way up the river to Wuzhou any month of the year, and the river was passable into Guangxi Province, at least as far as Nanning. Roads west to Wuzhou were still not in good condition, and the river remained the major means for transporting bulk commodities like iron ore, stone, and construction materials.

In the 1980s bridges, roads, and railroads transformed Zhaoqing's accessibility to the Delta area and even to the West. Although Zhaoqing had been a major river port and a county or prefectural capital since A.D. 111, it was not until May 1987 that a bridge spanned the river there, linking the city for the first time by road to the southern and southwestern portions of the prefecture, especially Yunfu and Luoding counties. The railroad west from Sanshui through Zhaoqing and Yunfu to Yaogu was opened by 1987, and when double tracking to the north was completed in 1988, goods could flow easily to Guangzhou and the north by train. It was to be at best 1990 before the railway to Maoming was completed, linking Zhaoqing by rail with southwestern China.

In the mid-1980s the completion of the bridge at Sanshui that ended the need for ferries on the road to Guangzhou, the new railroad link to Sanshui, and new five-hour hydrofoil service to Hong Kong were a great stimulus to industrial development. Expansion from Hong Kong did not affect Zhaoqing as quickly as it did Huizhou because Hong Kong was, in the late 1980s, three hours closer to Huizhou by motor vehicle, but Zhaoqing was close behind.

On the eve of reforms, Zhaoqing had very little industry. Until 1961 it had been only the county capital of Gaoyao County, under Jiangmen Prefecture, but in that year it was separated from the county to become a prefectural capital. As in Huiyang, the prefectural capital was located toward the end of the prefecture closest to Guangzhou, in order to provide easy access to Guangzhou and to enable cadres from the counties to stop at prefectural headquarters on the way to or from Guangzhou. As a prefectural capital, Zhaoqing's administrative infrastructure expanded, and supporting services followed. Zhaoqing had gained its new status, however, in the period of retrenchment from the Great Leap Forward, followed by the Cultural Revolution, and it therefore had no opportunity to develop a significant industrial base until reforms began. Up to that time its industry was essentially like a county town's, servicing agriculture by producing fertilizer, cement, and agricultural implements. Although Zhaoqing was important as a trading center for lumber products from its mountain counties and in guiding the development of Asia's largest sulphur iron ore deposits, the prefectural resources had not provided it an industrial base. The same was true for the marble being mined in Yunfu.

Although industrial investment in several counties, particularly Guangning, Luoding, and Yunan, aided the growth of Zhaoqing City in the late 1980s, those were far less important than the new links with the Inner Delta and Hong Kong. From 1980 to 1987 Zhaoqing had an annual industrial growth of 21 percent, compared to the provincial average of 16 percent. In 1980 Zhaoqing Prefecture's industrial production was valued at 160 million yuan, and by 1987 it surpassed 600 million yuan. Factories produced goods as diverse as beer (Dinghu Beer, a joint venture with Pabst Blue Ribbon), ink slabs for calligraphy, and electronic instruments. With nearby rich agricultural land, food processing developed rapidly. The greatest growth, however, was in machinery, electronics, textiles, and bicycles, and rapid increases in the production of communication equipment were expected. Unlike the Delta area, where collectives played the major role and small communities bubbled with entrepreneurial activity, in

Zhaoqing the advance was overwhelmingly in the state sector. By the end of the decade, however, more collective activity began to blossom as Zhaoqing began to copy Foshan, two hours to the east.

In preparation for the 1987 opening of the Zhaoqing station on the Sanshui-Maoming rail line, Zhaoqing set aside several hundred mou of land for an industrial development zone that would take advantage of its new links with Guangzhou, the Inner Delta, and Hong Kong. As labor rates in the Inner Delta began rising in the late 1980s, Zhaoqing and its counties were just beginning to attract processing contracts from Hong Kong by offering them lower wage rates.

Located further inland, with less overcrowding than the Delta counties, Zhaoqing had sent few emigrants to Hong Kong or overseas. But Zhaoqing had always been thoroughly a part of Cantonese culture, and it had the good luck to be the most popular site in all of Guangdong for Hong Kong tourists. The Seven Star Park (Qixingyuan), with seven striking mountain crags jutting up from an attractive lake in the middle of the city, reminded visitors of the more famous beauty spot of Guilin (Guangxi), and they flocked in daily by the bus, boat, and train load after the province reopened to the outside. As one Zhaoqing official concerned with joint ventures said, "We have almost daily contact with people coming from Hong Kong for vacations and thus have up-to-date information." It was not only the physical closeness to Hong Kong but the daily contact over a number of years with so many people from the Hong Kong area that enabled Zhaoqing to be in better touch with world markets, world technology, world fashion, and outside thinking than other localities equally close. As Hong Kong businesses began expanding their operations outside the Inner Delta in the late 1980s, Zhaoqing thus began very rapid growth and was poised to take further advantage of its opportunities.

## Shaoguan: The Burden of Heavy Industry

Located in northern Guangdong where the North River is formed, Shaoguan City was only a small town until World War II and then grew rapidly in the 1950s and 1960s. Four to five hours north of Guangzhou, it is nestled in a river valley, along which run the north-south rail lines and roadways. The surrounding mountains, although all under two thousand meters, have limey soil of low fertility. Three of Shaoguan's twelve counties are especially rocky and in the 1980s contained 100,000 Yao and substantial numbers of other minorities;[9]

otherwise the mountain villages are populated mostly by Hakka people. In 1986, Shaoguan City had a population of 372,000, and Shaoguan Metropolitan Region (until 1983, Prefecture), including the twelve counties, had 4,395,000.[10]

From 1937, when it fled from the Japanese, until 1945, the Guangdong government was located in the mountainous areas of Shaoguan. For a brief time the main offices were located in what became Shaoguan City, but for most of the period they were located in Lian County, a remote spot in the northwestern part of the prefecture, then already a model Kuomintang county, which even in the late 1980s still took seven hours to reach by car from Shaoguan. Many from the Pearl River Delta who depended on commerce or the government for their livelihood, or who wanted to educate their children free of Japanese domination, also fled to Shaoguan, Lian County, and surrounding areas. The Japanese tried to keep control of the north-south railway that passed through Shaoguan, but they considered Lian too remote to bother attacking.

Shaoguan thus grew suddenly during the war from a small town of scarcely ten thousand to a small city with a population of over fifty thousand. Those who moved in were largely Cantonese speakers from the Delta area. Some brought administrative expertise and higher education; others brought commercial skills that Shaoguan had previously lacked. Although most government officials returned to Guangzhou after 1945, some families from the Delta area remained and some single men married local women. Shaoguan City, though in a largely Hakka region, became a Cantonese outpost. After 1949 other outsiders, both northerners and Cantonese, were sent in, especially in the early 1950s when the city became the capital of Shaoguan Prefecture.

In 1949, this area had very little industry, and even at the end of the first five-year plan, in 1957, 64 percent of the prefecture's industry was in lumber and foodstuffs. As part of the Great Leap Forward, Dabaoshan, a large mountain just south of Shaoguan City, known for centuries to contain lead, zinc, and iron ore but little explored, was opened in 1958 for mining. That same year the Shaoguan Iron and Steel Plant, a "backyard steel plant," was built in Maba, a town twenty kilometers south of Shaoguan. Shaoguan zinc- and lead-refining facilities became among the most important in China. There were also three major coal mines (Quhua, Nanling, and Meitian) in the vicinity that also expanded, although it turned out that the quality of their coal was not high enough for producing steel.

Guangdong's key industries in the exposed Inner Delta that were moved in the late 1960s to the "little third front" within the province were primarily placed in Shaoguan.[11] Industrial electronics and military factories were moved to Lian County, heavy industry to Shaoguan and Maba. The Iron and Steel Plant, closed in 1962 after the Leap, was expanded and reopened in 1966, and machinery factories gradually opened nearby. From 1963 through 1970 heavy industry in Shaoguan Prefecture grew more than 20 percent per year and continued growing at an average annual rate of 14 percent from 1971 to 1975. By 1970 for the province as a whole, heavy industry formed about 40 percent of the industrial total; in Shaoguan Prefecture it represented 69 percent of the total.[12]

After 1979 officials tried to reduce the financial losses that had plagued so many of the third-front industries. Over ten area factories, far from supplies and markets and deeply in debt, were moved elsewhere. Some were shifted from remote rural areas like Lian County to Shaoguan City and elsewhere, and some went to Shenzhen, Foshan, and other locations in the Inner Delta. Others were consolidated. With some freedom to work where they chose, some of the technical talent that had been sent to Shaoguan for the third front flowed back to the Inner Delta and northern cities.

The effort to readjust these enterprises posed difficult issues. The six steel plants in Shaoguan were all deeply in debt. The biggest, the Iron and Steel Plant, had a cumulative deficit of 148 million yuan by 1979, almost as much as the 190 million invested in the plant. In 1979 a new management team was promoted from within, and in 1981 the other five steel plants, including four thousand workers, were amalgamated into it. The plant was given a three-year grace period in which to become profitable. It succeeded in this, in part because it was allowed to sell much of its product off state plan at higher prices. The most controversial aspect of the amalgamation was the inclusion of a specialty steel plant that had a very high technical level and a high esprit de corps. Incorporating the talented engineers from the specialty steel plant helped raise the level of expertise and the profitability of the Iron and Steel Plant, but it also eliminated all capacity to produce high-quality specialty steel within the province. Although the pressure to eliminate losses and adapt to market conditions was very strong, the need for specialty steel remained. In 1988, with the help of a factory in Heilongjiang, Shaoguan planned to establish a new, updated plant to produce specialty steel.

Despite readjustment and the province's overall plan to develop more light industry, Guangdong leaders decided that Shaoguan would remain a heavy industry center. Shaoguan suffered from its priority, which received relatively little new funding. From 1981 to 1985, with 6.9 percent of the province's population and 5.2 percent of its industrial output,[13] Shaoguan received only 3.7 percent of the province's investment. In the 1980s it still had the highest industrial product of the prefectural capitals except Maoming, which had a petrochemical complex. The costs of modernizing heavy industry in Shaoguan, moreover, were far beyond what the province could hope to finance in the foreseeable future.

Shaoguan officials recognized that light industry had faster growth potential and in the new era of greater local autonomy, local officials there as elsewhere tried to use locally generated funds and bank loans to develop the high-growth light industry areas of textiles and electronics. In the late 1980s, though considerably behind the Delta and even behind Huizhou and Zhaoqing, Shaoguan made a start in light industry.

Despite its problems, the Shaoguan Metropolitan Region moved ahead with new construction, market growth, and improvement in the local standard of living. Even without additional provincial funds, the region was able, because of the overall reforms and its own technical base in heavy industry, to expand into light industry. The railway trunk lines were used to send goods between Shaoguan and the north as well as the Inner Delta, and double tracking to the north and the new highways from Shaoguan to the north were expected to stimulate the Shaoguan economy. Although few people from Shaoguan had migrated to Hong Kong or overseas, Shaoguan had many cultural and personal links with the Cantonese in the Inner Delta dating from World War II and the third front migration, which facilitated the flow of information and trade. Shaoguan lagged behind the Delta area, but by ordinary standards it enjoyed a very substantial growth, thanks primarily to its own efforts to use its capital and technical talent from heavy industry in new, more dynamic sectors that required less investment.

## *Maoming: Marketing Byproducts of the Oil Refinery*

In 1983 Maoming became a metropolitan region (prefecture-level) capital when Zhanjiang Prefecture was split into two. From imperial and Republican times until the Communist period, the capital of the prefecture had been in Gaozhou County, just north of Maoming on the Jian River. Between 1949 and the early 1980s, however, three of Guangdong's prefectural capitals were relocated in response to economic factors: to Shantou and Haikou because of the growth of their ports, and to Maoming because of the growth of its large new petrochemical complex. Each had become the natural economic center of its region. When Maoming was first made a city in 1958, the total value of its annual industrial production was only 6 million yuan. By 1986, it was 1,863 million yuan,[14] and the city had a population of 450,000, of which 310,000 was rural and 140,000 urban. Maoming Metropolitan Region, including four counties, had a population of 4,650,000.[15]

Maoming was still a small town in 1955 when officials decided to mine the abundant local shale and produce oil from it. A large refinery was then built, and young petroleum engineers and managers were sent in from Beijing, Dalian, and elsewhere. Shale oil proved so expensive to produce that it was eventually decided not to mine it in large quantity. But because the oil-refining facility had already been established by then and had become the major refining facility in South China, it continued to grow, even during the Cultural Revolution, except for a brief respite during the retrenchment of the early 1960s. Its output grew more rapidly after the reforms, and by 1987 of the six million tons of petroleum refined in Maoming, only about 2 percent came from local shale; the rest was refined from crude oil brought mostly from elsewhere in China.

With the oil refining, a larger complex developed. A seventy-kilometer pipeline stretched from Maoming to the port of Zhanjiang, where the refined oil was shipped to Guangzhou and elsewhere. A railroad feeder was built from Maoming to Hechun, just north of Zhanjiang, linking Maoming to the railway from Zhanjiang to Guangxi and Southwest China.

The Maoming refinery, like other central government facilities at the mines of Shilu and Dabaoshan or the port of Basuo, established its own integrated community, not unlike an American military base. Beijing felt that personnel coming from afar needed their own housing, dining halls, restaurants, guest houses, schools and nurseries, movie houses, hospitals, bank branches, stores, and other services. Although most workers were recruited within the county, the large refining complex was in effect a separate political, economic, and social island within Maoming, directly under the central government.

Maoming City was laid out in the late 1950s by city planners with the cooperation of the central government. It was an integrated planned community, a more modest and cheaper precursor to Shenzhen, with wide boulevards, separated bicycle lanes, and greenery. In many cities officials had found it difficult to prevent local people from building their own facilities even when not in accord with the overall plan, but Maoming officials maintained tight control. Although pollution had not yet become a large issue when Maoming City was planned, living near oil refineries was already considered unpleasant, and the housing was therefore located across the river and at some distance from the industrial areas. By the standards of the 1980s the facilities built in the 1950s and 1960s seemed simple and rapidly aging, but compared to most cities in Guangdong, Maoming had very little run-down housing.

When, as part of the reforms after 1978, bureaus of the municipal government were made into integrated "controlling companies" *(zong gongsi),* turning the factories they had formerly supervised into their subsidiaries, they naturally turned their efforts toward their comparative advantage, the possible uses for byproducts of the oil company (Shiyu Gongsi). The Maoming Carbon Product Factory, already established in 1971, became such a subsidiary and by 1987, with almost seven hundred employees, was selling 80 percent of its product off plan, on the market. It had one basic product that had two uses in steel plants: to increase the temperature of the oven, and to mix steel to produce a desired consistency. Other plants used byproducts of oil refining to manufacture fertilizer, synthetic fibers, and other chemical products. Although the oil refinery remained a high-status separate central government island, it cooperated with Maoming officials to facilitate the use of its byproducts by local industry.

The rural hinterland in Maoming Metropolitan Region was below the provincial average in productivity. The northern part of the prefecture is hilly and mountainous, and the southern part sandy and subject to flooding. Until the late 1950s farming was often hampered by a shortage of water, but the Great Leap Forward, which stressed irrigation projects, made more of a contribution to Maoming than to many other areas. Crops adapted to the sandy soil, such as peanuts, cassava, and potatoes, had long played a larger role than in the more fertile parts of the province and were expanded with better irrigation and drainage.

After reforms, Maoming and Zhanjiang farmers, for whom the

urban markets of Hong Kong, Shenzhen, Macau, Zhuhai, and Guang-zhou were far away, had trouble, given the transportation problems of the day, breaking into the markets for fresh fish and fowl that Delta farmers found so lucrative. But improved transport and the expanding geographical scale of markets opened up another opportunity in the mid-1980s. Refrigeration was not yet widespread, and in the winter the lack of fresh vegetables and fruit was a serious problem in northern China. With the railway from Zhanjiang and the feeder line from Maoming, however, the farmers of semitropical Maoming and Zhan-jiang prefectures could send their fresh vegetables north by train. It often took three or four days for goods to be transported, and the farmers therefore produced eggplant, green peppers, squash, cucum-bers, and similar crops, which did not spoil easily. Those who had expanded their banana groves in response to high prices found that by the time their new trees had matured competition had lowered the local price of bananas, and they too therefore sought out northern markets.

Except in the very hottest season, when spoilage occurred too quickly, local communities arranged for trucks to collect the produce and carry it to the Maoming station, and contracted with northern cities, like Tianjin and Beijing, to handle the distribution once the produce arrived. Refrigerated cars were just beginning to be used as well, and venturesome local businesspeople and farmers began plotting how other vegetables like tomatoes might, if they could be kept cool en route, be profitably supplied to the north.

The semitropical climate was also suitable for producing rubber, and state farms had been established in Maoming and Zhanjiang in the 1950s to respond to national needs. After 1979 the state farms gradually revived rubber trees damaged by the Cultural Revolution but did not greatly expand the area cultivated (see Chapter 9). The effort of the state to acquire sugar by price incentives as well as by quotas, however, led to the rapid expansion of sugar crops in the Maoming and Zhanjiang areas. Until the 1970s sugar had been grown mostly in Delta counties like Panyu, Shunde, and Zhongshan, but with the advent of other ways to make money there, some farmers moved out of sugar. Maoming Metropolitan Region farmers helped fill this gap. Although it had virtually no base in sugar cane before reforms, in the 1980s sugar production in Maoming and Zhanjiang grew much more rapidly than in the Delta. Part of this increase may be attributed to Lin Ruo, then first secretary of Zhanjiang Prefecture's

Party Committee, who promoted sugar growing and helped with technology transfer from the Delta, but the price also proved attractive to Maoming and Zhanjiang farmers, who did not have the Delta's more rewarding alternative opportunities.

Maoming agriculture lagged one step behind Zhaoqing and Huizhou, and community industry in the late 1980s had not yet taken off. Industry making use of Maoming refinery products had prospered, but compared to Huizhou, Zhaoqing, and Shaoguan, Maoming was not yet affected by the dynamism of the Inner Delta. It still took twelve hours by truck to Guangzhou, and transport costs were still high. Nevertheless, even Maoming was affected by the growing markets elsewhere.

## Zhanjiang: Ocean Port and Gateway to the Southwest

Zhanjiang City, located in the southwestern corner of the province, has the finest natural harbor on Guangdong's long coast. Several islands protect the harbor from storms, and a long inlet, with a ninety-seven-kilometer coastline, could by the late 1980s accommodate ships of fifty thousand tons and with further construction could service still larger ones.

Until the Great Leap Forward, Zhanjiang Prefecture included four counties that were then handed over to Guangxi Province. This left Zhanjiang City with eleven counties, still too many for it to serve as an engine for county industrial development. In 1983 the prefecture's two eastern counties, Yangjiang and Yangchun, were assigned to Jiangmen Metropolitan Region. Four counties were incorporated into the newly created Maoming Metropolitan Region and the other five counties, three of which were in the Leizhou Peninsula, stretching down toward Hainan, were retained as Zhanjiang Metropolitan Region. In 1984, as Zhanjiang's port facilities progressed, it was named an open city, able to receive foreign investment. As the key port for southwestern China, for linking Hainan Island to the mainland, and for Maoming oil, and as a base for oil exploration, naval operations, and potentially for a major modern steel complex, it seemed poised to become an important regional center. Zhanjiang City proper had 947,000 people in 1986, 596,000 rural and 352,000 urban. The metropolitan region had 4,868,000.

Zhanjiang City is stretched along the west bank of the inlet, with potential for growth along much of the rest of its ninety-seven-kilometer coastline. Until 1984, the city's settlement had been primarily in two parts, separated by a hilly, relatively unsettled area with poor soil that covered about twenty-five square kilometers. Government offices had been built in the northern section, Chikan, in the 1950s, and the major port facilities were located in the southern section, Xiashan, where the old French port, a stopover point on the way to Vietnam, had been located in the latter part of the nineteenth century. The French had done relatively little development before being driven out by the Japanese in World War II, and by the mid-1980s there were virtually no remnants of their settlement other than a church, which was eventually reopened. Almost no one in Zhanjiang spoke French or was familiar with French culture, cuisine, or business. This was unlike northeastern China, where even in the 1980s many were still able to speak Japanese, learned under Japanese rule.

Only Beihai, in Guangxi, to the west of Leizhou Peninsula, was a competitor to Zhanjiang as a port serving China's southwestern provinces (Yunnan, Guizhou, Guangxi, and Sichuan), with a population in the late 1980s of two hundred million. Beihai, however, was smaller and its port facilities less adequate. In the mid-1980s Zhanjiang Port had three major terminals, rebuilt in stages that ran almost continuously for thirty years from the mid-1950s. The crude oil for Maoming entered through Zhanjiang, and the refined petroleum and other products came out through Zhanjiang. Guangxi's coal, timber, and nonmetallic ore came by rail to Zhanjiang for transport elsewhere in the province. In 1986, 50 percent of the port's cargo was oil, 14 percent iron ore, 9 percent nonmetallic ore, 6 percent bulk fertilizer, 6 percent coal, 5 percent steel, 4 percent grain, and 6 percent miscellaneous.[16]

Semitropical Leizhou Peninsula, just west of Zhanjiang City, produced rubber and sugar and had considerable potential for other tropical crops. As noted above, although rubber was produced almost entirely on state farms, Zhanjiang farmers, along with those in Maoming, were willing to produce sugar at state procurement prices when Delta growers became less interested. In 1986 Zhanjiang produced 4.4 million tons of sugar cane, far more than any other prefectural unit. It also produced oranges, bananas, and pineapples in considerable quantity and, lacking a large market beyond Zhanjiang City, shipped many fruits and vegetables to the north. With its Maritime Products College (Shuichan Xueyuan), one of four such institutes in the country, Zhanjiang was a longtime leader in the fishing industry, fish breeding, maritime products, and food processing. Its long coastal area was suitable for ocean fishing, and in the late 1980s it greatly expanded the cultivation of more profitable shrimp and shellfish.

Industry had been largely centered on food processing, including canning, and on textiles until the early 1980s. Although industrial growth increased rapidly in the 1980s, in 1986 the industrial production of the entire prefecture, including the city and its five counties, was roughly similar to that of one of the five leading counties in the Delta area, despite the excellence of Zhanjiang's natural harbor and its port facilities. One company, the Household Electric Appliances Corporation, famous for electric rice cookers and refrigerators, expanded quickly and by the late 1980s was by itself producing over one-fourth of the city's entire industrial output; it will be discussed in Chapter 10.

When plans were made for the expansion of oil exploration in the South China Sea in 1973, the China National Offshore Oil Corporation (CNOOC) split the territory into two parts, one to be explored by the Nanhai East Oil Corporation and the other by the Nanhai West Oil Corporation. When cooperation with foreign oil companies and oil exploration began in earnest, Nanhai East established offices in Guangzhou and set up oil exploration bases in Shenzhen and Zhuhai. Nanhai West established its offices and exploration base in Zhanjiang. Like other large central government facilities, it developed its own facilities and grew rapidly. By 1986 it had over ten thousand white-collar staff and workers, including facilities for foreign specialists and foreign companies that used the base for their oil exploration. Until 1983 hopes ran very high, but as the price of oil fell and the early exploratory efforts turned up less promising prospects than had been hoped for, optimism was tempered and some foreign investors gave up. Although Nanhai West had developed very modern facilities by the late 1980s, it had had little impact on the local economy at that point.[17]

In 1984, when Beijing announced that fourteen coastal cities, in addition to the special economic zones, would be opened for foreign investment, two were in Guangdong: Guangzhou and Zhanjiang. Although Zhanjiang's industry then lagged behind most of the others, it was included because of its potential importance. The city, prepared for the news, moved quickly to level the barren area between its two halves, and built a 7.4-kilometer modern road linking them. Like Guangzhou's Huangpu zone, developed near Huangpu Port about the same time, Zhanjiang's was called an "economic and technological development zone" and was to concentrate on technology and man-ufacturing, not on tourism and commerce. It established a number of factories that used local raw materials: carpets and wallpaper were made from hemp, plastic hose from rubber, and processed food from local crops. In addition, plans were made to attract export-processing factories linked with Hong Kong and to establish textile, apparel, electronics, and other factories. Hong Kong was still not immediately accessible; the trip by passenger boat took sixteen hours in the late 1980s.

The decision in 1987 to make Hainan Island into a separate province and to develop it rapidly promised to have a major impact on Zhan-jiang, which would eventually serve as an important way station and service center between Hainan and the mainland. A tiny port at the southern end of Leizhou Peninsula, Haian, only twenty kilometers from Haikou, was to be expanded, and plans called for the extension of the rail lines from Zhanjiang to Haian. Zhanjiang, however, was likely to remain the major port and to grow in importance as Hainan developed. Zhanjiang's future in the 1990s and beyond depended, of course, on how much oil might be discovered and whether higher-level officials decided to go ahead with plans for building one of China's largest modern steel plants.

Despite these developments, the fact that Zhanjiang was still behind Huizhou and Zhaoqing in industrial development in the late 1980s illustrated how critical Hong Kong had been in the short term for the development of the other areas. Yet many believed that as Hainan and southwestern China grew, Zhanjiang had the potential to become a major port and industrial city, surpassing these smaller cities nearer the Inner Delta.

## Shantou: The Slow Revival of a Major Commercial Port

Located along the coast in the northeast corner of Guangdong, where the Han River flows into the Taiwan Straits, Shantou (Swatow) Met-ropolitan Region was among the poorest in the province in the first reform decade. With a population in 1986 of 9,307,000, it was by far the most crowded prefecture in Guangdong, with an average of nine hundred people per square kilometer. It had almost 1 percent of the nation's population in 0.1 percent of the nation's area. Shantou City proper in 1986 had 774,000 residents, of whom 500,000 were not engaged in agriculture.

As noted in Chapter 4, Shantou experienced rapid growth in the twentieth century as a port and commercial center and by the 1930s was second only to Guangzhou in the province. After 1950, however, leaders were concerned about infiltration and attack from Taiwan, directly across the straits, and Shantou suffered from being sealed far more tightly against outside contact than the Pearl River Delta was.

For over a thousand years, until 1945, the capital of the prefecture, with its own government offices and examination halls, was Chaozhou. The "Chaozhou people," as they are still known, developed their own cuisine, opera, and dialect, and a reputation not only for feistiness and clannishness but also for producing many talented officials and fiercely loyal émigrés, many of whom had become successful Southeast Asian businesspeople. When the Communists came to power, they recognized that the port of Shantou had far outpaced Chaozhou City as the prefecture's economic and transport center and therefore made it their prefectural capital. Many of Chaozhou City's talented young people found their way to Shantou and elsewhere; the Shantou Metropolitan Region (formerly Prefecture) as a whole produced an unusually large number of high-level cadres.

Although Shantou had been primarily a commercial center before World War II, it had some industry as well, particularly in ceramics, embroidery, and needlework. The ordinary textile industry had continued after 1949, but embroidery and needlework, considered bourgeois, were curtailed. During the 1960s and 1970s some industry from Shantou was moved inland as part of the third front effort, to Liannan County in Shaoguan and elsewhere. Shantou, separated from Hong Kong by four hundred kilometers, was after 1950 very isolated from outside developments. As mentioned in connection with the Shantou SEZ, even before the twentieth century Shantou had developed a reputation as a good rice-producing area and a leading center for agricultural research. Although its rice yields were not quite up to Taiwan's levels after 1949, they were consistently the highest in the province, and Shantou agriculture became the favorite model for other areas to study. Because it was too distant from Hong Kong, Shantou could not sell economic crops to the outside and its agriculture therefore centered on rice and its well-known variety of mandarin oranges.

Until the late 1980s transport from Hong Kong was too difficult to make export processing a promising option. After several port facilities at Shantou were remodeled in the mid-1980s to accommodate ships of up to ten thousand tons and after the airport was opened in 1986 for flights to Hong Kong, Bangkok, and Singapore, Shantou, far behind the Pearl River Delta, slowly began to resume its trade with the outside world.

Hopeful local officials found that those of Chaozhou heritage in Hong Kong and Southeast Asia were too far away to develop the rapid and intimate contacts that linked Hong Kong and the Pearl River Delta. In addition, Chaozhou people who did well abroad were more often in banking than in industry, and thus Shantou received some help in finance from overseas Chinese in the 1980s but very little industrial investment. It happened that one of the two richest people in Hong Kong in the 1980s, Li Ka-shing, was from the Shantou Metropolitan Region, and in the 1980s he gave Shantou over three hundred million yuan to build the most modern university in Guangdong and contributed toward a bridge, a hospital, and the remodeling of an ancient Chaozhou temple. His contribution, more like that of other overseas Chinese than that of the small labor-intensive Hong Kong merchant, was very welcome, but it had little impact on the immediate development of the area.

Because of its remoteness from the outside world, poor transportation infrastructure, lack of electric power, and caution about using loans for financing investment, Shantou did not really begin industrial investment until 1983. Some of its growth after that lay in the revival of traditional industries. With contacts in Hong Kong, Shantou companies were particularly successful in adapting their traditional sewing techniques to produce beaded dresses, and they made excellent use of nearby rural communities, each with its own subspecialty, to renew their ceramics industry. They also began to expand in new areas like plastics, electronics, and magnetic tapes. Shantou hoped to tempt some well-trained scientific and technical people who had gone elsewhere to return to work in their native area. When Taiwan businesspeople were allowed to resume direct contact with China in late 1987, Shantou hoped that as the closest spot in Guangdong to Taiwan and with a local dialect related to the Taiwan dialect, within a few years it might receive a great stimulus in trade, investment, and technology.

By the late 1980s Shantou had broken into some sectors that required a high level of technology, particularly in ultrasound, including medical applications, and in photo materials. In both these areas the city enjoyed the support of officials in Guangzhou who regarded Shantou as the provincial champion in these areas. When the Shantou Photo Material Industry Corporation, already making black-and-white film, lost out in competition with a Fujian firm for national support to acquire equipment needed for a joint venture producing color film with Kodak, Guangdong Province decided to provide the necessary funds to allow the Shantou firm to enter a similar venture with Fuji Film. The Shantou firm moved rapidly to prepare to compete with the Fujian firm for national markets.

Unlike Shaoguan and Maoming, which were strong in heavy industry, Shantou's development in the 1980s was overwhelmingly in light industry. The ratio of light to heavy industry for the province as a whole varied in this period from about 60:40 to 70:30, but in Shantou the ratio was 80:20. Despite its commercial history, Shantou in the 1980s thus fell far behind Zhaoqing and Huizhou, capitals with far less commercial history but a step ahead of Shantou because of their closeness to the Delta. It was the one major area of Guangdong that even at the end of the first reform decade had not yet gained back its 1930s level. With its talent pool and proximity to Taiwan, however, Shantou had retained its potential for rapid growth and development of high technology, which was just beginning at the end of the decade.

## Meixian: Mountain Home of the Hakka

Meixian Metropolitan Region (until 1988, Prefecture) had long been and in the first reform decade remained by far the poorest area in continental Guangdong. The average annual per capita income in 1985 in Meixian Prefecture was 401 yuan; in Shantou Metropolitan Region, the second-poorest prefecture, it was 458 yuan. Three of the four poorest counties in the province (Wuhua, Fengshun, and Dapu) were in Meixian, and Meixian City itself, with an average income of 588 yuan per capita, was still by far the poorest of the prefectural capitals.[18] All six counties in the prefecture were largely mountainous, with very poor soil, and yet they were very crowded. In 1986 this prefecture, with only sixteen thousand square kilometers, had a population of 4,043,000. Meixian City (Meixian means "Mei County," and until 1983 Meixian City was a county) had a nonagricultural core of 174,000 people, although the city administrative boundaries included 575,000 rural people, a total of 749,000.[19]

Although the standard of living improved during the 1980s as markets opened and per capita grain rations rose above minimum food requirements, living conditions remained spartan. The light bulbs in street lights were small and the lights were far apart, as had been the case in other cities ten or fifteen years earlier. To buy a bicycle a typical family had to save for more months than elsewhere. Few could afford to go to the movies, let alone buy a television. Meixian residents ate more roots and leaves and less meat than people elsewhere. There were no towels for sale, because people used old clothes for towels. All other prefectural capitals by the late 1980s had at least one modern hotel; Meixian had none.

Hakka people, unlike the Chaozhou, have not in modern times been linked to one locality. Meixian, however, is the closest that they have to a homeland. Although physically indistinct from other Han peoples, the Hakka were a persecuted minority from northern China who escaped to the south in a series of migrations beginning in the Song Dynasty. Hakka (in Mandarin "kejia") means "guest people," that is, late arrivals to a locality. Since much of the plains was already occupied when they arrived, they settled mostly in the mountainous areas of Guangdong and neighboring provinces. They were looking for a haven safe from attack and in isolated, mountainous Meixian, they found it.

In the 1980s Meixian's county capitals were connected by paved roads, and a small antiquated railway ran from Meixian to Longchuan, but it remained the most remote of the prefectures. Many villages were unconnected by paved roads in the late 1980s, and Guangzhou was twelve hours from Meixian by car. The airport in Meixian was opened in October 1987, with a daily flight to and from Guangzhou. Meixian's links to Hakka elsewhere in China and overseas, nevertheless, gave it a certain cosmopolitan perspective.

Since the nineteenth century, when Meixian was already too crowded, success meant leaving. Meixian was the one inland area in Guangdong that sent out migrants continuously, to the United States, to Southeast Asia, and after 1949 to Hainan Island, to the army, to Shenzhen, and elsewhere in China. In the 1980s an estimated 1.8 million migrants overseas—more than twice the current population of Meixian City—could trace their ancestry to the prefecture. As mobility was proscribed in the 1960s and 1970s, population pressure became even tighter.

In contrast to the Inner Delta, overseas Chinese relatives had by the late 1980s not yet played an important role in the economic development of Meixian. Successful Hakka became soldiers, public officials, and teachers. Even before 1949 there was little local business activity, and few who left became wealthy entrepreneurs or bankers, and even for those who did go into business elsewhere, Meixian was far inland, making it difficult to visit. Few made the trip until air service was inaugurated. Moreover, the dilemma of the overseas businessperson was even more acute for those from Meixian. If overseas investors made money, they were seen as taking advantage of their homeland. If they did not, there was no sound business reason to invest, and a gift was a more effective way to gain local honor and appreciation. Hence Meixian emigrants who did invest in Meixian contributed to schools and public works. Indeed, the most successful venture in Meixian by an emigrant, Zeng Xuanze, owner of Gold Lion, Hong Kong's largest tie manufacturing company, brought many jobs to Meixian, but Zeng turned over all of his locally earned profits to Meixian.

Even after several generations overseas, most Hakka have kept their native dialect, which is closer to Mandarin than to Cantonese. With few distinctive beliefs or practices and little common culture, they are perhaps less an ethnic group than a category of people who at one point in history lived in mountainous areas. Hakka women never had bound feet and more commonly worked in the fields, men were more likely to become soldiers, and some Hakka had unique religious practices. But their folklore and family life were almost indistinguishable from that of other Han Chinese. Relations between Hakka in various places have been cordial but not intimate, with no special feelings of solidarity. Despite its respect for learning, Meixian had not developed research institutes by the late 1980s, and there were few books on Hakka history. The only real object of fierce loyalty in Meixian was their local soccer team, which youth participated in with passion and discipline. Hakka consider themselves able to endure difficulties, a quality that helped them adapt to their poor surroundings but also constrained their desire for change.

Hakka take pride in education, which had been almost the sole way out of their circumstances. Their top high school, Dongshan, the only nationally designated high school in the province, was recognized as one of the handful of best schools in the province. Although some prefectures had not yet established universities, Meixian, despite its poverty, upgraded a teachers' college into Jiaying University in 1985. But education remained even at the end of the decade more traditional in spirit, oriented toward passing examinations and toward classical subjects. Developmental opportunities in the first decade of reforms seemed to young people too limited to make it worthwhile to study applied subjects; few studied commerce, industry, or agriculture. Those who passed the examinations saw no reason to return to Meixian. In the late 1980s approximately 2,500 youths from the prefecture passed examinations to outside universities each year, but only about 100 a year returned after graduation. Some, not able to make the grade, became small businesspeople by default, but the locality was too poor to spawn prosperous entrepreneurs or financiers. In the late 1980s, the governor of Guangdong, Ye Xuanping, son of Marshal Ye Jianying, the preeminent Guangdong hero, was a Meixian Hakka, and about twenty high officials in Beijing of deputy minister rank or above were of Hakka extraction, an enormous success rate for the people's small numbers. But this achievement did not help Meixian development.

Until 1965 Meixian had been part of Shantou Prefecture, and its economy revolved around the supply of coal and other raw materials for Shantou industry. The total value of industrial production in 1965 was 110 million yuan, about 30 yuan per year of production per capita. Granted its own prefecture just on the eve of the Cultural Revolution, Meixian had little opportunity to develop industry before the reforms of 1979. What industry it had was designed to support agriculture and to provide the beginnings of heavy industry to make use of its coal and other ores. It was believed that Meixian had some promising deposits of coal and iron, but as of the late 1980s they had not yet been fully prospected and the coal did not seem to be of high quality.

Although the net effect of reforms since 1979 was beneficial to Meixian, the expansion of market forces created several new hardships for this backward area. The industries that it had developed in coal, metallurgy, machinery, chemicals, and car parts had all been operating at a loss, and because state enterprises were expected to be self-supporting, Meixian's situation became even more difficult. After the reforms, these industries, particularly coal mining, continued to drain provincial resources. In 1978 heavy industry in Meixian was 14.9 million yuan in the red, and by 1985 this had increased to 39.0 million yuan. Meixian had little money to invest, and the money it had it used mostly to pay for these losses. Its balance sheet began to improve by the late 1980s, but there was still very little local money to invest in either local collective or state enterprises.

Meixian also had problems in its electric power supply. After 1979 provincial officials developed a new financing procedure to increase electric power without taxing provincial funds. Counties made a contribution, and after the new power plants were built, they received a share of electric power according to their investment. Meixian, with few funds and pessimistic about its own growth rate, chose not to participate. In the mid-1980s, when it did begin to grow at a somewhat greater speed, it found itself short of electricity.

Nor did Meixian initially fare well under the new policy of financing by borrowing. When banks considered new issues such as the rate of return on investment, the speed with which money would be turned over, and the risk, Meixian did not appear promising. Local officials, lacking confidence in local markets and in their ability to repay loans, were reluctant to assume the burden of debt.

These problems began to improve slightly in 1984, as the national government adopted a policy of giving special aid to poor mountainous areas. Meixian received more funding for infrastructure, its industries were given preference in borrowing, and by then local officials, more familiar with how loans were used elsewhere, were more willing to apply.

Although parts of Meixian had little rainfall, the Meizhou River flooded about once every ten years. There were severe floods in 1960 and 1970, but the worst flood since 1949 was in July 1986, when the river overflowed its embankments and brought several feet of water to much of Meixian City and serious damage to four counties: Fengshun, Wuhua, Dapu, and Xingning. In the reconstruction process, Meixian City put up two large new bridges (the city had formerly had only one), and a third small supplementary bridge opened in 1987. The embankments along parts of the river were built up, and although much of the province by then had trouble getting laborers to work for just food, clothing, and housing, instead of wages, the need in this case was so obvious that each of the affected counties was able to recruit large numbers of workers, in the style of the Great Leap Forward, to help. With provincial aid, Meixian built some new roads, especially along the river. Although the face of Meixian was changed by these public works projects and they helped to defend against damage, they did little to stimulate the economy. Unfortunately, public funds were used more for erecting public buildings, offices, and cadre apartment buildings and for purchasing vans for city officials rather than for the modernization of industry.

The reforms alone were thus not enough to bring rapid growth to a poor mountainous area, though the new market flexibility and the special policy to assist mountain counties after 1984 did bring some progress. Industrial production between 1978 and 1986 rose from 514 million yuan to 920 million yuan. Meixian still lacked the margin of resources, the confidence, the entrepreneurial spirit, and the transport network it needed in order to grow as rapidly as other parts of the province.

## Prefectural Capitals: From Agriculture to Commerce and Industry

In the late 1980s these prefectural capitals were middle-sized cities with urban populations varying from 120,000 in Huizhou to 500,000 in Shantou. From imperial times, such cities had been used to help provinces collect taxes, keep order, and coordinate other activities in counties that were too numerous and distant for the province to manage directly. After 1949 these cities had expanded their administration in order to play a larger role in rural organization, agricultural development, and public health. They had supervised planning and collective organizations, helped deliver health care to the villages, and supervised schools in the countryside. Despite excesses in the Great Leap Forward, prefectures and counties had helped improve irrigation facilities and had helped develop some simple local industries to aid agricultural development.

After reforms began the prefectural capitals remained administrative cities, but the central issues of administration changed from a static economy centered in agriculture, rice quotas, and collective life to a dynamic one centered in commerce and industry, driven by the market. The prefectures helped guide the development of towns and cities and the introduction of new technology. Prefectural boundaries were redrawn to aid the process, and the position of prefectural Party and government officials concerned with industry was upgraded compared to those concerned with agriculture. The goal of industry was no longer to aid agriculture but to meet market demand, to satisfy consumers, and to increase efficiency and savings in order to pave the way for economic expansion. More officials felt their success would be judged by the growth and profitability of enterprises under their domain. More confidence in growth potential meant that more money was released to build up the infrastructure, including roads, electric power, public buildings, and services in the prefectural capitals.

Educators became more concerned with improving cadre training for their new role and with providing management and technical training to meet the needs of commerce and industry. Prefectural officials, with little prior contact with modern industrial society, looked to provincial leaders for advice and for financial and technical assistance. Those nearer Hong Kong began to look there for new investment, technology, markets, and information, but they often got this second-hand, through the Inner Delta. Most prefectures in the 1980s developed their own trading companies, with offices in Hong Kong under Yuehai (Guangdong Enterprises), to promote prefectural business interests.

By the late 1980s, with the exception of Huiyang Prefecture, where Dongguan's growth was faster than Huizhou's, the prefectural capitals had become the major sites in each prefecture for new investments in industrial plants and equipment. Counties in these areas were too remote to have many direct dealings with Guangzhou and Hong Kong, and they relied on the prefectural capitals for the same services for which the capitals in turn looked to Guangzhou and Hong Kong.

## From Prefecture to Metropolitan Region

The goal of guiding industrial and commercial development was at the heart of the 1988 administrative reorganization, the biggest since reforms began in 1978 (see the accompanying map, which may be compared with the map in the Introduction). Three of the prefectures were further divided to make smaller units that could better manage urban and industrial growth. These divisions paralleled the 1983 splitting of Foshan and Zhanjiang prefectures to establish metropolitan regions. Communist leaders, like imperial officials before them, originally conceived prefectural-level units not as independent units of government but as deputed branches of the province. Officially this remained true until they became metropolitan regions, but in fact their activities had multiplied and they had acquired some de facto independence. In the reorganizations of 1983 and 1988 the new metropolitan regions, which replaced prefectures, officially became an independent level of government. In the 1988 reorganization Hainan was made a separate province and Guangdong, which had fourteen prefectures and one hundred counties, passed on eighteen counties to Hainan. Some of the remaining twelve prefectural-level units were

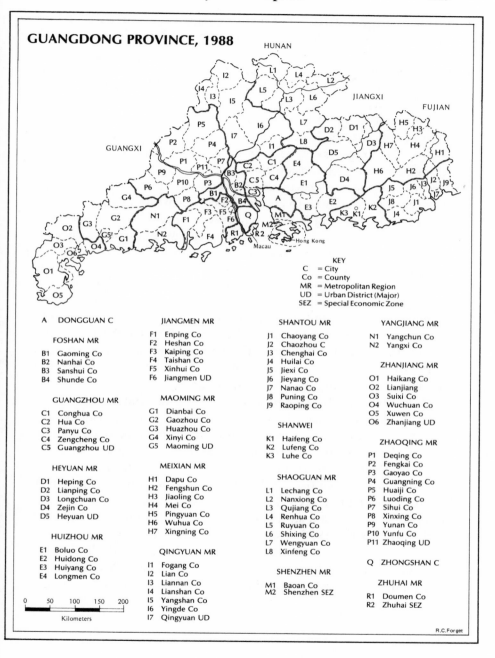

# GUANGDONG PROVINCE, 1988

HUNAN

JIANGXI

FUJIAN

GUANGXI

Hong Kong

Macau

KEY

C = City
Co = County
MR = Metropolitan Region
UD = Urban District (Major)
SEZ = Special Economic Zone

**A    DONGGUAN C**

**FOSHAN MR**

B1  Gaoming Co
B2  Nanhai Co
B3  Sanshui Co
B4  Shunde Co

**GUANGZHOU MR**

C1  Conghua Co
C2  Hua Co
C3  Panyu Co
C4  Zengcheng Co
C5  Guangzhou UD

**HEYUAN MR**

D1  Heping Co
D2  Lianping Co
D3  Longchuan Co
D4  Zejin Co
D5  Heyuan UD

**HUIZHOU MR**

E1  Boluo Co
E2  Huidong Co
E3  Huiyang Co
E4  Longmen Co

**JIANGMEN MR**

F1  Enping Co
F2  Heshan Co
F3  Kaiping Co
F4  Taishan Co
F5  Xinhui Co
F6  Jiangmen UD

**MAOMING MR**

G1  Dianbai Co
G2  Gaozhou Co
G3  Huazhou Co
G4  Xinyi Co
G5  Maoming UD

**MEIXIAN MR**

H1  Dapu Co
H2  Fengshun Co
H3  Jiaoling Co
H4  Mei Co
H5  Pingyuan Co
H6  Wuhua Co
H7  Xingning Co

**QINGYUAN MR**

I1  Fogang Co
I2  Lian Co
I3  Liannan Co
I4  Lianshan Co
I5  Yangshan Co
I6  Yingde Co
I7  Qingyuan UD

**SHANTOU MR**

J1  Chaoyang Co
J2  Chaozhou C
J3  Chenghai Co
J4  Huilai Co
J5  Jiexi Co
J6  Jieyang Co
J7  Nanao Co
J8  Puning Co
J9  Raoping Co

**SHANWEI**

K1  Haifeng Co
K2  Lufeng Co
K3  Luhe Co

**SHAOGUAN MR**

L1  Lechang Co
L2  Nanxiong Co
L3  Qujiang Co
L4  Renhua Co
L5  Ruyuan Co
L6  Shixing Co
L7  Wengyuan Co
L8  Xinfeng Co

**SHENZHEN MR**

M1  Baoan Co
M2  Shenzhen SEZ

**YANGJIANG MR**

N1  Yangchun Co
N2  Yangxi Co

**ZHANJIANG MR**

O1  Haikang Co
O2  Lianjiang
O3  Suixi Co
O4  Wuchuan Co
O5  Xuwen Co
O6  Zhanjiang UD

**ZHAOQING MR**

P1  Deqing Co
P2  Fengkai Co
P3  Gaoyao Co
P4  Guangning Co
P5  Huaiji Co
P6  Luoding Co
P7  Sihui Co
P8  Xinxing Co
P9  Yunan Co
P10  Yunfu Co
P11  Zhaoqing UD

**Q    ZHONGSHAN C**

**ZHUHAI MR**

R1  Doumen Co
R2  Zhuhai SEZ

0   50   100   150   200
Kilometers

R.C.Forget

divided to form sixteen metropolitan regions, which were in turn divided into seventy-seven counties, with two cities independent of these regions.

All the old prefectural capitals remained as capitals of the new metropolitan regions, but Shaoguan and Huizhou metropolitan regions passed on some of their counties to the new units. Since most of the counties they lost were poor ones, this was unlikely to affect their growth greatly. In addition, Guangzhou, Jiangmen, and Foshan metropolitan regions also lost one or more counties. Zhongshan and Dongguan, counties considered sufficiently urbanized and industrialized to manage their own development and closest to Zhuhai and Shenzhen, were allowed to become independent cities. Other counties (for example, Shunde) hoped eventually to attain the same status.

Four towns were selected to become capitals of the new metropolitan regions. All four were on key crossroads where market forces had already created opportunities for rapid growth. Two were port cities: Yangjiang, the leading port between Guangzhou and Zhanjiang in the west, and Shanwei, the leading port between Guangzhou and Shantou in the east. Both Yangjiang and Shanwei were port cities before 1949 but were virtually closed between the Korean War and the 1980s, and both were poised for growth in the 1990s. Yangjiang was seen as an outlet for the Si Yi, the heartland of overseas emigrants, and Shanwei for Haifeng, Lufeng, and the East River area. The other two new capitals were inland: Qingyuan, on the major rail and highway route halfway between Guangzhou and Shaoguan, and Heyuan, on the highway and the planned railway roughly halfway between Guangzhou and Meixian in the northeast. It was planned that they too would become urban centers for industrial development in their area.

Perhaps a half step behind the other prefectural capitals, these new metropolitan regions were assembling key officials, building new official headquarters, and attracting investment from elsewhere in China and abroad as the 1980s ended. Like other prefectural capitals, they were first becoming administrative cities and then gradually helping to attract industry, allowing commerce to develop and drive industrial development, and in turn assisting the development of counties under them.

# 8.

# *The Mountain Counties: Moving Development Uphill*

Although in 1979 leaders at all levels were prepared to allow increased inequalities for the sake of encouraging growth, they never abandoned China's basic goal of improving the life of peasants and workers. Some cadres had grown cynical and more absorbed with their own careers than with the people they served, but many leaders remained concerned about the living conditions of the poor. In Guangdong as in Beijing, some of the top political leaders had served as guerrillas in poor areas and were distressed that those areas that had contributed to the revolutionary struggle still suffered from poverty. In late 1984 Guangdong, without abandoning efforts to assist the more advanced areas, followed Beijing's lead and began a new approach to backward areas that was in the spirit of the reforms; in 1987 these efforts were carried a step further.

The most serious inequalities were those between mountainous areas and other localities. Under the 1978 reforms, the urban poor could improve their lot by engaging in individual enterprise. And in rural areas on the plains, the responsibility system distributed land-use rights within a given village relatively equitably. The crucial problem was therefore not inequalities within a village but between villages that had good land and access to markets and those in more isolated areas that did not. In Guangdong, as in many parts of China, the worst poverty was in the mountainous regions. Of the thirty poorest counties in the province in the late 1980s, twenty-seven were mountainous. (The other three, Chaoyang, Puning, and Huilai, were particularly crowded counties in Shantou Metropolitan Region, but because they were coastal areas they had new opportunities deriving from expanding markets.)[1] In many of Guangdong's mountain villages, population had roughly doubled since 1949 and food production had not been able to keep up with the increase. In 1987 it was estimated that in the nation as a whole, 4.4 percent of the households had per capita incomes of less than 150 yuan per year, but in Guangdong the figure was 6.2 percent, and these households were overwhelmingly in the mountainous areas.

Roughly 70 percent of Guangdong's land is mountainous or hilly. The tallest "mountain" in Guangdong, Shikengkong, is only 1,902 meters in elevation, but many areas are so steep or rocky that ordinary agriculture is impossible. Except for flatlands along major rivers, mountains and hills are almost continuous in Guangdong's north, northwest, and northeast. Guangdong's southern and coastal areas are generally flat, with only occasional hills jutting out of the plains. Mountains are also prominent in central and southern Hainan. "Hilly" *(qiu)* areas are sometimes distinguished from "mountainous" *(shan)* areas, but cadres have generally used "mountain counties" to mean either: (1) all counties with major areas covered by mountains (this usage in the reform decade included forty-seven counties, forty-eight after May 1987 when one Hainan county, Baoting, was divided); or (2) the poorest mountain counties (this usage, developed in 1985 for a special program, included thirty counties: six in Hainan Island, all seven counties in Meixian, five in Shaoguan, six in Huiyang, three in Shaoqing, two in Shantou, and one in Maoming prefectures). The forty-seven counties (see map) covered roughly 55 percent of Guangdong's area. In 1986 they had 21.6 million people, 34 percent of the provincial population.[2] They then produced only 9.2 percent of the gross value of production of the province, had only 5.4 percent of the basic capital investment, and took in only 8.3 percent of local fiscal income.[3]

Minority groups were among the poorest, least educated, and most isolated of Guangdong's mountain peoples. In the 1982 census, Guangdong counted 1,058,000 people of minority background. Some 811,000 were Li, who lived on Hainan, with 41,000 Miao. There were also 96,000 Yao, mostly in Lianshan, Liannan, and Ruyuan counties of Shaoguan Prefecture; 87,000 Zhuang, mostly near the Guangxi border; and far smaller groups of several other minorities.[4] These minorities spoke their own languages and were originally distinct from the Han majority. Although no precise figures have yet

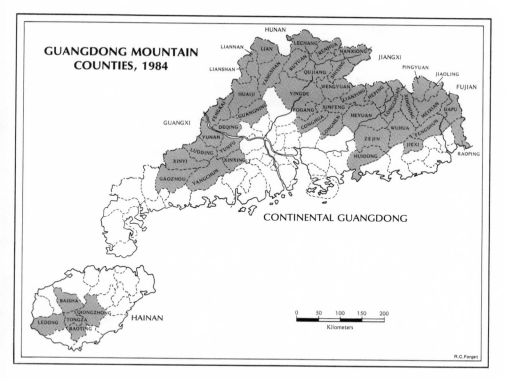

been available, at that time perhaps close to half of the mountain people, mostly in Meixian and Shaoguan prefectures, were Hakka.

The average mountain county had a population of four hundred thousand and was divided into twenty townships (before reforms, mostly commune headquarters). By the late 1980s there were paved roads linking every county seat to neighboring counties. A high proportion of the towns and larger settlements, even in mountain counties, were on or near the roads, but many of the smaller towns were connected only by dirt roads, many of which were unusable after rains. In 1987, of the roughly nine hundred administrative villages and towns in these forty-seven counties, twenty-five were not yet connected by even a dirt road. There were no data on the number of natural villages unconnected by roads, but many people in mountainous areas lived some distance from roads and could only walk or ride an animal, usually a water buffalo, between their homes and the nearest road.

It is impossible to use monetary terms to describe the conditions of people in these areas accurately, because they were largely self-sufficient and so little of their activity involved monetary exchanges. They usually grew their own crops and, if they could, raised their own fowl or pigs. In some areas the soil was very poor, as in areas covered with limestone in Shaoguan Prefecture. They tended to live in small homes, made of dried earthen bricks, that they built by themselves or with the help of neighbors. Many houses had mud floors. The homes protected villagers from the weather, but it was difficult to keep the bricks from crumbling. People gathered their own fuel, mostly brush or branches from trees. Many villages had electricity, but few could afford electric equipment other than a light bulb; few villages had plumbing.

By the latter part of the 1980s relatively few people suffered from malnutrition, but some had trouble getting enough food so that their stomachs felt full. Most of the people in these counties had enough clothes to keep warm in the winter, and the clothing was like that worn in the cities of the Delta a decade earlier, adequate but not very colorful. In the summer some, adults as well as children, went barefoot. Their precious cash was used to buy cooking utensils, Chinese medicine, salt, clothes, and food items they could not grow. Few felt they could afford fertilizer or Western-style medicine.

## Rural Reform, the Division of Land, and Reforestation

In mountainous areas the population was more widely dispersed than in the plains. Some villagers had built their homes in little ravines or valleys to take advantage of every bit of tillable land, and they were sometimes a great distance from those in the next ravine. Communes, brigades, and teams all had far fewer people on average than in the plains, yet they were spread over a larger geographical area. Even with a smaller number of people, all units found it more difficult to coordinate collective activity. The dispersion of the mountain villages, in addition to their poverty, encouraged officials to allow these villagers to switch to the household responsibility system for crop management before it was permitted elsewhere. The procedure used was fundamentally the same as later used all over the province.

Dividing up nontillable mountain land was more difficult. Boundaries were less clearly demarcated, and the issues of ownership and usage were more complicated, especially in mountain areas located near land claimed by state mines, state forests, and state farms. Even before reforms, some villagers had wanted to make use of items from nearby land that the state had claimed. The conflict between peasants and the state usually had a history. Residents had often long gathered goods in these areas before the state or collectives claimed them in the 1950s. They collected stones and gravel for construction, herbs for medicine, brush for firewood, and wild fruit, and cut down trees for lumber. When state preserves or mines were established it was impossible to keep guards on every part of the land, and it was not always clear where the property began; gathering brush, wild fruit, and herbs there was generally permitted.

As markets declined after collectivization, those who tried to sell items were accused of following the capitalist road and were punished severely by state officials. Most peasants were intimidated and desisted, but after 1978 with decollectivization, the relaxation of state authority, and new money-making opportunities in the new private markets, they were even more inclined to encroach on state land, thus intensifying conflicts between local villagers and the guardians of state property.

Thus around state mines (for example, Dabaoshan in Shaoguan, Yunfu in Zhaoqing, and Shilu on Hainan), in the 150 state farms (mostly for rubber growing on Hainan and in Zhanjiang Prefecture), in state forest preserves, and in state land near reservoirs, some nearby inhabitants were finding ways to take ore, rock, trees, or brush that might have commercial value. Rural cadres, aware of the difficulty of patrolling every square meter of the preserves, were sometimes sympathetic to poor farmers and resentful of central government institutions appropriating local resources, and they were often lax in keeping locals out. Before long, however, higher-level cadres were denouncing this as anarchy and calling for the preservation of state property.

The new forces at work in the 1980s among mountain dwellers and the state are illustrated in one of the best-known disputes at Dabaoshan ("Great Treasure Mountain"). (The disputes over state farms on Hainan are treated in Chapter 9.) The mining of iron ore on Dabaoshan, as noted in Chapter 7, had greatly expanded again in the late 1960s to provide ore for the Shaoguan Iron and Steel Plant.

Peasants had long been unhappy that they were not given more jobs in the Dabaoshan mines, which often hired army veterans and other outsiders. They had also long asked the mine for compensation for land appropriated, but the mine had refused. In the 1980s villagers took matters into their own hands and began stealing chunks of ore and selling it directly to plants. In response the mine assigned some employees to guard its property, whereupon the farmers took another tack. To get to the mine, workers ordinarily passed through what was officially village land. The peasants blocked the path, forcing miners to make a long circuitous walk of half an hour or more. When the matter was taken to a court composed of local officials, the court supported local residents against the mine, which was under central government jurisdiction. Incidents continued, however, until a child was shot in the arm by a guard at the mine. A local official called in the head of the mine and lodged a complaint, and other local Party and government officials also rallied behind the farmers. After considerable discussion, the mine agreed to make a substantial financial settlement to the child's family and to local people who had been using land the state had appropriated.

In the case of state forests, the issue of usage rights was complicated by the depletion of forests and consequent soil erosion, an urgent problem. Forests had been badly affected during the Great Leap Forward by the felling of trees used as fuel for industry. During the Gang of Four period, when the entire nation studied the Dazhai model of a mountain village that opened new land for planting, more of Guangdong's trees were felled. Forestry officials at various levels never gave up their efforts to control the cutting, but with the criticism and replacement of so many officials during the Cultural Revolution, forest management had grown very lax. In Zhaoqing Prefecture, which depended more on forestry than other prefectures did, not only forestry officials but the very highest leaders, county heads and Party secretaries, had given forest preservation high priority, and there they succeeded in preventing widespread destruction of forest land. But everywhere else the felling of trees had become a serious problem. In 1949 it was estimated that Guangdong had sixty-four million cubic meters of lumber in forests, and in 1980 it was estimated that this had declined to twenty-nine million.

The highest provincial officials acknowledged that tighter control over use of the woodlands and massive replanting of whole mountains were urgently needed. Leaders in Beijing, beginning with Zhao Ziyang, made controlling damage to state property and reforestation a high priority. In many ways the temptation to cut down trees was even greater after reforms because of the opportunity to sell timber on the open market to meet the demands of the province's burgeoning construction. Wood had long been in too short supply to use as a primary material in building, but it was used to make frames for placing bricks and to make doors and windows. For the poor farmers who lived at the edge of a forest, the chance to earn money was hard to resist.

Leaders therefore wanted to find a way both to give mountain dwellers some property rights that would allow them a source of income and to draw sharp lines to protect state property. Officials added a new category, "private mountain land" *(ziliushan),* and drew new boundaries to divide land into three categories: private mountain land, collective land, and state forests. In general the private forest land was located nearest people's homes, the collective land somewhat farther away, and the state farms were generally larger reserves with fewer nearby dwellings. This new division took place between 1981 and 1983, after the assignment of household responsibility for crop production.

Provincial-level officials, following meetings at their level, went down to the counties. There were no experimental areas for testing how to divide the land; instead, county officials simply picked a convenient commune and division was begun. The process of dividing mountain land in a county typically took about three months, and by 1983 the program had been completed in each of the forty-seven mountain counties.

In Huaiji County, for example, provincial officials began with county-level meetings and then divided up into work teams with local officials to go down to communes and then to brigades, where seven or eight officials spent two months. The work at the brigade level was divided into three stages.

First, the rights of land use were clearly delineated among production teams. Because boundary lines between teams in mountainous areas had not been drawn clearly, each team drew up its statement of land use and the higher officials adjudicated disagreements. This process took about one month.

Second, private mountain land was divided among households within the production team. In the Huaiji Commune, for example, the total amount of mountain land assigned to a team averaged about 13.5 mou per capita, of which about 1.0 mou per capita was assigned as private mountain land. (In localities with less land, officials still tried to give out close to 1.0 mou per capita as private mountain land

and reduce the amount given out as collective land.) The procedures for dividing up land within a team varied, but in the Huaiji Commune, for example, the households drew lots. Each household in turn was then allowed to select a plot of land of the size it was entitled to, and was given a large certificate, with an appropriate seal, awarding it the land for perpetuity. Having had land appropriated during collectivization and communization, many villagers lacked confidence in the stability of the policy and it took time to persuade many of them. To motivate peasants to keep down population growth, the government announced that the size of each household's plot assignment would be unchanged, no matter how many members it had. Villagers still had to get permission from village or township offices to cut down trees on their plots.

Third, responsibility for looking after the collective forest land was assigned down to the small group or household. In the Huaiji Commune the assignment was to last for thirty years, but it could be as much as fifty years. Permission for cutting down these trees also had to be obtained from village or township offices. Income from the collective plot was to go primarily to the household, with some accruing to the collective and some, usually about 7 percent, going to higher levels as a form of taxation.

Once these rights to use forests were clarified and mountain villagers given some source of income, controls were tightened. Workers on state forests were still paid salaries, but after reforms, to increase their motivation, responsibility for looking after the forest was subdivided and given to small groups and sometimes even to households of mountain villagers who lived on the edge of the forest.

The postreform approach to mine areas was similar. Villagers living nearby were given areas around a mine's edges that did not require state farm machinery or larger work groups, and they were allowed to sell the ore or rocks they mined to state factories or on the open market. But land beyond these areas was to be strictly controlled by the mines. These actions helped but did not end the problem, because the mines, whose costs were fixed, were unhappy that nearby farmers could undercut them on price, which created pressure on mines to lower prices.

These efforts did not end the problem of forest depletion. Some villagers, afraid that the government would change policy and again take away their land, rushed to cut the trees and sell them as soon as possible. Some venturesome young people, not afraid to run risks, still stole lumber from state land. But most villagers who were given their own forest plot were willing to stay off state land. Because the local village had been made responsible for the collective land, there were community sanctions against anyone who cut down trees. The government set up checks on key roads to make sure no unauthorized logs were being trucked out. The combination of giving villagers their own land, defining rights, and tightening controls transformed the problem from one involving many ordinary villagers to one involving a few determined lawbreakers.

As they developed greater confidence in the permanence of the private mountain plots, peasants by the mid-1980s basically adopted one of two strategies or some combination of both. One strategy, judged to be more profitable in some areas, was not to cut down trees but to use or sell only small brush, fallen tree limbs, and pine cones (sold to the state for making perfume). The other strategy was to select the most mature trees for sale each year and to replace them to ensure that an ample supply of trees would still be available indefinitely.

With tree cutting under control, officials could concentrate on the central problem that affected the long-range economic future of mountainous areas and provincial agriculture: reforestation. In 1984 officials, in line with national efforts for reforestation pushed by Hu Yaobang and Wan Li, launched a program aiming to replant all bald mountains with saplings by 1989. The provincial Party secretary, Lin Ruo, personally took responsibility for promoting the program. The Provincial Forestry Department set up a Greening Office (Luhua Bangongshi), with branches in the counties. Each county and town in mountainous areas developed an overall support structure for tree planting. They set up nurseries to grow saplings and distributed them to state farms and collectives, and they advised local villages on setting up their own tree nurseries. They made available specialists on tree planting and tree diseases. Two kinds of sapling that could help control soil erosion and that had some commercial potential were chosen: a pine tree that matured in about fifteen years and a cryptomeria (*shan,* sometimes translated as "Chinese fir tree") that matured in about twenty years.

Beginning in 1985, all cadres in mountain counties were expected to spend at least one week a year at tree planting. Sometimes cadres were organized to "green" *(luhua)* the county capital or areas nearby. Younger cadres were often sent either to backward communities that lacked labor power or to certain state farms for their week of planting. Usually they were allotted a certain number of holes, thirty or forty, to dig in a day. In some localities students were organized on Sundays or during their vacation to go to a mountain and dig holes for trees. Often the actual planting of the seedlings was left to a specialist team. Since the forestry division had a budget for greening, some counties used these funds to hire farmers during the two or three slack months of the agricultural year to work on planting. In Yangjiang County, for example, two thousand to three thousand young farmers were hired each year, and they received their final payments when it was clear that a high percentage of saplings, about 96 percent, had taken root.

Villages commonly set up their own nurseries to grow saplings for their collective land or to sell to individual households to plant on their private mountain land. Villagers paid a set fee per sapling, and the income from these individual payments plus some collective income was used to pay for the small number of people who worked part- or full-time for the collective nursery.

It was doubtful that every remote mountain in the province would be completely covered by 1989, especially in areas distant from public roads where high-level cadres were unlikely to visit. It was also not clear how well Guangdong would be able to solve the problem that had plagued other reforestation efforts in China, the low survival rate of seedlings. But a traveler in mid-1987 could already see from county roads mountain after mountain, previously barren of trees, covered with small seedlings.

With strict controls over cutting trees, in the short run income from felled trees was likely to be low. Some communities estimated that average per capita income from cut trees might be about forty yuan or so per year. But as more trees matured and could be harvested each year without causing deforestation, income was expected to increase substantially.

Reforestation was designed to solve problems of erosion, not to build up a lumber industry. Guangdong was prepared to accept that construction would rely more on bricks and cement than on wood, and that lumber would be used primarily for furniture and as a supplementary building material. In the late 1980s only a few counties in Zhaoqing Prefecture, near the Guangxi border, were making a serious effort to develop forests to be used for lumber.

## Growth of Mountain Markets

By the mid-1980s, with the growth of trucks and paved roads, goods could be easily transported from the cities of the Pearl River Delta and even from many other provinces to mountain county capitals. With the costs of highway construction and imported trucks and the long delays caused by crowded roads, transport continued to become more expensive at the same time that it had become more convenient. Transportation was still dominated by tiny individual enterprises, and truck transport was not yet rationalized to permit trucks to be fully loaded in both directions and loaded and unloaded quickly. By the late 1980s, however, most basic staple items were available in mountain counties at prices not greatly higher than elsewhere.

Within mountain counties, by the late 1980s transportation was mostly by motorbikes, diesel tractors, and "country bicycles" that had broad tires for bumpy roads and could carry heavier loads than city bicycles. Diesel tractors, produced in Guangdong, were not only far cheaper than trucks but could carry loads on dirt roads that trucks sometimes found impassable. Even though in mountainous areas one sometimes had to push a loaded bicycle up major hills, peasants found this a great advance over transporting the same load on carrying poles, which remained necessary only in very remote areas that lacked roads. The spread of diesel tractors, motorbikes, and country bicycles, combined with market reforms, stimulated mountain county market growth, which took three main forms: individual enterprises in larger towns, shops along roads, and periodic markets.

The county capitals, well connected by the transportation system, were in a sense the counties' "coastal areas," the first places to profit from the market expansion. Like prefectural capitals, they passed on information and technology from higher levels to more backward towns. In the county capitals and larger towns, households began to specialize in receiving goods transported from a distance and selling them locally. Some people even traveled on trains and buses or used their own vehicles to bring back goods from a distant location and sell them locally. In addition, local rural people brought their own produce, animals, and handicrafts to the daily markets in these larger towns. Commercial activity in mountain towns, though slightly simpler and more rustic, paralleled commercial activity in other towns in the province.

As the restraints on buying and selling were lifted, rural people located on main roads began selling goods along the road near their villages. Some started with mats and then little stalls, and the more successful gradually put up small shacks and then sturdier buildings. A village located, for example, a kilometer or so away from the road but whose land extended across the road would allow some of its villagers to use sites along the road. This pattern occurred throughout the province but was particularly important for mountain villages, because it provided additional income from increased road traffic passing through their areas. Although these new shacks served more than just local people, mountain residents could often find goods within easy walking distance that had previously been unavailable without a major trip. For some villages, this created a new shopping and work center away from the traditional living area; many people began to spend both their work and their leisure time along the road rather than in their original village center.

In county capitals, which typically had twenty thousand or more people even before 1949, the population had long been large enough to support regular stores that sold a variety of goods. In the Delta even before 1949 periodic markets had mostly been replaced with regular stores and daily shopping. In the smaller towns and villages of Guangdong, however, as in other parts of China where transport was more difficult and the population too dispersed to support large numbers of regular stores, people came together for rural markets on regular set days. The days were set by local custom according to the old lunar calendar, and they were commonly held every third, fourth, or fifth day. During the Cultural Revolution they atrophied, appearing every sixth, eighth, or tenth day or not at all, but after the reforms they blossomed again. In 1978 there were 1,936 periodic marketplaces in Guangdong, but by 1986 there were 3,300.[5] Provincial figures then showed a total annual turnover in periodic markets of almost ten billion yuan, some five times the turnover recorded in 1978. By that time sellers had to arrive at the designated market areas as soon as it was light in order to get a good place to spread their mats to sell their goods.

By the mid-1980s each township had on average two periodic markets. Most towns and large villages also had a small number of regular stores open daily, including the State Supply and Marketing Cooperative, in effect a rural version of a small department store, and other stores for hardware, dishes, pharmaceuticals, clothes, stationery, rice and food staples, plows, hoes, and other agricultural implements, as well as restaurants and tea shops. But on market days farmers brought in their own produce and crafts. Almost two-thirds of total periodic market sales were in food. In 1986, of the 9.38 billion yuan in total sales, 3.99 billion was in meat and eggs, 1.13 billion in fish and other aquatic products, and 0.60 billion in fruit.

Compared to rural Delta residents who used more manufactured goods, mountain dwellers used more inexpensive, locally made handicrafts. They wove chairs from reeds and bamboo, made their own mats, pounded out metal for kitchen utensils, twisted their own rope from hemp, and made nets from string and rope. There was a lively market in used goods—bottles, old rubber tires to be remade into shoes, pieces of scrap metal for making utensils, used clothes to be resewn, and plastic to make awnings and mats. Many mountain villagers in the late 1980s could not yet afford radios and sewing machines, let alone other household appliances. By the mid-1980s, people in the Delta area had begun to find it not worth their while to sew goods to put on the market, because manufactured goods were so widely available at low prices and they could make more money in other work. But in the mountain towns, many women still sewed for themselves and, after reforms, for the market. Bolts of cloth were common in periodic markets, and a sewing machine remained a key item for a bride to bring as part of her dowry.

Although dates of periodic markets were set by custom, local officials tried to bring some order so that markets in nearby towns occurred on different days. This enabled itinerant merchants from the county seat or even the prefectural capital to rotate between markets, taking manufactured goods to one periodic market each day. Officials also had to supervise these markets to avoid wild rises in prices, cheating, and poor hygiene. Market management committees in the towns endeavored to police the weights and measures, check up on fraud, and preserve standards of cleanliness, especially in the food and produce sections, much as market management committees did in the cities.

Although the amount and quality of goods could not compare with those sold in the Delta, for mountain villagers these markets brought in a range of previously unavailable goods, and competition had helped improve the quality—even of local handicrafts, which now had to compete with more state goods. Mountain dwellers with produce or crafts for sale could generate enough cash to buy goods they previously could not afford, and the opprobrium associated with being a small rural merchant gradually declined. By the late 1980s these periodic markets were as lively as they had ever been and were great social as well as business occasions.


## New Sources of Income and Their Limits

Paradoxically, policies that were aimed at helping the poor directly prior to the 1979 reforms did less to improve the livelihood of the mountain poor than did the post-1979 reforms, which specifically allowed others to get rich faster than those in the mountains. In the Inner Delta counties, most of the increase in rural income in the early years after reform came from industry and commerce. The mountain counties, despite their increase in income from forest products and mining, were still heavily agricultural; most of the increase in their income came from *zhong* and *yang,* planting crops and raising animals. Even after 1979 farmers were discouraged from reducing acreage in rice, but in marginal areas they significantly increased their "economic crops" like *ma* (hemp, ramie, flax) and fruit trees. Mountain dwellers increased the number of chickens, pigs, and goats they raised, and as Inner Delta areas gave up growing silkworms in order to produce more lucrative items, some in the mountains took their place in supplying the silk factories.

In addition to local handicrafts, pine cones, brushwood, and timber, some of the most lucrative products found in forest lands were the roots and herbs used for Chinese medicine. Some were sold to state procurement stations or, better still, sold directly in markets for somewhat higher prices. Despite all the years of collective life, herbs and roots were generally not cultivated systematically. They were treated, rather, somewhat like a pot of buried treasure, to be plucked from a secret place when no one was looking.

Increased construction throughout the province had created an enormous appetite for building materials of all kinds. Small boom towns sprang up in Yunfu, Luoding, Yingde, and Lian counties, which had marble deposits. Mountain dwellers in the Shaoguan area who had limestone rock (not just rocky soil) on their property, lived close to roads, and had access to trucks, could make what by their standards were high incomes. The same was true for those who could transport sand and gravel. Although modern construction equipment had come to the Inner Delta by the mid-1980s, it had rarely reached mountain counties at the end of the decade. Mountain villagers, sometimes women as well as men, used picks and hammers to break off rocks, and then chisels and hammers to break down the rocks into small stones to be used in making cement and laying roadbeds. Farmers who mined ore and stone around the edges of state mines used similarly primitive tools. There were many variations in the kind of stone dug up, with a wide range of prices, the highest of which went for stones useful for more attractive building surfaces.

Thus the degree to which the standard of living of a rural community progressed depended very much on whether it was located near appropriate resources that were accessible to the transport available. But no matter where they were located, mountain villagers had the opportunity to work on construction crews. This still meant carrying heavy loads, living in temporary shelters at work sites, and being covered with dirt. By the mid-1980s Inner Delta youth had found so many other job opportunities that few accepted ordinary construction work. Provincial and local leaders allowed those from the mountain counties to come to construction sites on temporary work permits.

Educational levels in the mountain counties remained low. One of the most troubling problems since reform was that the proportion of children in elementary schools throughout China had declined. Although the number of students in Guangdong senior middle schools, universities, and technical schools increased from 1978 to 1985, the number in elementary school declined from 8.32 million to 7.59 million, a decline of 1.1 percent in attendance rate, controlled for size of age cohort, and in lower middle school from 3.47 million to 2.66 million, a decline of 2.5 percent in attendance rate. In 1986 the number in lower middle school rose to 2.82 million.[6] The efforts since 1978 to increase the proportion of local financing for schools had led local communities to spend less for schools and this change was especially hard on the mountainous areas, which were more strained financially. More families had chosen to have their children forgo schooling to take advantage of economic opportunities, and since urbanites could no longer be ordered to the countryside, it was difficult to get qualified teachers there, especially in remote areas. In the 1980s mountain youth aged sixteen and above rarely qualified for skilled jobs and found manual labor their most promising source of income.

By 1987 officials estimated that over one million youth in the Inner Delta, in addition to the one million in Guangzhou and almost one million in Shenzhen and Zhuhai, were outsiders who had found work there since the reforms had begun. Although some were from nearby counties or distant provinces, about 60 percent were from mountain counties in Guangdong. By far the largest number worked on construction projects. Provincial construction officials decided in 1980 that to avoid increasing the state budget and to encourage market flexibility, they would keep a lid on the number of state construction workers and allow collective construction companies to expand to meet the demand instead. In 1980 there were 163,000 Guangdong construction workers working for the state. This expanded slightly to absorb the 20,000 construction workers discharged from military to civilian work in Shenzhen and some specialists, but by 1986, the number of state construction workers had increased to only 248,000.[7] In the meantime the number of collective construction workers increased from 180,000 to 720,000, and the number of short-term construction workers, though subject to more variation by season and demand, grew from almost none to about 400,000. Although no precise figures are available, in the late 1980s a typical mountain county had over 10,000 construction workers, and about one out of eight mountain county households at any one time had a son working on a construction crew.[8]

Collective construction workers became members of teams certified by county construction bureaus (Xinyi County Construction Company No. 1, No. 2, etc.). These teams, overwhelmingly from mountain counties, were organized by former cadres and included as core members some individuals with special technical expertise and former commune and brigade construction crew members. Others were recruited from the same or nearby townships as needed. At any one time a mountain county averaged several numbered teams. With this system, teams could be organized and expanded very rapidly to meet construction needs, all through local rural networks.

Mountain villagers reported that after the construction workers deducted their own living expenses, they all automatically sent back the rest of their income to their families in the villages. By the late 1980s a typical construction worker was earning close to two hundred yuan per month and turning over about half of that to his family. For households with a construction worker member, this meant roughly a doubling of the family income.

Because educational standards of the mountain areas had been so low, it was difficult to find locals capable of being team foremen and managers. By the mid-1980s, as the business stabilized, some of the more promising construction workers were sent to schools or special training programs to prepare for leadership positions. And even the mountain youth who did not rise to foreman had the opportunity to walk the streets of the city where they were working and get a sense of how things were done. In the West, where the gap between the cities and remote areas had long been reduced by modern communications and transport, this would have little significance. But for mountain areas in Guangdong in the 1980s, the exposure to life in the Inner Delta was perhaps as significant as the exposure of the Inner Delta to Hong Kong.

For mountain county cadres concerned about finding work for young people in the mid- and late 1980s, the availability of construction jobs made the placement of poor youth with low educational levels less troublesome than the placement of three other groups with more ambition: former brigade and team cadres, former soldiers, and qualified students not admitted to college.

Most brigade and team cadres whose positions had been abolished with decollectivization had opportunities to work in the new township governments or on the new village committees. Special efforts were made to find work in the towns for the older cadres, who had trouble engaging in physical work. In the more prosperous areas of the province, there were new companies led by local government units that could absorb the former rural cadres, who then often earned far more income than they had previously. But in the mountainous areas, perhaps one-fifth of former brigade and team cadres had no choice but to return to full-time agricultural production, which many of them considered quite a letdown.

Soldiers who had returned to the villages in previous years had often found positions as cadres. In the army they had often become members of the Communist Party or Youth League, and they were regarded as possessing patriotic virtue that should be rewarded with more than simple agricultural work. Veterans returning to their mountain villages after decollectivization, however, found no jobs as cadres and often had difficulty finding jobs that made use of the skills they had acquired in the army. After the reforms there was generally a decline in status for soldiers, because technical levels, salaries, and prestige in the army had not kept up with civilian economic advances, particularly in Guangdong. For veterans returning to their villages in the 1980s who had entered the army expecting much more, it was often a great disappointment to find there were no special opportunities.⁹ And yet they had nowhere else to go to get secure permanent employment; cities maintained tight household registration and generally permitted migrants to come in only for the poorer jobs with temporary registration.

With the return of the entrance examination system after 1977, schools had again begun to reorient their more able students for examination. Each county, including the mountain areas, usually had several "key point" elementary schools and at least one "key point" junior and senior high school—elite schools that the better students were able to attend and that served as models for the surrounding area. A few select students were then able to go on to a university, but at best this included only 2 to 3 percent of the age group across the whole province. The best schools in mountain counties could not begin to match the better urban schools, and therefore only a tiny percentage of their students qualified for university course work. Because the government, conscious of budget limitations, was trying to resist expansion and even to contract, and because there were few other opportunities in mountain communities, the rest of the better students had much greater difficulty in finding appropriate employment than less able students did. Some of the few opportunities lay in the new special economic zones in Shenzhen and Zhuhai. These areas gave preferential consideration to mountain youth, but they could absorb only a small portion of those who wanted jobs that did not involve construction or other unskilled labor.

For able young people in mountain counties whose opportunity to find nonlaborer jobs in the city was blocked, there was no easy answer. Some made their way in individual enterprises, and in their area the educational levels of those in individual enterprises tended to be much higher than elsewhere. But many of these mountain youths, seeing people with abilities like theirs prosper in the cities and the Delta, felt very frustrated.

Although mountainous areas thus contained relatively disadvantaged groups and clearly lagged far behind the Delta, their average income still went up rapidly after reforms. In 1978, the average annual per capita income from collective agricultural production in rural parts of Guangdong's mountain counties was 66 yuan. There are no comparable records for the mid-1980s because collective production had basically ended, but the total income per capita in these forty-seven counties in 1987 was 386 yuan. The figures are not comparable because there was not a great deal of noncollective income in 1978.

The extent to which progress in mountain counties lagged behind that in the province as a whole may be illustrated by comparing the available data for industrial and agricultural output (in billions of yuan):[10]

| | Guangdong Province | | | Mountain counties | | |
|---|---|---|---|---|---|---|
| | 1980 | 1985 | Percent change 1980–1985 | 1980 | 1985 | Percent change 1980–1985 |
| Industry | 24.3 | 52.0 | 213 | 2.9 | 4.7 | 162 |
| Agriculture | 12.2 | 17.5 | 140 | 3.8 | 5.6 | 145 |
| Total | 36.5 | 69.5 | 190 | 6.7 | 10.3 | 153 |

There were many reasons why the mountain counties had grown more slowly. As already noted, the government had earlier simply decided where to locate industry, regardless of market forces, and during the 1960s, when national defense had been an issue, some plants had been located in the mountains. The rationalization of these industries in the 1980s led to the closure of some factories. The big increase in industrial growth in the 1980s was in light industry, especially consumer industry, and investors in these industries chose sites in central locations with larger markets and better facilities and transportation. Since banks replaced government budget units as the source of funds, they were more concerned about whether an investment would pay off. Mountain areas, considered a poor risk, had difficulty attracting investment capital.

After reforms, a high proportion of town and village government income was generated by their own industries. Communities with more prosperous enterprises could generate enough income with very low tax rates. Poorer communities, which still had basic fixed educational and infrastructural expenses, had to tax their smaller number of enterprises more heavily to meet their needs. The heavier taxation of enterprises in backward areas made it more difficult for them to generate capital for reinvestment.[11] New policies giving local communities responsibility for more of their own funding also made it more difficult for poor communities to finance their infrastructure.

After reforms began, educated youth could no longer simply be ordered to serve in poor areas. At best they might accept brief assignments in mountain county capitals, but few were willing to remain. In 1986, for example, seventeen university graduates accepted assignments in Lianshan County, but two years later only one, promoted to be deputy head of the county in charge of industry, remained. Officials in most counties were trying what they considered the most promising method of gaining young administrators and teachers: they selected a few bright youth from their own county and offered to help finance their education in return for a pledge to return after graduation.

The problem of backwardness of the mountain areas was more than simply material. They had been so isolated and so accustomed to their limited opportunities that their whole way of thought and their patterns of relations were geared to that kind of existence. Some mountain people, when given opportunities in nearby towns to earn considerably more income, felt like outsiders in the towns and soon returned to their poorer native areas where they could live among friends and relatives who shared their way of life. In the Delta, where there was more margin above subsistence to spare, independent households were willing to take risks when opportunities for investment came. In mountain counties, where there was almost nothing to spare, fewer wanted to risk the little they had. Yet many mountain dwellers wanted a larger share of the new wealth coming to the province, and many leaders in Beijing and Guangzhou remained committed to the ideal of equal distribution and were troubled about the growing gap between prosperous and backward areas.

## The Program to Support the Poor Areas, 1987–1989

In September 1984, the Party Central Committee and the State Council issued a directive for a new program to "wipe out poverty" *(fupin)*. China would endeavor to eliminate its worst poverty during the seventh five-year plan (1986–1990) and ensure that all Chinese had a minimum of warmth and food *(wenbao)*. The directive acknowledged that despite considerable effort, programs to eliminate poverty had thus far had little success. The new approach followed the spirit of reform in other parts of the economy. Poor local communities, mostly found in mountainous areas, were to develop their own resources to produce goods that could be sold as commodities, and higher-level government and Party units would help local collectives and private organizations get the process started. Very poor areas would pay no agricultural tax for a period of five years starting in 1985 so that they could generate funds for local investment, but the hope was to improve productive capacity so that they could pay taxes later. In the meantime, higher levels would continue to help with roadbuilding and provide minimum financial assistance to help make elementary school training available for all young children.

In November, in line with national policy directives, Guangdong announced the formation of a "mountain area leading group" to speed up the work of improving mountain economies in thirty of the poorest counties of the province, twenty-seven of which were mountain counties and three of which (Lufeng and Hainan's Wanning and Dan) were old revolutionary bases. First Party Secretary Lin Ruo personally took an active role in the program and Ling Botang, the vice-governor in charge of agriculture, headed the group, which included representatives from the various commissions (agriculture, planning, economic, foreign economic, construction, science and technology, price) as well as from the Finance-Trade Office and the Civil Affairs Department. The group immediately began to devise various industrial projects and programs to build infrastructure.

In the early 1980s Guangdong had set its minimum standard for annual per capita income at 120 yuan per year. Beijing in 1984 set 150 yuan by 1990 as its national target, and in their new program Guangdong leaders decided to go one better, setting their target at 200 yuan by 1989. Although Guangdong's cost of living was higher than the national average, its targets were clearly higher than national ones. The province made some limited funds available, but the focus was on providing personnel to help local areas respond to the opportunity.

Five hundred young provincial cadres, divided into thirty teams, were assigned to the counties for a year or longer. Each team included provincial-level officials representing various branches of government, including highways, railroads, electric power, finance, industry, and agriculture, who could provide not only expertise but also liaison with provincial officials in their own field. Provincial commissions and offices *(wei ban)* divided up responsibility for supervising and coordinating the teams.

The teams of provincial officials went to live in county headquarters, where they worked with county officials in their respective areas to devise programs to raise productive levels and improve the standard of living. County officials, less familiar with the thinking of provincial departments, often did not know how to write proposals acceptable to higher officials, and the provincial insiders helped them package local programs and present them so that they could be funded by the province. Among the Economic Commission's 1987 programs, for example, were thirty-nine items for updating technology in mountain county factories, far more than in preceding years.

Provincial officials recognized that in most mountain counties only the county capitals had the infrastructure to be the site of substantial industrial projects, but they tried to find projects that would also benefit the surrounding countryside. In Lechang County, for example, provincial officials lent their support to building a very large ramie *(juma)* yarn plant that required an investment of twenty-seven million yuan, including the purchase of machinery from Murata in Japan. The plant not only employed several thousand people but enabled many farmers, including those in mountainous areas, to grow ramie, a product which was well suited to rocky soil and which brought a far higher return than the crops they had been growing. From virtually no land in ramie, by 1987 thirty-two thousand mou in Lechang were planted in ramie, with an increase to fifty thousand planned for 1988. The cooperation of officials, at both local and provincial levels, in areas of construction, electric power, industry, and agriculture reflected a growing ability within the province to manage large integrated projects.

In Guangning County, both a poor mountain county and an old revolutionary base, able local officials with support from higher levels put together an integrated industrial development program. They used local pine tree products and bamboo to make paper and locally grown plants to make ink, and built printing factories, thus making good use of local resources. With the cooperation of the province, they brought in modern machinery. They also developed a number of other products—glucose made from cassava, furniture, pressed wood, and ceramics—from local materials, which fit their concept of using industry to drive rural development in order to raise the income of mountain villagers.

As the province sent people down to the poorest counties, the prefectures and counties similarly sent comparable teams of officials down to the poorest towns and villages. In Shaoguan Prefecture, for example, forty of the poorest towns and villages were selected, and roughly one-third each year were made the center of a year-long effort by higher-level cadres who went to live in the villages.

One of the administrative villages selected by Shaoguan was Dongshan, located on the side of a mountain in Yangshan County. With its limestone soil, it was one of the poorest villages in the prefecture.

In 1987 Dongshan had a population of 11,658 with an average per capita annual income of 118 yuan. People consumed an average of 104 kilograms of unhusked rice a year, about one-third of the province's average consumption. At best the villagers averaged one bowl of rice per day, with various kinds of mixed grains for their other food. Their overall intake was below normal daily requirements. Of the natural villages in Dongshan, about 60 percent were connected by dirt road, the rest were not. About 20 percent of the population had electricity. Dongshan had telephone service, but none of the smaller natural villages did. Water had to be carried to the village from some distance.

Officials used their budget of eighty thousand yuan to help promote production in Dongshan in a variety of ways, several of which focused on agriculture. Villagers were supplied seedlings for planting trees. They were paid small amounts for management fees in the short run, and it was expected they would derive considerable income from the trees when they began harvesting them in ten to fifteen years. Villagers were also supplied chemical fertilizer and better seeds, appropriate for crops in their areas. They were given help in planting ramie for the factory that was starting in nearby Lechang. The income was expected to be more than enough to purchase additional rice from elsewhere to meet normal daily requirements. Officials also provided an incubator for hatching chicken eggs, in order to help villagers raise chickens, and gave technical advice on how to deal with some of the diseases that had killed their chickens earlier.

In an effort to increase nonagricultural income, approximately a hundred young men from the village were put in touch with outside construction crew jobs that would bring in cash to the village. To help meet fuel needs, assistance was given to obtain low-grade coal from nearby mines and provide simple machinery for making the coal into coal balls; this would allow cooking without having to cut down any more of their badly depleted woodlands. Nearby hydroelectric power and road construction projects, a separate budget item, were also expected to benefit Dongshan.

Cadres who took part in the program reported that one of the side effects of working in such a poor area was that they became less concerned about their own pay and perquisites.

At the end of 1987 provincial officials, in response to new Beijing guidelines, took steps to extend the poverty program. Officials in the local administrative villages were to keep a record of each household that had an annual per capita income below two hundred yuan and to work with the family to raise it up over the minimum by the end of 1989.

Such programs were not immune from manipulation. Some local officials initially collected statistics in such a way that their areas fell below minimum standards and qualified for assistance. As the program was implemented, the officials collected statistics to show that they had made the planned progress. It was impossible for higher officials to check such data, and it was unlikely that the long-standing bureaucratic talent for exaggerating progress in reporting to higher levels had disappeared with this particular program. It was doubtful that the problems of poverty would be eliminated by the end of the 1980s. Yet an observer could see that the combined effects of new market opportunities, the extension of road, electric power, water, and telephone infrastructure, and the work of some very dedicated officials were having a major positive effect on the standard of living in many of the poorer mountain villages.

The revenues that accrued to the provincial government as a result of a thriving economy elsewhere made it easier to finance these new projects. And though it is impossible to measure, the sense of accomplishing so much elsewhere undoubtedly made officials more optimistic and more resourceful in attacking the problems of the remote areas. These were not the first attempts that provincial officials had made to aid the mountain areas, and no one was under any illusion that the new efforts would be sufficient to alter life radically in mountain villages in the short run. Yet in contrast to their stagnant economy before reforms, substantial changes derived from increasingly linking mountain counties to the expanding commodity economy.

# 9.

# *Hainan Island:*
# *Accelerated Frontier Development*

Located thirty kilometers from Leizhou Peninsula, off the southwestern coast of Guangdong, Hainan is a tropical island with problems similar to those of mountain counties. With thirty-four thousand square kilometers it is slightly smaller than the other major Chinese island, Taiwan, whose success spurred Beijing in the 1980s to speed Hainan's development and, in 1988, to make it an independent province. Hainan is even hotter than Taiwan, with temperatures frequently reaching 40 degrees centigrade in the summer and rarely falling below 15 degrees in the winter, except in its higher elevations. It also has more mountains than Taiwan, mostly in its central and southern regions. Even much of the northern third of Hainan, which supports two-thirds of the island's population, is arid and bumpy. From November until May the virtual absence of rain in many parts of the island causes serious water shortages.[1]

Although Hainan has been romanticized as a "treasure island" and is well known through the sentimental poems of Su Dongbo, who once lived in Wugong Temple (Qiongshan County), in the 1980s even local people acknowledged that Hainan remained "backward" *(luohou)*. The buildings and stores found in Hainan were not totally dissimilar to those found in other parts of Guangdong, but they tended to be more rundown. Clothing was simpler and less stylish and until the late 1980s had more patches. Fewer people had watches. Even articles like glass, pots and pans, and plastic buckets were scarcer than they were elsewhere. In 1988, the average per capita income in Hainan, even including its cities and state facilities, was still little more than four hundred yuan per year, substantially below that of most other parts of Guangdong. Hainan had fewer roads, telephones, radios, and trucks than most of the province. By the late 1980s when most of Guangdong used cars as taxis, much of Hainan continued to use a sidecar attached to a motorbike, and many parts of the island could not be reached by bicycle, let alone motorized vehicle. Parts of the island still had no electricity. Its special circumstances, not yet known in the West, require some explanation to understand its changes after 1978.

## The Frontier before 1950

Beijing officials have long regarded Hainan as a frontier border society, to be defended by troops and guided by administrators sent from the mainland. Chinese emperors sent troops to Hainan, but they could not afford to send enough to defend the entire island. Therefore, as in other exposed frontier areas, they sent soldiers who retired there, receiving land on which to support themselves with the understanding that they were prepared to defend the country if need be.

In modern dynasties the capital *(fucheng)* of Hainan was located in the northeast, in Qiongshan, and magistrates sent out from the mainland held court there. In a nearby academy, which later became the site of a teacher training school, talented young people spent years preparing to take the examination for official service.

The first sizable Han Chinese migration came when the Ming Dynasty fell apart in the seventeenth century. Tens of thousands of defeated people from Fujian and northeastern Guangdong fled by boat to the northeastern portion of the Hainan wilderness. These immigrants pushed back those already on the island, tiny groups of Miao and larger groups of Li, to its mountainous areas.[2] These immigrants spoke the Minnan dialect of southern Fujian and the local adaptation of this dialect, known as Hainanese, became the basic language of the island. Hainan's port city, located at the Nandu River's mouth *(haikou)*, Haikou, gradually began to overshadow traditional, more cultured Qiongshan, just as Chaozhou on the mainland was overshadowed by Shantou (Swatow).

In the latter part of the nineteenth century Hainan's population growth outstripped its cultivated land resources, prompting emigration from its more settled northeast. At the same time that emigrants from Taishan and other mainland counties built the Chinatowns of the United States, youth from Wenchang and nearby counties in Hainan helped build the Chinatowns of Southeast Asia, in Thailand, Vietnam, Malaysia, and Indonesia.

The Kuomintang (KMT), like their imperial predecessors, maintained both troops and retired soldiers to keep the peace. They enjoyed a certain measure of support from local landlords, including the most prominent on Hainan, the Soong family of Wenchang County, which in the late nineteenth century produced three daughters, including one who married Sun Yat-sen and another who married Chiang Kai-shek.

The Japanese occupied Hainan for only six years, from 1939 to 1945. They did not have time to modernize agriculture or to establish industries as they had done in Taiwan from 1895 to 1945, but as soon as they arrived, they began to exploit Hainan's resources and to build several key bases to assist their military thrust into Southeast Asia. They opened up the iron ore deposits in Shilu, Changjiang County, in west central Hainan. Lacking a port, they mobilized twenty thousand workers from as far away as Hong Kong to build a large facility capable of receiving ten-thousand-ton transport ships. A fifty-kilometer railway was also built to link the iron ore mine to the port, and from 1943 through 1945 more than four hundred thousand tons of high-quality iron ore were exported from Shilu to Japan to meet wartime steel requirements.

The Japanese continued building the railway from Basuo around the southwest part of the island to Sanya, a project they had nearly completed when the war ended. In Sanya and Haikou they built modern harbors and established small military airfields. Although they did not build roads and did not penetrate the inner part of the island, the Japanese-built infrastructure remained relatively intact, with little improvement, until reforms began in the 1980s.

Hainan's Qiongyai Guerrillas were in 1950 the only Communist guerrilla force in Guangdong that could trace its history back to 1927. Because the island's mountains were so inaccessible, they had been able to survive and harass first the KMT, later the Japanese, and finally the KMT again. In 1950 the sixty thousand guerrillas were unable to win victory without the help of the Communist army, which invaded and routed the KMT in April. After the victory, the Communists, like their imperial and KMT predecessors, sent in large numbers of troops to provide long-range security. Like the locals before them, the proud

Hainan guerrillas were subordinated to the outsiders who came to rule. Still sparsely settled, the island had scarcely one million people. As a special frontier, with higher-ranking officials sent in, it was made an administrative region of Guangdong, halfway in status between a prefecture and a province.

## Rubber, Land Reclamation, and State Farms

In late 1949 Mao went to Moscow for consultations with Stalin. In the course of talks about the future of the Soviet bloc, they considered what strategic materials they needed. The Soviet Union had ample resources to meet their needs for iron, steel, and energy, but there was one important strategic material they lacked: rubber. With the Allied blockade that began with the Korean War, rubber became even more critical because China lost access to the exports from Malaysia. Mao and Stalin therefore decided to develop rubber production in China, the only nation within the Communist bloc that had areas with the appropriate climate. Knowing that rubber trees take five to seven years from planting to production, they prepared a long-range development program.

Specialists planned to develop the four most promising sites: Fujian, Yunnan, Guangdong's Leizhou Peninsula, and above all Hainan, because it had a better climate and more unsettled land and because some returned Chinese from Malaysia had already established small rubber farms there in 1919. By 1952, the Central South Land Reclamation and Cultivation Bureau (Huanan Kenzhiju, sometimes translated State Farm Bureau) was formally established in Guangzhou to direct rubber development in all four areas.

Over twenty Soviet advisors arrived in Hainan in 1951 to assist in the development of the rubber industry. Since the Soviet Union did not have a rubber industry or a tropical climate, the specialists were from such fields as forestry and agronomy and helped with general management and mechanization. Assigned to the Land Reclamation Bureau offices in Haikou and Dan County (see map), they worked closely with local specialists.

In 1952, two divisions of China's Fourth Field Army that had been responsible for forestry development, the first and second forestry divisions *(lin yi shi* and *lin er shi),* each with roughly three thousand men, were sent from Guangxi to Guangdong to begin reclaiming land

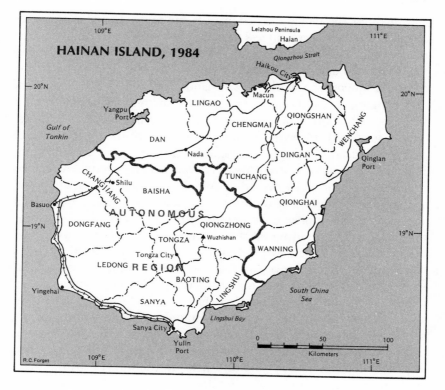

HAINAN ISLAND, 1984

and planting rubber trees. The second division was assigned to Lei-zhou, and the first division to Hainan. The first division sent out two brigades to the island's two original rubber farms at Nada and Qiong-hai, and from there they dispersed to twelve areas, where they recruited civilian workers and began planting rubber trees.

In 1953 the Chinese established their own Tropical Crops Research Center in Zhanjiang, headed by a talented forestry specialist, He Kang (later minister of agriculture in Beijing). In 1958 the headquarters was moved to a site near Nada, where state farms were more heavily concentrated, to strengthen liaison with those engaged in rubber cultivation. They also established a university to train specialists who could supervise the growing of rubber trees. As the Soviet specialists left in the late 1950s, the Chinese expanded their own efforts.

In the 1950s Chinese army engineers laid the first road through the mountainous center of the island all the way from Haikou to Sanya, and many of the newly opened state farms set up their headquarters along it. The engineers did less to maintain a smooth continuous road than would have been acceptable in an advanced country, yet, given the difficulties and the technology of the day, the road was a heroic accomplishment; the workers used hand picks and carried buckets of dirt hanging from shoulder poles. Over a hundred engineers and workers died in landslides, from snake bites, or from various illnesses.

Mao gave high priority to the establishment of these rubber farms and popularized the slogan "strengthening defense and consolidating Hainan" (*jiaqiang fangwei, gonggu Hainan*). The government helped the farms get started by providing initial equipment and funding and sending in rice and other food for the troops and workers while land was cleared and rubber trees were planted. The state could not bear the burden of supporting all the rubber workers for the seven years before the trees began to produce rubber, however, and the settlers were expected to start growing their own rice and other necessities as soon as possible. "Use the short to develop the long" (*yi duan yang chang*), went the slogan, meaning that one should grow short-term crops such as cassava and tea to bring in income while waiting for the rubber to mature. The twelve areas that had begun the planting and prospered became the nucleus for groups of state farms. Some failed and were consolidated as part of others. In the mid-1970s the management of state farms, like the management of most of the island, was divided into two parts, the southern, which had a large minority population, and the northern. By then there were forty-four state farms in the north and forty-six in the south, with a total population of over one million.

The local people in the surrounding area were called "farmers" (*nongmin*), but the employees of the state farms were known as "workers" (*nonggong*), which in the early days signified a more advanced stage of socialism. Most workers were assigned to care for rubber trees. Some work teams looked after the nurseries, where small rubber trees were cultivated until they reached maturity, and others collected the rubber from mature trees, which were ordinarily tapped every other day.

When the state farms were first established, the resistance of local farmers was not a problem. Population was so sparse, the land had been so unsuitable for ordinary crops, and transport and communication were so primitive that some residents encouraged the army to come to their locality. They hoped to find jobs, enjoy the benefits of electricity and better transport, and make it possible for their children to attend the schools that the army was beginning to establish.

From 1952 to 1954 the farms recruited workers among civilians, not only from the island but from other poor areas in Guangdong like Shantou and Meixian. But the leading nucleus of workers consisted of retired soldiers, who set the pattern and the tone of state farm life. By 1954–55, with the end of the Korean War, large numbers of soldiers were demobilized. Soldiers who had the opportunity to return to their native villages where they had close relatives and could earn a decent living did not consider settling elsewhere, but some who came from poorer areas and who had become accustomed to collective life chose to go to Hainan instead. In all, an estimated seventy thousand soldiers were settled onto Hainan state farms under the direction of the Land Reclamation Bureau. In the mid-1950s, 54 percent of the workers on state farms were military veterans, 28 percent were local civilians, and 22 percent were other civilians.

Compared to the individual family settlements in the surrounding communities, state farms retained the spirit of frontier military outposts. When state farms first started, people were awakened each day and called to work with bugles. Clothing and other necessities were issued. Workers, overwhelmingly male, worked in formations and followed orders in the spirit of military discipline. People lived in accommodations similar to barracks, which had large central halls where they ate, held meetings, and gathered for leisure activities. As in army camps and even more than in factories and universities in China, the state farms were complete communities. They had their own schools, hospitals and clinics, markets, stores, and movie theaters. They maintained their own army reserves ready to defend the island if need be. There was little reason for workers to go off the farm, and in fact they rarely did.

In 1952, China welcomed some seven hundred Malayan Chinese dissidents expelled by the Malayan government for supporting the Communist movement. Their forebears had originally emigrated from areas of grinding poverty in China, and in the 1950s there was still no opportunity for them in their families' native villages. Since they had come from warm climates and some even had experience as rubber workers, they were settled onto their own state farm, Xinlong, in Wanning County in southeastern Hainan. In the mid-1960s Xinlong opened its doors to overseas Chinese who escaped from persecution in Indonesia, and in the late 1960s and 1970s it admitted three thousand Chinese-Vietnamese refugees. As on the island's other state farms, these refugees concentrated on growing rubber, and because of their special refugee status, they received special help from the government to get established. After Xinlong, four more state farms composed of returned overseas Chinese were successfully established in Hainan. Although they did not have the martial spirit of the other state farms, they did have many of the same collective features. The supervision of these overseas farms shifted over the years from Overseas Chinese Affairs, to the Army Corps, to Land Reclamation, and, later, to the Agricultural Commission of the Hainan Regional Government, but their basic patterns of development did not change.

Many state farms had difficulty determining a common language and establishing a common culture. It was not uncommon to have on the same farm large numbers of workers whose native dialects were Chaozhouese, Hakka, Mandarin, Cantonese, and Hainanese, and it was often hard to coordinate them. Each state farm chose one dialect, usually Mandarin, to be its lingua franca. Problems were still acute, however, especially between the Hakka and those from Shantou. In 1954 and 1955 when demobilized troops could be used to come closer to fulfilling manpower needs, many of the quarreling Chaozhouese and Hakka who had been recruited earlier were sent back to their ancestral villages, even if they were overcrowded.

Nor were former soldiers always an ideal work force. Many from northern China found it difficult to adapt to a tropical climate, and in the late 1950s rubber workers were still in short supply. To meet the demand, various military districts in 1960 tried to send a hundred thousand veterans to Hainan, but fewer than sixty thousand could be mobilized to go. Of those who went, many, finding the climate inhospitable and conditions too difficult, asked to leave. Officials at first refused to grant permission, but before the end of the year some who insisted on leaving rebelled. The minister of land reclamation, Wang Zhen, had to be called to Hainan to negotiate a settlement, and ten thousand were permitted to return to northern China.

By the mid-1950s settlers began to marry and have children. Some soldiers received help from relatives in their native villages in finding wives; some found wives on Hainan, especially from Wenchang County, which always had a population surplus. The character of state farms gradually altered. In 1954 the system of supplying goods and food to everyone began to change to an accounting system in which people were paid wages, purchased their own daily necessities, and were allowed to cook food separately. Though family life replaced the barracks, work was still organized as in a state factory, with work brigades, set wages, and state social security system benefits.

Farming in the surrounding civilian economy, as elsewhere in China, had been collectivized in 1955 and communized in 1958. After 1961, with the production team as the basic accounting unit, ordinary farmers in the surrounding areas, unlike state farm workers, operated as a collective. A farmer's income was dependent on team income, with no regular state-set salaries, and he lacked the guarantees of the state system.

From the point of view of the state farms and of Land Reclamation, state farms were making a greater contribution to the nation than were the surrounding farms. They were producing a commodity of very high priority and opening up a wilderness area. In Haikou, officials in the Land Reclamation Bureau were considered to be of higher quality than those in the Hainan Island Regional Government. Workers on the state farms seldom had more than an elementary school education, but they were generally better educated than those in surrounding farm communities. State farms not only had tractors and other machinery but workers who knew how to operate and repair them. They had electricity and electricians, which surrounding production teams lacked. Perhaps more important, the local farmers had adapted to their climate and circumstances and did not have the state farm's determination to transform the environment. Tending rubber trees required special care, fertilizer, and knowledge about insects, the use of insecticides, and disease prevention. The rubber trees raised by surrounding farmers did not do nearly so well as those on state farms, and state farm officials discouraged farmers from growing rubber trees.

As the state farms continued to expand, they began to encroach more on land considered desirable by some of the surrounding farms. State farms argued that nothing had been previously planted there, but nearby farmers said that they used the land to graze their pigs and chickens. Some farmers would have been mollified if they or their children had been given regular jobs on the state farms, but the farms no longer had labor shortages or the capacity to absorb many more people. The disputes that arose over land use acquired an intensity that reflected the fundamental division between the locals and the outsiders on the state farms who did not speak the local language, used scarce resources like water, married many of the most attractive local women, and looked down on most locals. At the higher levels of bureaucracy in Haikou, these disputes were reflected in disagreements between the Hainan Island Regional Government, which supervised ordinary farmers, and the Land Reclamation Bureau, which almost rivaled the regional government in size.

The disputes were exacerbated by the anarchy of the Cultural Revolution, especially in 1969–1974, when state farms and surrounding communes were united under the Army Corps. Angry farmers, who felt that their land had been appropriated by state farms without any compensation, took the law into their own hands and cut down rubber trees on the state farms, and vigilantes from state farms burnt or attacked several of the surrounding villages, sometimes killing or wounding nearby farmers. After the Cultural Revolution, in a more lenient era, farmers demanded redress. In 1980 the disputes were so severe that officials, including Wang Zhen and Guangdong's first Party secretary, Xi Zhongxun, came to Hainan to mediate. After several years of strife, an agreement was reached in 1982. State farms were enjoined from expanding their territory any further and they were to make an effort to hire surrounding farmers as workers and to give the farmers technical advice and assistance in growing rubber and other crops they could sell on the market economy. Although minor disagreements continued, major ones subsided.

One of the reasons that state farms did not need additional labor during the Cultural Revolution was that they were asked to absorb one hundred thousand former Red Guards, educated urban young men and women, without work opportunities in their native cities. After 1968, as the Military Control Commission began to clamp down on the Red Guards and rebel cadres to bring order to the cities, it needed a place to send them. Universities were not yet completely reopened and the state farms, which still occupied territory not fully reclaimed, were expected to find places for more workers. Reclamation authorities in Haikou arranged for the assignment of the young people to specific farms.

Even though some had wanted to help their country, they went to Hainan because they had no choice, and many found living conditions very tough. By the time they were sent to the countryside, most had already become disillusioned by the crackdown on the Red Guards, which they once had been encouraged to join. Food on the farms was in short supply, in limited variety, and often not to their taste. Houses had dirt floors, insects were common, and sanitation left something to be desired. There were rarely any reading materials available except the works of Chairman Mao. And physical labor was not easy; loads were sometimes heavy, and the weather very hot. Most youth wanted to return to the cities, and many despaired of ever completing their educations. Some were still in the countryside in 1977, when examinations for higher schools and universities were held for the first time in over a decade, and they resented that they had not had the opportunity to prepare properly for the exams. Their careers, many felt, had been wasted, and they saw little future for themselves.

On the state farms, Army Corps officers and local cadres were sometimes cruel to the educated young people and abused the young women among them. Yet some farm workers and cadres were also kind to them, and many youth were sympathetic to local families in primitive living conditions. Many of those sent to Hainan took part in farm work, but others were called upon to be teachers, to bring higher levels of education to the farms. Regardless of their role, virtually all the youth left as soon as permission to return home was granted in the 1970s, and they quickly lost touch with the friends they had made. Only a handful who had married local people or who had some other special reason for staying remained behind. The youth who left were not replaced by new intellectuals assigned to state farms, and it proved difficult for the farms to sustain the higher standards in the schools that the educated youth had helped establish.

In one fundamental sense, the Cultural Revolution was different in Hainan state farms than in other parts of Guangdong. With the Vietnam War raging less than a half an hour by air to the west of the island, the soldiers demobilized to Hainan a decade or so previously were judged to require reinforcements. In 1968, on state farms as elsewhere, the Military Control Commission was sent in to examine the thought of leading cadres. But in 1969 the Army Corps (Bingtuan) was sent in directly from the Guangzhou Military Region to supervise military preparedness on the state farms. Several hundred corps members came to each farm, and they took over the management of the entire farm, including production. Since rubber production was considered urgent, trees that had been tapped every other day were sometimes tapped several times a day. On Hainan, Land Reclamation officials had learned that their trees could not really be tapped from November to March without damaging them, but the Army Corps ignored this. As a result it weakened the trees and made them even more vulnerable to typhoons, which destroyed a substantial portion of the rubber crop. It was a local replay of the excesses of the Great Leap Forward. People who were untutored in science and technology and who badly wanted rapid progress had the power to carry out policies that were out of keeping with reality, and by the end of the Cultural Revolution they had devastated the economy of the state farms and earned the enmity of local residents, including the earlier generation of soldiers who had become state farm workers.

## Li and Miao Minorities before Reforms

The relationship of the Li minority (810,000 by the 1982 census) to the Han majority of Hainan (then 5 million) was in many ways like Hainan's to mainland China. The Li were poorer, more backward, and had lower levels of education, and they were not welcome as workers on the state farms. The Li received some outside help, but few became cadres and, even if they did, the power lay elsewhere. Although some Han cadres made sincere efforts to develop good relations with Li, helping the Li was subordinate to other goals and most in fact looked down on the Li. The Li in turn looked down on the even more backward Miao (41,000 by the 1982 census), who mostly lived even farther up the mountainsides of Hainan.

Before army engineers built the road through central Hainan, the Li were quite isolated from other areas and eked out a living in the south by growing a kind of sweet rice in dry fields by slash-and-burn methods. They farmed fields in one spot for four or five years until the soil was depleted, and then moved their small bundles of belongings to another area, burnt the weeds to help enrich the soil, again grew crops for a number of years, and then moved on once more. Every twenty to twenty-five years they returned to their original area and began the cycle over again. The climate was mild enough that they could live through the winters without fuel, and thatched huts or caves protected them from the winds and rains.

The Li had long felt oppressed by the Han majorities, and a considerable number had joined with the Communist guerrillas in their long struggle that continued until 1949. This was particularly true for the many years that the Communist guerrilla forces made their base near the mountain Wuzhishan, deep in Li territory, where they worked closely with the Li.

After 1950, the Communists established the regional government, the Li-Miao Autonomous Region, in the southern half of the island and designated the old Li town of Yinggen as the capital. After the army engineers cut their new road, the Communists moved the capital southwest to an entirely new site on the road, not far from Sanya. As in many minority areas, the Communists found it easier to establish their rule in an entirely new city where they did not have to deal with tightly knit traditional communities. The new city, Tongza, became first an administrative center for the autonomous region (total population 1.9 million as of the 1982 census) and gradually a marketing and educational center as well. In addition to the region officials, Land Reclamation cadres moved to Tongza to direct the state farm work in the region, and their numbers in Tongza increased in 1974 when they became independent of the Land Reclamation Bureau in northern Hainan. While directing work in the southern half of the island, other government and Party officials in Tongza, however, remained under officials in Haikou who were responsible for all of Hainan.

In the 1950s and 1960s Han cadres flowed in to Tongza and to a lesser extent to the other counties in the autonomous region. The Communists there gave a certain position of honor to former Li guerrilla cadres and brought children of guerrillas and children of Li chieftains into the school systems, Youth League, and Communist training programs. Some were sent to special schools for minorities in Tongza, Haikou, and Guangzhou, to be trained for positions of leadership. Many Li cadres had become bitter by the mid-1950s, however, because they felt that they continued to be treated with condescension, that they were constantly discriminated against when it came to real power, and that Li children were not given equal opportunities to get ahead. This problem intensified during periods of crackdown on localism, as in 1957, and under some of the hardline policies of the Cultural Revolution. Han officials countered that Li were given special privileges, allowed to have more children, allowed to enter schools and training institutes despite having lower scores than Han, and that they were totally unprepared for leadership positions.

When the Han pursued an activist policy in the Li areas in the 1950s, they attempted to push the Li from slash-and-burn to settled agriculture, which they believed was more advanced and easier to manage. In some cases they helped irrigate new fields and establish rice-paddy agriculture. Some Li accepted the new life, but many preferred the taste of their sweeter "hillside" rice, and many continued to grow it and corn by traditional methods even if they had access to paddy fields. A few Li found new opportunities in Tongza, which had forty thousand people by 1985, and in the growing county capitals, as service personnel or as peddlers of produce. But most Li lived in more remote areas and continued to eke out a bare existence on the side of relatively barren mountains.

## Preparing the Infrastructure

Reforms and the new opening came to Hainan more slowly than elsewhere in Guangdong. Even as it began to open in 1980 Hainan remained more conservative and insular, the economy more primitive. Until the Vietnam conflict receded in the early 1970s, Beijing was so concerned about Hainan's vulnerability that it was kept more closed than other parts of Guangdong. Because Hainan was so backward, the effects of isolation were even more profound. In the late 1960s and early 1970s the few factories in Hainan had been mostly moved to the island's remote mountainous areas. There, cut off from specialists and good transportation, they tried to produce goods, but the results were even more disastrous than when mainland Guangdong industries were moved to Shaoguan.

Yet to achieve peaceful reunion with Taiwan, Beijing officials felt that they needed to show that they could manage their tropical island successfully.[3] By the late 1970s Taiwan had become a showcase of economic progress, with rising standards of living, improved educational standards, modern transportation and communication, and industrial power. Hainan was anything but a showcase, and officials in Beijing underestimated its disadvantages in the early 1980s in comparing it to Taiwan before its development took off. Taiwan in the 1950s had an infrastructure left by the Japanese, a basically literate population, massive inputs of American aid, and over a million outsiders, including tens of thousands of well-educated officials and thousands of American advisors. Cadres in Hainan in the early 1980s had very low levels of education and no experience with modern organization, let alone modern industry. Beijing did realize, however, that Hainan lacked leadership, that it could not suddenly advance to a market economy, and that outside aid and improvement in infrastructure were required.

Hainan officials were not necessarily receptive to help from outsiders, against whom they had long nourished resentments. They knew that they were "backward" and regarded as less capable. Their attitudes toward other Chinese were not unlike those of colonies complaining about colonialists. In Hainan's view, outsiders took high-quality iron ore from the mines at Shilu, rubber from the state farms, and salt from Yinggehai without proper repayments. The island had received some outside financial help, but it was niggardly, enough to create economic dependence on the outside without contributing to island development. In their view the mainland had sent the carpetbaggers who had subordinated the local guerrilla forces and in 1957 had cracked down on their localism and on their hero Feng Baiju for resisting. Even many outsiders acknowledged that Feng had been treated too harshly, but his honor was not restored.

Planning and reforms for Hainan lagged behind changes in other areas. At a lengthy conference on Hainan in Beijing in early July 1980, attended by Zhao Ziyang and other officials, it was decided first to improve relations between the state farms and the communes, to consolidate the agricultural base, and then to prepare for new construction. The sixth five-year plan, which began in 1981, already included a significant budget increase for Hainan's transportation and communication infrastructure. In 1982, Guangdong's first Party secretary, Ren Zhongyi, sent Lei Yu, an able subordinate who originally had come with him from Liaoning to Guangdong, to lead Hainan's Party and government. Lei Yu was still in his late forties and worked well with local Hainan cadres. He brought a sense of dynamism, he clearly had the ear of the provincial leadership, and yet, unlike earlier leaders who brought huge numbers of outsiders, Lei Yu came basically alone. For the most part local cadres found him sympathetic and were ready to work with him.

In January 1983 Zhao Ziyang led another forum on Hainan development, this time held on the island. Before two months had passed, other key national leaders also visited—Party General Secretary Hu Yaobang, land reclamation leader Wang Zhen, and go-between Gu Mu. On April 1, 1983, following these discussions, the Party Central Committee and the State Council sent out a directive that called for more rapid development in Hainan's agriculture, forestry, and rubber production and also helped lay plans for the beginning of industry. These plans were undergirded by a program of investment and tax credit, with help from Beijing and Guangzhou.

Because of the poor base for a commodity economy, the development of Hainan's infrastructure, unlike mainland Guangdong's, actually moved ahead of the growth of markets. By the mid-1970s Hainan had begun paving the two-lane highway from Haikou to Sanya that the army had built, and by the beginning of the sixth five-year plan much of the eastern and western highways around the edge of the island had also been paved. Work on these basic roads continued, and gradually the worst curves and bumps were ironed out. These roads supported every kind of transport: those on foot, bicycles, motorbikes, motorbikes with sidecars, cars, vans, tractors, trucks of all sizes, and buses. Travel from one end of the island to the other, a trip that took days in 1949, required only eight hours by the 1980s, barring unforeseen delays.

The outdated narrow-gauge railroad linking the iron-ore mine with the port of Basuo was replaced with a new wider-gauge track, and the line was extended around the southwestern part of the island between Basuo and Sanya. The port of Basuo was modernized so that it could handle several ships of up to twenty thousand tons at the same time. The silt in Haikou harbor had caused such problems that in 1980 it often took an hour just to dock the regular passenger ferry from Guangzhou. By the mid-1980s the harbor was dredged and deepened to over eight meters. By 1987, when a new wharf was completed, two five-thousand ton ships, two three-thousand ton ships, and a passenger ship could be docked. Haikou's new airport runway was extended to 2,500 meters, so that it could handle 150-passenger airplanes and begin regular international service to Hong Kong, Singapore, and elsewhere. Sanya's small military airport was opened to civilian traffic, with several flights a week to Haikou on a small forty-four seater.

Communication facilities were provided by NEC (Nippon Electric), with the cooperation of Hong Kong Cable and Wireless, and modern microwave service was installed in July 1987, linking Haikou and Hong Kong directly with service to Japan and the United States. Simultaneously, 940 channels were opened between Haikou and Sanya; these provided telephone linkage between the major cities and eight of Hainan's seventeen counties, with the expectation of introducing direct dialing and expanding service to the other counties before the end of the decade.

The area of infrastructure that lagged most behind was electric power. Over 90 percent of the 370,000 kilowatts available in all of Hainan in early 1987 (compared with 12,000,000 kilowatts then available in Taiwan) was from hydroelectric power. As demand increased, the lack of large reservoirs caused acute shortages of hydropower in dry seasons.

In the 1980s about one-third of Hainan investment was in Haikou City, even though its population was only 5 percent of the island's. Although there had been none in 1980, by the late 1980s there were five modern hotels and several modern cadre guest houses, and ten more hotels were either planned or under construction. From a poor overgrown town in 1980, Haikou began to take shape as a modern city with broad tree-lined boulevards. Haikou built hundreds of factories and multistory office buildings and greatly expanded its meager industrial base. With the exception of Shenzhen and Zhuhai and possibly Foshan, no city in Guangdong had undergone as much change relative to its size. But the source of change was more from state-led construction than from reforms and market forces.

## The Hainan Car Incident, 1984–85

Hainan had been granted specific approval by higher levels to import motorized vehicles and other goods for use on the island, and in early 1984 the administrative office director, Lei Yu, Hainan's highest government official (the post was unique to Hainan because of its special status), approved lower-level requests for the import of sixteen thousand vans.[4] From 1949 to 1984, aside from trucks, Hainan had imported only ten thousand vehicles. With their expanded budgets, however, units that wanted their own transportation could now use vans to carry eight to ten cadres on the newly paved roads.

The vans, purchased from Toyota by a Hong Kong Chinese businessman, were shipped directly to Hainan. As they began to arrive, virtually every major Party and government unit within Hainan began forwarding requests for the purchase of vans. Several lower officials in the regional government began to grant additional permission to import vans. Just as Lei Yu had clearly acted within the regulations, they were also within their rights in signing permission slips.

The problem was that some units purchasing vans found it more lucrative to sell them to units in mainland Guangdong and elsewhere that were not allowed to import them. It was not easy for higher officials, even within Hainan, to trace whether or not a unit had sold its vehicles. Foshan and other localities, earlier given special permission to import motor vehicles and other goods, had done some reselling without being punished. Many Hainan officials believed that bureaucrats in Beijing and Guangzhou, unable to budget enough to finance Hainan development, had at least implicitly expressed their willingness to look the other way so that profits from the resale of vans and some other goods could help finance Hainan development.

The amount of money that could be made by a Hainan unit in the resale of a car was far beyond anything they had ever known; for some, the opportunities were irresistible. Some of the units, starved for financial resources, did use the funds to expand the infrastructure development that was just beginning, but reports of other uses, including personal gain, began to reach higher-level officials. Units closest to the seats of power and information moved first to take advantage of the situation. Party, government, and army units, state farms, factories, stores, hotels, schools, and even kindergartens moved quickly to get their share of the profits. Within weeks, poor units farther away from Haikou also wanted their share. Of the first batch approved, 2,300 vehicles arrived in the first half of 1984 and 13,000 came in July, but by September, when higher officials called a firm halt, over 80,000 had been approved. At Hainan's level of development, it was an enormous expense. Leaders hesitated to stop the importing, both for fear that distant units, already disadvantaged, would claim that Haikou had once again looked after only itself and for fear that units that had gone into debt and made commitments to buy would not be able to pay what they owed if they did not get the vans they had ordered.

Personal relationships remain very important in China, and they are perhaps even more important in Hainan than in other parts of the country. Officials who were approached by their friends to purchase a car on their behalf found it difficult to refuse, and though some of these friends used the vehicles themselves, most sold them for profit. Hainan's highest-level native cadre was Chen Yuyi, deputy director of the island in charge of foreign economic work. He was approached especially by friends from his native Qiongshan County and by units from Qionghai County, where he had served as deputy Party secretary, and he personally approved 73,000 vehicles. Given the history of tensions between locals and outsiders, it was just as difficult for an outsider like Lei Yu, at forty-nine the youngest top leader Hainan had ever had, to risk ruining his relations with local cadres by criticizing his deputy Chen Yuyi. When Lei Yu, clearly acting on orders from higher provincial officials, finally went to the docks to stop boats carrying vans from Hainan to the mainland, he nonetheless encountered powerful local resistance. Even after the clampdown was ordered from above in September, over the next two weeks local officials, still consumed by desire, approved the import of 8,900 more vehicles in clear defiance of the order.

The Hainan purchases caused a crisis. They had used over $1 billion of China's hard-won foreign currency, and not only was there a shortage of hard currency for further purchases, but profiteering had ballooned out of control and attracted national and even international attention. Officials in Beijing felt they had no choice but to crack down. China's social order and reputation were at stake, and those high officials who had long opposed allowing such freedom in Guangdong were ready to embarrass the reformers if they did not take action. Top leaders in Beijing, approaching the problem cautiously, sent over one hundred officials from Beijing and Guangzhou in early 1985 to undertake a thorough two-month investigation. Their reports concluded that the entire arrangement was not basically in China's interest. If vans were to be imported at all, this should be done on more favorable terms, without so many middlemen, and in accordance with regulations about where and to whom they could be sold.

Higher levels therefore allowed no more van imports and required that vehicles already imported but still in the hands of Hainan middlemen be sold at a lower price. This meant a loss for some, but previous sales, impossible to trace, were allowed to stand, and some units had already enjoyed handsome profits. Lei Yu was dismissed as first secretary and reassigned to a lower-level position, deputy county Party secretary on the outskirts of Guangzhou, first in Hua and later in Zengcheng counties. In 1988 he again rose to become deputy mayor of Guangzhou and was put in charge of its new economic and technological development zone. He was found to be impeccably honest: all presents he had received had been turned over to units for public use, he had refused to accept even cigarettes personally, and he had bought no goods on his trips to Hong Kong. He was declared innocent of personal profiteering, but guilty of negligence. A few officials whose violations were particularly egregious were sent to jail, and many received minor criticism. Most decisions on punishments were announced soon after the investigation, in the hope that units could move on to more important work.

In an unintended outcome, however, Lei Yu became a hero. Having brought capable people to the fore in various parts of the island, he had provided far more dynamic direction than Hainan had ever known. Many high officials outside Hainan felt that the affair should have been handled more leniently in order to maintain the pace of development. In May 1986, 166 young cadres in Beijing, many of whom had gone to Hainan to investigate the case, signed a petition for Lei Yu's return to Hainan as administrative office director. Local cadres were even more upset. Though under pressure, he had refused to crack down on local cadres and was prepared to suffer personally for supporting them. Locals were bitter, believing that, as in 1957, Hainan was being unfairly punished. Foshan had not had to suffer for similar activities. If there was wrongdoing, why was no action taken against those who bought the vans? Punishing Lei Yu, some argued, was like arresting the nose ring after the bull had escaped. For locals who felt oppressed by outsiders, Lei Yu became their symbol.

The most unfortunate aspect of the episode was the loss of momentum for Hainan Island. It did not have a strong indigenous leadership, and just as one was beginning to develop, the Hainan incident nipped the new spirit in the bud. Cadres were again afraid to risk taking the initiative. On his visit to Hainan in January 1986, Zhao Ziyang tried to deal with the island's resentment and despair by offering financial help for twenty-four large projects, by allowing the sale of the remaining vans and other goods imported in 1984, and by assuring worried cadres that criminal charges would be brought against only the most flagrant violations.[5]

## State Farm Workers, Technical Progress, and Markets

One important goal of China's reform programs was to reinstate intellectuals and allow them to play a role in technical progress. The Tropical Crops Research Center, the only such center in China, had continued to make progress since moving to Hainan in 1958. Although the island had proved to be China's best natural rubber-growing area, it was not as warm as Malaysia. Malaysian rubber trees can be tapped all year long, but it had been hard to find varieties for Hainan that could be tapped more than eight months out of twelve. Various pests and local diseases affected the trees, but the biggest problem was the typhoons, mostly in August and September, that frequently devastated the groves.

He Kang had attracted an able and dedicated staff to the center, including Huang Zongdao, a young scientist on the faculty of Jinling University in Nanjing, and Pan Yanqing, a former student of Huang's. They spent thirty years developing more appropriate strains of rubber in what was, for China, a remote, rustic location. They also developed strains of eucalyptus and other trees that could be planted around the edges of the forests to shield the more tender rubber trees from the typhoons, and by 1980 they had basically solved the problems of pests. They then concentrated primarily on developing higher-yield varieties of seed.

During the Cultural Revolution, research was interrupted, people were sent to the fields, and the close contact between state farms and the center was essentially destroyed, especially during the Army Corps period of 1969–1974. After reforms, Huang became president of the center and its attached university and Pan the Party secretary. As state farms began to revive their neglected and damaged rubber trees, they sent their cadres to the university for special training programs. Although relations between the center (directly under Beijing), state farms, and Hainan agricultural officials still left much to be desired, a new group of university graduates was assigned to lead production work in most of the Hainan state farms and on rubber farms in Leizhou Peninsula, Yunnan, and Fujian as well.

Since the state farms in the southern part of Hainan were mostly opened later than those in the north, after new strains with yields comparable to Malaysia's (despite a shorter growing season) had been developed, they had planted trees with better yields. After the Cultural Revolution state farms in the north began to replace their older trees. The major constraint on accomplishing this speedily was the shortage of electric power to saw up the old trees so that the lumber could be sold, and planners worked to eliminate the bottleneck.

With better seeds and management Hainan increased rubber production from 50,000 tons in 1978 to 120,000 tons in 1986, about 60 percent of China's output. With strong demand, China still imported almost as much natural rubber in the late 1980s as it produced. Researchers were confident, however, that China would be able to double its natural rubber production between 1986 and 2000—from 200,000 to 400,000 tons per year—with Hainan's rubber production growing at roughly the same rate.

An agreement with the World Bank, completed in 1984, was expected to play a large role in increasing production and improving efficiency. The bank granted a no-interest, ten-year, $100 million loan for Guangdong rubber development, 20 percent to be used in mainland Guangdong and 80 percent in Hainan. As a result of this arrangement, various foreign specialists came to Hainan and helped make available foreign equipment and new management systems. In 1987 Thailand could deliver rubber to China for $5,000 a ton, while it cost China $6,100 a ton to produce it. Chinese wage rates were low, but the welfare burden on state farms, including education, health, and other benefits, was heavy. With international advice, leaders worked to improve management and responsibility systems in order to narrow the gap between local and international rubber costs.

In the 1970s virtually all income from state farms derived from rubber sold to the state at fixed prices, and the Land Reclamation Bureau remained focused on rubber production and processing. Although state prices were increased gradually, state farm income could only grow modestly on the basis of crude rubber sales. After reforms, to raise the standard of living, state farms tried to diversify their activities and increase the proportion of goods sold on the market. By 1988 the Land Reclamation Bureau included, in addition to its ninety-two state farms, two research centers and thirty-four separate companies and factories. Industrial activity, negligible in the 1970s, represented 15 percent of the value of its output by 1988 and was growing steadily. By then the Hainan bureau was allowed to retain roughly 30,000 tons of its 140,000 tons of raw rubber, and it had established small factories to produce rubber tires, rubber boots and athletic shoes, rubber gloves, and athletic balls. The wood from old rubber trees was processed into pressed wood, made into furniture, or used for shuttles for textile looms. The bureau also established its own cement, ceramics, marble-polishing, machinery, canned pineapple, and fruit juice factories. In the late 1980s they were still small and backward operations by international standards, but plans were being made to modernize and adapt them to international markets.

Collective life in the 1980s remained strong, with common facilities for education, health care, and recreation. To improve motivation on the state farms, however, collective and individual ownership came to be permitted in addition to state ownership. The changes were consistent with the natural trends toward separate family life that had already begun in the 1960s. In 1987 each worker was given a one-time supplement of seven hundred yuan to assist each family in building its own housing, which at the time cost an average of five thousand yuan. For a family containing two or three workers, therefore, roughly one-third of the expenses for building a new home were covered, and this led to a boom in private housing on state farms that replaced their dormitories and tiny apartments.

In 1987 individual families were allowed a total of 30,000 mou to grow their own rice and other crops, compared to a total of 3,600,000 mou used for rubber, 200,000 mou used for sugar, and 100,000 mou used for tea. Family initiative greatly helped the expansion of market-able tropical crops such as coffee, cocoa, pepper, coconuts, betel nuts, and varieties of Chinese medicine. In addition, nearly 30,000 tons of pork were produced each year on state farms, virtually all by individual households, about 40 percent of which was sold in the markets. Individuals were also allowed to buy shares in enterprises, and some were beginning to invest in those in the nearby towns. Even respon-sibility for growing rubber saplings and tapping and maintaining mature trees was contracted down to smaller groups and sometimes down to family units.

Young people on state farms had grown up very isolated. Even in the late 1980s they had not been exposed to television and had little knowledge about the rest of Hainan, let alone China. Except for a few who made their way into the army, migration was proscribed in the 1960s and 1970s and was still difficult in the late 1980s. Almost all youth expected that, like their parents, they would become workers on state farms. After private enterprise became acceptable in the early 1980s, however, some began to engage in more commercial and independent artisan activity. They set up shops in the areas near state farm entrances, which were transformed into small shopping centers. Some began to sell produce or make small articles for daily use. Allowed to buy tractors and motorbikes, a handful with the greatest access to funds started their own transport businesses. Slowly the most ambitious youth began to sense possibilities in the markets at the edge of their farms. In 1988 roughly one-third of state farm family income was private, and income per state farm worker was rising at a rate of about two hundred yuan per year, mostly from the increase in private income.

## Farmers and Production-Driven Markets, 1983–1988

Although an effort was made in the 1980s to break down the barriers between the state farms and the rest of the economy, they remained in the late 1980s essentially two separate economies, administered separately. It was acknowledged that Land Reclamation Bureau activities, including the state farms, were better planned than the rest of the island's economy and that the quality of their work force was higher.

Ironically, because the state farm economy was so heavily tied to rubber, which had administered prices, the rest of the economy grew more rapidly in the late 1980s. From 1950 to 1982 the central government had invested 5.3 billion yuan in Hainan, but in only four years from 1983 to 1987, it invested 4.8 billion yuan.[6] The proportion of the value of Hainan's agricultural and industrial output from the Land Reclamation sector, including state farms, fell in these four years from about one-third to one-fifth and was continuing to fall. Accordingly, per capita income off the state farms began to rise at a faster rate, though on average even in 1988 it was still about 80 percent lower than on the state farms.

As local leaders began to gain more perspective on the world economy, they began to consider what role Hainan might play in it. Hainan was still too far away for Hong Kong businesses to invest large amounts in processing factories. And it was still too poor and local entrepreneurs were too weak to expect that granting freedom to private individuals to form enterprises would bring a great advance to the economy anytime soon.

The obvious role for Hainan was to draw on its strength, the production of tropical crops and the mining of raw materials, and with outside help to develop local industries that used these resources. Since the island was too poor to generate effective demand, it would begin by producing for the outside. In line with new thinking about the role of the market in driving production, Hainan planners by the mid-1980s were thinking about how production of processed foods could in turn reorient and drive agricultural production. Although much of the soil in western Hainan was not terribly fertile, in 1987 over 80 percent of the island's population was in agriculture and the value of agricultural production, 4.1 billion yuan, was still far more than the value of industrial production, 2.4 billion yuan. Increasing agricultural income had to remain central to the island's plans.

The case of sugar was a good example. Since state procurement prices for sugarcane by the early 1980s were not rising rapidly enough to keep farmers in the Pearl River Delta interested in planting it, sugar-processing factories in that area were short of sugarcane. Hainan farmers were happy to produce and sell sugarcane at the same price.

Since sugarcane transport costs were expensive, it was better to let some processing factories in the Delta close down and be replaced by factories in Hainan. In the 1980s virtually every county in Hainan built sugar plants, and by 1987 there were thirty-nine; they produced 300,000 tons of sugar per year, one-sixth of Guangdong's total and two and a half times Hainan's production in 1983. Given the backwardness of Hainan transportation and the lack of funds, officials chose to build tiny factories far behind efficient world-class facilities. Some Hainan farmers found jobs in sugar factories but far more planted sugarcane to meet the rising demand from factories.

With imported machinery from Denmark and Italy, Hainan also began to expand its production of coffee. In 1987 it produced 350 tons of coffee beans, and production and sales were increasing rapidly. Many parts of Hainan were planning to begin growing Xinglong and Fushan coffee beans, the most promising strains developed in Hainan. A modest grant was also received from the World Bank to expand pineapple canning. Another World Bank grant was helping expand tea production, which by 1987 amounted to 4,400 tons, one-third of the province's production for the international market. On a smaller scale, demand in the domestic market was also prompting increases in other crops, especially pepper and Chinese medicine, but the cost of production and transport still made them noncompetitive on the world market.

Coconuts were one of the first great market successes. They were concentrated in the northeast corner of the island, not far from Haikou. About half of the trees were in Wenchang County, where commerce was more advanced than in most of Hainan. In early 1983 coconuts typically sold for 0.2 yuan each, but at the end of the year a number of coconut candy factories began expanding rapidly, which drove up the price to a peak of 0.8 yuan in 1984. Many factories consolidated because they could not compete individually, and by 1987 the price was down to 0.5 yuan. A small group of coconut middlemen had developed by then. They purchased coconuts from farmers, gathered them, and transported them to factories. They bargained with both the farmers and the factories to get the best price. Until the mid-1980s the hulls of the nuts were thrown away, but with new equipment purchased from West Germany, they were used to make floor mats, as is done in other parts of Southeast Asia. The floor mat plant, part of the most successful coconut candy factory in Wenchang, was formed by combining several smaller rural coconut factories; by 1987 it employed over five hundred people. In 1983 farmers began planting new coconut trees, which mature for seven years before bearing nuts. It was estimated that the number of coconut trees would expand from twenty-six million in 1980 to sixty million in 1990 to meet the demand created by factories.

The development of fish, lobster, shrimp, and other aquatic products along Hainan's east coast and in fresh-water ponds, though just beginning, also had great potential.

Hainan's highest officials also made an effort to respond to Hainan's complaints that it remained poor because all its resources were appropriated for use elsewhere. An obvious place to begin was in factories that used natural rubber. A rubber tire factory that in 1980 produced 140,000 tires expanded to a capacity of 300,000 by 1987, including 50,000 truck tires. It was allowed to import some Japanese machinery from Kobe Tekko with controls by Yokogawa, and it upgraded the machinery it used from domestic suppliers, made mostly in Dalian. Planners hoped to increase their tire production to 400,000 by 1990 and to 600,000 by 1995, which would still be less than 5 percent of the 14 million tires produced nationally in 1987. It was a modest goal for an island that supplied 60 percent of all the natural rubber produced in China and about 25 percent of all rubber, natural and artificial, used for rubber products in China. Other factories, also outside the Land Reclamation system, produced bicycle tires and rubber gloves with newly imported production equipment.

Laying the basis for a metal industry, in 1987 the State Council authorized the establishment of a steel plant to produce 350,000 tons a year, located near the iron-ore plant in Shilu. Coal was to be imported to fire the plant. At a cost of $8 million, used machinery was brought from a Ford factory in the Philippines to Hainan to help promote a car parts production plant that would eventually make use of the metal produced in Shilu. Ford engineers came to help install the machinery. At the time there were in all of Hainan only fifteen repair stations for repairing and installing spare parts in cars, tractors, and diesel engines, all on a modest scale. In addition, Hainan had only forty-three machinery factories. It was hoped that some of these repair stations could grow into auto parts producers, helping in turn to drive the development of Hainan's machinery industry.

In addition to building an industry around the island's own resources, Hainan planners also developed what was in effect a modest import substitution policy. At the beginning of the reforms a high proportion of Hainan residents could not afford manufactured clothing, but by the mid-1980s it was beginning to replace hand-sewn clothing except in the more remote areas. After the great success of the polyester fiber plants in Xinhui County, Guangdong had permitted the establishment of several such plants, including one in Haikou. Planning began in 1984 and production commenced in November 1986, using equipment from West Germany, England, and elsewhere. The plant received priority in electric supply and operated without interruption, producing polyester fiber in a world-class facility at the rate of five thousand tons per year.

A nearby textile plant actually opened slightly earlier, in December 1985, and by 1986 produced ten million meters of polyester cloth a year. In the fall of 1987 a dyeing facility opened, with the capacity to process twenty-one million meters of cloth per year. An additional part of the factory produced cotton yarn for export, to earn foreign currency. Both plants were highly automated, with modern equipment produced in various parts of China. The two plants were able to supply employment for three thousand local people and essentially allowed Hainan to produce its own clothing.

The breakthroughs in rubber, steel, metal, polyester fiber, textiles, and auto parts all required outside capital, technology, and management. Only the processing of tropical crops was managed mostly by local companies and grew up with indigenous leadership.

In the late 1980s, as the growth of local industry in Hainan quickened, it was constrained not only by the limited vision of local officials, accustomed to a static economy and inexperienced in markets, but by infrastructure problems. When there was a shortage of power, high-priority state factories received the supply. Lower-priority state factories received limited electricity, and factories not on state plans even less. Many thus had little opportunity to take advantage of the freedoms they had officially been granted. Locals and outsiders may have disagreed on whether Hainan had the local talent and skills to develop village and township enterprises and respond to market opportunities, but there was no way to test what was possible until they had more electric power.

## The Limited Reach of Early Reforms: The Minorities

The island's new construction, industrial growth, and lively markets were overwhelmingly concentrated in Haikou and, to a lesser extent, in three smaller port cities—Yangpu, Basuo, and Sanya. Because state

farms were tightly organized and linked to Land Reclamation planning, their new systems had an impact very quickly. Yet in the first
decade after 1978, reform had not reached many parts of the island,
especially the remote areas inhabited by the minorities.

The household responsibility system was introduced into the minority areas, and those there welcomed it, but generally the change
came later than in Guangdong's mainland mountainous areas. In 1982,
after the disputes between state farms and the surrounding areas had
subsided, the household responsibility system was tried in Ledong
County and then extended to other minority areas. Collective controls
had always been much looser among minorities, in any case, and
reorganization thus brought fewer changes. Market opportunities remained almost nonexistent.

Although minorities constituted roughly one-half the population of
the Li-Miao Autonomous Region, Han Chinese dominated jobs in
the new capital of Tongza. Of the 1988 population of forty-five
thousand, fewer than four thousand were Li or Miao. Five minority
towns and administrative villages were still unconnected to the outside,
even by unpaved roads. Isolated from other groups and surviving on
subsistence farming, the Li could not change their whole way of life,
of thinking, and of relating to other groups suddenly. Even in the late
1980s many minority families scarcely took part in the commercial
economy and did not feel comfortable visiting the towns. At best,
some minority families near towns and roads found some new opportunities to grow mangoes, pineapples, and bananas, or to collect
medicinal herbs for the market. But virtually none had bicycles or
money to ride the buses, and the goods they transported to market
were limited by what they could carry. The Li did not suffer from the
Hainan car scandal, for example, because information was so slow and
they were so poor that almost no Li units had bought vans to begin
with.

Almost no minorities owned radios, let alone television sets, and
literacy levels were so low that few read newspapers or other printed
materials. Li leaders estimated that illiteracy rates in 1988 for their
people were about 50 to 60 percent among those aged twelve to forty
and over 90 percent among those over forty. Although nearly 95
percent of Li children began elementary school at that time, fewer
than 60 percent completed it, and even those who finished received
very low levels of training. Parents had to buy books and other supplies
for their children, and this was a prohibitive expense. Teachers, whose
income came largely from local budgets, were paid far less than teach-

ers elsewhere, and few educated people were willing to go to these areas to teach. Teachers were allowed an average of 0.50 yuan a month to cover basic school supplies and often had to use some of their own low salary to meet minimal classroom needs. Although each county had a high school, and a handful of the brighter students went on for university training at minority institutes, not one Hainan Li had received technical training at the university level since 1950.

Few Han cadres had done much to improve minority life, and few minority leaders were in a position to change things. In Wanning County, for example, 16 percent of the population were Li but only 0.5 percent of the cadres were Li. In 1988 the autonomous region was abolished to unify administration, and much of its old area became part of Sanya City. Li officials felt that the abolition of the minority region and its own capital made little difference, since they had received so few benefits before.

In the mid-1980s a new effort was made to help poor rural areas by linking each state farm with a nearby poor village. Each state farm was to spend slightly more than 10 percent of its annual profits on programs, parallel to those in mainland mountain counties, designed to help the poor farm village learn how to grow tropical crops that had market potential. The programs were particularly important in the southern part of the island, where the villages were poorest and the largest number of villages were Li minorities. These efforts, though modest in scale, helped reduce the inequalities and the enmities between state farms and the surrounding farm families.

According to the best estimates of Li leaders, the number of Li below the poverty line decreased from about 500,000 in 1982 out of a total of 810,000 (measured as below 120 yuan per capita and 400 catties of grain per year) to 400,000 by 1988 (increasing the standard to 200 yuan per year, slightly more than price increases). By any standard, nevertheless, most Li remained marginal, too remote to be soon affected by the reforms. Even the urban centers of Tongza, Sanya, Yangpu, and Haikou had not yet in the 1980s expanded enough to pull in poorer migrants from Hainan's mountainous areas.

## Sanya Tourism

Hainan's climate is mild in the winter, and planners considering the island's potential naturally thought of tourism. Most promising of all was Sanya, on the southern tip near the Luhuitou ("The Deer Who

Looked Backward") Peninsula, whose name referred to the legend of the hunter who chased a deer to the end of the island, whereupon it turned into a maiden whom the hunter married. Sanya was known for its beautiful beaches, which stretched for thirty kilometers along the island's coast. Nearby were sharp cliffs covered with greenery, and large rock formations. The atmosphere was not polluted, and the clear water and colorful fish made it an attractive spot for swimming and snorkling. The Li-Miao Autonomous Region, less than an hour away, was also identified as a potential tourist attraction.

After 1950 the Luhuitou area had become a favorite winter spot for high-level cadres from Beijing and Guangdong, including Mao, Zhou Enlai, and Liu Shaoqi. Knowing Sanya's potential, Marshal Ye Jianying, who had spent some time there in early 1980, and Zhao Ziyang, who had visited on several occasions, became strong supporters of developing it for tourism.

In the early 1980s modest progress was made. A new cadre resort was established to give cadres an isolated private area and allow the larger Luhuitou area to be opened to the public. Zhao Ziyang decided that the naval base at Yulin could be moved to a spot some miles east, out of the way of tourist development. Sanya's tiny military airport was opened to the public. Permission was granted to build small new hotels. The government of Qiongyai County was reorganized, first as a municipal administration, Sanya City, and in 1988 as a metropolitan region. Even with relatively poor facilities, in 1986 49,000 foreign tourists and 180,000 Chinese vacationed there.[7] Five new hotels, with a thousand additional beds, were scheduled for completion by 1989.

Some had begun to talk of grander plans—of fifteen thousand hotel beds and 2.5 million tourists annually by the year 2000. But during the hiatus between 1983, when plans were made for Hainan expansion, and 1988, when Hainan became a province, no one locally had the experience, vision, or authority to plan and coordinate tourist development. Different scenic spots and even the bureaucratic structures for supervising hotels and other tourist facilities were under the jurisdiction of many separate organizations. It was almost impossible to ensure that even basic electricity, telephone, and other crucial services would be available when needed.

The director of Sanya tourism in 1987, Zhang Shan, stood out as one who tried to speed development. After it was announced that Hainan would become a province, more talented mainlanders were ready to move there, but before that Zhang Shan had been one of a

handful ready to forsake material comforts and attractive jobs elsewhere to help build up a backward area. As a Beijing official sent to
investigate the van scandal, he had been impressed with Sanya's potential. He and other young cadres in Beijing drew up a statement of
a vision for Hainan, and he went to Sanya to help achieve it.[8] There
he worked creatively to keep things going until Hainan became a
province and outside leaders could clear through jurisdictional boundaries and begin to provide more support.

Until 1988, for all its potential, Sanya was in fact still an impov-
erished-looking town where thirty thousand people of a very low
educational level eked out an existence and to which nearby farmers,
including Li, Hui, and Miao minorities, came to market their goods
and buy minimal necessities. Tourism was not yet large enough to
bring in any more wealth than in other poor towns.

## Hainan Province: Ambitious Goals and Formidable Obstacles

When China wanted to accelerate the development of Taiwan in 1887,
the Qing rulers made it a separate province. On August 28, 1987,
one century later, with similar goals, Zhao Ziyang announced that he
was proposing that Hainan be made a separate province. Although
Guangdong had made many efforts to accelerate development in
Hainan, Beijing felt that Guangdong was too large and had too many
other priorities to give Hainan the attention it needed for rapid development. Hainan officials welcomed the change because they gained
more independence from Guangdong and higher rank, higher salaries,
and more support from Beijing.[9]

Officials in Beijing and Haikou busied themselves in preparing new
guidelines for system reform, development, and outside investment.
Although many plans were similar to those made since 1983, everything was reconsidered and sped up. In 1986 a Japanese mission of
twenty-one specialists in areas such as transport, construction, mines,
finance, agriculture, tourism, and energy had, in collaboration with a
Chinese team under the State Council, drawn up very detailed scen-
arios for comprehensive development, published in eleven volumes in
May 1988.[10] But even this report was considered too conservative in
its projections by the time it came out, though it was useful for the
extensive background it provided. A team of specialists from the

Chinese Academy of Social Sciences came to Hainan for two months in early 1988 to make overall recommendations on issues that included system reform and personnel, not considered by the Japanese. At the same time the Rand Corporation was commissioned to do a study on Hainan system reforms that would be appropriate for interfacing with foreign businesses.

Officials wanted to make Hainan a special zone that would go beyond even the other SEZs in system reform. It was to have a "small government and large society," that is, very little state-operated enterprise and minimal government. Much like Hong Kong, it was to auction land-use rights to be leased for seventy years, to allow a free market for foreign exchange, and to operate primarily by market principles.

A talented team of outside leaders was brought in as a preparatory team in 1987 and assumed regular positions after Hainan became a province. These included First Party Secretary Xu Shijie, Governor Liang Xiang, and Vice-Governor Bao Keming. Xu was a widely respected urban reformist, originally from Chaozhou, who had served in Hainan from 1964 to 1971 before becoming Party secretary of the Zhaoqing Special District and of Guangzhou City. Liang Xiang had served in Guangzhou before becoming mayor of Shenzhen, where he played an entrepreneurial role in its development. Bao, a senior aeronautics planner in Beijing, was widely respected in national political circles. In addition to this top team, governmental branches in Hainan drew up a list of personnel needed for their new provincial status, and by mid-1988 had publicized on the mainland 4,500 openings for which no appropriate Hainan residents were available.

Haikou became a peculiar kind of boom town. Seeking new opportunities, boatloads of people arrived every day for months; it was estimated that Haikou received a hundred thousand people wanting jobs on the island. Some stayed only a few days, long enough to file an application and be interviewed for a formal position. Others, sensing the possibility of rapid growth, came as petty entrepreneurs. Many mainland units tried to lease land, either for operations they might want to establish or possibly to sell the lease to others later as prices rose.

Although direct contributions from the central government for Hainan development were modest, provinces were encouraged to send representatives, large state companies to establish branches, and banks to lend money. By late 1988 it was estimated that 1,500 companies from various parts of the mainland had representatives in Haikou. Commonly two or three individuals were sent who guaranteed to return a certain amount of profit to their home company after one or two years; they then sought out opportunities of all kinds. Although some focused on products and services related to the company's main work, others were given leeway to investigate any profitable activity, including buying and selling goods in short supply, opening up a free-swinging business atmosphere that more conservative leaders criticized for its speculative nature.

When Hainan became a province, various branches of government in Beijing and Hainan drew up a list of 250 projects for which they would seek foreign investment in the next few years.[11] These included efforts to build up appropriate physical infrastructure, industry, agriculture, and tourism. They envisioned industrial development in Haikou, Yangpu, and the west; agriculture in the east; and tourism in the unpolluted south and east. Thousands of overseas businesspeople came to investigate from Hong Kong, Japan, the United States, Southeast Asia, and even Taiwan, but they were cautious in making commitments. A few foreign ventures were arranged in 1988, but most potential investors felt that it was prudent to wait until more of the infrastructure was in place and until more decisions about system changes for the island had been spelled out and put into practice.

Some of the highest hopes were placed in the offshore oil and liquid natural gas (LNG) exploration off Hainan. In the late 1980s the most promising lead was the LNG discoveries by ARCO. Rather than pipe the LNG to Hong Kong, Hainan planners hoped to bring it onshore near Yinggehai and develop a petrochemical industry that would include fertilizer, then in short supply in Hainan and Guangdong. It was expected that if a satisfactory agreement was reached with ARCO, this multibillion dollar project would eventually dwarf in size any other development prospect then contemplated.

Many thought that the tourist industry was likely to take off first and that in the early 1990s, if run properly, its income could help finance expansion of infrastructure and industry. In early 1988 a team of urban planning leaders from Shanghai's Tongji University was sent to Hainan for two months by the State Council to draw up an overall conceptual plan (*guihua*) for tourist development as a basis for plans to be approved late that year. Places like Wanning and Qinglan Bay along the east coast and some of the colorful minority areas in the southeast were scheduled for development, but Sanya was the center.

An international airport was scheduled for completion in the early
1990s, after which Hong Kong would be only an hour away. Plans
were made to improve infrastructure, with every expectation that
Sanya would become one of the major winter tourist spots in Asia
before the end of the century.

Yet the leaders who were charting this development confronted
fundamental obstacles. One was the difficulty of overcoming bureaucratic barriers beyond their power to control. State farms remained a
separate system under the Land Reclamation Bureau in Haikou. Although the bureau was ready to adapt to markets, it was not ready to
give up its control over state farms. And the state's critical need for
rubber made many hesitate to permit an open market where prices
might get out of control or to expand factories so much that they
might threaten the profitability of the nation's advanced rubber factories in Shanghai and elsewhere. Other key national government
agencies were reluctant to open markets fully for the rest of Hainan's
critical resources: iron ore in Shilu, titanium off the east coast, and
salt in Yinggehai. Yet because these crops and resources made up a
major part of the Hainan economy, if they remained subject to planning controls, it would be difficult to have as free an economy as local
planners hoped. At the same time, granting freedom in the exchange
of currency and in import and export created the potential for abuse
by those from other provinces who were trying to escape controls in
their locality.

Acquiring adequate financing for desired infrastructure projects was
another problem. With the total value of Hainan's agricultural and
industrial output in 1987 only 6.7 billion yuan, about 5 percent of
Guangdong's, the vast needs in infrastructural development would not
be easy to finance. In 1988–89, the completion of Macun's thermal
electric power plant added 350,000 kilowatts of power and provided
relief for the most immediate electricity shortages, but it was not
nearly enough. Plans for the railway linking Haikou to Shilu, thus
creating a railway from Haikou to Sanya, moved ahead, with hope of
completion by 1991. But at best the island's first real container port
facilities were several years away, and the first superhighway from
Haikou to Sanya only began construction in 1988—and only half of
the highway, three lanes, could be paved because of the shortage of
funds. Many parts of the island were still not connected and even
people in the same city could not always call each other, despite new
microwave facilities that could be used to reach the outside world.
Some county bank branches in Hainan, concerned about getting their

capital back, were covertly investing in the Delta rather than in their own counties.

Although some outside cadres began to come to Hainan, the island faced another hurdle: integrating newcomers with local cadres. The gap in the standard of living between advanced and backward areas in 1988 was still so great that once the 1987–88 boom wore off, many in the Delta and northern cities with special skills were not prepared to go to Hainan, even if they were assigned. Few cadres who had originally gone from Hainan to other areas were willing to return. Some who agreed to move hoped to rise quickly or make money and were unprepared to endure the hardships they encountered. Few who came were willing to work anywhere but Haikou. And those who planned to come were often not released by their units. As of August 1988, of the first 3,800 outside applicants chosen by Hainan to fill its new cadre posts, only 1,584 had been able to get permission from their units to go to Hainan. And of those who had gone, over 200 had decided to return.

Many Hainan cadres did not hide their resentment against outsiders; nor did outsiders always conceal their lack of respect for locals. Worried that the newcomers might take their jobs or disrupt their routines, many local cadres continued to conduct all their business in Hainanese although they knew Mandarin. Outsiders new to Hainan found local cadres' conservatism, lack of awareness of the outside world, insularity, and sullen resistance difficult to endure. It would not be easy to bridge the gap.

Like earlier generations of mainland Chinese officials and former soldiers who had come to Hainan, outsiders in 1988 were confronting a backward frontier society. But unlike earlier generations who came to provide political rule and security, they were the first to concentrate on building a modern infrastructure and stimulating commerce and industry. Many doubted that their ambitious goals would be achieved in the early years of provincial status; neither attitudes nor objective conditions were yet ready. The freedom to engage in marketing had worked quickly in the Pearl River Delta, where a base of wealth, entrepreneurial skill, and nearby markets allowed the area to blossom. In contrast, the same freedoms in the early reform years had little impact in Hainan. Few doubted, however, that over the next several decades as a result of outside government-led initiatives Hainan would undergo a significant transformation that would expand its internal markets and strengthen its economic links with the rest of China and the outside world.

# PART III

# *Agents of Change*

# 10.

# *Entrepreneurs: Statesmen, Scramblers, and Niche Seekers*

Even after a decade of economic reforms, Guangdong did not have a fully developed free market economy. It did not have a fully open labor market or a capital market, and leaders could not choose to substitute capital or technology for labor. Basic goods were subject to planning, enterprises were under Communist Party leadership, and all major decisions were subject to review at higher levels of government. Yet there were entrepreneurs in China who would be recognizable in a free market society. They took risks, they organized production in creative new ways, and they brought great gains to the economy.

Considering the structure of the economy in 1979 and their lack of experience with free markets, these entrepreneurs achieved extraordinary results. They did not enjoy the charisma, special grace, and dedicated following accorded in the early 1950s to Guangdong's great wartime heroes. No matter how pleased consumers were, many considered economic success more a result of long overdue freedom than of wise leadership. Economic advances, in any case, did not have the aura enjoyed by victorious struggles against enemy troops and bourgeois exploiters. And after the excesses of the Mao era, the cult of the hero *(geren congbai)* was considered dangerous, and no Guangdong leader was glorified.

Yet amid the turmoil of the first decade of reform, as the old structure became unstuck and new ones were not yet in place, bold leaders played a major role in defining and taking advantage of new opportunities. This chapter presents examples of entrepreneurs, not only to show what they individually achieved but to help understand the structure of entrepreneurship in Guangdong during its first reform decade. Some worked within the government and Party bureaucracy, some managed cooperative enterprises and built large successful companies, and some led independent households. The three most prominent types may be characterized as statesmen, scramblers, and niche seekers.


## Elder Statesmen

Ren Zhongyi, first Party secretary in Guangdong from November 1980 until July 1985, was widely regarded as *the* great provincial entrepreneur of the reform period. When he assumed his position in Guangdong, he already enjoyed great leverage because of his seniority and his record of success in the Northeast. The extensive powers granted top local officials during the early stages of the special policy in Guangdong gave him considerable room for exercising political entrepreneurship. Beijing wanted a strong leader in Guangdong to launch reforms and deal with the outside world. Because of his stature he did not need to cultivate *guanxi* (personal relations) in Beijing; he worked with others to develop a vision for Guangdong development and concentrated on what was needed to achieve it. While informal with work associates, he had the sense of authority, calm, and concern for the correct policy and large public issues that people expect of their leaders. He was masterful in using Marxism-Leninism and in presenting policies to Beijing leaders in terms of their goals and guidelines in such a way that it was difficult for them to withhold approval.

Born near Tianjin (Hebei) in 1913, Ren Zhongyi and his wife, Wang Xuan, joined the December 9th movement of young intellectuals who fled from the Japanese to Communist-led border areas near Yanan in 1935. He was then just about to graduate from Zhongguo, a private university, where he had earlier joined the Communist Party.[1] After 1949, Ren rose quickly. He became first Party secretary in Harbin at age forty-three, and first Party secretary of Heilongjiang Province at forty-eight. The December 9th group, including Ren, was decimated by the Cultural Revolution, but its members reemerged afterward as among the best-educated and most powerful top Party leaders.

Ren had already won the respect of co-workers as a forceful and able administrator before he was transferred in 1977 to Liaoning, which Beijing considered one of its most troublesome provinces. There the Gang of Four had a following that was perhaps second only to Shanghai's, and Mao Zedong's nephew, Mao Yuanxin, arrested after his uncle's death, had built up a strong organization. Ren soon became first Party secretary and was able to smooth over the political difficulties, win the widespread support of cadres, and get the economy moving. Responsive to new ideas, he had already advocated an export-processing zone and system reforms while in Liaoning. He had been so successful that many considered him, along with Zhao Ziyang, a possible future premier, and he was said to have enjoyed the support of Deng Xiaoping and Hu Yaobang.

A key characteristic of successful top local leaders of the time was their willingness to accept criticism without blaming subordinates. People still felt vulnerable and were wary of leaders who, under pressure in the Cultural Revolution, had eased their own situation by criticizing those under them. At the time, nothing was more important in motivating and gaining the loyalty of cadres than a leader's reputation for protecting and standing behind those at lower levels. "Ren Zhongyi," said a close associate, "has strong shoulders." In 1982, when Guangdong was criticized for smuggling, and in 1984 when the province was under fire in the Hainan scandal, Ren Zhongyi was called on the carpet in Beijing. People who worked under him were convinced that he accepted the blame and defended his subordinates. They knew he was well versed in theory and policy and could effectively defend to his superiors what he asked his staff to do. He helped give cadres a sense of pride in Guangdong's economic successes, its new construction, the improvement of facilities and services, and its rate of growth. Their political flank protected, cadres could concentrate on the economic issues.

Like all new leaders at the provincial level, during his first few months in Guangdong Ren took trips around the province to become acquainted with local conditions and local leaders. He worked hard to ascertain the actual situation and get a sense of what was possible from front-line, basic-level cadres, who were the best informed on local developments. He soon identified physical infrastructure as a critical issue and by 1982 was pushing very hard on key roads and bridges, the railroad from Sanshui to Maoming, and electric power plants. Originally the railway and power plants were to be financed in good part by the central government, and Ren tried to prompt Beijing to move quickly. When it became clear that this was not possible, he worked to find funds within the provincial budget and through borrowing, from both domestic and foreign sources.

Ren managed to preserve room for local initiative in his relations with Beijing. "He was not a tape recorder," said one of his close associates, "but a transformer." As noted in Chapter 3, in Guangdong he pioneered the philosophy of pushing rules to the limits in order to get a job done. He quietly allowed new experiments and expanded those that worked well until they became policy, which made it difficult for conservative officials to oppose him. In 1982 Beijing, upset about decadence in Guangdong, told Ren to cut down on investment to avoid strains on limited national resources. Ren agreed that there were areas where investment should be slowed, and he cut in those areas. But, he argued, the policy should be applied with discretion, and he proceeded accordingly. Overall Guangdong continued to increase investment and to grow faster than some Beijing leaders had wanted. Local cadres loved his handling of the issue. Some believed he had even incurred the disapproval of more cautious Beijing leaders like Chen Yun and Peng Zhen for pushing local interests too vigorously.

By the time Ren came to Guangdong, the province was led not by a band of former local guerrillas but by a large complex administrative staff. Unlike Tao Zhu, he brought no team of northerners with him and he regarded local leaders as his allies. In contrast to the 1950s, when local cadres resented the northerners, in the 1980s local cadres happily followed Ren Zhongyi and other top administrators who were originally from other provinces. Although he had never worked in Guangdong before 1980, he became sufficiently attached that he made it his home after he retired in 1985.

Although Ren Zhongyi realized that the bureaucracy was overstaffed with marginally competent cadres, he wasted little time criticizing them. Instead he concentrated on identifying and encouraging those prepared to move things forward. Progress depended on many initiatives by many dedicated cadres, and he vigorously supported the entrepreneurs under him, including Governor Liang Lingguang, Vice-Governor Li Jianan, Shenzhen's Liang Xiang, Foshan's Yu Fei, and Hainan's Lei Yu. Ren was careful to avoid the personal publicity that might give the appearance of a developing cult of personality, but provincial cadres found him charismatic because of his skill in pushing policy to the limits, supporting new creative solutions to problems, and bringing economic improvement.

Liang Lingguang and some heads of municipalities and counties had an entrepreneurial style that resembled Ren's, as did Yuan Geng of Shekou, discussed in Chapter 4. As top officials in their locality, these statesmen all enjoyed considerable leeway. They were tested leaders who believed in reform, and they had the confidence of Beijing's top leaders, who had the same outlook. With their reputations, seniority, and solid support from above, they did not need to bother currying favor in Beijing, and they left detailed manipulation and bargaining to their underlings. They carefully studied and analyzed policy from above to know how far the bounds of acceptability could be pushed, and within that range they boldly pursued what they believed would work. They concerned themselves with the big issues that they thought would advance their localities and cultivated and protected good people under them who could put their plans into effect.

## Scramblers

Turmoil, stemming from the profusion of bewildering changes, was a key characteristic of organizational life in the first decade of reforms. Change proceeded more rapidly than established procedures to cope with it. Not only were there inadequate communication and transport, poor-quality goods, and bottlenecks from shortages, there were few established guidelines for resolving a whole host of complex economic issues never before confronted. Many officials, unsure how to proceed and afraid of making errors, were immobilized. Countless small problems were thus passed to a small number of higher-level officials who had the authority, confidence, and skill to resolve them.

In this situation, the successful entrepreneur was one who was flexible, resourceful, and quick in responding to any situation. He had to have a high degree of cooperation from key people in many different units who were willing and able to go beyond routines. At a critical juncture he might have to call on friends, make the necessary obeisances *(ketou)* to strangers, strike bargains that met the interests of the other unit as well as his own, or successfully apply pressure. Forward movement often required a certain audacity and a willingness to tolerate imperfections. Often these individuals began projects before everything was in place and then kept fighting to overcome whatever obstacles arose. The times required a bold and well-connected scrambler.

To be an entrepreneur, one had to have room to maneuver. Within the Party and government, Yu Fei and Lei Yu (discussed in Chapters 5 and 9, respectively), the province's best-known scramblers, had the needed leeway. But most state enterprises were so tied down in rules, quotas, and targets, so restrained by fixed personnel and equipment, and so dependent on set supply routes that there was no room for an entrepreneur, even a scrambler. However, some locally run enterprises, usually cooperatives, were flexible enough to permit some entrepreneurship. Two examples of unusually successful Guangdong entrepreneurs—one in a large collective enterprise, the other in a small state enterprise under local county management—illustrate the opportunities available and the different kinds of scramblers who took advantage of them. An example of one Hong Kong businessman helps illuminate further the structure of entrepreneurial opportunities in Guangdong in this reform decade.

*The Beginnings of a Modern Business.* Li Xiushen (Lei Sau Sum), a talented entrepreneur born in 1935 in Wuchuan, just east of Zhanjiang, developed the Zhanjiang Home Appliances Industrial Company.[2] He was already considered an outstanding student in elementary school, and in the fall of 1949, in a contest that included writing an essay in Chinese and giving a speech in both Chinese and English, he won first prize in a county with a population of five hundred thousand. Though most students in his school learned only Cantonese, he managed to teach himself Mandarin. In the spring of 1950, just a few weeks before he was to graduate from lower middle school, he responded to a call from the People's Liberation Army to serve as an interpreter between Mandarin and Cantonese forces in their invasion of Hainan.

Army officers, who respected his talents, gave Li introductions that led to work in Zhanjiang's Organization Department, the highly trusted branch of the Communist Party concerned with personnel. Soon a leader in Youth League work, he entered the Party in 1954, when he was nineteen. He became section chief at twenty-one and continued to rise in the Organization Department. He was selected for provincial Party school in Guangzhou in 1957, and then served on the Disciplinary Committee of the Party. In 1962, Li was assigned to the Zhanjiang branch of the People's Bank as Party secretary of its Organization Department.

A talented public speaker, Li was bold as well as eloquent. When criticized during the Cultural Revolution, he refused to admit errors. When an interrogator pressuring him said that if his name was Li and he was from Wuchuan he must be related to the Kuomintang leader Li Han-hun, he not only denied any relationship but answered back, "Since your name is Jiang you must be related to Chiang [which has the same Chinese character as Jiang] Kai-shek."[3] Li was made to do two and a half years of physical labor during the Cultural Revolution. He was officially still affiliated with the bank until 1972, but at that point, when allowed to return to work, he had such bitter memories of his former accusers there that he asked to be assigned elsewhere.

In May 1972 he was thus assigned to be Party secretary in a small collective hardware factory *(wujinchang)*. The factory had been formed in 1969 by the amalgamation of six small handicraft factories that made such diverse products as hoes, buttons, and rat traps. At the time the factory had almost four hundred workers but the value of its annual production was scarcely one million yuan. Many Party officials with backgrounds comparable to Li's would have regarded this job as a demotion, but Li felt that a collective factory had potential and considered it a challenge.

In 1973 Li saw an opportunity to sell fluorescent light fixtures to a state trading firm, which in turn sold them to Hong Kong, but he had trouble finding technically trained people who could help him get the product up to standards. He located an engineer, Ouyang Wen, a graduate of Wuhan's Jianghan University, who had the technical qualifications but had not been able to get satisfactory employment ever since the Korean War, when he had been investigated as a possible Kuomintang spy. Since Ouyang still had an "unclear history," ordinary factories were unwilling to hire him. But Li, after talking to him, was convinced that he could do the job and that he had not been a spy. He also hired a transformer specialist, Huang Riwu, who had had difficulty getting a job that was appropriate to his training ever since 1957, when he had been accused of being a rightist. Li placed full confidence in them and supported them to the hilt, and they in turn were prepared to put in far more than the usual effort for him.

It is unlikely that anyone would have then dared to hire such individuals without the connections in the Organization Department that Li had, and even he took a big risk. Indeed, in 1976, he came under suspicion when the tables turned in Beijing and Deng Xiaoping was under pressure for saying "Who cares if the cat is white or black if it catches the mouse?" A rival factory manager questioned Ouyang's basic loyalty and criticized Li for hiring such a person. When Li was given a brief chance to defend himself, he asked the manager, "How many ovens do you have in your no. 3 workshop?" When the manager couldn't answer, Li had embarrassed his accuser and made his point that he was minding production and doing his job while his accuser was not. Still, it took the support of the Public Security Bureau, which cleared Ouyang's name, and the special efforts of Sun Zhengshu, deputy Party secretary of Zhanjiang, to keep Li from getting into serious trouble over these two hirings. Though his name was officially cleared, he was ready to resign from the factory until his wife persuaded him to get the factory in good shape first. As it turned out, he followed her advice but never got around to leaving.

In the meantime, by 1974, with technical help from Ouyang, Li had been able to produce 12,000 fluorescent light fixtures, which he sold to the state trading firm and which were in turn sold in Hong Kong. Li applied himself not only to technology but to management and to markets. At a time when many others were afraid to accept the responsibility of going into debt, Li, like Yu Fei, had had enough experience with banks not to be worried. In addition, he had friends at the bank who were confident his company would be a good risk. Li imported new production equipment and, with his cheap labor and low price, expanded his sales to Hong Kong. By 1977 his company was selling 300,000 light fixtures a year and Japan's Matsushita, deciding that their sales of the product were no longer profitable there, pulled out of the Hong Kong market. By 1979 Li's product dominated that market, far outselling its Taiwan and Hong Kong rivals. By 1980 he was producing 1.5 million fixtures for that market a year, and before long his firm was one of those allowed to export directly to Hong Kong.

Convinced that the electric rice cooker, already popular in other countries of East Asia, would someday become popular in China, Li set out to develop appropriate technology. In 1980, when there were terrible electricity shortages, many companies were afraid to move into making family electrical appliances. Li, who always made it a point to get the best and latest information, found out that the central government had set up a hundred counties as experimental points for increasing the electricity supply and was allowing companies to produce consumer goods for them. With his market identified, in 1981 Li borrowed ten million yuan in financing from the People's Bank, an unusually large sum for a collective factory. By 1985 the loan was fully repaid, ahead of schedule.

In 1982, Li found out that a conference of commercial units from the one hundred counties was being held in Hunan at which family electric appliance factories could display their wares. Of the twenty-three household electronics companies that displayed such wares, the other twenty-two were state firms. Not only did Li have a product that was technologically ready to compete, but his associates had collected information on the prices to be offered by the other companies. At the meeting, he offered his goods at a price 10 to 20 percent below that of his competitors. He announced that while most other companies had only one size of rice cooker, he had a full line of sizes and that his company stood behind every product, a guarantee then almost unheard of in China. He swept the sales for rice cookers at the meeting and was on his way to becoming the dominant rice cooker producer in China at a time when the market was just developing. By 1987 his company was selling 3.5 million rice cookers a year and enjoyed roughly 50 percent of the Chinese market.

In 1979, to expand his production quickly, he arranged for many other factories to produce parts. Most of them were small machinery or electrical makers that were in financial difficulty. By 1987 Li presided over a "group" (*jituan*), a conglomerate, with fifteen factories under him, fourteen other suppliers, and three others in which his company was a partner. His managerial skills were important in coordinating these. The arrangement could not have been completed so quickly without the active cooperation of the administrators in Zhanjiang's industrial bureaus; nor could Li have undertaken the technological modernization of his factory without the support of the Provincial Economic Commission. They knew Li through Party and government circles and supported him because they had confidence in his ability to do the job.

From the time he was first allowed to contact Hong Kong businesses because they were buying his products, Li sought opportunities to learn from Hong Kong entrepreneurs because he believed they helped point the way for China's development. He began reading books on marketing; until then Chinese managers had little basis for estimating market demand, and he was ahead of his peers in considering how to predict it. He also took a special interest in reading the business history of well-known foreign companies like Toyota and Sanyo. He developed foreign contacts with Japanese business representatives in Guangdong and began going abroad to study technology and keep up with market trends. By 1987 he had already taken seven trips overseas, including three to West Germany and Italy. His son, a graduate of Guangdong's best engineering school, Huanan Engineering University, was then studying business management in the United States.

In 1986, with profits from fluorescent fixtures and rice cookers and with technical cooperation from Italian makers, Li began preparing to produce refrigerators; he made plans for producing 140,000 by 1988 and 400,000 by 1989. With substantial sales contracts already in hand, officials at all levels were confident of their success. In 1979 Li's company annual sales exceeded 2 million yuan, in 1986 they reached 200 million, and in 1987 250 million. It was expected that in 1988, with the new refrigerator line, they would reach 500 million yuan in sales, far surpassing any state factory in Zhanjiang.

*Traditional Connections and a Modern Product.* Li Jingwei founded Jianlibao, a company that manufactured a new drink for athletes by the same name that became a hit after the 1984 Olympics.[4] Li was born in 1937 in Sanshui County, northwest of Guangzhou. Placed in an orphanage at age ten, he completed only four years of elementary school, and at twelve years of age left to work in Guangzhou, first as a cook's helper and then at various odd jobs. He returned to Sanshui several years later, where he became head of a tiny print shop in 1957. A tall man, he played basketball and remained active in sports activities, becoming a deputy head of the Sanshui Sports Federation. Considered very sociable, he had a wide circle of friends. He became a member of the Youth League and later a member of the Communist Party.

In 1973 he went to work in a very small beer factory in Sanshui as an ordinary worker, but he gradually assumed managerial responsibility until he was selected as manager in the early 1980s. At the time the factory made about three thousand tons of beer a year and was losing money. In line with new efforts to make enterprises self-sufficient, Li Jingwei was expected to end the deficit.

When Li heard through a friend in early 1983 that the All-China Sports Federation wanted to prepare a sports drink for Chinese athletes in time for the 1984 Olympics, he sensed an opportunity for his factory and immediately inquired at the federation. From there he went to see Ouyang Xiao, a scientific technician at the Guangdong Physical Education Research Institute (Tiyu Kexue Yanjiusuo) who was carrying out scientific research to produce a health drink, and had just developed a tonic. Although the tonic had a bad taste, Li was delighted with its potential and hired Ouyang as an advisor. When Li ran into an old basketball friend, Jiang Weiji, then working as a technician in light industry in Guangzhou, he persuaded him to come back to Sanshui to experiment with liquids that could be mixed with the tonic to improve its taste.

Meanwhile the Provincial Sports Federation had approached several beverage plants in Guangzhou to develop a drink. The largest, Yazhou Qishuichang, proposed a development program costing one million yuan, which the federation considered too high. By then, after a hundred or more trials, Li and Jiang had come up with a formula, sweetened with honey, that seemed to have a good taste, and they began making their drink in Li's brewery. Their offer to develop it for the federation at no charge was accepted immediately.

At the same time Li and Jiang began to try their hand at publicity. They gave free samples to many sports groups, including the national women's volleyball team, whose members reported that they liked it. In May 1984 Li found out through another of his consultants, the deputy director of the Provincial Sports Federation, that the Asian Soccer Federation was having a meeting at the White Swan Hotel in Guangzhou, and Li hastened to send one hundred cartons of Jianlibao free of charge so that all at the meeting could sample it. With their help, Li was able to work through sports circles to get Jianlibao accepted as one of the drinks for the Los Angeles Olympics, along with drinks from Beijing, Liaoning, Hebei, and Sichuan.

By then Li had gotten permission from the county government to buy new production equipment worth $400,000 from Germany to produce cans, but it did not arrive in time to fill orders for the Olympic Games. But through a friend of Jiang Weiji who was working at the new Pepsi-Cola bottling plant in Shenzhen, they were able to obtain three hundred cartons, each containing two dozen unused Pepsi cans, fill them with Jianlibao, and get them to the Olympics on time. Li also paid for Ouyang to go to the Olympics to help with publicity.

At one of the press briefings before the Olympics, a Japanese reporter asked Ouyang about Jianlibao. He replied, "We'll see how good it is by the results of the women's volleyball team." When the team won the gold medal, the reporter wrote a small article in his newspaper calling Jianlibao the *"masui"* (in Chinese, *"moshui,"* the magic drink). Jianlibao used *"moshui"* in its ads, new stories appeared, and in China Jianlibao was a hit.

Li's factory bought a new and larger production line from West Germany and added facilities worth $2.8 million. When they borrowed money, one of their sponsors, CITIC, sent in a general accountant to straighten out their books. Jianlibao became an extremely profitable factory.

In fact Jianlibao was not particularly well managed and its staff not particularly efficient. Enough of the machinery was automated that very little work was required, however, and the drink's price was sufficiently high that the company made a very good profit.

These two examples represent opposite poles of one key dimension of enterprise entrepreneurs: traditional personal relations versus modern industrial organization. In the case of Jianlibao, traditional personal relationships were used to bring about success without modern concepts of efficiency, management, or organization. All important pieces of information were obtained through friends and acquaintances. There was a superficial overlay of modernism in the drink's publicity and the technology purchased by the plant, but human relations at Jianlibao remained in the traditional mold without high standards of performance.

The Zhanjiang Home Appliances Industrial Company made use of organizations, especially Party and government organs, but the content of its approach and the nature of its organization represented a fundamental change. The company was concerned with efficiency, product cycles, financial management, and changing market strategy to meet changing consumer demand. In the first reform decade it did not operate in a pure market context; it gained many of the people and goods it needed not from the market but through Party and government hierarchy. But the changing nature and demands of their markets forced the company to be responsive. Despite Li Xiushen's great talents, the company probably was not yet efficiently run by international standards of the late 1980s, but compared to China's starting point in 1978, it had moved in that direction with great speed.

*Foreign Expertise in Pursuit of Infrastructure.* During the first ten years of reform a number of foreign and Hong Kong businesspeople were important in individual Guangdong projects, but only one of them, Gordon Wu, played a major role in shaping the course of the province's development. To understand entrepreneurship in Guangdong in this period, it is instructive to consider his special involvement.

Gordon Wu's grandfather migrated to Hong Kong from just north of Guangzhou. Wu's father, born in Hong Kong in 1904, built up a huge taxicab fleet. He sent Wu to Princeton, where he was graduated in 1958 in civil engineering. After graduation, "I took the first plane back. I wanted to make as much money as I could and I thought

Hong Kong was the place to do it." Hong Kong was just then beginning its construction boom, putting up more tall buildings than any city in the world, and Wu managed to play a part in many of them. His company, Hopewell, became one of the most active in construction and in the bigger money maker, real estate development. Among wealthy Hong Kong residents, Wu was generally ranked just below the top handful in the 1980s. It was no accident, his acquaintances said, that though he could not build the largest building in Hong Kong, he managed to put up the tallest at the time, the sixty-four-story Hopewell Towers, with his office on the top. He had a taste for large, ambitious projects.

Even after decades in the business, Wu still worked on blueprints himself. He pioneered the development of "slipform," a technique for preparing building sites, but most progress in building construction came not from new technology but from better organization and management. In Hong Kong, with space and capital at a premium, it was essential to put up buildings quickly. When constructing tall buildings in the 1980s, Hopewell routinely added one floor every three days. As Guangdong began drawing on Hong Kong's experience in that decade, construction was high on its list and Wu made good use of the opportunities.

Wu was the developer of the China Hotel in Guangzhou. Before beginning site development in 1981, Wu insisted on the location immediately across from the trade fair in order to generate the traffic he considered necessary to make money. Guangzhou municipal planners refused, because they wanted to avoid excessive traffic in that area. Wu took the case to higher authorities, to the annoyance of Guangzhou officials, and won. The China Hotel, completed in 1984, proved more profitable than the other two major hotels built in the city in that period. Wu, convinced that it was absolutely essential to avoid blackouts, paid an additional sum for a guarantee of power from the province, although his hotel required what was then 2 percent of Guangzhou's supply of electricity.

Frustrated by the delays at China's busiest border crossing, Luohu, Wu conceived a new customs and immigration building, to be paid for by tolls collected at the border. He arranged for financing from Hong Kong and was awarded the contract. When the building was completed in 1985, Chinese officials, embarrassed at domestic criticism for collecting tolls for a foreign businessman, bought Wu out the following year.

While Wu was at Princeton, he had been deeply impressed by

Eisenhower's interstate highway program, which had been a great stimulus to local economic development. Wu envisioned a highway extending in a horseshoe shape around the Delta, from Hong Kong up through Guangzhou and down to Macau. He was given an opportunity to present his ideas on highways to Zhao Ziyang, who had at first wanted to concentrate on railways, which he believed cheaper and therefore more appropriate for China at its stage of development. Wu made the argument that roads were more flexible, that goods could move anywhere without interruption, and that therefore most developing countries were choosing highways. Zhao was persuaded and allowed Wu to arrange a loan package that China then repaid from the fruits of development sparked by the road.

From the beginning Wu advocated that the Chinese put up a six-lane highway. But Chinese leaders in the early 1980s consistently underestimated infrastructure needs, worried about costs, and chose conservative solutions. They finally accepted the idea of a two-lane highway to be built by the province in cooperation with Hopewell. Wu also proposed a highway ring around the city, the solution to urban traffic he had seen in the United States, but Guangzhou did not accept this idea until the late 1980s, when its major roads were strangling from traffic delays.

The highway project became bogged down because farmers and county governments were slow in giving up the necessary land. Although some in Hong Kong were skeptical, Wu insisted that his project was too large and important to risk easing the way by making illegal payoffs. Instead, he came up with an alternative. Originally 30 percent of the profits from road tolls were to go to the foreign investors, mostly American banks, and 70 percent to Guangdong. Wu proposed that Guangdong's 70 percent be divided between the province and county governments. Local officials lacked authority to decide, and Wu again had an audience with Zhao Ziyang. Zhao supported Wu, and counties quickly agreed to sell land rights. No sooner had the two-lane highway been completed in the mid-1980s than it was clear that it was inadequate. After a brief debate about whether to invest in such an expensive road in the most prosperous part of the province when many poor areas still had no paved roads, a genuine limited-access superhighway, six lanes wide, was under way, and Wu was again involved. Construction on the 256-kilometer superhighway around the Delta, from Hong Kong through Guangzhou to Macau and costing an estimated $1.3 billion, began in early 1987 and was scheduled for completion in 1990. It was expected to revolutionize transport in the Inner Delta area.

In 1979 Wu was convinced that inadequacies in power as well as in transportation would hold back development. After negotiations with Guangdong officials, he signed a letter of intent to build a large electric power plant. Further discussions soon broke down, however, because Guangdong insisted that the plant be oil-powered. Wu was convinced that China could not insulate itself from the world market in energy, that oil prices would remain high, and that China should follow international trends in going to coal. The project remained stalled until 1984, when the electricity shortage in Guangdong became so acute that Guangdong officials agreed to a coal plant. Construction projects in China had been notably slow by world standards in the 1970s, but the construction of the "Shajiao B," a 700,000-kilowatt, thermal-powered electric power plant just north of Shenzhen, was begun in February 1985 and completed twenty-one months later, in world-record time, faster than comparable Japanese and Korean power plants. Technology and equipment came from around the world, management expertise from Hong Kong, and labor from Guangdong. "Gordon Wu taught us," said a Hong Kong businessman, "that some things we thought were impossible are in fact possible."

Wu's opportunities arose from the fact that the skills he possessed were needed to develop Guangdong's infrastructure. He not only conceived plans essential for provincial development, but with a strong Hong Kong company he could arrange the financing and manage large, complex projects. He had the self-assurance, determination, and sense of history to persuade key leaders in Guangzhou and Beijing. Despite his many talents, the conditions under which he worked in Guangdong made it necessary for him to scramble to bring his projects to fruition. Many Guangdong officials give more praise to Hong Kong businessmen Henry Fok and Li Ka-shing, who made big financial contributions to Guangdong, than to Gordon Wu, who took substantial profits out of the province. Yet Wu played a far larger and more entrepreneurial role in Guangdong development.

## Petty Business Households: Protected Niche Seekers

Independent businesses were almost nonexistent from 1956 to 1978. Yet by 1986, 1.2 million of the province's 32.2 million workers were listed as working in 780,000 private enterprises *(geti hu)* in towns and cities.[5] And because data generally did not include part-time and temporary workers, the numbers were in fact much greater. In the first decade of economic reform these enterprises were tiny, organized around the household as the basic unit; even in Guangzhou in 1988, only 1,600 private businesses employed seven or more people.

In 1987, officials of the Individual Household Economy Division in Guangzhou estimated that of all private enterprises in Guangzhou, about 62 percent were engaged in commerce, 14 percent in drinking and eating establishments, 10 percent in handicrafts and industry, 3 percent in transport, with the rest distributed among service, repair, and construction. Many of those in handicrafts were in fact engaged in repair, and some of those engaged in commerce were in fact middlemen who transported goods as part of their activity. Towns and small cities had similar types of firms, in roughly the same proportions.

Little skill, technology, or capital was required. Entrepreneurs simply identified a market niche for which demand could be met easily and filled it. Those in commerce noticed which goods were in demand, arranged to acquire them cheaply, located themselves in a busy spot, priced their merchandise to make a profit, and decided how much to bargain. Almost anyone old enough and determined enough could perform the work, and few who began after 1978 had training or experience. Many arranged to obtain goods on consignment and even then the amount of goods was tiny. A shopkeeper rarely owned as much in assets as an entrepreneur in transport, whose largest investment was in a motorbike.

In the countryside, all farm households were in effect independent enterprises, but some, known as "specialized households" *(zhuanye hu),* managed to meet their grain quotas and still specialize in fruit, fish, ducks, geese, pigs, vegetables, or flowers.[6] A farm family might engage in a variety of commercial and transport activities as well, especially if it had a tractor or motorbike to collect goods from other families and transport them to market. When a family took its produce to market, it sometimes also acquired other items to buy and sell, even though it was not formally listed as an independent household. As in the towns and cities, few skills were usually required beyond those of an ordinary farm family.

Although most such operations remained tiny, many of the petty merchants earned far more than ordinary salaried workers. There were no accurate data on income in the late 1980s; some officials responsible for monitoring these households estimated that half or more of their income was not reported. A substantial number earned one thousand yuan or more a month, which was several times the highest salary paid to cadres, and an income of several hundred yuan a month was considered quite common for an individual entrepreneur.

Yet, despite their high income, those who ran these small businesses lacked security and prestige, and most who had an opportunity to get a regular job, especially in the government or a state enterprise, preferred that option. In the more advanced parts of Guangdong, where a high proportion of the population was able to go to good schools and get good government or state enterprise jobs, working as a petty entrepreneur was very much a second choice. In the more remote parts of the province, in contrast, where there were fewer opportunities, the more ambitious and better-educated youth often became petty businesspeople.

For a business to grow beyond a small individual household and take on other employees, as a few did, of course required further skills. These are best illustrated by examining three examples of independent businesses that grew: one from the countryside, and two different urban operations.

*Household in Tangzai Village, Gaozhou County.* Born in 1947 to a peasant family, Su Tongsheng left school at sixteen and found temporary work in the county capital, Gaozhou Town. He remained there two years as a helper in a Chinese pharmacy shop. In 1966 he followed in his elder brother's footsteps and joined the army, where he was able to get a job as a medical technician. Upon his discharge in 1971, he had trouble finding a satisfactory job and therefore went back to farming, but he was restless. He tried marketing a few goods on the side, but he did not expand on a large scale because he found he was criticized for not spending enough time on the collective fields.

In 1979, when some former army acquaintances came by to visit, they told him about new possibilities in the Shenzhen SEZ: money was being poured into the city, creating opportunities for all kinds of trades. Su took some herbs with him and set up shop in Shenzhen as a Chinese pharmacist, where his experience as a medic served him well. A friend from the army who worked in public security in Shenzhen arranged his household registration.

Pharmacies were completely unregulated at that time. Anyone could set up shop on the street, and those who lacked the funds to go to a regular doctor or the patience to wait in the long lines at a hospital or who simply preferred a Chinese pharmacist came by to get advice and buy medicine. Su did not charge high prices for his herbs, and his big financial breakthroughs came from several customers who had been told at hospitals that nothing could be done for them. Two or three individuals felt that Su had been responsible for saving their lives or at least for curing serious ailments. The traditional custom in such cases was to respond with the gift of a special red envelope containing money. Because many in Shenzhen were wealthy by Chinese standards, over the first two or three years Su received several envelopes with a thousand yuan or more, and one with three thousand yuan—more than a medical school professor would make in a year.

Su took on a second line of activity, selling nets for the women of his native village. Almost all the women in Tangzai wove fishnets, a traditional skill. The market for these nets had been limited in the 1960s and 1970s, but in the 1980s these nets became fashionable as shopping bags in Hong Kong and Shenzhen, and Su and his villagers responded to the demand. Although even by car the trip from Shenzhen to Gaozhou, just north of Maoming, took fifteen hours, Su came home from time to time to pick up a supply of fishnets to sell in Shenzhen. His success made him popular in the village as well as financially prosperous.

In 1984 Su added a new line that proved even more profitable, selling a variety of duck that had become a delicacy in Hong Kong and Shenzhen restaurants. These ducks were raised by a highly skilled specialist in Nanjing who had a sales outlet in Guangzhou. Su bought ducks there and brought them back to Shenzhen to sell to retailers. Once he proved trustworthy, the duck sellers in Guangzhou sometimes let him take a shipment of ducks on credit, paying after they were sold. With the capital he accumulated, Su not only invested directly in the company in Nanjing but flew there, bought ducks on his own, and flew back, bypassing the Guangzhou outlet. On his most successful single trip he came back with over 1,100 ducks and made a profit of over ten thousand yuan.

Su next branched out to breeding the expensive "American dove" on his family's Gaozhou farm, and eventually sold pairs for breeding purposes. He also began to raise high-priced turtles, another delicacy. The American doves, the turtles, and the even larger numbers of ordinary white pigeons he turned over to his family in Gaozhou to raise. He built a large new home on the farm for his mother and children; he and his wife stayed there too when in Gaozhou. He gave his elder brother, who lived next door and helped look after the animals, his used motorcycle when he purchased an even newer and bigger one. He and his wife, who shared his entrepreneurial activities with him, spent most of their time in Shenzhen. As of 1987 they had not yet found an appropriate reasonably priced house in Shenzhen to use both as a store and as living quarters, but they were shopping and expected to buy one before long. In the meantime they remained in an apartment and rented store space in Shenzhen.

*A Tailor Couple in Guangzhou.* A young couple, originally from Ningbo, moved to Guangzhou shortly before 1949 and worked there as tailors until 1955, when their shop was taken over by the local urban collective. The husband then found a job in a factory while his wife continued to work as a seamstress for a small tailor shop sponsored by the Residence Committee. As the years went by they raised two sons and three daughters.

The couple was among the first who applied in 1979 for permission to set up an independent business. The husband had just reached retirement age at his factory and figured he had nothing to lose. The Cultural Revolution had wiped out tailor shops, few ready-made garments were available, and those who could sew were in great demand. The couple set up a small tailor shop, the Changxing Shizhuangdian, and as business increased they gradually brought in the whole family, including their two daughters-in-law. They specialized in sewing low-cost clothes, and among their customers were many rural people living on the outskirts of Guangzhou. Because the couple had clearly demonstrated skills and sold their goods at a low price, they quickly became popular and were able to hire other people.

As business expanded, they were able to buy the small building where their shop was located and to open a second store some distance from their first. After one of their daughters went to Hong Kong with her husband, who was assigned there, they opened a third shop in Shenzhen that she managed, coming in regularly from Hong Kong.

The parents kept up good relations with officials and in 1986, for example, proudly paid more than fifty thousand yuan in taxes, a generous full payment, even though most small shops were known not to pay all they actually owed. After the shop was thriving, the husband served on local business household committees and gave occasional talks, sponsored by the local government, on how to run small enterprises. His Cantonese was not very good until he was asked to give speeches, but because of his new public role he took special lessons.

The couple received permission to import new sewing machines from Hong Kong, and they also set up what amounted to a small sewing factory where they produced ready-made goods to be sold in their stores. By the late 1980s in the main workshop the couple had about forty employees, who ate with the family members. The workers, including the two daughters-in-law, were paid regular wages. The firm had one van and one car, which were used by the owner and others as needed. Although the business remained very successful, some doubted whether there was much room for future expansion, owing to the fact that larger, well-funded collective factories had begun to produce more attractive ready-made garments of greater variety.

*A Guangzhou Specialty Restaurant.* A young man and woman, "intellectual youth," were sent down from Guangzhou to the countryside in the 1970s, and became engaged. When they were allowed to return to Guangzhou in 1980, they had difficulty finding regular jobs and therefore tried selling Chinese sausage in the large square between the statue commemorating the Guangzhou Uprising of 1927 and the old provincial athletic stadium.

The couple had no special skills or background, but they began experimenting with various recipes for flavoring the sausages until they hit upon one that became very popular. They did the same for roast goose. In 1982 they had earned enough to buy an old building on a little side street. Ordinarily small shops wanted to be located on a main road, but the couple had enough of a following that the side-street location, where the buildings were still affordable, did not hurt sales. His family name was He (river), hers was Lin (woods), and they called their place Helinji (House of Helin).

As the shop expanded, the wife's father, who by this time had retired, joined them to keep their books. They were able to buy a second store on a main road. They also decided to expand the first site, and were able to get permission from the district to build a three-story building, which they did immediately, and then waited for municipal approval to add on another three stories to be used as housing for relatives and workers. In the meantime they increased their staff to include over thirty workers. Still in their thirties, they had many dedicated customers.[7]

*Government Relations.* In the first reform decade only a tiny percentage of petty business households grew to the size of these three operations. In the early 1980s those who wanted to grow were discouraged from having more than seven nonfamily employees, and even after the mid-1980s, when cadres made it clear that there were no limits on the number of employees and announced a new title, "private enterprise" *(siying)*, for those with more than seven employees, very few operations grew to that size. The restraints on growth were more political than economic. The fact is that the reach of the local government and Party, in both the cities and the countryside, remained profound. The parts of government concerned with the economy still had great leverage over firms that grew beyond a certain size. Loans from government banks and cooperatives, land and building use, control over key resources and foreign currency, permission to engage directly in foreign trade, and access to information and new imported technology were all dominated by state and Party officials. Although local businesses were rarely subjected to criticism and punishment as they had been before 1978, local officials had leeway to ask successful enterprises to contribute to various local projects from which they might benefit, sometimes personally.

Successful petty businesspeople, therefore, often made local contributions and developed cooperative relations with local officials. Many independent entrepreneurs had relatives who were officials or Party members, which made it easier to get needed government cooperation. In one survey of highly successful petty business households *(wanyuan hu)* in the province, it was found that over 60 percent were led by former soldiers. These individuals had learned skills and gained information about distant localities through their military experiences, and they had also developed a network of relationships that included many Party members and government workers. As small businesses grew, many proprietors even volunteered to turn their business into a joint enterprise with the local unit of government in order to get a level of cooperation and protection otherwise not possible. As reform continued, more petty businesspeople found ways to reduce the risks of official interference, but throughout the first decade of reforms, entrepreneurial skills included managing relations with Party and state officials, and the reach of the government remained strong.

## Business Failures

Petty entrepreneurs had so little capital and so few goods that they were hardly big enough to fail. Those who did not find a good niche, were not skilled bargainers, produced goods or supplied services that did not satisfy their customers, or had a poor location sometimes generated only very modest incomes. But if they failed to sell or lost money, petty merchants took the small loss and started to sell other items or offer other services or changed their location. If the food produced one day failed to sell, a food shop did not necessarily go out of business; neither did a small retailer fail, if all his goods failed to sell.

It is easier to explain why some petty enterprises did not grow. Some were cautious in their approach and ventured little and gained little. Some ran into bottlenecks, energy shortages, lack of transportation, or limited funds that meant that no matter what they tried, the results could not be very impressive. Some had trouble finding a niche that was large enough to permit growth. Some failed to get the permission or tacit approval from higher levels that was necessary to accomplish their task.

State firms that did poorly often lost large sums of money year after year, but they rarely closed down. Some managers allowed workers to receive raises without increasing productivity or failed to make good use of the equipment they had. But were they in the red because of state pricing policy, shortages of materials and new equipment, and inability to find trained specialists, all beyond their power to affect, or were they in the red because of poor management? Despite efforts to assign enterprise responsibility, many factors were beyond the control of the enterprise, and government officials responsible for industrial production continued to subsidize inefficient operations. However, by the mid-1980s the enterprises that were not profitable were generally under pressure from the local level of government, and their salaries and worker facilities suffered as a result.

Entrepreneurial failures are easiest to define for collective enterprises, because they had significant investments and the autonomy to make decisions on their own, and most of their goods and services were bought and sold on the market. Certain problems were more common in Guangdong at this time than in other places. As they switched from producing for state plans to producing for markets, some failed to make the transition. As in capitalist societies, they made mistaken judgments about the market, or found that competitors had produced better or lower-priced goods or services. But many problems were familiar elsewhere in China. Some managers lacked the skills to get the cooperation of workers, lacked capital to make necessary investments at critical junctures, and made unwise decisions. Some firms that obtained new machinery from abroad or even from within China found that it was unusable because of lack of trained personnel or parts. Some firms lacked the connections with higher-ups or the priority to obtain the electric power, personnel, land, foreign currency, or new machinery they needed in order to be successful in the market.

## The Maturation of Entrepreneurship

The role played by the statesmen in this first decade of reform was shaped by peculiar historical circumstances. Beijing officials were so committed to economic progress that they granted regional leaders, especially in Guangdong, great leeway in achieving it. The new situation required leaders who not only understood Party policy well enough to push its flexibility to the limit but could quickly acquire enough sense of markets, the international economy, and of Guangdong's actual conditions that they could provide a firm sense of direction. In this first decade only a small number of top officials in a locality had the opportunity to become statesmen. Most cadres were too constrained by rules and procedures or personal caution to play such a role. Cadres were still sufficiently disciplined, however, that a few statesmen could move large organizations.

Ren Zhongyi, Liang Lingguang, and Yuan Geng fit the requirements for statesmen well. All were senior cadres, highly respected by the leaders in Beijing, who not only knew policy well but had an unusually good understanding of the world economy. Unlike Tao Zhu, who had become Guangdong's top leader in 1952 at age forty-six, they were all in their sixties when they arrived. Their goal was not to build a political machine but to cap off their careers by helping set up a system that after so many false starts would bring real economic progress to China. They had passionately believed in the need to change the system long before they were given the opportunity to do so, and they had a broad enough vision and sufficient faith in the direction to provide assurance to cadres under them who were less certain in the complicated and unfamiliar new age.

Scramblers were needed throughout the decade because of bureaucratic bottlenecks and shortages of capital, equipment, infrastructure, and trained personnel. To keep pace with the progress desired and the changes in the markets and market demands, they had to improvise. With the support of the statesmen above them, they dealt with bureaucrats in Guangdong and Beijing with a combination of obeisance, personal connections *(guanxi)*, and manipulation *(lihai guanxi)*. Their actions would make sense to politicians in the West, but in the fast-changing environment of Guangdong they had to move more quickly, and in a system that did not have formal democratic guarantees they were less restrained by interest groups and formal procedures.

Lei Yu, Yu Fei, and Liang Xiang were well suited to the scrambler role. Bright, quick, flexible, and confident, they were younger than the statesmen and they were willing to make deals. They had a masterful understanding of bureaucratic interests and personal relationships, which they were ready to use in the service of economic progress. They were troubleshooters who made tough decisions quickly. If the statesmen were heirs to the Confucian tradition, the scramblers were heirs to the legalist tradition. They were of course more controversial than the statesmen, and toward the end of the first decade, as they moved to new, higher positions, they personally tried to behave a little more like statesmen.

Successful prefectures, cities, and counties required some combination of the two—statesmen, who helped set overall policy and public tone, and scramblers, who did what was necessary to make things work. Sometimes the Party secretary behaved more like a statesman and allowed the administrative head of the locality or one of his deputies to behave more like a scrambler. Enterprise leaders who brought progress were also a combination of statesman and scrambler, but were more often scramblers. Li Xiushen and Gordon Wu were a mixture of the two, for example, but Li Jingwei was closer to being a pure scrambler.

Private businesses in this period were too small to confront the complex organizational issues of larger operations. They lacked the sophistication of businesses in mature market economies. The skill of the petty entrepreneur in this early era, therefore, lay in finding and quickly responding to a niche.

At the end of the first decade of reform, the nature of entrepreneurship had begun to change. As new systems began to take shape and the environment became more predictable, the statesmen who had been system builders were replaced by officials who behaved more like high-level managers. Beneath them, though infrastructure problems did not disappear and scramblers were still needed, enough systems were in place that many officials could guide progress while behaving more like mid-level managers. Petty niche seekers who had the business acumen and political cooperation to take advantage of the increased support for larger private enterprises faced new levels of complexity as their businesses grew larger. Like statesmen and scramblers, they too were beginning to acquire managerial skills.

In the first decade of reforms, entrepreneurial skills were learned mostly in the process of doing, and even those who were teaching management often lacked experience. In the second decade some skills will be learned in the classroom as well as in the market, as entrepreneurial successes are increasingly analyzed and their lessons taught to a new generation.

Despite its immaturity, entrepreneurship played a critical role in the 1980s in creating new policies, in making them work, and in filling niches to satisfy market demand. In the 1990s entrepreneurship is likely to lose some of its simple raw vitality and acquire more regularity and sophistication, which are urgently needed for China's domestic economy and for China's growing role in international trade.

# 11.

# *Reforming Foreign Trade*

JOHN KAMM

The journey to the Export Commodities Fair in Guangzhou during the Cultural Revolution was an eerie experience no business traveler was likely to forget. After boarding the Kowloon-Canton Railroad in the morning at Hong Kong's old Tsimshatsui terminal, one rode through the New Territories up to the border with China at Luohu. There the businessman left one world and entered—across a small but heavily guarded bridge—another, a world inimically hostile to capitalism and its representatives. Few made the trip.

Passport and visa inspection were strict; evidence of previous visits to Taiwan could lead to unpleasant scenes. Depending on the political climate, rigorous or not-so-rigorous customs inspections took place. Because the train for Guangzhou from the quiet border town, Shenzhen, did not depart for more than two hours, there was ample time for lunch—if the traveler had purchased the right ticket at the China Travel Service in Hong Kong. If there were other foreigners entering China that day, all ate together. If not, one ate alone, with nothing but nondescript food for company.

My memories of 1976 in Guangzhou are of grey buildings with huge red signs proclaiming the imminent liberation of Taiwan, dank interiors of run-down buildings that served as provincial headquarters for the state trading companies, the cold officiousness of the Public Security Bureau, and the omnipresent feeling of being watched. Foreigners were totally segregated from the local population and were accompanied everywhere by stiff and formal escorts. On Sundays, the one day of the week the trade fair closed, they signed up for staged visits to kindergartens, factories, communes, and, most dreaded of all, hospitals, where performances of stomach surgery under acupuncture anesthesia were laid on.

Foreigners ate well and cheaply, taking advantage of a totally irrational, heavily subsidized pricing system. The populace knew when it was trade fair time (April 15 to May 15, and October 15 to November 15) because rationing of foodstuffs became more severe. At the fair itself, Europeans and Americans were housed in a cavernous paean to Chinese Stalinist architecture, the Dongfang Hotel (room rate a mere fourteen yuan per day) and were looked after by the First Liaison Office. Japanese traders were put in the Guangzhou Hotel and were supervised by the Second Liaison Office. Hong Kong Chinese merchants occupied the Liu Hua and a score of other guest houses; they were looked after by the Third Liaison Office.

Across the street from the Dongfang Hotel was the Trade Fair Building, 110,000 square meters of exhibition halls and negotiating rooms whose massive entry was dominated by Chairman Mao's portrait. Here foreign merchants, surrounded by the paraphernalia of the Cultural Revolution, came face to face with China's foreign trade officials, representatives of a closed, stagnant economy struggling to emerge from a decade of turmoil and national loss.

## Emerging from the Cultural Revolution

The Cultural Revolution wreaked havoc on Guangdong's foreign trade. Purchases of commodities for export grew at less than 1 percent per year between 1966 and 1970. Overseas sales were carried out strictly in accordance with central policy and the national export plan. These stressed the primacy of grain, and as a result Guangdong became China's rice exporter. Before the Cultural Revolution, the province had exported 80,000 to 100,000 tons of rice per year. In 1975, exports hit 215,000 tons.[1] The model of foreign trade—enshrined at the 1976 spring fair as an exhibit in the Learn from Dazhai Hall at the Trade Fair Building—was Dongguan County, which exported more than 10,000 tons of rice in 1975 even though, unlike the triple-crop West River counties, it grew only two crops a year.

Cash crops or other economic activities that competed with grain—including, for example, Chaozhou tangerines, Hainan pineapples, and Dongguan woven mats—were under frequent attack in Guangdong between 1966 and 1976. Aquatic products suffered when fish ponds were filled in to plant more rice, a step taken in Shunde County and Panyu County in 1968 and 1969. In 1974 and 1975, a Communist Party secretary in Haikang County, Zhanjiang Prefecture, uprooted the citronella grass crop—the source of the prefecture's largest traditional export, citronella oil—and planted rice in its stead. Quotas and prices for subsidiary crops and output of sideline activities were lowered by state planners and price setters. Rural "periodic" markets—where such products as bamboo utensils and feathers and down entered the export procurement system—were either shut down or their schedules restricted. In 1974, militia were used to close these markets—a feature of the rural economy for more than a thousand years—and prevent itinerant peddlers from selling their wares.

Sometimes production of export commodities suffered as much from neglect as from politically directed sabotage. Guangdong had imported high-quality breeding sows from Europe in the early 1960s. Their offspring were fast-growing, lean pigs that were highly prized both within Guangdong and in the principal export markets of Hong Kong and Macau. Imports of breeding stock were stopped in 1967, however, and as the years went by, the crossbreeding of the European breeds with the local Guangdong species gradually led to inferior, excessively fat pigs. By the time this problem became apparent in the mid-1970s, Guangdong had slipped from being first among the provinces in exporting pork in the 1950s and 1960s to being only fifth in 1977. Exports of pigs from Guangdong fell by sixty thousand head in 1978 alone.

Guangdong's foreign contacts, modest in the 1960s, and the institutions that serviced them were reduced to a bare minimum during the Cultural Revolution. Branches of the national foreign trade corporations* were merged into a few "basket companies" (*yi lanzi*

---

*Throughout this chapter, "foreign trade corporation" refers exclusively to the dozen or so national corporations reporting to the Ministry of Foreign Trade in Beijing that handle all imports and exports of specified product lines. These bodies—for example, China National Chemicals Import and Export Corporation (SINOCHEM) and China National Machinery Import and Export Corporation (MACHIMPEX)—supervised branches in the provinces and municipalities and subbranches in the counties and prefectures. "Foreign trade enterprise," a term introduced later in this chapter, refers to any Chinese firm that is a member of the complete set of firms with foreign trade rights: that is, national foreign trade corporations and their branches, "local" foreign trade companies (for example, the Guangdong Province Foreign Trade Corporation), joint industrial-commercial foreign trade companies, and factories with direct export rights.

*gongsi)*, and virtually all of the Guangzhou municipal branches were shut down in 1970.[2] The Guangzhou Foreign Trade School was closed in late 1966, its faculty sent to labor in the countryside.

Private farmers and traders in Zhuhai County went out of business when border trade was brought under strict state control in May 1969. The flower trade with Macau withered and died, because the foreign trade corporations could not guarantee prompt and damage-free shipment. Baoan County, immediately north of Hong Kong, suffered even more than Zhuhai. The county's granite and sand resources offered the best potential for export earnings, but leftists opposed any sales of China's raw materials "to help build capitalism." By the end of the Cultural Revolution, the county's exports to Hong Kong—consisting of fruit, vegetables, and livestock—amounted to less than $5 million per year.

Many Cantonese traders and industrialists who remained in China after 1949 had been persecuted, even before the Cultural Revolution. Most of the founding members of the South China Industry and Enterprise Corporation Ltd., a model joint enterprise between the state and private interests established in 1951, were publicly humiliated; several committed suicide. Such joint state-private ventures, remaining active in Guangzhou for longer than elsewhere in China, managed a large segment of Guangdong's import and export trade before 1957. Relatives of those known as "patriotic capitalists" prior to the Cultural Revolution lived in shame and fear for years until, in the early 1980s, verdicts were reversed.

The Pearl River Delta branches of the Overseas Chinese Investment Corporation, which had been so effective in channeling money sent by Chinese abroad into housing and other construction projects throughout the early 1960s, were closed in 1967. Special retail outlets catering to relatives of overseas Chinese were closed at the end of 1966, and Guangzhou's Overseas Chinese Village—a residential district of luxury homes built with funds donated by Chinese abroad—was sacked in 1967. Everywhere properties were occupied, their lawful inhabitants driven out into cramped quarters shared with other unfortunates.

As word of their relatives' treatment reached Chinese communities abroad, the flow of remittances into Guangdong slowed, though it never entirely stopped. Since localities had been permitted to retain a portion of their nontrade earnings, the drop in the inflow of hard currency had a significant impact on import business. Coupled with the general crackdown on purchases of "things foreign," locally financed imports largely disappeared in counties with large populations of returned overseas Chinese and relatives of Chinese abroad (for example, Chaoyang near Shantou, and Taishan in the West River Delta).

The numbers of Hong Kong Chinese entering China to visit relatives gradually increased after 1970. Each "compatriot" returning to his or her home village was permitted to bring in some necessities (for example, knitting wool, 50 kilograms of foodstuffs) and a few select consumer goods (one watch, bicycle, radio, and sewing machine per family). And although food parcels—a boon to Guangdong during the 1961 and 1962 food shortages—were banned during the Cultural Revolution, medicine packages were permitted. A thriving if sometimes sad trade grew up in such items. On wintry nights before Chinese New Year, scores of small drugstores along Hong Kong's Jordan and Nathan roads were filled with shoppers organizing shipments of Chinese and Western drugs. Western intelligence kept tabs on medical conditions in Chinese cities by monitoring the trade.

As the country's point of contact with the representatives of international capitalism, the Guangzhou trade fair went through difficult days. Red Guards put up posters calling for the fair to be canceled, citing exploitation of Chinese workers by foreign firms. The spring fair of 1967 was threatened with disruption and was only saved by Zhou Enlai's intervention.[3] The autumn fair of 1967 opened a month late, and there were ugly "struggle sessions" against British traders. In the complex on Haizhu Square, foreign traders noticed the replacement of older, experienced Chinese negotiators with young ideologues, ignorant of world markets but well versed in Mao's thoughts. Many of the foreign traders remember the period from 1967 to 1972—"before the Americans arrived and ruined everything"—as the most difficult of periods in many respects, but also, ironically, as the most profitable time to be selling to China. Outsiders were confined, spied on, unable to communicate effectively with the outside world, but their efforts were very, very profitable. "All you had to do was be able to put up with a lot of political nonsense till the last few days of the fair. Then, Mr. Wang would throw you a piece of paper with the tonnage he needed to buy or sell according to the plan. That was your order, pretty much at whatever price you had quoted or bid weeks before," remembers a particularly successful European trader.

During the latter part of the Cultural Revolution, several positive developments took place that benefited Guangdong's postreform economic growth. In two important areas—commitment of production for export and encouragement of certain categories of imports—Guangdong's foreign trade cadres employed economic levers to achieve state targets. These experiments were often daring local initiatives, undertaken at a time when, elsewhere in the province, foreign trade was being openly attacked by autarkic zealots.

*The Foshan Experiment of Export Production Bases.* An expression used by Guangdong party officials in 1969 and 1970 aptly summarized the prevailing attitude toward export procurement : "Foreign trade departments can do without" *(waimao keyou kewu)*.[4] If there was a surplus of an item, it could be offered for export. If there was a deficit, first priority went to supplying local requirements. The subservience of foreign trade to domestic commerce resulted in an inability to meet export targets, which in turn translated into shortfalls of foreign exchange needed to purchase critical imports. Overseas buyers, including those in Hong Kong, lost confidence in China's ability to sustain long-term selling commitments.

There was a shortage of vegetables in Guangzhou in 1970, and as a result export procurement targets were not met. In that year, purchase of vegetables for sale to Hong Kong went like this: the provincial branch of the China National Foodstuffs Import and Export Corporation procured produce grown in Guangzhou from the municipal vegetables corporation under unified purchase contracts. These were annual contracts, covering all vegetables in the export plan. Based on the quantities specified therein, the municipal vegetables corporation then signed unified contracts with commune supply and marketing cooperatives, which in turn assigned quotas for vegetables to the production brigades. The foreign trade corporation was far removed from the producer.

In 1971, important changes in export procurement took place as efforts were made to improve the system. Foreign trade corporations began signing "three-cornered contracts," which linked them with both the municipal vegetables corporation and specific production brigades, and they also signed contracts directly and solely with production brigades. These contracts opened the way for the foreign trade corporations to influence the quantity and quality of export production. In 1973, Guangzhou Metropolitan Region achieved its fruit and vegetable export plan for the first time since 1966; more than 80 percent of 1974 export procurement came from production brigades under direct contract to the municipal or provincial export corporations. (Guangzhou foreign trade corporation branches were reestablished in 1972 and 1973.)

The export procurement contract was a simple document spelling out the parties' responsibilities; it incorporated the use of such incentives as "higher prices for better quality," advance payment, minimum-maximum procurement commitments, technical assistance to producers, and payment in kind with fertilizer, feedstuffs, and pesticides at subsidized values.

In 1972, a foreign trade conference in Nanhai County brought together economic cadres and commune leaders to address the problem of supplying the Hong Kong–Macau markets with fresh foodstuffs under the annual export plan, which had been sharply increased by Beijing in order to generate hard currency to pay for planned technology and equipment imports. The new export procurement contract system of 1971 was popularized and extended to both industrial (silk and rattanware) and agricultural (vegetables and pond fish) products.

Chen Yun had advocated the establishment of specialized export production bases in 1957, and quite a few had been established in the late 1950s and early 1960s in Guangdong. Export production bases were farms and factories dedicated entirely to making goods for export markets, notably Hong Kong. The program was a casualty of the Cultural Revolution, however, and by 1969 not a single one remained. In 1971 and 1972 the first linkages arising from the implementation of the new export procurement contract system led to the establishment of several dozen export production bases. The success of these bases in meeting export goals convinced Beijing's economic planners to extend and consolidate specialization, and in 1973 the Ministry of Foreign Trade designated Foshan Prefecture the country's first "unified export production base." To ensure that it received more foreign currency, Beijing had to make producing for export more attractive to local areas.

The immediate benefits to Foshan were substantial. Central allocations of raw materials (steel and fertilizer) at subsidized prices were increased, as was funding of improvements for ports and the transport system. Export producers could apply to local foreign trade corporation subbranches for allocations of "export production base foreign exchange." This was a special category of foreign exchange—drawn from a centrally administered fund—to be used exclusively to import machinery and specialty inputs (for example, chemical process aids) for export projects. In a daring experiment promoted by such officials as Yu Fei, then county chief of Nanhai, county bureaus and enterprises were granted allocations of the foreign exchange proceeds from the sale of specific export commodities that they produced. These funds were to become the principal component of local foreign exchange reserves *(difang waihui)*.

Subbranches of foreign trade corporations in Foshan City and in the county seats expanded in number, in the size and complexity of their commercial networks, and in the scope of their business. In each county three or four export procurement stations *(chukou shougou zhan)* of the foreign trade corporations handling foodstuffs and native produce were set up in the large market towns; these stations became the principal contractors for export procurement, working through export substations *(chukou shougou dian)* established in the communes. In Nanhai County, subbranches opened 230 "support agriculture link-up points"; they served as sources of capital, expertise, and raw materials while monitoring fulfillment of export procurement contracts.

After 1973, subbranches in Foshan made more and more direct sales and shipments to customers in Hong Kong and Macau (such sales doubled between 1971 and 1974). Specially favored firms—those designated distributors by the Beijing-controlled agencies in Hong Kong—were soon being invited to send representatives to Delta cities and towns to discuss regular export supply—a reassuring development after the confusions and uncertainties of the late 1960s.

In 1975, the Guangzhou branch of the Construction Bank of China began offering "export production special project loans." Denominated in renminbi, they were intended to help export enterprises expand production by making available funds not included in budgetary grants. This was a significant departure from the "iron rice bowl" system, in which state administrative organs covered all factory capital needs by grants and received, in turn, all factory profits. As with applications for "export production base foreign exchange," foreign trade corporations reviewed enterprise applications for export project loans, a process that once again drew the foreign trade departments more closely to the actual producers. The export project loans were a forerunner of the system of bank loans and credits that increasingly came to dominate the domestic financing of China's export trade.

The success of the Foshan experiment prompted Beijing to designate two other Guangdong prefectures—Zhanjiang and Huiyang—unified export production bases in 1976. In the same year, seventeen "single commodity production bases," which produced the mainstay agricultural products that were exported, were being run by provincial branches; in 1978 these bases accounted for one quarter of Guangdong's agricultural export production.

*Encouragement of Selected Imports.* Foreign trade planners have, since the early 1970s, sought to channel China's foreign exchange holdings into purchases of two kinds of goods—raw materials to be processed for export, and advanced technology and equipment. Allocations of *yijin yangchu waihui*—"using foreign exchange for importing to help exports"—have been made to factories out of the central government's annual foreign exchange disbursements to the provinces. Guangdong has been a principal beneficiary: its arts and crafts workshops alone have carved teak from Indonesia, jade from Burma, and ivory from Africa. *Jinliao jiagong*—processing of imported materials paid for with China's own foreign exchange into commodities for export—accounted for approximately 8 percent of Guangdong's export production in 1976.[5]

The subordination of customs houses under local foreign trade bureaus—the administrative organs at provincial and subprovincial levels that supervised foreign trade—made it easy to exempt raw materials for export industries from payment of import duties. (From 1963 to 1980 there was no national customs administration overseeing the customs bureaus or houses in the localities. Collection of tariffs—there was a national tariff code—was entirely the responsibility of the local houses.) Irish linen brought into Shantou for embroidering, for example, required no customs duties throughout the Cultural Revolution and still did not in the late 1980s.

Regulations governing the domestic pricing of imported goods had been promulgated in 1964 and were in force throughout the Cultural Revolution. In brief, these stipulated that imports for which domestic equivalents existed in China had to be priced at the domestic equivalents' ex-factory prices (prices before wholesale and retail markups), regardless of import cost. For imports without domestic equivalents—primarily foreign machinery and technology—a pricing formula was established whereby the domestic selling price was set at the landed price (tariff and industrial tax included, at official renminbi exchange rates) plus a markup of 103 percent. About 20 percent of imported goods were priced by the markup method in the early to mid-1970s.

In a move that significantly lowered prices for imported machinery and technology, the Ministry of Foreign Trade in Beijing lowered the import markup from 103 percent to 60 percent in 1975, the year Zhou Enlai established the four modernizations as state policy at the Fourth National People's Congress.[6] This new policy aided a surge in the import of capital equipment, complete plants, and technology.

The paucity of retained export earnings and the sharp drop in remittances from Chinese abroad after the Red Guard rampages of 1967 had led to a slowdown in import business financed with local foreign exchange, but Guangzhou-based foreign trade corporations continued to do a large import business during the Cultural Revolution because of a quirk in China's foreign trade system. In the Stalinist trade regimes of the Soviet Union and East European nations, all imports are centralized in the head offices of the national corporations, located in the country's capital city. In China during the Cultural Revolution, in contrast, the head offices of foreign trade corporations in Beijing, though continuing to monopolize and control imports, farmed out the national requirements for certain product lines to their "port corporations"—that is, to their branches in five port cities: Dalian, Tianjin, Qingdao, Shanghai, and Guangzhou. The Chemicals Corporation head office in Beijing designated Shanghai, for instance, to buy all medical instruments, and Guangzhou to handle all purchases of rubber products and rubber chemicals. This enhanced import efficiency and specialization and gave local officials experience in negotiating purchases from foreign firms.

Despite ideological strictures during this period against the ownership of foreign consumer goods, one luxury item continued to be offered for sale in Chinese department stores: Swiss watches. Orders were placed with Swiss manufacturers by the head office of the Light Industrial Products Import and Export Corporation for all parts of China save one: Guangdong Province, whose branch corporation made direct purchases of models especially popular with a more discerning population with wider foreign contacts. A few consumer goods manufactured in friendly socialist countries—cigarettes from Albania and North Korea, sugar from Cuba, and soap from Vietnam—could also be found in Guangzhou stores.

In addition to handling imports needed locally and, for specified product lines, those required nationally, the port corporations based in Guangzhou were entrusted with the work of exporting goods produced in six southern and southwestern provinces: Sichuan, Yunnan, Guizhou, Hunan, Jiangxi, and Guangxi Zhuang Autonomous

Region. Procurement of items for export from outside Guangdong was accomplished through contracts between the port corporations and "interior" corporations—foreign trade corporation branches that were prohibited from dealing directly with foreign firms.

Thus, despite the damage inflicted by the Cultural Revolution, Guangdong's foreign trade establishment expanded its contacts in the early 1970s and by the mid-1970s had emerged with vital foreign connections nurtured both by the trade fair and by knowledge gained from limited experimentation with contractual arrangements and material incentives in order to increase imports and exports. This experience was to prove useful when the "open policy" reforms brought on genuine decentralization and reliance on material incentives in 1978.

The growth of foreign trade after 1978 was not simple or straightforward; rather, the process was a complex, uneven one. It involved such conflicting developments as: freedoms granted by Beijing that it partially withdrew when problems arose; persistent efforts by reformers to chip away at bureaucractic practices that blocked progress; rearguard actions by bureaucracies and enterprises to protect interests enjoyed under the old system; responses to competitive environments involving new cost structures, markets, and transactors; and adaptations of existing businesses to take advantage of new opportunities.


## The 1978–1980 Boom

After the fall of the Gang of Four in 1976 there was an increase in China's exports and imports, and by 1978 this had become a boom. Foreign trade from 1978 to 1980, modest by international standards, was extraordinary for Guangdong. Purchases of export commodities produced both inside and outside the province grew from 2.8 billion yuan in 1978 to 4.8 billion yuan in 1980. Overseas sales rose roughly 50 percent, hitting $2.1 billion in 1980. The export sector took up 14 percent of the province's industrial and agricultural output in 1980, compared to 9 percent in 1978.[7] To assist direct trade between localities and the markets of Hong Kong and Southeast Asia, Guangdong opened nearly one hundred ports and "loading points" to foreign vessels in 1978 and 1979.[8] Foreign capital began reentering Guangdong in 1978, and by 1980 foreign investments totaling more than $200 million had been made, largely in rural, small-scale industry.

These changes had begun even before the new policy for Guangdong was formally enunciated in mid-1979.

Guangdong's foreign trade corporation officials remember 1978 and 1979 as the golden era of profitability. Export cost—the measure of how many yuan are required to create one U.S. dollar—remained stable throughout the 1978–1980 period. Profits rose when the markup on imported machinery sold by the foreign trade corporations to domestic end-users was raised in 1977 from 60 percent to 80 percent; locally financed imports increased from $200 million in 1978 to $300 million in 1980, as schemes to retain foreign exchange at the local level were implemented and overseas Chinese contributions of money and materials rose sharply. Bonus schemes for foreign trade corporation managers were tried out in 1979, and enterprise profitability was the chief determinant.

Foreign trade corporations were allowed to import certain consumer goods and sell them at unusually high markups. The biggest contributor to the profitability of the Light Industrial Products Import and Export Corporation in 1978 was undoubtedly the Japanese color television set, which appeared in Guangzhou retail outlets in the early spring. The first lots were quickly snapped up by the local populace, especially those with access to money from relatives overseas, despite price tags three to four times those prevailing in Hong Kong.[9] Official imports for resale in domestic retail outlets were limited to mainland-compatible sets, but around the same time that the sets were going on sale in Guangzhou, the Customs Administration in Shenzhen permitted returning overseas Chinese to bring in one television. Although most were mainland-compatible sets sold at special mainland department stores in Hong Kong, it was not long before Hong Kong–compatible sets were being brought in.

The television trade reflected the better treatment accorded to relatives of Guangdong's overseas Chinese, and this had a number of important consequences for the province's economy. First, there was a sharp rise in visits from Hong Kong and Macau Chinese as well as from Chinese residents in communities in Southeast Asia, Australia, Europe, and North America. These "tourists" spent heavily on feasts and made large contributions to repair graves and ancestral temples. Donations not only of televisions but of vans and trucks were made in startling numbers to villages and counties; a new business sprang up whereby one could order and pay for a Toyota van in Hong Kong or Macau, and relatives (or a unit with whom a special relationship existed) could pick it up in China. Returnees carried with them the maximum allowances of consumer goods, which resulted in a flood of luxury merchandise.

Second, there was a surge in deposits to accounts of relatives of overseas Chinese held by Bank of China subbranches in Taishan and throughout the Pearl River Delta. More than 90 percent of Guangdong's nontrade foreign currency receipts arose from personal expenditure by and remittances from the overseas Chinese communities of the Guangdong diaspora; remittances alone hit $400 million per year in 1979 and 1980.

Perhaps most important, the improvement in the lot of those with overseas connections created conditions for the first wave of foreign capital investments in China since 1949. Several hundred "compensation trade" and processing agreements were implemented in towns and villages all over Guangdong in 1978 and 1979. The first compensation trade arrangements—under which the foreign investor contributed equipment and received payment in output—were concluded in the late summer of 1978. All were between Hong Kong or Macau capitalists and provincial, municipal, or county enterprises. Far more numerous were the cut-and-sew garment factories or the plastic flower workshops, where scores of young village women worked as contract labor in processing arrangements.

The retailing of foreign consumer goods as a means to soak up the purchasing power of the population with relatives abroad and the absorption of foreign capital through "contractual" joint ventures and, later, "equity" joint ventures were thus two fundamental reforms introduced during Guangdong's foreign trade boom of 1978–1980. Four other reforms—foreign exchange retention by export producers and the creation of a limited market in foreign exchange; decentralization of import-export decision making; establishment of joint industrial-commercial companies; and liberalization of export procurement pricing—helped increase flexibility in the system.

*Foreign Exchange Retention.* China's central planners had for many years understood that sharing foreign exchange with local governments stimulated exports. Regulations put out as early as 1957 (largely discarded during the Cultural Revolution) allowed local governments to retain a share of the foreign currency proceeds from the sale of goods deemed not essential to national prosperity—known as "category three" goods—and as we have seen retention of overseas Chinese remittances and of export earnings—though limited to a few locales—was practiced in Guangdong in the early 1970s.

Prior to 1978 there was no unified system of foreign exchange retention in Guangdong, even though it was practiced in some localities. Foshan, in 1977, was retaining 15 percent of centrally managed export goods (with the exception of rice, cooking oil, and a few other items) and 20 percent of locally managed export goods, which covered the bulk of Foshan's light industrial, textile, and handicraft exports. Similar programs were in effect in Guangzhou Metropolitan Region and Baoan County.

In January 1978 Guangdong extended foreign exchange retention on an experimental basis to export producers in more product lines and in more locations.[10] Rates were raised to 20 percent for exports covered by the central plan and 30 percent for exports covered by the local plan. The effect of the new program was dramatic and soon caught Beijing's attention. In a speech at a national foreign trade conference that July, Yu Qiuli—one of China's top economic officials—endorsed sharing foreign exchange with localities. Bureaucrats began drafting national regulations, to be effected in January 1979, for local retention of trade and nontrade earnings.

As it turned out, the regulations were not promulgated by the State Council until August 1979 and had to be made retroactive to the first of the year. The delay reflected deep divisions within the central ministries over how far to go in loosening controls. In the summer of 1979 Yu Qiuli had tempered his support for local foreign exchange retention and added an important condition: national export targets sent down from Beijing had to be met before retention would be possible.

The new national rules covering retention of trade earnings were far from satisfactory as far as local governments were concerned. Retention formulas were activated only after export procurement targets were met, and the percentages locally retained—30 percent for centrally managed goods and 40 percent for locally managed goods—applied only to hard currency earnings arising from the sale of goods beyond the planned amount. Foreign exchange derived from sales of ten of the country's major export categories (grain, petroleum, coal, cement, etc.) could not be shared with local governments. And foreign exchange allocations were to be calculated only once a year, in the first quarter of the succeeding year. Thus the earlier a factory completed its procurement plan, the longer it had to wait to get its hands on the foreign exchange allocation it was due.

The rules governing the central-local split of nontrade earnings were more reasonable. No mention was made of plans; and percentages—

30 percent for overseas Chinese remittances, 40 percent for overseas Chinese construction funds, and up to 50 percent for tourist receipts—applied to the total nontrade earnings. The new sharing arrangements were especially timely for Guangzhou, where direct rail, air, and hovercraft services linking the city to Hong Kong were initiated in 1978 and 1979. In 1977 the first tourist ships were permitted to berth in Huangpu.

Fortunately for Guangdong, its special status was confirmed before the generally restrictive trade earnings retention system was implemented, and provincial officials had moved quickly to secure a special arrangement covering foreign exchange retention. This permitted Guangdong to receive a total foreign exchange allocation consisting of three parts: a sum of central foreign exchange covering the export production bases program, the "Importing to Help Exports" program, and other specific applications; a sum of locally retained foreign exchange from trade activities, equivalent to 70 percent of the export earnings above the 1978 export level ($1.4 billion); and a sum of locally retained foreign exchange from nontrade activities calculated by the terms spelled out in the national regulations. The system, which took effect on January 1, 1980, was guaranteed not to change for five years.

The Guangdong arrangement meant that the province accumulated far greater local foreign exchange reserves than did other provinces. The program to allow Guangdong a bigger U.S. dollar "bang" for its renminbi "buck" spurred export procurement sharply, and was a major cause of the 1978–1980 foreign trade boom.

As Guangdong's reserves grew, its enterprises and bureaus with allocations began undertaking import transactions on behalf of other provinces. A factory in Liaoning, for example, paid the Guangdong branch of a foreign trade corporation 2.5 million yuan in early 1980 for a piece of machinery which had been imported for $400,000, an effective exchange rate several times the official renminbi:dollar rate of 1.6:1.00. The Guangzhou port corporations scoured their procurement territories in the inland provinces, and the value of goods exported by Guangdong but produced outside the province increased to more than 700 million yuan in 1980.[11] These activities, though they seemed perfectly natural to those in Guangdong interested in making profits, engendered resentment elsewhere.

With more units obtaining foreign exchange allocations, a lively trade sprang up between the haves (many of whom had no particular need for imports) and the have-nots (who were far more numerous than the haves). Controlling this trade became a major headache for Guangdong. Although various rules and regulations were put out forbidding trade in "high-priced foreign exchange" (*gaojia waihui*), nothing was effective. Finally, toward the end of 1980, a foreign exchange trading room—the nation's first—was established in the Guangzhou branch of the Bank of China. Buyers and sellers of foreign exchange negotiated a price within a range of 2.8 yuan to 3.2 yuan per one U.S. dollar (the official exchange rate at the time was 1.5 yuan to one dollar); transactions were supervised and recorded by the bank. The trading room was the forerunner of the foreign exchange adjustment centers, the officially sanctioned "free markets" that by 1988 had come to play a pivotal role in the circulation of foreign exchange.

*Decentralization and Guangdong Initiatives.* With a greater share of the export earnings went greater freedom in deciding how much of which products to buy and sell. This devolution of decision-making power is usually referred to as decentralization, an overused and imprecise concept. It is not unusual, when charting the course of reforms in Guangdong, to notice that central controls were tightened for some products (as when export or import licenses issued by Beijing were required) at the same time that controls on others were loosened (as when items were taken off the central planners' list of mandatory control targets and placed on their indicative targets list). Decentralization to one unit could appear as recentralization to another. A good example of this occurred in 1983, when Foshan Prefecture was split into Foshan Metropolitan Region and Jiangmen Metropolitan Region. County foreign trade corporations established in 1980 and 1981 in Taishan and Xinhui felt strongly that their subordination to the Jiangmen foreign trade apparatus in 1983 represented a reversal of the decentralization process, because officials in Jiangmen were closer and more prone to "interference" than those in Foshan.

This said, the 1978–1980 period can still, on the whole, be considered as one in which the decentralization of China's foreign trade system from Beijing to the provinces received its first major push. One of the principal tenets of the central government's policy on Guangdong and Fujian was that the provincial governments were to take the leading role in the formulation of the import and export plans. Other provinces of China in 1981 were locked into a central planning system in which the State Planning Commission set targets for more than fifty key import items as well as fixing, by province and ministry, an astounding nine hundred export procurement and sale targets.[12]

The Guangdong branches of the national foreign trade corporations were, prior to the reforms of 1979 and 1980, subordinate to both the head offices in Beijing and the Guangdong Foreign Trade Bureau in Guangzhou, in what was referred to as "dual leadership" *(shuang-chong lingdao)*. The head offices exercised primary authority over the enterprise: setting targets, fixing prices, controlling negotiations, and issuing policy on all significant issues. The Foreign Trade Bureau ensured that resources were allocated as needed to fulfill the export procurement plan. It also staffed the junior and middle management positions in the branches; senior management was made up of officials assigned by Beijing.

As more and more foreign exchange flowed into provincial coffers and planning and pricing regimes were loosened, the power balance in the dual leadership system began to shift in favor of the province in 1979. This shift was accelerated by the central government's adoption of "flexible policies" for Guangdong and Fujian. Local Cantonese gradually took over the top management posts in the Guangdong foreign trade corporation branches, and it was not long before they developed their own strategies for imports and exports. The structure of the province's exports shifted from a mix dominated by agricultural commodities (rice, sugar, rubber) to a more diversified mix of agricultural, handicraft, and light industrial products. Rice exports, which had exceeded 215,000 tons in 1975, fell to roughly 140,000 tons in 1980. During the same period the value of garment exports shot up to $60 million from $16 million and sales of embroidered goods rose from $30 million to more than $100 million as the province cashed in on an American market eager for embroidered tablecloths and blouses.

As it acquired more power, Guangdong needed a commercial organization to represent its foreign trade interests. Under the old system, Guangdong had exercised its limited influence over the branch foreign trade corporations through the Guangdong Foreign Trade Bureau, a purely administrative body. The head office in Beijing was by contrast a corporation, a socialist legal entity with the capacity to enter into contracts with domestic and foreign parties.

In July 1980, the Guangdong Province Foreign Trade Corporation (GPFTC) was formally established, and six months later its subsidiary in Hong Kong, Guangdong Enterprises, opened for business. GPFTC was under the dual leadership of the Ministry of Foreign Trade and the Guangdong Foreign Trade Bureau, but the latter was given the upper hand. Aside from "strategic items"—category one and some category two goods—which were to be centrally managed and negotiated by head office personnel, GPFTC oversaw the sale of the bulk of the province's exports, the category three goods. It established branches in the prefectural capitals, and these bodies exercised "dual leadership" with the prefectural foreign trade bureaus over sub-branches in the counties. Shortly after its establishment, GPFTC instructed its subbranches to handle all aspects of the procurement and sale of 290 category three products, which freed the Guangzhou-based branches to concentrate on the bigger, more important exchange earners. It also established an import department in Guangzhou. Whereas GPFTC did not itself transact export business—procurement and sales were left entirely to the branches, subbranches, and joint industrial-commercial companies—it became, with Guangdong Enterprises, an active participant in the import trade, channeling provincial foreign exchange reserves into the purchase of advanced foreign machinery and raw materials to be used in the production of exports.

An organization to manage the province's investment program—the Guangdong International Trust and Investment Corporation (GITIC)—was created at the end of 1980. With a registered capital of two hundred million yuan and frequent infusions of provincial foreign exchange as a sort of "venture capital" reserve, GITIC represented provincial interests in joint stock companies in the province and abroad, notably in Hong Kong. Another institutional reform that began in 1980 was the establishment of economic courts. These courts, in effect ad hoc tribunals of the people's courts at various levels, had heard six hundred cases involving foreign investment disputes by the end of 1987—85 percent of all foreign investment litigation in China.[13] The Guangzhou Foreign Trade School, which had reopened on a limited scale in 1973, became one of China's four foreign trade institutes in 1980. As an institute it had a larger faculty, student body, and curriculum, and was graduating several hundred foreign trade cadres a year by the mid-1980s.

With their new freedom to set export prices and export plans, Guangdong's foreign trade cadres began experimenting with a number of promotional techniques to boost overseas sales. Advertising in provincial media became possible in 1978, and in April 1979 Diamond Shamrock, an American chemical company, placed the first ad for a foreign company's products in a Guangdong newspaper. The money spent by Guangdong export corporations on advertising in Hong Kong media far exceeded that of other provinces. The Guangdong branch of the Arts and Crafts Corporation staged its own trade show in Macau in 1978; provinces had previously been able to participate in overseas shows only under the banner of a central organization. In January 1980 Guangdong's foreign trade corporation branches mounted a large export fair in Hong Kong, a coordinated exhibition of all that the province had to offer.

The provincial authorities were to develop and implement their own policy in yet another area: registration and control of foreign offices within the province. By the time the State Council promulgated its national regulations controlling representative offices of foreign enterprises in October 1980, nearly forty American, Japanese, and European firms had established full-time presences in Guangzhou. Hong Kong firms operated even more offices, but their ability to conduct business more comfortably in a native environment made keeping track of their numbers difficult. Rather than put the national directives into effect and register the offices, the provincial government set out to develop its own rules, which appeared six months later, in May 1981. In general the authorities in Guangzhou were far more helpful to foreign offices, as well as appreciative of the positive roles they could play, than their counterparts in other cities. Hiring local staff was easier, office facilities were more modern and centrally located, and tax assessments more reasonable.

*Joint Industrial-Commercial Companies.* During the Cultural Revolution, the gap between international and Chinese prices, the virtual freezing of prices the state would pay to procure industrial export goods, and an effective ban on contacts with foreign firms had severely alienated Chinese industry from foreign trade. Delivery schedules for export goods were not met, quality control was lax, and lack of communication between industrial bureaus and foreign trade corporations led to the production of goods for which no foreign demand existed. The factories and their supervisory bureaus—their *popo*—resisted any increase in their export plans. Considering the trouble involved in making high-quality goods on schedule and the thin differentials in prices paid for these by the foreign trade corporations, industrial and agricultural producers preferred to sell their output on the domestic market.

The first steps to rectify this situation were taken in mid-1978. The "four uniteds, two opens" *(si lianhe, liang gongkai)* campaign, launched in Shanghai, was taken up quickly in Guangdong. Industrial departments and foreign trade corporations were exhorted to "work together, jointly arrange production, negotiate with foreign firms, and send study teams abroad." Foreign trade corporations were to disclose their selling prices and factories their costs, thereby reducing mutual suspicion and promoting cooperation. Just as foreign trade had been better linked to rural markets to promote agricultural markets, it was to be better linked to the industrial bureaucracy and factories to boost manufactured exports.

Shortly before the autumn 1978 trade fair, the State Council authorized the establishment of the China National Machinery and Equipment Import and Export Corporation (EQUIPEX). This corporation was, in effect, a joint venture between the Ministry of Foreign Trade and the First Ministry of Machine Building. It was given a monopoly over exports of machine tools, electric motors, and most industrial machinery. In March 1979 a provincial branch was established in Guangzhou.

From the outset there was friction between personnel assigned by the Foreign Trade Bureau (who had previously been employees of MACHIMPEX, the now-dismembered China National Machinery Import and Export Corporation) and personnel assigned by the industrial bureau. The procurement plan for EQUIPEX was developed by the industrial side; the export sales plan was developed and implemented by the foreign trade side. Coordination was poor. Moreover, the Ministry of Foreign Trade in Beijing refused to give EQUIPEX any power to import; MACHIMPEX retained sole rights to China's lucrative machinery import business.

Although EQUIPEX on the national level reported primarily to the foreign trade ministry and had a secondary reporting responsibility to the machine building ministry, in Guangdong the industrial bureau was able to wrest control of the provincial branch away from the Foreign Trade Bureau, which was reduced to providing support services. The seizure of foreign trade power from the old, rigidified foreign trade monopoly was immensely popular in industrial circles, and was an early indicator that reforms in Guangdong need not follow the exact course mapped out by Beijing.

In September 1980, Guangdong authorized the establishment of a branch of a foreign trade enterprise subordinate solely to an industrial department: the Metallurgical Import and Export Corporation. To avoid conflict with the Ministry of Foreign Trade's Minerals and Metals Corporation (MINMETALS), the new body's activities were limited to handling above-plan exports of metals. In other words, only after MINMETALS met its export plan was material made available for the industrial foreign trade enterprise to sell abroad. The Metallurgical Import and Export Corporation was also given responsibility for managing "Importing to Help Exports" business and cooperative ventures with foreign firms. It became the focal point for technical exchange programs with multinational mining companies.

Within a short period of time, fourteen industrial-commercial foreign trade enterprises were operating in Guangdong. The value of these companies' exports was $20 million in 1980, a figure that soared to more than $200 million in 1982.[14] Among the top exporters were the silk corporation and the aquatic products corporation, the latter benefiting from an ongoing effort to boost fresh-water fish sales to Hong Kong. Though the Foreign Trade Ministry in Beijing and the Foreign Trade Bureau in Guangdong tried to limit the joint industrial-commercial companies to above-plan export and processing or assembling business, it was not long before the new firms were openly competing with the long-established foreign trade corporations. Sometimes industrial bureaus successfully negotiated reductions in their export plans in order to increase sales made through their subordinate trade corporations. The ability of the joint industrial-commercial firms to carry on "Importing to Help Exports" business proved to be a big loophole through which all kinds of import business was conducted.

As their hold over import and export business loosened, the foreign trade corporations began competing with each other in areas where jurisdiction was unclear. Whereas in the past factories producing plastic articles for export had imported resins through the Chemicals Import and Export Corporation and exported finished products through the Light Industrial Products Import and Export Corporation, in 1980 they were able to place their import requirements through the same corporation that handled their exports. Although this change meant reduced costs and better coordination of imports and production, there were negative consequences as well. Because the pricing system had yet to be reformed, big profits could be made on certain imports while others continued to be subsidized at a loss. A good example in the early 1980s was pharmaceuticals. Large amounts of foreign medicines were imported and sold in Guangzhou at huge markups; many brands were counterfeit, others had expired shelf lives. Export corporations gladly undertook import business in profitable lines (for example, plastic resins and machinery) but shunned business in unprofitable lines. The latter were left to the corporations that held what had previously been monopolistic rights to a broad range of goods, both profitable and unprofitable.

Another consequence of the rise of competition among foreign trade enterprises was "parallel exports," colloquially known as "water goods" *(shuihou)*. On the procurement side, foreign trade corporations vied with each other to buy export goods, often paying producers the maximum differentials allowed for better export quality (without necessarily getting top-quality goods); on the export side, foreign trade corporations found themselves having to undercut their domestic competitors—notably the joint industrial-commercial companies—to make sales. The parallel goods problem became more and more serious as time went by and greater numbers of firms with foreign trade rights appeared. Particularly active were foreign trade enterprises registered in the special economic zones. Many were able to secure 100 percent foreign exchange retention of goods exported, regardless of source. They bought up goods all over China for renminbi and sold at whatever hard currency price they could get, causing confusion in markets and a deterioration in export profitability. On a local scale, in the Macau market for foodstuffs, profitability was destroyed by parallel goods, contributing to declines in the value of Guangdong's exports to the Portuguese enclave throughout the mid-1980s.[15]

A natural evolution of the policy to give industrial departments greater foreign trade exposure was granting factories the right to conduct direct exports. Initially, only factories generating a minimum of $750,000 in export earnings could apply. In November 1981 three factories—the Guangzhou Ramie Factory, the Jiangmen Wireless Radio Factory, and the Maoming Petrochemical Complex—were the first in Guangdong to be granted direct foreign trade rights.

As the established foreign trade corporations came under increasing threat from the joint industrial-commercial enterprises and factories with rights to conduct their own foreign commerce, several chose to turn the tables on their competitors by establishing their own farms and factories. Prior to 1980, foreign trade corporations had to procure export commodities from farms or factories under "arm's length" contracts described earlier. In 1979 and 1980, however, surging domestic demand for high-quality foodstuffs and consumer goods made it difficult to fulfill procurement plans. The response by the Zhongshan County Foodstuffs Export Corporation in Shiqi was to set up its own pigeon, chicken, and pig farms as well as a sausage factory. It structured a compensation trade arrangement with China's commercial entity in Macau—the Nanguang Company—under which it imported antibiotics, vaccines, and animal feed and in turn supplied the city with a large portion of its fresh meat requirements. The corporation was awarded the distinction of "model foreign trade corporation" by the Ministry of Foreign Trade in Beijing, prompting scores of other county and municipal subbranches to establish their own production facilities.

*Pricing of Export Goods.* The most effective incentives to spur factories to produce export goods—the ability of foreign trade corporations to pay higher prices for goods destined for foreign markets and the ability to raise prices if foreign market prices should rise—were absent in China for the duration of the Cultural Revolution and for a considerable period of time thereafter. The State Council had laid down rules covering the pricing of export commodities in November 1965; these took effect on January 1, 1966, and remained in force without significant modification until 1979. The regulations enunciated the general principle that export goods must be purchased by state trading corporations at the fixed domestic prices, either ex-factory (for industrial goods) or wholesale (for agricultural and handicraft goods). If there were significant quality or packaging improvements, an appropriate differential based on actual cost could be paid. If there were other extraordinary conditions—such as a domestic ex-factory price so high that it forced the state trading corporation to incur inordinately heavy export losses—the foreign trade corporation could negotiate a different price with the factory's administrative unit, but all such deviations had to obtain the approval of the State Pricing Bureau in Beijing. Specially approved exceptions became increasingly rare as the Cultural Revolution lurched forward from year to year, and by 1976 and 1977, manufacturers of export goods in Guangdong had been receiving the same prices from the foreign trade corporations for close to ten years.

Guangdong's senior officials, increasingly hamstrung in their efforts to boost exports, petitioned Beijing for greater flexibility in interpreting the 1966 export pricing regulations. In August 1979 the State Council authorized the State Pricing Bureau to issue a notice recommending modifications in the pricing of goods procured for export. Exceptions to the general rule of equivalent pricing for exports and domestic goods were enumerated, and more flexibility was given to foreign trade corporations to pay higher prices to factories that would otherwise incur losses on export production or that produced solely for exports. Most important for Guangdong, applications for price differentials for most goods could be approved by the Provincial Pricing Bureau, and no longer needed to be referred to Beijing.

Fresh-water fish, cultivated in ponds throughout the Pearl River Delta, were one of Guangdong's traditional exports to Hong Kong and Macau. Exports fell precipitously from 1975 to 1978, despite a rise in production and hectarage given over to fish rearing. The peasants, having no price incentive to sell to export corporations, either sold their fish on the free market or consumed them at the table. Meanwhile, Hong Kong consumers were willing to pay top dollar. Taking advantage of the new flexibility evident in the 1979 notice, the Guangdong government decided to try a truly novel approach to the problem of falling fish exports: it raised the procurement price of the most popular fish to reflect wholesale price levels in Hong Kong.[16] There was an immediate response, and procurement and sales rose almost immediately to pre–Cultural Revolution levels.

Fish exports to Hong Kong were profitable, but most Guangdong products were sold overseas at a loss. Guangdong's average export cost for all goods was 2.61 yuan to one U.S. dollar in 1979—a bit higher than the national average of 2.53 yuan to one U.S. dollar—and it remained stable in 1980 despite the sharp rise in export procurement prices. At this level, and given the prevailing official U.S. dollar:yuan exchange rate, the state was selling at an average of 35–40 percent below cost to earn foreign exchange. (National regulations prohibited exports at greater than 70 percent loss.) Part of the reason for the stability in export cost was the generally weak U.S. dollar in the latter years of the Carter presidency. But Guangdong's foreign trade technocrats also contributed by successfully applying to the Provincial Taxation Bureau or the Ministry of Finance to rebate commercial-industrial taxes on goods procured for export and to the Customs Administration to eliminate export tariffs. Both moves substantially reduced export costs. Tariff reductions and tax rebates, first tried out in 1978–1980, were employed once again in 1986 as key elements of Guangdong's export drive.

## Stagnation and Decline, 1981–1984

One consequence of restrictions on foreign trade during the Cultural Revolution was the decline in the percentage of Guangdong's total exports dedicated to the Hong Kong–Macau market. In the early sixties, more than half of the province's exports were destined for Hong Kong and Macau. By 1970 this had dropped to 42 percent, reflecting poor rice export prices and Beijing's decision that Shanghai and Beijing would supply Hong Kong with light industrial and textile products.

Immediately on obtaining its special status, Guangdong's foreign trade establishment turned its attention to boosting sales to Hong Kong. In 1980 sales to Hong Kong and Macau exceeded half of total exports for the first time in ten years. The degree of dependence increased further, to 60 percent, in 1984.

It is not difficult to understand why overdependence occurred. The quickest way to improve the bottom line in any business is to sell next door; this is especially true for commodity business, where freight is a large component. Hong Kong's tastes in foodstuffs were the tastes of its fellow Cantonese, and Guangdong's export producers were quick to shift out of grain and into pond fish, chickens, pigeons, and vegetables. In the industrial area, as much as 90 percent of foreign investment in new, export-devoted capacity in Guangdong was made by Hong Kong or Macau capitalists, and the lion's share of the output of these deals found its way to the same territories for consumption or re-export.

In the late 1980s, many in Guangdong complained about overdependence on Hong Kong, but not a single official had proposed a coherent program to do anything about it. Any marketing manager can explain the danger of putting too much reliance on any one market; there is lots of money to be made when times are good, but when times are hard, the firm really suffers. Hong Kong went through very trying times in 1981–1984. First, the short but sharp American recession led to a 5 percent drop in Hong Kong foreign trade in 1982. Then, as recoveries in industrial economies began showing impressive gains in 1983 and 1984, Hong Kong found itself in the grips of a serious confidence crisis: its economy was characterized by a weak currency, low property prices, and little investment in capital equipment. For the entire period from 1981 to 1984, Hong Kong ran a persistent trade deficit. Though never a serious threat to the economy, this deficit limited the extent to which Hong Kong could import more Guangdong products.

Guangdong's exports grew at an average rate of less than one percent per annum during the 1981–1984 period. The worst year was 1982, when overseas sales fell by 7 percent. As a percentage of industrial-agricultural output, the value of export procurement fell for three consecutive years (1982–1984), hitting a low of 9 percent in 1984. When foreign trade cadres were asked about the poor performance, they cited the weak Hong Kong market and the poorly developed trade infrastructure of the province. Transport was abysmal in the Delta. A trip from Jiangmen to Guangzhou, roughly a hundred kilometers, took close to eight hours in 1982 and 1983. At the Jiujiang River, trucks, buses, cars, and every other conceivable form of conveyance queued for two hours or more before being able to cross. It was here that some of the most blatant payoffs were exacted, and local trucks jumped to the head of the line with mysterious regularity. In the 1970s, at all crossings there were signs stipulating that vehicles carrying export commodities were to be given priority on the ferries. These signs disappeared in the early 1980s, and transport fees—a large component of export cost—then rose sharply.

Lack of energy was a major headache for foreign investors, each of whom had to negotiate quotas for power usage. Blackouts and brownouts were common. During the summer months some factories in Guangzhou operated only two or three days a week. Communications, similarly, were extremely poor. International direct dial service from Guangzhou to Hong Kong was not possible until 1984; most municipalities—Foshan, Jiangmen, Shiqi—had to wait until 1986 before direct dial and telex links were in place.

In retrospect, there should have been much greater investment, much earlier in the reform process, to improve trade-related infrastructure. Guangdong paid a heavy price in sales lost because of its backwardness in transport, communications, and energy.

Another negative phenomenon that affected investment trends was the large expenditure on tourist facilities, nearly all with Hong Kong/ Macau capital, in the early 1980s. In the same period foreign equity investment in manufacturing showed meager gains. In 1984, Guangdong absorbed $24.6 million in foreign investment in joint venture factories; by comparison $19.5 million went into the building of tourist hotels.[17] Hotels depreciate quickly and make lots of foreign currency in the high seasons, but they do nothing for the development of long-term export earnings.

*Recentralization.* As more and more of the provinces adjacent to Guangdong won foreign trade autonomy, the amount of goods Guangdong could procure in other provinces declined. In 1981, the volume of export commodities purchased by Guangdong foreign trade corporation branches from producers outside of Guangdong plunged nearly five hundred million yuan. Years of resentment over Cantonese trading practices translated into the quick cut-off of many long-standing supply chains. In February 1982, national leaders criticized the Guangdong corporations at a conference in Guangzhou. They were accused of offering export producers in adjacent provinces inflated procurement prices and thereby driving up the prices of agricultural sideline produce.

The annoyance Beijing felt about Guangdong in 1982 manifested itself in several ways. A State Council announcement in January provided that branches of foreign trade corporations in Guangdong were to submit to the decisions of the head office for all commodities that required "central coordination." Three months later, the newly expanded Ministry of Foreign Economic Relations and Trade (MOFERT) sent teams of one hundred cadres to set up Special Representative Offices in Dalian, Tianjin, Shanghai, and Guangzhou. Their functions included "supervising and leading" coordination work for key export commodities—decisions related to major changes in markets, volumes, customers, and prices were relayed to Beijing for decision—and issuance of import and export licenses.[18]

Concerned with rampant smuggling, Beijing further tightened its grip on Guangdong in August when it forbade Guangdong and Fujian enterprises from importing seventeen luxury goods for resale to inland provinces. All movements of imported automobiles, television sets, and refrigerators out of Guangdong to other parts of China had to be covered by a special transport permit issued by Beijing.

At the same time that Guangdong was being cut down to size, restrictions were being placed on foreign trade activities in and through Shenzhen. A chemicals minifair held in Shenzhen in the latter half of 1981 was subsequently declared "illegal" because it had not been sanctioned by MOFERT. Moreover, all contracts made at the fair were declared null and void, which seriously damaged the reputation of the Chinese sellers, many of whom were new to the export trade.

A strengthened Customs Administration—reconstituted in 1980 as a ministry-level organ reporting to the State Council—gradually took over the role of watchdog for the central government throughout the province. MOFERT's special representative was situated in Guangzhou and had no outposts elsewhere in Guangdong, whereas there were customs houses in nearly all major trade centers. The Customs Administration had great power it could bring to bear. In 1983, for example, I was advised of an impending breakthrough in foreign trade: subbranches at the county and municipal level were to be permitted to sign import contracts with foreign (that is, American, British, etc.— not just Hong Kong and Macau) firms. But one year and no contracts later, I went back to the subbranches in one Delta town and found out what had happened. "We'd gotten all the approvals to proceed . . . the foreign trade corporation in Guangzhou, the bank, the local foreign trade bureau . . . everyone except Customs." Customs wouldn't sign off, and it wasn't until 1986 that American firms were selling directly to subbranches in Guangdong.

The revitalized Customs Administration affected the business of foreign trade corporations in other ways. Since 1963 the corporation branches and subbranches had been the collectors of customs duties, and this revenue had been a major part of corporation profits. After 1980 the Customs Administration assumed collection of duties, and all revenues were sent to Beijing. The impact of this change on corporation profitability was tremendous. According to an official estimate, China's national foreign trade corporations earned trading profits and taxes totaling 4.61 billion yuan in the seventeen-year period from 1963 to 1980. Of this sum, customs duties represented 2.98 billion yuan. After the Customs Administration began collecting duties, corporation losses, already mounting due to rising export costs, exploded. For China as a whole, foreign trade corporation losses amounted to 3.18 billion yuan in 1980.[19]

Many cadres saw Beijing's tightening of controls as a reversal of the special powers granted to Guangdong in 1979—in effect, a campaign of recentralization. There was growing disillusionment with the reforms and a feeling among export producers that they had been misled with respect to foreign exchange retention. A newspaper article published in late 1980 echoed complaints heard in the factories and on the farms: "Commencing this year, regulations stipulate that a division of the above-1978 export earnings will take place, but first approximately 50 percent of the amount to be shared is subtracted as 'export support fees' paid to the foreign trade corporations. Of the remaining funds, 30 percent is sent up to the central government, leaving 70 percent for division within the province. The actual amount of foreign exchange entitlement for the factory is only 10 percent [of the above-1978 export level minus export support fees]. Moreover, to actually get its hands on this money, the enterprise must apply through many levels, regardless of the amount involved. Such a system will do little to motivate enterprises to export."[20]

*The Dual Exchange Rate and the Agency System.* China introduced an "internal" exchange rate of 2.8 yuan to one U.S.dollar on January 1, 1981 (when the official rate was 1.6 yuan to one dollar). The internal rate was employed, as the name suggests, in foreign trade transactions between domestic Chinese firms, that is, in the pricing and accounting of import and export goods. All dealings involving foreigners—opening of letters of credit, valuation of foreign-contributed assets of joint ventures, cashing of traveler's checks—were still calculated at the external rate set by the People's Bank of China and posted daily in Beijing.

The rationale behind the move to establish a dual exchange-rate system, common in Eastern Europe but never before attempted in China, was twofold: to stimulate exports by making them profitable— the national average export cost was 2.5 yuan to one U.S. dollar when the internal rate was set up—and to restrict imports by making them costly. The experiment was a flop. Shortly after Ronald Reagan became President in 1981, the dollar began a sharp and steady upward gallop. Month by month the gap between the external and internal rates closed while export cost continued its upward spiral.[21] Guangdong's average export cost exceeded 3.0 yuan per dollar in early 1983, meaning that producers who sold their products to foreign trade corporations at a yuan:dollar rate of 2.8:1.00 once again lost money on the deals.

Late in 1983 world attention was directed to China's dual exchange-rate system when American textile manufacturers filed a countervailing duty petition with the U.S. Department of Commerce on the grounds that adoption of the 2.8 yuan rate amounted to an export subsidy. In early 1984, a Chinese internal directive—noting that national export cost now exceeded 2.8 yuan to one U.S. dollar—abandoned the use of the rate in pricing imported machinery and technology.[22] On January 1, 1985, Beijing discontinued the dual exchange-rate system altogether.

The sharp rise in export cost after 1980 was a national phenomenon, but in the 1981–1983 period it affected Guangdong's ability to boost exports more than it did that of other provinces and municipalities. During these three years an experimental "financial guarantee" system was in effect. Guangdong guaranteed the central government a fixed sum of foreign exchange each year. Aside from this, the province was free to develop its overseas sales, provided that its enterprises be solely responsible for subsidizing their export losses. Other provinces continued to receive central subsidies to offset rising export costs resulting from domestic inflation and the strengthening U.S. dollar.

With the burden of subsidization shifted to Guangdong, a series of measures were announced to eliminate big export losers—defined in 1981 as items whose export cost exceeded five yuan to one U.S. dollar. These measures curtailed production not only of old, inefficiently made items but also of new products with high start-up costs. A study by leading foreign trade economists in Guangzhou contends that the shift of subsidization to the province for this three-year period was the principal reason for the stagnation of Guangdong's exports during the sixth five-year plan (1981–1985).[23] The financial guarantee system was scrapped at the end of 1983, and in 1984 the central government once again began allocating subsidies to partially offset export losses.

Guangdong's foreign trade cadres would have preferred to stick with the guarantee system, had the internal rate been allowed to devalue, but the State Council decided against letting the 2.8 yuan to one dollar rate float downward. (Why is anyone's guess: at the time the internal rate was introduced, it was stated that it would be subject to change.) In the absence of devaluation, Guangdong was left with a simple strategy to conduct foreign trade profitably: reduction of export cost and accumulation of import profit. This strategy was pursued vigorously in 1983.

Some localities worked hard that year to become more profitable. Foshan achieved a 10 percent reduction in its average export cost in September and October 1983 by ceasing sales of big export losers, enforcing export procurement plans of low-cost, high-profit items, reducing inventories, and cutting export procurement prices.[24] Guangzhou's export corporations successfully negotiated price reductions of sixty-seven export commodities with domestic factories and farms in

1983, which reduced the municipality's export cost by 12.5 million yuan.[25] Nevertheless, some of these gains were offset by the growing incidence of waste and spoilage in many localities.[26]

Cutting prices paid to export producers just when domestic market prices are rising is not a winning business strategy in the long run. In early 1984 producers were being asked both to take cuts and to raise quality at the same time, and naturally they grumbled. Opposition to these tactics was so strong that foreign trade enterprises yielded and stopped applying to the Pricing Bureau to reduce export commodity prices in 1984 and concentrated on offsetting their inevitable export losses with newly reinstated export subsidies and accumulated import profits. It was the single-minded pursuit of profit that lay at the root of the Hainan car scandal of 1984; although this was the most spectacular case, it was symptomatic of Guangdong's large purchases of foreign consumer durables, all carrying big renminbi sales tags, throughout 1984 and the first half of 1985. Profits from these import deals were often used by the foreign trade enterprises to fund more export procurement of profitable goods; the local government's share of profits was devoted to capital investment projects and public welfare.

After April 1983, when the central government adopted the policy of accelerated development for Hainan, substantial sums of both renminbi and foreign currency were allocated to the island, and strictures on foreign trade were loosened. Late that year, as described in Chapter 9, the island's leadership hit upon the aggressive strategy of obtaining large sums of renminbi by trading in foreign cars and consumer durables. Renminbi loans were raised by county and municipal enterprises from local branches of the island's banks. Using these funds, a total of $570 million in foreign exchange was purchased at free-market rates from units in twenty-one provinces; 81 percent of the amount was purchased in Guangdong. Provincial organs sold $115 million, while enterprises in Foshan and Shenzhen each sold more than $80 million.[27]

The $570 million was put to work importing eighty-nine thousand vehicles and large quantities of television sets, stereos, motorcycles, refrigerators, and the like. The bulk of the profit was reinvested in purchasing raw materials available in China and crucial to Hainan's development such as steel, cement, and coal. When the business was fully exposed in August 1985, the extent of Hainan's crimes were judged to be little more than violations of the 1982 regulations against transporting imported consumer goods out of Guangdong and irregularities arising from the bank loans and foreign exchange transactions. Yet officials all over China were scandalized by the size of the transactions and the pervasiveness of involvement by cadres at all levels of government.

In late 1980, as the introduction of the dual exchange rate was being mooted in Beijing, another important reform of the foreign trade system was being promoted by Vice-Premier Yao Yilin and his supporters: adoption of the agency system in foreign trade. Use of the internal exchange rate to make exports more profitable to producers and the switch to agency business were linked reforms designed to further entice manufacturers—as opposed to traders—into the export business.

In agency business the foreign trade enterprise's role is solely one of a commission agent. It works on an indent basis for a commission agreed to in advance with its principal, usually 1.5 to 3.0 percent of the contract's value. Prior to the agency system's introduction, foreign trade enterprises worked exclusively on a resale basis, that is, they bought and sold for their own account. This way of doing business is referred to in the Chinese foreign trade lexicon as *jiying jinchukou* (self-managed importing and exporting). In resale business the profit and loss on a foreign trade transaction is on the foreign trade enterprise's account; in agency business the manufacturer makes the profit or suffers the loss.

Following a call by Beijing at the end of 1983, Guangdong's corporations launched a big drive to popularize and increase agency business. The *Nanfang ribao* revealed that, in a two-week period in February 1984, Guangdong export deals worth 320 million yuan were concluded by means of the agency system.[28] Altogether about 20 percent of the province's export procurement was directed to agency sales in 1984.

The agency system was largely unsuccessful in Guangdong, however, and many factories that tried it in the 1981–1984 period abandoned it in favor of selling products to foreign trade enterprises at freely negotiated prices, and letting them resell them abroad at whatever prices they can get. With the imposition of import license controls in 1984, exporters that were selling products at a loss to gain foreign exchange allocations found their ability to buy foreign consumer goods severely constrained. (Foreign trade corporations had much freer access to licenses that were granted by their supervisory units, the foreign trade bureaus.) Also, foreign trade enterprises refused to take physical title to goods sold under agency contracts, so that if there was any delay caused by the buyer's failure to open a letter of credit or perhaps by difficulty in finding a vessel, the export producer suffered from high inventory and tied-up capital. These difficulties were compounded by the general disenchantment of export manufacturers with the operation of the foreign exchange retention system.

*The Underground Economy.* With the inception of the open economic policies in 1978 came a subterranean economy of corruption and back-door deals based on a huge smuggling trade. The currencies of this trade were China's gold, silver, antiques, traditional medicines, and pearls in exchange for the opiates of the twentieth century—television sets, stereos, flashy watches, beer, and cigarettes.

There is no way to estimate with any accuracy the size of Guang-dong's underground economy at any given time over the years 1978–1987, but 1981 and 1982 were perhaps the worst. Driving by car from Shantou to Shanwei, the traveler passed roadside stands loaded with every brand of American cigarettes imaginable and stacked cartons of San Miguel beer, Hong Kong's finest. Shantou itself was a beehive of illicit trade; 587 major seizures were made in 1981 and the total haul was estimated at forty-seven million yuan.[29] Seizures were a minuscule percentage of the total value of smuggled goods working their way through Shantou's economy. A cadre in the prefectural government remarked that in 1980 and 1981, the amount of foreign exchange represented by the value of smuggled luxury goods far exceeded the local foreign exchange expended on imports of machinery, equipment, and technology.

Guangdong's export trade in musk ambrette—an expensive raw material used to manufacture perfume—virtually collapsed in 1980, when the smugglers hit upon the product as an ideal currency for the outward run to Hong Kong. Out of secret caches that had escaped the attention of the Red Guards came a flood of silver dollars— American trade dollars of the 1870s and 1880s, Spanish and Mexican coins, the popular Dragon Dollar, and the more common Yuan Shikai and Republican coins. More than a million coins left China, mostly through Guangdong. The treasure spilled out and wound up in wicker baskets lining the back alleys of Aberdeen, the big fishing port on Hong Kong's southern coast.

So vast and profitable was the smuggling business that many, probably most, of Hong Kong's fishing fleet abandoned fishing altogether.

This is reflected in the precipitous fall in saltwater fish sales to Hong Kong and Macau: from 10,500 tons in 1980 to 3,500 tons in 1982. Vegetable trucks operated by export truckers in Zhuhai and Zhongshan smuggled the bulk of the priceless antiques that exited China via Macau in the early 1980s.

Corruption and high-level complicity in black market and smuggling operations were rife, and perhaps understandably, cadres in charge of foreign trade enterprises or their administrative organs were frequently fingered. Three of the biggest cases involved senior management of newly established joint industrial-commercial companies. Published revelations of ethically spineless, corrupt newcomers on the trade scene did little to encourage Beijing to countenance establishing more joint industrial-commercial companies. Not until 1985 was the practice of granting batches of enterprises foreign trade rights resumed.

Other problems that caught the attention of provincial and national leaders were the upsurge in exports of parallel goods, the misuse of foreign exchange certificates—introduced in 1980—for black market transactions, and wastage arising from mismanagement and malfeasance. First-generation Hong Kong clones of personal computers flooded into Guangdong, only to pile up in warehouses. When they broke down, as was very frequent, they were usually not serviceable by the Hong Kong firm. Hundreds of taxis were imported—many by the Dongfang Hotel under very questionable circumstances—but somebody neglected to arrange for imports of spare tires. At one point I counted forty-eight blue Japanese taxis sitting on blocks outside the Dongfang. They had been cannibalized for tires and parts to enable the remaining fleet to operate.

The impatience of Beijing's conservative wing with these shenanigans was reflected in the 1982 measures slapping controls on Guangdong and Fujian's freewheeling external economy. By the spring of that year the response had been insufficient and smuggling and corruption had not appreciably waned. Officials therefore decided to take further steps.

In the summer, calls were heard for stiffer penalties, and shortly thereafter smugglers and corrupt officials began receiving longer jail terms. Finally, in the summer and fall of 1983, numerous leaders of the underground economy met their fate at the hand of the executioner during the swift, sharp campaign against lawlessness that swept Guangdong (where there were more than one thousand executions out of a national total of approximately ten thousand). Though not the sole reason—better coordination with the Hong Kong authorities and the depletion of silver reserves in private hands were other factors—the imposition of capital punishment had a chilling effect, and smuggling and related crimes of bribery and fraud showed signs of leveling off in 1984.

## Second Wind, 1985–1988

The year 1985 is referred to in Guangdong trade circles as the "new liftoff," and indeed the province's import and export performance in the four years ending in 1988 was outstanding. Exports rose 180 percent from $2.5 billion in 1984 to more than $7.3 billion in 1988, growth that compares favorably with that registered by any of the newly industrializing economies of Asia. In 1984, Guangdong ranked a poor fifth among China's provinces and municipalities in exports. Two years later Guangdong became China's number one exporter for the first time, and in 1987 and 1988 it widened its lead. In the highest of compliments, Shanghai's top leaders led a large delegation to the province in early 1988 to learn how to do business from the Cantonese.

During 1985–1987, Guangdong's imports that were financed with its own foreign exchange soared, more than doubling, from $1 billion to nearly $2.6 billion (see Appendix, Table A.6). Purchases of this scale brought Guangdong increasing attention as a market in its own right. American, European, Japanese, and of course Hong Kong businesspeople devoted more and more time to the province in order to explain the advantages of their products and technologies. More than two thousand delegations and study groups left Guangdong for foreign destinations in 1987, and many went to view the best the West had to offer.

In short, foreign trade moved further away from the periphery and closer to the center of Guangdong's economic development strategy after 1985. The province became externally oriented to a degree unknown elsewhere in China. Export procurement as a percentage of provincial agricultural and industrial output rose to more than 17 percent in 1986, but in a number of townships the export sector came to represent fully a third to a half of industrial output. Everywhere, export-processing zones blossomed. In Foshan Metropolitan Region alone, six such zones—offering a bewildering variety of "favorable conditions and policies" to foreign investors—were operating in early 1988. These zones and a great many export-oriented townships became centers of production for particular industries, attracting and building on pools of capital, labor, and management. Taiping Township in Dongguan Municipality was a center of the toy industry. Zhencheng Township, in Guangzhou Metropolitan Region, became known as the "blue jeans capital" of Guangdong. In addition to scores of factories churning out piece goods and garments for overseas consumers, the township itself was a huge denim market from one end to the other, with hundreds of shops, stalls, and street vendors offering piles of blue jeans.

A belt of export-processing satellite towns sprang up within a 150-mile radius of Hong Kong. They fed the territory and its export markets and incorporated technologies and materials in concentrated centers of expertise. Guangdong passed a number of local laws to encourage businessmen in Hong Kong to shift processing work into the province, and the response was significant. The prosperity that ensued in the externally oriented townships was perhaps the most visible achievement of the 1985–1987 import-export surge.

Excluding the processing business, which showed healthy growth in export earnings year after year, Guangdong's foreign investment performance in this period was mixed. With all its teething problems, the Chinese investment environment simply could not compete with those of Southeast Asia and Taiwan in the eyes of foreign firms. New contracts for foreign investment in Guangdong fell from 13,700 in 1985 to 9,500 in 1986 and 7,000 in 1987 (see Table A.7). The precipitous fall in commitments by foreign investors—in Guangdong and throughout China—prompted Beijing to issue in October 1986 what became known as the "twenty-two points" to encourage more foreign investment. (Guangdong and many of its townships put out supplementary regulations—often the merest refinements of the basic principles—throughout 1987.) Despite taking several steps in the right direction—most notably, allowing greater access to China's domestic market for products manufactured by joint ventures—the twenty-two points were only partially successful. Guangdong enjoyed an increase in the value of new commitments in 1987, but actual investment, that is, projects commissioned, declined to $1.23 billion in 1987 from $1.45 billion in 1986.

These statistics hide, however, some important trends. More than 40 percent of the foreign capital used in 1986 consisted of foreign bank loans. These funds—a hefty $632 million—were put largely into infrastructural improvements. Good examples were the loans granted by Scandinavian banks to finance improved telecommunications in the province; beginning in mid-1986, more than a dozen townships gained international direct dialing and telefax service in a twelve-month period. Other loans were applied to railroads—two major lines were under construction in late 1987 and three were being mapped out—and bridges. In 1987 it became possible to drive from Hong Kong to Macau via Guangzhou without using a ferry. Many of the new bridges throughout the Pearl River Delta were to be paid for with tolls from Hong Kong's and Guangdong's fast-growing motor vehicle fleet.

Alarmed by the percentage of foreign investment devoted to non-productive sectors, cadres in municipalities, townships, and counties stopped authorizing establishment of service joint ventures. A Jiangmen official in charge of approving foreign investment projects related that nineteen service joint ventures were put to him for approval in the latter half of 1986—gasoline stations, a hotel, video game parlors, taxi companies, and the like. Not a single one was approved. Provincewide, investments in manufacturing and energy accounted for nearly 95 percent of all foreign capital inflows in 1987, up from 86 percent the year before. One of the most impressive projects that was commissioned in 1987 was the world-class Shekou Float Glass Plant, a $100 million joint venture involving American, Thai, and Chinese interests.[30] Yet another key project that commenced operation in 1986 was the Shajiao Power Station in Dongguan County; the plant, erected by Hong Kong's Hopewell Group in record time, was a principal reason behind the steady improvement in power supply—and the sharp reduction in downtime by export factories—that characterized the Guangdong economy from the middle of 1986 to early 1988.

Aside from the flourishing processing and assembly business (which generated more than $250 million in foreign exchange earnings in both 1986 and 1987), the use of foreign loans to finance infrastructural projects, and the start-up of a few world-scale plants, Guangdong's explosive export growth owed surprisingly little to foreign capital. Imports of raw materials and equipment by foreign equity ventures far exceeded the value of their exports in 1986. State-owned enterprises led Guangdong's post-1986 export growth, accounting for 83 percent of provincial exports in 1987 (versus 67 percent in the previous year).[31] Three initiatives enabled Guangdong's state sector to surge ahead of other provinces after 1985: a renewed commitment to decentralized foreign trade and investment decision making; the encouragement of competition in foreign trade services; and a comprehensive overhaul of export incentives, including major reforms of the foreign exchange retention systems.

By the middle of 1984 both the national campaign against "spiritual pollution" and the provincial campaign against economic crime had largely run their course. Deng Xiaoping had expressed his support for the Shenzhen experiment, and Premier Zhao Ziyang, with nearly twenty years of experience working in Guangdong, was concerned about the stagnation of the southern province's external trade. The climate was right for new moves to decentralize and otherwise reform import, export, and investment decision making. In June 1984, Guangdong's provincial government issued regulations that defined, for the first time, the limits of authority within which administrative units down to the county level could make decisions on key capital construction projects without having to seek higher approval. The projects could be funded by joint ventures, foreign bank loans, and/or the locale's own foreign exchange reserves. Guangzhou was permitted to approve and implement projects up to $10 million in value; Zhanjiang, Shantou, Zhuhai, Foshan, and Jiangmen, $5 million; other municipalities and bureaus under direct provincial control, $3 million; county-level municipalities (for example, Zhongshan), $1.5 million; and counties, $1 million.

The new regulations were popular with officials throughout the province. The more enterprising among them, as discussed in Chapter 10, often found ways to circumvent the limits by dividing larger projects into several small pieces. Yu Fei, at the time mayor of Foshan, was a strong advocate of this approach, and sometimes broke large deals into four or five pieces to avoid troublesome and time-consuming submissions to provincial and central organs.

Moves to decentralize authority over other imports (for example, raw materials and consumer goods) were stalled by the nationwide drive to reduce China's spiraling trade deficit, a movement that dates to mid-1985. A vast array of measures was adopted by Beijing to curb imports: import licenses were introduced, special import surcharges imposed, certificates of import approval by industrial ministries adopted, and rigorous inspection procedures for imports implemented. In late 1984 Guangdong established a "leading group" in the

Foreign Economic and Trade Commission to screen and coordinate imports of all products subject to national and, increasingly, provincial controls.

Despite these import restraints, Guangdong took a decisive step toward further decentralization in November 1985, when it established rules whereby county foreign trade enterprises could both import and export goods. Subbranches began making imports in January 1986. In 1987 exports handled by county foreign trade corporations (the subbranches) accounted for 70 percent of the province's total exports (exclusive of sales by joint ventures).[32]

Having authority to import without having adequate foreign exchange to pay for purchases is of little use. In late 1984 the province scrapped the foreign exchange system that had been in place since 1980. Effective January 1, 1985, use of the 1978 base year for calculation of allocations was discontinued; the province and its constituent administrative units were henceforth eligible to retain 30 percent of total export earnings. In certain instances—for example, for processing and assembly business and for nontrade earnings—higher percentages were permitted. Of the 30 percent retained, the bulk went initially to the export enterprises' administrative organs, but as of January 1, 1986, producers were granted the lion's share of these earnings. And in 1987 producers of electrical machinery and instruments—a high-priority export industry for China—were made eligible for 100 percent foreign exchange retention, subject to application. This move presaged other industry-specific retention schemes; light industrial products, arts and crafts, and garment exporters were granted access to 70 percent of their foreign exchange earnings in January 1988.

Although serious problems remained in implementing the retention schemes, rewarding export producers with greater and greater shares of the foreign currency proceeds generated by sales of their products was the cornerstone of the export promotion drive begun throughout the province in the first quarter of 1986. Other export incentives offered at the time were the linking of export procurement prices with export sales prices in order to pay domestic producers of profitable goods higher prices; rebates of industrial-commercial taxes; and direct rewards of 0.10 yuan for every U.S. dollar exported above the planned figure. The latter payments were used primarily to fund bonus programs in export factories and foreign trade enterprises.

Hand in hand with decentralization went deregulation. Beijing made efforts in both 1985 and 1986 to curb the astonishing rise in the number of Guangdong firms engaging in foreign trade, but to little avail. By the end of 1987 nearly nine hundred foreign trade enterprises—foreign trade corporations in MOFERT's sphere, "local" foreign trade companies, joint industrial-commercial enterprises, and export factories—had won foreign trade rights.[33] A number of these enterprises reorganized themselves into holding companies, establishing numerous subsidiaries that in turn obtained import and export business permits from industrial-commercial administrative bureaus after being approved by the foreign trade bureaus. At the same time, Guangdong sought to implement horizontal integration and sanctioned the establishment of quasi-official export associations, akin to chambers of commerce for specific product lines.

Counties that supplied more than 10 million yuan in export goods or earned in excess of $2 million in foreign exchange annually were authorized to conduct direct foreign trade in 1987, while factories with annual export sales in excess of $1 million were eligible to apply for direct selling rights. Below the level of enterprises with foreign trade rights was another tier of firms with licenses to distribute or handle foreign trade goods. In August 1987, Guangdong did away with the requirement that firms obtain business licenses to distribute import or export goods, and shortly thereafter strictures against private enterprises handling imported products were eased.

These changes opened up a multitude of channels through which enterprises in Guangdong could import or export products. No longer could foreign trade enterprises operate as monopolies. They had to hustle for business by offering improved service and lower commissions. Some did far better than others, and within a very short period of time small foreign trade "tigers"—mostly county foreign trade corporations—were roaming the Delta and, once again, localities outside Guangdong in search of opportunities to buy and sell. They made "internal" joint ventures with enterprises in the interior.

Other foreign trade enterprises sought to bolster their competitive position by establishing companies overseas, and at the end of 1987, approximately 125 overseas companies established with Guangdong capital were up and running. Though located primarily in Hong Kong and Macau, Guangdong-owned firms could be found in the United States, Canada, Australia, Europe, and the Middle East. Guangdong investment even made its way to such faraway places as Saipan in the Western Pacific, where it came to play a major role in textiles manufacturing and construction in the Commonwealth of the Northern Marianas. A Guangdong official estimated that there were several hundred companies in Hong Kong and Macau controlled by enterprises in the province but not officially sanctioned by or registered with the provincial government.

In nearly all other service-related businesses, deregulation took hold. Banks arose to challenge the Bank of China's monopoly on foreign exchange dealings and aggressively offered loans under favorable terms and letters of credit that were free of the stifling strictures that had delayed many settlements in previous years. Foreign exchange adjustment centers were set up in Shenzhen (1985), Zhuhai (1986), and Shantou (1986) to supplement the Guangzhou center; enterprises with unwanted allocations shopped around to find the best free-market rates. Even when local governments sought to impose upper limits on the exchange rate there was little impact on the ever-deteriorating value of the renminbi.[34] Buyers and sellers simply made side agreements outside the center to cover "services" not reflected in the rate. In another service sector opened to competition, ports were forced to compete with each other for business, promising faster turnaround times and cut-rate tonnage dues to snare cargoes of prospective shippers.

Deregulation of foreign trade and ancillary services resulted in important efficiencies, but overall the cost of producing foreign exchange rose steadily in 1985–1987. This was the principal difference between the booms of 1978–1980 and 1985–1987. In 1987 the provincial cost of creating one U.S. dollar hit 5.37 yuan, obliterating the beneficial effects of China's two-step devaluation of the official renminbi-U.S. dollar rate that was carried out in early 1986 (the official rate was set at 3.7 yuan to one U.S. dollar in April 1986 and remained there throughout 1986, 1987, and 1988). The major cause of the rise in export cost was sharply higher procurement prices. At 1986 plan prices, Guangdong's export procurement value should have been 10.9 billion yuan. In prices actually paid, export procurement totaled 13.5 billion yuan, more than double the actual value recorded in 1985. This doubling of procurement brought only 40 percent more hard currency.

Cost inflation was also spurred by a strong dollar in 1985 and 1986. Since 30–40 percent of Guangdong's exports consisted of processed imports by 1986—a figure far greater than in 1980—every time the dollar rose, export cost went up. Another big difference between

1978–1980 and 1985–1987 was that export producers were far less trusting, by 1985, of state promises to allow them to retain greater shares of foreign exchange earnings.

Beijing reacted with concern at the growing subsidization of Guangdong's exports. The State Pricing Commission and MOFERT, through the head offices of the foreign trade corporations in Beijing, sought to establish upper limits on prices to be paid to export producers. In August 1987 a notice was issued that strictly prohibited the payment of procurement prices above these limits and at the same time attempted to control unhealthy competition among enterprises, which bid up prices of goods offered by export factories. Monopolies were reimposed over several Guangdong export products (for example, cassia, which was to be handled only by the native produce corporation) and, in a draconian move to eliminate big losers altogether, MOFERT forbade the procurement and sale of a number of Guangdong's traditional export commodities, including varieties of herbal medicines and animal byproducts. Throughout 1986 and 1987, Beijing also brought more and more products under the export licensing scheme. By the end of 1987 more than 250 export items required licenses before they could be sold overseas. Soy sauce manufactured in Guangdong had to be covered by an export permit; the same product made elsewhere in China could be shipped abroad without a license.

The attempt to reduce subsidization and to lower export costs—an effort made more pressing by China's application to rejoin the General Agreement on Tariffs and Trade (GATT)—gave impetus to the introduction of the "responsibility system" for foreign trade corporations in 1987. Under the responsibility system as initially practiced in Guangdong, provincial branches received three "macro" targets from the Beijing head office: total exports; total enterprise profitability; and average export cost (that is, the enterprise's average cost of creating one U.S. dollar). These targets were further refined by the branches and were then sent down to their various sections and subbranches, sometimes all the way to individual managers and salespeople. Only enterprises and individuals who fulfilled their targets were to be eligible to receive bonuses out of a fund administered by the head office.

As with earlier Beijing-mandated reforms, the responsibility system as practiced in 1987 was far from a success. There were the inevitable implementation problems associated with operating a complex system of targets across so many product lines. Members of the bicycles export section of the light industrial products foreign trade corporation might exceed their targets but receive meager bonuses because of overall corporate performance. At the same time, in the same corporation, members of the watch and clock section—traditionally a big export loss-maker—might receive no bonus at all because one out of three targets was missed, even though this was an improved performance over the past. There was no way for the center to monitor, let alone control, the situation.

In contrast, some branches of the foreign trade corporations were able to negotiate good bonuses with their head offices by fulfilling two of their three targets, namely overall exports and total enterprise profit/loss. This was not difficult to achieve in such product lines as chemicals and machinery, because large import profits were possible as a means of offsetting losses arising from the overfulfillment of the export plan. Even if the head office withheld approval of a bonus, it was not uncommon for county subbranch personnel to receive bonuses from local governments. These governments had a vested interest in maximizing exports, regardless of cost, in order to maximize their allocation of foreign exchange. It was these same governments that operated their own non-MOFERT foreign trade enterprises—the county-level "local" foreign trade companies—and very few of these operated under export cost constraints in 1987.

The rise in export cost was reflected in the settlement rates at the foreign exchange adjustment centers, where ever-increasing volumes of foreign exchange allocations were traded in the mid-1980s. Guangzhou's center operated at a rate roughly 10 percent over the export cost of creating one U.S. dollar. Enterprises seeking to export with imported raw materials factored into their cost the rate of creating one additional dollar, and this in turn led to still higher export costs. More and more of Guangdong's productive capacity was being consumed to produce the same value in hard currency. I calculated that at an old-style electric battery factory in Jiangmen in April 1986 the cost of producing one dollar was in excess of ten yuan.

Spiraling export costs and the attendant rise in free-market foreign exchange rates had important consequences for the management of Guangdong's external debt. By the end of 1987, enterprises in Guangdong had borrowed $1.5 billion from foreign banks; the lion's share of funds had been lent by foreign and Chinese banks in Hong Kong. Though small by developing country standards, Guangdong's external debt was concentrated in two or three municipal regions in the Pearl River Delta. For these localities—Foshan prominent among them—

the size and servicing of hard currency borrowings emerged as important constraints to additional infrastructure growth during 1988; Hong Kong banks became increasingly cautious and lent funds far more sparingly. Foshan and Jiangmen had export costs higher than the provincial average in 1987, a cause for concern. To pay back loans from Hong Kong banks Foshan borrowers had to buy their U.S. dollars from units with foreign exchange entitlements at rates among the highest in Guangdong.

Another challenge confronting Guangdong's foreign trade cadres was how to manage the foreign exchange windfall that resulted from the new retention system introduced in January 1985. Vast quantities of consumer durables were bought with state funds in 1985—335,000 color televisions, 263,000 stereos—and many more were carried into the province by overseas Chinese paying visits to relatives and friends, though there was a significant slowdown in 1987 when Guangdong's Party secretary, Lin Ruo, banned the reception and viewing of Hong Kong television programs.

In 1987 the consumer durable enjoying the greatest demand in the Delta was the air conditioner. So many units were imported that hard-won gains in power generation were threatened by the surge in consumption. To slow the trade, the Customs Administration announced in July 1988 a doubling of the import tariff on air conditioners to one thousand yuan per unit. Rumors of the impending tariff hike—widespread in the weeks prior to the official announcement—helped fuel growing anxiety over price increases. These worries exploded into a short but severe panic in Guangzhou and neighboring cities late in June 1988, as mentioned in Chapter 3. For the first time since 1949, depositors rushed to the banks to withdraw their money and caused several to shut their doors. There was panic buying of foodstuffs and daily necessities.[35] An official who had to deal with this decried Guangdong's growing import dependence; there was dismay among cadres that tariff hikes could set off such reactions.

Examples of irrational imports abound. Guangdong, a major toy exporter, spent more than $30 million importing children's playthings in 1986. Large quantities of second-hand clothing, much of it originally made in China, were imported before a customs ban was imposed in mid-1985. Guangdong's substantial monosodium glutamate industry—producing the concoction used widely in Chinese restaurants around the world—was decimated in late 1987 by a flood of foreign product, which caused prices to drop by as much as 40 percent.[36]

Provincial industries cried out for restrictions on imports, and the

1985–1987 period was one of increasing reliance on administrative measures to protect Guangdong's factories and farms. China's import licensing system gave the Provincial Foreign Trade Bureau responsibility for issuing permits for thirty-five of forty-nine controlled goods (as of early 1988), and cadres at the bureau exercised considerable discretion in deciding whether or not to issue permits. In addition to centrally controlled items, Guangdong developed its own list of banned imports. Items for which import approval would be withheld by the province's "leading group" in the Foreign Economic and Trade Commission included such products as marble, nylon zippers, and yeast as of October 1986. Fruit was added to the list in July 1987, killing in one stroke what had been a growing market for American citrus producers.

Yet if products were required in Guangdong and there were no provincial industries to supply them, the province generally preferred to import them from abroad rather than buy them from other parts of China, for reasons of both quality and price. This was true even when Beijing imposed strict national import controls to force customers to "buy Chinese." Guangdong proved adroit at evading the rules.

Under national regulations promulgated in 1987, agrochemicals, fertilizers, and construction materials that were donated by overseas Chinese to their home counties could be brought into China without the need to obtain import licenses or pay customs duties. A roaring trade in pesticides, which were controlled by the Ministry of Chemical Industries in Beijing by a certificate of approval scheme, sprang up in and through Guangdong. Hong Kong firms "donated" hundreds of tons of insecticides, herbicides, and fungicides that were subsequently resold by the recipients. Resale of donated products for profit contravened the regulations, but there were very few instances of successful interdiction.[37] The Hong Kong donors profited immensely by obtaining rights to buy scarce products from their home districts at heavily discounted prices.

Duplication of equipment and technology imports was another concern of Guangdong's planners, as was continued import of products that could, at least in theory, be produced by newly imported and commissioned plants. Although given impetus by Guangdong's implementation of the "twenty-two points" to encourage foreign investment, import substitution gained a life of its own in 1987 with the publication by provincial authorities of three lists of approved substitutes. After products were certified as substitutes for imports and had been in production for at least one year, they could be sold for U.S. dollars within Guangdong (though not necessarily in other provinces).

*The Growing Hong Kong–Guangdong Trade Nexus.* Economic integration between Guangdong and Hong Kong accelerated after the conclusion of the Sino-British Joint Declaration on the territory's future, which brought in its wake both opportunities and problems. There is no question that Hong Kong's tremendous growth after 1984 greatly contributed to Guangdong's export surge. Best estimates were that 75 percent of all Guangdong's exports went to or through Hong Kong, and that, in 1986 and 1987, 80–90 percent of all foreign investment in the province originated in Hong Kong. Various figures have been cited for the number of Guangdong workers in the employ of Hong Kong capital; figures released by Hong Kong sources point to an employment of at least 1.5 million at the end of 1987—more than the number of workers in Hong Kong's own industrial sector (900,000). The Christian Industrial Association, a Hong Kong pressure group, documented more than 120 instances in 1987 alone of Hong Kong factory owners abruptly shutting down facilities in the territory and reopening them in China. No compensation was usually offered to those thrown out of work.

Guangdong's dependence on Hong Kong has taken many forms, some of them quite unusual. China introduced daylight savings time in 1986, and the whole country moved its clocks forward in April. In Foshan and Zhongshan, however, few enterprises complied, and it became important, when setting appointments, to specify whether the time was "local" or "Hong Kong." After sharp curbs on its use in 1983 and 1984, the Hong Kong dollar regained its role as Guangdong's second currency in the 1985–1988 period. A Guangzhou bank source estimated that, at the end of 1987, HK$4–6 billion worth of Hong Kong dollar notes and coins were circulating in private hands in Guangdong, equivalent to 15–20 percent of the territory's total notes and coins in circulation. When Hong Kong's textile quotas ran out in 1986 and 1987, unscrupulous merchants teamed with gullible if not conniving Guangdong textile producers to forge China quotas and certificates of origin, in turn "using up" China's quotas that were supposed to have been administered by MOFERT's port offices. The ensuing uproar nearly resulted in the breakdown of the vital U.S.–China Textiles Agreement. And in another example of the dangers of overdependence, Guangzhou's aggressive trading arm in Hong

Kong—Yuexiu Company—reportedly lost heavily in the worldwide stock market crash of October 1987. It had bought into Hong Kong equities, a decision that nearly proved fatal when the territory's exchange closed for four days. Positions were honored, however, and six months later Guangdong's extensive holdings in Hong Kong, especially in the property sector, were looking very healthy again.

## Into the Future

Guangdong's road to the top of China's foreign trade in the first decade of reforms was neither straight nor easy. It grappled with subtle but real policy shifts, the unforeseen consequences of well-intentioned reforms, the effects of rapid depreciation of the renminbi, and the growth of a pervasive and shadowy underground economy. Against this backdrop, its achievements were impressive: more than $5 billion in foreign investment where a decade before there had been none, a ten-year growth in exports that rivaled those of the Asian newly industrializing economies, and the creation of a market for imports that was reasonably open and vibrant. What is one to conclude about this period of Guangdong's foreign trade?

Perhaps most obviously, Guangdong's experience in foreign trade was very different from the experience of the newly industrializing economies, which makes comparisons difficult. Officials in Singapore, Taiwan, South Korea, and even Hong Kong (which prides itself on noninterference by government) have placed exports at the core of their economies' development. Industry has served exports. In Guangdong, the percentage of gross domestic product dedicated to export production in the late 1980s was far smaller than in any of these economies.

Most cadres continued to view foreign trade as subservient to and supportive of agriculture and industry. The need for a fundamental change in attitude was stressed by Zhao Ziyang on a tour of the Pearl River Delta in late 1984, and his words still rang true for many parts of Guangdong five years later: "In seeking to enter the international market, export bases for agricultural products and processed goods must change the structure of agricultural production in accordance with the needs of export markets. For these districts, the direction of policy should be 'trade–industry–agriculture' not 'agriculture–industry–trade.' It's not a case of your planting what you want, processing what you want and then making available for export what you can spare; quite the opposite, based on the international market you both plant and process."[38]

In some respects, Guangdong simply came too late to the party. By 1979–80, the first full years of Guangdong's reform program, the vital American market had already been penetrated by the products of East Asian exporters. Niches had been established, textile quotas taken up. It would have been difficult to dislodge such competition under the most favorable conditions. In any case, the American recession of 1981–82 gave rise to a prevailing mood of protectionism, sharply limiting the ability of new suppliers to enter the market. If Guangdong is to maintain strong export growth in the future, it will need to find new, rapidly growing markets that can play the role the U.S. market played for Singapore, Taiwan, South Korea, and Hong Kong.

Although the American consumer's seemingly insatiable appetite for the export products of East Asia fueled the economic engines of these four economies, it is instructive to note that none of the four ever relied on any one country for more than 50 percent of its overseas sales. Governments encouraged, with considerable success, diversification of export markets. Guangdong, by comparison, remained heavily dependent on one export market, Hong Kong's, and it was hard to envision how the province's officials would be able to lessen dependence in the short-to-medium term.

Other dissimilarities include Guangdong's slow infrastructural development, its depreciating instead of appreciating currency, and, ironically in view of China's reputation as a tough market to penetrate, its ineffective control over the import of nonessential goods. In the late 1980s Guangdong exhibited neither the commitment to independent research and development nor the emphasis on quality control that typified the export sectors of Singapore, Taiwan, South Korea, and Hong Kong. And, in the final analysis, Guangdong lacked their autonomy and freedom of maneuver. The province was still very much a part of China, and what Beijing ordained, Guangdong (generally) obeyed.

Rather than conceptualizing Guangdong as a separate export-oriented powerhouse—an emerging "little dragon"—it is far more useful to think of it as a component part of a Cantonese newly industrializing economy (NIE), centered in Hong Kong. The concept of the NIE—as opposed to the largely discarded term NIC (newly industrializing country), which defines economic entities in purely national terms—enables us to explore the structure of something as complex and interdependent as the economies of Hong Kong, Macau, the neighboring SEZs, Guangzhou, and the Inner Delta taken as a whole. The Cantonese newly industrializing economy, to which we will return in Chapter 13, is the practical expression of the one country, two systems formula. With all its flaws and problems, at the end of the 1980s it was clearly a viable, rapidly growing force in both regional and global terms. Hong Kong's hinterland, the critical mass that fueled its industrial, commercial, and financial engines, might be constrained politically by Beijing, but it was responding economically to the rhythm of Cantonese expansionism.

Guangdong's surge to the top of China's foreign trade and its ability to remain there have been dependent, then, on the health of the Hong Kong economy and on the degree of support enjoyed by the province at senior levels in Beijing. As we have seen, the ideologues and bureaucrats of central departments can create great difficulties for Guangdong, even to the extent of effectively reversing key components of the "special policy." When tepid support in Beijing is coupled with a slowdown in Hong Kong growth, the consequences for Guangdong can be serious indeed, involving such dislocations as unemployment and runaway inflation.

Guangdong in 1988 found itself blessed with an unusually strong body of supporters in Beijing. Party General Secretary Zhao Ziyang and President Yang Shangkun had both served in the southern province and were sympathetic to Guangdong initiatives for accelerated development. Guangdong's corps of supporters pushed through a ten-point comprehensive economic reform program in January 1988. The stated purpose of the program, approved by the State Council in January 1988 (implemented in the eighteen municipalities of Guangdong in April), was to reinforce Guangdong's role as an economic laboratory where experiments are tried out first and, if successful, applied elsewhere in the country. The program consisted principally of extending and expanding reforms already in place; in foreign trade, it called for enhancing the network of foreign exchange adjustment centers (all large and medium-sized cities were eventually to have one), greater competition among banks, and more authority at the local level over approval of projects and issuance of import-export licenses. Municipalities in Guangdong could now approve export-oriented capital construction projects involving up to $20 million in hard currency expenditure (Guangzhou's upper limit was $30 million), provided the products themselves were not covered by the central import-export plan.[39] There were only nine import goods still managed solely by Beijing in mid-1988.

Just as the municipalities were lining up new projects, China's overheated economy prompted Beijing to order a slowdown in economic growth in September 1988. Enterprises had been pursuing cheap credit for large construction projects, and banks, especially the newer ones established through deregulation of the banking system, had obliged by pumping money into local economies. This in turn fueled a strong inflation that ran at a 40–50 percent per year clip in urban centers of Guangdong during the summer. At a Provincial People's Congress session in August, Guangdong's leaders were criticized by angry delegates for letting price rises get out of hand. Half of the people in the cities were actually worse off than a year earlier, some claimed.

Bank runs, panic buying, and hyperinflation were the phenomena that led to the decision to limit China's real growth to 7 percent per year for a readjustment period of three to five years. In Guangdong growth will slacken and even suffer temporary reverses as interest rates are raised, banks become more conservative in granting loans, and products are brought back into the central import-export plan. Granting of direct export and import rights to enterprises will be done more selectively and at a slower pace. Controls over the issuing of import and export licenses will be tightened. In a well-publicized case, the central government sharply criticized Guangdong for issuing excessive export permits for pig iron in late October, and the Province Foreign Economic and Trade Commission announced the suspension of all licenses and a prohibition on procurement and export of the commodity immediately thereafter. Another device to rein in uncontrolled foreign trade growth will be modification of foreign exchange retention schemes. After January 1, 1989, enterprises in the special economic zones were no longer able to obtain 100 percent allocations of their hard currency earnings from exports, and had to surrender 20 percent to the central government.

During this period of "rectifying the economic environment," authorization limits for capital construction projects will be revised downward and even temporarily suspended. In Guangdong during the autumn of 1988 all projects already approved but not yet implemented were frozen and subjected to a process of "reexamination and approval." Among the first casualties were thirteen joint venture hotels, cancelled in October.

In mid-December 1988 a meeting of key provincial and municipal officials in charge of economic planning, capital construction, and foreign trade was convened in Guangzhou. The meeting set criteria for reexamining and reapproving new investment projects. First, there had to be sufficient funds in hand; funding with bank loans was to be discouraged. Second, the project had to produce goods that were in short supply. Investments in such industries as cement, characterized by overcapacity, were to be stopped. Finally, projects funded in whole or in part with foreign exchange had to employ "realistic" exchange rates in calculating the return on investments. This meant that the foreign exchange component of the total project cost was to be converted to renminbi at different rates, according to the source of the foreign exchange. U.S. dollars made available by the central government were to be converted at 3.7 yuan to the dollar, those allocated by the province were to be translated into renminbi at 5.5 yuan to the dollar, and foreign exchange allocated by the municipality was to be converted at 6.2 yuan to one U.S. dollar. If an enterprise still needed foreign exchange, it would have to buy it at the foreign exchange adjustment center at a rate greater than 7.0 yuan to the dollar. Although cadres were reassured that projects could now go ahead provided these criteria were met, there were expressions of bewilderment and frustration at the use of multiple foreign exchange rates.

The increased exercise of central powers, tighter credit policies by local banks and governments, power and raw material shortages, and a softening of Hong Kong demand pointed to an unprecedented drop in Guangdong's exports of more than 20 percent in 1989. While serious, Guangdong officials generally felt that this recessionary phase of the reform cycle would be short and, after 1989, fairly mild. Modifications and downward adjustments were anticipated, but not wholesale or even fundamental reversals of policy. It was generally assumed that Guangdong would still be permitted growth above the national average, that foreign trade in particular would continue to be emphasized, and that foreign investments would still be welcomed and encouraged in priority areas—energy, raw materials, and transportation. The majority of cadres in economic departments in Guangdong's municipalities believed that Guangdong would be permitted a rate of inflation higher than elsewhere in China, and that the price freeze on key materials announced by Beijing in September 1988 would not prove a major impediment.

In granting Guangdong the requisite doses of autonomy, Beijing has been constrained by three things: competition from other coastal regions and open cities, resentment by interior provinces of Guangdong's wealth, and responsibilities incumbent upon China in its quest for its rightful place in world commerce. When China is eventually readmitted to the GATT it will become eligible for Generalized Scheme of Preference treatment in the U.S. market, a privilege withdrawn from the manufactured products of Hong Kong, Singapore, South Korea, and Taiwan as of January 1989. It will also become eligible for most favored nation status in about twenty-five countries with whom China has yet to conclude bilateral trade agreements. As a contracting party to the GATT, China must ensure that its foreign trade policies and practices are uniform throughout the country. After the secretary general of the GATT visited Beijing in October 1987, he visited Guangzhou. There he held discussions with provincial officials on areas of possible divergence between China's national foreign trade regime and that of Guangdong.

It is likely that, over time, Guangdong will have to compete with other provinces for economic prominence on an increasingly even playing field. To stay one step ahead, Guangdong will need to become more efficient in carrying out foreign trade and more attractive to foreign investors able to play a decisive role in the modernization of the province's industry. In the late 1980s much work still needed to be done on these fronts. The average cost of producing one U.S. dollar was higher in Guangdong than China's national average in 1988 and this had been true for at least ten years, reflecting higher procurement costs and higher service fees (despite deregulation, Guangdong's transport cost inflation was the highest in China in 1987). The speed and breadth of the reforms that had taken place in the foreign trade system at times contributed to export cost, as when changes in buying and selling channels or in ways business was handled (as in the introduction of the agency system) resulted in excessive inventories and hence high interest and warehousing charges.[40]

Guangdong's incentive system to increase exports remained administratively unwieldy and, to the factories that were supposed to benefit from it, a source of bewilderment, frustration, and confusion. A good example of capricious bureaucracy at work occurred in late 1987, when the Guangzhou municipal government engineered a fall in the foreign exchange adjustment center rate by enjoining enterprises with foreign exchange entitlements but no approved import plans to put their allocations on the market. Those enterprises that balked had access to their allocations frozen by the Bank of China. A more serious abuse took place in 1988. Early in the year the province's joint industrial-commercial foreign trade enterprises were benefiting from a special arrangement in which 20 percent of the firm's foreign exchange earnings were sent up to Beijing and 30 percent to the provincial or metropolitan *popo;* this left 50 percent as the firm's entitlement. As recentralization gathered steam late in the year the scheme was scrapped and all allocations held by the enterprises were appropriated by the administrative organs at local and central levels.

In the area of foreign investment, enterprises with foreign equity continued to experience discriminatory treatment vis-à-vis domestic firms. The incentives that enabled the state-owned sector to achieve large exports in 1986 and 1987 were initially denied to joint ventures, and many of the benefits—including direct rewards based on dollars earned—were still not available to all foreign investors in 1988. The only major exception to the general trend of expanding the foreign trade rights of enterprises in recent years was the prohibition, announced in late 1984, of joint venture factories importing and exporting products not manufactured by themselves.[41] This denied joint ventures an important source of income. Foreign investors in 1988 were still complaining about the opacity of the investment environment—in a well-known case a modern joint venture pig farm foundered because the foreign partner was not familiar with the provincial export license system—and "price gouging" was still common. In 1986 and 1987, twenty-one strikes by disgruntled workers broke out in foreign-owned factories in Shenzhen alone. Strikes are discouraged by the Chinese Constitution and are rare occurrences in the state-owned sector: there were fewer than one hundred instances nationwide in 1987.

Despite impressive gains in electricity generation, Guangdong's power grid could not keep up with demand. Many foreign factory owners in Guangzhou and Shenzhen were only able to operate their plants for three days a week at the end of 1988, despite promises and guarantees made at the time of their investments that power supplies would be ample. Raw material shortages were as serious as power outages for some export industries as interior provinces like Hunan refused to ship their produce for value-adding in Guangdong.

Not only had the growth in foreign trade given Guangdong great prosperity in a relatively short period of time, but the interaction with the outside world had set off changes in organization, technology, and thinking that continually pushed Guangdong ahead. As the first decade of reforms ended the leadership had realized that there were serious issues involved, and it was tackling them with a "try, try again" attitude.

A new responsibility system for foreign trade enterprises was announced in 1988 and put into practice in 1989. It covered all foreign trade enterprises, and under it their targets had to be fulfilled or the firm risked its import-export license being revoked. In 1989, the three targets Guangdong foreign trade enterprises "contracted for" *(cheng-bao)* with either the head office in Beijing (in the case of foreign trade corporations and some joint industrial-commercial enterprises) or the local government foreign trade bureau (for "local" foreign trade companies) were changed from those originally established in 1987. Foreign trade enterprises now had to achieve these three targets: total exports, foreign exchange handed over to Beijing or the local government, and *net* export cost, that is, total export cost minus profits from import business and sales of export products on the domestic market. As with enterprise profitability under the responsibility system as practiced in 1987 and 1988, the target of net export cost was much easier to achieve than export cost as the foreign trade enterprises could generate big profits from the resale of imported goods. Few Guangdong foreign trade enterprises were concerned about making their targets—and keeping their licenses—after the responsibility system was modified.

To answer complaints about the administration of the foreign exchange retention system, the Bank of China in early 1988 announced that exporting enterprises could have immediate access to 70 percent of their estimated allocations, with the remainder available upon bank confirmation of the exact entitlement. The president of the People's Bank of China, Chen Muhua, announced China's intention to do away with the application procedure whereby an enterprise obtains access to its allocation. Although the statement was received well in Guangdong, most exporters remained skeptical that this reform would take place before the end of the 1980s.

Efficient creation and consumption of foreign currency and attraction of foreign capital can only come about through continued provincial investment in infrastructure and human resources. Far more emphasis was being placed on the former in Guangdong than on the latter at the end of the first reform decade, but the development of individuals skilled in the ways of world commerce and finance was at least as important to the province's future as, say, the addition of the Daya Bay nuclear power plant. The principal constraint on the pursuit of foreign trade rights by more enterprises and counties was the dearth of individuals who could use English to negotiate and execute contracts and who at the same time had mastered the intricacies of global communications and data handling.

In 1988 Guangdong was the best example to date of an underdeveloped, third world economy shackled by a Stalinist, centrally planned foreign trade system making a decisive move in the direction of a market-oriented, competitive economy. Those who attended the Guangzhou trade fairs of the 1970s needed to spend only a couple of days in Guangdong's capital in the late 1980s to judge the impact—the success—of the reforms. People were visibly better off, and foreign trade had been largely responsible for this. Maintenance of the province's leading position in foreign trade would continue to require constant experimentation with new ways of resolving problems like overdependence on Hong Kong or inefficiencies of export production, but no barriers would be insurmountable in the years to come if Guangdong's fledgling entrepreneurs maintained the same resolve and spirit that had carried them through the first ten years of reform.

# PART IV

*Perspectives on Change*

# 12.

# Society in Transition: Between Planning and Markets

Even leaders who supported the reforms and the opening to the outside worried about the impact these changes would have on their society. They were proud that they had overcome the rampant prostitution, gambling, extortion, and decadence that had plagued China before 1949. They dreaded a return to the unrestrained pursuit of personal gain, the neglect of public responsibility, the growth of economic inequalities, and the exploitation of the poor by the rich. How much selfishness and social disorder would they have to tolerate to revitalize the economy and raise the standard of living? Would the expansion of markets revive the worst excesses of capitalism and veer out of control? Would market opportunities entice officials into using their positions to enrich their friends and relatives? Was it possible, they wondered, to make the transition from socialism to a market economy and yet retain the gains they had made? Before looking at the problems of personal relations and corruption, we will first examine the static nature of Guangdong socialist organization on the eve of reform and the basic social structure after reform. A consideration of possible guidelines for the second reform decade will conclude the chapter.

## From a Cellular Society to a Commodity Society

Despite the trumpeting of revolutionary ideology and despite whatever gains were made by the socialist order from the completion of collectivization until reforms, social changes in Guangdong from 1956 to 1978 were, paradoxically, less revolutionary than those in Taiwan, which was promoting a conservative Confucian ideology. In Taiwan, as the economy grew and adapted to world markets, work and family life underwent basic changes. Young people in the countryside moved freely to towns and cities to take advantage of new work opportunities. As factories introduced new machinery, work organization changed radically. Urban workers frequently left their jobs to find new ones or to start their own firms. New housing made it possible for young couples to "split the hearth" and establish new family units. Increased mobility and a rapid rise in the standard of living gave people more choices about their style of life and loosened old social bonds. Exposure to the outside world through travel and new media reinforced and hastened the transition to a more open, individuated urban industrial society.

In Guangdong, from 1956 to 1978, despite the turmoil of the Great Leap Forward and the Cultural Revolution, membership in social units, including families, villages, workplaces, and urban neighborhoods, was remarkably stable, even in the Inner Pearl River Delta.[1] Except in 1958 when investment greatly expanded, authorities blocked the influx of rural migrants for fear that urban areas could not provide grain, housing, employment, and services for all who wished to live in them. Aside from the very few accepted by universities and the army, rural youth could not get urban household registration and were dissuaded from moving not only by their fear of being caught but by their inability to obtain employment and ration books for rice, oil, meat, and cloth.

There was also little turnover in employment. State enterprises and collectives almost never closed down, and there was almost no private enterprise. Workers rarely asked to transfer and few who applied were given permission. The large workplace, like the rural village, was a small, all-embracing society *(xiao er quan)*. It was as if Guangdong was sharply divided into tiny cells with little movement between them.

The difficulty of exiting from the cell gave the local unit and its leader great leverage over the individual, who had little choice but to adjust. Since most young couples commonly continued to live with or near their parents, they naturally came under their sway. Conservative family and sexual mores and the subordination of the individual to the group, backed up by higher-level cadres and the media, constrained everyone. In rural areas, the production team controlled the individual's life and work. Since spending time on private plots or marketing was discouraged for fear that workers would neglect collective tasks, villagers had no means of livelihood if they did not yield to the team leader. In the cities, employees of larger enterprises lived in compounds under the control of the work unit, and enterprise managers were similarly worried about workers spending too much time away from their unit. Urban dwellers depended on their units not only for their jobs but for housing, child care, medical care, subsidized food, and other services. Urban workers, like rural villagers, thus had few options if they lost access to its facilities.[2]

In these cells individuals had a sense of belonging, and they knew that many in their neighborhood or work unit were prepared to offer help when needed. Yet the economy was stagnant and people felt excessively restricted. They had trouble acquiring goods not made locally, raising their level of education, or improving their skills. Ambitious rural youth felt trapped, and urban students and workers resented the stultifying atmosphere created by political activists and "guides" who stood ready to criticize "improper" behavior.[3] As reforms began critics acknowledged that the lack of a market economy, low levels of education, and an authoritarian political structure had perpetuated within the cells some of the worst aspects of feudalism.[4]

Reform and opening to the outside gave rise to many of the individuating currents found in Taiwan during its economic takeoff. Cells that had been almost autonomous began to open as people and commodities began to move across old geographic and bureaucratic boundaries with increasing frequency. In this first decade Guangdong did not become a full-scale market society since the markets for land and capital were not yet really operating, the labor market was only partially opened, and even commodity markets, while flourishing, were not yet fully mature. Though Guangdong at the end of the first ten years of reform had the largest, most advanced commodity markets in China, by comparison with modern industrial societies it still had a long way to go in breaking down market barriers. Guangdong in this period might best be characterized, therefore, as an "early stage commodity society."

The movement to later stages of commodity society in the 1990s can be seen as a progressive breaking down of social and political barriers to the free flow of goods, labor, and capital. Further reforms were planned for the second decade of reform, but even without them, forces had already been set loose that had a dynamic of their own. In the early stage of a commodity society, there are many tiny, new private firms with small and restricted markets, but in later stages these markets will grow. Initially goods remain in short supply and state firms producing many products can charge high prices, "monopoly rents," but as goods become more available, competition will make this more difficult. When transport is limited, prices vary considerably by locality, but in a later stage, these differences are likely to decline further. And as tiny firms grow, specialization, economies of scale, and size are all likely to expand.

## Patterns of Employment and Life-Style

The freer flow of commodities and of labor had a profound impact on society, but the self-contained units, closed for decades, did not all open quickly when reforms began. Among the units that changed least in the decade were the large units administered directly by the central government: the state farms in Hainan and western Guangdong; the large mines of Dabaoshan, Shilu, and Yunfu; and the large petrochemical complex at Maoming. All these exchanged goods with the outside, and the complexity of their tasks required high levels of contact outside the community, but social life remained extraordinarily self-contained. Cellular life remained strong in large state factories as well. Mountain communities not yet linked by roads to the outside also remained self-contained, but their internal economies and social organization were far simpler and the levels of internal communication and literacy far lower.

The greatest social changes occurred in the rural areas on the plains and in the private and collective sector in the towns and cities. Here individual producers and workers in small enterprises responded to outside market forces by making rapid internal changes as well. With the decline of food rationing, the demise of cloth rationing, and the increase in scale and diversity of consumer purchasing in the early 1980s, the individual consumer was also much more integrated in the commodity economy.

Strong resistance to the opening of social cells came from those who feared the loss of economic security and the loss of power. Employees in state offices and enterprises enjoyed special perquisites that were in danger of disappearing if markets were fully opened. Bureaucrats who had political power in their own sphere *(xitong)* or in supervising enterprises under them were reluctant to give up their power. But by the late 1980s the commodity markets opened by farmers, petty businesspeople, collectives, and consumers had developed a strong attraction that was already affecting the edges of even the most self-contained communities and the most powerful independent kingdoms. It was the evolution of this powerful draw as well as new policy initiatives that ushered in more advanced stages of commodity society at the end of the 1980s.

The conditions of employment created in the 1980s three major patterns of life for workers and their families: the state employees, least integrated into the commodity economy; collective employees, partially integrated into the commodity economy; and the self-employed, including farmers, most fully integrated into the market economy. The workers were classified as follows:[5]

|  | 1978 | (%) | 1986 | (%) |
|---|---|---|---|---|
| State enterprises | 4,428,400 | (17.7) | 5,558,700 | (17.3) |
| Other units (joint state-foreign, etc.) | 0 | | 122,500 | (.3) |
| Collectives (cities and towns) | 1,529,000 | (6.1) | 2,181,100 | (6.8) |
| Rural workers (including farm) | 18,989,000 | (76.0) | 23,156,700 | (72.0) |
| Private | 30,000 | (0.1) | 1,166,900 | (3.6) |
| Total employed | 24,976,400 | (100.0) | 32,185,900 | (100.0) |
| Total population | 55,930,000 | | 63,463,000 | |

In this early stage commodity society most people in Guangdong still lived in rural areas and were engaged in agriculture, but by 1986, according to the best data available, 5,068,000 rural workers, almost one-fourth, were employed in collective or individual enterprises. The private and collective sectors in towns and cities constituted a small portion of the overall economy and provided only about one-tenth of provincial employment, but they had begun to grow. Employment in the state sector declined only marginally and still included about one-sixth of provincial workers, well over half of the nonrural work force.

*State Employees.* State employees had the greatest security, the most generous perquisites, and were the most insulated from the markets. Whether at the province, municipal, region, county, or town level, employees of state offices and enterprises were essentially guaranteed employment until retirement, which in most units was at sixty for men and fifty-five for women. They received a set monthly salary, were covered by health insurance, and even after retirement were paid a stipend, about 85 percent of their salary after thirty years' service.[6] Housing was ordinarily supplied at several yuan a month, a small fraction of what it would have cost on the open market. The worker's family was usually permitted to eat in the unit dining room, shop at the unit's stores, and get services and repairs in its shops, commonly at below-market prices. Many of these were opened to outsiders by the end of the 1980s, albeit at higher prices, as a way of increasing incomes—an illustration of the lure of the commodity markets.

State employees were part of a national system. They were divided into broad categories (administrative cadre, staff person, or worker) and within the category assigned a rank. Enterprises and work units were ranked hierarchically; in general the higher the level of government supervising an enterprise, the better the facilities and perquisites and the higher the rank of officials who could be hired according to its table of organization. The category and rank determined not only salary range but perquisites described above, and, for higher-level cadres, use of cars or vans, invitations to banquets, performances, and opportunities to travel. Because perquisites were so important, salary differentials, even for those separated by two or three ranks, had little impact on style of life or work incentives. Government office workers received no bonuses, but even in enterprises bonuses became so predictable that they were in effect part of one's salary.

State workers' salaries rose moderately during the first reform decade, but not nearly as fast as those of private entrepreneurs. Salaries rose more rapidly in enterprises than in state organs, but even in enterprises there were set salary ceilings, regardless of productivity improvements. There was an egalitarian pressure for wage increases in state firms that managers were unable to resist, and few officials in Guangdong received a total salary of over four hundred yuan a month even at the end of the decade, but as noted in Chapter 10, much higher incomes were common among private entrepreneurs. Yet individuals with a choice of getting a regular state job or earning more as an independent entrepreneur generally wanted to work for the state. They considered entrepreneurs subject to the risks of unpredictable government policy, arbitrary officials, and markets. They knew that state enterprises were almost never allowed to fail and that even if that occurred, they would be assigned employment elsewhere. They and their families were thus insulated from the market and also enjoyed greater prestige. It was easier for a state sector employee to attract a desirable spouse. Even the state contract workers still expected to be renewed at the end of their period of employment.

In short, although salaries and perquisites of state employees improved, the basic pattern and terms of employment were unaffected by reform. Reformers had tried to open up some of the perquisites, such as housing, to market forces, but when this occurred, state employees lost not only some security but their special privileged position vis-à-vis workers elsewhere. Because state employees dominated the positions of power, such reforms proved difficult.

*Collective Employees.* Collective *(jiti)* enterprises were in fact run by the local government—by a county, town, administrative village, or an urban district. Rural community enterprises *(xiangzhen qiye)*, which were, until 1983, commune, brigade, and team enterprises, were classified as part of rural society, separate from urban collectives, but the ownership principle was the same. Employees in collective enterprises were linked to the local community; they could not be transferred to another area and had no security if the enterprise failed. And yet the local community accepted responsibility for their welfare and tended to open new enterprises to provide work if one failed. Local welfare benefits were rarely as generous or as secure as those given a state employee. Even if the collective provided medical service, the clinics or hospitals were usually of lower quality. If the finances of the locality were inadequate, retirement benefits were almost nonexistent. The "iron rice bowl" was the local community, not the nation.

Because collective enterprises were unprotected by state plans, a collective enterprise manager trying to improve performance of workers in the 1980s had several advantages over a manager in a state factory. Because collective enterprises were not on state plans, had less restrictive regulations, and less supervision by state bureaus, managers had fewer reports to file and greater flexibility in hiring, promoting, and organizing work. Because employee salary and perquisites were linked so directly to the enterprise's success, employees were readier to cooperate to make it successful. The employer was freer to use financial incentives, and the employee, having fewer perquisites, was more responsive to them. Collective enterprises thus tended to be more dynamic.

When the reforms made it possible for enterprises to find their own supplies and market their own products, the collectives responded more quickly and more effectively than state enterprises, albeit sometimes using questionable practices such as making private payments to state officials to get supplies. Successful state factories could not ordinarily pay salaries higher than those offered by unsuccessful ones, which also raised salaries to the limit, but successful collective factories could offer higher wages, though rarely more perquisites, than state enterprises could. With these advantages, successful collective enterprises grew more rapidly, and workers in collectives were more optimistic about their future. Some young people, cadres as well as workers, began to prefer working in collectives, thus upsetting the traditional hierarchy. In sum, though the management of collective enterprises was closely linked to local governments, collective workers and their families were far more responsive to the commodity economy than state employees and their families were.

*Self-Employed Households.* In the countryside, except for remote areas where it had not yet penetrated, the commodity economy fundamentally transformed peasants from employees of a collective to members of a household oriented toward markets. Rural families enjoyed the freedom to farm, make handicrafts, market their products themselves, and seek other temporary employment as they chose. In remote areas the largest part of a household's income still derived from meeting its quotas for the state, but in other areas, especially in the Inner Delta, rural families became in effect independent business households, with various members assigned to farming, marketing, and rural industry. Although no precise figures are available, during the 1980s perhaps over a third of these families in the Inner Delta had invested in the ultimate in rural household security—a new home.

Most of those who were self-employed in cities and towns originally chose that route because they saw no opportunity of obtaining state employment. Some workers in collective enterprises, however, confident of their own abilities, left and formed their own enterprise. The variation in standard of living among the self-employed, between the very small-scale operators who marketed their own farm products and barely eked out a living and those with substantial property, was far greater than among state or collective employees. Because independent entrepreneurs received none of the perquisites of state employees, those who did not live with their parents had to find their own housing. Since they provided their own medical care and saved for their own retirement, these expenses absorbed much of their higher average incomes.

Although rural youth migrated to towns and cities, few entire households left the villages in the 1980s. When they needed help, they still turned not only to friends and relatives but to their former collectives, some of which had retained welfare, though not productive, functions. In the urban area independent households, lacking a work unit to provide a sense of belonging and services, often tried to develop their own looser networks of friends and acquaintances. Some began to bond together to form mutual aid groups to provide welfare benefits. Among larger urban households, it was not uncommon for a family to try to combine the best of all worlds: to have one family member who belonged to a state work unit that provided security and perquisites, and then to have one or more self-employed members who could add a great deal of income to the household. In some households, young independent entrepreneurs who brought in substantial income lived with their parents, who had kept their housing after retirement. Whatever strategy the self-employed used, because of their responsiveness to market forces they played a crucial role in filling the demand for goods and services and in raising standards of efficiency and service.

*Reducing Gaps by Market Forces.* The growth of a commodity society not only changed farm households into petty entrepreneurs, created a new class of independent households, and expanded collective employment more rapidly than state employment; it reduced and sometimes reversed the gap in style of life that once separated those who worked for the state from those who did not. Because collective enterprises were more responsive to markets and made more gains in efficiency in the decade, salaries of collective workers rose far more rapidly than did salaries of state employees; incomes of independent entrepreneurs rose even more rapidly. Collective workers and independent entrepreneurs in urban areas, overwhelmingly young people, achieved a standard of living as high as or even higher than that of state workers their age, except for housing, which ordinarily remained beyond their means. They could achieve high salaries quickly while state employees had to wait for increases based on seniority. Technical and commercial high schools were just developing; in urban areas, most entrepreneurs left school and learned through doing; virtually all college graduates, in contrast, went to the state sector.

The collective worker and independent household gradually began to gain in prestige. In 1978, when reforms began, independent entrepreneurs were held in low esteem, a sentiment that preceded but was intensified by Communist disrespect for petty capitalists. It reflected the disdain of stable rural and urban workers for the marginal people in their society. Until the mid-1980s, the behavior of the nouveaux riches *(baofa hu)* could be dismissed as crude. But gradually some of them acquired a new style of life. They ate out more and in better restaurants, listened to tape recorders, watched videotapes, went to discos, rode motorbikes, and traveled—activities they could afford more easily and that quickly came to have broader appeal, especially among the young. Their social position, like that of small entrepreneurs in Taiwan and elsewhere, gradually rose until it provided an alternative life-style that could be expected to broaden in appeal as the commodity society matured. In short, though the commodity economy had not eliminated the attractiveness of state employment, it had greatly reduced the gaps in prestige and standard of living between state employees and the rest of society.

## Migration and the Softening of Cellular Authority

One of the most profound changes generated by reforms was the increase in opportunities for migration from the countryside to towns and cities and from one job to another. These changes came from the reforms in agriculture, the new willingness of towns and cities to accept temporary migrants, and new employment opportunities.

Only the lowest level of urban employment—temporary jobs and small independent businesses—were opened to rural residents; permanent jobs and in some cases the registration of independent businesses for fixed locations required regular urban household registration, and this was still not granted to new migrants. The restrictions were similar to those in many countries against immigrants, and the rationale was the same. Cities accepted some measure of responsibility for their residents' food, housing, security, and welfare, but on a limited budget no city could hope to provide permanent housing and other services for all who wished to move there. Cities therefore gave permanent registration only to those migrants who could show that they had come to fill long-term positions that could not be filled by registered urban residents. With this policy, Guangdong was able to avoid the squatter settlements that characterized Hong Kong, Taipei, Seoul, and many cities in Latin America and elsewhere at similar stages of development. The system of a partially opened labor market and limited social mobility discriminated against the abler rural youth and protected better jobs for urban residents; the control of migration cushioned the transition to a more open society and limited social disorder. It was impossible to record their numbers accurately, but by the late 1980s in the special economic zones, Guangzhou, and the

Inner Delta county towns there were perhaps three million new temporary migrants.

These new options for migration and for private enterprise helped reduce the arbitrary nature of cadre authority in the countryside. With decollectivization villagers were no longer subject to daily assignments and supervision, nor did they need permission to migrate to the cities. Though rural cadres lost what for some had amounted to their own independent closed kingdom, many found new economic opportunities. Those who remained as cadres learned to forge new relationships with the villagers. As one seasoned rural leader put it, "the weakened power of rural cadres has improved their relationship with the people and made their life much easier."

Cadre authority in the cities had already loosened with the questioning of the Communist Party after the Cultural Revolution and the growing awareness of the success of non-Communist countries. In state enterprises, the low rate of exit maintained the authority of leading cadres more than in rural locations. But in areas like the Inner Delta where there were so many new opportunities, even state enterprise cadres found their personal authority weakened by the ability of workers to find attractive work in collectives or to start their own enterprises. Though not many workers left, the option to leave made them freer to resist arbitrary cadre authority.

## *Guanxi* and Dynamic Imperfect Markets

The cultivation of personal connections (*guanxi*), long a prominent feature of Chinese society,[7] was moderated beginning in the late 1970s by the new concern for universal standards, but at the same time *guanxi* blossomed to play a new instrumental role for entrepreneurs taking advantage of market opportunities. Confucian texts had long extolled greater loyalty toward one's relatives and friends than toward society at large, and the limited base of universal trust in the turbulent decades before 1949 had led many to rely more heavily on family and friends for business relationships than in many societies. Participants in the early Communist movement had tried to overcome this particularism by expanding the universal base of trust to all their fellow Communist comrades (*tongzhi,* literally, those with the same ideals). After 1949 leaders initially tried to extend universal comradeship to all citizens of good standing.[8] They made some progress in this direction, but the attacks on people of "bad class" backgrounds created social cleavages that were later hard to bridge. And at the time of political campaigns, when some were targeted for attack, people tended to seek allies among friends and relatives. Within social cells, moreover, the core of Party leaders often used their monopoly of official authority to appoint, promote, and favor people who were loyal to them personally.

On the eve of reform, top leaders in Guangdong as well as Beijing saw that China needed to break down barriers to universal standards in order to select and promote its ablest people. Local leaders could not be allowed to appoint only their friends. Those at the top also realized that to lay the groundwork for modern markets and infra-structure, they needed to mend some of the social cleavages caused by particularism and create a universal basis of trust and a broader base for political legitimacy. From the late 1970s, high-level officials in the province as well as in the center waged a continuous struggle to overcome the forces that led people to work through personal connections. They tried to reduce antagonisms between different groups and to adopt achievement-based criteria for admission to ed-ucational institutions and for appointments and promotions within government offices and enterprises.

Beginning in the late 1970s leaders encouraged the reintegration of rightists, intellectuals, capitalists, landlords, and those with overseas connections and tried to heal the wounds that had kept them from filling needed positions in society. The healing process required enor-mous effort by leaders at both higher and lower levels and was not yet complete after ten years of work, but considering the depth of scars and alienation in these groups in 1976, they had made consid-erable progress.

The greatest advance in universal standards came in 1977 with the reestablishment of examinations as the basic criterion for admission to outstanding secondary schools and major institutions of higher learning. In preceding years, local units had made recommendations for admission, a practice that, though ostensibly to reward virtuous workers, led in fact to wholesale recommendation of friends and relatives of unit leaders. Entrance exams thus represented a major dramatic change, a reassertion of the traditional meritocratic basis for selecting officials. Within a few years this meant that most newly appointed officials had passed these exams and had then received advanced training, and this helped legitimize officials in the eyes of the public. Parents and lower-level schools began to strengthen the preparation of students for future entrance exams. Although some schools still accepted candidates on the basis of personal introductions, major institutions admitted entirely or almost entirely on the basis of examinations. In addition, after 1977 almost no students were prevented from taking examinations or attending universities because of family background or political attitude. Entrance exams had almost a sacred quality; cheating was rare and subject to stiff punishment.

In government offices and enterprises, the effort to establish universal standards in appointment and promotion met with less success. Minimum standards of education and work experience were introduced, and it became difficult to appoint relatives or friends who did not meet those standards. Entrance examinations were introduced for hiring in some government offices and in state enterprises, but they were easier and administered more casually than in educational institutions. This allowed room for discretion on the part of personnel officials as long as candidates met basic standards. The appointment of friends and relatives was widely attacked in the media and by youth who resented the advance of others they considered less able than themselves. Some officials became more cautious in appointing friends or relatives and even avoided close contact with their native area. But many found ways, without exceeding the bounds of what was tolerated, to help friends and relatives who met minimal qualifications. It was not uncommon, for example, for official A to appoint a relative of official B and for official B in return to arrange an appointment for a relative or friend of official A. Or official C, believing the connection would be useful, sometimes hired a relative of high official D without any intervention by official D.

In the early 1980s many state enterprises, to encourage workers to retire, agreed to hire their child or close relative in their place *(dingti)*. Although this practice was officially banned in 1983, in various informal guises it continued to exist, because work units were reluctant to force senior workers to retire against their will from stable jobs.

Despite the sincere efforts of many officials to create an open system where merit was rewarded, in fact the children of high officials were still more likely to attend the better schools and to obtain desirable jobs in Hong Kong, in the special economic zones, and in foreign trade branches and joint ventures with foreign firms in major Chinese cities. In Guangdong, as elsewhere in China, many of the young officials selected for top positions in the 1980s were the children or relatives of leading officials or martyrs in the Communist movement who were believed to have a deep commitment to the Party and to be able to gain respect and cooperation of fellow workers. The situation was not totally different from that of other societies and was subject to similar debates on whether good jobs resulted from natural ability, hard work, and family-supported training, or from favoritism. A few young people, desirous of making it on their own merit, refused to make known their connections with high officials, but many, believing that there were far more able people than good jobs and that using connections was necessary, were still willing to use personal relationships to gain attractive positions.

For official appointments, the use of *guanxi* was thus more constrained by concerns for qualifications and equity than had been true before the reforms, but before 1979 private enterprise had been so moribund that the use of *guanxi* in business relationships was essentially nonexistent. With the new dynamism after 1978, the use of *guanxi* for these purposes blossomed. *Guanxi* covered a broad continuum from casual acquaintances to close blood relatives, and people used the full range of relationships. But *guanxi* by definition involves some degree of relationship that goes beyond an immediate financial transaction. With the growth of a commodity economy, however, some substituted cash and short-term casual relationships for deeper personal relationships, especially in transacting business beyond their local community. Within the local community, although authority was softened, there was sufficient continuity of personnel that entrepreneurs still cultivated long-term relationships.

There is a subtle difference between doing something to help friends and using friends to accomplish something else. People arranged employment in a government office or enterprise to help friends, but after reforms, entrepreneurs in government and business also went through friends to achieve work-related goals. Within a given government office or jurisdiction there was clear authority, and things could move quickly without *guanxi*. But despite great efforts in the late 1980s to develop new "horizontal" connections between jurisdictions, routines were not yet in place for easy coordination of unprecedented problems. A factory that, for example, wanted electric power quickly often had no choice but to use personal connections. One unit followed orders to reduce its entertainment allowance, but it found that key tasks were not getting accomplished because it had difficulty greasing the wheels to make things run smoothly. Even those who wanted to move toward universal standards found that in the short run it was useful to promote individuals with influential relatives and friends who could help their work unit.

At a later stage, if goods and services become more readily available at standard prices in the market and standard procedures come to provide easy coordination between jurisdictions, *guanxi* will be less necessary. But in Guangdong in this early but dynamic stage of commodity society, when markets were not yet fully opened, the new desire to make things happen led many entrepreneurs to use *guanxi* to achieve what was otherwise impossible.

## Corruption: Gatekeepers and Impatient Customers

As helpful as *guanxi* was for entrepreneurs in accomplishing goals in imperfect markets, it often shaded into corruption that posed serious problems for those who wanted to expand universal standards and maintain popular support for the Party and government. From the time reforms began in 1978, corruption was sufficiently serious to be a major worry for foreign businesspeople, the Chinese media, leaders in Guangdong and Beijing, and concerned Chinese citizens. Officials accepted personal gifts in exchange for public goods and services, pressed private businesses for funds and favors, diverted public goods for private use, and gained positions for unqualified friends and relatives. Private individuals engaged in bribery, smuggling, trafficking in foreign currency, speculating, and illegal profiteering.

What was new was not the existence of corruption, but its nature. During the Cultural Revolution, some untrained youth suddenly acquired almost unrestrained power over people under them, and under the cloak of Maoist rhetoric, they promoted friends and attacked enemies. Public goods were used for private pleasure, but the private business sector was so small that those in power found little to extort. Perhaps the most common economic crime was black marketeering; so little commercial activity was permitted that the simplest kinds of transactions were regarded as illicit. When careers could be made or broken by political decisions, people were more concerned about escaping political criticism than about acquiring household appliances. Corruption involved the use of appointments and the selection of political targets in exchange for political support; it was far more political than economic.

After 1978 many public officials, like other citizens, passionately sought goods and pleasures long denied them. When the Maoist world view collapsed and sacrifice lost its meaning, the moral basis for resisting temptation was eroded. Given their modest salaries, few had much hope of bridging the enormous gap between their own standard of living, barely above subsistence level, and the alluring life-style of Hong Kong, dangled before their eyes in advertisements on television, by overseas visitors, and during their own visits. Many sought to acquire goods quickly and with little effort. There were means to be found within China, but with the expansion and freeing of foreign trade, there were many more opportunities, on a far larger scale, through Hong Kong and overseas acquaintances.

The central problem of corruption in Guangdong in the reform decade occurred at the intersection of market forces and officialdom, between officials and businesspeople. With the increase in economic activity, private business had acquired wealth that it had lacked before, but officials still controlled access to many scarce goods and services. The problem arose when the private businessperson, impatient with regular procedures, used his wealth to gain the special cooperation of the public official who controlled the gate to the resources.

Gatekeepers could be found everywhere that there was official discretion in making critical decisions involving desired resources or permits in short supply. They were found among customs officials who used discretion in charging duties. They were found among policemen who discovered smuggling and had the option of deciding how seriously to treat the crime. They were found among inspectors who decided whether a building site met standards or who granted land-use permits. They were found among tax officials who determined levies, and among industrial bureaus that decided whether a plant could be built and under what kind of arrangements. They were found among factory officials who decided where products in short supply would be shipped. They were found among public security officials who decided whether a person or family should receive urban registration. They were found among officials responsible for: assigning housing; deciding which plants would receive how much electricity or telephones; allocating limited space on freight cars; assigning limited hotel, airline, or train beds or seats; determining who would travel abroad; hiring and promoting; granting loans; and setting prices. And with the collapse of the old moral order, loss of pride in their position, and thirst for goods they could not otherwise hope to acquire, many gatekeepers were ready to bargain.

Impatient customers could also be found at all these gates. They had a variety of options, depending on their status, their long-term strategy, and the item involved. If the issue was large enough, then those with access to highest officials could sometimes break through the logjam without giving special gifts. If the customer had good *guanxi* with certain individuals, he might call on this *guanxi* to solve a problem, even without special payments. If the customer needed repeated or long-term assistance, he might give frequent presents or favors. If he needed a one-time service, he might offer a specific present.

Just how widespread these practices were was difficult for anyone, including the most skilled public security investigators in China, to discern precisely. Interviews with foreign and Hong Kong business-people and reports from the Hong Kong and mainland press suggest that the situation in the late 1980s was as follows.

The highest provincial and municipal officials rarely accepted gifts of significant size but did allow their children to receive opportunities for education, training, and desirable jobs, especially in the foreign trade sector. High officials received, by Chinese standards, a good salary and many perquisites and enjoyed security and positions of honor, which they were not tempted to jeopardize by accepting large presents. What they did value highly were foreign education and jobs for their children. Unlike leaders in Hong Kong and many other countries, they did not earn enough to pay for their children to study abroad, and the chance of winning a scholarship was minuscule.

The highest officials did not personally seek opportunities for their children; this was a serious offense. Hong Kong and foreign business-people, however, believed that it was useful to hire or provide foreign scholarships to the children of high-level cadres. These offspring often had family and former elite school classmates who had risen high in the Chinese bureaucracy and could provide useful information, advice, and connections. Private companies in Hong Kong dealing with the mainland hired many such individuals. In fact, a significant proportion of the Chinese employees in firms that traded with China were children or relatives of top cadres in Beijing and Guangzhou, including such Hong Kong companies as CITIC, Everbright, and Kanghua. By the late 1980s, however, indignation against children of high cadres was sufficiently strong among those who had risen without such connections that a request by a child of a high cadre for bureaucratic assistance in China did not always succeed and could even hurt more than it helped.

There was also a large gray area in which the giving of small gifts and favors to officials at all levels was very widespread. The offering of favors to keep up good relationships is so rooted in Chinese society that the scope of what is considered proper has always been larger than in many Western societies. Banquets to which a large number of people are invited, New Year's gifts, gifts of cigarettes and liquor when visiting, and paying for hotel and other services for Chinese visiting Hong Kong or abroad have been so common that, within bounds, they are considered not corruption but kindnesses or, at worst, the annoying costs of maintaining a relationship. The sense of what is proper is also colored by the fact that the Hong Kong or overseas friend or relative is so much richer; some on both sides consider it only human for the one who has so much to share with the one who has so little.

In the 1980s outside travelers were ordinarily allowed to bring one large consumer item when they came into China. They were also permitted to carry in some other items duty free. Many brought sizable presents almost automatically for certain business partners, and sometimes specific requests were made. Hong Kong businesspeople often paid the expenses of business partners who came to Hong Kong for negotiations, and sometimes "expenses" included a per diem used in part to enjoy pleasures while in Hong Kong or to purchase sizable presents to bring back home.

It was sometimes hard to specify precisely when boundaries between courtesies and greed or between custom and corruption were crossed. If a Chinese engineer traveled abroad for training needed by a joint venture in China, few regarded this as corruption. If a Chinese individual traveling abroad on a small per diem allowance arrived in a city and canceled the hotel reservation his host had made for him in order to stay with a Chinese friend and saved the per diem to buy a few foreign books or videotapes, this too was perhaps not corruption. What if the engineer acquired enough abroad to bring back a personal computer for his work? Or a videocassette recorder for his home? Or for resale? What if in the tour group, in addition to several specialists and engineers, there were one or several administrative and Party officials who had no specialized knowledge, and they too acquired gifts to bring back?

Certain gatekeepers offering services in China did demand specific payments, which might be used by the unit or the people in it. A classic problem for foreign businesspeople investing in China was that once the agreement was made, the foreigner found new, unanticipated charges. He might discover that to hire workers he had to pay extra fees to the "labor service bureau," which then paid low wages to the Chinese workers and kept a sum sometimes several times the amount that went to the workers. Sometimes he was expected to reimburse the institution that had trained or released the employee he planned to hire. Putting up a building on former farm land might mean hiring those displaced from the land, regardless of their qualifications. Sometimes compensation had to be paid to local agricultural bureaus that had to do without the production of goods on those fields. Sometimes special fees had to be paid to units in charge of construction, electric power, and sewage in order to get work done in a timely fashion. "It seems," said one foreigner, "that anyone who has the power to stop a project has his hand out."

Because government, Party, and army units were permitted in the 1980s to use their own facilities to earn funds to supplement the budget allotted them, many of them used land in prime locations to open restaurants, stores, and other facilities that they operated for profit. Some of these units were able to procure state goods at lower prices and thus increase their margin of profit. These commercialized operations operated in effect like private businesses, and they too could supply funds to the friendly gatekeepers in the units above them who helped provide the necessary permissions and access.

Although many officials refused to accept gifts of significant size and others were working to crack down on corruption, the problem was sufficiently large that it attracted serious opposition from foreign businesspeople, some of whom withdrew their investment or decided not to invest; from those who lacked the opportunity or refused to accept such gifts; from those waiting in line for scarce goods and services; and from high-level officials concerned with the overall moral state of society. Corruption was not unique to Guangdong; serious problems of corruption also occurred elsewhere in China. If anything, Guangdong officials were tougher in prosecuting crimes than in many other locales. In 1982–83 alone, over a thousand people in the province were executed for economic crimes. Leaders thus sought to keep the lid on a problem that had deep roots in the transitional system in which socialist planning and organization coexisted with dynamic, partially opened markets.

## Proposed Guidelines for the Future

It was unprecedented for a socialist province to move so far toward a market economy, and thus it is not easy for anyone, in China or elsewhere, to provide useful guidelines for Guangdong's future. From the vantage point of 1988, the cutoff date for this study, we might consider where Guangdong is headed and how leaders might shape the forces they have unleashed. Considering the broad social, economic, and political changes of the first decade of reform, what goals might a foreign social scientist suggest to help guide the province during the second reform decade and beyond?

*Creating a Realistic Time Framework for Expectations.* Filled with revolutionary fervor, leaders launching the Great Leap Forward and the Cultural Revolution wanted to accomplish everything at once. Some reformers and consumers, when given new opportunities in the late 1970s, were just as impatient, just as lacking in time perspective, and just as frustrated by failure to acquire what they wanted instantly.

Since reforms were experimental, it was not possible to have a well worked-out agenda and time frame. Plans still provide some perspective for coordinating parts of the economy, but with new market forces operating and change coming so rapidly, government units, enterprises, and ordinary citizens have had more difficulty coordinating their activities. What is needed is not more planning but a greater effort to understand and analyze the new forces of markets and their interconnection in Guangdong to arrive at realistic estimates of future growth and needs that can be made publicly available; unlike plans, which are difficult to adjust, estimates can be easily and regularly revised. With realistic estimates, government units, localities, firms, and ordinary citizens can adjust their expectations and take appropriate initiative on their own. For example, consumers who had a more realistic estimate of when they might acquire certain items would be less frustrated, and educational institutions would be able to gear their training to the likely needs of the economy and society. Attention to actual trends would help officials and ordinary citizens gain a longer-term perspective and give them a clearer idea of what resources, investment, technology, manpower, and infrastructure are needed at each stage before goals can be achieved.

*Management of Price Decontrol and Inflation.* Guangdong officials recognize both the importance of decontrolling prices to open markets further and the dangers of the inflation that may result. In particular, they are highly sensitive to the importance of controlling inflation in order to prevent social unrest, and they are preparing to give substantial help to low-paid salaried workers to tide them through the transition. They realize that though this contributes to inflationary pressure, their support is necessary to effect further price decontrol. They are also trying to provide adequate supplies of the key goods that people rush to buy whenever they fear price increases.

One of the biggest dangers of decontrolling prices before markets are fully developed is that state enterprises that are the only producers of certain goods will begin to behave like monopolies in a market society; they will be able to raise prices without feeling pressure to become more efficient and without improving services to the consumer. The market in the next decade will not always be strong enough to create independent enterprises that are sufficiently large and strong to compete with some of the biggest state firms. Price decontrols thus need to be coordinated with the creation of competition in a sector to reduce the danger of monopoly behavior. This is also true for service companies, originally government units, which act like monopolies under little pressure to change.

As a way of keeping down inflation during this period, the government may also have to take action to prevent cartels from raising prices more in certain sectors than in others. Although cartels eventually may be controlled by regulations, before these rules are well developed, various government agencies will have to play an administrative role in ensuring the benefits of more open competition.

Because inflation and cost-of-living subsidies have such a powerful effect on the public mood, it may sometimes be necessary to tighten price controls until goods become plentiful enough that market competition can keep down prices. The government, however, cannot afford large subsidies to tide workers through the transition to price decontrol. Nevertheless, given public anxieties, it is important that people be carefully prepared for the elimination of subsidies.

*Developing Market Rules and Regulations.* Just as the United States and other countries found imperfections in markets and gradually developed a variety of regulations to deal with them, so Guangdong will have to expand the role of custom and law to control the potentially harmful side effects of market competition. It will need to expand rules that fulfill the functions of regulating risks to health from food and drugs, preventing restraint of trade, and avoiding conflicts of interest. Not all these problems necessarily require the legal mechanisms that North America and Western Europe use; some can be achieved by custom and administrative management, as in other East Asian countries, as long as public decisions can be divorced from the concerns of private gain.

*Loosening State Employees' Dependence on Their Units.* Officials are quite aware of the many restraints on labor mobility. State employees are so dependent on their units for housing and other services that the units therefore behave almost as if they own their employees *(danwei suoyouzhi)*. Even if new units are willing to hire someone and arrange for household registration, the old unit is rarely willing to release the person.

To achieve greater labor mobility between state units, at least two major changes are required: housing must be available outside work units, and social security, welfare, and health benefits must extend beyond units. Beginnings have been made in this direction, but they require such massive financial outlays and restructuring that only moderate progress can be expected in the next decade.

Short of these structural changes, the government could at least find ways of making it more difficult for units to hold on to workers who wish to move to an attractive position in a new unit. Rapidly growing collective enterprises, able to offer higher salaries and challenging positions, are becoming more attractive to able employees in state enterprises. Allowing them the freedom to leave would place pressure on state enterprises to make better use of their talents. Since state enterprises have more political power than collectives, it will take some effort on the part of higher officials to ensure that they do not block such moves.

At the same time that mobility between companies becomes easier, salaries need to be geared to long-range company success, and long-range career development programs need to be expanded to provide the worker with some incentive for improving overall company performance. Many collectives have already created the sense that their competitiveness in the marketplace will affect their workers' livelihood, but this attitude is rarely found in state firms. Companies need to develop enough stability so that individual career lines are predictable and to promote talented workers in such a way that it is perceived as fair by others. Although social attitudes make it very difficult to close down state firms or former state firms, wage increases, if contingent on profitability, can have a strong effect on incentives. With career development programs, not only salary but training can be integrated with long-term career development. Higher identification with the firm and the recognition that it is not invulnerable will help reduce the feeling among employees that the state firm is so rich that they can waste or pilfer resources without being personally affected.

*Increasing Information Available to the Public.* Enormous progress was made in the first reform decade in upgrading public understanding, but much remained to be done. Before 1978, even the most basic information about local population, production, and average income and salaries was often not only unavailable to the general public but considered a state secret. Even academics and researchers often lacked access to the simplest of government statistics.

In the 1980s better information gradually replaced vacuous abstract statements and simple propaganda releases as vast amounts of documents were publicly released for the first time. Literature became much franker and a new genre, reportage *(baogao wenxue)*, allowed more open airing of public issues. The range of discussion permitted in the media greatly expanded, libraries were opened with new materials readily accessible, and new adult education courses became increasingly informative, but progress was uneven. Sometimes documents made public contained more information than others not released. Some books released publicly were published in such small quantities that even researchers could not obtain them, and some documents stamped "secret" *(neibu)* were in fact on sale publicly. Some officials were willing to share information informally with the interested public, but most wanted to avoid the bother and the risk of criticism. Something as basic as the province's seventh five-year plan (1986– 1990) was not publicly released. Yet many officials began to realize that more information was needed by the public in order to perform various tasks, and they found that its release did not cause the disasters they originally feared. Public understanding of technology, management, and policy still lags far behind levels in other East Asian countries, and therefore requires continued efforts by officials to expand information available to the public.

*Further Adaptation to World Markets.* China, and especially Guangdong, faces a critical period in the early 1990s. It is advantageous for China to join the GATT, but to do this it must stop subsidizing its foreign exports, as discussed in Chapter 11. Since many goods for export are now highly subsidized, changing this is likely to require some devaluation of the Chinese yuan. Export processing, already competitive in international markets, is unlikely to be adversely affected, and agricultural produce from Guangdong, already competitive, is likely to remain so. Because of their large market and its unfulfilled demand, Guangdong firms are able to sell profitably in the domestic market without having to meet the higher competitive standards of the international market. Yet China badly needs to earn foreign currency in order to import new machinery. In the years ahead, moreover, with deficiencies in the supply of coal and other domestic resources and their high costs, Guangdong may need to import more resources from abroad, further increasing the need for exports to balance accounts.

It is possible that within several years the competition in the domestic market for certain products, like electric fans, will become so intense that firms producing them will become competitive internationally. It is possible that more products can be found, like the high-speed, lightweight bikes produced in Shenzhen, not suitable for Chinese roads and hence having little domestic market, that will force companies to adapt to international standards. It is possible that Chinese construction crews, like Korean crews in earlier years, can be sent abroad to places like Hong Kong and Japan, which are short of labor, to earn foreign currency. But policies will be needed nevertheless to prod companies to compete in international markets and gain the experience, in Hong Kong and elsewhere, that will help a broader range of managers and workers understand how to cope with foreign competition. The experience of Taiwan, South Korea, and other rapidly growing economies has been that continuous external pressure is needed to force ongoing change in management and work style to bring fundamental improvement of efficiency.

*Restraining Inequality by Investing in Backward Areas.* Just as coastal provinces in China grew more rapidly than inner provinces after reforms, the most serious problems of inequality in the 1980s were between prosperous coastal areas and remote mountain areas. Within prosperous areas, inequalities narrowed because the new opportunities for private marketing and temporary work for those with low incomes grew faster than the benefit package for the more privileged, salaried state employees. The most striking contrast is between the Inner Pearl Delta area and the forty-seven mountain counties, as can be seen by comparing their industrial and agricultural growth (in billions of yuan, controlled for price increases):

| | Inner Pearl River Delta | | | Mountain counties | | |
|---|---|---|---|---|---|---|
| | 1980 | 1985 | Percent change 1980–1985 | 1980 | 1985 | Percent change 1980–1985 |
| Industry | 5.4 | 16.1 | 297 | 2.9 | 4.7 | 162 |
| Agriculture | 2.9 | 3.7 | 126 | 3.8 | 5.6 | 145 |
| Total | 8.3 | 19.8 | 239 | 6.7 | 10.3 | 153 |

The remote areas grew rapidly and the increase in value of their agricultural output exceeded that of the Delta, but the industry in the Delta grew far faster. And survey data in the plains and mountain counties at the end of 1986, for example, showed a marked difference in the distribution of consumer goods (per one hundred households):[9]

| | Plains | Mountains |
|---|---|---|
| Bicycles | 155 | 107 |
| Sewing machines | 65 | 50 |
| Watches | 191 | 157 |
| Electric fans | 84 | 51 |
| Television sets | 22 | 11 |
| Washing machines | 0.9 | 0.3 |

More needs to be done, therefore, to speed up development in the mountain areas. Nothing is more critical there than building roads and increasing the supply of electricity. When the infrastructure is in place, investment in industries that make use of local products—hemp and flax for cloth, stone for cement, herbs for Chinese medicine—will be expanded by market forces.

The greatest frustration in these remote areas is among those with greater talent, education, skills, or experience. They are not allowed to move to the cities while unskilled laborers can find temporary work in various urban locations. Although officials agree that it would create too much disorder to allow the free movement of such people to the cities, more needs to be done to provide them challenging opportunities within their home counties. The development of new infrastructure and industry would in turn enlarge the service sector. One important prerequisite, however, is the upgrading and expansion of educational facilities.

*Restructuring Educational Costs.* The development of human resources in Guangdong still lags behind that of Taiwan and South Korea at comparable stages of development, and the quality of education outside the better schools of the cities is a serious problem. Financing is a key bottleneck, especially in the poorest areas, because the local communities bear such a large share of schooling costs. It can be argued that in the initial period of reforms it was necessary to give priority to industry in order to generate an economic base, but the lack of expertise among employees is such a critical problem at the end of the decade that a higher portion of the budget needs to be spent on training.

As noted in Chapter 8, school attendance actually declined in Guangdong during the reform decade. From 1975 to 1982, the percentage of primary school graduates going on to junior high school declined from 92 percent to 74 percent, and the percentage of junior high graduates going on to senior high dropped from 67 to 44 percent.[10] Although about 20 percent of the population was estimated to be illiterate in the 1982 census, elementary school attendance was almost universal in the larger towns and cities and approximately 90 percent in rural areas. Literacy levels were still too low for a modernizing country.

The educational system needs urgent attention to avoid even further inequalities and to help the population move toward more productive work. Because it is almost impossible to get talented urban youth to go to backward areas, upgrading schools and teacher salaries in these areas could help make use of the talent in rural areas now frustrated by their lack of opportunity. The poorest counties will require more help from the province in order to make the needed improvements.

*Maintaining Local Collective Support Networks.* In Guangdong, although many rural families continued to have two children, few women in the towns and cities by the early 1980s were giving birth to more than one child. In an earlier era parents with several children encouraged them to choose varying specialties and live in different locations, in the hope that at least one of them might help support them in their old age. After reforms, urban parents placed all their attention on their single child, making children the best-dressed people in China. Many intellectual and cadre families, despite their meager income, purchased pianos and provided their son or daughter with music lessons. Families worked hard to help prepare their child for entrance examinations. Newspapers and advice columns warned of the danger of treating children like "little emperors," who would later find it difficult to accept physical labor and army service. This attention to education and training will in a generation greatly raise the cultural standards of the urban population, but as parents age it will also create new problems for the one child, who will not possibly be able to provide adequate care for two sets of grandparents.

State units originally provided medical facilities and retirement benefits for sick and aged employees and their families. However, the national budget, given rising costs and China's economic base, cannot continue to provide adequate benefits for all state employees, let alone for growing numbers of retirees and nonstate workers. Since rural collectives no longer produce crops jointly, great effort will have to be made to maintain their vitality in order to provide a welfare network for the sick and aged. China is fortunate in having active urban neighborhood associations, which have played a key role in controlling crime and promoting family planning. As mobility between work units increases, it will become all the more important to use these urban neighborhood associations and rural collectives to help provide the needed welfare network.

*Redefining the Role of the Communist Party.* It is widely recognized that the Party should increasingly remove itself from daily affairs and microeconomic management and concentrate on policy and macroeconomic management. It is necessary to give the Party a more positive role than simply relinquishing its role to others. In the Confucian tradition, factions were considered improper; modern complex societies, however, demand political brokering to achieve goals. As new interest groups and units develop in the modernizing economy, Communist Party organizations could be in a position to broker these interests. The Party has attracted people who are experienced in mediating between different interests, and, somewhat like traditional magistrates, Party leaders at each level, if they had a good understanding of the needs of modern society, could make decisions, balancing the claims of various groups. This would require a new vision that aimed to broker interests in line with economic progress, and some of the best Party secretaries are in fact moving in this direction. Rather than allow it to happen by default and reinforce the worst aspects of feudalism, it would be better to pursue a positive vision—expanding public discussion of controversial issues, sponsoring meetings with representatives of interest groups, and creating new ground rules for resolving issues, consistent with a public sense of fairness.

*Containing Corruption.* There are some reasons to believe that forces already in motion will help contain corruption in the next decade.

As more markets are opened up, and available goods and services are distributed according to market forces, gatekeepers will automatically have less leverage and their role should decline. If permits for setting up a stall, for example, become widely available for a fixed fee, then there will be no need to form a special relationship with an official who controls such permits. Guangdong is moving very rapidly to upgrade the quantity and quality of the most desired consumer goods. In 1981–82, for example, tens of thousands of television sets, watches, and other consumer goods were reportedly smuggled in. As Chinese-made televisions and watches improved in quality and quantity, however, the smuggling of foreign sets decreased. As market rules are established and regulations publicized and enforced, opportunities for official profiteering should decrease as well. In the construction industry, for example, since there were few rules concerning bidding, contracting, permits, or charges for services, bidders for contracts had nothing to protect them from officials who chose to exploit their position. Gradually, however, more rules are being created.

In the early stages of market reforms, higher-level officials were prepared to tolerate a certain amount of corruption and profiteering to avoid suffocating business activity, but they remain committed to controlling these excesses in the long run. Foreign businesspeople report that, unlike their experience in some Southeast Asian countries, they have seen almost no cases of senior political leaders involved in corruption in Guangdong.

Despite these favorable factors, Guangdong begins its second decade of reform with serious problems of attitude and structure that, if not changed, could make real progress against corruption very difficult to achieve. One of the most serious problems stems from the low morale of cadres who feel that despite their superior training and dedication they are losing out to private entrepreneurs their age who already earn far higher incomes and enjoy far more consumer goods. The problem is severest in the most prosperous localities, where officials are paid set national wages, where cost of living has risen rapidly, and where many independent businesspeople and even some collective workers earn far more than the highest-paid cadres. Higher-level officials, aware of the relative decline in cadre life-style, are reluctant to clamp down on underlings who find ways to attend sumptuous banquets, ride in vans and limousines, engage in moonlighting, and accept gifts. Since these activities erode public respect for officialdom, however, some other means of addressing the problem of cadre living standards and pride in their status is required. Although there are restraints on official income because of national salary scales, improved cadre housing facilities and local cost-of-living allowances could make a significant difference. To reduce the growing income gap between salaried workers and independent entrepreneurs, other steps, such as a gradual increase in taxation of private business, is desirable, for these businesses are sufficiently well established that such measures will no longer destroy their vitality.

Because many government units carry on commercial activities to supplement their budgets, it is also important to draw sharper lines between those involved in these ventures and those officials who should be insulated from opportunities to profit personally from them. Officials in Taiwan learned to keep some distance from businesspeople, and the same approach is now desirable in Guangdong.

Using moral teachings and severe punishment against corruption will not solve the problem unless markets are expanded further, clear new rules and regulations are established, cadre life-style is improved, tolerance for extra income is reduced, and government and commercial activities are sharply separated.

*Reestablishing a Cultural and Moral Base.* In order to vitalize the economy and society, Guangdong's reformers were willing to unleash the population's suppressed lusting for material belongings, but they never wanted those desires to define society in the long run. In the late 1980s, enthusiastic as they were about the province's dynamism, the fathers of reform did not find it fully satisfying. It was too self-centered, too superficial, too lacking in regard for others and for the society as a whole. They realized that acquisitiveness would not end in the next ten years, but they were looking for other directions.

The better-educated public and higher cadres would like to see a return to a greater sense of dedication to the public good. Perhaps it will take several more years before the cynicism of the Cultural Revolution wears off and people become willing to rally to a new commitment to civic morality. At the beginning of the second reform decade, no group in Guangdong seems able to define this new direction and give it conscious shape. Most who served earlier in propaganda work are too bound to an old content and an old style to play an important new role. They faithfully fashioned and memorized slogans and passed them on, but their past experience has been too restricted to prepare them for a role in helping define the shape of society in the new age. In Beijing there are new groups of writers and researchers who, with considerable spirit, are trying to define a new culture, new philosophies, and a new literature. In Guangdong, however, although some individuals are trying to do similar work, there is not yet a critical mass, a community of people who together have the vision and determination to pursue such goals.

Into the vacuum, during the first decade, swept popular culture from Hong Kong. It was impossible for cultural conservatives in Guangdong to stop the flow. They could take down some antennae that received Hong Kong programming, they could ban certain publications, or proscribe certain types of writing, but Guangdong was too open and the desire for modern outside currents too great. Yet thoughtful people in and out of government do not find this popular culture fully satisfying. Their quest clusters under two rubrics: socialist humanism and a modern Cantonese culture.

Leaders in Guangdong have no trouble admitting the failures of the Great Leap Forward and the Cultural Revolution, but they still believe there was much value in what they have done and what they have fought for—what has been called "socialist humanism." The question is how to better define the values of a modern socialist humanism so that it both expresses their sentiments and provides useful guidelines for the future.

It is still perhaps easier for Guangdong leaders to define the faults of capitalism: the all-out pursuit of personal gain, the high rate of crime, the treatment of workers like ciphers, to be fired quickly when a company is in the red. They want to reduce anxiety about employment, and they do not want to force employees to move as the economy changes. They seek a system that considers the needs and desires of the worker. They want to acquire modern technology and expertise to ease the work and bring greater comfort for their people. They want to provide security and medical care, even though they recognize that they have to put this on a sound financial base. They want to create more equality between different groups, and especially to bring their poorest citizens up to minimum standards. All these are values most thoughtful cadres aspire to, but the question of the next decade will be how to refine these goals, gain public support for them, and find a system that preserves them while allowing the market an increasing role.

It is just as difficult to define a modern Cantonese "culture." Cantonese opera is still viable, and there will undoubtedly be more adaptations of traditional arts. In 1988 a new museum for Guangdong's historical relics was built in Guangzhou. But in the late 1980s Guangdong is just beginning to think, as Hong Kong did in the late 1960s, about how to build civic cultural centers. For political as well as social reasons, the new definition of Cantonese culture cannot be detached from Chinese culture or, given its appeal, from modern Hong Kong culture. Guangdong can, however, give attention to the development of its own history, architecture, literature, and art. This effort has hardly begun and deserves more attention. Both of these projects, discussing and defining a desirable socialist humanism and a modern Cantonese culture, despite the low priority they have had, are sufficiently important to deserve the attention of a community of leading cadres and intellectuals in the 1990s.

# 13.

# *The Takeoff of the Guangdong–Hong Kong Region*

The world has become well aware of the remarkable economic takeoffs of Japan and the newly industrialized economies of East Asia. Guangdong's takeoff, beginning in the mid-1980s, was the first instance of this pattern in a socialist country. Having detailed the origins and the growth of Guangdong's new dynamism from the special economic zones through the Pearl River Delta to the rest of the province, we may now seek to place these developments in broader perspective. How did other East Asian industrializing economies take off and how did Guangdong's initial pattern compare with theirs? As Guangdong and Hong Kong, still two separate worlds in the early 1980s, became intertwined at the end of the decade, what was the nature of the emerging Guangdong–Hong Kong region and where was it heading? Finally, what significance do these developments have for the rest of China and for the socialist world?

## Takeoffs in Japan, Taiwan, and South Korea

To gain perspective on Guangdong's growth since 1978, no comparisons are more illuminating than those with three recently developed economies of East Asia: Japan, South Korea, and Taiwan. They are from the same cultural area and of comparable size. Japan's population is only twice Guangdong's, South Korea's two-thirds, Taiwan's about one-third, and the geographical areas of the four rank in the same order. Hong Kong and Singapore, East Asia's other newly industrializing economies, are city states with no rural base and similar in size only to the city of Guangzhou; they face problems very different from those faced by Guangdong and the others. Guangdong is not an independent political unit, but with its "special policy," it has had enough autonomy since 1979 to be confronted with most of the major issues faced by Japan, South Korea, and Taiwan. Although the province began with a far lower base, its rate of growth during the reform decade was similar to Japan's rapid growth that began in the early 1950s, to Taiwan's in the late 1950s, and to Korea's in the early 1960s. What were the common features of their takeoffs?

*Spurt of "Late Late" Development.* The "late developing countries"—Germany, Russia, and, to some extent, France and Italy—began the industrial revolution with bigger spurts in industrial investment and growth than did the early developers, England and the United States. To bridge the gap with early developers, late developers assembled more funds for initial investments and made greater leaps in technology. They engaged in more conscious borrowing of technology and expertise and developed more centralized and more formal training programs; the earlier developers had developed more gradually from within. As a consequence, late developers required more coordination by the government and created more centralized institutions for borrowing and development.

In the late twentieth century, when the "late late developers," first Japan and later South Korea, Taiwan, Hong Kong, and Singapore, made their leap to fully modern industry, the gaps between the advanced industrialized economies and the less industrialized economies were still greater. Even greater increases in investment and technology were required in order to catch up, and in this period world trade was much more extensive. The late late developers followed patterns similar to those of the late developers except in more extreme form, and they felt a greater urgency to break into the world market, for fear of being inundated with products from other countries before they had a chance to develop.

*Intimate Contact with and Support from an Advanced Economic Power.* The substantial borrowing of funds, technology, and broad-based knowledge to make these breakthroughs required a high level of cooperation and assistance from an advanced industrialized country. During the cold war, the United States, concerned about the strength of the anti-Communist front and confident of its own economic prowess, was prepared to provide unique assistance to its allies.

From 1945 to 1952, hundreds of thousands of Americans served in Japan, and advisors in every major field worked closely with their Japanese counterparts. The Japanese had an opportunity to learn in every major field, economic, political, and cultural. In the case of Taiwan, after the Kuomintang retreated there from mainland China in 1949, the United States sent in tens of thousands of troops and advisors to help in the early stages of its modernization. And after the end of the Korean War in 1953, large numbers of American troops and advisors remained in or were sent to Korea to assist in the reconstruction.

The level of American effort and spending in these areas was far higher than in other lesser developed economies. Because these countries were considered to be on the front line of the battle against communism, great military aid was also deemed necessary. During the two major wars after 1945, in Korea and Vietnam, the American need for rear services in Japan and later in other East Asian countries was a terrific boon to the host economies.

Although U.S. aid was substantial, it was of relatively minor importance compared to the close personal contact people in these economies had with American advisors. Such links enabled them to learn firsthand about the latest American thinking in agriculture, industry, commerce, science, and technology, then the best in the world. This intensive contact began over a decade before industrial takeoff: in Japan, which already had a modern industrial economy before World War II, contact began in 1945, and rapid industrial takeoff began in the 1950s; in Taiwan, contact accelerated when mainlanders withdrew there in 1949, over a decade before industrial takeoff; and in South Korea, close contact with advisors began in 1953, some seven years before plans for takeoff began. The rapid transfer of technology and knowledge was also facilitated by the new means of communication, particularly television, which made it possible for the masses of people in one country to learn about the patterns of thought and organization that underlay the technology and industry of the more advanced countries.

South Korea and Taiwan, developing later, also learned a great deal from Japan. Both had been its colonies and under it had developed some degree of infrastructure in railroads, highways, electrical power, and telecommunications. Both also received training in discipline and, in Japanese-run schools, a high level of fluency in the Japanese language and an intimate understanding of Japanese ways. Japanese colonialism was harsh, but it was also oriented toward modernization and extended more thoroughly into the daily lives of the local people than colonialism elsewhere. Although the colonial experience left scars and a legacy of ill will, it enabled those trained under the Japanese to have easy access to and solid understanding of Japan's industrial strategy and technology.

*Powerful National Drives.* All these economies had a promethean desire to acquire new technology and expertise, and this spurred them to make good use of their opportunity for learning. The drive for success had an economic basis, but it also had a psychological and political base that was nourished by leaders seeking popular support for their programs. The economic basis lay in the necessity of importing to meet their basic requirements. In the mid-nineteenth century Japan was still self-sufficient, but by the 1930s its agricultural production was not enough to support its population, and this was even more true after World War II, when six million Japanese soldiers and civilians returned from overseas. With no colonies from which to extract agricultural goods, Japan had to export in order to pay for imports of food, energy, and other natural resources, and the urgency of its situation was well publicized and instinctively understood by its citizens. The same was true for South Korea and Taiwan.

The fear of outside domination also played a crucial role. As an island with a unique language, history, and racial stock, historically more distinct than any other major country, Japan has had a natural basis for unity. Its citizens have been driven by the desire to catch up and overtake the occidental civilization that threatened to dominate them in the late nineteenth century. South Koreans have been driven by a resentment of Japanese cruelties and a determination to break out from under Japanese domination. And as parts of divided countries, fresh from civil war, both Taiwan and South Korea have feared invasion. At the time of Taiwan's initial economic breakthrough, Communist China was preparing to invade the island, a threat taken seriously by Taiwan and heightened by the battles in the Taiwan Straits in 1958. Citizens were prepared to work together in order to maintain their security.

These factors provided a powerful underpinning for the drive to succeed in modernization. People were willing to work hard, to accept sacrifices, to undertake fundamental disruptive changes, and to accept authoritarian leaders who helped the nation realize its goals.

*A Stable Authoritarian Government.* Although all three economies experienced strong pressures for further democratization in the 1980s, such demands were very weak at the beginning of their industrial takeoff. At that time their public, influenced by a Confucian tradition in which the people were subjects and not citizens, was not clamoring to play a major role in determining government policy.

The governments in these nations were sufficiently stable that economic policy could continue without any great disruptions. In Japan, under Yoshida Shigeru and his "school" of successors, the Liberal Democratic Party dominated from 1955 on, despite individual and factional changes. In Taiwan, the leadership by Chiang Kai-shek and his son Chiang Ching-kuo continued from 1949 until 1988, providing great continuity. In Korea, after the student demonstrations that led to the fall of Syngman Rhee in 1960, there were two military coups, first by Park Chung Hee and later by Chun Doo Hwan, but despite these violent changes and some fragility, the nation's leaders remained in office for many years and exercised forceful leadership with basic continuity.

In their early years, Taiwan and Korea had a strong secret police and military and did not hesitate to crack down to maintain order. After military rule was in place and stability achieved, military suppression generally remained in the background and leaders endeavored to adopt a softer authoritarian style. Compliance was high not only because of fear and force but because many people believed strong leadership was necessary to prevent chaos, to respond to the Communist threat, and to preserve the gains in the standard of living. In a stable, predictable environment, it was easier for private businesspeople to undertake investment. This predictability was further enhanced by the close cooperation between authoritarian leaders and the bureaucracy.

*Powerful, Meritocratically Selected Bureaucrats.* All three economies relied on elite bureaucrats who achieved their positions on the basis of examinations and proven ability. This was consistent with the East Asian classical tradition from China, Korea, and Japan, but the content of the bureaucrats' training, even before the economic takeoff, was distinctly modern, including modern political economy, national economic strategy, international relations, science, and technology. The training provided more historical perspectives and context than the focused, pragmatic training of American law and business schools. The elite bureaucrats had some specialized training but were essentially generalists, responsible for thinking more about the broad picture than about how they performed some specific role.

Tokyo University, Seoul National University, and Taiwan National University were set up primarily to train government officials, and some of each society's most talented young people, as measured by national examinations, were selected by and educated in these institutions. Their best students, in turn, were selected for the national bureaucracy. This procedure was important not only to ensure that some of the ablest people in the society were determining governmental policy but also to accord them legitimacy in the eyes of the public.

*Government Guidance of the Economy, with Strong Private Enterprise.* In Japan, South Korea, and Taiwan, the top leaders and bureaucrats played a central role in reaching a consensus about basic industrial policy, in ensuring that the necessary finance, technology, personnel, and infrastructure were available to businesses, in subsidizing key sectors until they became internationally competitive, and in clearing away obstacles to business growth. Although the size of the core elite government bureaucracy was relatively small, the bureaucrats had many key points of leverage over firms—in helping get concessionary loans, granting a variety of approvals, and in determining taxes—that they could use to enforce enterprise compliance with their strategy. But except for a small number of critical public firms, enterprises were overwhelmingly in private hands. Companies were ordinarily held responsible for their own profits and losses, and workers tended to link their personal well-being with their company's success, which provided a strong overall motivation to work hard for their company.

*Emphasis on Manufactured Goods for World Markets.* Unlike many Latin American and African countries, Taiwan, Japan, and Korea did not supply agricultural products or raw materials to the major powers, nor did they have powerful interests closely linked to agriculture and resources that could prevent labor from being pulled away to industry. Basically all sectors of society benefited from industrial growth, which brought great breakthroughs in improving the standard of living.

In economies that follow only a policy of import substitution, trying to produce locally what they formerly imported, local industries are not under such intense pressure to gain world levels of efficiency. These East Asian economies, however, were much more ambitious. They wanted to sell goods competitively in the world market, and the pressure to do this made companies sensitive to international markets and apprehensive lest they slip slightly behind. Sensing how vulnerable exporters could be to changes in the world market, they moved quickly to keep up with world markets by relentlessly increasing efficiency and quality. All three nations protected their infant industries, especially those that, though not yet competitive, were expected to be important in the future. But they also gradually, albeit reluctantly, liberalized import restrictions as their own products became internationally competitive.

*A Strategy of Changing Comparative Advantage.* The old Ricardian notion that dominated Western economic thinking about comparative advantage was illustrated by England, whose cool climate and rolling hills were suitable for sheep herding, and Portugal, whose warmer climate was suitable for grapes. If England traded its wool for Portugal's wine, they would both be drawing on their competitive advantage to their mutual benefit.

At the end of World War II, Japanese leaders considered Ricardo's explanation, but they found its conclusion troubling. If Japan, with so few resources, simply accepted its comparative advantage, cheap labor, it would be doomed to poverty. Leaders who hoped to enrich the nation could not accept such a static view, and chose instead to pursue an activist program of constantly changing their comparative advantage.

They used Japan's comparative advantage of cheap labor to produce textiles and low-grade electronics, but then used the profits to buy and develop more modern technology and upgrade skills to develop a comparative advantage more in the country's long-range interest. The government saw its role as working with the private sector to ensure that whatever was required for the next stage would be available. It provided the coordination, the stimulation, and when necessary the assistance to ensure that the necessary capital, technology, and manpower were in place. Japanese companies gradually went up ladders of changing comparative advantage from simple electronics, to television, to higher electronics; from shipbuilding to steel to automobiles; from lower to higher technology; from labor-intensive and energy-intensive to knowledge-intensive and research-intensive industry; from manufacturing to service industries.

Although less powerful, Taiwan and South Korea followed in Japan's footsteps. They began with labor-intensive industries as Japanese labor costs went up and gradually moved to capital-intensive and technology-intensive industries that were competitive in world markets. Individual industries in these economies sometimes ran into problems, as when Japan overexpanded its shipbuilding capacity, for example, or Korea suffered losses from overextending heavy and chemical industries, but on the whole all three managed the transition to higher comparative advantage successfully. Favorable conditions in international markets and internal discipline and training helped support the overall strategy.

*Temporary Sacrifices for an Initial Breakthrough.* Initially all of these economies, to speed up and expand investment and to meet the competition in international markets, restrained personal consumption. In the early stages of industrialization, wage rates went up more slowly than increases in productivity, and the state, concentrating on productive capacity and efficiency, provided low levels of welfare services and did little to control pollution. Although the standard of living increased more slowly than foreign sales and productivity increases, it still rose quickly enough that people could look forward to continuing rapid improvements. Japan was able to work out various formulae for pacing wages and the standard of living with economic growth as early as the mid-1950s. South Korean leaders, however, demanded more sacrifices, because Korea had started from such a low capital and technical base. It was not until the late 1980s that Korean workers insisted on more rapid improvement and forced management to make more concessions. Taiwan, which was not as ambitious in heavy industry, did not strain as hard as South Korea, but its citizens also made sacrifices to develop an infrastructure and capital-intensive industry before distributing or, in the case of small businesses, taking substantial benefits.

*High Investment in Human Resources.* All these economies expected high levels of discipline at work, and workers knew that their jobs were at risk if they did not perform. Children were trained from their early years to be respectful of authority, to work hard, and to be prompt. Schools were regarded as places to train children in skills rather than to help them express themselves or find their own individuality. Teachers expected all students to meet high minimum standards, and the fact that students had to take achievement-based exams for admission to higher schools and universities was used as an outside pressure to keep up the level of effort.

By 1900 basically all Japanese children were receiving an elementary school education, and by World War II most children in Korea and Taiwan were also attending elementary school. After World War II all three economies expanded educational facilities at explosive rates. In the late 1940s Japan extended compulsory education from six to nine years, and by the late 1970s 94 percent of Japanese young people were finishing high school (compared to less than 80 percent in the United States) and by the mid-1980s almost half were going on for postsecondary training. In the 1950s Taiwan began moving in the same direction, and after the Korean War, South Korea followed suit. The investment in human resources was less a huge financial investment than a thorough-going commitment to standards, but the governments did finance a very rapid expansion of educational institutions as the demand for higher training grew. High standards of basic education were extended almost universally throughout the society. Students performed well on standardized international tests in science and mathematics. Company training programs, national news media, and periodicals could assume a high level of education and therefore provide high levels of information.

Young workers in Japan, South Korea, and Taiwan were accustomed to putting out great effort. Enterprises drew on their habits of disciplined study to demand high levels of performance. Labor unions, with a few important short-range exceptions, basically cooperated with management to achieve common goals of gaining competitiveness in world markets. Management was paternalistic, accepting some responsibility for looking after the welfare of the workers, and the workers accepted their responsibility to exert themselves on behalf of the company. All these economies also developed national manpower plans closely related to anticipated future demands for various skills. Training programs, for example, were geared to the changing requirements of enterprises.

## The Special Features of Guangdong's Takeoff

When it began reforms at the end of 1978, Guangdong had many disadvantages in comparison to the other three developing economies at the time of their takeoffs. The province had a bloated, poorly trained bureaucracy, a rigid system of planning, and no experience in guiding a market economy. Its intellectuals were disaffected, its work force poorly disciplined. Compared to the other three governments, which exercised independent political rule, Guangdong, as part of China, was subject to far more political and economic constraints. With abundant resources in China, Guangdong did not feel the desperate need to export in order to survive that served as such a stimulus to unity and adaptation for the other developing economies. And with the cold war over and the possibility of military action remote, Guangdong could not mobilize the fear of outside military action that had earlier served to unite and mobilize the citizenry in the other three.

Furthermore, the international climate in the 1980s, when Guangdong began to take off, was far less supportive and receptive to exporters than it had been in earlier decades. After its withdrawal from Vietnam and the thaw in world affairs, the United States was no longer so concerned about the threat from the Soviet Union that it was prepared to send massive amounts of military and technical aid. Nor in the mid-1980s was the United States, the world's greatest importer, able, with its large trade deficits, to absorb the vast portion of the world's manufacturing exports or to expand imports as it had when the other three began their takeoffs. By then strong exporters in other countries were already competing eagerly for the American market, and no other countries had replaced the United States to provide such a huge market for industrial exports. Thus Guangdong's challenges were greater.

And yet despite these problems, Guangdong had begun to grow at explosive rates by the mid-1980s, at least as rapidly as the other newly industrializing economies at their peak of growth. How did Guangdong manage this and how did its pattern of development compare with the other three?

*Spurt of "Late Late" Development.* Guangdong too grew in a great spurt. Having been so closed to outside technology, Guangdong had fallen decades behind. The introduction of new technology and management systems from the outside, even though not generally at the most advanced world levels, brought great spurts of growth. As in the early years of takeoff in the other East Asian economies, the spurt came not from large investments in heavy industry but from large numbers of small investments. Perhaps the most important area of investment for development was in modern production equipment. Some export-processing factories, making labor-intensive products like apparel, toys, and low-grade electronics, introduced only the bare minimum of modern equipment. Other domestic-oriented factories brought in more equipment, however, in order to produce light consumer goods such as electric fans, drinks and processed foods, textiles, radios, refrigerators, washing machines, bicycles, and pharmaceuticals. This new equipment, even without modern systems of management and without high levels of efficiency, led to great spurts of growth.

Some of the spurt came indirectly from investment in new infrastructure, particularly roads, bridges, trucks, electric power, and tele-communications. This investment made it possible for large numbers of small factories and farmers producing agricultural cash crops and inexpensive manufactured goods to be linked to markets, both do-mestic and foreign, for the first time. The funds for investment came from domestic savings generated by the sale of agricultural and in-dustrial products on the newly opened markets, from tourism, and from small Hong Kong companies.

*Intimate Contact with and Support from Hong Kong.* Not only did Guangdong lack access to the massive amounts of American aid and technical assistance once received by the other economies, but, in contrast to Taiwan and South Korea, its people lacked an understand-ing of Japanese language and society to enable it to profit directly from Japanese technology and skills. Guangdong had a unique op-portunity, however, in its special access to Hong Kong and overseas Chinese. Hong Kong could not directly offer the range of advice that the United States had given other East Asian nations in agriculture and industrial technology, but it had high general management skills, a well-developed financial and service sector, and perhaps most im-portant, an excellent information network that opened access to tech-nology and markets around the world. In one sense using Hong Kong was almost too easy, because it did not force Guangdong officials and businesspeople to have direct intimate contact with the major powers of the world. In effect, Hong Kong was a shortcut, a cushion, that made it possible to acquire skills and information with relatively little effort.

*Powerful Individual Drive for Material Acquisition.* Lacking an omi-nous military threat or a fear of being cut off from needed imports, Guangdong had more difficulty developing a sense of crisis to help bring higher levels of internal cooperation and rapid adaptation of the political and economic structure. The Cantonese have strong local pride, but this alone was not strong enough to cause the people of the province to unite effectively or to drive them to modernize.

The real passion for change resulted from Guangdong's opportunity to see what had happened in Hong Kong during the decades that the border had been closed. The awareness of Hong Kong's progress ended whatever nagging doubts Guangdong might have had that modernization was beyond the grasp of the Cantonese. If its Can-tonese cousins in Hong Kong could do it, what was to stop Guang-dong? But more important, by flaunting the benefits of their economic progress, Hong Kong made people in Guangdong acutely dissatisfied with their state of backwardness, mobilizing them to pursue what their brethren across the border had achieved.

The passion for change did not arise full blown with the first real opening to Hong Kong in the 1970s. The world of Hong Kong then seemed too foreign, its way of life too different. Hong Kong seemed too wasteful, too superficial, its level of living beyond Guangdong's grasp and even beyond its hopes. But ways of doing things that first seemed distant and foolish gradually became familiar and even attractive. Most people's desires were at first surprisingly modest, but goods that in the late 1970s seemed unnecessary and even ridiculous gradually came to appear enticing and even essential. A sense of relative deprivation fueled a powerful materialistic acquisitive drive. The drive had a long history in the Pearl River Delta area, but after decades of suppression, it took several years for it to reignite. And in remote areas of Guangdong, never before linked to the province transport system except by foot, the acquisitive drive of the 1980s went far beyond anything they had previously known.

*A Large but Unwieldy Authoritarian Government.* Not only was the government of Guangdong intertwined with Beijing, but it had more layers and was less tightly centralized than governments in other East Asian economies. Despite the turmoil in the Communist Party during the Cultural Revolution and the fundamental questions raised by concerned citizens about its legitimacy, thereafter its control of positions of power was never in doubt. The Communist Party in Guangdong reached more directly into more organizations and more localities than did any of the political parties in other East Asian economies. With a membership including 4 percent of the population and with leverage everywhere in controlling important appointments, the Party could command a measure of obedience everywhere. In 1952 Guangdong had 540,000 employees in government and Party units and in state enterprises, and in 1978 it had 4,430,000, over 10 percent of the adult population.[1] Paradoxically, smaller political structures in the other economies, with more modern means of communication, better information, clearer rules, more finely tuned procedures, and a more disciplined staff, made decisions more efficiently and implemented policy more rapidly and thoroughly than did Guangdong.

Because it was so large, poorly coordinated, and subject to personal variations, the Party and government of Guangdong provided a less predictable environment for businesses and even for local government units. But on critical issues the Party could mobilize support anywhere. Enterprising political leaders at various levels in Guangdong were with great effort able to use personal connections to achieve on occasion a high level of coordination and rapid response.

*From a Loyalty-Based to a Meritocratic Bureaucracy.* Until 1977, many bureaucrats had come from poor peasant and worker families, because they had been favored over those from rich families. Educational levels were low, and in the favored social classes they were still lower. Except for the 1961 to 1966 period, when merit was given more attention, political dedication was generally valued over merit. The average educational and technical level of Guangdong cadres was, prior to 1977, far below that in Japan, South Korea, and Taiwan.

The changes beginning with entrance examinations in 1977 may be seen as a return to the tradition of selecting Guangdong officials on the basis of merit, a tradition that had been very much alive during the takeoff of other East Asian economies. As part of the reforms, Guangdong leaders, like those elsewhere in China, took steps to improve qualifications of officials by retiring older, less competent officials, setting higher minimum educational standards for appointment and promotion, and expanding training programs. But because the bureaucracy in China was so bloated and because less competent officials could not be easily dismissed, Guangdong had only a small group of highly talented, meritocratically selected officials, often on a fast track, who still worked in large offices with many others who were less able. Even at the end of the decade Guangdong had serious problems in coping with feudalistic patterns of clientalism and poorly trained officials.

*Reducing Direct Economic Management by the Government.* From 1956 until the reforms in 1979, the government directly managed state firms and maintained tight controls over collectives. Planning, production and sales targets, procurement quotas, and state-set prices dominated the economy. The first decade of reforms decreased these direct controls and increased the role of markets, thus moving Guangdong farther in the direction of the other East Asian economies. Guangdong officials aimed in the second decade of reforms to reduce further the government role to that of formulating and coordinating macroeconomic policy, thereby granting far greater autonomy to private enterprises.

Guangdong achieved considerable success in this transition to a commodity economy, especially in the consumer goods sector and in enterprises run by towns and villages. Materials in short supply and large state enterprises were still subject to tight government controls, but these controls were much reduced. The legacy of the earlier management style made it tempting to return to controls when problems arose. The Communist Party still had an important role in guiding local overall policy and in approving personnel decisions. Yet by the end of the first reform decade, towns and villages, as well as individual enterprises, had enough freedom from higher-level planning that even if they were subject to supervision by local Party and government officials, they were able to begin responding to new economic opportunities much as enterprises in the other newly industrializing economies did.

*Ease in Selling to the Domestic Market.* Because levels of quality and efficiency in internal Chinese markets lagged behind those in the international market, Guangdong producers, by acquiring modern foreign technology and expertise more rapidly than other regions, could sell easily in the domestic market. As noted in Chapter 11, during this first decade of reforms, most Guangdong manufacturers were insulated from the pressures of international competition both by a foreign trade bureaucracy and by the separation of procurement prices from international prices. By the end of the decade, provincial officials were trying to remove the foreign trade bureaucracy as an intermediary in order to increase the responsiveness of firms to international markets and to eliminate indirect export subsidies. The huge domestic market gave Guangdong greater security than those in the other developing economies and helped drive rapid growth. Removed from international pressures, however, Guangdong's enterprises did not raise their standards of efficiency and quality as rapidly as those in other industrializing economies at comparable stages.

*A Strategy of Acquiring New Production Equipment for Light Industry.* Because of resources and markets available within China, Guangdong leaders, unlike those in Japan, South Korea, and Taiwan, did not feel the need in the early reform years to generate foreign currency sufficient to buy large amounts of natural resources. Rather, they sought to buy only enough to import technology to make their industry more efficient, and they allowed some high-priced foreign-made consumer products in because they profited from high duties on the goods. By the late 1980s, as their growth outpaced the availability of local resources, many Guangdong enterprises were confronted with the necessity of buying high-priced foreign resources and passing on higher prices domestically, which made domestic competition more difficult. During the first decade of reform, however, cash crops sent to Hong Kong and labor-intensive products exported through Hong Kong provided the needed foreign currency to achieve what provincial leaders considered most important, the purchase of modern equipment for light industry.

The new technology purchased from abroad, particularly new production machinery, brought vast increases in productivity. Since most industry was still in state factories, many of them were able to double and triple production even without greatly changing worker motivation and concepts of efficiency.

When they had begun to develop their new policies after 1978, Guangdong's leaders, more isolated than leaders in other East Asian economies at the same stage, overestimated their ability to attract foreign companies to build state-of-the-art factories in China. Observing Japan, South Korea, and Taiwan ahead of them, they passionately wanted to jump to higher and higher stages of comparative advantage, but they found it difficult to supply the skilled manpower, the infrastructure, a predictable environment, low costs, and the assurance that a foreign company's profits could be repatriated. They had to accept the fact that changing their comparative advantage would be at best a slow process, and that it would take some time before they would have many products, beyond those produced by labor-intensive processing industries, that were competitive on the world market. Even at the end of the first decade, though they had a desire to upgrade their comparative advantage, they did not yet have the control over standards, efficiency, and technology to be able to turn the desire into a realistic strategy. In the meantime even when their goods were not competitive on the international market, foreign trade officials often were allowed to operate at a loss in the 1980s in order to gain the foreign currency needed to purchase modern technology from abroad.

*Reluctance to Sacrifice for an Initial Breakthrough.* In Guangdong, as in the rest of China and in many other countries as well, there has always been some tension between acquisitiveness and higher ideals, particularly dedication to one's community and society. But with the discrediting and collapse of the Maoist world view after the Cultural Revolution, Guangdong had a weak public ethic with which to counter the passion of individuals, families, and small groups of friends for materialistic acquisition. The drive for possessions was strong enough to sustain many people who had first appealed for gifts and resorted to clever schemes and then learned that they could succeed only by achieving in competitive markets. During these early years many came to see the links between hard work, efficiency, and income for the first time.

In 1979, as in the rest of China, state government offices and enterprises in Guangdong already had in place what was, given the economic base at the time, a generous benefit package for state workers, including housing, health, and social services. After two decades of sacrifice without improved standards of living, and with the new awareness of how far their standard of living lagged behind Hong Kong and other East Asian economies, it was unrealistic to expect people to give up what seemed comparatively modest benefits. Workers were in no mood to heed calls for more sacrifice. Leaders had no choice but to help improve the standard of living even before they greatly increased investment. Fortunately, economic growth in Guangdong was so rapid that productivity rose even while the standard of living also rose rapidly. However, the benefit packages, unstoppable worker demands, and low levels of efficiency in their state enterprises discouraged Guangdong leaders, who worried about competition from economies where workers had made more sacrifices in the early stages of breakthrough.

*Effort to Overcome Inadequate Investment in Human Resources.* Cut off from contact with the world's advanced technology and management practice and devastated by attacks on people of talent during the Cultural Revolution, Guangdong on the eve of reform had educational levels, technical and management skills, and worker discipline far below those of other economies at comparable stages. Since 1977, by starting entrance examinations, reviving key point schools with high standards, sending people abroad for advanced training, establishing new universities in each prefecture, expanding "spare time" schools and universities, upgrading television news and information programs, and raising minimal job requirements, Guangdong officials made vigorous efforts to overcome the inadequate investment in human resources. But it was not easy to overcome decades of deficient training, political attacks on intellectuals, and poor discipline. With one-fifth of the province's adults illiterate and many more semiliterate, managers could not assume high levels of basic information or capacity to absorb new information and skills. They had no choice but to provide considerable on-the-job training for new workers and to allow the establishment of many enterprises that did not require high levels of education and skill. It may take decades before Guangdong's human resources catch up to the levels that other East Asian economies had when they launched their takeoffs.

Nevertheless, Guangdong found ways to compensate for its weaknesses in order to push the economy forward. Despite its problems and disadvantages, the province's industrial-agricultural output grew 14 percent a year between 1978 and 1988. Individual companies and the bureaucracy were still far from a smoothly functioning operation with a well-developed understanding of efficiency, but perspectives had undergone fundamental change. Seeing what progress could bring, officials began to take pride in increased productivity in their jurisdictions, and their superiors rewarded them for it. Gradually they began to learn more about what they needed to do to achieve growth.

## The Emergence of the Guangdong–Hong Kong Region

The intertwining of the Guangdong and Hong Kong economies began in the late 1970s and accelerated throughout the next decade, especially after the 1984 agreement on the return of Hong Kong to China. Border procedures were simplified, and Hong Kong citizens passed across quickly and easily. By 1988 ten thousand commercial vehicles crossed the border from Hong Kong into Guangdong each day. Tens of thousands of managers and employees from Hong Kong commuted across the border to Guangdong to work, and tens of thousands more crossed each weekend for recreation. Trains, airplanes, ferry boats, and above all, trucks linked Hong Kong with the towns and cities of Guangdong. By 1988 citizens from China, who until then had difficulty getting permission to visit Hong Kong unless they had special business reasons, were allowed to travel there in tour groups.

By late 1988, as mentioned in Chapter 2, officials from Hong Kong's Xinhua News Agency estimated that two million people in Guangdong were employed directly by Hong Kong manufacturers, more than all such enterprises employed in Hong Kong itself. Shenzhen and nearby counties in Guangdong had become in effect the new suburbs and outskirts of Hong Kong, as businesses located their plants there in order to obtain cheaper land and labor.

By the late 1980s enterprises and government agencies from Guangdong and other parts of China played a major role in Hong Kong.

Plans for Hong Kong's second tunnel were made after a Hong Kong government team visited Guangdong and consulted with its officials, and a Chinese corporation, CITIC, played a major role in organizing its financing. Guangdong officials estimated that as many as one thousand enterprises with home bases in Guangdong had offices in Hong Kong. Guangdong Enterprises (Yuehai), in effect the provincial trading company, in 1988 employed 1,500 people in Hong Kong, managing a variety of business activities in industry, hotels, restaurants, finance, and trading. To be sure, some of these were companies in name only *(pibao gongsi)* to cover for various kinds of transactions, and many Guangdong companies, new to capitalist business, were not necessarily faring well in the world of open competition. But their numbers and their business skills were continuing to increase.

Even during the height of the Cultural Revolution, Guangdong kept its agreement to supply water to Hong Kong. By the late 1980s there were joint Guangdong–Hong Kong governmental discussions to plan transportation systems. There was joint planning to estimate electric power needs and to finance the Daya Bay nuclear facility and other power stations. The Hong Kong Cable and Wireless Company was well integrated into all the planning for telecommunication facilities in Guangdong and Hainan. Plans for airports and shipping facilities required consultation and adjustment on both sides of the border. As noted earlier, private Hong Kong companies were deeply involved with the construction of highways and with the construction and management of hotels, restaurants, and factories in Guangdong. Hong Kong's Chinese University and Hong Kong University had regular faculty and student exchanges with Shenzhen University and Zhongshan University, and their faculties were engaged in joint projects. Soccer matches between Hong Kong and Guangdong teams were a regular highlight of the annual sports season. In short, by the late 1980s social, economic, political, and educational contacts were flowing across the border almost as if it no longer had great meaning.

Hainan, though officially detached from Guangdong in April 1988 to become an independent province, continued to expand commercial and social links with Hong Kong and Guangdong. It may someday become part of the region, but as a still-distant island, at the end of the decade it was not yet integrated into the region's economy. Macau, though centrally located in the region, had too small an economy to play a major role. In essence, therefore, the region centers on the Guangdong–Hong Kong axis.

Despite all these trends toward the formation of a single economic region, the existence of two systems, two currencies, wide disparities in standard of living, and two separate government administrations made coordination of the Guangdong–Hong Kong region cumbersome. Negotiations with Hong Kong were conducted by Beijing more than by Guangdong, and even on issues negotiated by Guangdong, the province had to consider the views of Beijing. Even within Guangdong, Shenzhen had its own separate administration, a separate economic and political framework, and an intermediate standard of living. Hong Kong remained and will remain after 1997 more oriented to world markets and more independent of Beijing than Shenzhen and the rest of Guangdong are. In the 1980s, with less than one-tenth of Guangdong's population, Hong Kong had a higher gross national product and far more foreign trade. The gaps in political and economic systems and standard of living were being reduced, but their existence still created great difficulties for timely decisions and their implementation.

By the early 1980s, businesspeople on both sides of the border, with a common interest in stability, had begun to negotiate directly, and loosened governmental control over their activity in Guangdong made this easier. The Communist Party already played an important role in Hong Kong and Macau, as well as in Shenzhen, Zhuhai, and Hainan, and it was the one organization that could provide political linkages across these different boundaries and systems. The Party was by no means a monolith and the Party's local units reflected the differences of the localities, but it remained the organization with the greatest potential to bring effective coordination to different systems of the region.

As in the United States, where the District of Columbia is the political capital and New York the business capital, Guangzhou remained the major political center of the region while Hong Kong became the center for information, finance, international trade, and business. With the upgrading of industry in Guangdong, Hong Kong was also becoming a center for higher technology and industrial engineering; its new university, Hong Kong Polytechnic, was becoming a major training center for Guangdong.

The speed of structural change in the Guangdong–Hong Kong economy was staggering. Hong Kong was a center of low-wage, labor-intensive industry for almost thirty years, but Shenzhen's wages rose so quickly that it passed through that stage in less than a decade.

During the 1980s, Hong Kong companies moved their manufacturing across the border at a frightening speed, not always with adequate consideration for their Hong Kong workers. In a number of cases taken to court, Hong Kong workers showed up at work in the morning to find the factory empty, the machinery having been moved across the border during the night. Even Inner Delta counties by the late 1980s felt pressure to introduce new production equipment to upgrade their labor productivity, for as their wages rose and the transportation system improved, they needed to compete with counties further away offering lower wage rates for labor-intensive process industries.

Despite its complexity and the uncertainty surrounding the future of Hong Kong after 1997, the new Guangdong–Hong Kong region had become one of the most dynamic in the world by the late 1980s. Hong Kong had flourished as a financial center even before renewing its links with Guangdong, but in the mid-1980s when Singapore, the other East Asian city state, was suffering from a serious recession, Hong Kong was booming all the more because of its new links with Guangdong. Although this may be seen as a return of Hong Kong to its traditional entrepôt role, it is on a scale far beyond anything in its past. At the end of the 1980s many people in Hong Kong remained nervous about their personal future and about Hong Kong's future, and over fifty thousand a year were leaving. But perhaps the best indication of expectations could be seen in Hong Kong's property and stock markets: both were booming.

In the thirteen years from 1965 to 1978, Guangdong's economic growth was slower than that of China as a whole. Because Guangdong lagged behind other provinces in industrial skills when reforms first began, other provinces—Jiangsu, for example—that had more skilled labor, a better-developed industrial base, and a forward-looking provincial leadership were able to move faster. Yet overall, during the 1978–1986 period Guangdong moved up from sixth to fifth position nationally in overall industrial-agricultural output, from sixth to second place in overall construction, and from second to first place in overall commercial turnover. By 1986 it was first in the nation not only in the value of its rubber, sugar, fruit, and sea products but in a number of consumer products, such as household refrigerators. By 1987, the accumulated effect of moving faster in reforms and having an economy more intertwined with Hong Kong enabled Guangdong to spurt ahead. In 1987 Guangdong's 33 percent industrial growth was far greater than that of any other province. It kept up the pace in 1988 and leaders were confident that even calling off major projects to avoid overheating the economy would not greatly alter its path of progress. All of China had grown rapidly in response to reform opportunities, but by the end of the decade Guangdong had begun to accelerate far more rapidly.[2]

In technological levels, productivity, and educational levels, Guangdong in the late 1980s was still substantially behind the newly industrializing economies, but its growth rates compared favorably with those of Taiwan and South Korea at the peak of their growth. Hong Kong, a world-class information, financial, and transport center, and the Guangdong hinterland, supplying Hong Kong with agriculture and low-cost labor, were a natural combination for competing in international markets. As one of Hong Kong's Chinese business leaders put it, "With Hong Kong and Guangdong working together, we are ready to take on any of the newly industrializing economies."

## The Impact of Guangdong's Reforms beyond Its Border

In October 1987 China's Thirteenth Party Congress strongly reaffirmed the reform program as pursued in Guangdong and elsewhere. But even more than the Thirteenth Party Congress, the symbol of Guangdong's success came at the Sixth All-China Games held in Guangdong in November 1987. Held every two years, the Games bring together teams from every province as well as from the army and other national institutions. In the 1987 Games, Guangdong scored more points than any other province, but more important, it demonstrated its modernity to the visiting teams and dignitaries. It displayed a beautiful new stadium and modern electronic equipment, modeled closely and successfully after those at the Los Angeles Olympics. It housed the athletes in a brand new world-class hotel. For a province so recently mired in struggles, poverty, and inefficiency, it was a dazzling, albeit costly, display of progress. The highlight of the Games for Guangdong came when the representative of the National Sports Federation praised the province for its first-class organization and services.

At the Games the representative from Sichuan, a province with a population of over one hundred million that initially boasted great reforms under Zhao Ziyang, accepted the torch as the site for the

1989 contest, but he expressed concern whether his province could match Guangdong; a few weeks later he sadly reported that Sichuan could not properly host the next Games. Even two years later only Shanghai or Beijing could hope to provide facilities comparable to Guangzhou's in 1987. In early 1988 Guangdong was designated a national model for its experiment in comprehensive reform, and other provinces were encouraged to study its example.

Part of Guangdong's impact in China stemmed simply from awareness of its success. Guangdong residents traveling in the late 1980s to other parts of China reported a new level of interest in and respect for Guangdong—even in Shanghai, which traditionally looked at Guangzhou with disdain. Young people elsewhere followed the latest fashions from Guangdong and sang the latest songs, some even in the original, though poorly pronounced, Cantonese. Some northerners who had or were seeking business contacts in Guangdong and Hong Kong began to study Cantonese. Consumers elsewhere sought products from Guangdong because they assumed that they were more likely to incorporate the latest foreign technology. People from other provinces gave gifts from Guangdong. Virtually every province and many cities in China had offices not only in Hong Kong but in Shenzhen, in Zhuhai, and in Guangzhou. They used them not only to market their provincial products but to help their province follow new developments in technology and management to arrange for joint ventures with Guangdong to speed the transfer of technology and skills. Jealousy and criticism of Guangdong remained strong in other provinces and in Beijing because of concern over Guangdong's ability to buy desirable goods and resources, but that did not slow down Guangdong's influence.

Part of Guangdong's impact came from market forces. Wuzhou, the Guangxi city bordering Guangdong on the West River, informally began to be called "Guangxi's Shenzhen." It brought in new ideas and new products from Guangdong, and the area around Wuzhou, benefiting from Guangdong trade, became more prosperous than other parts of Guangxi. Southern parts of Fujian, on Guangdong's northeastern border, and southern parts of Hunan, on the northern border, began to flourish because of their trade with Guangdong. Although this trade had its most immediate impact on nearby areas, it gradually stretched to other parts of China as well. To persuade Guangxi to provide electric power, Guangdong helped finance a major new hydroelectric power plant in Guangxi, and to get needed resources from other parts of China, Guangdong was negotiating agreements with other provinces to invest in development projects in exchange for guaranteed supply of output.

As labor costs began to rise in Taiwan and South Korea, their labor-intensive industries became increasingly envious of Hong Kong's investments in Guangdong. For Taiwan the major potential partner was not Hainan, which was far away and had a smaller population base, but nearby Fujian, which spoke Taiwan's Fujianese dialect and had a much larger population than Hainan. The organizational base was already in place in the special policy that covered Fujian as well as Guangdong and in Xiamen's special economic zone. After the Taiwan government began to allow its citizens to visit their relatives on the mainland in 1987, some Taiwanese businessmen, while on family visits, invested in mainland plants. In Fujian they found receptive hosts; in that year, in fact, Fujian officials had announced that they had not used the special policy as well as Guangdong had, and they resolved to do better in emulating Guangdong's example. As South Korea drew closer to Communist countries to ensure their attendance at the 1988 Seoul Olympics, Korean businesses developed a lively interest in the China market. In the short run they rushed to establish connections in Hong Kong to pave the way for investments in Guangdong, but they showed greater long-range interest in Shandong and northeastern China, which are located near Korea and contain Korean-speaking minorities.

It is unlikely that Guangdong's success played a significant role in the Soviets' basic decision to carry out reforms of their economic system. But officials from the Soviet Union and Eastern Europe had taken a keen interest in China's economic reforms, and each year since 1978 several major delegations from Eastern Europe and the Soviet Union have visited Guangdong to observe the course of reforms. Delegations included senior planning officials and leading members of academies. Visitors were impressed with the scope and speed of Guangdong's development and acknowledged that some reforms—in price reform, for example—had proceeded much further in Guangdong than elsewhere in China. The Soviet Union took a special interest in Shenzhen, and by 1988 was considering establishing a special economic zone in Vladivostok. On a smaller scale, Estonia was beginning to think about links with Finland similar to Guangdong's with Hong Kong, and areas in the Soviet Union near Austria and other West European localities were also stimulated to consider a variety of regional links with the outside. At the very least, reports of the successes of reform in Guangdong and other parts of China were used in the internal debate in the Soviet Union to support and help shape the course of their reforms. That a large socialist province could grow so rapidly was a source of considerable encouragement. Socialist nations in Asia—Vietnam, Cambodia, and even North Korea—began to follow China's progress very closely.

## A Large Step Ahead

In 1988, most of Guangdong's leaders no longer suffered from illusions. They knew that by international standards their province remained poor and backward, that it had too many people for its resources, that its infrastructure lagged behind its needs, that it had high rates of inflation and corruption and low levels of education and efficiency—problems with no easy solutions. But the pace of change gave them a momentum and a measure of optimism in wrestling with those issues. They could see that they had built a solid base for continued progress that would outlast worries about inflation and restraints from Beijing to keep the economy from overheating.

In the first two decades of Communist rule, the ability of Guangdong's leaders to manage the economy wisely lagged behind their ability to expand their political power. In the third decade of rule, disastrous internal political struggles set them back even further. But in the fourth decade a new group of leaders, with encouragement and support from Beijing, acknowledged the seriousness of their past policy failures and embarked on a new course that began to transform their province. The 1980s may well be seen as a turning point in socialist history, when leaders in many countries acknowledged that the socialist system had not achieved the economic progress they had sought. At a time when some were beginning to draw on lessons from the capitalist world to overcome their economic stagnation, Guangdong's leaders enabled their province to take full advantage of its special opportunity to walk a step ahead.

*Appendix*

*Notes*

*Selected Bibliography*

*Acknowledgments*

*Index*

# Appendix

## Provincial Structure and Statistics

Table A.1.  Levels of government in Guangdong Province

| | Before reforms | | After early reforms | | 1988 |
|---|---|---|---|---|---|
| Chinese | English | Chinese | English | Chinese | English |
| sheng | province | sheng | province | sheng | province |
| xingzhengqu | administrative region[a] | xingzhengqu | administrative region | sheng | province |
| diqu, zhuanqu, shi | special district, prefecture, metropolitan region[b] | diqu, shi | prefecture, metropolitan region | shi | metropolitan region |
| zizhizhou | autonomous region[c] | zizhizhou | autonomous region | (abolished) | |
| xian[d] | county | xian | county | xian | county[e] |
| zizhixian | autonomous county[f] | zizhixian | autonomous county | xian | county |
| shi | city | shi | city | shi | city |
| gongshe | commune | zhen, qu | township,[g] district[h] | zhen | township |
| dadui | brigade | xiang | administrative village[i] | xiang | administrative village |
| shengchandui, xiaodui | production team, team | cun | village[j] | cun | village |

*Note:* The number of units underwent constant change; a particular unit from an earlier stage was not always replaced by a single unit that covered precisely the same geographical area. See also the maps of Guangdong in the Introduction and Chapter 7.

a. "Administrative region" was a term used only for Hainan Island. It was a level of government similar to, but officially one-half step higher than, a prefecture. It was abolished when Hainan became an independent province in 1988. Elsewhere before reforms prefectures were directly under the province. In 1978 only Guangzhou was a metropolitan region. Other prefectures were changed into metropolitan regions at various times during reform. In 1983, for example, Meixian, Huiyang, and Zhaoqing were still classified as prefectures (*diqu*) while all the other prefectures had become metropolitan regions, reorganized to guide modern urban and industrial development. In the remaining prefectures, the prefectural capitals were classified as cities under the prefecture. In 1988 all remaining prefectures became metropolitan regions.

c. The Li-Miao Autonomous Region was part of the Hainan Island Administrative Region and included seven of its sixteen counties. It was abolished in 1988 when Hainan Island became a province; all sixteen counties then came directly under the province.

d. In Chinese the name of a county is also sometimes used to refer to the county seat.

e. In 1985 two former counties, Zhongshan and Dongguan, were renamed cities but had essentially county-level status. (Note that the Chinese term *shi* is the same for both city and metropolitan region though their functions are different.)

f. Three counties (Lianshan Zhuang-Yao, Liannan Yao, and Ruyuan Yao) were classified as autonomous counties because of their high proportion of minorities. In 1988 they were made counties.

g. In Chinese the name of a township is also sometimes used to refer to the town that is its headquarters.

h. The urban areas of metropolitan regions, cities, and large towns were further divided into "urban districts" (*shihequ* or *shiqu*). When cities were absorbed into metropolitan regions, the geographical area that formerly constituted the city became known as an urban district.

i. An administrative village (*xiang*) was much larger than a village (*cun*) and usually composed of several villages (*cun*).

j. Roughly three production teams were combined to make a single village (*cun*). Even after reforms some rural people still continued to call their locality by the old production team, brigade, or commune terminology.

Table A.2.   Statistical overview of Guangdong. Population figures are given in millions; all others are in billions of yuan. Not all columns sum correctly due to rounding.

|  | 1978 | 1980 | 1985 | 1986 |
|---|---|---|---|---|
| *Population* |  |  |  |  |
| Total population | 55.9 | 57.8 | 62.5 | 63.5 |
| Working population | 25.0 | 26.0 | 30.0 | 32.2 |
|   Industry | 2.7 | 2.9 | 4.6 | 5.0 |
|   Agriculture | 18.5 | 19.4 | 18.2 | 18.2 |
|   Other | 3.8 | 3.7 | 7.2 | 9.0 |
|   Agric. as % of Agric. + Ind. | 87.4% | 87.1% | 79.7% | 78.3% |
| *Gross output*[a] |  |  |  |  |
| Industry[b] | 20.7 | 23.8 | 54.9 | 64.9 |
| Agriculture[c] | 9.6 | 13.9 | 27.6 | 31.5 |
| Construction | 2.4 | 3.6 | 13.6 | 15.1 |
| Transport-communication | 1.6 | 2.1 | 4.0 | 4.7 |
| Commercial turnover | 2.9 | 5.1 | 11.2 | 12.4 |
|   Total | 37.3 | 48.4 | 111.4 | 128.6 |
| *Net industrial output breakdowns*[d] |  |  |  |  |
| Heavy industry | 8.1 | 8.6 | 15.5 | 16.9 |
| Nonvillage light industry | 11.4 | 13.9 | 30.6 | 35.8 |
| Village (*cun*) industry | 1.2 | 1.7 | 5.9 | 7.3 |
|   Total | 20.7 | 24.2 | 52.0 | 60.0 |
| State industry | 14.2 | 15.4 | 27.7 | 29.9 |
| Collective industry | 5.3 | 6.6 | 15.6 | 18.3 |
| Village (*cun*) industry | 1.2 | 1.8 | 5.9 | 7.3 |
| Other industry | 0.0 | 0.4 | 2.8 | 4.4 |
|   Total | 20.7 | 24.2 | 52.0 | 60.0 |

Table A.2.    *(continued)*

|                        | 1978 | 1980 | 1985 | 1986 |
|------------------------|------|------|------|------|
| *Investment*[a]        |      |      |      |      |
| By the state           | 2.4  | 2.9  | 14.3 | 16.1 |
|   Basic      | 2.1  | 2.6  | 10.4 | 11.4 |
|   Industrial renovation | 0.3 | 0.4 | 3.4 | 4.5 |
|   Other      | 0.0  | 0.0  | 0.5  | 0.2  |
| By collectives         | 0.1  | 0.2  | 2.5  | 2.8  |
|   Cities, towns | 0.0 | 0.1 | 1.4 | 1.7 |
|   Rural      | 0.0  | 0.1  | 1.1  | 1.1  |
| By individuals         | 0.0  | 0.0  | 3.1  | 3.4  |
| Total investment[c]    | 2.4  | 3.1  | 19.9 | 22.3 |
| *Other financial data* |      |      |      |      |
| Bank savings           | 7.1  | 10.3 | 33.2 | 46.7 |
| Bank lending           | 10.9 | 16.1 | 53.9 | 68.1 |

*Source:* For population, *Guangdongsheng tongji nianjian* (Guangdong Province statistical yearbook) (Guangzhou: Zhongguo Tongji Chubanshe, 1987), pp. 34, 95; for output, ibid., pp. 42, 159; for investment, ibid., p. 217; for savings and lending, ibid., p. 369.

a. Gross output data *(shehui zongchanzhi)* and investment data are not adjusted for inflation.

b. Average increase per year between 1978 and 1987 was 16.0 percent (*Guangdongsheng tongji nianjian,* 1988, p. 14).

c. Average increase per year between 1978 and 1987 was 7.0 percent (*Guangdongsheng tongji nianjian,* 1988, p. 14).

d. Net industrial output *(gongye zongchanzhi)* deducts the cost of production materials consumed during production. Data for 1978 are controlled for price increases starting in 1970; after 1980 they are controlled for price increases starting in 1980.

e. Average increase per year between 1979 and 1987 was 24.9 percent (*Guangdongsheng tongji nianjian,* 1988, p. 16).

Table A.3.  Output of key products in Guangdong

|  | 1978 | 1980 | 1985 | 1986 | 1987 |
|---|---|---|---|---|---|
| **Agricultural** | | | | | |
| Grain (million tons) | 16.2 | 18.0 | 17.3 | 17.1 | 18.4 |
| Sugarcane (million tons) | 9.0 | 9.0 | 22.4 | 19.4 | 16.0 |
| Fruit (million tons) | 0.3 | 0.3 | 1.2 | 2.0 | 2.8 |
| Beef, pork, lamb (million tons) | 0.5 | 0.7 | 1.1 | 1.2 | 1.3 |
| Marine products (million tons) | 0.7 | 0.7 | 1.2 | 1.5 | 1.7 |
| Edible oil (thousand tons) | 388.9 | 531.5 | 615.7 | 656.6 | 586.8 |
| Tea leaves (thousand tons) | 10.9 | 11.9 | 22.6 | 26.1 | 28.6 |
| **Industrial** | | | | | |
| Electric power (billion kw hrs) | 9.6 | 11.3 | 17.5 | 19.0 | 23.0 |
| Steel (million tons) | 0.4 | 0.4 | 0.7 | 0.8 | 0.9 |
| Cement (million tons) | 3.9 | 4.1 | 11.5 | 12.8 | 15.1 |
| Bicycles (millions) | 0.6 | 1.0 | 2.1 | 2.2 | 2.8 |
| Sewing machines (millions) | 0.5 | 0.7 | 1.6 | 1.6 | 1.6 |
| Watches (millions) | 0.5 | 0.9 | 8.8 | 23.6 | 20.9 |
| Washing machines (millions) | 0.0 | 0.0 | 0.8 | 1.1 | 1.4 |
| Television sets (millions) | 0.0 | 0.0 | 1.3 | 1.3 | 2.0 |
| Tape recorders (millions) | 0.0 | 0.1 | 5.1 | 4.6 | 4.7 |
| Electric fans (millions) | 0.0 | 1.4 | 13.1 | 12.9 | 15.1 |

*Source:* For agriculture, *Guangdongsheng tongji nianjian* (Guangdong Province statistical yearbook) (Guangzhou: Zhongguo Tongji Chubanshe, 1987), p. 34, for 1978–1986 data; ibid., 1988, p. 5, for 1987 data. For industry, *Guangdong tongji nianjian*, p. 35, for 1978–1986 data; ibid., 1988, p. 7, for 1987 data.

Table A.4.  Annual increase in Guangdong consumer price index. For each year, 100 is the base price index of the previous year.

| | |
|---|---|
| 1978 | 100.4 |
| 1979 | 103.0 |
| 1980 | 108.5 |
| 1981 | 109.3 |
| 1982 | 102.3 |
| 1983 | 100.7 |
| 1984 | 101.2 |
| 1985 | 113.6 |
| 1986 | 104.8 |
| 1987 | 111.7 |

*Source: Guangdongsheng tongji nianjian* (Guangdong Province statistical yearbook) (Guangzhou: Zhongguo Tongji Chubanshe), 1984, p. 267; 1986, p. 288; 1987, p. 313; 1988, p. 254.

Table A.5.  Basic data on Guangdong counties. Population figures are given in thousands, output in millions of yuan, and income in yuan. Administrative divisions are as of 1984.

| | Population | | Non-agricultural population | Industrial output[a] | | Agricultural output | Average per capita income[b] |
|---|---|---|---|---|---|---|---|
| | 1983 | 1986 | 1986 | 1983 | 1986 | 1986 | 1985 |
| Foshan Metropolitan Region | | | | | | | |
| Foshan City | 292 | 323 | 254 | 1,375 | 2,808 | 30 | 3,286 |
| Gaoming County | 220 | 230 | 49 | 43 | 100 | 111 | 660 |
| Nanhai County | 833 | 862 | 215 | 777 | 2,434 | 380 | 1,646 |
| Sanshui County | 427 | 313 | 86 | 147 | 661 | 148 | 1,273 |
| Shunde County | 824 | 859 | 247 | 1,014 | 2,658 | 372 | 1,645 |
| Zhongshan City | 1,047 | 1,073 | 245 | 884 | 2,495 | 519 | 1,429 |
| Guangzhou Metropolitan Region | | | | | | | |
| Conghua County | 386 | 404 | 50 | 98 | 171 | 115 | 513 |
| Fogang County | 239 | 252 | 15 | 28 | 53 | 76 | 454 |
| Guangzhou City | 3,170 | 3,359 | 2,650 | 10,887 | 15,283 | 330 | 2,602 |
| Hua County | 441 | 441 | 100 | 150 | 560 | 140 | 664 |
| Longmen County | 255 | 268 | 43 | 47 | 62 | 76 | 434 |
| Panyu County | 683 | 712 | 162 | 449 | 1,106 | 325 | 1,123 |
| Qingyuan County | 916 | 959 | 135 | 131 | 249 | 285 | 531 |
| Xinfeng County | 195 | 202 | 24 | 140 | 300 | 50 | 431 |
| Zengcheng County | 587 | 619 | 86 | 100 | 246 | 187 | 586 |

Table A.5.  (continued)

| | Population | | Non-agricultural population | Industrial output[a] | | Agricultural output | Average per capita income[b] |
|---|---|---|---|---|---|---|---|
| | 1983 | 1986 | 1986 | 1983 | 1986 | 1986 | 1985 |
| **Hainan Administrative Region** | | | | | | | |
| Chengmai County | 385 | 402 | 59 | 28 | 61 | 92 | 469 |
| Dan County | 622 | 648 | 127 | 37 | 69 | 161 | 626 |
| Dingan County | 254 | 265 | 38 | 28 | 39 | 63 | 442 |
| Haikou City | 269 | 300 | 218 | 233 | 398 | 24 | 1,338 |
| Lingao County | 321 | 333 | 48 | 26 | 41 | 79 | 423 |
| Qionghai County | 384 | 392 | 50 | 38 | 100 | 157 | 668 |
| Qiongshan County | 515 | 522 | 80 | 48 | 97 | 143 | 458 |
| Tunchang County | 214 | 222 | 36 | 16 | 23 | 49 | 502 |
| Wanning County | 422 | 448 | 53 | 18 | 41 | 118 | 472 |
| Wenchang County | 479 | 485 | 67 | 33 | 83 | 140 | 584 |
| *Hainan Autonomous Region* | | | | | | | |
| Baisha County | 145 | 150 | 20 | 10 | 34 | 33 | 820 |
| Baoting County | 204 | 218 | 54 | 19 | 10 | 30 | 617 |
| Changjiang County | 175 | 189 | 55 | 128 | 175 | 47 | 1,197 |
| Dongfang County | 275 | 288 | 54 | 18 | 34 | 73 | 515 |
| Ledong County | 387 | 405 | 55 | 39 | 62 | 98 | 510 |
| Lingshui County | 255 | 267 | 38 | 9 | 19 | 61 | 423 |
| Qiongzhong County | 192 | 197 | 36 | 16 | 20 | 36 | 634 |
| Sanya City | 308 | 324 | 75 | 20 | 51 | 64 | 594 |

| | | | | | | | |
|---|---|---|---|---|---|---|---|
| **Huiyang Prefecture** | | | | | | | |
| Boluo County | 637 | 656 | 89 | 83 | 156 | 198 | 494 |
| Dongguan County | 1,176 | 1,230 | 265 | 589 | 1,962 | 650 | 1,482 |
| Haifeng County | 801 | 865 | 190 | 57 | 141 | 224 | 486 |
| Heping County | 387 | 312 | 39 | 29 | 45 | 66 | 299 |
| Heyuan County | 564 | 583 | 92 | 136 | 104 | 123 | 460 |
| Huidong County | 526 | 550 | 107 | 40 | 114 | 134 | 502 |
| Huiyang County | 170 | 188 | 122 | 194 | 113 | 149 | 827 |
| Huizhou City | 434 | 455 | 65 | 40 | 257 | 23 | 618 |
| Lianping County | 298 | 312 | 39 | 17 | 38 | 59 | 281 |
| Longchuan County | 685 | 716 | 74 | 83 | 73 | 120 | 297 |
| Lufeng County | 1,096 | 1,170 | 198 | 135 | 224 | 215 | 279 |
| Zijin County | 580 | 600 | 57 | 33 | 68 | 131 | 328 |
| **Jiangmen Metropolitan Region** | | | | | | | |
| Enping County | 381 | 392 | 81 | 122 | 281 | 167 | 851 |
| Heshan County | 313 | 319 | 54 | 124 | 289 | 106 | 743 |
| Jiangmen City | 219 | 240 | 177 | 877 | 1,338 | 26 | 2,595 |
| Kaiping County | 592 | 607 | 117 | 230 | 532 | 203 | 883 |
| Taishan County | 945 | 951 | 148 | 293 | 893 | 300 | 790 |
| Xinhui County | 818 | 837 | 195 | 542 | 1,440 | 305 | 913 |
| Yangchun County | 836 | 868 | 109 | 159 | 266 | 241 | 398 |
| Yangjiang County | 1,171 | 1,213 | 227 | 194 | 461 | 426 | 508 |
| **Maoming Metropolitan Region** | | | | | | | |
| Dianbai County | 1,118 | 1,166 | 118 | 74 | 287 | 253 | 400 |
| Gaozhou County | 1,120 | 1,160 | 98 | 121 | 245 | 362 | 422 |
| Huazhou County | 946 | 991 | 95 | 72 | 178 | 321 | 465 |
| Maoming City | 418 | 450 | 140 | 1,404 | 1,864 | 87 | 2,187 |
| Xinyi County | 868 | 883 | 67 | 67 | 153 | 229 | 382 |

Table A.5. (continued)

| | Population | | Non-agricultural population | Industrial output[a] | | Agricultural output | Average per capita income[b] |
|---|---|---|---|---|---|---|---|
| | 1983 | 1986 | 1986 | 1983 | 1986 | 1986 | 1985 |
| **Meixian Prefecture** | | | | | | | |
| Dapu County | 447 | 458 | 55 | 40 | 79 | 69 | 310 |
| Fengshun County | 521 | 542 | 56 | 31 | 74 | 100 | 349 |
| Jiaoling County | 199 | 203 | 34 | 38 | 591 | 496 | 509 |
| Meixian City | 722 | 745 | 174 | 233 | 445 | 159 | 588 |
| Pingyuan County | 214 | 220 | 29 | 30 | 578 | 100 | 482 |
| Wuhua County | 878 | 918 | 87 | 43 | 85 | 156 | 280 |
| Xingning County | 925 | 954 | 127 | 178 | 297 | 168 | 401 |
| **Shantou Metropolitan Region** | | | | | | | |
| Chaoyang County | 1,723 | 1,802 | 196 | 218 | 488 | 319 | 331 |
| Chaozhou City | 1,186 | 1,227 | 270 | 457 | 1,045 | 286 | 609 |
| Chenghai County | 655 | 679 | 118 | 134 | 293 | 175 | 489 |
| Huilai County | 705 | 734 | 106 | 58 | 107 | 169 | 340 |
| Jiexi County | 621 | 645 | 92 | 90 | 167 | 152 | 369 |
| Jieyang County | 1,298 | 1,333 | 149 | 218 | 574 | 281 | 453 |
| Nanao County | 60 | 62 | 16 | 8 | 17 | 16 | 486 |
| Puning County | 1,212 | 1,264 | 94 | 75 | 288 | 189 | 341 |
| Raoping County | 760 | 787 | 131 | 84 | 210 | 162 | 366 |
| Shantou City | 733 | 774 | 500 | 846 | 1,649 | 60 | 973 |

| | | | | | | | |
|---|---|---|---|---|---|---|---|
| **Shaoguan Metropolitan Region** | | | | | | | |
| Lechang County | 415 | 444 | 146 | 197 | 241 | 122 | 656 |
| Lian County | 433 | 449 | 80 | 74 | 113 | 134 | 475 |
| Liannan Auton. County | 130 | 133 | 20 | 178 | 26 | 35 | 431 |
| Lianshan Auton. County | 91 | 95 | 16 | 141 | 67 | 138 | 652 |
| Nanxiong County | 400 | 411 | 64 | 56 | 115 | 150 | 569 |
| Qujiang County | 334 | 343 | 64 | 48 | 107 | 108 | 571 |
| Renhua County | 150 | 160 | 51 | 40 | 59 | 54 | 734 |
| Ruyuan Auton. County | 168 | 175 | 28 | 44 | 43 | 47 | 536 |
| Shixing County | 205 | 212 | 31 | 45 | 51 | 66 | 524 |
| Wengyuan County | 303 | 317 | 42 | 36 | 88 | 117 | 613 |
| Yangshan County | 414 | 432 | 38 | 51 | 67 | 138 | 481 |
| Yingde County | 836 | 865 | 128 | 189 | 242 | 293 | 616 |
| **Shenzhen Metropolitan Region** | | | | | | | |
| Baoan County | 228 | 257 | 49 | 89 | 552 | 139 | 1,600 |
| Shenzhen SEZ | 177 | 257 | 216 | 631 | 3,108 | 153 | 5,188 |
| **Zhanjiang Metropolitan Region** | | | | | | | |
| Haikang County | 969 | 1,017 | 116 | 86 | 178 | 331 | 503 |
| Lianjiang County | 1,023 | 1,064 | 124 | 130 | 356 | 300 | 464 |
| Suixi County | 639 | 665 | 67 | 112 | 232 | 259 | 577 |
| Wuchuan County | 634 | 670 | 99 | 81 | 267 | 116 | 386 |
| Xuwen County | 483 | 505 | 71 | 109 | 156 | 146 | 522 |
| Zhanjiang City | 878 | 947 | 352 | 509 | 1,041 | 151 | 871 |

Table A.5. *(continued)*

| | Population | | Non-agricultural population | Industrial output[a] | | Agricultural output | Average per capita income[b] |
|---|---|---|---|---|---|---|---|
| | 1983 | 1986 | 1986 | 1983 | 1986 | 1986 | 1985 |
| **Zhaoqing Metropolitan Region** | | | | | | | |
| Deqing County | 301 | 308 | 38 | 56 | 101 | 144 | 561 |
| Fengkai County | 363 | 374 | 43 | 54 | 133 | 136 | 557 |
| Gaoyao County | 713 | 734 | 90 | 128 | 362 | 508 | 866 |
| Guangning County | 454 | 469 | 49 | 60 | 129 | 143 | 425 |
| Huaiji County | 634 | 655 | 51 | 61 | 110 | 205 | 349 |
| Luoding County | 789 | 805 | 66 | 148 | 340 | 291 | 501 |
| Sihui County | 348 | 357 | 72 | 134 | 326 | 149 | 825 |
| Xinxing County | 364 | 373 | 39 | 55 | 129 | 186 | 580 |
| Yunan County | 393 | 408 | 54 | 79 | 191 | 138 | 517 |
| Yunfu County | 437 | 459 | 62 | 50 | 181 | 169 | 664 |
| Zhaoqing City | 171 | 194 | 152 | 230 | 424 | 18 | 1,278 |
| **Zhuhai Metropolitan Region** | | | | | | | |
| Doumen County | 247 | 260 | 50 | 155 | 282 | 159 | 1,138 |
| Zhuhai SEZ | 139 | 165 | 100 | 129 | 431 | 69 | 2,751 |

*Source: Guangdongsheng tongji nianjian* (Guangdong Province statistical yearbook) (Guangzhou: Zhongguo Tongji Chubanshe), 1985, pp. 376–380, 381–385; 1986, pp. 438–442; 1987, pp. 473–477, 478–482.

a. In that year's prices.

b. Calculated by province; based on total value of production divided by population.

Table A.6. Guangdong's export and import performance (in millions of yuan and U.S. dollars)

| | 1978 | 1980 | 1982 | 1983 | 1984 | 1985 | 1986 | 1987 |
|---|---|---|---|---|---|---|---|---|
| Export procurement | ¥2,833 | ¥4,375 | ¥5,322 | ¥5,260 | ¥5,107 | ¥6,527 | ¥13,477 | ¥17,942 |
| Gross value of industrial and agricultural output (GVIAO) | ¥31,900 | ¥36,539 | ¥41,499 | ¥45,506 | ¥57,031 | ¥69,449 | ¥78,686 | ¥100,140 |
| Export procurement as a percentage of GVIAO | 8.9% | 12.0% | 12.8% | 11.6% | 8.9% | 9.5% | 17.1% | 17.9% |
| Exports from Guangdong ports | $1,397 | $2,233 | $2,274 | $2,399 | $2,515 | $3,035 | $4,290 | $5,560 |
| Imports by Guangdong foreign trade enterprises | $204 | $314 | N.A. | $937 | $1,210 | $2,812 | $2,625 | $3,693 |

*Source: Guangdongsheng tongji nianjian* (Guangdong Province statistical yearbook) (Guangzhou: Zhongguo Tongji Chubanshe), various years.
*Note:* N.A. = not available. All renminbi values are at 1980 constant prices. Exports are on an FOB Guangdong Port basis; imports are on a CIF Guangdong Port basis. Import data include purchases financed with central foreign exchange and local foreign exchange. Exports and imports include transactions by state-owned enterprises as well as by joint ventures. Exports and imports for 1987 include Hainan.

*Appendix*

Table A.7.   Guangdong's intake of foreign funds (in millions of U.S. dollars)

|  | 1980 | 1983 | 1984 | 1985 | 1986 | 1987 |
|---|---|---|---|---|---|---|
| Number of contracts | 5,082 | 11,365 | 17,594 | 13,896 | 9,444 | 7,024 |
| Value of contracts signed | $1,385 | $736 | $1,590 | $2,619 | $1,843 | $2,031 |
| Foreign funds actually used | $209 | $410 | $654 | $921 | $1,459 | $1,226 |
| Loans from foreign banks included in previous category | 0 | 0 | $4 | $268 | $664 | $395 |

*Source: Guangdongsheng tongji nianjian* (Guangdong Province statistical yearbook) (Guangzhou: Zhongguo Tongji Chubanshe), various years.

*Note:* Figures are for all forms of foreign investment: processing, compensation trade, cooperative production, joint-equity ventures, wholly foreign-owned ventures, and bank loans.

# Notes

## Introduction

1. Data from *Nanfang ribao* (Southern daily) (Guangzhou), August 1, 1988.

## 1. The Cultural Revolution

1. The most comprehensive account of the Cultural Revolution in Guangdong, focusing on the mass movement, is Stanley Rosen's *Red Guard Factionalism and the Cultural Revolution in Guangzhou (Canton)* (Boulder: Westview, 1982). A good general account of the Cultural Revolution by a young Guangdong intellectual is Liu Guokai, "A Brief Analysis of the Cultural Revolution," in *Chinese Sociology and Anthropology: A Journal of Translations,* ed. Anita Chan (Winter 1986–87). For personal accounts by participants, see Gordon A. Bennett and Ronald N. Montaperto, *Red Guard* (New York: Doubleday, 1971), and Ruth Earnshaw Lo and Katharine S. Kinderman, *In the Eye of the Typhoon* (New York: Harcourt Brace Jovanovich, 1980). For an account of the strategies of political and military groups in the early years, see my *Canton under Communism: Programs and Politics in a Provincial Capital, 1949–1968* (Cambridge, Mass.: Harvard University Press, 1969), pp. 321–349.

2. Anne F. Thurston, *Enemies of the People: The Ordeal of the Intellectuals in China's Great Cultural Revolution* (New York: Knopf, 1987), pp. 214–215, 148–149.

3. Rosen, *Red Guard Factionalism,* pp. 147–161.

4. Thurston, *Enemies of the People,* p. 133.

5. *Zhengming* (Contending) (Hong Kong), March 1979, p. 48.

6. See Jonathan Unger, "China's Troubled Down-to-the-Countryside Campaign," *Contemporary China* (1979): 79–82.

7. See Stanley Rosen, ed., "The Rehabilitation and Dissolution of 'Li Yizhe,'" *Chinese Law and Government* 14, no. 2 (Summer 1981). See also Anita Chan, Stanley Rosen, and Jonathan Unger, eds., *On Socialist Democracy and the Chinese Legal System: The Li Yizhe Debates* (Armonk, N.Y.: M. E. Sharpe, 1985).

8. Lu Xinhua et al., *The Wounded: New Stories of the Cultural Revolution, 1977–1978,* trans. Geremie Barmé and Bennett Lee (Hong Kong: Joint Publishing Co., 1979). Richard King, "'Wounds' and 'Exposure': Chinese Literature after the Gang of Four," *Pacific Affairs* (Spring 1981): 82–99. For an account of the role of fiction in Guangdong at the time, see Perry Link, "Fiction and the Reading Public in Guangzhou and Other Chinese Cities, 1979–1980," in *After Mao: Chinese Literature and Society, 1978–1981,* ed. Jeffrey C. Kinkley (Cambridge, Mass.: Council on East Asian Studies, Harvard University, 1985).

9. *Guangdongsheng tongji nianjian* (Guangdong Province statistical yearbook) (Guangzhou: Zhongguo Tongji Chubanshe, 1984), pp. 52, 264.

10. See Barry Naughton, "The Third Front," *China Quarterly* (September 1988): 351–386.

## 2. Hong Kong

1. An account of Hong Kong's hinterland is that of Gregory Eliyu Guldin, "The Invisible Hinterland: Hong Kong's Reliance on Southern Guangdong Province," typescript, 1987.

2. Perry Link, "Fiction and the Reading Public in Guangzhou and Other Chinese Cities, 1979–1980," in *After Mao: Chinese Literature and Society, 1978–1981,* ed. Jeffrey C. Kinkley (Cambridge, Mass.: Council on East Asian Studies, Harvard University, 1985).

3. Data from U.S. Consulate, Hong Kong. In the tables, as in the rest of the text, all data without specific citation are from internal statistics and interviews. Basic data on Guangdong, all from published sources, may be found in the Appendix.

4. An account of the negotiations leading to the Joint Declaration is Frank Ching, *Hong Kong and China* (New York: Foreign Policy Association, 1985).

## 3. A Decade of Reforms

1. *Zhengming* (Contending) (Hong Kong), August 1981, pp. 56–59.

2. *Zhengming,* February 1981, pp. 10–12.

3. For major statements on these four principles in Guangdong see *Nanfang ribao* (Southern daily) (Guangzhou), April 4, 1981, trans. Foreign Broadcast Information Service (hereafter FBIS) (Washington, D.C.), April 13, 1981, pp. 1–4. *Nanfang ribao,* May 15, 1981, in FBIS, June 1, 1981, pp. 1–5.

4. See Melinda Liu, "The Role of the Overseas Chinese in the Four Modernizations," in *Doing Business in China* (Hong Kong: American Chamber of Commerce in Hong Kong, 1980).

5. An account of his earlier career is found in David M. Lampton, *Paths to Power* (Ann Arbor: Center for Chinese Studies, University of Michigan, 1986), pp. 107–148.

6. *Zhonggong Guangdongsheng guanyu fahui youyue tiaojian, kuoda duiwai maoyi, jiakuai jingji fazhan de baogao* (The Communist Party, Guangdong Province, announcement on giving full play to favorable conditions, expanding foreign

trade, and accelerating economic development) (Guangdong: Provincial Party Committee, 1979).

7. Ibid.

8. See Donald W. Klein and Anne B. Clark, *Biographic Dictionary of Chinese Communism, 1921–1965*, 2 vols. (Cambridge, Mass.: Harvard University Press, 1971), s.v. Hsi Chung-hsun (Xi Zhongxun) and Yang Shang-k'un.

9. For a description of this period, see my *Canton under Communism: Programs and Politics in a Provincial Capital, 1949–1968* (Cambridge, Mass.: Harvard University Press, 1969).

10. *Zhengming*, December 1980, pp. 48–49.

11. Ibid. See Chapter 10 for a fuller description of Ren Zhongyi.

12. See, for example, *Nanfang ribao*, January 22, 1981, in FBIS, February 12, 1981, pp. 2–4.

13. See, for example, *Nanfang ribao*, August 21, 1981, in FBIS, September 1, 1981, pp. 1–3; Guangzhou Radio, March 26, 1981, in FBIS, March 27, 1981, p. 1.

14. For an account of the method of determining revenues elsewhere, see Michel Oksenberg and James Tong, "The Evolution of Central-Provincial Fiscal Relations in China, 1950–1983: The Formal System," typescript, February 1987.

15. *Guangdongsheng tongji nianjian* (Guangdong Province statistical yearbook) (Guangzhou: Zhongguo Tongji Chubanshe, 1984), p. 107.

16. Ibid.

17. Ibid. Dazhai was a "model" production brigade singled out by Mao for its successes (later exposed as fraudulent) in boosting grain production despite its poor soil and climate.

18. Ibid., p. 114.

19. John P. Burns, "Rural Guangdong's 'Second Economy,' 1962–1974," *China Quarterly*, no. 88 (December 1981): 629–644. For a chronology of the reforms emanating from Beijing, see Gao Shangchuan, *Jiunianlai de Zhongguo jingji tizhi gaige* (Nine years of Chinese economic system reform) (Beijing: Renmin Chubanshe, 1987), and *Zhongguo jingji tizhi gaige jishu* (A collection on Chinese economic system reform) (Beijing: Chunqiu Chubanshe, 1987).

20. Burns, "Rural Guangdong's 'Second Economy.'"

21. Ibid.

22. Calculated on the basis of data in *Guangdongsheng tongji nianjian*, 1984, p. 107.

23. See, for example, Radio Guangzhou, January 21, 1979, in FBIS, January 24, 1979.

24. Shengfu Zijinxian Diaochazu, "Sheng Diaochazu Huibao Cailiao" (Reference materials from the report of a provincial investigation group) (Zijinxian), June 28, 1980 (document for internal circulation); Du Ruizhi, "Guangdongsheng Nongye Weiyuanhui" (Guangdong Province agricultural commission) (Guangzhou), July 15, 1980 (document for internal circulation).

25. "Zhonggong zhongyang guanyu jiakuai nongye fazhan ruogan wenti" (The Central Committee of the Communist Party on some problems of accelerating agricultural development) in *Jingji tizhi gaige shouce* (Economic system reform handbook), ed. Wang Jiye and Zhu Yuanzhen (Beijing: Jingji Ribao,

1987), p. 65. For a general account of the spread of the household responsibility system nationally, see David Zweig, "Household Contracts and Decollectivization, 1977–1983," in *Policy Implementation in Post-Mao China,* ed. David M. Lampton (Berkeley: University of California Press, 1987), and Kathleen Hartford, "Socialist Agriculture Is Dead: Long Live Socialist Agriculture," in *The Political Economy of Reform in Post-Mao China,* ed. Elizabeth Perry and Christine Wong (Cambridge, Mass.: Council on East Asian Studies, Harvard University, 1985). Rural cadres in Guangdong did not draw a sharp line between passing down some responsibilities *(baochan daohu)* and all responsibilities *(baogan daohu).*

26. Zhonggong zhongyang yinfa, "Guan jinyibu jiaqiang he wanshan nongye shengchan zerenzhi de jige wenti de tongzhi" (An announcement on some problems of further strengthening and perfecting the agriculture production responsibility system), in *Jingji tizhi gaige shouce,* p. 75.

27. Graham E. Johnson, "The Production Responsibility System in Chinese Agriculture: Some Examples from Guangdong," *Pacific Affairs* (Fall 1982): 430–451.

28. *Guangdongsheng tongji nianjian,* 1984, p. 320.

29. *Guangdong jingji tizhi gaige yanjiu* (Research on Guangdong's economic system reform) (Guangzhou: Zhongshan Daxue Chubanshe, 1985), p. 127.

30. See, for example, *Guangjiaojing* (Wide-angle lens) (Hong Kong), November 1984, pp. 27–33.

31. *Guangdongsheng tongji nianjian,* 1984, p. 87.

32. See B. Michael Frolic, "Flying Kites on White Cloud Mountain," in idem, *Mao's People: Sixteen Portraits of Life in Revolutionary China* (Cambridge, Mass.: Harvard University Press, 1980), pp. 257–265.

33. *Guangdong jingji tizhi gaige yanjiu,* p. 129.

34. William A. Byrd and Lin Qingsong, eds., *China's Rural Industry: Structure, Development, and Reform* (Washington, D.C.: World Bank, in press). See also Jean Oi, "Commercializing China's Rural Cadres," *Problems of Communism* 35 (October 1986): 1–15.

35. Ibid., p. 87. See also *Guangdongsheng tongji nianjian,* 1986, p. 133.

36. *Renmin ribao* (People's daily) (Beijing), December 8, 1979, in FBIS, October 18, 1979.

37. Ibid., and Radio Guangzhou, June 21, 1980, in FBIS, June 17, 1980.

38. Qingyuanxian Jingji Weiyuanhui Bangongshi, ed., *Guangdong Qingyuanxian gongye guanli tizhi gaige* (Qingyuan County of Guangdong Province on economic system reform of industrial management), mimeo, July 1981. Zeng Muye, "Zi yige xian de fanweinei shixing jingji tizhi gaige de jingyan" (The experience of a county in carrying out economic system reform), in *Guangdong jingji tizhi gaige yanjiu,* pp. 141–162.

39. Janos Kornai, "The Hungarian Reform Process: Visions, Hopes, and Reality," *Journal of Economic Literature* (December 1986): 1687–1737. For Kornai's impressions of Chinese reforms, see J. Kornai and Z. Daniel, "The Chinese Economic Reform—As Seen by Hungarian Economists," *Acta Oeconomica* 36 (1986): 289–305.

40. For a fuller discussion of wage reforms at the national level, see Andrew G. Walder, "Wage Reforms and the Web of Factory Interests," *China Quarterly,*

no. 109 (March 1987): 22–41. See also Andrew G. Walder, *Communist Neo-Traditionalism: Work and Authority in Chinese Industry* (Berkeley: University of California Press, 1986) and idem, "Factory and Manager in an Era of Reform," *China Quarterly* (in press).

41. *Guangdong jingji tizhi gaige yanjiu,* p. 125.

42. Guangzhou Radio, November 12, 1980, in FBIS, November 5, 1980.

43. *Guangdong jingji tizhi gaige yanjiu,* p. 120.

44. Ibid., p. 125.

45. Ibid.

46. See, for example, FBIS, March 3, 1982, p. 2.

## 4. Special Economic Zones

1. *Zhengming* (Contending) (Hong Kong), April 1985, p. 27.

2. Two studies of rural villages are Anita Chan, Richard Madsen, and Jonathan Unger, *Chen Village: A Recent History of a Peasant Community in Mao's China* (Berkeley: University of California Press, 1984), and Richard Madsen, *Morality and Power in a Chinese Village* (Berkeley: University of California Press, 1984).

3. *Shenzhen jingji tequ zuzhi renshi zhidu gaige shixian yu tansuo* (An exploration of the system reform of the administrative personnel system in Shenzhen special economic zone) (Shenzhen: Haitian Chubanshe, 1986), p. 45.

4. *Shenzhen tequ jingji de diaocha yu yanjiu* (An investigation and study of the economy of Shenzhen's special economic zone) (Beijing: Qiushi Chubanshe, 1987), p. 3.

5. See, for example, *Zhengming,* April 1985, pp. 16–27.

6. A summary of reforms by the head of the Municipal Policy Research Office is *Shenzhen tequ jingji de diaocha yu yanjiu,* p. 109.

7. *Zhuhai jingji nianjian* (Zhuhai economic yearbook), 1979–1986 (Guangzhou: Guangdong Renmin Chubanshe, 1986); *Zhuhai tequ shouce* (Handbook of the Zhuhai special economic zone) (Zhuhai: Xinhua Chubanshe, 1985).

8. R. D. Cremer, ed., *Macau: City of Commerce and Culture* (Hong Kong: UEA Press, 1987).

## 5. The Inner Delta Counties

1. *Zhujiang sanjiaozhou jingji kaifangqu touzi zhinan* (An investment guide to the Pearl River Delta economic development zone) (Hong Kong: Xinhuashe, 1986).

2. For studies of a Delta village at the time of Communist victory, see C. K. Yang, *Chinese Communist Society: The Family and the Village* (Cambridge, Mass.: Massachusetts Institute of Technology Press, 1959). For studies of pre-1949 Guangdong society, based heavily on the Delta area, see Maurice Freedman, *Chinese Lineage and Society: Fukien [Fujian] and Kwangtung [Guangdong]* (London: Athlone Press, 1966); Maurice Freedman, *Lineage Organization in South-eastern China* (London: Athlone Press, 1958).

3. *Zhujiang sanjiaozhou jingji kaifangqu touzi zhinan.*

4. Calculated on basis of data in *Guangdongsheng tongji nianjian* (Guangdong Province statistical yearbook) (Guangzhou: Zhongguo Tongji Chubanshe, 1986), pp. 433–437.

5. *Zhujiang sanjiaozhou jingji kaifangqu touzi zhinan,* p. 32.

6. Ibid., p. 15.

7. Ibid., p. 32.

8. Two important national studies of township and village enterprises, containing a wealth of statistical data, are: William A. Byrd and Lin Qingsong, eds., *China's Rural Industry: Structure, Development, and Reform* (Washington, D.C.: World Bank, in press), and Yok Shiu Lee, "Rural Nonfarm Activities in China: Growth and Effects of Township Enterprises, 1978–1987" (Ph.D. diss., Massachusetts Institute of Technology, 1988). Byrd and Lin include Nanhai County as one of their four fieldwork sites. Lee did extensive fieldwork in Taishan County in addition to collecting national data. One important community study of Xinhui County includes information on township and village enterprises: Helen Siu, *Agents and Victims: Accomplices in Rural Revolution in South China* (New Haven: Yale University Press, forthcoming).

9. Byrd and Lin, *China's Rural Industry.*

10. Ibid.

11. *Guangdongsheng tongji nianjian,* 1987, p. 482.

12. *About Foshan* (Beijing: Hongqi Chubanshe, 1985). Other basic information is contained in *Zhujiang sanjiaozhou jingji kaifangqu touzi zhinan.*

13. *Guangdongsheng tongji nianjian,* 1986, p. 438.

14. A broad-gauged history of Xinhui County is found in Siu, *Agents and Victims.*

## 6. Guangzhou

1. Guan Qixue and Liu Guangpu, eds., *Lun jingji zhongxin: Guangzhou* (A discussion of the economic center: Guangzhou) (Guangzhou: Guangdong Gaodeng Jiaoyu Chubanshe, 1987), p. 132. An excellent basic statistical source on Guangzhou is *Guangzhou nianjian* (Guangzhou yearbook) published in Guangzhou beginning in 1985 by Guangdong Renmin Chubanshe; in 1983 and 1984 its predecessor was published as *Guangzhou jingi nianjian* (Guangzhou economic yearbook). A bimonthly journal of research and theory about Guangzhou is *Guangzhou yanjiu* (Guangzhou research), published by the Guangzhou branch of the Chinese Academy of Social Sciences. In 1988, a new annual, *Guangzhou tongji nianjian* (Guangzhou statistical yearbook), was begun.

2. *Guangzhou jingji shehui fazhan zhanlue* (A development strategy for Guangzhou's economy and society) (Guangzhou: Kexue Puji Chubanshe, Guangzhou Fenshe, 1986), p. 352.

3. Ibid., p. 112.

4. Ibid., p. 113.

5. Ibid., p. 370.

6. Ibid., p. 365.

7. Guan Qixue and Li Guangpu, eds. *Lun jingji zhongxin,* p. 124.

8. *Guangdongsheng tongji nianjian* (Guangdong statistical yearbook) (Guangzhou: Zhongguo Tongji Chubanshe, 1986), pp. 438f.

9. Yu Xiuqiang and Li Ya, "Wailai laodong yu chengshi fazhan chutan" (A preliminary study of temporary migration and Guangzhou development), Zhongshan University and Hong Kong University Geography Department's International Conference on the Pearl River Delta, Guangzhou, August 1988.

## 7. Prefectural Capitals

1. *Guangdongsheng tongji nianjian* (Guangdong statistical yearbook) Guangzhou: Zhongguo Tongji Chubanshe, 1987), p. 198.

2. Ibid., 1987, p. 197.

3. Ibid.

4. Ibid., 1984, p. 324; 1987, p. 424.

5. Ibid., 1987, pp. 406, 432.

6. For a stimulating discussion of Chinese urban centers and their role in the urban network, see the work of G. William Skinner, ed., *The City in Late Imperial China* (Stanford: Stanford University Press, 1977). A regional economic geography that describes Guangdong in that frame of reference is the work by Robert Silin and Edward Winckler, *China: Provincial Economic Briefing Series,* vol. 5, *South/Southeast China* (Hong Kong: BA Asia, 1982).

7. *Guangdongsheng tongji nianjian,* 1987, p. 78.

8. See, for example, Graham Peck, *Two Kinds of Time* (Boston: Houghton Mifflin, 1950).

9. *Guangdongsheng disanci renkou pucha baogaoshu* (Guangdong Province report of the third census) (Guangzhou: Guangdong Renkou Pucha Bangongshi, 1986), pp. 127–128. For a description of the Yao and Zhuang minorities in Shaoguan Municipal Region, see *Liannan Yaozu Zizhixian gaikuang* (An overview of the Liannan Yao Autonomous County) (Beijing: Minzu Chubanshe, 1985); *Lianshan Zhuangzu Yaozu Zizhixian gaikuang* (An overview of the Lianshan Zhuang-Yao Autonomous County) (Beijing: Minzu Chubanshe, 1986); and *Ruyuan Yaozu Zizhixian gaikuang* (An overview of Ruyuan Yao Autonomous County) (Guangzhou: Guangdong Renmin Chubanshe, 1985).

10. *Guangdongsheng tongji nianjian,* 1987, pp. 474–475.

11. See Barry Naughton, "The Third Front," *China Quarterly,* no. 115 (September 1988): 351–386.

12. One of the few prefectural yearbooks in Guangdong, pulling together a great deal of historical as well as factual material, is *Shaoguan nianjian* (Shaoguan yearbook) (Shaoguan, Guangdong: Shaoguan Nianjian Bianjibu, 1986).

13. Calculated on the basis of data in *Guangdongsheng tongji nianjian,* 1986, p. 195.

14. *Guangdongsheng shidixian gaikuang* (An overview of Guangdong Province's cities, prefectures, and counties) (Guangzhou: Guangdongsheng Ditu Chubanshe, 1985), p. 255.

15. *Guangdongsheng tongji nianjian,* 1987, pp. 77–78.

16. Zhanjiang Harbor Bureau, *Zhanjiang gang* (Zhanjiang Port), pamphlet for internal circulation, Zhanjiang, 1986.

17. For more information on the role of Nanhai West, see Kenneth Lieberthal and Michel Oksenberg, *Policy Making in China: Leaders, Structures, and Processes* (Princeton: Princeton University Press, 1988).

18. *Guangdongsheng tongji nianjian,* 1986, p. 441.

19. Brief history and data can be found in *Meixian gaikuang* (An overview of Meixian), ed. Meixianshi Difangzhi Bianxuan Weiyuanhui, pamphlet for internal circulation, Meixian, 1987.

## 8. The Mountain Counties

1. *Guangdongsheng tongji nianjian* (Guangdong Province statistical yearbook) (Guangzhou: Zhongguo Tongji Chubanshe, 1987), p. 50.

2. Ibid.

3. Ibid.

4. *Guangdongsheng disanci renkou pucha baogaoshu* (Guangdong Province report of the third census) (Guangzhou: Guangdongsheng Renkou Pucha Bangongshi, 1986), pp. 127–136.

5. Zeng Guangxian, "Guangdongsheng jingji gaige jiunian huigu" (A review of nine years of economic reform in Guangdong Province), *Gaige* (Reform) (Beijing), no. 2 (1988): 119.

6. *Guangdongsheng tongji nianjian,* 1987, pp. 441–442; *Zhongguo renkou: Guangdong Fence* (China's population: Guangdong) (Beijing: Zhongguo Caizheng Jingji Chubanshe, 1988), p. 387.

7. Ibid., 1985, p. 93; 1987, p. 106.

8. The estimate of over ten thousand per county is from mountain county officials. The estimate of one out of ten is derived from the fact that a typical county had six hundred thousand people, and the average household had slightly more than five members. In the 1982 census, 61 percent of Guangdong mountain households had five or more members, compared to 54 percent of plains dwellers and 40 percent of city families. See *Guangdongsheng disanci renkou pucha baogao,* p. 78.

9. See, for example, *Zhengming* (Contending) (Hong Kong), January 1985, pp. 22–24; May 1985, pp. 14–16.

10. *Guangdongsheng tongji nianjian,* 1986, pp. 64, 68, and Provincial Statistical Bureau data.

11. These issues are explored more fully in *China's Rural Industry: Structure, Development, and Reform,* ed. William A. Byrd and Lin Qingsong (Washington, D.C.: World Bank, in press).

## 9. Hainan Island

1. Basic geographical information is contained in Catherine Schurr Enderton, "Hainan Dao: Contemporary Environmental Management and Development of China's Treasure Island" (Ph.D. diss., University of California at Los Angeles, 1984). Since there is little historical information on Hainan in English, I have included more historical background here than for other parts of Guangdong.

2. For an account of Hainan's Li and Miao minorities, see *Hainan Lizu*

*Miaozu Zizhizhou gaikuang* (An overview of the Hainan Li-Miao Autonomous Region) (Guangzhou: Guangdong Renmin Chubanshe, 1986).

3. See, for example, the central government directive on Hainan development, "Jiakuai Hainandao kaifa jianshe wenti taolun jiyao" (Minutes of the discussion on problems of accelerating Hainan Island's development), *Zhongfa*, no. 11, March 12, 1983, p. 34.

4. In addition to interviews, the above account draws on several written accounts. Deng Jiaying and Zhang Shengyou, "Mingyun kuangxiangqu" (A rhapsody of fate), in *Zhongguo zuojia shuangyuekan* (Chinese writers' bimonthly) (Beijing), no. 5, 1986, pp. 124–153; Li Yu, "Shijie diyi shangpin" (The world's number one commodity), *Dangdai shuangyuekan* (Contemporary era bimonthly) (Beijing), no. 5, 1986, pp. 194–203; and *Zhengming* (Contending) (Hong Kong), 1984–85, passim. A good English summary of the basic facts of the incident is José Santiago L. Sta Romana, "Hainan and China's Opening to the World: A Case Study of Hainan Island, 1979–1985" (M.A. thesis, Tufts University, Fletcher School of Law and Diplomacy, 1987).

5. See *Guangjiaojing* (Wide-angle lens) (Hong Kong), March 1986, pp. 18–19.

6. *Hainandao de touzi huanjing* (The investment climate of Hainan Island) (Haikou: Zhongguo Duiwai Jingji Maoyi Zixun Gongsi et al., December 1987), p. 44.

7. *South China Morning Post* (Hong Kong), June 1, 1987.

8. *Guanyu jianshe Sanya guoji luxingcheng de zongti gouxiang he kexingxing yanjiu baogao* (A research report on the overall concept and feasibility of developing Sanya into an international tourist city) (Beijing: Shoudu Qingnian Zhishi Fenzi Zhiyan Hainan Jianshe Lianhehui, May 1986).

9. The basic plan, with detailed background statistical information on development, is contained in *Hainandao de touzi huanjing*. A brief introduction to facilities in the new province, in English as well as Chinese, is: Haikou Provincial Preparatory Group, *Hainan Province: A Glittering Pearl on the South China Sea* (Haikou: Haikou Provincial Preparatory Group, 1986).

10. This report is presented in Nipponkoku Kokusai Kyooryoku Jigyoodan, *Chuuka Jinmin Kyoowakoku, Hainantoo: Soogoo kaihatsu keikaku choosa* (Hainan Island, People's Republic of China: Research report on an overall development plan), 11 vols. (Tokyo, May 1988).

11. Hainan Province Planning Department, ed., *Hainansheng touzi zhinan* (Investment guide to Hainan Province) (Haikou: Hainan Renmin Chubanshe, 1988).

## 10. Entrepreneurs

1. For a study of this group, see John Israel and Donald W. Klein, *Rebels and Bureaucrats: China's December 9ers* (Berkeley: University of California Press, 1976).

2. Some of the basic information about Li and his company are contained in *Lu: Guangdong Zhanjiang Jiaodian Gongsi baogao wenxueji* (The path: Zhanjiang Guangdong Home Appliances Industrial Company reportorial literature), Decem-

ber 1986; *Gongye jingji guanli* (Industrial economics management), Zhongguo Shehui Kexueyuan Gongye Jingji Yanjiusuo, December 1986; and *Biaojun jiliang yu zhiliang* (Management of evaluation of standards and quality), Guangdongsheng Zhiliang Guanli Xuehui, June 1986.

3. Li Han-hun was governor of Guangdong during World War II, when the government was exiled to Shaoguan. Li Han-hun's son, Victor Li, has been director of the East-West Center of the University of Hawaii for many years.

4. The basic information, though hardly objective, can be found in *Jianlibao wenji 1984–1987* (Collection of materials on Jianlibao, 1984–1987), Jianlibao County, 1987.

5. *Guangdongsheng tongji nianjian* (Guangdong Province statistical yearbook) (Guangzhou: Zhongguo Tongji Chubanshe, 1987), p. 95. See also Zeng Guangxian, "Guangdongsheng jingji gaige jiunian huigu," *Gaige* (Reform) (Beijing), no. 2 (1988): 119.

6. Kathleen Hartford, "The Dilemmas of Socialist Reform," typescript, November 1986, includes nationwide information on such rural households.

7. Other examples of Guangzhou petty entrepreneurs may be found in *Guangjiaojing* (Wide-angle lens) (Hong Kong), April 1985, pp. 14–17.

## 11. Reforming Foreign Trade

1. *Guangdongsheng tongji nianjian* (Guangdong Province statistical yearbook) (Guangzhou: Zhongguo Tongji Chubanshe, 1984), p. 281.

2. *Guangzhou jingji nianjian* (Guangzhou economic yearbook) (Guangzhou: Guangzhou Jingji Nianjian Bianji Weiyuanhui, 1983), p. 300.

3. For an account of Zhou Enlai's speech on the trade fair, given to Red Guard representatives on April 14, 1967, see John Collier and Elsie Collier, *China's Socialist Revolution* (New York: Monthly Review Press, 1973), pp. 150–154.

4. Guangdongsheng Nanhaixian Duiwai maoyiju, "Yikao dangwei chujin shengchan gaosudu fazhan duiwaimaoyi" (Relying on the Party Committee to accelerate production and develop foreign trade at a high rate), in *Quanguo caimao xue Daqing xue Dazhai dianxing huiyi cailiao xuanbian* (Collection of articles from the nationwide finance and trade "learn from the Daqing and Dazhai models" conference) (Beijing: China and Economy Press, 1978), p. 265.

5. Tan Yinghua, "Zhengque hesuan waimao jinliao jiagong de jingji xiaoyi" (Correctly account for the economic benefits of importing materials with state foreign exchange for export processing), in *Yijiubasan nian kuaijixue lunwenxuan* (A collection of essays on accounting for 1983) (Beijing: China Finance and Economy Press, 1985), p. 279. Chinese foreign trade workers distinguish *jinliao jiagong*—importing materials paid for by state foreign exchange for export processing—from *lialiao jiagong*—importing materials contributed by a foreign firm for export processing. The latter business only started up after 1978, whereas the former has been practiced without interruption since 1949.

6. *Jiagexue* (Study of prices) (Beijing: People's University Press, 1982), pp. 502–503.

7. *Guangdongsheng tongji nianjian*, 1984, pp. 46, 279.

8. A listing of Guangdong ports and "loading points" open to foreign trade can be found in *Yangcheng wanbao* (Yangcheng evening news), August 16, 1981.

9. John Kamm, "Foreign Consumer Goods Now Available," *Canton Companion* (Hong Kong), no. 2 (1978): 8–9.

10. John Kamm, "Local Trade in Kwangtung [Guangdong]," *Canton Companion, no. 2,* p. 20.

11. "Guangdongsheng tongjiju guanyu Guangdongsheng yijiubayi nian guomin jingji jihua zhixing jieguo de gongbao" (Guangdong Province 1981 economic plan), *Nanfang ribao* (Southern daily) (Guangzhou), May 12, 1982.

12. *Zhongguo jihua guanli wenti* (Problems of managing China's planning) (Beijing: China Railway Press, 1984), pp. 471–472.

13. He Chaoming, "Some Legal Problems Concerning Economic Disputes Involving Hong Kong and Macao," in Ren Jianxin et al., *Legal Aspects of Foreign Investment in the People's Republic of China* (Hong Kong: China Trade Translation Co., 1988), p. 230.

14. *Guangdongsheng tongji nianjian,* 1984, p. 279; *Guangzhou jingji nianjian,* 1984, p. 321.

15. John Kamm, "Macau's Economic Role in the West River Delta," in *Macau: City of Commerce and Culture,* ed. R. D. Cremer (Hong Kong: UEA Press, 1987), p. 174.

16. *Nanfang ribao,* April 16, 1980.

17. *Guangdongsheng tongji nianjian,* 1985, p. 276.

18. "Duiwai Jingji Maoyibu Guanyu Zai Zhuyao Kouan Sheli Tepaiyuan Banshichu he 'duiwai jingji maoyibu tepaiyuan banshichu zanxing tiaoli' de Qingshi" (The Ministry of Foreign Economic Relations and Trade instructions on the establishment of special representative offices in major coastal ports), *Zhonghua renmin gongheguo xianxing fagui huibian* (A collection of current laws of the Chinese People's Republic) (1949–1985) (Beijing: Waishi Waijingmao Zhuan, People's Press, 1987), pp. 34–35.

19. *Jiagexue,* p. 496.

20. *Guangzhou ribao* (Guangzhou daily), August 28, 1980.

21. The national average export cost rose from 2.50 yuan to $1.00 in 1980, to 3.22 yuan to $1.00 at mid-year 1983. See Thomas M. H. Chan, "Reform in China's Foreign Trade System," in *China's Economic Reforms,* ed. Joseph C. H. Chai and C. K. Leung (Hong Kong: Hong Kong University Press, 1987), p. 435.

22. "Guojia Wujiaju guanyu gaijin jizhong jinkou shangpin guonei zuojia banfa de baogao" (State Pricing Bureau report on changing certain pricing methods for imported commodities), *Guangdongsheng wujia nianjian* (Guangdong Province pricing yearbook) (Guangzhou: Guangdong Pricing Bureau Press, 1985), pp. 380–381.

23. Liu Jianxiang and Guan Qixue, *Guangdong duiwai jingji guanxi* (Guangdong's external economic relations) (Guangzhou: Guangdong Higher Education Press, 1988), pp. 86–87.

24. *Yijiubasi nian caimao jingji guanli jingyan xuanbian* (Collection of materials on finance and trade economic management experience of 1984) (Beijing: People's Press, 1984), p. 172.

25. *Guangzhou jingji nianjian,* 1984, p. 330.

26. *Waimao qiye xiandai guanlixue* (Studies on modern management in foreign trade enterprises) (Beijing: China Foreign Trade and Economy Press, 1986), p. 28.

27. Statistics on the scale of the Hainan car incident are from the Central Investigation Team's report. *Nanfang ribao,* August 1, 1985.

28. *Nanfang ribao,* March 1, 1984.

29. *Nanfang ribao,* June 1, 1982.

30. Martin Weil, "The Guangdong Float Glass Company," *China Business Review* (January–February 1987), pp. 20–21.

31. "Guangdongsheng Tongjiju guanyu yijiubaqi nian guomin jingji he shehui fazhan de gongbao" (Guangdong Province State Statistical Bureau statistical report on 1987 economic and social development), *Nanfang ribao,* March 24, 1988. See also *Guangdongsheng tongji nianjian,* 1987, p. 329.

32. *Renmin ribao* (People's daily), February 2, 1988.

33. Wu Mingguang, "Guangdongsheng duiwaijingmao de huigu yu zhanwang" (Retrospectives and perspectives on Guangdong Province's foreign economic relations and trade), in *Guangzhou Duiwaimaoyi Xueyuan xuebao* (Journal of the Guangzhou Foreign Trade Institute), no. 1 (1988): 7.

34. When the first official "free trades" of yuan for U.S. dollars took place in Guangzhou in late 1980, the rate was approximately 3.0 yuan to $1.00. The rate deteriorated steadily and was roughly 6.0 yuan to $1.00 at the Guangzhou foreign exchange adjustment center during the last quarter of 1987. By the middle of 1988 the rate at which state-regulated free trades were taking place was between 6.5 and 7.0 yuan. Hong Kong dollar note purchases, spurred by the flight to Hong Kong currency during the panic of June 1988, were taking place on the black market (the unregulated free market) at the rate of HK$1.00 to 1.2 yuan, an equivalent U.S. dollar:renminbi rate of U.S. $1.00 to 9.2 yuan.

35. *Mingbao* (Enlightenment daily) (Hong Kong), August 13, 1988, quotes estimates of a net reduction in Guangdong city and township deposits of 135 million yuan during the last two weeks of June 1988 as compared to the corresponding period of 1987. In light of the huge increase in money supply in China, the actual outflow of deposits throughout the province probably approached 500 million yuan.

36. *Xinxi shibao* (Information times), April 12, 1988.

37. The misuse of the donation permit system, involving the resale of 1,500 tons of imported steel, is illustrated in *Renmin ribao,* July 20, 1988. A MOFERT investigator was sent to southern provinces in July and, as part of a crackdown beginning in August, a Guangxi official was sentenced to death for issuing fraudulent donation permits. See *Dagongbao* (Daily worker) (Hong Kong), August 19, 1988.

38. *Renmin ribao,* December 26, 1984.

39. "Guangdong's Pioneering Economic Reform Program Approved," *China Economic News,* April 11, 1988.

40. *Mingbao,* August 13, 1988. Changes in the structure of export production-procurement-sale resulted in tied-up capital and increased state subsidization estimated at 3 billion yuan during the first half of 1988.

41. *Nanfang ribao,* November 22, 1984.

## 12. Society in Transition

1. For an account of rural life in Guangdong on the eve of the takeover, see C. K. Yang, *Chinese Communist Society: The Family and the Village* (Cambridge, Mass.: Massachusetts Institute of Technology Press, 1959).

2. See, for example, Martin King Whyte, *Small Groups and Political Rituals in China* (Berkeley: University of California Press, 1974).

3. See, for example, Susan Shirk, *Competitive Comrades* (Berkeley: University of California Press, 1982).

4. Among the more famous critiques of feudalism, widely read at the time, were: Su Shaozhi, "Zhengzhi tizhi gaige chuyi" (My humble opinion on reforms of the political system), *Dushu* (Reader) (Beijing), no. 9 (1986); Li Honglin, "Xiandaihua he minzhu" (Modernization and democracy), *Shijie jingji daobao* (World economic herald) (Shanghai), June 2, 1986; and Dai Qing, "Guanyu fan fengjian de yixie sikao—Fangwen Li Shu" (Some reflections on opposing feudalism: An interview with Li Shu), *Guangming ribao* (Enlightenment daily) (Beijing), June 16, 1986.

5. *Guangdongsheng tongji nianjian* (Guangdong Province statistical yearbook) (Guangzhou: Zhongguo Tongji Chubanshe, 1987), p. 95; *Guangdong nianjian* (Guangdong yearbook) (Guangzhou: Guangdong Renmin Chubanshe, 1987), p. 150. Percents for 1978 do not sum to 100 due to rounding.

6. For a fuller treatment of this issue, see Deborah Davis-Friedmann, *Long Lives: Chinese Elderly and the Communist Revolution* (Cambridge, Mass.: Harvard University Press, 1983).

7. See, for example, Morton Fried, *The Fabric of Chinese Society* (New York: Athlone, 1954).

8. See Ezra F. Vogel, "From Friendship to Comradeship," *China Quarterly*, no. 21 (January–March, 1965): 46–60; Thomas B. Gold, "After Comradeship: Personal Relations in China since the Cultural Revolution," *China Quarterly*, no. 104 (December 1985): 657–675.

9. *Guangdongsheng tongji nianjian*, 1987, p. 432.

10. *Zhongguo renkou: Guangdong fence* (China's population: Guangdong) (Beijing: Zhongguo Caizheng Jingji Chubanshe, 1988), p. 387.

## 13. The Takeoff of the Guangdong–Hong Kong Region

1. *Guangdongsheng tongji nianjian* (Guangdong Province statistical yearbook) (Guangzhou: Zhongguo Tongji Chubanshe, 1984), p. 95.

2. Wang Zhuo, "Juyou Guangdong Tese de Shinian Gaige Kaifang" (Certain special characteristics of Guangdong's ten years of opening and reform), Paper presented to Guangdong Gaige Kaifang Zonghe Shidian Lilun yu Duice Yantaohui (Seminar on Guangdong's Comprehensive Experiment in Reform and Opening), September 1988. *Guangdong nianjian* (Guangdong yearbook), (Guangzhou: Guangdong Renmin Chubanshe, 1987), p. 510.

# Selected Bibliography

This bibliography includes all major known works on Guangdong since 1949 and important general works on China that help shed light on developments in Guangdong. The list is divided into seven sections: the Cultural Revolution; Hong Kong; reforms; special economic zones; other works on Guangdong; general works on Chinese society, economy, and politics; and periodicals and newspapers.

## Cultural Revolution

Ahn, Byung-joon. *Chinese Politics and the Cultural Revolution*. Seattle: University of Washington Press, 1976.

Bennett, Gordon A., and Ronald N. Montaperto. *Red Guard: The Political Biography of Dai Hsiao-ai*. New York: Doubleday, 1971.

Blecher, Marc J., and Gordon White. *Micropolitics in Contemporary China: A Technical Unit during and after the Cultural Revolution*. White Plains, N.Y.: M. E. Sharpe, 1979.

Chan, Anita. *Children of Mao: Personality Development and Political Activism in the Red Guard Generation*. Seattle: University of Washington Press, 1985.

Chan, Anita, Stanley Rosen, and Jonathan Unger. "Students and Class Warfare: The Social Roots of Red Guard Conflict in Guangzhou." *China Quarterly*, no. 83 (September 1980): 397–446.

Chan, Anita, Stanley Rosen, and Jonathan Unger, eds. *On Socialist Democracy and the Chinese Legal System: The Li Yizhe Debates*. Armonk, N.Y.: M. E. Sharpe, 1985.

Dittmer, Lowell. *Liu Shao Ch'i and the Chinese Cultural Revolution: The*

*Politics of Mass Criticism.* Berkeley: University of California Press, 1974.

Domes, Jurgen. *China after the Cultural Revolution: Politics between Two Party Congresses.* Berkeley: University of California Press, 1977.

Gao, Yuan. *Born Red: A Chronicle of the Cultural Revolution.* Stanford: Stanford University Press, 1987.

Goldman, Merle. *China's Intellectuals: Advise and Dissent.* Cambridge, Mass.: Harvard University Press, 1981.

Karnow, Stanley. *Mao and China.* New York: Viking Press, 1972.

Kau, Michael Ying-mao. *The Lin Piao Affair: Power Politics and Military Coup.* White Plains, N.Y.: International Arts and Sciences Press, 1975.

Kwong, Julia. *Cultural Revolution in China's Schools, May 1966–April 1969.* Stanford: Hoover Institution, 1988.

Lee, Hong Yung. *The Politics of the Chinese Cultural Revolution: A Case Study.* Berkeley: University of California Press, 1978.

Leys, Simon. *Chinese Shadows.* New York: Viking Press, 1977.

Liu, Guokai. "A Brief Analysis of the Cultural Revolution." *Chinese Sociology and Anthropology: A Journal of Translations,* ed. Anita Chan (Winter 1986–87).

Lo, Ruth Earnshaw, and Katharine S. Kinderman. *In the Eye of the Typhoon.* New York: Harcourt Brace Jovanovich, 1980.

Lu Xinhua et al. *The Wounded: New Stories of the Cultural Revolution, 1977–1978,* trans. Geremie Barmé and Bennett Lee. Hong Kong: Joint Publishing Co., 1979.

MacFarquhar, Roderick. *The Origins of the Cultural Revolution.* 3 vols. New York: Columbia University Press, 1974, 1983, and forthcoming.

Oksenberg, Michel, Carl Riskin, Robert Scalapino, and Ezra Vogel. *The Cultural Revolution: 1967 in Review.* Ann Arbor: Michigan Papers in Chinese Studies, 1968.

Raddock, David. *Political Behavior of Adolescents in China: The Cultural Revolution in Kwangchow [Guangzhou].* Tucson: University of Arizona Press, 1977.

Rosen, Stanley. "Guangzhou's Democracy Movement in Cultural Revolution Perspective." *China Quarterly,* no. 101 (March 1985): 1–31.

——— *Red Guard Factionalism and the Cultural Revolution in Guangzhou (Canton).* Boulder: Westview Press, 1982.

Thurston, Anne F. *Enemies of the People: The Ordeal of the Intellectuals in China's Great Cultural Revolution.* New York: Knopf, 1987.

Witke, Roxane. *Comrade Chiang Ch'ing.* Boston: Little, Brown, 1977.

Yue, Daiyun, and Carolyn Wakeman. *To the Storm: The Odyssey of a Revolutionary Chinese Woman.* Berkeley: University of California Press, 1985.

Zweig, David. *Agrarian Radicalism in China, 1968–1981.* Cambridge, Mass.: Harvard University Press, 1989.

## Hong Kong

Aijmer, Goran. *Atomistic Society in Sha Tin.* Göteborg, Sweden: Acta Universitatis Gothoburgensis, 1979.

Aijmer, Goran, ed. *Leadership on the China Coast.* London: Curzon Press, 1984.

Baker, Hugh D. R. *Sheung Shui: A Chinese Lineage Village.* London: Frank Cass, 1968.

Bonavia, David. *Hong Kong 1997: The Final Settlement.* Hong Kong: South China Morning Post, 1985.

Catron, Gary. "China and Hong Kong, 1845–1967." Ph.D. diss., Harvard University, 1971.

Cheng, Joseph. *Hong Kong in Transition.* New York: Oxford University Press, 1987.

Ching, Frank. *Hong Kong and China.* New York: Foreign Policy Association, 1985.

Domes, Jurgen, and Yuming Shaw, eds. *Hong Kong: A Chinese and International Concern.* Boulder: Westview Press, 1988.

Dwyer, D. J. *Asian Urbanization.* Hong Kong: Hong Kong University Press, 1971.

Endacott, G. B. *Government and People in Hong Kong, 1841–1962.* Hong Kong: Hong Kong University Press, 1964.

——— *A History of Hong Kong.* London: Oxford University Press, 1958.

Faure, David, James Hayes, and Alan Birch. *From Village to City: Studies in the Traditional Roots of Hong Kong Society.* Hong Kong: Hong Kong University Press, 1984.

Grantham, Sir Alexander. *Via Ports: From Hong Kong to Hong Kong.* Hong Kong: Hong Kong University Press, 1965.

Guldin, Gregory Eliyu. "The Invisible Hinterland: Hong Kong's Reliance on Southern Guangdong Province." Typescript, 1987.

Harris, Peter. *Hong Kong: A Study in Bureaucratic Politics.* Hong Kong: Heinemann, 1978.

Hayes, James. *The Rural Communities of Hong Kong: Studies and Themes.* Hong Kong: Oxford University Press, 1983.

Ho, H. C. Y. *The Fiscal System of Hong Kong.* London: Croom Helm, 1979.

*Hong Kong.* Hong Kong: Hong Kong Government Information Services, annual.

Hopkins, Keith, ed. *Hong Kong: The Industrial Colony.* Hong Kong: Oxford University Press, 1971.

Hughes, Richard. *Borrowed Place, Borrowed Time: Hong Kong and Its Many Faces.* London: Andre Deutsch, 1968.

Ikels, Charlotte. *Aging and Adaptation: Chinese in Hong Kong and the United States.* Hamden, Conn.: Shoestring Press, 1983.

Jarvie, I. C., and Joseph Agassi, eds. *Hong Kong: A Study in Transition— Contributions to the Study of Hong Kong Society.* London: Routledge and Kegan Paul, 1969.

Johnson, Graham E. "1997 and After: Will Hong Kong Survive?" *Pacific Affairs* (Summer 1979): 237–254.

Jones, John F. *The Common Welfare: Hong Kong's Social Services.* Hong Kong: Chinese University Press, 1981.

King, Ambrose, and Rance Lee, eds. *Social Life and Development in Hong Kong.* Hong Kong: Chinese University Press, 1981.

Lau, Siu-kai. *Society and Politics in Hong Kong.* Hong Kong: Chinese University Press, 1982.

Lethbridge, David, ed. *The Business Environment in Hong Kong.* Hong Kong: Oxford University Press, 1980.

Lin, Tzong-biau, Rance P. L. Lee, and Udo-Ernst Simonis, eds. *Hong Kong: Economic, Social and Political Studies in Development.* White Plains, N.Y.: M. E. Sharpe, 1979.

Miners, Norman. *The Government and Politics of Hong Kong.* Hong Kong: Oxford University Press, 1981.

Potter, Jack M. *Capitalism and the Chinese Peasant: Social and Economic Change in a Hong Kong Village.* Berkeley: University of California Press, 1968.

*Report of the Advisory Committee on Diversification, 1979.* Hong Kong: Hong Kong Government Secretariat, 1979.

Sit, Victor, ed. *Urban Hong Kong.* Hong Kong: Summerson, 1981.

Turner, H. A. et al. *The Last Colony, But Whose? A Study of the Labour Movement, Labour Market and Labour Relations in Hong Kong.* Cambridge: Cambridge University Press, 1980.

Watson, James L. *Emigration and the Chinese Lineage: The Mans in Hong Kong and London.* Berkeley: University of California Press, 1975.

Youngson, A. J., ed. *China and Hong Kong: The Economic Nexus.* Hong Kong: Oxford University Press, 1983.

*The Reform Movement*

Barnett, A. Doak. *China's Economy in Global Perspective.* Washington, D.C.: Brookings, 1981.

Barnett, A. Doak, and Ralph N. Clough, eds. *Modernizing China: Post-Mao Reform and Development.* Boulder: Westview Press, 1986.

Burns, John P., and Stanley Rosen, eds. *Policy Conflicts in Post-Mao China:*

*A Documentary Survey, with Analysis.* Armonk, N.Y.: M. E. Sharpe, 1986.

Byrd, William. *China's Financial System: The Changing Role of Banks.* Boulder: Westview Press, 1983.

Byrd, William et al. *Recent Chinese Economic Reforms: Studies of Two Industrial Enterprises.* Washington, D.C.: World Bank, 1984.

*China Briefing.* Boulder: Westview Press and New York: China Council of the Asia Society, annual.

Colton, Timothy J. *The Dilemma of Reform in the Soviet Union.* New York: Council on Foreign Relations, 1986.

Fei, Hsiao Tung et al. *Small Towns in China: Functions, Problems and Prospects.* Beijing: New World Press, 1986.

Goldman, Marshall. *Gorbachev's Challenge: Economic Reform in the Age of High Technology.* New York: Norton, 1987.

Harding, Harry. *China's Second Revolution: Reform after Mao.* Washington, D.C.: Brookings, 1987.

Hartford, Kathleen. "The Dilemmas of Socialist Reform." Typescript. November 1986.

Ho, Samuel P. S., and Ralph Huenemann. *China's Open Door Policy: The Quest for Foreign Technology and Capital.* Vancouver: University of British Columbia Press, 1984.

Howard, Pat. *Breaking the Iron Rice Bowl: Prospects for Socialism in China's Countryside.* Armonk, N.Y.: M. E. Sharpe, 1988.

Johnson, Graham E., "The Production Responsibility System in Chinese Agriculture: Some Examples from Guangdong." *Pacific Affairs* (Fall 1982): 430–451.

——— "Responsibility and Reform: Consequences of Recent Policy Changes in Rural South China." *Contemporary Marxism,* nos. 12–13 (1986): 144–162.

——— "Rural Transformation in South China? Views from the Locality." Typescript, 1988.

Kinkley, Jeffrey C., ed. *After Mao: Chinese Literature and Society, 1978–1981.* Cambridge, Mass.: Council on East Asian Studies, Harvard University, 1985.

Kornai, Janos. *The Economics of Shortage.* Amsterdam: North-Holland, 1980.

Lampton, David M., ed. *Policy Implementation in Post-Mao China.* Berkeley: University of California Press, 1987.

Lee, Hong Yung. "The Separation of the Party from the Government and the Issues of Personnel Management." Paper presented to the annual meeting of the Association for Asian Studies, Berkeley, March 1988.

Lee, Peter N. S. *Industrial Management and Economic Reform in China, 1949–1984.* New York: Oxford University Press, 1988.

Lee, Yok-shiu. "Rural Nonfarm Activities in China: Growth and Effects of Township Enterprises, 1978–1980." Ph.D. diss., Massachusetts Institute of Technology, 1988.

Link, Perry. *Roses and Thorns: The Second Blooming of the Hundred Flowers in Chinese Fiction, 1979–1980*. Berkeley: University of California Press, 1983.

Morse, Ronald A., ed. *The Limits of Reform in China*. Boulder: Westview Press, 1983.

Perry, Elizabeth J., and Christine Wong, eds. *The Political Economy of Reform in Post-Mao China*. Cambridge, Mass.: Council on East Asian Studies, Harvard University, 1985.

Reynolds, Bruce, ed. *Chinese Economic Reform: How Far, How Fast?* Boston: Academic Press, 1988.

——— *Reform in China: Challenges and Choices*. Armonk, N.Y.: M. E. Sharpe, 1987.

Saith, Ashwani, ed. *The Reemergence of the Chinese Peasantry*. London: Croom Helm, 1987.

Schram, Stuart. *Ideology and Policy in China since the Third Plenum, 1978–1984*. London: Contemporary China Institute, 1984.

Siu, Helen F., and Zelda Stern, eds. *Mao's Harvest: Voices from China's New Generation*. New York: Oxford University Press, 1983.

Stavis, Benedict, ed. "Reform of China's Political System." *Chinese Law and Government* (Spring 1987).

Tidrick, Gene, and Chen Jiyuan, eds. *China's Industrial Reform*. New York: Oxford University Press, 1987.

Tong, James, ed. "Urban Economic Reforms in Sichuan under Zhao Ziyang." *Chinese Law and Government* (Fall 1987).

Tsou, Tang. *The Cultural Revolution and Post-Mao Reforms*. Chicago: University of Chicago Press, 1986.

U.S. Congress. Joint Economic Committee. *China in the 1980s*. Washington, D.C.: GPO, 1986.

——— *China under the Four Modernizations*. Washington, D.C.: GPO, 1982.

——— *China's Economy Looks toward the Year 2000*. 2 vols. Washington, D.C.: GPO, 1986.

### Special Economic Zones

Falkenheim, Victor C. "China's Special Economic Zones." In U.S. Congress, Joint Economic Committee, *China's Economy Looks toward the Year 2000*. Vol. 2. Washington, D.C.: GPO, 1986.

*Guangdong jingji tequ yaolan* (A guide to Guangdong's special economic zones), 1983–84. Guangzhou: Guangdongsheng Jingji Tequ Yanjiu Zhongxin, 1985.

Jao, Y. C., and C. K. Leung. *China's Special Economic Zones: Policies, Problems and Prospects.* Hong Kong: Oxford University Press, 1986.

Oborne, Michael. *China's Special Economic Zones.* Paris: OECD, 1986.

*Shenzhen jingji tequ nianjian* (Shenzhen special economic zone yearbook). Shenzhen: Jingji Tequ Nianjian Bianji Weiyuanhui, 1985, 1986.

*Shenzhen jingji tequ zuzhi renshi zhidu gaige shixian yu tansuo* (An exploration of the system reform of the administrative personnel system in the Shenzhen special economic zone). Shenzhen: Haitian Chubanshe, 1986.

*Shenzhen tequ fazhan de daolu* (The road to Shenzhen special economic zone development). Zhonggong Shenzhen Shiwei Bangongting. Beijing: Guangming Ribao Chubanshe, 1984.

*Shenzhen tequ jingji de diaocha yu yanjiu* (An investigation and study of the economy of Shenzhen's special economic zone). Beijing: Qiushi Chubanshe, 1987.

Wong, Kwan-yiu, ed. *Shantou SEZ: An Agent for Regional Development.* Hong Kong: Centre for Contemporary Asian Studies, Chinese University, 1985.

——— *Shenzhen Special Economic Zone: China's Experiment in Modernization.* Hong Kong: Hong Kong Geographical Association, 1982.

Wong, Kwan-yiu, and David K. Y. Chu, eds. *Modernization in China: The Case of the Shenzhen Special Economic Zone.* Hong Kong: Oxford University Press, 1985.

Zhou, Wei Ping, and Xu Long, eds. *Zhongguo jingji tequ fazhan xinjieduan* (The new stage of development of China's special economic zones). Liaoning: Caijing Daxue Chubanshe, 1986.

*Zhuhai jingji nianjian* (Zhuhai economic yearbook), 1979–1986. Guangzhou: Guangdong Renmin Chubanshe, 1986.

## Guangdong

Bennett, Gordon. *Huadong: The Story of a Chinese People's Commune.* Boulder: Westview Press, 1978.

Bernstein, Thomas P. *Up to the Mountains and Down to the Villages: The Transfer of Youth from Urban to Rural China.* New Haven: Yale University Press, 1977.

Chan, Anita, Richard Madsen, and Jonathan Unger. *Chen Village: A Recent History of a Peasant Community in Mao's China.* Berkeley: University of California Press, 1984.

*Foshanxing* (About Foshan). Zhongguo Chengshi Gaige congshu. Beijing: Hongqi Chubanshe, 1985.

Frolic, B. Michael. *Mao's People: Sixteen Portraits of Life in Revolutionary China.* Cambridge, Mass.: Harvard University Press, 1980.

Guan, Qixue, and Liu Guangpu, eds. *Lun jingji zhongxin: Guangzhou* (A discussion of the economic center: Guangzhou). Guangzhou: Guangdong Gaodeng Jiaoyu Chubanshe, 1987.

*Guangdong jingji fazhan zhanlüe yanjiu* (Research on a development strategy for Guangdong's economy). Guangzhou: Guangdong Renmin Chubanshe, 1986.

*Guangdong jingji tizhi gaige yanjiu* (Research on Guangdong's economic system reform). Guangzhou: Zhongshan Daxue Chubanshe, 1985.

*Guangdong nianjian* (Guangdong yearbook). Guangzhou: Guangdong Renmin Chubanshe, annual, beginning 1987.

*Guangdongsheng difangxing fagui huibian* (Guangdong Province compendium of local laws), December 1979–June 1986. Guangzhou: Guangdong Renmin Chubanshe, 1986.

*Guangdongsheng disanci renkou pucha baogaoshu* (Guangdong Province report of the third census). Guangzhou: Guangdongsheng Renkou Pucha Bangongshi, 1986.

*Guangdongsheng renkou zhuangkuang fenxi yu yuce* (Guangdong Province's population structure: Analysis and forecasts). Guangzhou: Zhongshan Daxue Chubanshe, 1986.

*Guangdongsheng shidixian gaikuang* (An overview of Guangdong Province's cities, prefectures, and counties). Guangzhou: Guangdongsheng Ditu Chubanshe, 1985.

*Guangdongsheng tongji nianjian* (Guangdong Province statistical yearbook). Guangzhou: Zhongguo Tongji Chubanshe, annual, beginning 1984.

*Guangdongsheng xingzhengquhua jiance* (A handbook of Guangdong Province administrative divisions), 1986. Guangzhou: Guangdong Lüyou Chubanshe, 1987.

*Guangzhou jingji* (Guangzhou economy). Guangzhou: Zhongshan Daxue Chubanshe, 1987.

*Guangzhou jingji jishu kaifaqu touzi falu yibaiwen* (One hundred questions and answers on investment rules of the Guangzhou economic and technological development zone). Guangzhou: Jingji Jishu Kaifaqu Weiyuanhui, 1987.

*Guangzhou jingji nianjian* (Guangzhou economic yearbook) (after 1985, *Guangzhou nianjian*). Guangzhou: Guangzhou Jingji Nianjian Bianji Weiyuanhui, annual, beginning 1983.

*Guangzhou jingji shehui fazhan zhanlue* (A development strategy for Guangzhou's economy and society). Guangzhou: Kexue Puji Chubanshe, Guangzhou Fenshe, 1986.

*Guangzhou tongji nianjian* (Guangzhou statistical yearbook), 1988. Guangzhou: Zhongguo Tongji Chubanshe, 1988.

Guldin, Gregory Eliyu. "Urbanizing the Countryside: Hong Kong,

Guangzhou, and the Pearl River Delta." Paper presented to the annual meeting of the Association for Asian Studies, Berkeley, March 1988.

*Hainandao de touzi huanjing* (The investment climate of Hainan Island). Haikou: Zhongguo Duiwai Jingji Maoyi Zixun Gongsi, 1987.

Kamm, John. "Macau's Economic Role in the West River Delta." In *Macau: City of Commerce and Culture,* ed. R. D. Cremer. Hong Kong: UEA Press, 1987.

Lee, Peter N. S. "The Economic Bureaucracy and Industrial Policy in Guangdong during the Post-Mao era, 1979–1983." Paper presented at the Workshop on Economic Bureaucracy in Seven Chinese Regions, East-West Center, Honolulu, 1984.

Madsen, Richard. *Morality and Power in a Chinese Village.* Berkeley: University of California Press, 1984.

Nipponkoku Kokusai Kyooryoku Jigyoodan. *Chuuka Jinmin Kyoowakoku, Hainantoo: Soogoo kaihatsu keikaku choosa* (Hainan Island, the People's Republic of China: Research report of an overall development plan). 11 vols. Tokyo, May 1988.

Nolan, Peter. *Growth Processes and Distributional Change in a South Chinese Province: The Case of Guangdong.* London: Contemporary China Institute, 1983.

Parish, William L., and Martin K. Whyte. *Village and Family in Contemporary China.* Chicago: University of Chicago Press, 1978.

Rosen, Stanley, ed. "The Rehabilitation and Dissolution of 'Li Yizhe,'" *Chinese Law and Government* 14, no. 2 (Summer 1981).

Ruddle, Kenneth, and Gongfu Zhong. *Integrated Agriculture-Aquaculture in South China: The Dike Pond System of the Zhujiang Delta.* Cambridge: Cambridge University Press, 1988.

*Shaoguan nianjian* (Shaoguan yearbook). Shaoguan, Guangdong: Shaoguan Nianjian Bianjibu, 1986.

Shirk, Susan. *Competitive Comrades.* Berkeley: University of California Press, 1982.

Silin, Robert, and Edward Winckler. *China: Provincial Economic Briefing Series.* Vol. 5, *South/Southeast China.* Hong Kong: BA Asia, 1982.

Siu, Helen. *Agents and Victims: Accomplices in Rural Revolution in South China.* New Haven: Yale University Press, forthcoming.

Sun, Ru. "A General Survey and Forecast of Guangdong Economic Development." Paper presented at the Workshop on Economic Bureaucracy in Seven Chinese Regions, East-West Center, Honolulu, 1984.

Teiwes, Frederick C. *Provincial Party Personnel in Mainland China, 1956–1966.* New York: East Asian Institute, Columbia University, 1967.

Tuan, Chyau, Danny S. N. Wong, and Chun-sheng Ye. *Guoren chuang-*

*yezhe yanjiu: Xianggang yu Guangzhou diqu de ge an fenxi* (Chinese entrepreneurship under capitalism and socialism: Hong Kong and Guangzhou cases). Hong Kong: Centre of Asian Studies, Hong Kong University, 1986.

Unger, Jonathan. *Education under Mao: Class and Competition in Canton Schools 1960–1980*. New York: Columbia University Press, 1982.

Vogel, Ezra F. *Canton under Communism: Programs and Politics in a Provincial Capital, 1949–1968*. Cambridge, Mass.: Harvard University Press, 1969.

Whyte, Martin King. "Inequality and Stratification in China." *China Quarterly*, no. 64 (December 1975): 684–711.

——— *Small Groups and Political Rituals in China*. Berkeley: University of California Press, 1974.

Whyte, Martin King, and William L. Parish. *Urban Life in Contemporary China*. Chicago: University of Chicago Press, 1984.

Wu, Yuwen, ed. *Guangdongsheng jingji dili* (Guangdong Province economic geography). Beijing: Xinhua Chubanshe, 1985.

*Zhongguo renkou: Guangdong fence* (China's population: Guangdong). Beijing: Zhongguo Caizheng Jingji Chubanshe, 1988.

*Zhujiang sanjiaozhou jingji kaifangqu touzi zhinan* (An investment guide to the Pearl River Delta economic development zone). Hong Kong: Xinhuashe, 1986.

## General Works on Chinese Society, Economy, and Politics

*Asia Yearbook*. Hong Kong: Far Eastern Economic Review, annual.

Barnett, A. Doak, with a contribution by Ezra Vogel. *Cadres, Bureaucracy, and Political Power in Communist China*. New York: Columbia University Press, 1967.

*China: Long-Term Development, Issues and Options* (6 annexes). Washington, D.C.: World Bank, 1985.

*China: Socialist Economic Development*. 3 vols. Washington, D.C.: World Bank, 1983.

Davis-Friedmann, Deborah. *Long Lives: Chinese Elderly and the Communist Revolution*. Cambridge, Mass.: Harvard University Press, 1983.

Dittmer, Lowell. *China's Continuous Revolution*. Berkeley: University of California Press, 1987.

Domes, Jurgen. *The Government and Politics of the PRC: A Time of Transition*. Boulder: Westview Press, 1985.

Falkenheim, Victor, ed. *Citizens and Groups in Contemporary China*. Ann Arbor: Center for Chinese Studies, University of Michigan, 1987.

Funahashi, Yooichi. *Neibu: Aru Chuukoku hookoku* (Inside story: A report from China). Tokyo: Asahi Shinbunsha, 1983.

Goldman, Merle. *Literary Dissent in Communist China*. Cambridge, Mass.: Harvard University Press, 1967.

Guillermaz, Jacques. *The Chinese Communist Party in Power, 1949–1976*. Boulder: Westview Press, 1976.

Harding, Harry. *Organizing China: The Problem of Bureaucracy, 1949–1976*. Stanford: Stanford University Press, 1981.

Henderson, Gail E., and Myron S. Cohen. *The Chinese Hospital: A Socialist Work Unit*. New Haven: Yale University Press, 1984.

Kraus, Richard Curt. *Class Conflict in Chinese Socialism*. New York: Columbia University Press, 1981.

Lardy, Nicholas R. *Agriculture in China's Modern Economic Development*. Cambridge: Cambridge University Press, 1983.

Lewis, John, ed. *The City in Communist China*. Stanford: Stanford University Press, 1971.

Lieberthal, Kenneth, and Michel Oksenberg. *Policy Making in China: Leaders, Structures, and Processes*. Princeton: Princeton University Press, 1988.

Liu, Alan P. L. *How China Is Ruled*. Englewood Cliffs, N.J.: Prentice Hall, 1986.

MacFarquhar, Roderick, and John K. Fairbank, eds. *The Cambridge History of China*. Vol. 14, *The People's Republic of China, Part 1: The Emergence of Revolutionary China, 1949–1965*. New York: Cambridge University Press, 1987.

Nathan, Andrew J. *Chinese Democracy*. New York: Alfred A. Knopf, 1985.

Nee, Victor, and David Mozingo, eds. *State and Society in Contemporary China*. Ithaca: Cornell University Press, 1983.

Parish, William, ed. *Chinese Rural Development: The Great Transformation*. Armonk, N.Y.: M. E. Sharpe, 1985.

Perkins, Dwight H. *China: Asia's Next Economic Giant?* Seattle: University of Washington Press, 1986.

Perkins, Dwight H., and Shahid Yusuf. *Rural Development in China*. Baltimore: Johns Hopkins University Press, 1984.

Pye, Lucian. *The Dynamics of Chinese Politics*. Cambridge, Mass.: Oelgeschlager, Gunn and Hain, 1981.

Rozman, Gilbert, ed. *The Modernization of China*. New York: Free Press, 1981.

Shue, Vivienne. *Peasant China in Transition: The Dynamics of Development toward Socialism, 1949–1956*. Berkeley: University of California Press, 1980.

——— *The Reach of the State: Sketches of the Chinese Body Politic*. Stanford: Stanford University Press, 1988.

Skinner, G. William, ed. *The City in Late Imperial China*. Stanford: Stanford University Press, 1977.

Solinger, Dorothy J. *Chinese Business under Socialism: The Politics of Domestic Commerce, 1949–1980.* Berkeley: University of California Press, 1984.

Townsend, James R., and Brantly Womack. *Politics in China.* 3d ed. Boston: Little, Brown, 1986.

Walder, Andrew G. *Communist Neo-Traditionalism: Work and Authority in Post-Revolution China.* Berkeley: University of California Press, 1986.

White, Lynn T., III. *Careers in Shanghai: The Social Guidance of Personal Energies in a Developing Chinese City, 1949–1966.* Berkeley: University of California Press, 1978.


*Periodicals and Newspapers*

*Asian Wall Street Journal,* daily, Hong Kong.

*Far Eastern Economic Review,* weekly, Hong Kong.

*Foreign Broadcast Information Service* (FBIS, translations), Washington, D.C.

*Guangjiaojing* (Wide-angle lens), monthly, Hong Kong.

*Guangzhou ribao* (Guangzhou daily), Guangzhou.

*Guangzhou yanjiu* (Guangzhou research), monthly, Guangzhou.

M. E. Sharpe translations:
  *Chinese Economic Studies,* 1967–.
  *Chinese Education,* 1968–.
  *Chinese Law and Government,* 1968–.
  *Chinese Sociology and Anthropology,* 1968–.

*Mingbao* (Enlightenment daily), Hong Kong.

*Joint Publications Research Service* ( JPRS, translations), Washington, D.C., 1957–.

*Nanfang ribao* (Southern daily), Guangzhou.

*Qishi niandai* (The seventies); after 1980 retitled *Jiushi niandai* (The nineties), monthly, Hong Kong.

*Union Research Service* (URI), Hong Kong, 1955–1975.

U.S. Consulate General, Hong Kong:
  *Current Background* (CB), 1950–1977.
  *Supplement to SCMP and SCMM,* 1960–1973.
  *Survey of China Mainland Magazines* (SCMM), 1955–1977.
  *Survey of China Mainland Press* (SCMP), 1950–1977.

*Yangcheng wanbao* (Yangcheng evening news), Guangzhou.

*Zhengming* (Contending), monthly, Hong Kong.

*Zhongguo jingmao wenti* (China economic and trade news digest), weekly. Hong Kong: CERD Consultants.

# Acknowledgments

My greatest thanks go to the members of the Economic Commission of Guangdong Province, for their unflagging cooperation and friendship and for allowing me the freedom to write the story of their province completely in my own way. My invitation to spend seven months in Guangdong came from Vice-Governor Yang Li. Yang, Zhang Gaoli, director of the Provincial Economic Commission, and Huang Cun, director of foreign affairs of the province, were all kind and gracious hosts. Deputy Director Yang Mai, extraordinarily dedicated and knowledgeable, patiently answered endless questions. I was fortunate to have Dou Shengyuan assigned as my research assistant, and he went beyond the call of duty both in setting up appointments and in teaching me about matters large and small. For a briefer time I was assisted by another able and well-informed official, Tan Yangbo. Their colleagues in the provincial, prefectural, and county economic commissions and many other officials at various levels were wonderfully hospitable and informative. A researcher could not ask for more. They bear no responsibility, however, for the final product, which is a Western social scientist's attempt to relate and analyze the recent experiences of Guangdong for a Western audience.

My wife, Charlotte Ikels, accompanied me on both major field trips to Guangdong, in 1980 and 1987. Although she was studying Cantonese families and the elderly, we shared a broad base of intellectual interests. She was unusually patient with a single-minded workaholic husband and properly determined in her efforts to save me from misinterpretations.

In my first fieldwork in Guangdong, for three months in 1980, my wife and I were the guests of Zhongshan University and received great help from our friends Xia Shuzhang and Qian Manli and their staffs. For that research I received a grant from the Committee on Scholarly Communication with the People's Republic of China.

Since 1980, when the American Consulate was established in Guangzhou, I have had the help of a succession of talented consul generals—Weaver Gim, Jerry Ogden, Mark Pratt, Richard Williams—and their staff members, particularly Barry Friedman, Ying Price, Steven Schlaikjer, and Nora Sun. I have also enjoyed the friendship of two Japanese consul generals in Guangzhou, Taguma and Hasumi.

At Harvard I have had the benefit of working closely with Ding Xueliang and Su Wei, young leaders in bridging the intellectual gap between China and the West. Officially they were research assistants, but in fact they were my teachers and my friends.

My administrative assistant, Laurie Scheffler, a China specialist in her own right, is my de facto manager. She has cheerfully looked after everything from daily details and Chinese transliteration to the theoretical structure of my arguments. Nancy Hearst, who has worked creatively for years to make Harvard's library collection on contemporary China one of the best, has called many materials to my attention. I have benefited from the stimulation of the Harvard China community, especially from colleagues K. C. Chang, Paul Cohen, Bernard Frolic, Merle Goldman, Kathleen Hartford, Donald Klein, Arthur Kleinman, Philip Kuhn, Stanley Lubman, Roderick MacFarquhar, Patrick Maddox, Suzanne Ogden, Jean Oi, Dwight Perkins, Lucian Pye, Benjamin Schwartz, Terry Sicular, the late Judith Strauch, James Thomson, Wei-ming Tu, Andrew Walder, James Watson, Ellen Widmer, Edwin Winckler, Christine Wong, and David Zweig. In various stages of my research I have also been ably assisted by Treacy Curlin, Fan Gang, Gong Xiaoxia, Li An, Qian Ruxiang, Judy Shen, David Tsui, and especially Edward Chan and Anna Laura Rosow, who worked with me on *Canton under Communism*. I received advice on the maps from Clifton Pannell and Katharyne Mitchell, and they were prepared by Robert Forget.

John Kamm, whom I have known from the time he was a graduate student in East Asian studies at Harvard in the early 1970s, has been an ideal collaborator, tough-minded but generous, invariably prompt, excited by our findings, and full of ideas and information. He thanks his research assistants, Simon Lui Ming Ha and Raymond Kan, who uncovered so much new material on Guangdong's foreign trade.

The handful of dedicated Pearl River Delta field-workers generously shared with me their unpublished papers: William Byrd, Gregory Guldin, Graham Johnson, Yok-shiu Lee, and Helen Siu. In my work on Chinese society I have been enriched especially by the intellectual and personal friendship of Thomas Bernstein, Doak Barnett, John Berninghausen, Deborah Davis, Albert Feuerwerker, Thomas Gold, Marion Levy, Kenneth Lieberthal, Perry Link, Richard Madsen, Andrew Nathan, William Parish, John Pelzel, Gilbert Rozman, William Skinner, Douglas Spellman, Philip West, Lynn White, and Martin Whyte.

Like all other Western China scholars I have found invaluable the world's great center for materials on contemporary China, the Universities Service Center of Hong Kong, which was in 1988 transferred to the Chinese University. The Center was nourished for thirteen years by John Dolfin, who used his unique resources to serve scholars all over the world. At Chinese University, where my wife and I lived for some months in 1982–83, I am especially grateful for the intellectual stimulation and personal kindness of F. C. Chen, Ambrose King, and Byron and Carolyn Weng. In Hong Kong, while working on this book, I also benefited from the wisdom of Governor David Wilson, Vice-Chancellors Wang Gong Wu and Ma Lin, Victor Fung, Melinda Liu, the late Sidney Liu, Robert Silin, and consul generals Donald Anderson, Burton Levin, David Osborn, Thomas Shoesmith, and their staffs.

In revising the manuscript, I was fortunate to receive comments on earlier drafts from Thomas Bernstein, Edward Chan, Gregory Chow, Timothy Colton, Thomas Elmore, Victor Falkenheim, Deborah Davis, Thomas Gold, Merle Goldman, Gregory Guldin, Arthur Hummel, Graham Johnson, John Kamm, Philip Kuhn, C. K. Leung, Kenneth Lieberthal, Stanley Lubman, Dwight Perkins, Mark Pratt, Andrew Walder, Martin Whyte, Barrie Wiggham, and David Zweig. These friends contributed an amazing amount of time and thought to save me from egregious errors and provide me with new information and new interpretations. I only wish I had the answers to all the penetrating questions they raised.

# Index

Agricultural Bank of China, 114, 115, 169, 172, 184

Agriculture: production teams in, 91, 92, 94; communes in, 91, 93, 95, 97–98, 283; Dazhai model in, 91, 256, 339; rice production in, 92, 93, 109, 163, 167, 339, 340; mechanization in, 92, 159, 164; during Cultural Revolution, 92, 339; quotas vs. contracts in, 93–94, 96; responsibility system linked to output, 94; borrowing of land in, 94–95, 96; cash crops in, 167–168, 188, 339, 440; sugar crops in, 235, 237, 298–299; from, to commerce and industry, 247–248; ramie production in, 272, 273; specialized households in, 328; and foreign trade, 384. *See also* Reforms: in agriculture; Responsibility system, household; Shantou special economic zone: agriculture in

Akers-Jones, David, 54

All-China Games, Sixth, 446

All-China Sports Federation, 322, 446

Alley, Rewi, 7

Anhui Province, 86

Anti-rightist campaigns, 10, 18

Anticipatory socialization, two-way, 73–75. *See also* Hong Kong

Architects, 135, 139–140, 188

Army Corps (Bingtuan), 282, 284, 285, 295

Army Engineer Corps (Gongcheng Bing), 137–138

Arts and Crafts Corporation, 174, 356

Asian Soccer Federation, 323

Association of Southeast Asian Nations (ASEAN), 57

Baiyun Mountain (Guangzhou), demonstration on, 99

Bank of China, 29, 46, 64, 83, 184, 350, 353, 378, 390, 391

Banks, 109, 114–116, 152, 208, 223, 246, 320, 387; runs on, 113, 381, 387. See also *individual banks*

Bao Keming, 306

Baoan County, 156, 161, 164, 176, 190, 193; and Shenzhen, 130, 131, 136–137, 154, 225; exports from, 192, 351; and Cultural Revolution, 341

Baoting County (Hainan), 252

Basuo, 233, 277, 290, 301

Beihai (Guangxi), 237

Beijing: in Cultural Revolution, 21, 22, 23, 24, 25, 30, 31, 34; and reforms, 68, 80, 83, 87, 89–90, 96, 98, 102, 104, 113, 121, 129, 140; and Guangdong, 207, 233, 235, 323, 447; and foreign trade, 362

Bo Yibo, 128

Cambodia, 132, 449

Canton, *see* Guangzhou

Canton Trade Fair, *see* Export Commodities Fair

*Canton under Communism* (Vogel), 6, 7

Capitalism, 5, 11, 89, 135, 449; hostility to, 20, 338, 403; fear of excesses of, 45, 395, 424; euphemisms for, 100; state, 128
Carter, Jack, 54
Cathay Pacific Airways, 65
Central South Land Reclamation and Cultivation Bureau (Huanan Kenzhiju; State Farm Bureau), 278
Changjiang County, 277
Chaoyang County, 251, 342
Chaozhou, 55, 276, 306, 339
Chaozhou people, 48, 157, 158, 226, 243. *See also* Shantou
Chen Caidao, 25
Chen Muhua, 391
Chen Shuihong, 190, 191
Chen Yun, 77, 128, 316, 344
Chen Yunkang, 191
Chen Yuyi, 292
Chiang Ching-kuo, 430
Chiang Kai-shek, 3, 277, 319, 430
China: and the West, 43, 76; overseas business leaders of, 57; and Canada, 60; and Taiwan, 125–126, 305; as market, 143; strikes in, 390; children in, 420–421; welfare network in, 421. *See also* Soviet Union: and China; United States: and China
China International Trade and Investment Corporation (CITIC), 64–65, 411, 443
China International Trust and Investment Company, 114
China Merchants Steamship and Navigation Company (CMSN) Ltd., 46, 64, 130, 131, 132, 133, 154
China National Chemicals Import and Export Corporation (SINOCHEM), 340n, 347, 358
China National Foodstuffs Import and Export Corporation, 343
China National Machinery and Equipment Import and Export Corporation (EQUIPEX), 357
China National Machinery Import and Export Corporation (MACHIMPEX), 340n, 357
China National Offshore Oil Corporation (CNOCC), 238
China Resources, 46, 64
China Travel Service, 64
Chinese Academy of Social Sciences, 306

Chinese University (Hong Kong), 443
Christian Industrial Association, 383
Chun Doo Hwan, 430
Civil Affairs Department, 271
Clavell, James, 51
CMSN, *see* China Merchants Steamship and Navigation Company, Ltd.
Collectivization, 95–96, 99, 258, 283; and reforms, 10, 40, 93, 97, 170, 396; market declines after, 163, 255
Commission for Restructuring the Economy, *see* Economic System Reform Commission
Communist Party, 3, 10, 81, 287, 314, 437–438, 444; victory in 1949, 3–4, 16; control by, 5, 45, 164, 313, 333; disillusionment with, 17, 40, 405; Propaganda Department of, 21; and economic system, 40–41, 78, 79; in Hong Kong, 64, 73, 444; thirtieth anniversary of victory of, 79; Central Committee of, 84, 85, 126, 130, 270, 289; rectification campaign of (1983), 116; Party Organization Department of, 117, 318, 319; International Liaison Department of, 132; soldiers in, 267; and universal comradeship vs. personal connections, 405–409; redefining role of, 421, 439. *See also* Cultural Revolution: Communist Party in
Communist Party Liaison Department (Guangdong), 62
Communist Youth League, 267, 287, 318, 322
Confucianism, 53, 336, 396, 405, 421, 430
Conghua County, 28, 36
Construction, 1, 2, 35, 114, 136, 208–209, 387, 422; in Hong Kong, 58, 132, 135; financing of, 115, 136, 387; in special economic zones, 132, 135–140, 150, 155, 210; in Inner Delta, 165, 170, 179–180, 220, 265; workers in, 266
Consumer goods, 76, 110, 170, 197, 207, 220, 320, 342, 435, 438; and Cultural Revolution, 30, 164, 165; smuggling of, 147, 422; demand for, 171, 359–360, 381; imported, 347, 349–350, 439
Corruption, 120–121, 170, 409–413, 421–423, 449; and children of officials, 411

Cult of personality, 313, 316
Cultural Revolution, 7, 15–42, 43, 72, 99, 127, 162, 228, 233, 396, 414; reforms after, 10, 30, 77, 79, 80, 81, 84, 167, 187; class struggle in, 17, 19, 20, 41; struggle sessions in, 18, 21, 23; in Guangdong, 19–34, 443; revolutionary rebels in, 21, 22; Communist Party in, 21–23, 116, 117, 314, 437; revolutionary alliance in, 23, 26–27; military takeover in, 23–27; armed clashes in, 24–26; suicides in, 25, 26; end of, 27, 34–35, 40–42, 76, 125; economy in, 28–31; agricultural policy in, 29; Production Group in, 29; leadership in, 31; reassessment of, 31–34, 89, 405, 424; costs of, 35–40; distribution of power during, 39; and Hong Kong, 52, 64; failures of, 62, 85; and overseas Chinese, 83, 201; victims of, 87, 106; state factories in, 102; financial controls during, 114; effects of, 163, 182, 235, 423, 440, 441; forest management during, 256; and local leaders, 315, 318–319; Export Commodities Trade Fair during, 25, 338–339, 348; effect of, on foreign trade, 338–348, 350, 356, 360, 362; corruption in, 409. *See also* Guandong–Hong Kong region; Red Guards; *individual counties*
Cultural Revolution Group, 22
Currency, foreign, 83, 85, 86, 109, 126, 218, 223, 308, 335; and Hong Kong, 44, 46, 68, 132, 383; and overseas visitors, 127, 200; in Shekou, 134; in Shenzhen, 139, 140, 141, 148; retention of, 141, 174–175, 350–353, 376; need for, 144, 146, 147, 211, 418, 439, 440; in Foshan, 184; and trade fairs, 202; and import business, 341, 344–345, 350; and investment, 388, 391. *See also* Hainan car incident
Customs Administration, 361, 365, 381

Dabaoshan mines (Shaoguan), 230, 233, 255–256, 398
Dalian, 212, 233, 300, 347, 364
Dan County, 271, 278
Dapu County, 242, 246
December 9th movement, 314
Democracy, bourgeois, 79, 87–88
Democracy Wall, 33, 40–41

Deng Hanguang, 206, 207
Deng Xiaoping, 27, 33, 70, 195, 315, 319; reforms of, 2, 77–89, 106, 116, 129; speech at Eleventh Party Congress, 32, 41; and special economic zones, 128, 155, 375
Denmark, 132, 134, 299
Development: "five wheels of," 188; "late late," 427, 435–436
Dianbai County, 25
Ding Sheng, 31, 88
Dongguan, 161, 175–181, 187, 190, 192, 193, 195, 217, 225, 226; emigration from, 164; as independent city, 165, 250; and Huiyang Prefecture, 166, 248; as model of foreign trade, 339; toy industry in, 373; Shajiao Power Station in, 374. *See also* Inner (Pearl River) Delta
Doumen County, 130, 154, 156, 161, 192, 193
Du Ruizhi, 95

East River Guerrillas, 22, 131, 182
East Wind, 24, 31
Eastern Europe, 3, 41, 108, 198, 347, 366, 448
Economic System Reform Commission (Jingji Tizhi Gaige Weiyuanhui), 78
Economic zones, special (SEZs), 11, 88, 125–160, 306, 426; guidelines for, 86, 144–145; criticism of, 127–128; and treaty ports, 127, 157; commission, 155; foreign trade enterprise in, 359, 387; migrants in, 404–405. See also *individual economic zones*
Education, 35, 244–245, 248, 265, 430, 449; reform in, 5, 118; during Cultural Revolution, 37–38; return of examination system in, 268, 285, 406–407, 438, 441; restructuring costs of, 419–420; in Japan, 433–434; in South Korea, 434; in Taiwan, 434. *See also* Universities
Eighth Party Congress, Eleventh Plenum of, 19
Eighth Route Army, 87
Electronics Enterprise Group (Dianzi Jituan), 153
Eleventh Party Congress: Third Plenum of, 32, 35, 41, 77, 84, 87, 122, 126; Fourth Plenum of, 96
Employees: state, 399–401, 403, 416–

Employees: state *(continued)* 417, 421; collective, 399, 401–402, 403; in self-employed households, 399, 402–403

Enping County, 130, 161, 164, 166, 193, 194

Enterprises: collective, 8, 99, 100–101, 186, 334, 401–402, 403, 416; individual, 8, 99, 100, 101, 187, 251, 261, 268, 328, 398; state, 99, 100, 101–106, 110, 114, 141, 186, 194, 207, 223, 245, 318, 400, 405, 407, 415, 416, 439, 441; "private" category, 100, 333, 336, 337, 431; taxation of, 104; managers of, 105, 334; rural, 120; third front, 142; failures of, 333–335

Entrepreneurs, 11, 49, 51, 63, 100, 101, 105–106, 157, 313–337; with peasant background, 174; as elder statesmen, 314–317, 335, 336, 337; as scramblers, 317–327, 335–336, 337; as niche seekers, 327–333, 336–337; future of, 392; incomes of, 400, 402, 403, 423; lifestyle of, 403–404. *See also* Enterprises

Everbright (firm), 65, 154, 411

Export Commodities Fair (Guangzhou), 25, 201, 338–339, 342, 348, 392

Export processing, 125, 126, 158, 175–181, 372–373, 378–379, 418, 435. *See also* Economic zones, special

Exports, 125–129, 143, 146, 148, 163, 308, 355, 429; traditional, 190, 361, 379; during Cultural Revolution, 339–343; direct from factories, 359; parallel ("water goods"), 359; and tariffs, 361, 381; self-managed, 369; rise in (1985–1988), 372–384; subsidizing of, 379, 417–418; drop in (1989), 388. *See also* Economic zones, special; Export processing; Foreign trade; Foshan

Factories, 1, 2, 27, 35, 36, 63, 211, 319; state, 8, 101, 104–105, 171, 174, 204, 398; textile, 47–48, 59, 134, 186–187, 240, 301; in Hong Kong, 48; changes in, 111, 396; direct exports from, 122, 340n, 359; construction of, 136, 440; in Shenzhen, 142, 152; in Zhuhai, 156; in Shantou, 159, 240; in Inner Delta, 164, 165, 175, 177–180, 186–188; women workers in, 177, 180; ceramics, 187, 218, 240, 241, 296; large modern, 189–

192, 223; third front, 231, 240, 288; beverage, 322–323. *See also* Wages: factory

Farms, 8, 109, 169; state, 255, 257, 280–282, 294–297, 303, 308; and foreign trade corporations, 359–360. *See also* Agriculture; Markets

Feng Baiju, 289

Fengshun County, 242, 246

Finance-Trade Office, 271

First Ministry of Machine Building, 357

Fishing industry, 167, 237, 340, 361, 362

Five-year plan: first, 77, 230; fourth, 28, 208; sixth, 211, 289, 290, 367; seventh, 210, 211, 270, 417

Fogang County, 216

Fok, Henry, 63, 203, 327

Foreign Affairs Ministry (Guangdong), 62

Foreign Economic Relations and Trade Commission, 155, 376, 382, 387

Foreign Investment Control Commission, 128

Foreign trade, 3, 9, 91, 122, 127, 163, 201, 439; effect of Cultural Revolution on, 338–348, 350, 356, 360, 362; reforms in, 338–392; encouragement of selected imports, 346–348; customs houses in, 346, 365; 1978–1980 boom in, 348–361; and foreign exchange retention, 350–353, 359, 375, 376, 381, 387, 391; decentralization in, 353–356, 375, 376; dual leadership system in, 354, 355; economic courts in, 355; and advertising, 355–356; and joint industrial-commercial companies, 356–360, 371, 377, 390, 391; and "four uniteds, two opens" campaign, 357; pricing of export goods in, 360–361; stagnation and decline (1981–1984) in, 362–372; recentralization in, 364–366, 390; dual exchange rate in, 366–369; agency system in, 366, 369–370; financial guarantee system in, 367; from 1985 to 1988, 372–383; "twenty-two points" in, 373, 382; and deregulation, 377–378; Hong Kong–Guangdong nexus in, 383–384; future of, 384–392; in 1989, 388; and human resources, 391–392

Foreign trade corporations, 340–349, 353–366, 379–380, 391

Foreign trade enterprises, 340n, 359, 368, 391

Forests, *see* Reforestation
Foshan, 116, 161, 181–189, 190, 193, 195, 210, 215, 224, 229, 231, 250, 316; in Cultural Revolution, 182, 183; factories in, 185–189; and foreign trade, 291, 367, 368, 372, 375, 380, 381, 383; experiment of export production bases, 343–348; and retention of exports, 351; communications in, 363
Foshan Metropolitan Region, 166, 181–189, 216, 353
Foshan Prefecture, 119, 163, 182, 248, 294, 353
Four managements, 89
Four modernizations, 77, 130, 347
Four olds, 20, 21
Fourth Field Army, 278
Fourth National People's Congress, 347
Fujian Province, 48, 162, 242, 276, 364, 371, 447, 448; "special policy" for, 80, 82, 83–84, 88, 353, 354; rubber production in, 278, 295
Fujian Provincial Party Committee, 85

Gan Ziyu, 84
Gang of Four, 25, 27, 32, 33, 92, 100, 116, 256, 315, 348
Gaoming County, 130, 161, 166, 193, 194
Gaoyao County, 228
Gaozhou County, 233, 329, 330
General Agreement on Tariffs and Trade (GATT), 379, 389, 417
Goh Keng Swee, 137
Gorbachev, Mikhail, 3
Government's Legislative Council and Executive Council (Hong Kong), 55
Grantham, Sir Alexander, 54
Great Britain, 3, 24; and Hong Kong, 43, 44, 45, 46, 49, 51, 52, 54, 56, 57, 70, 89, 131
Great Leap Forward, 29, 228, 230, 231, 236, 246, 256, 396; results of, 7, 76, 77, 95; failures of, 10, 62, 85, 424; and Communist Party, 40, 117; and irrigation projects, 234, 247; policies of, 286, 414
Gu Mu, 84, 85, 121, 128, 140, 183, 186, 289
Guangdong Enterprises (Yuehai), 64, 248, 354, 355, 443

Guangdong Foreign Trade Bureau, 354, 355, 357, 358
Guangdong–Hong Kong region, 11, 385–386, 426–427, 442–446
Guangdong International Trust and Investment Corporation (GITIC), 355
Guangdong Physical Education Research Institute (Tiyu Xexue Yanjiusuo), 322
Guangdong Province: 1984 map of, 4; 1988 map of, 249; in 1973, 1; transportation in, 1, 2, 222–223, 253, 261, 265, 363; fieldwork in, 1–11; as economic laboratory, 2, 5, 386; and economic reforms of 1980s, 2, 251, 385–392; reforms in, compared with *perestroika,* 3; characteristics of, 3; migration overseas from, 3, 82; and Communist Revolution, 4–5; links with Massachusetts, 6; Cultural Revolution in, 19–34, 339–343, 347, 348; land reform in, 45; reopening of, 60–66; "special policy" for, 80–87, 354, 386; meritocratic bureaucracy in, 438; government-led growth in, 223–224; seven centers of regional growth in, 224–247; communications in, 363, 374; future of, 414–425; economic takeoff of, 426, 434–442; impact of reforms in, on China, 446–449. *See also* Guangdong–Hong Kong region; Guangzhou; Hong Kong: and Guangdong; Reforms
Guangdong Province Foreign Trade Corporation (GPFTC), 340n, 354
Guangdong Province System Reform Office (Tizhi Gaige Bangongshi), 90
Guangdong Provincial Party Committee, 85
Guangning County, 25, 228, 272
Guangxi Province, 25, 162, 167, 168, 227, 233, 236, 237, 252, 260, 278
Guangxi Zhuang Autonomous Region, 347–348
Guangzhou (Canton), 11, 55, 196–219, 220, 250; map of, 199; 1970s vs. 1980s in, 1, 92, 338–339; Cultural Revolution in, 21–40, 201, 205, 210; Military Region of, 31, 285; travel between Hong Kong and, 60, 155, 212, 338, 352; and Hong Kong, 62–66, 68, 198, 200, 202, 203, 212, 325, 326, 362, 436; and Shenzhen, 147, 155, 209, 214, 338; bureaucracy in, 162, 196, 198, 214; emi-

Guangzhou (Canton) *(continued)*
gration from, 164; population of, 166,
182, 184, 196; food in, 167, 362; housing in, 196, 197, 198, 201, 210–211,
218, 219; per capita income in, 188;
factories in, 189, 197–198; during Cultural Revolution, 197, 198, 331; facilities for overseas visitors in, 200–203; reviving commerce in, 203–208;
rebuilding, 208–211; Donghu Xincun
(East Lake New Village) project in, 210;
economic and technological development
zone in, 212; Municipal Party Committee of, 214; Administrative Committee
(Guanli Weiyuanhui), 214; development
of counties, 215–219; petty business in,
331–333; Public Security Bureau in,
338; foreign trade in, 347, 364; modern
culture in, 423–425; civic cultural centers in, 424–425. *See also* Guangdong
Province; Inner (Pearl River) Delta
Guangzhou Foreign Trade School, 341,
355
Guangzhou Metropolitan Region, 166,
215–216, 217, 343, 351
Guangzhou Overseas Chinese Affairs Office, 201
Guangzhou Ramie Factory, 359
Guangzhou Revolutionary Committee, 26
*Guanxi, see* Personal connections, cultivation of
Guilin (Guangxi), 229
Guizhou Province, 237, 347


Haifeng County, 24–25, 226, 250
Haikang County (Zhanjiang Prefecture),
95, 340
Haikou City (Hainan), 224, 233, 239,
276, 279, 287, 301, 303, 305, 309; Japanese occupation of, 277; land reclamation in, 283, 284; communications in,
290; investments in, 291; as boom
town, 306–307, 308. *See also* Hainan car
incident
Haikou County, 192, 278
Hainan car incident (1984), 134, 291–
294, 302, 315, 368–369
Hainan Island, 102, 141, 217, 224, 225,
236, 275–309, 316, 318; map of, 279;
as separate province, 11, 239, 248, 305,
307, 443; state farms in, 27, 255, 278–

286, 294–298, 302, 303, 308, 398; reform in, 121, 288, 305, 368; infrastructure in, 221, 288–291, 292, 301, 307,
308; migrants to, 243; minorities in,
252, 286–288; poor counties in, 271;
per capita income in, 275–276; before
1950, 276–278; transportation in, 276,
290, 291; Japanese occupation of, 277;
rubber production in, 278–286, 294–
297, 300; Agricultural Commission of,
282; Regional Government of, 283,
284; land reclamation in, 283–284; Cultural Revolution in, 284, 285, 286, 287,
295; minorities in, 286–288, 302, 303;
Li-Miao Autonomous Region in, 287,
302, 304; communications in, 290, 443;
housing in, 296–297; agriculture in,
298–300, 339; Luhuitou Peninsula in,
303–304; tourism in, 303–305, 307;
goals and obstacles for, 305–309; investment in, 307; and off-shore oil and
LNG exploration, 307; and foreign
trade, 368; Communist Party in, 444;
and Taiwan, 448. *See also* Hong Kong:
and Hainan
Hakka people, 48, 230, 242–247, 282. *See
also* Meixian; Minorities
Handicrafts, 110, 170, 187, 263, 264,
328, 402
Hangzhou, 225
Harbin, 314
He Kang, 279, 295
Hebei Province, 314, 323
Heilongjiang Province, 231, 314
Heping County, 95
Heshan County, 130, 161, 166, 193, 194
Heyuan County, 95, 250
Hong Kong (Xianggang), 9, 10, 11, 43–
75, 82, 125, 167; and Guangdong, 2,
10–11, 41, 60–66, 229, 248, 320, 338,
436; and Inner Delta, 11, 162, 163,
166, 174, 175, 176–181, 186, 187,
190, 192, 193–195, 248; émigrés from
mainland to, 33, 39, 44–45, 68, 131,
164, 404; population of, 43–44, 46,
166; loss of hinterland, 44–47, 56; industrial growth in, 47–49; growth of
manufacturing in, 47–52; Western community in, 50; land prices in, 50, 132,
149; housing in, 51–52, 53; common
civic culture in, 52–56; education in,
53; income in, 53; business leaders of,

55–56, 57–58, 63–64, 66, 71, 73, 105, 125–126, 139, 321, 324–327, 412; as global city, 56–60, 156; shipping in, 58, 132–133; influence of, 62–66, 198, 200, 225, 410, 424, 425; new entrepôt trade in, 66–70; and labor supply, 68–69, 418; 1984 agreement on return to China, 70–75, 126, 132–133, 442; and mainland reform, 81, 83, 85, 89, 111; tourism in, 127, 134; technology from, 174, 175, 444; and Hainan, 290, 298, 306; and reform of foreign trade, 348, 356, 362, 383–384, 385–386, 389; late development of, 427. *See also* Guangdong–Hong Kong region; Guangdong Province; Shenzhen special economic zone

Hong Kong Cable and Wireless Company, 443

Hong Kong Polytechnic University, 444

Hong Kong University, 51, 443

Hopewell Group (Hong Kong), 325, 374

Household Electric Appliances Corporation (Zhanjiang), 238

Housing, 35, 137, 234, 396, 400, 403, 416. *See also individual counties*

Housing Management Bureau, 201

Hu Yaobang, 195, 259, 289, 315

Hua County, 36, 216, 293

Hua Guofeng, 76, 77, 82, 88

Huaiji County, 257–258

Huanan Engineering University, 213, 322

Huang Riwu, 319

Huang Yongsheng, 23, 31, 88

Huang Zongdao, 295

Huangpu, 212, 213, 217, 238

Huangpu (Whampoa) Military Academy, 3

Huaxia Department Store (Guangzhou), 207

Hughes, Richard, 52

Huilai County, 251

Huiyang Development Company, 226

Huiyang Prefecture, 166, 180, 225, 226, 228, 248, 252, 345. *See also* Huizhou

Huizhou, 224–226, 232, 236, 239, 242, 247, 248, 250; and Hong Kong, 226, 228. *See also* Inner (Pearl River) Delta

Human resources, investment in, 433–434, 441–442

Humanism, socialist, 423–425

Hunan Province, 110, 128, 133, 167, 168, 321, 347, 390, 447

Ikels, Charlotte, 9

Imports, 343, 346–348, 369, 372, 375, 384, 387

Income, per capita, 1, 2, 35, 93, 97, 164, 169–170, 252; in state vs. private employment, 400–401. *See also individual counties*

Independent Commission against Corruption (ICAC; Hong Kong), 55

Individual Household Economy Division, 328

Indonesia, 57, 277, 281

Industrial-Commercial Bank of China, 114, 115, 184

Industrial-Commercial Friendship Association (Gongshang Lianyihui), 206

Industrial goods, 110, 113. *See also* Price controls

Industrialization, 10, 119, 204, 433

Industry: heavy, 35, 76, 110, 197, 211, 219, 231, 232, 242, 245; light, 83, 88, 194, 211, 219, 232, 242, 269, 439, 440; military, 111; loans for, 115; village and town, 115, 170, 171–175, 264; role of prefectural capitals in, 247; and foreign trade, 384. *See also* Economic zones, special; Factories

Inflation, 108, 109, 112, 113, 114, 121, 387, 388, 414–415, 449

Information, public, 417

Inner (Pearl River) Delta, 11, 161–195, 218, 220, 231, 396, 405; map of, 130; economic zone, 161; Cultural Revolution in, 164, 165; reopening of, 164–166; per capita income in, 164, 216, 252, 264; and Hong Kong, 165, 175, 176, 248, 267, 445; and markets in agricultural products, 166–170; rural families in, 168–170, 402; housing in, 169, 179, 182; township and village industry in, 170, 171–175, 264; export processing in, 175–181, 192, 193; layers of change in, 192–195; transport and market expansion in, 221–223, 327; and mountain counties, 418–419

Intellectuals, 18, 22, 28, 37, 41, 294, 314

Italy, 229, 321

Iwateya Department Store (Fukuoka, Japan), 207

Japan, 10, 48, 49, 50, 65, 76, 125, 327, 349, 418; occupation of China, 46, 47,

Japan *(continued)*
  237; business leaders of, 55, 56, 57, 58;
  comparison with Hong Kong, 57, 68,
  69; and Chinese economic zones, 145,
  159; purchase of machinery from, 272,
  300; mission to Hainan, 305, 306; eco-
  nomic takeoff of, 426–434, 438, 439.
  *See also* War of Resistance
*Japan as Number One* (Vogel), 6–7
Jardine Matheson & Company, 71
Jiang Qing, 19, 25, 33
Jiang Weiji, 322, 323
Jianghan University (Wuhan), 319
Jiangmen City, 118, 161, 193, 195, 224;
  and foreign trade, 363, 374, 375, 380,
  381
Jiangmen Metropolitan Region, 166, 183,
  193, 236, 250, 353
Jiangmen Prefecture, 156, 194, 228
Jiangmen Wireless Radio Factory, 359
Jiangsu Province, 73, 172, 182, 445
Jiangxi Province, 347
Jianlibao (beverage plant), 322–324
Jiaying University (Meixian), 244
Jinling University (Nanjing), 295
Johnson, Graham, 96

Kader Industries, 134
Kaiping County, 130, 161, 164, 166, 193,
  194
Kang Yuwei, 3
Kanghua (firm), 411
Kaohsiung (Taiwan), 126, 127
Kissinger, Henry, 60
Korean War, 43, 45, 163, 250, 278, 281,
  319, 428
Kuomintang (KMT), 20, 45, 87, 108,
  119, 121, 131, 230, 319; supporters of,
  in Hong Kong, 44–45, 61; in Guang-
  zhou, 198; in Hainan, 277; in Taiwan,
  428

Labor: cost of, 44, 144, 147, 149, 158,
  194, 432, 448; supply of, 48, 68, 156,
  179; rural, 92–93, 188; mobility of,
  416. *See also* Wages
Labor unions, 45, 46, 64, 434
Land Reclamation Bureau (Hainan), 278,
  281, 282, 283, 284, 285, 287, 296,
  298, 300, 302, 308
Language: Mandarin, 6, 9, 57, 73, 244,
  282, 309, 318; Cantonese, 9, 57, 158,

230, 244, 282, 318, 331, 447; Portu-
  guese, 59; English, 59, 392; Chaozhou
  (Tiuchew), 157, 282; Hakka, 244, 282;
  Minnan dialect, 276; Hainanese, 276,
  282, 309; Japanese, 428, 436; Fujianese
  dialect, 448
Lechang County, 28, 192, 272, 273
Ledong County, 302
Leftists, 18, 24, 89, 128
Lei Yu, 214, 217, 218, 289, 291, 292–
  294, 316, 318, 336
Leizhou Peninsula, 236, 237, 239, 275,
  278, 279, 295
Lenin, New Economic Policy of, 125
Li Han-hun, 319
Li Hao, 84
Li Hung-chang, 131
Li Jianan, 316
Li Jingwei, 322, 323, 336
Li Ka-shing, 63, 241, 327
Li Peng, 78
Li Tieying, 78
Li Xiannian, 195
Li Xiushen (Lei Sau Sum), 318–322, 324,
  336
Li Yizhe, 25, 33, 88
Lian County, 27, 230, 231, 264
Liang Lingguang, 6, 87, 316, 335
Liang Qichao, 3
Liang Sicheng, 138
Liang Xiang, 137, 140, 306, 316, 336
Liannan County, 240, 252
Lianping County, 225
Lianshan County, 252, 269
Liaoning Province, 88, 289, 315, 323, 352
Light Industrial Products Import and Ex-
  port Corporation, 347, 349, 358
Light industry bureaus, 100
Lin Biao, 17, 19, 25, 27, 31, 32, 33, 88,
  92
Lin Ruo, 235, 259, 271, 381
Ling Botang, 271
Linkage, horizontal, 120, 152–153, 408
Liu Shaoqi, 32, 65, 154, 304
Liu Xingyuan, 31
Lo Ruiqing, 87
Longchuan, 221, 243
Los Angeles Olympics (1984), 322, 323,
  446
Lu Dingyi, 87
Lu Xinhua: "Shanghen" (The scar; The
  wounded), 33–34

Lufeng County, 226, 250, 271
Luoding County, 227, 228, 264

Macau, 83, 85, 154, 164, 167, 326, 359, 443; compared with Hong Kong, 58–59; travel from, to Guangzhou, 60; return to China, 82, 126, 160; and special economic zones, 127–128, 129, 154, 155, 158, 160, 341; population of, 166; and Inner Delta, 192, 193; Communist Party in, 444
Machinery, 1, 170, 185, 189, 191, 198, 211; imports of, 299, 300, 301, 323, 334–335, 418, 440
Macun (Hainan), 308
Malaysia, 57, 277, 278, 281, 294, 295
Management, macroeconomic, 98, 108
Mao Yuanxin, 315
Mao Zedong, 3, 5, 61, 98, 182, 304, 410, 440; death of, 2, 10, 27, 76, 315; and Cultural Revolution, 15–19, 23, 27, 31, 32, 33, 34, 37, 39; and personality cult, 16–17, 313, 339; *Thoughts* of, 16, 28, 79, 285, 342; criticisms of, 18, 62, 79; and rubber production, 278, 280
Mao Zhiyong, 128
Maoming, 221, 224, 227, 229, 232–236, 237, 242, 315, 330
Maoming Carbon Product Factory, 234
Maoming Metropolitan Region, 233, 236
Maoming Petrochemical Complex, 359, 398
Maoming Prefecture, 252
Maritime Products College (Shuichan Xue-yuan), 237
Markets: food, 1, 2, 8, 29, 83, 93, 97, 168, 204–205, 263; international, 11, 64, 126, 142, 150, 163, 384–385, 417–418, 431–432, 439; in Cultural Revolution, 41, 163; of Hong Kong, 58; expansion of, 78, 79, 93, 98, 107, 108–111, 261, 308, 398; in China, 143, 321, 439; black, 147–148; in agricultural products, 166–170; growth of mountain, 261–264; Hong Kong–Macau, 362–364, 371, 385; commodity, 397, 399, 400, 402–404, 438; regulation of, 415–416; and comparative advantage, 432–433, 440
Marxism-Leninism, 79, 80, 90, 128, 314
Massachusetts, Commonwealth of, 6
May Seventh Cadre Schools, 27–28, 30

Mei County, 162, 221, 242. *See also* Meixian
Meide Electric Fan Factory, 174
Meihua Yuan, 23
Meixian, 48, 224, 242–247, 250, 281
Meixian Metropolitan Region, 242–247
Meixian Prefecture, 242–247, 252, 253
Metallurgical Import and Export Corporation, 357, 358
Metropolitan regions, 119–120, 149, 248–250
Migration, 33, 39, 44–45, 65, 131, 164, 404–405. See also *individual counties*
Military Control Commission, 284, 285
Minerals and Metal Corporation (MIN-METALS), 358
Mines, 8, 35, 230, 233, 245, 255, 258. See also *individual mines*
Ming Dynasty, 182, 198, 276
Ministry of Aeronautics, 153
Ministry of Chemical Industries, 382
Ministry of Communications, 130, 132, 151
Ministry of Finance (Beijing), 361
Ministry of Foreign Economic Relations and Trade (MOFERT), 364, 379, 380, 383
Ministry of Foreign Trade (Beijing), 340n, 344, 347, 355, 357, 358, 360
Minorities: Yao, 229, 252; Zhuang, 252; Li, 252, 276, 286–288, 302, 303, 305; Miao, 252, 276, 286–288, 302, 305; and early reforms, 301–303; Hui, 305. See also Chaozhou people; Hakka people
Modernization, 62, 82, 116, 119, 200, 429, 436; of agriculture, 92, 159, 164; of Chinese Navy, 131; of industrial plants, 185, 189, 389
Mountain counties, 11, 251–274, 398; map of, 253; poverty in, 251–252, 254; population of, 252, 253; minorities in, 252–253; reforms in, 254–260, 268, 269; growth of markets in, 261–264; sources of income in, 264–270; construction workers in, 266–267; and Inner Delta, 267, 418–419; program to support poor areas, 270–274. *See also* Reforestation
Multinational companies, 51, 57, 59, 68, 72, 143
Municipal Commercial Bureau (Guang-zhou), 205, 207

Municipal Consumers' Council, 207

Nanfang Department Store (Guangzhou), 30, 189, 205–207
Nanfang Electronics Factory, 174
*Nanfang ribao*, 369
*Nanfeng chuang* (The window to the South Wind), 63
Nanguang Company (Macau), 360
Nanhai County, 130, 161, 166, 182, 183, 190, 193, 194, 195, 217, 344, 345
Nanhai East, 138
Nanhai East Oil Corporation, 238
Nanhai West Oil Corporation, 238
Nanning, 227
Nanshan Development, 138
Nantse (Taiwan), 126, 127
National People's Congress, 144
National Sports Federation, 322, 446
Newly industrializing country (NIC), 385
Newly industrializing economy (NIE), 385–386
Nie Yuanzi, 19
1911 Revolution, 3
Ningpo, 58, 59
Ninth Party Congress, 27
Nippon Electric (NEC), 290
Nixon, Richard, 60
North Korea, 449

Oil production, 233, 236, 237, 238, 307
Opium War, 3, 24, 70, 127, 129, 180
Ou Jianchang, 173–174
Ouyang Wen, 319–320
Ouyang Xiao, 322, 323
Overseas Chinese, 3, 82–83, 189–190, 194, 200–201, 341, 342, 352; and Hong Kong, 63, 83; and reforms, 84; and consumer goods, 147, 349–350, 381; investment from, 158, 241, 243–244; on state farms, 281–282; gifts from, 382, 412
Overseas Chinese Affairs, 282
Overseas Chinese Investment Corporation, 341

Pan Yanqing, 295
Panyu County, 130, 161, 164, 166, 192, 193, 216, 217, 235, 340
Pao, Y. K., 58
Park Chung Hee, 430
Pearl River, 162, 197, 198, 201, 205, 212

Pearl River Delta, 96, 196, 230, 298, 350, 361, 380, 384, 426, 437; Greater, 161; formation of, 162; emigration from, 164. *See also* Inner (Pearl River) Delta
Pearl River Delta economic development zone, 161. *See also* Inner (Pearl River) Delta
Peasant Training Institute (Canton), 3
Peihua ("Cultivation of China") Foundation, 64
Peng Pai, 25
Peng Zhen, 87, 316
People's Bank of China, 113, 114, 115, 318, 320, 366, 391
People's Construction Bank of China, 114, 115, 345
*People's Daily,* 19
People's Insurance Company, 114
People's Liberation Army, 318
*Perestroika,* 3, 448–449
Personal connections, cultivation of (*guanxi*), 292, 314, 405–409, 411
Philippines, 57
Pige Furniture Company, 174
Pingzhou Commune, 1, 2
*Popo* (*zhuguan;* supervisory government bureau), 118, 120, 356, 390
Prefectures, 119–120; capitals of, 220–250; changes from, to metropolitan regions, 248–250
Price controls, 77, 86, 92, 96, 98, 108, 112–114, 122, 381, 387, 388, 414–415
Pricing Bureau, 112, 368
Profiteering, 293. *See also* Hainan car incident
Provincial Agricultural Commission, 95
Provincial Economic Commission, 5, 8, 104, 185, 189, 190, 195, 272, 321
Provincial Finance Bureau, 104
Provincial Foreign Economic and Trade Commission, *see* Foreign Economic Relations and Trade Commission
Provincial Foreign Trade Bureau, 382
Provincial Forestry Department, 259; Greening Office (Luhua Bangongshi), 259
Provincial Military Control Commission, 23, 25–26
Provincial People's Congress, 387
Provincial Pricing Bureau, 361
Provincial Revolutionary Committee, 26, 28–29, 31

Provincial Sports Federation, 323
Provincial System Reform Office, 107
Provincial Taxation Bureau, 361
Public Security Bureau, 320
Puning County, 251

Qing Dynasty, 3, 119, 129, 131, 198
Qingduo, 347
Qinghua University, 138
Qingyuan County, 103–104, 107, 118, 216, 218, 250
Qionghai County, 279, 292
Qiongshan County, 275, 276, 292
Qiongyai County, 304
Qiongyai Guerrillas (Hainan), 277

Railroads, 60, 155, 163, 221, 226, 227, 235, 308, 326, 374
Reagan, Ronald, 366
Red Flag, 24
Red Guards, 15, 17, 18, 33, 201, 284, 347, 370; launching of, 19–20; attacks on Party leaders, 21–23; and military, 23–24, 31; and Guangzhou trade fair, 25, 342
*The Red Lantern* (opera), 72
Reforestation, 256–260
Reform, system vs. structural, 78
Reforms, 2–3, 10, 11, 31, 75, 76–122, 317, 348; after 1978, 5, 34–40, 41, 42, 251, 434–435; 1977–1979 period of, 10, 76–78; launching of, 87–90, 164; in agriculture, 91–98, 122, 404; in pricing, 92, 96, 99, 112–114, 122; in increasing markets, 93, 107, 108–111; and government reorganization, 97–98, 99, 118–120, 122, 247–250; in enterprise management, 98–106, 122; wage and employment, 99, 106–107, 122; in finance systems, 99, 114–116; in planning, 107–111, 112, 122; role of the Communist Party in, 116–118; benefits of, 170; of 1988, 386–392, 435; impact of, on society, 395–413, 446–449. *See also* Economic zones, special; *individual counties*
Ren Zhongyi, 81, 87, 88, 89, 90, 289, 314–317, 335
Responsibility system, household, 92–97, 99, 109, 166, 169, 170, 251, 254, 257, 302. *See also* Agriculture
Rhee, Syngman, 430

Rightists, 18, 20, 128
Rong Yiren, 64
Rosen, Stanley, 24
Ruayuan County, 252
Rubber production, 278–286, 294–297, 300
Rural Credit Cooperative, 115, 169

Saige, *see* Electronics Enterprise Group
Sanshui County, 163, 166, 182, 216, 221, 227–228, 229, 315, 322, 323
Sanshui Sports Federation, 322
Sanya City, 277, 279, 287, 290, 301, 303; tourism in, 303–305, 307–308
Seoul National University, 431
SEZ Economic Commission, 155
SEZs, *see* Economic zones, special
Shajiao Electric Power Station, 180
Shandong Province, 448
Shanghai, 207, 212, 315, 447; and Hong Kong, 47–48, 55, 62, 68; and reform, 83, 84, 89; and Shenzhen, 140, 142, 147, 149; and foreign trade, 347, 357, 362, 364, 372
Shantou (Swatow), 157, 224, 233, 239–242, 247, 281, 282; and foreign trade, 342, 346, 370, 375, 378
Shantou Metropolitan Region, 251
Shantou Photo Material Industry Corporation, 241–242
Shantou Prefecture, 225, 246, 250, 252
Shantou special economic zone, 127, 129, 157, 159, 168, 222; location of, 4, 158; compared with Shenzhen and Zhuhai, 157–158, 159, 160; agriculture in, 159, 240
Shanwei, 250, 370
Shanxi Province, 212
Shaoguan City, 162, 163, 224, 229–232, 236, 240, 250, 264
Shaoguan Iron and Steel Plant, 230, 231, 255
Shaoguan Prefecture, 221, 250, 252, 253, 254, 272; relocation of factories in, 36, 102, 288; Economic Commission of, 104; synthetic fiber plants in, 192; heavy industry in, 231, 242
Shaoqing Prefecture, 252
Shekou Float Glass Plant, 374
Shekou industrial zone, 129, 130–135, 151, 152, 154, 213, 317; Chiwan docks in, 133, 138

Shenzhen City, 223, 224, 225, 231, 265, 266, 291, 306, 316, 327, 368
Shenzhen Metropolitan Region, *see* Baoan County
Shenzhen special economic zone, 11, 126, 127, 129–153, 198, 220, 225, 243, 250, 323, 447; and Hong Kong, 65, 154, 160, 195; experiments in, 107, 151–153; urban planning in, 135–140, 188, 234; population of, 135, 166; links with inner China, 140–143; links with outside capital, 143–146; recession in, 146–148; readjustment in, 149–151; employment and labor payments in, 151; simplification of economic bureaucracy in, 151–152; democratic restraints on management in, 152; enterprise autonomy in, 152; banking services in, 152; horizontal linkage in, 152–153; freedom in land use in, 153; changing role of, 153; and Zhuhai, 154, 155–156, 157, 159–160; compared with Guangzhou, 212–213; and oil exploration, 238; jobs in, 268, 329, 330, 331; Customs Administration in, 349; and foreign trade, 364, 375, 378, 390, 418, 444; Soviet Union's interest in, 448. *See also* Shekou industrial zone
Shenzhen Municipal Planning Bureau (Shenzhenshi Guihuaju), 135
Shenzhen University, 443
Shilu mines (Hainan), 233, 255, 277, 289, 300, 308, 398
Shipping, 131, 132–134
Shiqi, 360, 363
Shunde County, 94, 130, 161, 166, 173, 190, 193, 194, 195, 235, 250, 340
Sichuan Province, 31, 86, 234, 323, 347, 446–447
Singapore, 10, 79, 125, 136, 137, 241, 290, 445; and Hong Kong, 47, 56, 57, 58, 60, 69; and foreign trade, 384, 389; compared with Guangdong, 426–427
Sino-British Joint Declaration on the Question of Hong Kong (Sept. 1984), 70–71, 383
Sino-British Joint Liaison Group, 71, 73
Sino-Soviet split (1960), 36
Snow, Edgar, 7
Socialism, 3, 10, 40, 41, 79, 100, 128, 280, 449

Soldiers, returned, 267, 281, 282. See also *individual counties*
Song Dynasty, 225, 243
Soong family, 277
South China Industry and Enterprise Corporation, Ltd., 341
South Korea, 41, 49, 56, 125, 327, 384, 404, 418, 419, 448; compared with Hong Kong, 57, 58, 68; and United States, 385, 389, 428; economic takeoff of, 426–434, 436, 438, 439, 446; and 1988 Seoul Olympics, 448
Southbound Work Team, 87
Soviet Union: reform in, 3; and China, 10, 41, 43, 60, 92, 128, 198, 278; Stalinist foreign trade system of, 347, 392; and Guangdong reforms, 448–449
Special economic zones, *see* Economic zones, special; *individual zones*
State Capital Construction Commission, 84
State Council: and economic reforms, 84, 85, 87, 106, 107, 270, 289, 386; and special economic zones, 126, 128, 130, 140; and poverty program, 270; and Hainan Province, 289, 300, 305, 307; and foreign trade, 351, 356, 357, 360, 364, 365, 367
State Farm Bureau, *see* Central South Land Reclamation and Cultivation Bureau
State farms, *see* Farms
State Planning Commission, 353
State Pricing Bureau (Beijing), 360–361, 379
State Supply and Marketing Cooperative, 262
Steel production, 111, 132, 133
Su Dongbo, 225, 275
Su Tongsheng, 329–331
Sun Yat-sen, 3, 277; Three Principles of, 53
Sun Yat-sen Memorial Hall, 24, 88
Sun Zhengshu, 320
Swatow, *see* Shantou
System Reform Office (Beijing), 90


Taichung (Taiwan), 126, 127
Taiping rebels, 28
Taishan County, 130, 161, 163, 164, 166, 193, 194, 277, 342, 350, 353

Taiwan, 9, 10, 41, 79, 83, 157, 164, 320, 338, 404, 418, 423; and Hong Kong, 46, 47, 49, 53, 57, 58, 61, 68, 71, 125–126, 131, 448; business leaders in, 55, 56; and Beijing, 82; and Shantou, 240, 241, 242; compared with Hainan Island, 275, 288, 290; Japanese occupation of, 277, 288; and Qing rule, 305; and foreign trade, 373, 384, 385, 389; social change in, 396, 397; human resources in, 419; economic takeoff of, 426–434, 436, 438, 439, 446

Taiwan National University, 431

Tanaka Kakuei, 60

Tang Dynasty, 182

Tangshan earthquake, 137

Tao Siling, 21

Tao Zhu, 16, 21, 32, 87, 90, 103, 316, 335

Technology, 5, 226, 272, 321, 390, 424; and reform, 5, 76, 83, 89; in special economic zones, 125, 134, 140, 141, 142, 143, 146, 148; borrowing of, 174, 427, 429, 435; in Guangzhou, 213, 214–215; in Shantou, 241–242. *See also* Hong Kong: technology from

Television, 65–66, 349, 381, 422, 428, 441

Thailand, 57, 241, 277, 296

Thatcher, Margaret, 70, 82, 132

Thirteenth Party Congress (1987), 3, 113, 122, 446

Tianjin, 83, 140, 142, 149, 154, 212, 235, 314, 347, 364

Tokyo University, 431

Tong Mengqing, 182

Tongi University (Shanghai), 307

Tongza (Hainan), 223, 224, 287, 288, 302, 303

Tourism, 127, 134, 154, 158, 200–203, 303–305, 307–308, 363–364, 436

Trade fair, *see* Export Commodities Fair

Transportation Bank of China, 114

Tropical Crops Research Center (Zhanjiang), 279, 294

Tucker, Robert, 16

Tung, C. Y., 58

Underground economy, 370–372, 384

Unemployment ("youth awaiting employment"), 99, 149, 204

United Nations, 45, 70

United States: and China, 43, 58, 60, 79, 322, 366, 444; business leaders in, 56; Carter presidency in, 361; recession of 1981–82 in, 385; Generalized Scheme of Preference treatment in, 389; market regulation in, 415; aid to allies, 427–428, 435, 436

Universities, 118, 150, 189, 268, 431, 441; and Cultural Revolution, 1, 19, 28, 37–38, 284; of Hong Kong, 51, 58, 63–64

Urban planning, 135–140, 153, 234

U.S. Chamber of Commerce (Hong Kong), 57

U.S.-China Textiles Agreement, 383

Vietnam, 277, 282, 449

Vietnam War, 36, 43, 57, 132, 285, 288, 428, 435

Wages: reforms in, 86, 102, 106–107, 151; and bonuses, 106, 107, 151, 400; piece-rate, 106, 177, 178; contract system for, 107, 151; in Shenzhen, 147, 150; factory, 178–180, 187, 188. *See also* Employees

Wan Li, 86, 259

Wang Guangying, 65, 154

Wang Xuan, 314

Wang Zhen, 282, 284, 289

Wang Zhuo, 90, 107

Wanning County, 271, 281, 303, 308

War of Liberation, Huai-Hai battle in, 131

War of Resistance, 20, 22, 230

Warlords, struggles against, 20

Wei Guoqing, 31, 121

Wenchang County, 277, 282, 299

Western Europe, 60, 299, 321, 323

Wilson, David, 69

World Bank, 171, 295–296, 299

World War II, 47, 50, 57, 87, 108, 125, 135, 190, 229, 232, 240; destruction of railroads in, 163; and Japan, 237, 428, 429, 432, 433

Wu, Gordon, 324–327, 336

Wu Liangyang, 138

Wu Nansheng, 140

Wuhan Incident, 25

Wuhua County, 242, 246

Wuzhou (Guangxi), 227, 447

Xi Zhongxun, 31, 85, 87, 88, 121, 284
Xiamen (Fujian) special economic zone, 88, 127, 129, 157
Xingning County, 221, 246
Xinhua News Agency, 62, 69, 73, 442
Xinhui County, 130, 161, 164, 166, 189–192, 193, 301, 353; polyester fiber plant in, 189, 191–192
Xinlong state farm, 281–282
Xintang, 217
Xinyi County, 266
Xu Jiatun, 73
Xu Shijie, 306

Yanan, 314; Shensi-Gansu Border Region in, 87
Yang Deyuan, 183
Yang Li, 6, 84–85
Yang Shangkun, 31, 87, 88, 121, 386
Yangchun County, 166, 236
Yangjiang County, 25, 166, 236, 250, 260
Yangpu, 301, 303, 307
Yangshan County, 272–273
Yangtze River, 47
Yao Wenyuan, 19
Yao Yilin, 369
Yazhou Qishuichang (beverage plant), 323
Ye Jianying, Marshal, 79, 245, 304
Ye Xuanping, 245
Yingde County, 28, 264
Yinggehai (Hainan), 289, 307, 308
Yoshida Shigeru, 430
Youth, rustication of, 27–28, 33, 38, 41, 99, 218, 284–285
Yu Fei, 182–186, 188, 316, 318, 320, 336, 345, 375
Yu Qiuli, 351
Yuan Geng, 131–132, 133, 134, 151, 152, 317, 335
Yuexiu Company, 384
Yuexiu Stadium, 24
Yuhua Department Stores, 64
Yuhua Electric Fan Factory (Yuhua Dianfengshanchang), 173–174
Yulin, naval base at, 304
Yunan County, 228
Yunfu County, 227, 228, 264
Yunfu mines (Zhaoqing), 255, 398
Yunnan Province, 237, 278, 295, 347

Zeng Sheng, 22, 131, 132
Zeng Xuanze, 244

Zengcheng County, 130, 161, 166, 193, 194, 217–218, 293
Zhang Gaoli, 6
Zhang Shan, 304–305
Zhanjiang City, 221, 224, 233, 234, 236–239, 250, 279, 318, 320, 321, 322; transportation in, 235; economic zone, 238; and foreign trade, 375
Zhanjiang Home Appliances Industrial Company, 318, 324
Zhanjiang Metropolitan Region, 236
Zhanjiang Prefecture, 119, 222, 224, 232, 235–236, 248, 255, 315
Zhao Ziyang, 78, 315, 326; on reform in socialist countries, 3; in Cultural Revolution, 21, 23, 31, 33; and reform in Guangdong, 83, 95, 121, 183, 195, 386; reforms of, in Sichuan, 86, 446; and special economic zones, 127, 128; encouragement of cash crops, 167; on export processing, 181; and reforestation, 256; and Hainan, 289, 294, 304, 305; and foreign trade, 375, 384
Zhaoqing, 224, 225, 226–229, 232, 236, 239, 242, 306; Seven Star Park (Qixingyuan) in, 229
Zhaoqing Prefecture, 156, 224, 227, 255, 256, 260
Zhongguo University, 314
Zhongshan County, 161, 165, 166, 190, 193, 194, 195, 250; escapees to Hong Kong from, 164; sugar growing in, 235–236; smuggling in, 371; and foreign trade, 375, 383
Zhongshan County Foodstuffs Export Corporation, 360
Zhongshan University (Guangzhou), 6, 24, 26, 443
Zhou Enlai, 25, 27, 87, 304, 342, 347
Zhu Shenlin, 213, 218
Zhuhai City, 223, 224, 250, 265, 291, 371, 375, 378, 444, 447
Zhuhai County, 341
Zhuhai Metropolitan Region, *see* Doumen County; Zhuhai special economic zone
Zhuhai special economic zone, 11, 126, 153–156, 157, 159–160, 195, 209; area of, 127, 129; and Shenzhen, 154, 155–156; industrial zones in, 155; population of, 156, 166, 220; and oil exploration, 238; jobs in, 268
Zijin County (Huiyang Prefecture), 95, 96